SOCIAL MEDIA AND CRISIS COMMUNICATION

Edited by Lucinda Austin and Yan Jin

 Routledge
Taylor & Francis Group

NEW YORK AND LONDON

First published 2018
by Routledge
711 Third Avenue, New York, NY 10017

and by Routledge
2 Park Square, Milton Park, Abingdon, Oxon OX14 4RN

Routledge is an imprint of the Taylor & Francis Group, an informa business

© 2017 Taylor & Francis

Library of Congress Cataloging-in-Publication Data
A catalog record for this title has been requested

ISBN: 978-1-138-81199-7 (hbk)
ISBN: 978-1-138-81200-0 (pbk)
ISBN: 978-1-315-74906-8 (ebk)

Typeset Bembo
by Apex CoVantage, LLC

SOCIAL MEDIA AND CRISIS COMMUNICATION

Social Media and Crisis Communication provides a unique and timely contribution to the field of crisis communication by addressing how social media is influencing the practice of crisis communication. The book, with a collection of chapters contributed by leading communication researchers, covers the current and emerging interplay of social media and crisis communication, recent theories and frameworks, overviews of dominant research streams, applications in specific crisis areas, and future directions.

Both the theoretical and the practical are discussed, providing a volume that appeals to both academic-minded readers and professionals at the managerial, decision-making level. The audience includes public relations and corporate communication scholars, graduate students studying social media and crisis communication, researchers, crisis managers working in communication departments, and business leaders who make strategic business communication planning. No other volume has provided the overarching synthesis of information regarding the field of crisis communication and social media that this book contains. Incorporated in this volume is the recent social-mediated crisis communication model developed by the editors and their co-authors, which serves as a framework for crisis and issues management in a rapidly evolving media landscape.

Lucinda Austin is an assistant professor at the University of North Carolina at Chapel Hill, where she researches social media, health and crisis communication, and publics' perspectives in CSR and relationship building. Austin has published in journals including *Communication Research*, the *Journal of Applied Communication Research, Health Communication,* the *Journal of Public Relations Research,* and *PR Review.* She has been awarded AEJMC's Promising Professors and SuPRstar Awards, Arthur Page Center's Legacy Educator and Scholar Awards, and NCA's PRIDE Award.

Yan Jin is an associate professor at the University of Georgia. Her research focuses on crisis communication, social media, and the role of emotions in strategic conflict management _____ ticles and 20 book chapters. She has presented _____ ved 14 top paper awards at national and inte _____ has been awarded AEJMC's Krieghbaum Und_____ e Arthur W. Page Society.

CONTENTS

CONTRIBUTORS

Editors

Lucinda Austin (Ph.D., University of Maryland College Park) is an assistant professor at the University of North Carolina at Chapel Hill. Her research focuses on social media, health and crisis communication, and publics' perspectives in CSR and relationship building. She has published in journals including *Communication Research, Applied Communication Research, Health Communication, Public Relations Research,* and *PR Review.* Austin has been awarded AEJMC's Promising Professors and SuPRstar Awards, the Arthur Page Center's Legacy Educator and Scholar Awards, and NCA's PRIDE Award.

Yan Jin (Ph.D., University of Missouri–Columbia) is an associate professor of public relations and associate director of the Center for Health and Risk Communication at the University of Georgia. Her research focuses on crisis communication, social media, and the role of emotions in strategic conflict management. She has authored more than 50 peer-reviewed journal articles and 20 book chapters. She has presented over 100 research papers and received 14 top paper awards at national and international research conferences. Jin has been awarded AEJMC's Krieghbaum Under-40 Award. She is a member of the Arthur W. Page Society.

Chapter Authors

Norshima Bte Abdul Aziz (MMC, Nanyang Technological University) is the deputy director of Corporate Communications at Yayasan MENDAKI, a non-profit organization with the mission to empower low-income families through education. Prior to public relations, Norshima had 15 years of experience in the broadcasting world and was the program director of Radio Singapore International.

William L. Benoit (Ph.D., Wayne State University) is a professor of communication studies at Ohio University. He developed image repair theory (*Accounts, Excuses, Apologies: Image Repair Theory and Research*, 2nd ed., 2015). He has applied this theory to instances of image repair in political discourse, corporate discourse, discourse in sports and entertainment, and international discourse.

Kati Tusinski Berg (Ph.D., University of Oregon) is associate professor of strategic communication in the Diederich College of Communication at Marquette University. Her research focuses on public relations ethics, lobbying, social media, and corporate social responsibility. Her research has been published in the *Journal of Mass Media Ethics*, the *Public Relations Journal*, *Case Studies in Strategic Communication*, *PRism*, and various edited books. Her professional experience includes work in nonprofit and agency public relations.

Bruce K. Berger (Ph.D., University of Kentucky) is professor emeritus of advertising and public relations at the University of Alabama. He serves as research director for the Plank Center for Leadership in Public Relations Research at the University of Alabama. Previously, Berger was a public relations professional and executive for The Upjohn Company and Whirlpool Corporation for 20 years. His research focuses on communication management and leadership, employee communications, and power relations inside organizations. He has authored or edited four books and more than 80 book chapters and scholarly and professional articles.

Shannon A. Bowen (Ph.D., University of Maryland) is a professor at the University of South Carolina. Her research focuses on ethical decision making within organizations. Dr. Bowen has more than 100 publications on ethics in public relations and has won numerous awards for her research. Dr. Bowen is author of the recent books *An Overview of the Public Relations Function* and *Excellence in Internal Communication Management*, published by Business Expert Press.

Ross Buck (Ph.D., University of Pittsburgh) is a professor of communication and psychological sciences at the University of Connecticut. His research explores nonverbal communication and emotional expression with a focus on aspects such as the evolution of human behavior, communication, and social structure. Dr. Buck has published over 100 journal articles, chapters, and books, including *Human Motivation and Emotion*, *The Communication of Emotion*, and *Emotion: A Biosocial Synthesis*. He is currently working on the neuroscience of emotional and cognitive empathy using fMRI.

Glen Cameron (Ph.D., University of Texas at Austin) is a professor and the Maxine Wilson Gregory Chair in Journalism Research at the Missouri School of Journalism. Cameron has a joint appointment in family and community medicine to study patient-centered outcomes research. He has received many academic awards and honors. Cameron's research includes studies of public relations and news production, information processing of news and commercials, and tailored health news.

Zifei Fay Chen (Ph.D. candidate, University of Miami) is an assistant professor in the Department of Communication Studies at University of San Francisco. With a focus on public relations, her research interests involve corporate communication, corporate social responsibility, crisis communication, new media, consumer psychology, and relationship management. Professionally, Chen has worked as an analyst at Ketchum Global Research and Analytics in New York City and has worked in marketing analysis and communications at Fiserv in Atlanta, Georgia.

Yang Cheng (Ph.D. candidate, University of Missouri) is an assistant professor at North Carolina State University. Her research interests include public relations and social media and crisis communication. Some of her publications have appeared in *New Media & Society*, the *International Journal of Communication*, *Public Relations Review*, and the *Asian Journal of Communication*, among others. She has also received many awards, such as the Grunig PRIME Research Fellowship, Best Student Paper from the International Communication Association, the Peter Debreceny Corporate Award, and the Kaiser Graduate Students of Color Award.

Samuel Chua (MMC, Nanyang Technological University) is a communications practitioner in Singapore with over a decade experience in both private and public sectors. His interests are in corporate communications, social media strategy, and user experience design.

An-Sofie Claeys (Ph.D., Ghent University) is an assistant professor at the Institute for Media Studies at KU Leuven in Belgium. She received the 2015 Young Scholar Award from the Netherlands-Flanders Communication Association (NeFCA). Her research on crisis communication has appeared in journals such as the *Journal of Communication*, *Public Relations Review*, the *Journal of Business Research*, and the *Journal of Applied Communication Research*.

W. Timothy Coombs (Ph.D., Purdue University) is a professor in the Department of Communication at Texas A&M University and an honorary professor in the Department of Business Communication at Aarhus University. His primary area of research is crisis communication. He has received the Jackson Jackson & Wagner Behavioral Research Prize from PRSA and the 2013 Pathfinder Award from the Institute of Public Relations. His research appears in *Management Communication Quarterly*, *Public Relations Review*, *Corporate Reputation Review*, the *Journal of Public Relations Research*, and the *Journal of Communication Management*.

Stephen M. Croucher (Ph.D., University of Oklahoma) is a professor and head of the School of Communication, Journalism, and Marketing at Massey University,

New Zealand. He researches immigrant cultural adaptation, religion, communication, statistics, and conflict. He has also explored how religion influences communication behaviors.

Ratna Damayanti (MMC, Nanyang Technological University) has more than a decade of communications experience in both the public and private sectors. She has taught mass communication to polytechnic students, specializing in communication research, organizational behavior, consumer behavior, and cross-cultural communication. She recently started a market research company based in Singapore focusing on advertising and public relations campaigns. Her academic research interests include crisis communication, image management and repair, and public relations.

Audra Diers-Lawson (Ph.D., University of Texas at Austin) is a senior lecturer in public relations in the Faculty of Business and Law at Leeds Beckett University in Leeds, UK. Her research focuses on crisis communication and the exploration of the influences of attitudes, engagement, and message effects.

Marcia W. DiStaso (Ph.D., University of Miami, APR) is an associate professor and chair of the Public Relations Department at the University of Florida. She is the director for the Institute for Public Relations Digital Media Research Center and a research consultant for the Arthur W. Page Society. She won the Silver Anvil and MarCom awards and was recognized as a promising professor and an emerging scholar by AEJMC. Her research focuses on exploring and informing the practice of social media.

Elina Erzikova (Ph.D., University of Alabama) is a professor of public relations in the department of journalism at Central Michigan University. Erzikova's research interests include the role of power in the state—media relations, professional ethics and leadership, and cultural aspects of journalism and public relations. She has published in *Political Communication*, *Mass Communication and Society*, the *International Communication Gazette*, *Journalism Studies*, *Public Relations Review*, and the *Public Relations Journal*.

Julia Daisy Fraustino (Ph.D., University of Maryland) is an assistant professor in the Reed College of Media at West Virginia University, where she is co-director of the Public Interest Communication Research Lab in the Media Innovation Center. Fraustino researches strategic communication and public relations with a focus on community resilience, particularly within the intersections of risk and crisis communication, ethics, and social and mobile media. Her research, teaching, and leadership have won several regional, national, and international awards.

Karen Freberg (Ph.D., University of Tennessee) is an associate professor in strategic communications at the University of Louisville. Freberg's research has been published in several book chapters and in academic journals such as *Public Relations Review*, the *Journal of Public Relations Education*, the *Journal of Contingencies and Crisis Management*, and *Health Communication*.

Lisa Gandy (Ph.D., Northwestern University) is an assistant professor of computer science at Central Michigan University. Her research interests include text mining, text informatics, natural language processing and machine learning. She has worked on a diverse array of text-mining applications, from using the text of bills to detect when and where U.S. senators are receiving campaign donations to creating software to automatically merge biomedical data. Dr. Gandy's work has been published in esteemed conferences such as AAAI (Association for the Advancement of Artificial Intelligence), ICWSM (International Conference of Weblogs and Social Media) and WWW (World Wide Web Conference).

Nathan Gilkerson (Ph.D., University of Minnesota) is an assistant professor of public relations and strategic communication at Marquette University. His research interests include political communication and public relations, social media and political activism, and public relations measurement and evaluation. He teaches courses on media writing, principles of public relations, public relations strategies, and campaign development and implementation. Gilkerson worked professionally in the fields of political communication, advertising and public relations, and has published research in a variety of academic journals.

Mark Glantz (Ph.D., University of Missouri) is an assistant professor of communication and media studies at St. Norbert College. His research interests include image-repair discourse, new media, and political communication. His work has been published in outlets such as *Public Relations Review*, the *Journal of Communication Inquiry*, and *American Behavioral Scientist*.

Michael B. Goodman (Ph.D., SUNY Stony Brook) is a professor and director of the master's in corporate communication at Baruch College, the City University of New York, and director of CCI Corporate Communication International. He is visiting professor at Aarhus University (Denmark), Hong Kong Polytechnic University, and Universita IULM (Italy). He has published widely, including *Corporate Communication: Critical Business Asset for Strategic Global Change* and *Corporate Communication: Strategic Adaptation for Global Practice*. He has been a consultant to more than 40 corporations and institutions on corporate communication, managerial communication, problem solving, new business proposals, change, and corporate culture.

Jeanine Guidry (Ph.D. candidate, Virginia Commonwealth University) is an assistant professor in the Richard T. Robertson School of Media and Culture at the Virginia Commonwealth University. Her research interests are focused on the use of visual social media platforms Instagram and Pinterest in the area of health communications. Her work has been published in academic journals like *Vaccine*, *Health Communication*, *Public Relations Review*, and the *Journal of Social Marketing*.

Sherry Holladay (Ph.D., Purdue University) is a professor in the Department of Communication at Texas A&M University. Her research interests include crisis communication and corporate social responsibility. Her research appears in *Public Relations Review*, *Public Relations Inquiry*, *Management Communication Quarterly*, the *Journal of Communication Management*, and the *International Journal of Strategic Communication*. She is co-author of *It's Not Just PR: Public Relations in Society*, *Public Relations Strategies and Applications: Managing Influence*, and *Managing Corporate Responsibility: A Communication Approach* and co-editor of *Handbook of Crisis Communication*.

Chun-Ju Flora Hung-Baesecke (Ph.D., University of Maryland) teaches at Massey University in Albany, New Zealand. Her research interests include organization-public relationships, CSR, social media, employee communication, and issues and crisis management. She is the 2014–2016 Arthur W. Page Legacy Scholar. She presents her research at international conferences and publishes in various refereed journals. She is the special overseas board member of the Public Relations Society of China and is on the academic committee of the China International Public Relations Association.

Øyvind Ihlen (Ph.D., University of Oslo) is a professor at the Department of Media and Communication, University of Oslo, and co-director of POLKOM, Centre for the Study of Political Communication. He has published over 60 journal articles and book chapters and written or edited nine books, including *Public Relations and Social Theory: Key Figures and Concepts* (2009) and the award-winning *Handbook of Communication and Corporate Social Responsibility* (2011). Ihlen is president of the European Public Relations Education and Research Association (EUPRERA).

Melissa Janoske (Ph.D., University of Maryland) is an assistant professor at the University of Memphis, head of the public relations major, and assistant director of graduate studies in the Department of Journalism and Strategic Media. Dr. Janoske has published research on both crisis and social media, including best practices in crisis communication, social media activism, and online communities and social networking.

Yi Grace Ji (Ph.D. Candidate, University of Miami) is an assistant professor in the Richard T. Robertson School of Media and Culture at the Virginia Commonwealth University. Her research interests center on social-mediated public relations, including stakeholder online engagement, big data application in public relations research, stakeholder decision making, and relationship management.

Hua Jiang (Ph.D., University of Maryland) is an associate professor of public relations at S.I. Newhouse School of Public Communications, Syracuse University. Her major research areas include employee and internal communication, social media and leadership, environmental communication and health communication, and segmentation of publics. Dr. Jiang has published more than two dozen manuscripts in peer-reviewed communication and public relations journals.

Dean Kruckeberg (Ph.D., University of Iowa, APR, fellow PRSA) is a professor at the University of North Carolina at Charlotte. He is co-author of *This Is PR: The Realities of Public Relations* and *Public Relations and Community: A Reconstructed Theory*. His honors include the PRSA Atlas Award for Lifetime Achievement in International Public Relations, the PRSA Outstanding Educator Award, the Pathfinder Award of the Institute for Public Relations, and the Jackson Jackson & Wagner Behavioral Research Prize. He has lectured and performed research worldwide.

Kenneth A. Lachlan (Ph.D., Michigan State University) is an associate professor of communication at the University of Connecticut, and editor-in-chief of *Communication Studies*. His research interests include crisis and risk communication, new media technologies, and the use of social media in estimating attitudes and behaviors.

Abbey Levenshus (Ph.D., University of Maryland) is an assistant professor of strategic communication at Butler University. Her research on government communication, risk and crisis communication, and social media has been published in books and top communication journals like the *Journal of Applied Communication Research* and the *Journal of Public Relations Research*. Levenshus's professional experience includes serving as communication director for a U.S. congressman, political technology company, and a government consulting firm in Washington, DC.

Cong Li (Ph.D., University of North Carolina) is an associate professor in the School of Communication at the University of Miami. His research interest is centered on the effect of personalized information. He has authored two books and a number of journal articles.

Eric Wei Lim (MMC, Nanyang Technological University) is senior executive for corporate communications and CSR at Mitsui Chemicals Asia Pacific, Ltd., the regional headquarters of one of Japan's largest petrochemical groups. He formulates strategies for internal communications at Mitsui Chemicals Asia Pacific, and is commencing strategies for global employer branding for Mitsui Chemicals Group.

Rachael Song-Qi Lim (MMC, Nanyang Technological University) is a strategic communications practitioner who specializes in formulating information strategies and policies, as well as designing public relations and engagement plans in the public sector. She was also a writer with one of Singapore's longest-circulating magazines.

Xialing Lin (Ph.D., University of Kentucky) is an assistant professor of corporate communication at Pennsylvania State University–Worthington Scranton. Her research interests include social media; intercultural, emergency and crisis communication; and corporate communication.

Brooke Fisher Liu (Ph.D., University of North Carolina) is an associate professor at the University of Maryland. Her research investigates how communication helps people respond to and recover from disasters. Liu leads the Risk Communication & Resilience Program at the DHS Center of Excellence and serves on the FDA's Risk Communication Advisory Committee. She also serves on a National Academy of Sciences committee examining the future of alerts and warnings. Liu has authored more than 50 articles and chapters in some of the field's leading outlets.

Jiangmeng Liu is a doctoral student from the School of Communication at the University of Miami. Her research interests include corporate social media use for advertising and public relations purposes and word of mouth on social media. She is also interested in social media effects in terms of civic engagement, the acculturation process, and psychological well-being.

Yi Luo (Ph.D., University of Maryland) is an associate professor in the School of Communication and Media at Montclair State University. She has conducted research in the areas of organizational change, sense making, leadership, social media and communication management, activism, organizational justice, and global public relations. Dr. Luo teaches a variety of courses in organizational communication and public relations, such as cases and campaigns, communication theories, communication research, global public relations, public relations ethics, new media application in organizations, and others.

Tina McCorkindale (Ph.D., University of Miami, APR) is the president and CEO of the Institute for Public Relations. She taught as a professor for 15 years and has more than 10 years of experience working in corporate communication and analytics. She has more than 100 presentations and academic publications in books and journals with her research broadly focusing on aspects of digital media. She is active in several industry groups and serves on the editorial review board of several academic journals.

Nance McCown (Ph.D., University of Maryland) serves as department co-chair and associate professor of communication at Messiah College in Grantham, PA.

Earning her Ph.D. from University of Maryland–College Park in 2008, McCown focuses her research on nonprofit crisis communication, internal public relations, leader-employee relationship building, and public relations education. Prior to her academic career, she held various strategic communication roles in higher education and managed a thriving freelance business.

Juan Meng (Ph.D., University of Alabama) is associate professor of advertising and public relations at the University of Georgia. Her current research focuses on leadership in public relations, talent management and leadership development, trust in reputation management, and organizational culture and employee engagement. Meng has published her research in leading scholarly journals in public relations and communication management. Meng is the co-editor of the scholarly book *Public Relations Leaders as Sensemakers: A Global Study of Leadership in Public Relations and Communication Management*.

Marcus Messner (Ph.D., University of Miami) is an associate professor at the Richard T. Robertson School of Media and Culture at Virginia Commonwealth University. His main research focus is on the influence and adoption of social media in journalism and public relations. He has presented more than 70 research papers at national and international conferences and has published more than 30 articles in academic journals and various books.

Michael North (Ph.D., University of Miami) researches how businesses use social media to reach stakeholders with a specific emphasis on Twitter. He currently teaches public relations writing and social media strategy at Central Connecticut State University.

Michael J. Palenchar (Ph.D., University of Florida), an associate professor at the University of Tennessee, has three decades of professional and academic public relations experience. Research interests include risk communication, crisis communication, and issues management. He has over 100 journal articles, book chapters, and conference papers, including his first book with co-author Robert L. Heath titled *Strategic Issues Management*. He has presented his research and conducted workshops throughout the United States, China, Germany, Turkey, Norway, Spain, the United Kingdom, Australia, New Zealand, Mexico, Canada, and Denmark.

Augustine Pang (Ph.D., University of Missouri) is an associate professor and program director of the master's of mass communication at Wee Kim Wee School of Communication and Information, Nanyang Technological University. He specializes in crisis management and communication, image management and repair, media management, and public relations. He publishes actively in refereed books and journals and is thankful for the multiple research awards won at top international conferences such as the International Communication Association (2015), among others.

Bryan H. Reber (Ph.D., University of Missouri) is C. Richard Yarbrough Professor of Crisis Communication Leadership and assistant department head in the Department of Advertising & Public Relations in the Grady College of Journalism and Mass Communication at the University of Georgia. His research focuses on public relations theory, practice, and pedagogy, especially as it relates to crisis and health communication. Prior to joining the Grady College, Dr. Reber worked in public relations at Bethel College, Kansas.

Stacey Rodrigues (MMC, Nanyang Technological University) is a content producer who spent 12 years in the publishing industry in Singapore before crossing over to public relations. She is especially interested in evolving digital communication platforms and change management.

Stefania Romenti (Ph.D., International University of Languages and Media) is an associate professor in corporate communication and strategic public relations at IULM University, Milan, Italy. She is adjunct professor of communications, KPIs, and intangibles at IE Business School. Dr. Romenti has written over 50 international publications in communication management and public relations. She is director of the executive master's in public relations management at IULM University and head of the Scientific Committee of the European Public Relations Education and Research Association (EUPRERA).

Melony Shemberger (Ed.D., Tennessee State University) is an assistant professor of journalism and mass communication at Murray State University in Murray, Kentucky. She previously worked in university public relations. Her PR work was recognized consistently by the Tennessee College Public Relations Association and the Council for Advancement and Support of Education (CASE). Before entering academia, Shemberger had award-winning reporting careers in west Kentucky. Shemberger earned a doctorate in administration and supervision, with a concentration in higher education, from Tennessee State University.

Patric Spence (Ph.D., Wayne State University) is an associate professor and director of business communication in the School of Information Sciences at the University of Kentucky. His research interests include emergency and risk communication, organizational communication, and social robotics.

Patricia Swann (M.S., Syracuse University, APR) is the author of *Cases in Public Relations Management: The Rise of Social Media and Activism*. She is a professor of public relations and journalism and former dean of the School of Business and Justice Studies at Utica College.

Elizabeth Yingzhi Tan (MMC, Nanyang Technological University) is a communications practitioner specializing in internal communications. She has executed programs that clinched PR industry awards for communication excellence and effectiveness. She manages a multichannel internal communication suite to communicate strategic messages to 3,800 employees of a leading utility and networks company in Asia. She also curates, authors, and develops content for various communication platforms.

Chiara Valentini (Ph.D., University of Jyväskylä) is an associate professor in public relations and corporate communication at Aarhus University, School of Business and Social Sciences, Denmark. Her research interests focus on public relations, corporate communication, crisis communication, political communication, and social media. Her work has appeared in numerous international peer-reviewed journals, international handbooks, and volume contributions. She is currently the chair of the Public Relations Division at the International Communication Association (ICA) and serves as reviewer and editorial board member of several international journals.

Xiuli Wang (Ph.D., Syracuse University) is an associate professor in the School of Journalism and Communication at Peking University. Her research focuses on social media and international public relations. She has published in both English and Chinese journals such as the *Journalism and Mass Communication Quarterly* and *Computers in Human Behavior*. Her recent published books are *China in the Eyes of Japanese* and *Social Media for Social Good: Cases and Best Practices*.

Yi Wang (Ph.D., University of Connecticut) is an assistant professor of communication at the University of Louisville. Her research explores the cognitive and emotional factors in the processing and effectiveness of health and risk messages. She teaches visual and video communication and also studies the role of emotion and other factors in shaping the virality of media content.

Yue Wu (Ph.D., University of Connecticut) is an instructor in the School of Journalism & Communication at China Youth University of Political Studies. His research interests include the influence and effects of digital media, especially in popular culture and subcultures, intercultural studies, and political communication.

Jueman (Mandy) Zhang (Ph.D., Syracuse University) is an associate professor in the Department of Communication Arts at New York Institute of Technology. Her primary research areas include uses and effects of digital media, health and crisis communication, and journalism. She has published in journals such as *Health Communication*, *Vaccine*, *JMIR mHealth and uHealth*, the *Journal of Consumer Health on the Internet*, and the *Chinese Journal of Journalism & Communication*.

INTRODUCTION

Lucinda Austin and Yan Jin

How to effectively engage with publics via both traditional and social media in different types of crises with different forms of communication channels has been a critical question for both media professionals and communication scholars. Crisis communicators facing high-stakes threats have an increasing need for evidence-based guidelines for crisis information to ensure the safety and welfare of publics and organizations and aid in crisis recovery. Scarce theory-grounded research explores how publics receive, seek, and share crisis information via social media.

Media plays an essential role in crisis communication. Crisis information production and dissemination are critical for crisis preparedness, crisis response, and crisis recovery, as many have witnessed, from man-made disasters, such as the Boston Marathon bombings and the recent Paris terrorist attacks, to corporate crises that endanger societal well-being, such as the BP oil spill. Although media professionals and communication scholars recognize the importance of engaging publics via different forms of media, how to effectively engage with publics via both traditional and social media has been a struggle.

This edited volume, *Social Media and Crisis Communication*, provides a unique and timely contribution by addressing how social media are influencing the practice of crisis communication across different organizations and industry areas. To date, no existing book covers comprehensively the joint topic of social media and crisis communication as a specialty applied communication area. This volume covers current and emerging issues in social media and crisis communication, overviews of dominant research streams, emerging theories and frameworks, areas for special consideration (including characteristics of crises, organizations, audiences, and communication), future directions, and applications in specific areas of crisis, including health, disaster, corporate, nonprofit and philanthropic, political, sports, and other specific crises. Chapters represent a variety of perspectives including theoretical, empirical, review, and case study perspectives. We believe the volume not only enriches the body of knowledge in crisis communication but also provides research-based insights for crisis communication practice at both managerial decision-making and strategic response optimization levels.

This volume begins with an "Overview of Social Media Research in Crisis Communication." First, authors Cheng and Cameron walk us through an analysis of articles published in public relations and communication journals from 2002 to 2014 featuring social media and crisis communication as major areas of focus. Cheng and Cameron's analysis suggests the need for more global approaches to social media and crisis communication research, improved sampling frames, an emphasis on different phases, and a need for better metrics and measures of effectiveness. Cheng and Cameron's chapter sets the stage nicely for the remainder of the book, as many of the other chapters focus on these areas. Also in the overview of social media and crisis communication is Coombs' chapter on revising situational crisis communication theory (SCCT) to focus more on the influence of social media. As Coombs' crisis communication work is so foundational for much of the public relations research in crisis today, this chapter provides a pivotal overview of the development of this foundational research and SCCT's evolution in the age of social media.

Following the overview is a section on "Current Issues of Social Media and Crisis Communication." First, Goodman discusses the need for reputation, issues management, and crisis management for sustainable companies, providing recommendations for various crisis stages. Next, Valentini, Romenti, and Kruckeberg provide a thorough overview of social media and crisis communication as it relates to stakeholder crisis awareness and sense making, as well as organizational crisis preparedness. Valentini and colleagues call for the need for more research from stakeholder perspectives and consideration of dialogic approaches to crisis communication. Last, in this section, Hung-Baesecke and Bowen discuss ethical engagement in crises via social media through examination of the case of Dolce & Gabbana's photo ban crisis. Their findings reveal that the lack of ethical communication, including disrespecting stakeholders, providing misleading information, justifying through false store policies, and shifting blame, led to a greater crisis that damaged the organization's reputation.

The section on "Foundations and Frameworks" is divided into three parts: (a) organizational approaches and considerations, (b) audience-oriented approaches and considerations, and (c) characteristics and types of social media. First, under "Organizational Approaches and Considerations," the three chapters here focus on organizational leadership, organizational spokespeople, and organizational crisis message response types. Meng and Berger discuss the role of effective public relations leadership in effective management of social media in crisis. Findings from a global study of public relations professionals reveal that, in an age of social media, the most important factors in crisis communication leadership were dealing with the volume and speed of information, being prepared to effectively deal with crises, and managing social media. Next, Damayanti, Rodrigues, Chua, and Pang discuss the importance of spokespeople in times of crisis and suggest the importance of a social media–specific spokesperson training for crises. Important factors for spokespeople include optimizing the strengths of the specific social media platform while having a consistent message across platforms. Chen and Reber then examine the effectiveness of various message response strategies in both the United States and China based on a fictional plane crash. Based on Chen and Reber's findings, apology and compensation, across the board, were perceived more positively and communicated about more positively via word of mouth; however, different message strategies had no effect on negative online crisis communication. Chinese participants had higher negative online reactions for all message strategies than did U.S. participants.

Second, under "Audience-Oriented Approaches and Considerations," the two chapters here provide an overview of audience-oriented approaches and activist strategies and tactics. Fraustino and Liu identify four main categories of audience-oriented approaches and research including organization-public relationships, audience and publics segmenting, emotion and coping, and two-way communication and cocreation. Fraustino and Liu call for further research on ethics, crisis metrics, cultural multiplicity, and multivocal theoretical frameworks. Gilkerson and Berg discuss social media activism by activist publics through the use of "hashtag hijacking" and provide case studies and recommendations for organizations in similar situations.

Third, under "Characteristics and Types of Social Media," the three chapters here focus on various aspects and characteristics of social media that help and hinder communication in crises. Coombs, Claeys, and Holladay discuss effects of social media in crises, as previous research has suggested a unique channel effect when communicating via social media. Coombs, Claeys, and Holladay suggest that, instead, we cannot rule out that social media may have a "stealing thunder" effect, where an organization is the first to release the crisis information and thus receives fewer negative outcomes. Glantz and Benoit examine image-repair discourse via Twitter, exploring how this discourse is different in three types of Twitter messages: tweets, retweets, and replies. Glantz and Benoit found that accused parties used tweets to put forward their initial defense, retweets to strengthen their persuasive defense, and replies to directly address tweets that attack them. Freberg and Palenchar provide a review of characteristics of new and innovative types of wearable technology, reality applications, and gamification, in relation to crisis communication and show how these tools can help organizations to build trust, engage and collaborate, provide transparency, and help publics embrace uncertainty during crises.

The section of "Areas of Application" is divided into six categories: (a) corporate, (b) nonprofit, (c) health, (d) disaster, (e) political, and (f) sports. Under the corporate category, North, Li, Liu, and Ji examined how Fortune 500 companies used Twitter for crisis communication and found companies primarily used the rebuild message strategy, followed by the diminish and deny strategies. Replies on Twitter during crises increased and skewed negative. Zhang, Y. Wang, Wu, X. Wang, and Buck examined frames, emotions, behavioral intentions, corporate reputation, and country image in the Malaysia Airlines crisis. They found that doubt was the strongest evoked emotion and was likely to lead to negative word-of-mouth communication; anger was also significantly associated with negative word-of-mouth communication, as well as negative perceived corporate reputation.

Under the nonprofit category, Shemberger explores how social media influence crisis communication for nonprofit organizations and introduces three nonprofit organization case studies as examples. Shemberger suggests that social media are a more effective tool of dialogic communication for nonprofits and have enabled nonprofits to implement crisis communication at critical moments, giving nonprofits the potential for greater impact. McCown explores the case study of Christian humanitarian nonprofit World Vision in its gay hiring and reversal decision crisis. McCown finds that factors contributing to the crisis include World Vision's limited knowledge of stakeholder values, lack of transparency, low online engagement, and failure to anticipate a potential crisis.

Under the health category, R. Lim, Tan, W. Lim, Aziz, and Pang present a social media pandemic communication model combining the World Health Organization's continuum of pandemic phases with the health belief model; their model provides recommendations for crisis communication via social media at each stage of pandemic. Guidry and Messner examine how vaccine safety is communicated via Pinterest and find that the majority of Pinterest posts represent an antivaccine stance, although posts with a provaccination stance are "repinned" more and received more favorably. According to their findings, pediatric health organizations on Pinterest largely do not respond to antivaccine concerns and are limited in any discussion of vaccines.

Under the category of disaster, Fraustino, Liu, and Jin provide an overview of social media use during disasters, examining how and why publics use social media during disasters. Fraustino, Liu, and Jin suggest that publics use social media during disasters because of convenience, social norms, and personal recommendations and because they are seeking humor; timely, unique, and unfiltered information; connections with friends, family, and community; a place to share updates and mobilize; and emotional support and healing. Lachlan, Spence, and Lin discuss how Twitter is used for stakeholder communication during natural disasters and suggest that Twitter may be especially useful for dialogic communication or at least creating the perception of dialogue. Janoske discusses the impact of visuals in recovery from disasters and finds that visuals helped individuals recovering from Hurricane Sandy to survey and process the damage, vent emotionally, and provide support.

Under the political category, Gandy and Erzikova explore how expanded social media visibility for politicians and public figures has altered crisis communication through a look at how one-time presidential candidate Herman Cain responded to accusations of sexual harassment. Gandy and Erzikova find that Twitter conversation was shifted away from Cain's platform and to the scandal through Cain's poor social media engagement strategy and negative attitudes displayed by Twitter users. Swann's chapter explores how activists use social media platforms for political and social activism and illustrates that social media allow mobilizing and sharing resources (organizational, financial, and human) and building awareness, allowing activists to gain power and pressure organizations more effectively.

Last, under the sports category, Diers-Lawson and Croucher discuss sports, culture, and financial crisis through a cross-cultural comparison of social media responses in the United States and the United Kingdom. Their findings suggest that communication strategies for sports crises must be considered within the context of the national culture for effective crisis response. McCorkindale and DiStaso examine the controversy over the U.S. National Football League Washington Redskins' controversial name through examination of social media posts from stakeholders; they find that engagement is spurred by media-driven stories, and conversation across social media platforms follows the same general trend pattern with some slight variations.

The last major section of the book, "Emerging Frameworks and Future Directions," suggests new areas of research for social media and crisis communication. Ihlen and Levenshus discuss the potential of and need for more dialogic approaches to crisis communication via social media, which is a theme highlighted through many of the preceding chapters in the book. Jiang and Luo put forth a preliminary model for measurement of social media engagement in crisis communication, again another theme highlighted through many of the preceding chapters, as metrics and methods of evaluation for crisis outcomes have been limited in prior research. Last, Austin, Fraustino, Jin, and Liu put forward discussion of the social-mediated crisis communication model, an emerging model that combines many of the areas of the preceding foundations and frameworks chapters, including audience- and organization-oriented approaches and characteristics of social media types and sources.

As illustrated in the chapter descriptions, this volume includes a variety of global and international perspectives with authors based in countries including Belgium, China, Denmark, England, Finland, Hong Kong, Italy, New Zealand, Norway, Singapore, the United States, and more. Although many chapters of the book are written primarily from a U.S.-based perspective, we hope the structure and content of this volume will make it highly relevant to non-U.S. readers (both scholars and practitioners). First, the theoretical frameworks of social media and crisis communications, as the foundation of this scholarly book, can be applied to different countries and cultural origins. Second, specific sections and chapters are dedicated to the influence of culture and global media on how social media, in various forms and embedded in different contexts, influence the life cycle of crisis communication. Third, examples and cases associated with social media and crisis communications outside of the United States are included, which we hope will be relevant and relatable to international readers.

In conclusion, we hope this book will appeal to public relations and corporate communication scholars and educators, graduate students studying social media and crisis communication, communication researchers, and crisis managers working at agencies and in-house communication departments. We believe this book should also be of interest to business leaders and management team members who make strategic business communication planning and implementation decisions in both crisis and noncrisis situations. We hope this collected work will stimulate further research innovation and collaboration in theory development and practice enhancement in the emerging field of social media and crisis communication.

Overview of Social Media Research in Crisis Communication

1

THE STATUS OF SOCIAL-MEDIATED CRISIS COMMUNICATION (SMCC) RESEARCH

An Analysis of Published Articles in 2002–2014

Yang Cheng and Glen Cameron

Introduction

The 21st century has witnessed the rapid diffusion of various *social media* (e.g., Twitter, Pinterest, and Facebook), which are defined as "a group of Internet-based applications that build on the ideological and technological foundations of Web 2.0, and that allow the creation and exchange of user generated content (UGC)" (Kaplan & Haenlein, 2010, p. 61).

Contrasted with traditional media (e.g., the television) where users are passive recipients, social media provide an interactive and updated platform for active social participation, which has transformed the way of sending and receiving information. On the one hand, "gatewatchers" on social media not only play the role of publishing news like "gatekeepers" but also revise and republish news based on collective online comments (Bruns, 2005). On the other hand, massive and diverse stakeholders can easily get access to social media and directly communicate with organizations. The proliferation of channels and decentralization of audiences form a selective, immediate, and interactive way of communication between organizations and public. Online activities such as the crowdsourcing or collective intelligence may assist effectively the crisis-communication community (Howe, 2008), while at the same time, generate the possibility for intensive crises or risks (Hallahan, 2009).Viruses or rumors online can easily trigger crises and cause financial costs. Studies show that almost 40% of crises in 16 countries, such as the United States and China, result from either negative publicity on new media or digital security failures (Burson-Marsteller & PSB, 2011).

Given this, what may be the effective strategy or response form utilized on social media in crisis communication? How should organizations manage the image and organizational-public relationship online? How should crisis information through social media platforms be sought? These questions have triggered heated discussions among scholars from all over the world, such as Cheng (2016); Jin and Liu (2010); Liu, Jin, and Austin (2013); Taylor and Perry (2005); and Utz, Schultz, and Glocka (2013). Their research has mainly focused on the field of *social-mediated crisis communication*, which refers to the social-mediated "dialogue between the organization and its publics" (Fearn-Banks, 2002, p. 2) or "dialogue within organizations or publics." *Crisis* here can be initialized or transmitted through social media, and it refers to "a major occurrence with a potentially negative outcome affecting the organization, company, or industry, as well as its publics, products, services, or good name" (Fearn-Banks, 2002, p. 2).

Considering the large amount of relevant literature on social-mediated crisis communication (SMCC) in the field of public relations or communication, pressing concerns that need to be addressed include the following:

- What is the general trend of SMCC research, in terms of the theoretical framework and methodological approach?
- What types of SMCC research have been studied (i.e., research focus, crisis type, time, and region)?
- What are the forms of SMCC practice (i.e., crisis communication strategy, forms of response, and crisis management effectiveness)?

The study took a synthesized review of how global scholarship examined the realm of social media research in crisis communication and provided insights for the theoretical implications from two dimensions: (a) to enrich the theories of crisis communication by placing social media research in crisis communication at a higher theoretical level, an extensive literature review on the state of this field (SMCC) and how the field has evolved, including theoretical perspectives on crisis communication, crisis types, and crisis phases, is presented; and (b) to reflect and direct future research, a scholarly assessment tool for the SMCC research is provided.

Data and Framework of Analysis

In order to present a comprehensive overview of the SMCC research, ten Social Sciences Citation Index (SSCI) academic journals, mainly in relevant academic disciplines such as public relations or communication, were selected for full screening, ranging from 2002 to 2014. Five highly ranked journals based on five-year impact factors from the SSCI in the field of communication (i.e., the *Journal of Communication* and *Communication Research*, which were a common outlet for the communication research; the *Journal of Computer-Mediated Communication, Cyberpsychology and Behavior*, and *New Media & Society*, which particularly focused on new media in communication) were first identified. Then, two representative journals in the public relations field were chosen (i.e., the *Journal of Public Relations Research* and

Public Relations Review). Three journals relevant to the field of applied communication were added (i.e., the *Journal of Applied Communication Research*, the *Journal of Contingencies and Crisis Management*, and *Management Communication Quarterly*). The keyword screening method was applied to filter related articles. Articles with any of the following keywords, either in titles, abstracts, or keywords, were selected for review: "social media," "new media," "online," "Internet," "social network," "social networking," "blog," "microblog," "video," "Web," "Facebook," "Twitter," "crisis," and "crises." A total of 69 articles in ten journals exclusively focusing on SMCC were confirmed as directly relevant with the purpose of this study and short-listed for final content analysis. A total of 18 articles (26%) were randomly selected for a reliability check, and the result of composite intercoder reliability reached 0.91 by applying Krippendorff's alpha (Hayes & Krippendorff, 2007).

Table 1.1 provides an overview of the number of published articles in the journals. Among the total 69 articles drawn from the 10 journals, 38 articles (55%) were in *Public Relations Review* and 10 articles (14.5%) in the *Journal of Public Relations Research*, serving as major outlets for SMCC research. Findings also demonstrated an increasing attention to "SMCC" over the past 13 years, with only 9 articles (13%) published between 2002 and 2005, 32 articles (46%) published between 2007 and 2010, and a vast number of articles published from 2011 to May 2014 (28 articles, 41%).

TABLE 1.1 The Number of SMCC Research Articles in Each Journal

Source	No. of Articles			Total	%
	2002–2006	2007–2010	2011–2014		
Communication Research	–	1	–	1	1.5
Cyberpsychology & Behavior	–	1	–	1	1.5
Management Communication Quarterly	–	–	1	1	1.5
New Media & Society	2	1	1	4	6
Journal of Applied Communication Research	–	3	1	4	6
Journal of Communication	–	–	2	2	3
Journal of Computer-Mediated Communication	1	3	1	5	7
Journal of Contingencies and Crisis Management	1	–	2	3	4
Journal of Public Relations Research	–	7	3	10	14.5
Public Relations Review	5	16	17	38	55
Total	9	32	28	69	100

The Status of SMCC Research

Theoretical Framework

Findings suggested that 53 out of 69 (77%) articles applied a specific theory, among which the most frequently examined theory was image-repair theory (24%), followed by situational crisis communication theory (SCCT; 19%), frame theory or agenda-setting theory (15%), blog-mediated or social-mediated crisis communication model (10%), excellence theory (5%), attribution theory (4%), media system dependency theory (3%), users and gratifications (3%), diffusion of innovation (3%), contingency theory (3%), and others such as selective exposure theory and crisis leadership theory (11%).

Data also showed that, from 2002 to 2014, increasing studies applied either research questions (RQs) or hypotheses (Hs) or both. Generally, "RQs" (31 articles, 45%) was the most prevalent one, followed by "neither RQs nor Hs" (21 articles, 30%), "RQs and Hs" (11 articles, 16%), and "Hs" (6 articles, 9%).

Methodological Approach

Among the 69 articles listed in the SSCI, case studies (51 articles, 74%) dominated SMCC studies, with 41 (83%) single-case studies, and 10 (17%) multiple-case analyses. Some scholars conducted longitudinal studies with a sample of 92–120 cases (e.g., Schwarz & Pforr, 2011; Taylor & Perry, 2005). Most studies (66%) only used relatively basic statistical analyses (e.g., frequency, mean, and *SD*) instead of multivariable analyses (e.g., regression, MONOVA, and social network analysis). For research method, quantitative research was relatively more prominent in SMCC studies (46 articles, 67%) than qualitative research (21 articles, 30%). Mixed methods didn't appear until the year 2013 (2 articles, 3%). Specifically, quantitative content analysis (34%) and qualitative content analysis (24%) were the dominant methods, whereas experiment (13%), survey (13%), textual or discourse analysis (4%), interview (3%), focus group (3%), and multiple methods (6%) were not frequently shown.

Types of Research

Types of research refers to research focus, crisis type, time, and region. *Research focus* means the main subject of specific research (An & Cheng, 2007). In 2002–2006, articles in SSCI journals largely focused on the evaluation of crisis situations (e.g., the context, information processing, and whether the crisis is managed well or not; see, e.g., DiNardo, 2002), and suggestion of organizational crisis communication practice (strategies, form and source, and relationship; see, e.g., Taylor & Perry, 2005). After 2007, research subjects became more diverse and new focuses included the examination of effectiveness of crisis communication practice (e.g., Coombs & Holladay, 2009), media framing in crises (e.g., Hong, 2007; Littlefield &

Quenette, 2007), and building models and theories (e.g., Jin & Liu, 2010). Most importantly, greater interest was shown toward the "public." Public perception and media use (e.g., Cho & Hong, 2009) became the most dominant area (28 articles, 41%) in SMCC research. Discussions emphasized the public motivation for online media use, public strategies, emotions, engagement, identification, and generated online content in crises (Choi & Lin, 2009; Fortunato, 2011; Stephens & Malone, 2009; Tai & Sun, 2007).

As for *crisis type, time, and region*, data showed the most frequently studied crisis type was managerial misconduct crisis (20 articles, 29%), such as Mattel's product recall in 2007 and the melamine-contaminated milk powder of Sanlu in 2008. Other types included natural crises (e.g., Hurricane Irene in 2011; Hurricane Katrina & Rita in 2005), public health crisis (e.g., SARS in 2003; the flu pandemic in 2009), terrorism (e.g., September 11, 2001), rumors or hoaxes (e.g., Domino's YouTube crisis in 2009), business and economic crisis (the financial crisis in 2008), and technological failure (e.g., Y2K). These crises occurred from 1999 to 2011 and mostly took place in the United States (42 articles, 54%).

The Forms of SMCC Practice

For *crisis communication strategy* (CCS), several clear features manifested: first, the CCS spectrum, such as image-repair strategies (Benoit, 1997), crisis-response strategies (Coombs, 2007), and the corporate communication response model (Bradford & Garrett, 1995), still dominated SMCC research. Scholars frequently applied the traditional CCS, including denial (e.g., Veil, Sellnow, & Petrun, 2012), reduction of offensiveness (e.g., Schwarz, 2012), modification (e.g., Cho & Cameron, 2006), and excuse (Moody, 2011).

Second, strategies such as enhancing and transferring (Kim & Liu, 2012), stakeholder-based strategies such as diverting attention and ingratiation (Brown & Billing, 2013), and stakeholder-desired emotional and informational support strategies (Stephens & Malone, 2009) were added. The pattern of CCS has been particularly increasing with specific cases explored in China. Different from the recommended "two-way" symmetrical relationship in Western societies (Grunig, 1992), organizations in China tended to maintain a dominant and asymmetrical relationship with stakeholders (Tai & Sun, 2007; Veil & Yang, 2012). Strategies such as deception, lying, and offering briberies were utilized to cover up crises, manipulate the public, and reduce negative media exposure in crises such as the SARS epidemic and the Sanlu milk contamination crisis.

In sum, in both Western and Eastern contexts, SMCC research has realized the empowering function of social media (Tai & Sun, 2007; Veil & Yang, 2012). An accurate, transparent, and symmetrical "interact" strategy was suggested to accommodate the more involved public agenda. Scholars advised that in a two-way interaction model, organizations can effectively utilize certain characteristics of social media by connecting links of other stakeholders, paying more attention to citizen-generated content, adopting stakeholder-desired strategies, cultivating opinion leaders on social media, or creating textual or video responses online in the same way as the hoax was distributed for organizational legitimacy (Choi & Lin, 2009; Greer & Moreland, 2003; Stephens & Malone, 2009; Veil & Yang, 2012).

Forms of Response

Three traditional forms of response (i.e., timely, consistent, and active response forms) (Huang & Su, 2009) were frequently mentioned in the SMCC research. For instance, Liu and colleagues (2013) suggested that once a crisis began, organizations should proactively and immediately encourage key publics' participation in sharing crisis information published in television messages. Greer and Moreland (2003) showed that because of its well-designed webpage, United Airlines could respond immediately and consistently to the terrorist attacks of September 11, 2001.

Furthermore, "interactivity" was intensively discussed in 17 out of the 69 articles (25%). As social media allowed for interpersonal communication and emotional support, scholars recommended that organizations should have interactive dialogues with member of key publics online to improve crisis communication effectiveness (Gilpin, 2010; Macias, Hilyard, & Freimuth, 2009; Moody, 2011; Yang, Kang, & Johnson, 2010). For example, Yang and colleagues (2010) found dialogic communication could enhance public engagement in crisis communication, which, in turn, led to positive postcrisis perceptions.

Crisis Communication Effectiveness (CCE)

Among the several measurements for CCE (Huang, 2012), it was found that reputation was most frequently used (36%), followed by media publicity (31%), revenue reputation (11%), cost reduction (11%), and organizational-public relationship (11%).

Meanwhile, new measurements of CCE emerged from three dimensions. First, social media publicity was explored, including the number of posts or comments about crisis by valence; the number of visitors, followers, Rich Site Summary (RSS) subscribers, or crisis-related links to and from other sites; attributes of comments and posts; and word of mouth (e.g., Jin & Liu, 2010; Veil & Yang, 2012). Second, organizational-public relationship was extended by adding the organization-blogger relationship, blogger-follower relationship, and blogger-issue relationship. Finally, the economic value involved the reduction of negative public emotion (e.g., anger, confusion, fear, and sadness), increased account acceptance, key public awareness, and public engagement.

Reflection

In summary, findings reflected the situation that SMCC gradually made its way onto the academic agenda from 2002 to 2014. Studies focused on the

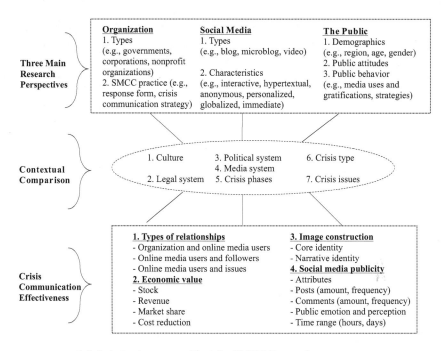

FIGURE 1.1 A Scholarly Assessment Tool for SMCC Research

"stakeholder." Characteristics of social media were advised to be utilized in a two-way interaction response form, and an accurate, transparent, and symmetrical CCS was suggested to accommodate the increasing powerful public agenda (Greer & Moreland, 2003).

Based on the review of relevant articles, we also found several weaknesses in the SMCC research, including a narrow content of research perspectives and sampling frames, a lack of emphasis on crisis phases or extending models and theories, and biased measure of CCE. As follows, critiques, suggestions, and a scholarly assessment tool (as shown in Figure 1.1) were offered for future studies in the field of SMCC.

To Add Types of Organizations, Social Media, and Stakeholders

Organizations, social media, and stakeholders, as three major research perspectives were clearly identified in the SMCC research (see Figure 1.1). For the types of organizations, it was found that governments or corporations were mostly discussed, whereas only 4 out of 69 articles (6%) discussed nonprofit organizations. Concerning to the types of social media, blog, Twitter, and Facebook were most discussed, whereas few scholars analyzed photos (e.g., Flickr), videos (e.g., You-Tube), virtual game worlds (e.g., World of Warcraft), and virtual social worlds (e.g., Second Life). Stakeholders in the SMCC research were frequently defined as homogeneous individuals (e.g., Stephens & Malone, 2009). Under this situation, more types of organizations should be added in. Future research should discuss how different types (e.g., YouTube or Twitter) or features (e.g., interactive, hypertexts, semi-public) of social media influence the crisis communication practice. We also suggest that the stakeholders with more diversified demographic information could be investigated in studies.

To Emphasize the Variable of Crisis Phases

It was found that only 12 out of 69 articles (17%) discussed time or phases in previous research, although in the practice, crisis time or phases played an important role in the crisis communication. Taylor and Kent (2007) suggested that real-time monitoring and proper strategies applied within a certain time or phase could effectively prevent a "look like" crisis or a "paracrisis" (Coombs, 2014; Coombs & Holladay, 2012). Especially with the rapid dissemination of information on social media, the length of crisis–response time of organizations has been greatly shortened. Given this, some scholars recommended an immediate time range of responses (Muralidharan, Dillistone, & Shin, 2011; Veil & Yang, 2012); Liu, Jin, Briones, and Kuch (2012) established a model suggesting how responding strategies varied in phases of rumor (i.e., generation, belief, rebuilt, and recovery). For example, instructing and adapting information should be applied in the earlier phase of rumor phases (generation); deny, diminish, reinforce, and punish in the middle phase (belief and transmission); and rebuild (compensation, apology) in the last phase (crisis recovery). However, little empirical research specifies a critical response time in the real scenario of crises. A longitudinal study to test the stability of existing patterns and possible changes over time becomes necessary. How the response time and strategy vary before, during, and after crises deserves more exploration.

To Improve the Measures of Crisis Communication Effectiveness (CCE)

As Crisis Communication Effectiveness (CCE) was an essential component of crisis communication research, scholars (Jin & Liu, 2010; Veil & Yang, 2012) continually provided insights for some new measures such as types of organizational-online public relationships, statistics traced through social media applications, and content analyzed variables (e.g., public engagement, account acceptance, key public awareness etc.). Future studies are encouraged, from the four dimensions as shown in Figure 1.1 (i.e., social media publicity, economic value, image construction, and relationships), to continuously look for a comprehensive measurement of CCE.

To Extend Models or Theories

By examining the impact of social media in crisis communication, scholars continuously contributed to the SMCC research: for instance, Choi and Lin (2009) added two types of emotion (attribute dependent and independent) into the SCCT model. Moody (2011) extended the image repair theory to the area of social media and found that, still, traditional image-repair strategies were applied to succeed. Based on the "networked crisis communication model," Utz and colleagues (2013) argued that the impact of media channels on the effectiveness of crisis communication were stronger than the effects of crisis types; blog-mediated crisis communication (BMCC; Jin & Liu, 2010) and SMCC models generated a strategic approach to understand the organization and audience via social media in crises (Austin, Liu, & Jin, 2012; Liu et al., 2012). However, the existing theoretical research (e.g., Austin et al., 2012) was either limited by having students serve as the sample elements or constrained with artificial experiment environments or a small sample size. Future research should advance the theoretical framework of SMCC within real case studies and help explore interesting research themes such as the interaction of traditional and social media for diffusion of information, the impact of word-of-mouth communication on public opinion, and the exact influence of a dialogic (positive or negative messages transmitted) communication on the crisis communication practice.

To De-Westernize the SMCC Research in a Global Context

By examining the variables such as crisis region or author's institutions, it was found that only 6 out of 69 articles (9%) discuss social media in crisis communication within a non-Western context (e.g., China, Korea); few authors belong to institutions from the Asian area. In contrast, large quantities of studies (91%) have primarily been developed in North American or European cultural contexts.

We thus suggest a de-Westernized approach in future SMCC research: first, as Cheng (2014) suggested, the Western (e.g., the United States) and non-Western countries (e.g., China) may differ in four dimensions, including cultural values (individualism vs. collectivism), political system (democracy vs. communism), media landscape (liberal vs. transitional), and level of public dependency on the Internet (low vs. high). These unique contextual factors may bring new theoretical perspectives with non-Western characteristics. For example, during the credibility crisis triggered by the Guo Meimei incident that occurred in the Chinese microblog, Cheng, Huang, and Chan (2017) extended the theorization of crisis communication strategies and the effects of agenda building by adding information about Chinese political and cultural characteristics.

Second, applying a de-Westernized approach does not mean rejecting or imperializing SMCC research. Instead, we are suggesting an equal dialogue between West and East and a mutual enriching chance to advance SMCC research in a cosmopolitan environment. As increasing crises occur in a global context with the widespread use of social media, it is expected that more cross-contextual or cross-cultural case studies could be conducted in the future and advance the theoretical or methodological framework in international communication (Cheng, 2014).

References

An, S. K., & Cheng, I. H. (2007). *Crisis communication research in public relations literature in 1975–2006.* Paper presented at the annual meeting of the National Communication Association, Chicago, IL.

Austin, L., Liu, B. F., & Jin, Y. (2012). How audiences seek out crisis information: Exploring the social-mediated crisis communication model. *Journal of Applied Communication Research, 40*(2), 188–207.

Benoit, W. (1997). Image repair discourse and crisis communication. *Public Relations Review, 23*(2), 177–186.

Bradford, J. L., & Garrett, D. E. (1995). The effectiveness of corporate communicative responses to accusation of unethical behavior. *Journal of Business Ethics, 14,* 875–892.

Brown, A. N., & Billings, A. C. (2013). Sports fans as crisis communicators on social media websites. *Public Relations Review, 39*(1), 74–81.

Bruns, A. (2005). *Gatewatching: Collaborative online news production.* New York: Peter Lane.

Burson-Marsteller, & PSB (Penn Schoen Berland). (2011, August). Reputation in the cloud era digital crisis communications study. Retrieved from http://www.slideshare.net/bmasia/bursonmarsteller-digital-crisis-communications-study

Cheng, Y. (2016). How social media is changing crisis communication strategies: Evidence from the updated literature. *Journal of Contingencies and Crisis Management.* doi: 10.1111/1468-5973.12130.

Cheng, Y. (2014, May). *The status of online crisis communication research in 1999–2013: A review and critique.* Paper presented in the 64th annual conference of the International Communication Association (ICA), Seattle, USA.

Cheng, Y., Huang, Y. H., & Chan, C. M. (2017). Public relations, media coverage, and public opinion in contemporary China: Testing agenda building theory in a social mediated crisis, *Telematics and Informatics, 34*(3), 765–773. doi:10.1016/j.tele.2016.05.012

Cho, S., & Cameron, G. T. (2006). Public nudity on cell phones: Managing conflict in crisis situations. *Public Relations Review, 32*(2), 199–201.

Cho, S., & Hong, Y. (2009). Netizens' evaluations of corporate social responsibility: Content analysis of CSR news stories and online readers' comments. *Public Relations Review, 35*(2), 147–149.

Choi, Y., & Lin, Y. (2009). Consumer responses to Mattel product recalls posted on online bulletin boards: Exploring two types of emotion. *Journal of Public Relations Research, 21*(2), 198–207.

Coombs, W. T. (2007). Protecting organization reputations during a crisis: The development and application of situational crisis communication theory. *Corporate Reputation Review, 10*(3), 163–176.

Coombs, W. T. (2014). State of crisis communication: Evidence and the bleeding edge. *Research Journal of the Institute for Public Relations, 1*(1), 1–12.

Coombs, W. T., & Holladay, S. J. (2009). Further explorations of post-crisis communication: Effects of media and response strategies on perceptions and intentions. *Public Relations Review, 35*(1), 1–6.

Coombs, W. T., & Holladay, S. J. (2012). The paracrisis: The challenges created by publicly managing crisis prevention. *Public Relations Review, 38,* 408–415.

DiNardo, A. M. (2002). The Internet as a crisis management tool: A critique of banking sites during Y2K. *Public Relations Review, 28*(4), 367–378.

Fearn-Banks, K. (2002). *Crisis communications: A casebook approach.* Mahwah, NJ: Lawrence Erlbaum Associates.

Fortunato, J. (2011). Dancing in the dark: Ticketmaster's response to its Bruce Springsteen ticket crisis. *Public Relations Review, 37*(1), 77–79.

Gilpin, D. (2010). Organizational image construction in a fragmented online media environment. *Journal of Public Relations Research, 22*(3), 265–287.

Greer, C. F., & Moreland, K. D. (2003). United Airlines' and American Airlines' online crisis communication following the September 11 terrorist attacks. *Public Relations Review, 29*(4), 427–441.

Grunig, J. E. (1992). *Excellence in public relations and communication management.* Hillsdale, NJ: Lawrence Erlbaum Associates, Inc.

Hallahan, K. (2009). Crises and risk in cyberspace. In R. L. Heath & H. Dan O'Hair (Eds.), *Handbook of risk and crisis communication.* (pp. 415–448). New York: Routledge.

Hayes, A. F., & Krippendorff, K. (2007). Answering the call for a standard reliability measure for coding data. *Communication Methods and Measures, 1,* 77–89.

Hong, T. (2007). Information control in time of crisis: The framing of SARS in China-based newspapers and Internet sources. *Cyberpsychology & Behavior, 10*(5), 696–699.

Howe, J. (2008). *Crowdsourcing: Why the power of the crowd is driving the future of business.* New York: Crown Business.

Huang, Y. H. (2012). Gauging an integrated model of Public Relations Value (PRVA): Scale development and cross-cultural studies. *Journal of Public Relations Research, 24,* 243–265.

Huang, Y. H., & Su, S. H. (2009). Determinants of consistent, timely, and active responses in corporate crises. *Public Relations Review, 35,* 7–17.

Jin, Y., & Liu, B. F. (2010). The blog-mediated crisis communication model: Recommendations for responding to influential external blogs. *Journal of Public Relations Research, 22*(4), 429–455.

Kaplan, A. M., & Haenlein, M. (2010). Users of the world, unite! The challenges and opportunities of social media. *Business Horizons, 53*(1), 59–68.

Kim, S., & Liu, B. F. (2012). Are all crises opportunities? A comparison of how corporate and government organizations responded to the 2009 Flu Pandemic. *Journal of Public Relations Research, 24*(1), 69–85.

Littlefield, R. S., & Quenette, A. M. (2007). Crisis leadership and hurricane Katrina: The portrayal of authority by the media in natural disasters. *Journal of Applied Communication Research, 35*(1), 26–47.

Liu, B. F., Jin, Y., & Austin, L. L. (2013). The tendency to tell: Understanding publics' communicative responses to crisis information form and source. *Journal of Public Relations Research, 25*(1), 51–67.

Liu, B. F., Jin, Y., Briones, R. L., & Kuch, B. (2012). Managing turbulence online: Evaluating the blog-mediated crisis communication model with the American Red Cross. *Journal of Public Relations Research, 24,* 353–370.

Macias, W., Hilyard, K., & Freimuth, V. (2009). Blog functions as risk and crisis communication during Hurricane Katrina. *Journal of Computer-Mediated Communication, 15*(1), 1–31.

Moody, M. (2011). Jon and Kate Plus 8: A case study of social media and image repair tactics. *Public Relations Review, 37*(4), 405–414.

Muralidharan, S., Dillistone, K., & Shin, J.-H. (2011). The gulf coast oil spill: Extending the theory of image restoration discourse to the realm of social media and beyond petroleum. *Public Relations Review, 37*(3), 226–232.

Schwarz, A. (2012). How publics use social media to respond to blame games in crisis communication: The love parade tragedy in Duisburg 2010. *Public Relations Review, 38*(3), 430–437.

Schwarz, A., & Pforr, F. (2011). The crisis communication preparedness of nonprofit organizations: The case of German interest groups. *Public Relations Review, 37*(1), 68–70.

Stephens, K. K., & Malone, P. C. (2009). If the organizations won't give us information . . . : The use of multiple new media for crisis technical translation and dialogue, *Journal of Public Relations Research, 21*(2), 229–239.

Tai, Z., & Sun, T. (2007). Media dependencies in a changing media environment: The case of the 2003 SARS epidemic in China. *New Media & Society, 9*(6), 987–1009.

Taylor, M., & Kent, M. L. (2007). Taxonomy of mediated crisis responses. *Public Relations Review, 33*(2), 140–146.

Taylor, M., & Perry, D. C. (2005). Diffusion of traditional and new media tactics in crisis communication. *Public Relations Review, 31*, 209–217.

Utz, S., Schultz, F., & Glocka, S. (2013). Crisis communication online: How medium, crisis type and emotions affected public reactions in the Fukushima Daiichi nuclear disaster. *Public Relations Review, 39*(1), 40–46.

Veil, S. R., Sellnow, T. L., & Petrun, E. L. (2012). Hoaxes and the paradoxical challenges of restoring legitimacy: Dominos' response to its YouTube Crisis. *Management Communication Quarterly, 26*(2), 322–345.

Veil, S. R., & Yang, A. (2012). Media manipulation in the Sanlu milk contamination crisis. *Public Relations Review, 38*(5), 935–937.

Yang, S.-U., Kang, M., & Johnson, P. (2010). Effects of narratives, openness to dialogic communication, and credibility on engagement in crisis communication through organizational blogs. *Communication Research, 37*(4), 473–497.

2

REVISING SITUATIONAL CRISIS COMMUNICATION THEORY

The Influences of Social Media on Crisis Communication Theory and Practice

W. Timothy Coombs

In the fall of 2008, an online advertisement for Motrin offended a number of mothers. The offended parties expressed their displeasure on Twitter by the hundreds. Johnson & Johnson responded by removing the advertisement from the Internet and apologizing to the people the company had offended (Learmouth, 2008). Originally called a Twitterstorm, the "Motrin Moms" eventually came to exemplify the concept of a social media crisis. A social media crisis is an event that transpires in or is amplified by social media (Owyang, 2011). Unfortunately, the definition of social media is far too vague and ultimately problematic for many crisis experts and researchers. However, the idea that social media are altering crisis communication is a reality (Coombs, 2015). The influences of social media on crisis communication should cause us to reflect upon existing crisis communication knowledge to determine if and how that knowledge should be updated.

Situational crisis communication theory (SCCT) is one of the dominant theories in crisis communication research (Avery, Lariscy, Kim, & Hocke, 2010). This chapter provides insight into how social media have influenced recent efforts to revise SCCT. The two primary points of intersection between social media and SCCT involve the increasing public nature of the precrisis phase and the selection of channels for crisis communication. Social media have exposed to public view once-private efforts to manage certain crisis risks. The visibility of crisis risk management warrants an extension of SCCT to the precrisis phase. With the proliferation of channels, the topic of channel selection becomes salient. However, before we can discuss how and why social media lead to modifications in SCCT, it is prudent to first consider the basic elements of SCCT.

Development of SCCT

The development of SCCT began in 1995 (Coombs, 1995) with publication of a decision tree for crisis communication in *Management Communication Quarterly*. The ideas were refined, and the first use of the title SCCT appeared in 2002 (Coombs & Holladay, 2002). The dates are relevant because the initial development and testing of SCCT predates the explosion of social media channels online. Hence, social media were not a part of the original conceptualization for SCCT. This book is a testament to the effect of social media on crisis communication. The current efforts to revise SCCT are cognizant of social media's effects on crisis communication.

Origins of SCCT

SCCT was driven by Benson's (1988) observation that we did not have a serious and systematic means of connecting crisis-response strategies (what crisis communicators say and do during a crisis) and crisis situations. By the late 1990s, researchers had identified lists of both crisis-response strategies and crisis types. What had yet to emerge was a theoretical framework to link crisis-response strategies and crisis types in a systematic manner. SCCT draws upon attribution theory to make the connection between crisis-response strategies and crisis types. Attribution theory holds that people seek reasons for events, especially negative events. People seek to understand why something has occurred. People attribute events to either external factors (situational concerns) or internal factors (something about the people involved in the event; Weiner, 1986). For instance, a favorite sports team loses. Was the loss a result of poor play and coaching (internal) or weather conditions and improper officiating (external)? The attributions are important because they shape how people feel about and react to the event (Weiner, 1995). SCCT argues that crises are negative events that lead people to make attributions about the crisis responsibility of the organization involved in the crisis.

Crisis responsibility, the degree to which stakeholders attribute responsibility for the crisis to the organization in crisis, is *the* pivotal variable in SCCT. SCCT posits that the amount of crisis responsibility generated by the crisis situation determines the nature of the crisis response that will be appropriate for the crisis. An appropriate response serves to protect the organization from reputational damage and from the desire of customers to stop using a product or service (Coombs, 2007).

SCCT recommends that crisis communicators examine the crisis type and the intensifying factors to assess the probable crisis responsibility stakeholders will attribute to the organization in crisis. Obviously, the crisis responsibility attributions will not be uniform across all stakeholders, but a general assessment of crisis responsibility can be established. The crisis type is the frame being used to interpret the crisis situation. Crisis types can be divided into three categories: minimal crisis responsibility, low crisis responsibility, and high crisis responsibility. Table 2.1 presents a more detailed list of the crisis types. Intensifying factors cause people to increase

TABLE 2.1 SCCT and Crisis Types

Minimal crisis responsibility

- Workplace violence: an attack on coworkers by current or former employees
- Malevolence: an outside attack on the organization such as product tampering or terrorism
- Natural disasters: operational disruptions from acts of nature
- Misinformation: harmful but inaccurate information about the organization in circulation among stakeholders

Low crisis responsibility

- Technical-error accidents: an accident created by a failure in technology
- Technical-error product harm: a defect and potentially dangerous product created due to a failure in technology

High crisis responsibility

- Human-error accidents: an accident created by the human error of employees
- Human-error product harm: a defect and potentially dangerous product created due to the human error of employees
- Organizational misdeed or management misconduct: stakeholders knowingly placed at risk or laws or regulations knowingly violated by managers

---

their attributions of crisis responsibility. Crisis history (whether or not an organization has had similar crises previously) and prior reputation (was the organization perceived unfavorably before the crisis) are proven intensifying factors (Coombs, 2007, Elliot, 2010). A history of crises or an unfavorable precrisis reputation will intensify stakeholder attributions of crisis responsibility. Intensifying factors matter most with crises that involve low levels of crisis responsibility. An intensifying factor would shift a crisis with a low level of crisis responsibility to crisis with a high level of crisis responsibility, thereby causing a significant shift in the appropriate crisis-response strategy. Both crises with minimal and low levels of crisis responsibility utilize similar response strategies requiring little shift of crisis-response strategies for crisis managers as one moves from minimal to low levels of crisis responsibility.

The revision of SCCT includes a reconceptualization of crisis types. Crisis management was designed to address operational concerns—the organization's ability to produce goods or deliver services. Sohn and Lariscy (2014) have documented a rise in reputational crises. The rise in reputational crises is due in large part to social media (Coombs, 2015). A reputational crisis is about situations that can erode an organization's reputation (Booth, 2000; Sohn & Lariscy, 2014). Obviously, operational crises create reputational damage, and reputational crisis might disrupt operations. However, there are conceptual and responsive differences between the two macrocategories of crisis types. In Table 2.1, only the misinformation crisis is a reputational crisis while the rest are operational crises.

The crisis-response strategies can be divided into instructing information, adjusting information, and reputation repair (Holladay, 2009; Sturges, 1994). Instructing information helps stakeholders to cope physically with a crisis. Product recall statements and evacuation signals are examples of instructing information. Adjusting information helps people cope psychologically with a crisis. Expressions of sympathy, corrective actions, information about the crisis event, counseling services, and to some degree compensation are examples of adjusting information (Holladay, 2009; Holladay & Coombs, 2013). SCCT refers to the combined use of adjusting and instructing information as the ethical base response. The ethical base response should be used any time a crisis creates victims, or those who suffer from the crisis in some way, and should be the first response offered by crisis managers (Coombs, 2015). For crises with minimal to low crisis responsibility, the ethical base response alone should be the appropriate response for protecting organizational assets.

There are three primary reputation-repair strategies presented in Table 2.2: denial, diminish, and rebuild. Denial strategies seek to disconnect the organization from the crisis. If the organization has no responsibility for the crisis, the crisis should not harm the organization (Benoit, 1995). Denial should be reserved for misinformation crises—when false information is being spread about an organization. Diminish strategies attempt to reinforce the view that the organization has low responsibility for the crisis. Rebuild strategies seek to create positive information about the organization and include apologies and compensation. Bolstering is considered a

TABLE 2.2 SCCT Crisis-Response Strategies

Denial

- Attack the accuser: confront those saying negative things about the organization
- Denial: deny any responsibility for the crisis
- Scapegoating: blame some other party for the crisis

Diminish

- Excuse: minimize organizational responsibility by denying the intention to do harm or denying the ability to control the situation
- Justification: attempt to minimize the perception of the damage inflicted by the crisis

Rebuild

- Compensation: give victims aid, material goods, or money
- Apology: publicly take responsibility for the crisis and ask for forgiveness

Bolstering

- Reminding: remind stakeholders of past organizational good works
- Ingratiating: praise stakeholders for helping during the crisis
- Victimage: indicate the organization is also a victim in the crisis

secondary strategy that should not be used alone. Bolstering involves attempts to flatter those who have helped with the crisis or to remind stakeholders of past good works by the organization (Benoit, 1995). As with rebuild strategies, the bolstering strategies attempt to create positive perceptions of the organization.

SCCT recommends that crisis managers match the crisis response to the attributions of crisis responsibility. As noted earlier, when attributions of crisis responsibility are minimal to low, the ethical base response is an effective crisis response. Diminish strategies can be added to crises with low crisis responsibility but add little to reputational protection. Diminish strategies have limited utility as they work best in technical-error accidents or product-harm crisis. There are very few accidents or product crises that are predominantly caused by technical errors. Rebuild strategies should be reserved for crises that generate strong attributions of crisis responsibility due to the high cost of those response strategies for the organization (Coombs, 2007; Tyler, 1997). Bolstering can be used in combination with any of the three primary crisis-response strategies.

SCCT was developed for the crisis-response phase of the crisis with an emphasis on organizational reputation as the primary outcome. However, SCCT also has used purchase intention, emotions, and negative word of mouth as outcome variables (Coombs, 2007). Channel selection and social media are not part of the original conceptualization and presentation of SCCT. In the next section, we consider why social media ferments the need for inclusion in and revision of SCCT.

Visibility of the Precrisis Phase

Historically, the precrisis phase was private and not viewed by the public. Precrisis activities include preparation and prevention or mitigation efforts. Crisis management plans typically are considered confidential documents, and external stakeholders will know little about crisis team training or even most mitigation efforts. However, social media have made certain types of prevention and mitigation efforts visible to external stakeholders due the increased occurrence of paracrises. For instance, stakeholders' claims that an organization is acting irresponsibly are becoming public events (Coombs & Holladay, 2012b).

Paracrises appear to be crises but are actually crisis risks that are being managed in public (Coombs & Holladay, 2012b). A paracrisis emerges when a crisis risk becomes public knowledge. Organizations are then faced with the decision of whether or not to engage the crisis risk and how to address the crisis risk if they decide to engage. There are three forms of paracrises: challenges, organizational faux pas, and angry customers.

The Challenge Paracrisis

Challenges emerge when stakeholders, often an activist group, publicly claim that an organization is operating in a socially irresponsible manner and should change that behavior. Lerbinger (1997) was the first to discuss crises that were based on challenges from external stakeholders. Initially these were called "challenge crises" (Coombs, 2015). However, the concept of the challenge crisis was underdeveloped until the articulation of the paracrisis. This section attempts to elaborate on the challenges that trigger paracrises and reveals the complexity of challenges.

Stakeholders have been questioning the practices of corporations since the advent of large corporations. Even excellence theory notes how, at times, activists must confront organizations in order for managers to realize the situation warrants their time and attention (Grunig & Grunig, 1992). Stakeholder challenges are on the rise (King, 2011), and social media make the challenges visible to other stakeholders, hence the emergence of paracrises. Prior to social media, activists would utilize media advocacy to pressure corporations. Media advocacy are attempts to attract traditional media coverage of the activists' concerns (Ryan, 1991). The problem is that the traditional media showed little interest in activists. Because they were marginalized, activists had to resort to extreme actions to garner media coverage. The problem with extreme media-advocacy efforts is that the media might cover the action but not discuss the concerns or issues behind the action, a common problem with uncontrolled media. For instance, the news might report on people hanging a banner from a building but not report on the reason for hanging the banner—the issue of concern to the activists (Coombs & Holladay, 2010).

The digital environment, especially social media channels, permits activists to use controlled media in their attempts to challenge corporations. Now activists could control how and when their messages would appear. The Greenpeace Detox campaign is a perfect illustration of the paracrisis. Greenpeace wants garment makers to stop using certain hazardous chemicals in their supply chains. Greenpeace uses YouTube videos, Facebook posts, tweets, and in-person protests to focus attention on garment makers that are using hazardous chemicals and that need to detox. Greenpeace has been very successful in getting large corporations to agree to detox after Greenpeace has initiated efforts to create paracrises (Coombs, 2014). We need to examine the paracrisis process more closely to determine why paracrises are on the rise, why they can succeed, and how they fit with SCCT.

Managers now accept that reputations are a valuable yet intangible assets (e.g., Deephouse, 2000; Turban & Cable, 2003). Management invests heavily in building positive reputations. Public relations is part of the reputation-building efforts of organizations (Hutton, Goodman, Alexander, & Genest, 2001). Managers seek to protect, as well as to build, reputations. Increasingly, corporate social responsibility (CSR) is a critical element of the corporate reputation. CSR accounts for over 40% of the corporate reputation and this percentage is likely to increase (CSR, 2012, Smith, 2012).

For a challenge to be a threat, current organizational behaviors must be redefined as irresponsible. Irresponsibility is a critical label because connecting the organization to irresponsible actions damages its reputation by questioning its commitment to CSR. Lange and Washburn (2012) argue that perceptions of irre-sponsibility are explained by attribution theory. Their model is called the model of corporate social irresponsibility attributions. The model begins with the basic assumption that people spontaneously make causal attributions and assign blame predicated upon those causal analyses, the same foundation found in SCCT. There are three parts to the model of corporate social irresponsibility: (a) stakeholders realize there is an undesirable outcome, (b) stakeholders attribute responsibility for the undesirable outcome to the corporation, and (c) stakeholders believe that the victims of the undesirable outcome could do nothing to prevent its occurrence. A challenge begins with stakeholders identifying an undesirable social outcome, such as child slave labor. Then the stakeholders seek to link the undesirable out-come to the organization's current behavior. For instance, current cocoa-sourcing practices facilitate child slave labor among cocoa plantations and are allowed to exist because corporations still buy from these abusive suppliers. Finally, stakehold-ers must argue that the victims are helpless to prevent the undesirable outcome. In our example, the children and their families cannot stop the child slave-labor practices. If these three steps are successful, people will attribute irresponsibility to the organization, thereby potentially damaging its reputation. This is the exact process Green America used to link the Hershey Company to child slave labor in its cocoa supply chain (Coombs, 2014).

The perception of irresponsibility is an attributional process and shares a natural connection with the attribution theory roots of SCCT. Charges that a corporation is acting irresponsibly can become a threat to corporate reputation. If stakeholders think the organization is acting irresponsibly, the organization's reputation can be damaged. This is similar to corporate reasoning for wanting favorable media cov-erage and seeking to reduce or avoid negative media coverage (Cancel, Cameron, Sallot, & Mitrook, 1997).

As with traditional media coverage, negative comments in social media can be damaging to corporate reputations (McCorkindale & DiStaso, 2013). Social media can be used as a direct route to the corporate reputation as it replaces the indi-rect route through traditional media gatekeepers. Again, merely employing social media to criticize corporate behavior does not guarantee other stakeholders will see, care about the message, or add to the call for change culminating in corporate reform (Coombs & Holladay, 2010). However, the paracrisis creates a different dynamic for the challenge by adding public visibility to managing a crisis risk.

Organizational crises can be reputational, as well as operational (Coombs, 2015; Sohn & Lariscy, 2014). Charges of corporate irresponsibility promoted in social media are a risk that could escalate into a reputational crisis. Having stakeholders perceive a corporation as irresponsible does damage to the corporate reputation. The confluence of the value of CSR as a component of reputation and social media as forums for presenting claims of irresponsibility provides the ideal environment of incubating paracrises. When faced with public charges of irresponsibility, man-agers must decide how best to respond to the situation. If the threat is too low, managers can simply ignore the challenge. But the question becomes, how does a challenge create a serious enough crisis threat to warrant a reaction from the organization under attack?

Challenges related to irresponsibility are designed to pressure organizations into changing their operations. Stakeholders want certain practices or policies, such as irresponsible raw material sourcing, to be changed. To create change, the challenge must pose a serious enough threat to the organization's reputation to warrant consideration. Challenges are predicated on organizations seeking to protect reputations and avoiding the label of irresponsible. Organizations will modify their operations when the valued organizational reputation asset is at risk (Coombs & Holladay, 2002). Informed by Mitchell, Agle, and Wood's (1997) criteria for stakeholder salience, reputational threats can be defined as a function of power, legitimacy, and urgency. Power is the ability of the stakeholders to threaten a reputation. Can the challenging stakeholders really damage the organization's reputation? Legitimacy is the willingness of other stakeholders to accept the challenge as worthy of their support and the recognition of the challenger's right to advance the challenge. Will other stakeholders support the challenge? Urgency is the level of commitment the stakeholders have for the challenge and the spread of the challenge to other stakeholders. Is the challenge being effectively pushed to other stakeholders? These three factors are used to unpack the four primary elements of paracrises: challenging stakeholders, the challenge, the challenged organization, and the challenge response.

Both contingency theory and Internet contagion theory (ICT) inform the analysis of challenges and stakeholder salience. Contingency theory examines a multitude of internal and external factors that shape how organizations respond to conflicts with stakeholders. The responses vary from accommodative (give stakeholders what they want) to advocacy (arguing against the stakeholder demands; Cameron, Pang, & Jin, 2008). The external factors used to assess threats are applicable to challenges. ICT explains how stakeholders utilize online communication resources in attempts to change their power relationship with organizations. ICT can be used to explain how stakeholders can leverage online communication to push organizations into changing policies or behaviors (Coombs & Holladay, 2012a). Table 2.3 provides summary of the four key variables in a challenge and their connections to power, legitimacy, and urgency (the threat assessment). Table 2.3 includes the relationship to each element of contingency theory and ICT, as well as others to be used when assessing the threat posed by a challenge and a list of response options. The ideas of stakeholder salience, threats from contingency theory, and ICT provide insights into four factors that compose the challenge dynamic.

Challenging stakeholders are the ones initiating the paracrisis. Power, legitimacy, and urgency are all important to the challenging stakeholders. If challenging stakeholders do not establish their power, organizations are likely to ignore them. Table 2.3 presents the contingency theory and ICT factors that are relevant for

TABLE 2.3 Contingency Theory and Internet Contagion Theory Influences on Challenges

Challenge Variables	Core Threat Factors	Contingency Theory	ICT	Constraints	Response Options
Challengers	Power	• Number of supporters • Past success • Hired communication consultants	• Number of communication channels • Structure of communication channels		
	Legitimacy Urgency	• Credibility • Commitment to the issue • Willingness to dilute the cause			
Challenge	Legitimacy		• Quality of messages • Utilization of legitimacy resources	Type of challenge • Expose • Organic	
	Urgency		• Crossover to traditional and in-person • Communicative skill		
Challenged Organization	Power	• Power relative to challenger power		Constraints • Cost • Strategy • Feasibility • CSR use	
Corporate Response					• Refusal • Refutation • Reform • Recognition or Reception • Repression • Revision

establishing the power of challenging stakeholders. Power is enhanced through the number of supporters, past successful challenges, the hiring of communication consultants, and the number and variety of communication channels utilized. Legitimacy involves the connection between the challenger and the issue—does it seem appropriate that the challenger is representing a particular social or environment issue (Coombs, 1998)? Contingency theory refers to this as credibility. Urgency is the commitment to the issue, unwillingness to dilute the cause, crossover into traditional media and in-person activities, and skill in structuring the communication effort. If a challenger will not yield, the threat could be long term because of the commitment to the cause (Cameron et al., 2008).

The challenge is the actual cause or concern being raised by the challengers. The challenge is the behavior or policies that have been identified as being irresponsible. Legitimacy is the core of the challenge. Other stakeholders must accept that the challenge worthy of their support—that is, they must believe the behavior or policy is irresponsible. As noted in Table 2.3, challenger legitimacy is a function of message quality and utilization of legitimacy resources. If a message is unprofessional, people are likely to dismiss it without too much analysis. Hence, a quality message is one that is professionally presented. For example, the posts are not poorly written or do not include misspellings. Legitimacy resources are the various ways to build legitimacy, including endorsements from legitimate sources, use of logical evidence (statistical data) to support claims, and the emotions evoked from concern. Child slave labor can be used as an example. A respected source from the United Nations could endorse the concern, data about the number of children in slave labor worldwide establish logical support, and the emotional stories of those in child slave labor reinforce the importance of the concern—that is, they give people another reason to care about the concern.

The challenge can affect urgency, too. Crossover to traditional media expands the number of stakeholders exposed to the challenge and increases the potential for reputational damage. In-person activities demonstrate commitment to the cause (Coombs & Holladay, 2012a). The challenge paracrisis can be organic (Coombs, 2010). An organic challenge arises over time as the values and beliefs of stakeholders change, leading them to expect different behavior from the corporation. This is a natural process wherein corporate behavior can lag behind stakeholder expectations as the stakeholders and corporations drift apart in terms of expectations.

The challenged organization is the target for the challenge. The two critical factors are the relative power of the organization and its prior use of CSR in building its reputation. An organization that is much more powerful than the challenger stands a better chance of convincing stakeholders to accept its side of the cause (Cameron et al., 2008). If the organization uses CSR to build its reputation, a challenge of social irresponsibility is more urgent because it is a greater threat to the reputation. An organization that professes to back CSR creates certain expectations. The challenge can indicate a violation of expectations, and that can create a crisis (Sohn & Lariscy, 2015).

Challenged organizations are bound by at least four constraints: strategy, cost, feasibility, and prior CSR efforts. Management does not want to change practices or policies that deviate from their core strategy. If the challenge requires an organization to shift strategy, management is likely to reject the challenge (Coombs, 2010). Cost is a common driver in risk management. Organizations do not pursue risk reduction that is too costly or a risk reduction effort that lacks feasibility. Risk reduction needs to be at the right price and have a strong likelihood of being effective (Coombs, 2015). Similarly, organizations will reject challenges that will be cost prohibitive or problematic, from their perspective, to enact. Finally, CSR efforts create expectations for future actions. Managers must make every effort to be consistent with their CSR claims or risk offending stakeholders by being hypocritical. Organizations that have little invested in CSR do not generate the same type of expectations (Sohn & Lariscy, 2015). Creating expectations for being socially responsible is a constraint for a challenge that is CSR based.

When faced with a challenge crisis, managers have six broad strategic responses: refusal, refutation, repression, recognition or reception, revision, and reform. Refusal is when managers ignore the challenge and offer no response. Refutation seeks to demonstrate the challenge is invalid; managers argue that they are compliant with key stakeholder expectations. The substrategies are denial with evidence and dispute. Denial with evidence claims there is no violation and provides evidence of how the corporation is meeting important stakeholder expectations. Perhaps the situation is a result of a lack of awareness or a misinterpretation of actual organizational behaviors. Dispute can involve debating the merits of the expectations. The corporate managers argue that the expectations are invalid—that most of their stakeholders do not hold the violated expectations. Hence, no change is necessary because the violated expectation is limited to small group of stakeholders who lack salience. Part of the dispute response includes efforts to marginalize the challenging stakeholders. It is important to note that any denial will intensify the reputational damage if the expectation violation is later proven to be true.

Repression involves efforts to stop the challenge from spreading. Managers take actions to prevent challengers from communicating about the concern. Lawsuits are a typical strategy organizations use to silence critics (Coombs & Holladay, 2010). People fear the cost of a lawsuit, hence the mere threat of a lawsuit can silence challengers. Repression, however, can be a pyrrhic victory. Repression precludes the free flow of ideas, a foundational element of free speech and democracy. Repression tactics can create a backlash as other stakeholders express their displeasure over such a harsh response.

Recognition or reception is when managers acknowledge the concerns expressed by stakeholders and that a problem exists. However, the organization takes no action designed to address the problem. Revision involves managers making minor modifications that are consistent with the demands being made by the challenging stakeholders. Moreover, managers do not acknowledge the challenges when they discuss the revisions. There is a purposeful attempt not to mention the challenge that precipitated the changes.

Reform has managers note there is a problem and that they are working with stakeholders to overcome the expectation violation. The violation is legitimized and the corporation is taking action to change behaviors. By partnering with the stakeholders who identified the violation, other stakeholders can have increased confidence that the solution will indeed correct the expectation violation.

Organizational Faux Pas

Faux pas are a second form of paracrisis and are unrelated to challenges. Managers often misuse social media, create messages that offend stakeholders, or both. We can call these paracrises organizational faux pas (Coombs, 1995). For instance, American Apparel uses a hashtag related to Superstorm Sandy to advertise a sale. These are embarrassing situations that have some potential to become crises. However, the response can be simple if the organization apologizes and promises not to repeat the mistake. The situation is an issue of competence. Research demonstrates that apology is an extremely effective response to competency-based problems (Kim, Ferrin, Cooper, & Dirks, 2004).

Angry Customers

Customers can get angry when a product or service violates their expectations. This is commonly known as a customer complaint. The customer relations literature informs us that an organization should seek to resolve the complaint in order to retain the customer (Davidow, 2003; Tax & Brown, 1998). Hence, the response to a paracrisis related to customer service is an attempt to resolve the complaint. Customers are even angrier when they seek revenge. With revenge, the customer just wants to hurt the organization in some way and is not looking to have his or her complaint resolved (Grégoire, Laufer, & Tripp, 2010). Recognition or reception is about the only option that is viable. By recognizing the problem, the organization may help to reduce the anger to some degree.

Summary

Paracrises have altered the crisis-communication process by making crisis risk management visible to stakeholders. The organization has to decide whether or not to engage in a crisis risk, and how they decide to address the risk can be performed in public view. SCCT has been modified to include a new section that examines paracrises. As with crisis responses, the nature of the paracrisis is used to help determine the paracrisis response that should best mitigate the crisis risk. Table 2.4 presents a summary of the SCCT recommendations for paracrisis responses along with the SCCT recommendations for crisis responses.

TABLE 2.4 SCCT Communication Recommendations

For paracrises

- Customer service: corrective action and apology
- Customer revenge: recognition or reception by acknowledging the concern
- Faux pas: corrective action and apology
- Challenge
  - Refusal: for use when stakeholders have no salience
  - Refutation: for use when there is a need to protect the current practices
  - Repression: for use only when there is a need to stop the flow of inaccurate information
  - Reform: for use when it is cost effective, consistent with organizational strategy, and feasible
  - Recognition or reception: for use when an organization wants to acknowledge a problem but cannot take action on the problem due to constraints, especially feasibility
  - Revision: for use when it is cost effective, fits strategy, and feasible

For crisis response

- The ethical base response is used any time there are victims.
- Diminish strategies *can* be added when the attributions of crisis responsibility are minimal.
- Apology or compensation *should be* added to the ethical base response when attributions of crisis responsibility are likely to be strong.
- Denial is used *only* when there is a misinformation crisis.
- Bolstering can be used in combination with any other strategy.
- Victimage should only be used when the crisis is caused by some external factor.

Channel Selection

Channel selection is a common topic in corporate communication that is relevant to public relations, advertising, and marketing communication. SCCT did not explicitly examine channel selection. It was assumed that crisis managers would utilize traditional media coverage (the focus on media relations) and controlled channels, such as websites, during a crisis (Taylor & Kent, 2007). Given the variety of channels that are emerging in the digital world, SCCT should provide a more direct discussion of channel selections. The channels discussion needs to consider the general goals of public safety and welfare and reputation repair found in crisis communication. Public safety and welfare combines the goals of protecting stakeholders physically and psychologically from a crisis because the two often are intertwined (Holladay, 2009).

Public safety and welfare seek to protect stakeholders from the myriad ways in which a crisis might harm them. Channel selection for public safety and welfare should, as a rule, use every channel available. The goal is to help stakeholders, and organizational messages cannot help stakeholders if stakeholders do not encounter the message. True, a shotgun approach will lead to overlap of target audiences and people receiving messages multiple times. But overlap and repetition is a good thing given the objective of protecting stakeholders. Moreover, the relatively low cost of social media channels should encourage the use of all these new channels during a crisis. Why refrain from using any channel if that channel might help protect even a few more people from the crisis?

Reputation repair creates a situation where crisis managers can be more selective in channel selection. Reputation messages should appear in channels that the target stakeholders are most likely to use. For instance, customers often use Twitter, so a Twitter feed might be a place for a reputation-repair message. The problem is that Twitter is limited to 140 characters. All crisis communication involving social media should use a hub-and-spoke design. The organizational website is the hub. The website is a controlled medium and can contain massive amounts of information if necessary. The social media channels should be the spokes. Links should be provided in the social media channels that take the stakeholder to the more detailed information on the website. Although Twitter has character limits, the other social media channels have conventions for writing that may not permit long discussion of key issues in the crisis. Hence, any social media channel might find the use of links for more information valuable.

SCCT offers the following channel recommendations:

1. When the communication objective involves public safety and welfare, use every channel at the organization's disposal.
2. When the communication objective is reputation repair, use the channels that are best for reaching the target stakeholders.
3. A hub-and-spoke design is ideal for crisis communication, with the organization's website serving as the hub and social media channels as the spokes.

Conclusion

If we return to the Motrin Moms example from the introduction, it becomes clear this situation is a paracrisis rather than a crisis. The example demonstrates the need for managers to address crisis risks publicly. The public exposure of crisis-risk mitigation efforts was a key driver for SCCT revisions presented in this chapter. The first revision involved SCCT being extended to the precrisis phase. The types of paracrises were analyzed and linked to response strategies. The same focus on situational factors determining effective responses from SCCT was utilized in the precrisis extension of SCCT.

The second revision to SCCT presented in this chapter involved an explicit statement of social media selection as part of the crisis response. Crisis managers must be cognizant of their social media choices and utilization during a crisis. The two revisions to SCCT reflect the growing importance of social media in crisis communication. Crisis managers must integrate social media into their crisis communication efforts or they will fail to maximize the value communication can add to crisis management efforts.

References

Avery, E. J., Lariscy, R. W., Kim, S., & Hocke, T. (2010). A quantitative review of crisis communication research in public relations from 1991 to 2009. *Public Relations Review, 36*(2), 190–192.

Benoit, W. L. (1995). *Accounts, excuses, and apologies: A theory of image restoration.* Albany: State University of New York Press.

Benson, J. A. (1988). Crisis revisited: An analysis of strategies used by Tylenol in the second tampering episode. *Communication Studies, 39*(1), 49–66.

Booth, S. A. (2000). How can organisations prepare for reputational crises?. *Journal of Contingencies and Crisis Management, 8*(4), 197–207.

Cameron, G. T., Pang, A., & Jin, Y. (2008). Contingency theory: Strategic management of conflict in public relations. In T. L. Hansen-Horn & B. D. Neff, (Eds.), *Public relations: From theory to practice* (pp. 134–155). Boston, MA: Pearson.

Cancel, A. E., Cameron, G. T., Sallot, L. M., & Mitrook, M. A. (1997). It depends: A contingency theory of accommodation in public relations. *Journal of Public Relations Research, 9*(1), 31–63.

Coombs, W. T. (1995). Choosing the right words: The development of guidelines for the selection of the "appropriate" crisis response strategies. *Management Communication Quarterly, 8,* 447–476.

Coombs, W. T. (1998). The Internet as potential equalizer: New leverage for confronting social irresponsibility. *Public Relations Review, 24,* 289–304.

Coombs, W. T. (2007). Attribution theory as a guide for post-crisis communication research. *Public Relations Review, 33,* 135–139.

Coombs, W. T. (2010). Sustainability: A new and complex "challenge" for crisis managers. *International Journal of Sustainable Strategic Management, 2,* 4–16.

Coombs, W. T. (2014). *Applied crisis communication and crisis management.* Thousand Oaks, CA: Sage Publications.

Coombs, W. T. (2015). *Ongoing crisis communication: Planning, managing, and responding* (4th ed.). Thousand Oaks, CA: Sage Publications.

Coombs, W. T., & Holladay, S. J. (2002). Helping crisis managers protect reputational assets: Initial tests of the situational crisis communication theory. *Management Communication Quarterly, 16,* 165–186.

Coombs, W. T., & Holladay, S. J. (2010). *PR strategy and application: Managing influence.* Malden, MA: Wiley-Blackwell.

Coombs, W. T., & Holladay, S. J. (2012a). Internet contagion theory 2.0: How Internet communication channels empower stakeholders. In S. Duhé (Ed.), *New media and public relations* (2nd ed., pp. 21–30). New York: Peter Lang.

Coombs, W. T., & Holladay, J. S. (2012b). The paracrisis: The challenges created by publicly managing crisis prevention. *Public Relations Review, 38*(3), 408–415.

CSR is not dead, it is just mismanaged. (2012). Retrieved from http://www.reputation institute.com/thought-leadership/csr-reptrak-100

Davidow, M. (2003). Organizational responses to customer complaints: What works and what doesn't. *Journal of Service Research, 5*(3), 225–250.

Deephouse, D. L. (2000). Media reputation as a strategic resource: An integration of mass communication and resource-based theories. *Journal of Management, 26*(6), 1091–1112.

Elliot, J. D. (2010). How do past crises affect publics' perceptions of current events? An experimental testing corporate reputation during an adverse event. In W. T. Coombs & S. J. Holladay (Eds.), *The handbook of crisis communication* (pp. 205–220). Malden, MA: Wiley-Blackwell.

Grégoire, Y., Laufer, D., & Tripp, T. M. (2010). A comprehensive model of customer direct and indirect revenge: Understanding the effects of perceived greed and customer power. *Journal of the Academy of Marketing Science, 38*(6), 738–758.

Grunig, J. E., & Grunig, L. (1992). Models of public relations and communication. In J. E. Grunig (Ed.), *Excellence in public relations and communication management* (pp. 285–325). Hillsdale, NJ: Lawrence Erlbaum Associates.

Holladay, S. J. (2009). Crisis communication strategies in the media coverage of chemical accidents. *Journal of Public Relations Research, 21*, 208–215.

Holladay, S. J., & Coombs, W. T. (2013). Successful prevention may not be enough: A case study of how managing a threat triggers a threat. *Public Relations Review, 39*(5), 451–458.

Hutton, J. G., Goodman, M. B., Alexander, J. B., & Genest, C. M. (2001). Reputation management: The new face of corporate public relations?. *Public Relations Review, 27*(3), 247–261.

Kim, P. H., Ferrin, D. L., Cooper, C. D., & Dirks, K. T. (2004). Removing the shadow of suspicion: The effects of apology vs. denial for repairing ability- vs. integrity-based trust violations. *Journal of Applied Psychology, 89*(1), 104–118.

King, B. G. (2011). The tactical disruptiveness of social movements: Sources of market and mediated disruption in corporate boycotts. *Social Problems, 58*(4), 491–517.

Lange, D., & Washburn, N. T. (2012). Understanding attributions of corporate social irresponsibility. *Academy of Management Review, 37*(2), 300–326.

Learmouth, M. (2008). How Twittering critics brought down Motrin moms campaign. Retrieved from http://adage.com/article/digital/twittering-critics-brought-motrin-mom-campaign/132622/

Lerbinger, O. (1997). *The crisis manager: Facing risk and responsibility.* Mahwah, NJ: Lawrence Erlbaum.

McCorkindale, T., & DiStaso, M. (2013). The power of social media and its influence on corporate reputation. In C. Carroll (Ed.), *The handbook of communication and corporate reputation* (pp. 497–512). Malden, MA: Wiley-Blackwell.

Mitchell, R. K., Agle, B. R., & Wood, D. J. (1997). Toward a theory of stakeholder identification and salience: Defining the principle of who and what really counts. *Academy of Management Review, 22*(4), 853–886.

Owyang, J. (2011). Social media crises on rise: Be prepared by climbing the social business hierarchy of needs. Retrieved from http://www.web-strategist.com/blog/2011/08/31/report-social-media-crises-on-rise-be-prepared-by-climbing-the-social-business-hierarchy-of-needs/

Ryan, C. (1991). *Prime time activism: Media strategies for grassroots organizing*. Boston, MA: South End Press.

Smith, J. (2012). The companies with the best CSR reputation. Retrieved from http://www.forbes.com/sites/jacquelynsmith/2012/12/10/the-companies-with-the-best-csr-reputations/

Sohn, Y. J., & Lariscy, R. W. (2014). Understanding reputational crisis: Definition, properties, and consequences. *Journal of Public Relations Research, 26*(1), 23–43.

Sohn, Y. J., & Lariscy, R. W. (2015). A "buffer" or "boomerang?"—The role of corporate reputation in bad times. *Communication Research, 42*(2), 237–259.

Sturges, D. L. (1994). Communicating through crisis: A strategy for organizational survival. *Management Communication Quarterly, 7*, 297–316.

Tax, S. S., & Brown, S. W. (1998). Recovering and learning from service failure. *Sloan Management Review, 40*(1). Retrieved from http://sloanreview.mit.edu/article/recovering-and-learning-from-service-failure/

Taylor, M., & Kent, M. L. (2007). Taxonomy of mediated crisis response. *Public Relations Review, 33*, 140–146.

Turban, D. B., & Cable, D. M. (2003). Firm reputation and applicant pool characteristics. *Journal of Organizational Behavior, 24*(6), 733–751.

Tyler, L. (1997). Liability means never being able to say you're sorry: Corporate guilt, legal constraints, and defensiveness in corporate communication. *Management Communication Quarterly, 11*(1), 51–73.

Weiner, B. (1986). *An attributional theory of motivation and emotion*. New York: Springer Verlag.

Weiner, B. (1995). *Judgments of responsibility: A foundation for a theory of social conduct*. New York: Guilford Press.

SECTION II

Current Issues of Social Media and Crisis Communication

3

COMMUNICATING STRATEGIC CHANGE

The Continuum of Reputation, Issues Management, and Crisis Management Is Built on a Positive Corporate Culture

Michael B. Goodman

The ability to adapt to change is clearly apparent in the way a corporation manages events and situations that are beyond its control. These events reveal the manifestations of the corporation's culture along a continuum of strategies, from reputation management to issues management to crisis management. In the face of uncertainty, the leaders of corporations now look internally for the strategies to maintain their companies as high-performing organizations. For example, they create a strong customer-centric culture, promote agility and flexibility in their organizational design to reflect rapidly changing business needs, create and maintain a culture of accountability, support a culture of innovation and entrepreneurship that learns from failure, empower employees to make appropriate decisions and execute effectively, and raise employee engagement to drive productivity (Ray, 2015). Social media offer an additional, powerful management tool to implement reputation, issues, and crisis messages and initiatives. Each one of these functions is related to the others and they often blend into one another. The success of each of these communication management initiatives is built on the foundation of a positive corporate culture.

Corporate Culture and Sustainable Change Management

Terrence Deal and Allen Kennedy popularized the term "corporate culture"[1] in 1982 with the publication of their book *Corporate Cultures: The Rites and Rituals of Corporate Life*. The assumptions that form the foundation for a corporate culture are often intuitive, invisible, or just below the level of awareness. Human groups, in an anthropologist's terms, by their nature have a culture—the system of values and beliefs shaped by the experiences of life, historical tradition, social or class position, political events, ethnicity, and religious forces. In this context, a corporation is no exception. Its culture can be described, understood, nurtured, and coaxed in new directions. But rarely can a corporate culture be created, planned, or managed in the same way that a company creates a product or service. Analyzing the culture of a corporation, when appropriately done, offers powerful insights into the organization's beliefs, values, and behavior.

In analyzing a corporation's culture, they provided the following descriptive terms:

- *artifacts and patterns of behavior*, which can be observed but whose meaning is not readily apparent;
- *values and beliefs*, which require an even greater level of awareness; and
- *basic assumptions* about human activity, human nature, and human relationships, as well as assumptions about time, space, and reality.

For corporate communication executives, the central functions of the corporation remain, but they are in the hands of a greatly reduced central staff—much like an orchestra—surrounding the CEO. The management "span of control" numbers are greatly increased. The challenges, mitigated by the ubiquity of the Web and digital communication, remain:

- To create a unified culture and vision for the corporation that can be shared by increasing numbers of specialists, complicated by the globalization forces over the last three decades that have negated the contract between the individual and the corporation—much as the "job for life" has disappeared for two generations of corporate employees.
- To motivate the corporation through career opportunities, rewards, and recognition; these traditional human resources (HR) functions now seem more difficult when employees owe no loyalty to the corporation, but their effort is critical to the organization's success.
- To create a structure that can get work done with a mobile workforce spread over many time zones.
- To create managers who understand that the new communication environment has long since abandoned the "command and control" model of internal communication for the "inform and influence" model and the "be informed and be influenced" model that can work with new forms of social media and the Web.

What is the source of successful organizations that have sustained performance over a long period? The economy? Luck? Corporate excellence?

In this environment of forces that buffet corporations constantly, the sustainable companies are resilient. Such corporations set goals and meet them through professional performance and execution of strategies, supported by a workforce that understands its common vision and shared values. They align their employees with a common purpose. They understand that to accomplish that, they must reinvent themselves as the environment demands and recruit and retain people who are resilient and drive for renewal. This process is illustrated in "Case Study: Ethnography, Corporate Culture, and Transformation" in Goodman and Hirsch's (2015) book, *Corporate Communication: Critical Business Asset for Strategic Global Change* (p. 178–179). In an interview, Pierre Beaudoin, CEO of Bombardier, explains how he transformed his engineering-driven aerospace company into a world-class culture by focusing on customer expectations, teamwork, and continuous improvement (Simpson, 2011). Beaudoin explained that first, he gained consensus among his management team about the definition of the problem. Then he surveyed his employees to understand how to talk to them about the problem so they could know clearly what the organization valued. He also had to change the management culture so that people would be able to confront facts and face up to issues without blaming one another. To accomplish this, change involved breaking down silos, as well as replacing the "culture where we valued the 'firefighter,' the person who would step on everybody but get the job done in a crisis" with one that valued teamwork. He recognized that aerospace is, as Deal and Kennedy called it, a "bet-the-company" culture, one that involves very long-term thinking. He then set three priorities: "creating a rewarding and safe workplace, providing superior customer service, and reducing waste in everything we do." He also identified four leadership skills to make that happen: "people first, teamwork, continuous improvement, drive for results."

This example from Bombardier illustrates that to become sustainable, companies must create and nourish viable corporate cultures, as well as robust processes and metrics to monitor their success, and take corrective actions when needed. Corporations and organizations shape and influence the behavior of individuals in subtle, yet powerful, ways. These forces, like the wind and the tides in natural environments, are often unseen and unnoticed themselves, but their effects can easily be observed. These forces combine to create the culture of a corporation.

Reputation Management[2]

Over the past two decades, most multinational corporations have established formal or semiformal systems of reputation management. However, there is a wide divergence in how individual companies define reputation management and the processes they use for doing so. Although it is not the most commonly observed model, reputation management properly includes both defensive and offensive elements. Defensive actions, such as crisis communication, mean the ways in which some companies use careful monitoring of emerging issues to plan actions designed to avoid any negative impact on the company's reputation. Offensive actions are all those methods that companies use to enhance their corporate reputations.

It is very important that reputation management not become a passive, box-checking exercise. Although it is clearly of some value to management leaders to be able to show their boards of trustees improving numbers on widely read reputation lists, such as Fortune's "Most Admired Companies," performance improvement in reputation requires a more hands-on approach.

A "campaign" approach to reputation is preferable, and the campaign should be reviewed and refreshed annually. The review process forces those people responsible for reputation in the corporation to be very specific about their objectives. Putting a schedule in place for the campaign helps make this possible. Reputation management goals and objectives can be put in the corporate strategic plan for the coming fiscal year as part of the same corporate planning cycles for revenue growth, new product launches, and profitability targets. Having annually revised reputation goals also helps keep such programs fresh and attuned to changing market realities.

Various reputation measurement metrics are in use today. Most of them are based on asking a select subgroup of stakeholders their opinion about a range of the company's activities and scoring their responses, both positive and negative, on a fixed scale and arriving at a weighted number for an aggregate reputation score. Quantitative opinion metrics are frequently augmented with focus group research. Other systems use market value (i.e., shareholder opinion) as a proxy for the opinion of all stakeholders. Here are some of the criteria used to measure corporate reputation:

- Ease of doing business
- Consumer friendliness
- Good fiscal management
- Long-term growth orientation
- Product or service innovation
- Ethical business practices
- Social responsibility
- Long-term investment
- Global competitiveness
- Employee engagement
- Quality of products or services

Issues Management

Another part of defensive reputation management is issues management.[3] It is made up of several elements. These include the following:

- Proactive monitoring of issues, such as the environment, human rights, or corporate governance, in which changing trends could cause the company's policies to be singled out for criticism;
- Building and maintaining relationships with nongovernmental organizations and other potential critics so that the companies' positions are well understood and it gets early warning of changing trends; and

- Designing and implementing an effective issues-response system to ensure that crises are quickly and expertly managed.

The quality of the offensive component of a company's reputation management effort is usually a direct product of how rigorously those efforts are measured and how specific they are in seeking to achieve meaningful goals. Reputation management targets should be designed for each key stakeholder audience:

- Employees
- Customers or consumers
- Shareholders
- Communities
- Business partners
- Regulators

Although reputation in the aggregate might appear to be an intangible quality, the more specific the desired outcomes with respect to an individual stakeholder group, the more powerful the potential effect. For example, a strong reputation for product innovation with business partners is a generally positive outcome, but much more powerful is seeking to increase the likelihood that a business would look positively on a joint venture because of the original company's innovativeness. Similarly, most companies attempt to improve their standings in surveys that purport to measure how positively employees evaluate them as a "good place to work." More specific metrics, however, such as the perceived value of the company's training, its working environment, and its career-building culture, are more likely to support positive business outcomes, such as strength of recruitment and low turnover.

Although many crises appear to come out of nowhere, in most instances missed warning signals could have alerted the organization to an impending problem. This is why one of the first principles of effective crisis management[4] is sound planning to identify risks and put in place protective plans to manage a crisis should one occur. This process needs to take two distinct but equally important pathways.

In the issues-mapping process, the planning team looks at every discrete activity of the organization and maps all of these activities against evolving trends in the global environment. The purpose of this planning exercise is to identify hidden threats and vulnerabilities that, if ignored, have the potential to create a crisis. Some of these vulnerabilities exist in plain sight. A coal mine obviously needs to have highly developed safety and materials-handling procedures and a process for responding to any breach of mine protocol. A pizza company, however, might not have thought through the ramifications of their on-time delivery guarantee in a sales model that relies on independent delivery contractors.

In one well-known example, a national pizza company offered a delivery guarantee, which created the unintended incentive for its drivers to drive too fast while at the same time imposed the costs of maintaining the vehicles on the independent contractors—the drivers themselves. An analysis of the company's basic business model could have indicated the gradual, then accelerating increase in the number of accidents involving pizza deliveries.

The issues-mapping process creates a robust picture of the threats and vulnerabilities faced by the organization. Once this process is complete, crisis communication planners can determine which of them require changing the way the organization behaves and which require careful monitoring and messaging. The issues identified should form the basis of a keyword-search-monitoring system to help give the organization early warning of media interest in these topics. Traditionally, these monitoring systems have focused on print and television media, but today organizations should also be monitoring websites, search engines, blogs, and podcasts, as well as video content on social networking sites.

Crisis communication defines that area of communication that comes into play when an organization's reputation—as well as its human, physical, financial, and intellectual assets—comes under threat. This threat can be sudden and abrupt, as in an airline accident, or remain dormant for a long time before bursting into public view. The latter form of crisis might be a long pattern of employee harassment by a manager that finally comes to light, or a technical incident of financial fraud that is only revealed as the result of an investigation into an unrelated matter.

Regardless of the cause, each crisis requires rapid and consistent decision making and communication with all affected stakeholders, and the company response occurs under stressful conditions in which fundamental ethical questions are often in play. As a result of this interplay of factors, organizations can sometimes exacerbate the reputational impact of a crisis through poor communications. From time to time, communications themselves can cause a crisis.

At the same time, the planning team should also be conducting a crisis-communication planning exercise. This consists of identifying the individuals in the organization who would need to participate in any crisis response and the ways to quickly convene them in the event of a crisis. Once the individuals have been identified, a communication and decision-making structure appropriate to that organization needs to be created in order to create an effective crisis response. In most crises, rapid information gathering and decision making can be the deciding factor that separates success from failure.

Another key step at this stage of the process is to pre-position company data and messaging in all of the communication channels available. This could include background materials explaining the company's value chain, as well as websites hidden from view that can be activated at a moment's notice.

The final step in crisis communication preparedness should be a drill that puts the system through its paces. A good drill will help accustom the participants to their roles and unearth hidden limitations to the crisis communication plan. At one German refinery, the crisis communication drill revealed the fact that, in an actual emergency, all of the phone lines in and out of the facility were shut down except the line to police and fire and safety centers, posing a significant problem for communicators trying to deal with other stakeholders in a crisis.

Even with effective preparedness and a careful issues-mapping process, a crisis can take hold with lightning speed and come from any direction. Sometimes the first news an organization has of a crisis brewing is a call from a reporter. In other situations, the crisis is already being covered on every TV channel and across the Web before management has become aware of it.

Regardless of where the first news originates, the crisis-response team should be immediately called into action. In the early minutes and hours of the crisis, this team needs to develop the clearest possible view of how the crisis is likely to unfold. The team needs to quickly answer some key questions. These include the following:

- What steps still need to be taken to manage the crisis itself?
- Who has been harmed, and what actions will make them feel the organization has responded effectively?
- Who should speak on behalf of the organization, how frequently, and in what forum?
- Which third-party entities—academics, think tanks—can be enlisted to speak up in defense of the organization?

These questions are designed to help steer the organization toward a successful and credible public perception in the midst of a crisis. In effective crisis communication, the key determinants are not the severity of the crisis itself, but how the crisis is being handled and how well the company involved is communicating about it. This means that in the early hours and days of a crisis, even before the facts are clear, companies that understand crisis response set up a system by which they can deliver regular updates to the media and other stakeholders. Even if there is little fresh information to share, the mere fact of offering to communicate has beneficial effects: it expresses confidence that the organization can handle the crisis and implicitly accepts the proposition that "the public has a right to know" what's going on.

At the same time, companies need to be aware of "dribbling out" new information. If one of the key goals of any crisis communication effort is to get the story off the front page, then releasing small amounts of new information simply has the effect of providing the media with fresh details to cover for another news cycle. This does not mean the organization under attack shouldn't be communicating. In fact, one of the most valuable tasks to be performed by the crisis teams is to identify the impact of the crisis on various stakeholders and prepare messaging that is specific to each one. In the wake, for example, of a spectacular business loss, the media will be simultaneously pursuing stories about the impact on investors, employees, the communities in which the company has major operations, the philanthropic organizations the company has supported, and so on.

Being ahead of the game by having reached out to these stakeholders and having appropriate messaging sends a strong signal that the management team understands the ramifications of what has happened and is not just thinking about themselves and the fate of the company but is sensitive to the entire community. One frequently neglected stakeholder group in a crisis is employees. Sharing unfolding events with internal audiences in a timely fashion is one of the hallmarks of good crisis communication.

Each crisis has its own rhythm, but there is often a moment of stasis in mid-crisis when an organization takes or doesn't take the steps that will be required to ensure long-term recovery of its reputation. This is the phase in the crisis when the immediate danger is usually over, when the broad outlines of the crisis and what might have caused it are clear, and there has been wide coverage of the events involved in the crisis.

Having survived the intense heat of the acute phase of a crisis, decision makers often mistakenly believe that the worst is over. This moment, however, is precisely the moment that recriminations begin and the public—regulators, the media, analysts, depending on the crisis—are looking for answers. Astute crisis managers understand that this is the moment when decisions with long-term consequences need to be made. The kinds of questions that come up in this phase include the following:

- Do we need to retain an independent panel of experts to assess the origins of this crisis and recommend solutions?
- Do we need to close this business unit or fire the CEO?
- Do we need to fundamentally reshape our relationship with our customers?
- Do we need to recall the product?

History is replete with examples of companies that failed to act aggressively at this stage of the crisis. The consumer products company, for example, that decided to stop shipping their products but didn't announce a recall. What happened? Retailers simply removed the products from the shelves themselves. The company that announced the CEO would retire but not for three months? The CEO was gone within two weeks.

At the other end of the spectrum are companies that act too rapidly in their anxiety to find a scapegoat and fire midlevel or lower level employees before the dust has even settled. This is rarely an effective move because it short-circuits the period in which the media and the public are still deciding whether there was a fundamental defect in the company's systems that needs to be repaired. Such actions usually evoke negative reactions even when, objectively, a firing might have been justified.

Once the acute crisis is over, there are still enormous reputational dangers that lurk in the waters. Even when the news is off the front page, the media and the public will still be looking to see whether the organization has fully understood the nature of the crisis and, as appropriate, changed its behavior to reflect that understanding. This usually involves changing company policy, increasing training programs, replacing aging equipment, or agreeing to independent monitoring of its activities for some period of time. (See the sidebar "Lessons Learned from 'Scandal!' ")

LESSONS LEARNED FROM "SCANDAL!"

Investigative reporter for *The New York Times* Ralph Blumenthal and Michael B. Goodman team-taught a graduate seminar titled "Scandal!: Communicating with the Media in the Midst of Crisis." It investigated the management of issues, reputation, and damage control, as well as the media practices of investigative journalism, ethical and unethical. The discussion focused on well-known recent categories and cases, for example:

- Celebrity bad behavior: Tiger Woods (background), Lance Armstrong
- Financial crisis: Drexel Burnham Lambert, AIG (background), rogue traders (Adoboli, UBS 2012; Jerome Kerviel, Societe Generale 2008)
- Insider trading: Martha Stewart (background); Galleon, Rajaratnam, and Gupta (McKinsey)
- Accounting fraud: Enron
- Self-inflicted crises: Toyota (Audi 5000 background); BP; Hewlett Packard (HP); Apple; Walmart
- Illegal and unethical actions: News Corp, BBC
- Supply chain: Apple and Foxconn (electronics); Walmart and Tazreen Fashions; H&M and the Rana Plaza factory complex (Bangladesh, garments)

Guest experts included investigative journalists and corporate executives who discussed the cases from their unique perspectives as participants. Here is a list of lessons learned generated by the seminar participants:

- It is best to tell the media the truth.
- Treat everyone with respect and always get back to reporters. Build your credibility and relationships with reporters.
- If you hurt other people, it's only worse and lasts longer. (i.e., Lance Armstrong's bullying)
- Every scandal is unique. Even if you have the best crisis communication strategy, you still have to change and adapt new ideas.
- No matter how you prepare, you are never quite ready.
- Know the facts before you speak.
- Apologize if you've done something wrong.
- Keep employees in the loop.

- Never say, "No comment."
- Announce your own bad news and tell your own story.
- Reputation can take years to build up and can disappear in a matter of hours.
- Watch how you behave (power of social media).
- Trust yourself.
- Analyze the risks.
- Don't just say it; back it up with action.
- Have an outside counsel to confide in and help advise you.
- No corporate communicator ever represents the company by themselves.
- Build alliances.
- Never burn a reporter.
- Never say, "Mistakes were made." Say, "We made mistakes."
- Cultivate a culture of responsibility.
- "When you eat shit, don't nibble."
- "Rip the Band-Aid off."
- Utilize third-party validators.
- There is no right way to do the wrong thing.

In Goodman and Hirsch (2015) *Corporate Communication: Critical Business Asset for Strategic Global Change.* NY: Peter Lang, (61–62).

To the extent that management changes have been part of the solution, the new management still needs to demonstrate that the conditions that enabled the crisis have been changed and periodically remind stakeholders that changes have been made. Sometimes, this process can take several years. One well-known casual dining chain was the target of dozens of lawsuits charging systemic racism in the workplace tolerated by management. After this crisis blew up, the leadership of the organization made long-term pledges to ensure that minority employees and diners would be treated equitably. The company continued to report on its progress in this effort for many years to come, winning plaudits from the community for its efforts and its perseverance.

The Culture Is Key

One of the key findings on the 2013 *CCI Corporate Communication Practices and Trends Study* noted that:

> There is a renewed emphasis placed on building positive corporate culture and employee engagement (corporate character) in response to volatile

global economic conditions, changing business and media models, "big data," and the networked enterprise. This internal focus acknowledges the essential role that employees play in the networked enterprise, and it continues to drive the need to boost employee morale.

(Goodman, Genest, Bertoli, Templo, & Wolman, 2013)

The 2015 *CCI Corporate Communication Practices and Trends Study: United States* (Corporate Communication International, 2015) found that "integrity, trust, and comprehensive understanding of the business and its constituencies are among the main success factors for reputation management." In interviews for that study, communication officers and thought leaders said that to manage the corporation's reputation successfully, the company values must be emphasized internally by a communication leader who understands the business environment. The 2015 CCI study asked corporate communication officers if the corporate communication department was primarily responsible for internal communication, and if it did not oversee internal (employee) communication, what department (HR, information technology, marketing and sales, office of the CEO, office of a C-suite executive other than the CEO, public affairs, a dedicated employee-engagement department that oversees internal communication, a dedicated internal communication department, or something else, in which internal communication tasks are decentralized and conducted by individual departments or divisions) had that responsibility. *None* of the respondents indicated that they did not oversee internal communication—that is, 100% of the respondents were responsible for overseeing internal communication.

For the chief communication officer of a Fortune 50 company, success is "obviously, a clear understanding of your culture, and your purpose. A reputation isn't made by communicators. A reputation is made by [your] people. A reputation is the sum of all perceptions that people have of your organization. Our role is to help build a strong culture, to help align our values with broadly held social values." (Goodman, 2016, p. xi)

Another CCO observed that it was "alignment because everybody has to be clear on what direction we're going in, what we're really trying to accomplish." And another added,

> Leadership support and participation . . . preparedness . . . you can't anticipate every crisis that's going to come along, maybe you can't anticipate any of them. You can be in the position to respond effectively by understanding the fundamentals of what makes effective crisis communication. And that is filling the vacuum, don't let other people fill the vacuum. And being nimble. The world moves really, really fast, and you have to be in a position where you can react in minutes, not just hours or days, to changes in the market, to announcements by the government or what's happening on Wall St., or allegations of some scandal.

(Goodman, 2016, p. xi)

The 2015 CCI study noted that blogs, social networks, and websites have become important vehicles of communication with key external stakeholders of the company. From a list of 13 social media channels, chief communication officers identified the ones they used as official channels of communication. A large majority, more than three quarters, used LinkedIn, Twitter, Facebook, and YouTube. The study also found that from among nine choices, at the company, a large majority (77.8%) indicated the corporate communication officer has access to and is authorized to use such channels of communication. Asked if their company has a formal policy on the personal use of social media by employees, more than 95% indicated that they did.

This internal focus acknowledges the essential role that employees play in the networked enterprise, and it continues to drive greater employee engagement. Even in well-run organizations, issues simmer and then erupt at any time. With a foundation of a strong, positive corporate culture, a careful crisis-response system in place, and a commitment to monitoring issues and emerging threats, most organizations can come through a crisis with their reputation intact and sometimes even enhanced.

The key ingredients for good crisis communication are essentially no different from good communication in any setting—openness, clarity, and putting yourself in the other person's shoes, whether that person is an employee, a customer, a shareholder, or a member of the community. The challenge in a crisis is that our natural instinct is to do the opposite—control information, circle the wagons, protect our own, and attack the enemy.

Overcoming these built-in reactions and looking to the long-term outcomes for the organization are the hallmarks of a true crisis communicator who is the product of a positive corporate culture. Those are the qualities and capabilities that define an effective corporate culture and drive a sustainable company. And the 2015 *Corporate Communication Practices and Trends Study* (CCI Corporate Communication International, 2015) also found that "social Media, no longer a novelty, becomes another part of the strategic management of corporate communication."

Notes

1 Foundational works on the analysis of corporate culture are anthropologist Edward T. Hall's works *The Silent Language* (New York: Doubleday, 1959), *The Hidden Dimension* (New York: Doubleday, 1966), and *Beyond Culture* (New York: Doubleday, 1976). In *Communication Within the Organization: An Interpretive Review of Theory and Research* (New York, NY: Industrial Communication Council, 1972), W. Charles Redding articulated his concept of managerial climate, which emphasized organizational supportiveness; participative decision making; trust, confidence, and credibility; openness and candor; and an emphasis on high performance goals. Edgar Schein's body of work (*Organizational Culture and Leadership*, 4th ed., 2010; *The Corporate Culture Survival Guide*, 1999, revised 2009) demonstrates how national, organizational, and occupational cultures influence organizational performance. Terrence Deal and Allen Kennedy's *Corporate Cultures: The Rites and Rituals of Corporate Life* (Reading, MA: Addison-Wesley, 1982) is discussed here

for its wide use and accessibility. We also recognize Geert Hofstede's seminal work *Cultures and Organizations: Software of the Mind* (2nd ed.) with his son Gert Jan Hofstede (New York, NY: McGraw-Hill, 2005); his student Fons Trompenars's *Riding the Waves of Culture: Understanding Cultural Diversity in Business* (New York: McGraw-Hill, 1993); and the GLOBE Study, *Culture, Leadership, and Organizations* (Eds. R. J. House, et al., Thousand Oaks, CA: Sage, 2004). We have found useful tools to unlock corporate cultures in *Ethnography and the Corporate Encounter: Reflections on Research in and of Corporations*, Ed. Melissa Cefkin (New York: Berghahn Books, 2010); J. Steven Ott's *The Organizational Culture Perspective* (Pacific Grove, CA: Brooks/Cole Publishing, 1989); and J. Keyton's *Communication and Organizational Culture: A Key to Understanding Work Experiences* (Los Angeles: Sage, 2011). We discuss corporate culture at length in M. B. Goodman and P. B. Hirsch's *Corporate Communication: Strategic Adaptation for Global Practice* (New York, NY: Peter Lang, 2010); and in my *Intercultural Communication for Managers* (New York, NY: Business Expert Press, 2013).

2 In chapter 5 of M. B. Goodman and P. B. Hirsch's *Corporate Communication: Critical Business Asset for Strategic Global Change* (New York: Peter Lang, 2015), there is a discussion of reputation management, and chapter 9 includes an analysis of Ron Alsop's *The 18 Immutable Laws of Corporate Reputation: Creating, Protecting, and Restoring Your Most Valuable Asset* (New York: Free Press, 2004). In 2001, in "Reputation Management: The New Face of Corporate Public Relations?" (*Public Relations Review* 27, 2001, 247–261), Jim Hutton and I, with Jill Alexander and Christina Genest, discuss the growth in reputation management and the issues concerning consensus about its definition, reputation measures, and when and how (and even whether) reputation can be "managed." The debate began with Charles Fombrun's articles in *The Harvard Business Review* and the *Academy of Management Journal* in the early 1990s and his book *Reputation: Realizing Value From Corporate Image* (Boston, MA: Harvard Business School Press, 1996). There are numerous journals on the subject, including *Corporate Reputation Review* and *Reputation Management*. Some of the books on the subject include John Doorley and Helio Fred Garcia's *Reputation Management: The Key to Successful Public Relations and Corporate Communication* (New York, NY: Routledge, 2007), John M. T. Balmer and Steven A. Greyser's *Revealing the Corporation: Perspectives on Identity, Image, Reputation, Corporate Branding, and Corporate-Level Marketing* (New York, NY: Routledge, 2003), Pekka Aula and Saku Mantere's *Strategic Reputation Management: Towards a Company of Good* (New York, NY: Routledge, 2008), Gary Davies's *Corporate Reputation and Competitiveness* (New York, NY: Routledge, 2003), and Fraser P. Seitel and John Doorley's *Rethinking Reputation: How PR Trumps Marketing and Advertising in the New Media World* (New York, NY: Palgrave Macmillan, 2012).

3 According to the Public Affairs Council (n.d.), "Issues management involves prioritizing and proactively addressing public policy and reputation issues that can affect an organization's success. Many large companies use issues management techniques to keep their external relations activities focused on high-priority challenges and opportunities." The Issue Management Council (http://issuemanagement.org/learnmore/professional-standards/) defines it this way:

> An issue exists when there is a gap between stakeholder expectations and an organization's policies, performance, products or public commitments. *Issue management is:* . . . the process used to close that gap . . . a formal management process to anticipate and take appropriate action on emerging trends, concerns, or issues likely to affect an organization and its stakeholders . . . an outside-in cultural mindset and linkage between an organization and its stakeholder ecosystem. This linkage enhances responsiveness to change and acknowledges and attempts to balance the myriad expectations of affected entities and individuals . . . genuine and ethical long-term commitment by the organization to a two-way, inclusive standard of corporate responsibility toward stakeholders . . . Issue management involves but does

not solely focus on the following disciplines: Public relations, lobbying or government relations; Futurism, trend tracking or media monitoring; Strategic or financial planning; Law. *Issue management is not:* One-way control of public policy issues; Spin or damage control; Defensive delay and deflection activities to crush opponents; Reactive fire-fighting in a crisis mode; superficial imposition of a set of values and way of doing business on an institutional culture that neither understands nor embraces it.

4 Historically, the way Johnson & Johnson managed the Tylenol poisoning crisis in early 1986 set the benchmark for crisis communication and management. One of the first books on the subject was *When It Hits the Fan: Managing the Nine Crises of Business* (Boston, MA: Houghton Mifflin, 1986) by Gerald C. Meyers, former chairman of American Motors. Cases for corporate crises appear regularly in the pages of *The New York Times, The Wall Street Journal*, and the *Financial Times*. Our focus is on mitigating crises in the first place by understanding the continuum from a positive corporate culture to a strong reputation and through a robust issues-management practice. Among the wealth of publications on crisis communication and crisis management are *Handbook of Risk and Crisis Communication*, eds. Heath, Robert L. and H. Dan O'Hair (New York, NY: Routledge, 2009); Coombs, W. Timothy, *Ongoing Crisis Communication: Planning, Managing, and Responding*, 3rd ed. (Thousand Oaks, CA: Sage, 2012); Crandall, W. R., Parnell, J. A., & Spillan, J. E. (2014). *Crisis management: Leading in the new strategy landscape*, 2nd ed. (Thousand Oaks, CA: Sage, 2014); Ulmer, Robert R., et al., *Effective Crisis Communication: Moving From Crisis to Opportunity* (Thousand Oaks, CA: Sage, 2011); *Crisis Communication: Practical PR Strategies for Reputation Management and Company Survival*, ed. Peter Anthonissen (London, UK: Kogan Page, 2008); Harmon, Jon F., *Feeding Frenzy: Trial Lawyers, the Media, Politicians and Corporate Adversaries: Inside the Ford-Firestone Crisis* (New York, NY: Eloquent Books, 2009).

References

Alsop, R. (2004). *The 18 immutable laws of corporate reputation: Creating, protecting and repairing your most valuable asset.* New York: Free Press.

Anthonissen, P. (Ed.). (2008). *Crisis communication: Practical PR strategies for reputation management and company survival.* London: Kogan Page.

Aula, P., & Mantere, S. (2008). *Strategic reputation management: Towards a company of good.* New York: Routledge.

Balmer, J. M. T., & Greyser, S. A. (2003). *Revealing the corporation: Perspectives on identity, image, reputation, corporate branding, and corporate-level marketing.* New York: Routledge.

Corporate Communication International (CCI). (2015). *2015 CCI Corporate Communication Practices and Trends Study: United States.* Retrieved from http://www.corporatecomm. org/wp-content/uploads/2016/04/Key-Findings-CCI-Study-2015-29Oct15.pdf

Cefkin, M. (Ed.). (2010). *Ethnography and the corporate encounter: Reflections on research in and of corporations.* New York: Berghahn Books.

Coombs, W. T. (2012). *Ongoing crisis communication: Planning, managing, and responding* (3rd ed.). Los Angeles: Sage.

Crandall, W. R., Parnell, J. A., & Spillan, J. E. (2014). *Crisis management: Leading in the new strategy landscape* (2nd ed.). Los Angeles: Sage.

Davies, G. (2003). *Corporate reputation and competitiveness.* New York: Routledge.

Deal, T., & Kennedy, A. (1982). *Corporate cultures: The rites and rituals of corporate life.* Reading, MA: Addison-Wesley.

Doorley, J., & Garcia, H. F. (2007). *Reputation management: The key to successful public relations and corporate communication.* New York: Routledge.

Fombrun, C. J. (1996). *Reputation: Realizing value from corporate image.* Boston: Harvard Business School Press.

Goodman, M. (2016, June.) *An introduction: Transformation of the corporate communication profession – Leading practices 2016.* Proceedings of the CCI Conference on Corporate Communication 2016, New York, NY.

Goodman, M. B. (2013). *Intercultural communication for managers.* New York: Business Expert Press.

Goodman, M. B., Genest, C., Bertoli, K., Templo, S., & Wolman, L. (2013). *Corporate communication practices and trends 2013: United States executive summary of final report.* Retrieved from http://www.corporatecomm.org/wp-content/uploads/2013/06/Corporate-Communication-Practices-and-Trends_2013-U.S.-Study_Exec.-Summary.pdf

Goodman, M. B., & Hirsch, P. B. (2010). *Corporate communication: Strategic adaptation for global practice.* New York: Peter Lang.

Goodman, M. B., & Hirsch, P. B. (2015). *Corporate communication: Critical business asset for strategic global change.* New York: Peter Lang.

Hall, E. T. (1959). *The silent language.* New York: Doubleday.

Hall, E. T. (1966). *The hidden dimension.* New York: Doubleday.

Hall, E. T. (1976). *Beyond culture.* New York: Doubleday.

Harmon, J. F. (2009). *Feeding frenzy: Trial lawyers, the media, politicians and corporate adversaries: Inside the Ford-Firestone crisis.* New York: Eloquent Books.

Heath, R. L., & O'Hair H. D. (Eds.). (2009). *Handbook of risk and crisis communication.* New York: Routledge.

Hofstede, G., & Hofstede, G. J. (2005). *Cultures and organizations: Software of the mind* (2nd ed.). New York: McGraw-Hill USA.

House, R. J., Hanges, P. J., Javidan, M., Dorfman, P. W., & Gupta, V. (Eds.). (2004). *Culture, leadership, and organizations: The GLOBE study of 62 societies.* Thousand Oaks, CA: Sage Publications.

Hutton, J. G., Goodman, M. B., Alexander, J. B., & Genest, C. M. (2001). Reputation management: The new face of corporate public relations? *Public Relations Review, 27*(3), 247–261.

Keyton, J. (2011). *Communication and organizational culture: A key to understanding work experiences.* Los Angeles: Sage Publications.

Meyers, G. C. (1986). *When it hits the fan: Managing the nine crises of business.* Boston: Houghton Mifflin.

Ott, J. S. (1989). *The organizational culture perspective.* Pacific Grove, CA: Brooks/Cole Publishing.

Public Affairs Council. (n.d.). Issues management. Retrieved from http://pac.org/issues_management

Ray, R. (2015, February 4). *The CEO challenge: Creating opportunity out of adversity . . . building agile and innovative people-driven organizations to beat the slow growth economic blues.* CCI Corporate Communication International Briefing at Baruch College/CUNY. Retrieved from http://www.corporatecomm.org/event/the-ceo-challenge-and-its-implications-for-human-capital/

Redding, W. C. (1972). *Communications within the organization: An interpretive review of theory and research.* New York: Industrial Communication Council.

Schein, E. H. (2009). *The corporate culture survival guide.* San Francisco, CA: John Wiley & Sons.

Schein, E. H. (2010). *Organizational culture and leadership* (4th ed.). San Francisco, CA: John Wiley & Sons.

Seitel, F. P., & Doorley, J. (2012). *Rethinking reputation: How PR trumps marketing and advertising in the new media world.* New York: Palgrave Macmillan.

Simpson, B. (2011, March). Flying people, not planes: The CEO of Bombardier on building a world-class culture. *McKinsey Quarterly,* Interview, March 2011. Retrieved from http://www.mckinsey.com/business-functions/organization/our-insights/and-8220flying-people-not-planes-and-8221-the-ceo-of-bombardier-on-building-a-world-class-culture

Trompenars, F. (1993). *Riding the waves of culture: Understanding cultural diversity in business.* New York: McGraw-Hill.

Ulmer, R. R., Sellnow, T. L., & Seeger, M. W. (2011). *Effective crisis communication: Moving from crisis to opportunity.* Los Angeles: Sage.

4

HANDLING CRISES IN SOCIAL MEDIA

From Stakeholder Crisis Awareness and Sense Making to Organizational Crisis Preparedness

Chiara Valentini, Stefania Romenti, and Dean Kruckeberg

Introduction

During the past 10 years, social media have played an increasingly important role in the lives of people worldwide, affecting the ways in which people relate, communicate, and share opinions with one another—including about crises. Valentini and Kruckeberg (2012a) defined *social media* as conversational platforms in which individuals with common interests, relations, and passions can gather to discuss, share, and exchange ideas and opinions. A stream of public relations research has examined crises and crisis communication, increasingly so within the milieu of social media. Coombs (2013a) defined a *crisis* as the perception of an unpredictable event that threatens important expectations of stakeholders and that can seriously impact an organization's performance and generate negative outcomes. The interest in social media for crisis communication and management is related to the fact that, today, social media have become the milieu in which many crises are discussed, if not formed. There is a general increase in social media use by publics during crises, and these publics tend to give more credibility to social media coverage than to traditional news media coverage (Jin, Liu, & Austin, 2014), thereby impacting other forms of crisis-related communications. Hence, crisis communication is more often occurring online. Since early 2000, many organizations from a range of industries have used the Internet, together with traditional media, as a channel to communicate their crisis-response actions (Perry, Taylor, & Doerfel, 2003). More recent studies (e.g., Liu & Kim, 2011; Muralidharan, Rasmussen, Patterson, & Shin, 2011) have contributed specific understandings of how social media are used by different organizations in different critical situations.

This chapter reviews major concepts, models, and theories to better understand how to handle crises in social media and how social media affect crisis development and management. The chapter discusses how social media influence stakeholder knowledge about a crisis, as well as these stakeholders' understanding of a crisis and their actions upon it. The authors argue that organizations should focus on integrating social media management into crisis preparedness activities. They examine the importance of mapping stakeholders who are online and of adopting communication strategies based on dialogue. Although no prescriptive guidelines are provided, the major aspects of which organizations and crisis managers must be aware are explored. Examples are offered throughout the discussion, and the authors conclude with recommendations for future research.

How Social Media Change Crisis Dynamics

There is a growing consensus in the literature that social media are changing crisis dynamics by speeding up the development of critical situations and by potentially forming new types of crises (cf. Pang, Hassan, & Chong, 2014; Valentini & Kruckeberg, 2015). Social media speed the development of critical situations because they enable rapid sharing of information on a hugely unimaginable scale in real time. People use social media to seek updated information on critical situations, to share experiences, and to get emotional support (Austin, Liu, & Jin, 2012). Thus, during critical situations, public-to-public conversations play a key role in shaping social media networks' awareness (Mei, Bansal, & Pang, 2010), in understanding and acting upon critical situations, and thus in enhancing the escalation of the crisis itself. Furthermore, online conversations constitute discursive practices that make publics aware of critical situations about which they may or may not have otherwise known. For instance, most of the recent political upheavals in the Middle East have become known to international audiences because of online videos and posts in social media, even before they were reported in the mainstream media (Pang et al., 2014; Valentini & Kruckeberg, 2012b). The implications of this speed are that managers of organizations that are affected by a crisis have less time to plan and to implement actions to solve these crises and, thus, to restore their reputations, with even less time to monitor how publics perceive and discursively talk about these organizations' actions in their online networks.

Furthermore, social media conversations can trigger crises (Pang et al., 2014) by spreading rumors that can affect "real-world" threats to organizations' reputations (Laurence, 2011, July 6). Coombs and Holladay (2012) defined this type of crisis as a *paracrisis*—that is, "a publicly visible crisis threat that charges an organization with irresponsible or unethical behavior" (p. 409). Often, a paracrisis is an expression of stakeholder dissatisfaction with how an organization is handling an issue that stakeholders are experiencing. Yet, paracrises can turn into real crises if not promptly dealt with. An example is the case of United Airlines breaking a Canadian singer's guitar and refusing to reimburse him for the damage. The singer responded by creating a YouTube video mocking the airline. The video attracted millions of viewers and, by doing so, damaged the reputation of the company (Tran, 2009, July 23).

Other times, online rumors may not be true but nevertheless represent accusations that could hinder the image of an organization. Typically, these are generated by trolls—that is, individuals who post inflammatory, extraneous, or off-topic messages with the intent to provoke individuals into emotional responses or to disrupt a conversation (Noble, Noble, & Adjei, 2012) appearing in specific issue arenas (Luoma-aho & Vos, 2010), such as dedicated forums, blogs, and online communities. An example is the case of Barilla, the Italian pasta manufacturer that was supposedly alleged by an Italian professor to have produced and sold low-quality products, which resulted in diverse online communities calling to boycott the company. The allegations circulated via e-mail, in Facebook, and in other social media. Yet, the message was a hoax, and the named professor denied being involved in orchestrating this online boycott (Becerra, 2012, December 20). Although the hoax was shortly discovered, the troll who had created this content touched upon common public perceptions and shared meaning of "good quality food" among publics, enabling the troll to reach a larger group of people.

Social media conversations challenge organizational responses to critical issues because these conversations are not confined on a specific network but can move from arena to arena and can even spread to offline arenas. In their study of the blogosphere and news media, Messner and DiStaso (2008) found the existence of a source cycle between journalists and bloggers, indicating that journalists were also influenced by online discussions. Similarly, Pang et al. (2014) argue that "it has becoming more difficult for mainstream media to ignore content originating from social media" (p. 97). Yet, even if hoaxes rarely find their way to mainstream media, paracrises or critical situations that are discussed in social media may potentially seed into news media agendas.

The problem with this critical content is that it is often publicly available and visible throughout the world through social media (Coombs & Holladay, 2012). When publics become aware of this content, online conversations serve as a mechanism to discursively shape and construct public opinions on the critical situation by sharing and discussing such content, giving meaning to critical experiences that publics directly or indirectly face (Jin et al., 2014). Thus, a process of sense making occurs, in which online sources can shape the opinions of others who do not directly experience the crisis. Recent studies indicate that people's attitudes are more favorable to accepting persuasive messages when they perceive shared characteristics with the source of the message (Aldoory, Kim, & Tindall, 2010). People within a close network of friends, family, colleagues, and professionals tend to trust one another (Putnam, 2000). This means that the likelihood to follow influential stakeholders' "sense of the crisis" is higher in those networks. Such network voices can juxtapose not only with official, often organizational, voices, but also with many other online sources from different arenas. It is through this multivocal discursive practice that many critical situations form and develop into crises (Frandsen & Johansen, 2013) or simply develop a "double-crisis," also known as a communications-crisis—that is, "a crisis, where the original crisis is superposed by a communications-crisis, as the organization fails in managing the communication processes that should have contributed to the handling of the original crisis" (Johansen & Frandsen, 2007, p. 79). Given that social media discourses have a central role in shaping publics' crisis awareness and perceptions, social media have changed the way in which many crises form and develop and have lifted the role of communication from a tool to implement crisis management into a fundamental activity for pre-, during, and postcrisis management. Organizations should pay particular attention to crisis preparedness to be prepared in handling social media if a crisis occurs. They also should use social media monitoring as a routine activity to foresee the emergence of possible critical discussions and to engage in conversations with online publics to assure that critical discussions and false information do not develop into a real crisis.

Crisis Preparedness and Social Media: Educating, Monitoring, and Collaborating

Social media's potentialities are rapidly becoming acknowledged as being central to effective crisis preparedness, including all communication and management activities through which an organization's leaders should develop robust plans to prevent crises or to manage them effectively if they occur (Taneja, Pryor, Sewell, & Recuero, 2014). During crisis preparedness, organizations must develop an efficient online monitoring alert system to intercept "negative rumors" that are generated by trolls before these rumors spread throughout the Web (Noble et al., 2012), as well as to be warned about critical issues that can threaten online (and potentially offline) reputations of organizations.

Crisis preparedness obviously cannot eliminate any risks and uncertainties surrounding organizations, but such preparation represents a vital part of the management tool kit, because it makes organizations less vulnerable to crises and preserves their vitality, as well as their stability, during a crisis (Coombs, 2012). Crisis preparedness includes a range of activities, such as the development of risk assessment, preparation and continual review of a crisis manual, a communication plan, a training plan, as well as the selection of the members of the crisis management team (González-Herrero & Smith, 2008). Each mentioned activity should be integrated with the social media environment. During the risk assessment activity, online issues would be prioritized on the basis of their probability of occurrence and their potential impact on the organization. A crisis manual must include an updated list of links of sources of information to monitor, such as blogs, activists' websites, online communities, as well as clear guidelines to properly use social media if a crisis occurs. Scholars recommend that organizations have in their crisis management manuals specific indications about the most appropriate tone and language to address online critics.

Given that social media conversations can affect crisis awareness and interpretation among stakeholders, social media management has been recognized as an important element of crisis management, especially in supporting the education of employees about social media. Employees need to be up to date about new trends in communication technology, and these employees should possess adequate communication and social media skills to participate in stakeholders' conversation networks. Organizations are recommended to support employees' training activity, for instance, by delivering live online seminars and by creating Web-based libraries that employees can access.

Before and during crises, social media also foster collaboration and support for coordinated actions. For instance, wikis can allow internal and external people to access updated reports, crisis manuals, plans, and contact lists (González-Herrero & Smith, 2008). Guth and Alloway (2008) argued that social media could also identify partners who will support organizations during crises. The authors mentioned partners, such as those having graphic, video, and audio skills who can update content on interactive media, when the crisis begins. Partners could also include an organization's Facebook fans, because if these fans are continually informed about a crisis, they can share updates with their online and offline personal networks and, thus, they can support the dissemination of official crisis information. Hence, organizations should map digital publics and prioritize those that could potentially become "communication partners" if a crisis occurs, but these organizations also should monitor those potential "developers" of crises.

Identification of Key Social Media Stakeholders

A fundamental aspect of crisis management is understanding stakeholders—that is, how they (could) perceive a crisis, as well as their information-seeking and forwarding behaviors (Kim & Grunig, 2011) and their shared experiences (Aldoory et al., 2010). Such understanding allows organizations to foresee stakeholders' communicative behaviors because information-seeking and -forwarding behaviors of stakeholders in relation to a possible or existing crisis can be dissimilar. Furthermore, in social media, not all online claims are legitimate and require actions because many online conversations about critical issues are simply rumors that are generated by trolls (Noble et al., 2012) or are paracrises (Coombs & Holladay, 2012). Because organizations have limited resources, they should focus their communicative efforts toward those online stakeholders who are active in social media and who are influential, have legitimate claims, have high centrality in the network, and can potentially be the catalysts of shared experiences (cf. Aldoory et al., 2010). These online stakeholders can work as amplifiers of organizational messages, what Kim and Grunig (2011) referred to as information-forwarding behavior, by helping organizations reach victims or potential victims to whom they do not have direct contact. But such people can also work as attenuators, or even as saboteurs, of organizational messages by claiming other causes, responsibilities, and consequences of the crisis. This online behavior has consequences, not only for the reputation of organizations under crisis, but also for the effectiveness of a crisis-response action, because people can become more confused by the presence of diverse instructing and adjusting information. Hence, it is important to identify influential stakeholders in different networks and to understand their information-seeking and -forwarding behaviors.

Sedereviciute and Valentini (2011) developed a model to identify and to prioritize unknown online stakeholders based on a social network analysis of online content (cf. Scott, 2000) and the prioritization of online stakeholders according to the stakeholder salience model (Mitchell, Agle, & Wood, 1997). The model identifies four typologies of online stakeholders: *unconcerned lurkers, concerned lurkers, unconcerned influencers,* and *concerned influencers.* Concerned influencers are those online stakeholders to whom organizations need to pay particular attention during critical situations because these stakeholders have an important position in the social media network (high centrality) and great interest (in terms of urgency and legitimacy of posting) in an organization. They have the potential to set the tone of conversations about an organization's culpability and appropriateness of response, and they influence how victims and other publics perceive a crisis. Organizations have the opportunity to engage these concerned influencers through different types of collaboration and direct communication, for example, by developing crisis content that could be shared or by promoting a network coproduction model of word of mouth (Kozinets, de Valck, Wojnicki, & Wilner, 2010), in which influencers are invited to produce messages based on inputs that are provided by organizations.

Crisis Communication Management: From Informing to Communicating Dialogically

Crisis communication research has typically focused on informing and *communicating to* stakeholders and on understanding the impact of such communications on stakeholder attitudes and behaviors—that is, in how they cope with instructive messages (Coombs, 2013b). But the online environment requires addressing the medium's interactivity and the user-generated nature of online content, as González-Herrero and Smith (2010) suggested. Recent studies have sought to tackle these aspects by investigating stakeholders' discursive interactions in social media to indirectly understand how crisis meaning is managed (Meer & Verhoeven, 2013; Schultz, Kleinnijenhuis, Oegema, Utz, & van Atteveldt, 2012).

Limited knowledge exists about *communicating with* stakeholders in a more dialogical manner during crises, and even less research exists on dialogic communication via social media during crises. Dialogue is crucial to establish credibility, trust, and believability around an organization, its mission, and its behaviors (Coombs, 2012). Dialogue is also an important mechanism to make the voices of stakeholders heard by the crisis perpetuators and to create solutions that meet the needs of the victims and stakeholders at large. By cultivating dialogue processes with publics, an organization can nurture two-way communication that is suitable to co-orientate organizational aims and public interests and to create an acceptable equilibrium among the different stakeholder and organizational interests. But how can organizations implement dialogue? Does a unique kind of dialogue exist? Or can different strategies of dialogue be used? If so, what are the most effective dialogue strategies that crisis communication managers could employ?

Mei et al. (2010) new media crisis communication model is among the first attempts to leverage the interactive nature of social media by suggesting that organizations monitor and track conversations about potential issues and answer queries and comments proactively. Similarly, Jin and Liu (2010) developed a blog-mediated crisis communication model that includes monitoring the blogosphere and identifying key bloggers to help organizations respond adequately to critical situations that arise in the online environment. That model proposes response strategies to circumvent rumor generation, belief, and transmission on and through influential blogs but does not consider dialogue as a possible alternative communication strategy during crises. From a stakeholder's point of view, dialogue can work as a catharsis for releasing negative emotions and helping victims overcome unpleasant and traumatic experiences. Dialogue can generate positive feelings because it shows the organization's willingness to listen and to learn. Dialogue can boost authenticity and inclusiveness in what an organization intends to do to resolve a critical situation, and, as a result, it can enhance organizational trust and credibility. During crises, dialogue becomes a mechanism that supports participatory and collaborative patterns, both outside and within organizations, to solve problems that are caused by a crisis. Romenti, Murtarelli, and Valentini's (2014) *Crisis Communication Strategic Planning* includes suggestions for a dialogic approach in crisis communication management via social media that is based on four typologies of dialogue strategies: concertative, transformative, framing, and generative. Framing and concertative dialogue strategies are aimed at seeking public consensus of organizational actions during a crisis; thus, with the creation of convergent opinions, transformative and generative dialogue strategies call for new assumptions or ideas about the implementation of existing organizational strategies and policies (transformative) or for new actions based on public perspectives and points of view (generative).

When a crisis occurs, the choice of the most adequate dialogue strategy to adopt is situational. For instance, the level of organizational responsibility toward a crisis can affect the propinquity of using dialogue and the choice of dialogue strategy. If its responsibility is low, an organization can pursue consensus or prominence goals by respectively using concertative and framing dialogue strategies. But if the organization is perceived as the main cause of a crisis, the generative and the transformative approaches to dialogue are recommended. Generative and transformative dialogue strategies are perceived by stakeholders as being more genuine attempts to do something to recover from the crisis, and when organizations are responsible of the crisis, these strategies show organizational willingness to change those behaviors that are considered to be the main causes of the crisis itself.

The choice of a dialogue strategy during a crisis is also influenced by its organizational dialogue history. *Dialogue history* can be defined as "an organization's record of using dialogue strategies in internal and external communications with stakeholders" (Romenti et al., 2014, p. 11). Thus, if an organization frequently uses generative online dialogue strategies, but during a crisis, for which it is responsible switches to a framing strategy, its stakeholders would not favorably engage in conversations with the organization that simply seeks consensus with the organization's own crisis-response actions. Following corrective actions would be the best approach, yet those corrective actions should also be cocreated by engaging publics in online conversations. An organization would recover faster and more effectively from a crisis if it is open to others' opinions about which behaviors should be changed (generative dialogue), rather than, for instance, insists on its own specific argumentations (framing dialogue). A concertative strategy, on the other hand, would be more suitable in low responsibility situations, in which organizations are not directly responsible for the crisis, but in which stakeholders expect the organization to act and to protect stakeholders' interests by providing instructive measures. Concertative dialogue can, thus, be used to assure public consensus on instructive messages on how to cope with the crisis situation.

Conclusion

This chapter is intended to be an entry into a continuing conversation to better understand how social media affect crisis development and how organizations must engage stakeholders in crisis situations. Social media greatly affect crisis dynamics by speeding up critical situations or developing new crises, and, thus, social media cannot be ignored or relegated to a secondary status in crisis communication. Indeed, social media management must be completely integrated in an organization's crisis management planning and execution from the earliest crisis-preparedness phase.

This integration includes the constant monitoring of the online environment, and digital issues must be prioritized and online stakeholders must be accurately mapped (Sedereviciute & Valentini, 2011). These activities should be performed with the full understanding that the online environment has its own rules and that specific crisis planning and management must be addressed. This chapter has discussed how social media have changed crisis dynamics and how online conversations can fuel new types of crises. The authors have discussed the importance of focusing on online conversations to learn more about how stakeholders make sense of a critical situation in social media conversations. It is through a better understanding of these online sense-making processes that organizations can learn what stakeholders already know, what they have misunderstood about the situation, what they care the most about, and what expectations they may have of these organizations. This knowledge allows organizations to plan effective crisis responses that meet stakeholders' information-seeking and -forwarding behaviors. The authors urge organizations to recognize that the online environment privileges a relational and dialogic model of communication rather than approaches that are based solely on information exchange. The chapter has illustrated Romenti et al. (2014) model of online dialogue strategies (framing, generative, transforming, and concertative), which can be adopted to help organizations recover from crises, as well as to proactively prevent them. Future research should help organizations to better understand how social media can be used during specific crisis situations. Such research should test the effectiveness of online dialogue strategies during specific crisis situations and in organizations that have different characteristics and communicative histories. Future research should also examine how social media are altering the ways in which stakeholders perceive critical situations and how these situations can become crises through online sense making. Without continuing focused attention by scholars and by practitioners, organizational crises—inappropriately addressed—can only be exacerbated in an online environment of stakeholders who are greatly influenced by the social media conversations.

References

Aldoory, L., Kim, J.-N., & Tindall, N. (2010). The influence of perceived shared risk in crisis communication: Elaborating the situational theory of publics. *Public Relations Review, 36*, 134–140.

Austin, L. L., Liu, B. F., & Jin, Y. (2012). How audiences seek out crisis information: Exploring the social-mediated crisis communication model. *Journal of Applied Communication Research, 40*(2), 188–207.

Becerra, A. (2012, December 20). Barilla e il grano ammuffito: Arriva la seconda puntata di una bufala diffusa in rete. La smentita ufficiale. *Il Fatto Alimentare.* Retrieved January 15, 2015, from www.ilfattoalimentare.it/bufala-barilla-grano-ammuffito.html

Coombs, W. T. (2012). *Ongoing crisis communication: Planning, managing and responding.* London, UK: Sage Publications, Inc.

Coombs, W. T. (2013a). Crisis and crisis management. In R. L. Heath (Ed.), *Encyclopedia of public relations: Volume 1* (pp. 216–219). Thousand Oaks, CA: Sage Publications, Inc.

Coombs, W. T. (2013b). Crisis communication. In R. L. Heath (Ed.), *Encyclopedia of public relations: Volume 1* (pp. 221–224). Thousand Oaks, CA: Sage Publications, Inc.

Coombs, W. T., & Holladay, S. J. (2012). The paracrisis: The challenges created by publicly managing crisis prevention. *Public Relations Review, 38*(3), 408–415.

Frandsen, F., & Johansen, W. (2013). Rhetorical arena (Crisis theory). In R. L. Heath (Ed.), *Encyclopedia of public relations: Volume 2* (pp. 797–800). Thousand Oaks, CA: Sage Publications, Inc.

González-Herrero, A., & Smith, S. (2008). Crisis communications management on the Web: How Internet-based technologies are changing the way public relations professionals handle business crises. *Journal of Contingencies and Crisis Management, 16*(3), 143–153.

González-Herrero, A., & Smith, S. (2010). Crisis communication management 2.0: Organizational principles to manage crisis in an online world. *Organizational Development Journal, 28*(1), 97–105.

Guth, D. W., & Alloway, G. A. (2008). Untapped potential: Evaluating state emergency management agency web sites 2008. *Online report.* Retrieved January 15, 2015, from www.dguth.journalism.ku.edu/WebVersionEMA.pdf

Jin, Y., & Liu, B. F. (2010). The blog-mediated crisis communication model: Recommendations for responding to influential external blogs. *Journal of Public Relations Research, 22*(4), 429–455.

Jin, Y., Liu, B. F., & Austin, L. L. (2014). Examining the role of social media in effective crisis management: The effects of crisis origin, information form, and source on publics' crisis responses. *Communication Research, 41*(1), 74–94.

Johansen, W., & Frandsen, F. (2007). *Krisekommunikation: Når virksomhedens image og omdømme er truet.* Frederiksberg, DK: Forlaget Samfundslitteratur.

Kim, J.-N., & Grunig, J. E. (2011). Problem solving and communicative action: A situational theory of problem solving. *Journal of Communication, 61,* 120–149.

Kozinets, R. V., de Valck, K., Wojnicki, A. C., & Wilner, S. J. (2010). Networked narratives: Understanding word-of-mouth marketing in online communities. *Journal of Marketing, 74*(2), 71–89.

Laurence, D. (2011, July 6). A digital crisis is coming your way: Are you ready? *Forbes.* Retrieved January 15, 2015, from http://www.forbes.com/sites/forbesleadershipforum/2011/07/06/a-digital-crisis-is-coming-your-way-are-you-ready/

Liu, B. F., & Kim, S. (2011). How organizations framed the 2009 H1N1 pandemic via social and traditional media: Implications for US health communicators. *Public Relations Review, 37*(3), 233–244.

Luoma-aho, V., & Vos, M. (2010). Towards a more dynamic stakeholder model: Acknowledging multiple issue arenas. *Corporate Communications: An International Journal, 15*(3), 315–331.

Meer, T. G. van der, & Verhoeven, P. (2013). Public framing organizational crisis situations: Social media versus news media. *Public Relations Review, 39*(3), 229–231.

Mei, J. S. A., Bansal, N., & Pang, A. (2010). New media: A new medium in escalating crises? *Corporate Communications: An International Journal, 15*(2), 143–155.

Messner, M., & DiStaso, M. W. (2008). The source cycle: How traditional media and weblogs use each other as source. *Journalism Studies, 9*(3), 447–463.

Mitchell, R. K., Agle, B. R., & Wood, D. J. (1997). Toward a theory of stakeholder identification and salience: Defining the principle of who and what really counts. *Academy of Management Review, 22*(4), 852–886.

Muralidharan, S., Rasmussen, L., Patterson, D., & Shin, J. (2011). Hope for Haiti: An analysis of Facebook and Twitter usage during the earthquake relief efforts. *Public Relations Review, 37*(3), 175–177.

Noble, C. H., Noble, S. M., & Adjei, M. T. (2012). Let them talk! Managing primary and extended online brand communities for success. *Business Horizons, 55,* 475–483.

Pang, A., Hassan, N. B. B. A., & Chong, A. C. Y. (2014). Negotiating crisis in the social media environment: Evolution of crises online, gaining credibility offline. *Corporate Communications: An International Journal, 19*(1), 96–118.

Perry, D. C., Taylor, M., & Doerfel, M. (2003). Internet based communication in crisis management. *Management Communication Quarterly, 17*(2), 206–233.

Putnam, R. D. (2000). *Bowling alone.* New York, NY: Simon & Schuster.

Romenti, S., Murtarelli, G., & Valentini, C. (2014). Organisations' conversations in social media: Applying dialogue strategies in times of crises. *Corporate Communications: An International Journal, 19*(1), 10–33.

Schultz, F., Kleinnijenhuis, J., Oegema, D., Utz, S., & van Atteveldt, W. (2012). Strategic framing in the BP crisis: A semantic network analysis of associative frames. *Public Relations Review, 38*(1), 97–107.

Scott, J. (2000). *Social network analysis: A handbook* (2nd Ed.). Thousand Oaks, CA: Sage Publications.

Sedereviciute, K., & Valentini, C. (2011). Towards a more holistic stakeholder analysis approach: Mapping known and undiscovered stakeholders from social media. *International Journal of Strategic Communication, 5*(4), 221–239.

Taneja, S., Pryor, M. G., Sewell, S., & Recuero, A. M. (2014). Strategic crisis management: A basis for renewal and crisis prevention. *Journal of Management, 15*(1), 79–85.

Tran, M. (2009, July 23). Singer gets his revenge on United Airlines and soars to fame. *The Guardian* (London). Retrieved January 15, 2015, from www.theguardian.com/news/blog/2009/jul/23/youtube-united-breaks-guitars-video

Valentini, C., & Kruckeberg, D. (2012a). New media versus social media: A conceptualization of their meanings, uses, and implications for public relations. In S. Duhe (Ed.), *New media and public relations* (pp. 3–12). New York, NY: Peter Lang.

Valentini, C., & Kruckeberg, D. (2012b). "Iran's Twitter Revolution" from a publics (sic) relations standpoint. In A. M. George & C. B. Pratt (Eds.), *Case studies in crisis communication: International perspectives on hits and misses* (pp. 383–402). London: Routledge.

Valentini, C., & Kruckeberg, D. (2015). The future role of social media in international crisis communication. In A. Schwarz, M. Seeger, & C. Auer (Eds.), *The handbook of international crisis communication research* (pp. 478–488). London: Wiley-Blackwell.

5

ETHICAL ENGAGEMENT AT A TIME OF CRISIS IN THE SOCIAL ERA

Chun-Ju Flora Hung-Baesecke and Shannon A. Bowen

Numerous studies have been done on using social media in public relations (e.g., DiStaso, McCorkindale, & Wright, 2011; Wright & Hinson, 2008), crisis communication (e.g., Austin, Liu, & Jin, 2012; Jin, Liu, & Austin, 2014), public engagement (Men & Tsai, 2013), and ethical guidelines (Bowen, 2013). A Pew Internet study (Rainie, Smith, & Duggan, 2013) revealed that social-networking site users are checking in more frequent than ever before. Yet, DiStaso and Bortree's (2014) study showed corporations usually are not actively communicating with stakeholders via social media, though many conversations among social media users are about them. Organizations therefore have to participate and engage actively with publics in the social context.

Moreover, Solis (2014) contended that social media are not lawless and the behaviors on social networking sites should be "guided by aspiration, grounded in virtues, and packaged in respect" (p. xvii). Echoing the same view, DiStaso and Bortree (2014) advocated for ethical considerations in conducting effective social media campaigns. Austin, Liu, and Jin (2012) and Procopio and Procopio (2007) found stakeholders tend to view social medial as more credible than traditional media. Therefore, it is important to ensure clarity and transparency of information disseminated through social media channels to stakeholders during a crisis.

Coombs (2008) considered social media to be an effective tool for organizations to detect crises and issues, identify warning signs, send and update messages, and provide an interactive tool for communication with stakeholders during a crisis. Reasons for audiences relying on social media during a crisis include emotional support (Choi & Lin, 2009), real-time information updates (Procopio & Procopio, 2007), and the ability to obtain information that stakeholders are unable to obtain elsewhere (Sutton, Palen, & Shklovski, 2008). Consequently, social networking sites have become useful crisis-information communication channels for both crisis managers and stakeholders (Austin et al., 2012).

Scholars have pinpointed keywords for ethical communication online and offline: duty, dignity, respect, intention (Bowen, 2013), transparency (DiStaso & Bortree, 2012; Rawlins, 2009), openness, disclosure (Waters, 2014), authenticity (Henderson & Bowley, 2010), honesty, candor, and openness (Veil, Buehner, & Palenchar, 2011). Bowen (2013) summarized the principles of ethical communication and developed guidelines for social media. Yet, no study has examined the importance of ethical guidelines in dealing with *crisis communication* via social media. In this chapter, we seek to examine one crisis case and the use of social media, including its ethics, in order to help fill that void in the literature.

Overview of Social Media Use in Public Relations

In a longitudinal study of social media, Wright and Hinson (2013) found that "those who practice public relations believe social and other emerging media continue to improve in terms of accuracy, credibility, honesty, trust and truth telling" (p. 14). Among the respondents, 15% reported spending more than half of their workday on social media initiatives. Clearly the use of social media is changing the core communication channels that public relations practitioners use to reach their stakeholders. Berg and Sheehan (2014) found that stakeholders are coming to rely more heavily on social media for all sorts of communication from organizations, and indeed beginning to demand it. Senior public relations executives, among them Eberwein (2010), Kelly (2009), and Olson (2013), explained that the microblogging site Twitter is often the first source to provide stakeholders, and even news reporters, with information about major news events, crises, or catastrophes.

With the development of technology, digital, mobile, and social media allow more simultaneous information exchange and sharing. Information can be considered "published" as soon as it is posted to a microblog such as Twitter, and the role of traditional gatekeepers and editors is practically nonexistent on social media. Such rapidly available and easily disseminated and redistributed information has created a heightened need for public relations professionals to communicate rapidly during a crisis—but with an even greater emphasis on accurate and ethical communication.

Crisis Communication Ethics

Review of Crisis Communication Theories

Coombs (2015) contended that a crisis brings negative impact on stakeholders physically, emotionally, psychologically, and sometimes financially. Hence, this situation provides the opportunity for stakeholders to think negatively about the organization; a reputational threat to the organization thus arises.

Situational Crisis Communication Theory (SCCT)

The development of the situational crisis communication theory (SCCT) offers the framework guiding organizations' strategic communication development for maximizing the reputational protection at the time of a crisis (Coombs, 2007a). In this chapter, we focus on the discussions of ethical crisis communication during a crisis. As a result, we will only focus on the discussion on factors in SCCT for understanding the importance of applying ethical principles in handling crises. In SCCT, after a crisis happens, people would search for the reasons and responsibilities that caused the crisis. When a person attributes responsibility for a crisis, certain kinds of emotions, usually anger or sympathy, will be developed. Coombs posited that the responsibility attribution and emotions provide the motivations for stakeholders to take actions (Coombs, 2007a, 2015). SCCT analyzes the possible reputational threat brought by a crisis so that a crisis manager can devise crisis-response strategies accordingly (Coombs, 2007a). Yet, in choosing crisis-response strategies, an organization needs to be aware of its ethical responsibilities in responding to a crisis—to address the physical, psychological, and emotional concerns of the affected stakeholders first, instead of fixing an organization's reputation first. In addition, effective crisis management should seek to evoke positive responses from stakeholders by meeting their information needs or providing appropriate responses to those needs within media coverage (Coombs, 2007b).

Social-Mediated Crisis Communication (SMCC) Model

Jin and Liu (2010) first developed the blog-mediated crisis communication (BMCC) model in illustrating the context of how influential blogs as opinion leaders affect their followers and indirectly affect nonfollowers. With the effects of the media and word of mouth via interpersonal communication, blog followers pass crisis information to non-blog followers. As Coombs (2015) contended, websites were only the starting point for utilizing online communication tools in affecting how organizations communicate and manage crises. In responding to this rapid change in the online environment, the BMCC model was expanded to the social-mediated crisis communication (SMCC) model, which portrayed a wider range of the social media channels and how information can be shared online and offline (for detailed discussions on this model, please see Austin et al., 2012; Jin et al., 2014).

The elements of the SMCC model include (a) the types of publics producing and consuming the crisis information (influential social media creators, social media followers, and social media inactives); (b) forms, or how the crisis information is conveyed (Facebook, Twitter, YouTube, blogs, traditional media, etc.); (c) sources, or who, either the organization or a third party, sends out the crisis information; and (d) five considerations that would affect how organizations respond to crises: crisis origin, crisis type, infrastructure, message content, and message form.

In different studies, researchers found out that informational and emotional needs were the major motivations for using social media during crises (yet traditional media were still perceived as a more credible source of information; Austin et al., 2012). Effects of internal crisis origin included publics tending to have stronger crisis emotions and expecting more accommodative crisis responses and if the crisis information was disseminated by a third party via social media; when the original of a crisis was external, people would tend to accept evasive responses from an organization (Jin et al., 2014).

Synthesis

In the discussions of the SCCT and the SMCC model, we consider the interplay of these two theories, which helps provide the context in the case we are analyzing for this chapter. For example, SCCT will explain how stakeholders react when they attribute the cause of a crisis to the organization and the crisis-response strategies the organization adopts in the crisis situation. Studies from the SMCC model show more contextual factors as to why publics use social media to disseminate crisis information, and how multiple channels are employed that further escalated a crisis situation.

Ethical Crisis Communication

DiStaso and Bortree (2014) contended that, for effectively using social media strategically, organizations should have ethical considerations in their practices in engaging dialogically with their stakeholders. Very little research has been published that deals specifically with the ethics of managing a crisis, especially in the social media domain. We give a brief overview of this topic so that we can also examine the ethical nature of the organizational response in the crisis case we discuss later in this chapter.

Consequentialism: Utilitarianism

One major school of thought in moral philosophy uses the outcomes, or potential outcomes, of actions to determine the ethics of the decision. Using the consequences of an action to weigh its ethical impact does not examine the moral principle supporting the action but rather the impacts on stakeholders of those actions. The consequentialist approach allows the public relations manager to effectively evaluate the potential effects on stakeholders of organizational actions.

We refer to this consequentialist school of thought as utilitarianism, the most commonly used consequential approach. It is useful in helping determine how stakeholders may view organizational decisions from their own perspectives, before the organization commits to a particular course of action.

Using a consequentialist, utilitarian approach requires the public relations manager to make relatively accurate predictions about the outcomes of future events, as well as the responses of key publics. The more information one uses in that decision analysis, the better the understanding of the situation and potential future consequences. Still, accuracy is difficult and requires industry knowledge and experience. Another pitfall of utilitarianism is that the majority always carries the decision: because moral principle is not involved in evaluating the decision, the minority might have an extremely compelling argument based on moral principle that goes ignored by the utilitarian approach. Therefore, for a more morally rigorous approach, decisions need to be augmented with a nonconsequentialist, moral-principle-based approach.

Nonconsequentialism: Deontology

A nonconsequentialist approach is based purely on moral principle, meaning that consequences of a decision are no longer the driving factor—universalism, reversibility, and good intention are. Although this approach does not ignore consequences, they are but one factor in the decision, equal among many.

Kant's deontology ordered the moral duties and obligations that all rational beings are obligated to act under into the three forms of his categorical imperative test (Sullivan, 1989). Form 1 tests the universality of a decision, asking the decision maker to act only on the action that he or she would want to be a universal law in all similar situations. Form 2 tests reversibility by asking the decision maker if the potential action maintains dignity and respect of all involved. And, form 3 asks if the decision is made from goodwill alone, testing the moral intention of the decision maker. If an act can pass all three tests of deontology, it is ethical. A more full explanation of these ethical tests as applied to public relations and issues management can be found in Bowen (2004), and a practical application of deontology in public relations was offered in Bowen (2005).

Both utilitarian and deontological schools of thought provide rational means for moral analyses of problems. Each school of thought has strengths and weaknesses, so they are often best used in conjunction, to complement one another and offer a multiplicity of insights into ethical problems. The combination of utilitarian and deontological analysis was first presented as a model for public relations analysis in Bowen and Gallicano (2013) and will be used later in this research as a means to apply rigorous ethical tests to the crisis cases under study.

Ethical Digital Engagement in Crisis

Ethics and Ethical Guidelines for Digital Engagement

Due to the rapidity of information dissemination in a digital environment, ethical guidelines for crisis communication in the digital realm are an urgent consideration. In any case, a crisis situation demands response—with both rapid and ethical examination as foremost considerations.

TABLE 5.1 Ethical Guidelines for Using Social Media

#	Guideline	Rationale/Implementation★
1	Be fair and prudent.	Consider fairness, justice, and access. Consider the right to know.
2	Avoid deception.	If it is deceptive, even arguably, simply do not do it.
3	Maintain dignity and respect.	Ensure that the communication maintains the dignity and respect of the involved publics.
4	Eschew secrecy.	Barring trade or competition secrets, if an initiative warrants secrecy, something needs ethical examination.
5	Consider reversibility.	How would you feel on the receiving end of the message? Is it still ethical then?
6	Be transparent.	Paid speech should be transparently identified as such by "Endorsement," "Paid Message," or similar phrasing.
7	Identify clearly.	Personal speech and opinion versus speech as a representative of the organization should be identified.
8	Analyze rationally.	Examine messages from all sides. How would it look to other publics? How could it potentially be misconstrued?
9	Emphasize clarity.	Even if the source or sponsorship is clear, make it clearer.
10	Disclose.	Be transparent in message creation, facts, and data needed for an informed decision.
11	Verify sources and data.	Be consistently credible. Do not use rumor or speculation.
12	Establish responsibility.	Does the message maintain your responsibility to do what is right?
13	Examine intention.	Is your decision made with goodwill alone?
14	Encourage the good.	Does your message help build connectedness, engagement, and community?
15	Be consistent to build trust.	Consistency allows publics to know and understand you, and you can meet their expectations.

★The level of analysis can be changed by using the words "campaign" or "initiative" instead of "message," which is used here for simplicity.

Bowen (2013) conducted research on ethical lapses and exemplars in social media and, based on applying moral philosophy to those situations, constructed 15 ethical guidelines centering around the deontological obligations for honesty, universal decisions, respect, and good intention. The rationale for each ethical standard is explained in Table 5.1, but the 15 guidelines later used to analyze the case in this study encourage fairness and prudence, avoiding deception, dignity and respect, eschewing secrecy, reversibility, transparency, identification, rationality, clarity, disclosure, verification, responsibility, good intention, encouraging the good, and being consistent to build trust. Using those guidelines in social media can not only help an organization ethically respond to a crisis, but also help avoid crises in the first place.

Authenticity in Ethical Crisis Communication

The Arthur W. Page Society (2012) defined *authenticity* as "conforming to fact and therefore worthy of trust, reliance, or belief" (p. 15) and considered that one of the values public relations contributes to an organization was to help it be authentic when communicating with stakeholders. The development of the concept of authenticity has been done in different disciplines. In psychology, self-determination theory (Deci, 1980) and the fully functioning individual (Rogers, 1961) are the major approaches in viewing authenticity. Per the self-determination theory, an individual is authentic when he or she is autonomous and self-determining. In the fully functioning individual approach, an authentic individual is one who can fully take charge of his or her life, making decisions about life autonomously. In extrapolating the meanings of authenticity to ethics, an individual is autonomous in making decisions about his or her behaviors, is responsible for the consequences, and ensures his or her words conform to his or her actions.

Bowen (2010) considered authenticity to be a core construct essential to ethical communication and defined *authenticity* as "being the same on the inside as one appears to be on the outside, in the sense of a genuine and true relation" (p. 579). For her, authenticity illustrates three different concerns: transparency, genuineness, and truthfulness. Her insights on transparency in authenticity are also shared by Rawlins's (2009) and Shen and J. Kim's (2012) studies on how open communication can lead to authentic public relations. Edwards (2010) viewed authenticity and integrity to be important steps for public relations to achieve credibility and trust. Stoker and Rawlins (2010) posited that authenticity in public relations could be obtained when practitioners "achieve moral congruity among internal beliefs, conscious commitment, and external actions" (p. 67). Molleda (2010) contended authenticity should be reviewed by the messages, actions, and how these are perceived from the stakeholders' point of view.

In summary, we believe that ethics serves as an important foundation for organizations' ability to conduct authentic communication. Without ethics, the meaning of authenticity is lost, as organizations do not have an ethical conscience to guide their behaviors, and what organizations consider to be authentic behaviors will still be deemed unethical.

Synthesis

During a crisis, publics, affected stakeholders, and the media are eager to attribute responsibilities for the crisis. Opinion leaders, such as influential social media creators, share and disseminate crisis information to their followers and indirectly to the inactive publics online and offline. Organizations that cause crises ought to understand the dynamic context of how information can be created and disseminated via different channels. With an ethical conscience, organizations causing crises should evaluate the best approach in responding to crises, making sure publics' interest should be at least as important as the organizations' (J. Grunig, 2001) in ensuring transparent, open, and accountable communication behaviors on different forms of communication channels.

In the following section, we are using the case of Dolce & Gabbana's photo ban crisis that was escalated by corporate arrogance and lack of respect for stakeholders and the information shared online and offline in various forms of communication channels.

Case: Dolce & Gabbana Photo Ban Crisis

Overview of the Case

The photo ban saga started in December 2011, when some stakeholders in Hong Kong complained on the Internet that the security staff at the Dolce & Gabbana (D&G) Harbour City store prevented them from taking photos in front of the store. Reporters from the local newspaper, *Apple Daily*, went to D&G's stores on January 4, 2012, to find more information and were also told not to take photos. The response from D&G was that it had to protect its intellectual property.

On January 5, 2012, *Apple Daily* published a story on the front page, titled "Mainland Chinese Guests Are Allowed to Take Photos. Hong Kongers Get Lost. D&G Flagrantly Bullies Hong Kongers." A photographer from this newspaper reported that a security guard from the D&G store stated only mainland Chinese or foreign tourists were allowed to take photos outside the store and that this security guard threatened to break the photographer's camera (Booker, 2012). Within hours, angry Hong Kongers left hundreds of messages on D&G's Facebook wall and created a Facebook event "10,000 People Photograph D&G Event," protesting D&G discriminating behaviors. By 10 p.m. on the same day, more than 3,000 Facebook users had agreed to participate in this event. However, D&G restated that the company's consent was required for taking photos in front of the stores.

During the following days, local newspapers continued reporting this incident, with more Hong Kongers showing their protest by joining the event Facebook event and taking photos in front of D&G stores. On January 8, more than 1,000 angry protesters gathered in front of the D&G Harbour City store, taking photos and carrying signs with various slogans like "D&G, Dust & Garbage," "D&G Go Home," and "Shame." The protest—an overwhelming victory—forced D&G and nearby stores to close doors early on that day. Still, D&G refused to apologize and issued an unsigned statement on the same day, saying,

> Controversial statements reported in the Hong Kong press have not been made by Dolce & Gabbana nor its staff, and we strongly reject any racist or derogatory comments.

> It is regrettable that Dolce & Gabbana has been brought into this matter, but we wish to underline that our company has not taken part in any action aiming at offending the Hong Kong Public.

As noted by *Forbes*, such statements could not assuage public anger. Hong Kong residents used Facebook to either share information online or offline and create "boycott D&G" groups and write protesting and furious comments on the brand's official page. Still, D&G did not seem to be aware of the seriousness of the crisis. To make things worse, one employee from the same store accused on her own Facebook page the Hong Kong protesters of having "mental problems" and a "herd mentality" (Booker, 2012). Though she later apologized, more protesters joined the "10,000 People Photograph D&G Event" and organized another demonstration outside the D&G store.

On January 11, the Equal Opportunities Commission in Hong Kong expressed concerns on the different treatment of Hong Kongers and mainland Chinese. No response or reply was received from D&G. Up to January 12, more than 22,000 people had joined the Facebook event, which continued to encourage people to take photos outside the D&G store with the flash on. Between January 13 and 15, two more protests outside the D&G store were launched and the number of people joining the Facebook event exceeded 24,000.

Finally, facing great pressure and a boycott from Hong Kong protesters, D&G issued a formal apology to Hong Kong, saying it had learned from the scandal and would listen to the views of people from different sectors in society.

Analysis of the Case

We analyze this case with a view on how the crisis information was disseminated via different communication channels by using the SMCC model and how D&G violated the ethical principles in this crisis.

Crisis Communication Behaviors

First of all, the crisis started when D&G, the originator of the crisis, adopted two different standards in treating Hong Kongers and mainland customers in the issue of photography. This story was shared and reported by influential social media creators (e.g., the Facebook user who created "10,000 People Photograph D&G Event") and the traditional media (*Apple Daily*). Social media followers then received the information via the various communication channels, online and offline, and joined the actions. From D&G viewpoint, corporate arrogance prevented the company from accepting the responsibility, and had it take a defensive approach to handling the crisis. What D&G failed to do in time was to utilize different social media communication tools to detect the issue and to identify the warning signs in the business environment. Worse, the company did not take

advantage of the interactive nature of social media in communicating with stakeholders despite there being extensive discussions and growing anger in the society.
Coombs's (2007a) and Austin and her colleagues' (2012) studies have pointed out
that responsibility attribution, emotions, and informational needs are the motivations for publics to take actions and use social media during crises. Their points
were well reflected in this case, in which angry protestors used social media to
share and obtain more information and to organize protest against the company.

Ethical Crisis Communication Principles

D&G violated (disregarded) each form of ethics considered in this chapter. It violated the "greater good for the greatest number" principle by refusing to permit
those who cannot afford the designer clothes to simply take a keepsake photo. It
also violated the universal nature of deontology because other D&G stores could
obviously not follow such an outlandish rule. It violated the dignity and respect
owed to stakeholders, indeed the Hong Kong fans of the brand (someone not a
fan of the brand would not want a photo there in the first place), as well as the
equality owed to mainland Chinese and Hong Kongers. Finally, it did not act with
good intention. In fact, it took D&G two full weeks to respond to the crisis in
an apology; responses before that did not acknowledge the problem and therefore
exacerbated it. Coombs (2014) explained, "A repression response to a challenge
risks backlash when the organization cannot justify stopping a message" (p. 136).
D&G seemed unaware of the ethical implications or severity of the crisis it caused
or the backlash from its lack of response.

  In looking at Bowen's 15 guidelines for ethical social media, it is difficult to
find a single standard that D&G upheld. One could argue that trade secrets make
the no-photograph policy of the storefront necessary, but that argument becomes
absurd when rationally examining the purpose of the displays in storefront win-
dows. Therefore, D&G fails on all 15 ethical standards for action, in that they did
not respond to the social media outcry, did not consider the implications of their
policy, and so forth. This case is an excellent one for examining how a total lack
of ethical examination can cause an organizational crisis.

Authenticity in Crisis Communication

Molleda (2010) viewed that authentic communication means organizations
should offer access to genuine and substantial dialogue with stakeholders by providing truthful information and respecting the views of stakeholders. In D&G's
case, there was no access provided for engaging in dialogues with stakeholders.
The company provided false information by stating that it was the company's
policy of protecting intellectual property for not allowing Hong Kongers to take
photos outside the store. Furthermore, the criticism by the D&G employee of
the angry stakeholders further worsened the situation. The first statement issued

by the company was full of shifting blame, denying responsibilities, and offering no apologies. It was only when the company faced great pressure that it finally apologized to Hong Kong. However, this delayed apology made the company lose credibility and could not been seen as an authentic apology.

Conclusion

The case reviewed herein offers several valuable lessons for the ethical management of crises. D&G's behavior reveals that inattention to ethics, lack of fairness and transparency, misleading stakeholders, justification of its own behavior by false store policy, shifting responsibilities, and dismissive intention in treatment of stakeholders can create a major crisis and damage the reputation.

When planning crisis-response strategies in the era of social media, organizations should not ignore the importance of engaging with stakeholders in the digital sphere. It is clear that stakeholders use those channels to both complain and to organize. By ignoring their importance, D&G exacerbated the crises. The role and impact of digital engagement will only continue to grow, and by using the ethical standards offered herein as a means of analysis, organizations can both prevent crises and respond to them confidently. Since this crisis, D&G has handled difficult ethical and social issues with grace and appears to have managed issues effectively—it appears they have learned much from this crisis.

References

Austin, L., Liu, B. F., & Jin, Y. (2012). How audiences seek out crisis information: Exploring the social-mediated crisis communication model. *Journal of Applied Communication Research, 40*(2), 188–207.

Berg, K. T., & Sheehan, K. B. (2014). Social media as a CSR communication channel: The current state of practice. In M. W. DiStaso & D. S. Bortree (Eds.), *Ethical practice of social media in public relations* (pp. 99–110). New York: Routledge.

Booker, A. (2012, January 12). What luxury brands should learn from Dolce & Gabbana's Hong Kong PR disaster. Retrieved from http://www.forbes.com/sites/china/2012/01/12/what-luxury-brands-should-learn-from-dolce-gabbanas-hong-kong-pr-disaster/

Bowen, S. A. (2004). Organizational factors encouraging ethical decision making: An exploration into the case of an exemplar. *Journal of Business Ethics, 52*(4), 311–324.

Bowen, S. A. (2005). A practical model for ethical decision making in issues management and public relations. *Journal of Public Relations Research, 17*(3), 191–216.

Bowen, S. A. (2010). The nature of good in public relations: What should be its normative ethic? In R. L. Heath (Ed.), *The Sage handbook of public relations* (pp. 569–583). Thousand Oaks, CA: Sage.

Bowen, S. A. (2013). Using classic social media cases to distill ethical guidelines for digital engagement. *Journal of Mass Media Ethics: Exploring Questions of Media Morality, 28*(2), 119–133.

Bowen, S. A., & Gallicano, T. D. (2013). A philosophy of reflective ethical symmetry: Comprehensive historical and future moral approaches in the excellence theory. In K. Sriramesh, A. Zerfass, & J. N. Kim (Eds.), *Public relations and communication management* (pp. 193–209). London: Taylor & Francis.

Choi, Y., & Lin, Y.-H. (2009). Consumer responses to Mattel product recalls posted on online bulletin boards: Exploring two types of emotion. *Journal of Public Relations Research, 21*(2), 198–207.

Coombs, W. T. (2007a). Protecting organization reputations during a crisis: The development and application of situational crisis communication theory. *Corporate Reputation Review, 10*(3), 163–176.

Coombs, W. T. (2007b). Attribution theory as a guide for post-crisis communication research. *Public Relations Review, 33*, 135–139.

Coombs, W. T. (2008). Crisis communication and social media. *Institute for public relations.* Retrieved from http://www.instituteforpr.org/crisis-communication-and-social-media/

Coombs, W. T. (2014). Nestle and Greenpeace: The battle in social media for ethical palm oil sourcing. In M. W. DiStaso & D. S. Bortree (Eds.), *Ethical practice of social media in public relations* (pp. 126–137). New York: Routledge.

Coombs, W. T. (2015). *Ongoing crisis communication: Planning, managing and responding.* Thousand Oaks, CA: Sage.

Deci, E. L. (1980). *The psychology of self-determination.* Lexington, MA: Heath.

DiStaso, M. W., & Bortree, D. S. (2012). Multi-method analysis of transparency in social media practices: Survey, interviews and content analysis. *Public Relations Review, 38*(3), 511–514.

DiStaso, M. W., & Bortree, D. S. (2014). *Ethical practice of social media in public relations.* New York: Routledge.

DiStaso, M. W., McCorkindale, T., & Wright, D. K. (2011). How public relations executives perceive and measure the impact of social media in their organizations. *Public Relations Review, 37*, 325–328.

Eberwein, E. (2010). What Southwest Airlines learned about media use during the "Landing on the Hudson." *Remarks to the public relations executive forum,* Chicago. May 6.

Edwards, L. (2010). Authenticity in organizational context: Fragmentation, contradiction and loss of control. *Journal of Communication Management, 14*(3), 192–205.

Grunig, J. E. (2001). Two-way symmetrical public relations: Past, present, and future. In R. L. Heath (Ed.), *Handbook of public relations* (pp. 11–30). Thousand Oaks, CA: Sage.

Henderson, A., & Bowley, R. (2010). Authentic dialogue? The role of "friendship" in a social media recruitment campaign. *Journal of Communication Management, 14*(3), 237–257.

Jin, Y., & Liu, B. F. (2010). The blog-mediated crisis communication model: Recommendations for responding to influential external blogs. *Journal of Public Relations Research, 22*(4), 429–455.

Jin, Y., Liu, B. F., & Austin, L. (2014). Examining the role of social media in effective crisis management: The effects of crisis origin, information form, and source on publics' crisis responses. *Communication Research, 4*(1), 74–94.

Kelly, G. (2009). Remarks to the Arthur W. Page society. Chicago. September 15.

Men, L. R., & Tsai, W. S. (2013). Towards an integrated model of public engagement on corporate social network sites: Antecedents, the process, and relational outcomes. *International Journal of Strategic Communication, 7*, 257–273.

Molleda, J. (2010). Authenticity and the construct's dimensions in public relations and communication research. *Journal of Communication, 14*(3), 223–236.

Olson, J, (2013, unpublished manuscript). US Airways and the "miracle on the Hudson" landing. In S. Bowen (Ed.), *Strategic communication management: Public relations for competitive advantage.* New York: Pearson Allyn and Bacon.

Page, A. W. (Ed.). (2012). *The authentic enterprise.* New York: The Arthur W. Page Society.

Procopio, C. H., & Procopio, S. T. (2007). Do you know what it means to miss New Orleans? Internet communication, geographic community, and social capital in crisis. *Journal of Applied Communication Research, 35*(1), 67–87.

Rainie, L., Smith, A., & Duggan, M. (2013). Coming and going on Facebook. Retrieved from http://www.pewinternet.org/2013/02/05/coming-and-going-on-facebook/

Rawlins, B. (2009). Give the emperor a mirror: Toward developing a stakeholder measurement of organizational transparency. *Journal of Public Relations Research, 21*, 71–99.

Rogers, C. (1961). *On becoming a person: A therapist's view of psychotherapy.* New York: Houghton Mifflin Company.

Shen, H., & Kim, J.-N. (2012). The authentic enterprise: Another buzz word, or a true driver of quality relationships? *Journal of Public Relations Research, 24*, 371–389.

Solis, B. (2014). Foreword: Social media is lost without a social compass. In M. W. DiStaso & D. S. Bortree (Eds.) *Ethical practice of social media in public relations* (pp. xv–xxiv). New York: Routledge.

Stoker, K., & Rawlins, B. (2010). Taking the BS out of PR: Creating genuine messages by emphasising character and authenticity. *Ethical Space-International Journal of Communication Ethics, 2*(3), 61–69.

Sullivan, R. J. (1989). *Immanuel Kant's moral theory.* Cambridge: Cambridge University Press.

Sutton, J., Palen, L., & Shklovski, I. (2008, March). *Backchannels on the front lines: Emergent uses of social media in the 2007 southern California wildfires.* In F. Fiedrich & B. Van de Walle (Eds.), Proceedings of the 5th International ISCRAM Conference, Washington, DC.

Veil, S. R., Buehner, T., & Palenchar, M. J. (2011). A work-in-process literature review: Incorporating social media in risk and crisis communication. *Journal of Contingencies & Crisis Management, 19*(2), 110–122.

Waters, R. (2014). Openness and disclosure in social media efforts: A frank discussion with Fortune 500 and Philanthropy 400 communication leaders. In M. W. DiStaso and D. S. Bortree (Eds.) *Ethical practice of social media in public relations* (pp. 3–20). New York: Routledge.

Wright, D. K., & Hinson, M. D. (2008). How blogs and social media are changing public relations and the way it is practiced. *Public Relations Journal, 2*(2). Retrieved from http://www.prsa.org/SearchResults/download/6D-020203/0/How_Blogs_and_Social_Media_are_Changing_Public_Rel

Wright, D., & Hinson, M. (2013). An updated examination of social and emerging media use in public relations practice: A longitudinal analysis between 2006 and 2013. *Public Relations Journal, 7*(3), 1–39. Retrieved from http://apps.prsa.org/intelligence/PR Journal/Documents/2013_WrightHinson_2013.pdf

SECTION III
Foundations and Frameworks

SECTION III-A
Foundations and Frameworks

Organizational Approaches and Considerations

6

THE ROLE OF PUBLIC RELATIONS LEADERSHIP IN EFFECTIVE SOCIAL MEDIA AND CRISIS COMMUNICATION MANAGEMENT

Juan Meng and Bruce K. Berger

Introduction

Over the course of the last decade, public relations scholars have become increasingly convinced that the deliberate identification of leadership functions is crucial for maximizing the power influence and effectiveness of public relations practice (Berger & Meng, 2010). Given the importance we attribute to leadership in many realms of life, it's not hard to argue that leadership is critical in a variety of communication situations that involve strategic desicion-making. Researchers have developed many approaches and theories to explain and predict leadership effectiveness and organizational performance. These approaches encompass leader traits, styles, skills, and behaviors; leader power and influence; situational determinants of leader behavior; and leadership as an attributional process (e.g., Bass, 1990; Conger, 1999; Dansereau, Graen, & Haga, 1975; Fiedler, 1978; House, 1971; Stogdill, 1948; Yukl, 1989). However, limited research has specifically focused on the role of public relations leaders and the application of leadership when social media have radically altered the information-gathering and processing procedure in professional practice. More crucially, such leadership challenge is leveraged when facing the call for effective crisis communication.

Although the capacity of leadership in facilitating effective public relations practice is recognized, only a small body of theory-driven research addresses the potential roles of communication and public relations executives as crucial informal leaders (or formal ones in certain situations; Broom & Dozier, 1986; Dozier & Broom, 1995). At the empirical level, we see growing interests in designing research that explores public relations executives' leadership roles in addressing communication value, achieving effectiveness in and for organizations, developing and managing ethical practice, and helping organizations make strategic choices (e.g., Aldoory & Toth, 2004; Berger, Reber, & Heyman, 2007; Choi & Choi, 2009; Lee & Cheng, 2011; Meng & Berger, 2013; Meng, Berger, Gower, & Heyman, 2012; Werder & Holtzhausen, 2009, 2011).

To continue our research efforts in confirming the critical role of leadership to public relations executives when emerging issues, such as risks, crises, and the prevalence of social media, present great challenges in finding effective responsive solutions and strategies, in this chapter, we offer a unique perspective to explore strategies and actions to effectively manage social media and diverse types of crises by looking at the role of public relations leadership and its critical dimensions in social media and crisis management. We believe emerging issues or situations create particularly unique contingencies, constraints, and opportunities for communication leaders to explore leadership and its effectiveness in those contexts.

To guide our efforts, we begin this chapter with reviews and reflections on research perspectives in public relations that have directly or indirectly explored leadership. Guided by this review, we articulate the importance of leadership in different contextualized situations in public relations practice. From this base of understanding, we begin a detailed explanation on a global research project on public relations leadership and issues management, which highlights the identified emerging needs of managing social media and crises effectively by public relations practitioners all over the world. We then discuss how critical leadership dimensions can support or produce effective responses. Throughout, we seek to highlight the unique influences that various dimensions of public relations leadership can have on the issues-management processes with the hope that this knowledge may inform more refined approaches in managing social media and crises.

Literature Review: Perspectives in Leadership-Centered Research in Public Relations

Though leadership has been little explored directly by public relations scholars, it seems likely that the assumption of excellence in public relations has its roots in leadership and organizational studies. Both public relations professionals and scholars have recognized the importance of applying appropriate leadership style in practice. Overall, there are six major perspectives emerged in leadership-centered research in public relations, which include the excellence and role theories, the contingency theory, the power relations theory, gender and leadership in public relations, ethical leadership, and the behavioral approach.

Excellence and Role Theories

As one of the most comprehensive research projects completed in the field of public relations, the excellence study provides a conceptual framework for understanding the functions of public relations (J. E. Grunig, 1992; L. A. Grunig et al., 2002). Results of the excellence study implicitly recognize the importance of leadership and its application in the scope of excellence in communication management (J. E. Grunig, 1992). Specifically, researchers suggest that organizations must empower public relations as a critical management function, and relevant managerial role activities should be carried out (Broom & Dozier, 1986; Dozier, 1984, 1992; Dozier & Broom, 1995).

The role theory (Dozier, 1992) identifies managerial role activities reflecting characteristics and values that a public relations unit should present as a managerial function, which can contribute to organizational effectiveness (Dozier & Broom, 1995). Excellence theory and role theory highlight certain traits (visionary, managerial view), skills (communication knowledge and expertise), and behaviors (model two-way communication) of public relations leaders. The theories also underscore the influence of organizational culture and structure (power, hierarchy, dominant coalition) on practice and leadership and the need for diversity and equal opportunities for women and minorities.

The Contingency Theory

The contingency theory focuses on establishing strategic and conflictual relationships between an organization and its publics (e.g., Cameron, Cropp, & Reber, 2001; Reber & Cameron, 2003). It specifies the role of public relations leaders in helping their organizations scan the external environment, identify crucial issues, and interpret what they mean and then make appropriate strategic choices based on those issues and actors. This view suggests that "leadership is best not conceived as a universal trait, but as situationally-sensitive management and strategic (even tactical) options" (Shin, Heath, & Lee, 2011, p. 172).

Public relations leaders must be able to assess external threats and opportunities, make strategic choices, and advocate for those situationally sensitive choices with organizational leaders, based on their close analysis of the issue and the strategic choice continuum. Through this process, public relations moves the organization "to be outer directed and to have a participative organizational culture" (Heath, 2006, p. 76). Contingency theory in public relations research reflects the situational approach in leadership theory (Waller, Smith, & Warnock, 1989): context affects what leaders pay attention to and what they do. This approach recognizes the rich and complex diversity of issues with which organizations must deal, such as employee issues, stakeholder activities, public policy matters, organizational cultural and structural factors, societal culture and political-economic realities, and so forth.

Power Relations Theory

Empowerment is a principle goal of leadership (Conger & Kanungo, 1988; Kirkman & Rosen, 1999), as empowering leadership involves sharing power with a view toward enhancing employees' motivation and engagement in their work, providing participation in decision making, conveying confidence in the significance of the work, and removing bureaucratic constraints (Ahearne, Mathieu, & Rapp, 2005). In discussing empowerment in the profession, public relations researchers find that some practitioners failed to gain power and influence inside organizations not only due to the devaluation of organizational executives but also because of the lack of self-empowerment capabilities. The lack of professional expertise, leadership skills, organizational knowledge, and inexperience with organizational politics and power relations impede the empowerment process (Berger & Reber, 2006).

Berger and Reber (2006) built on this power-control perspective and explored how power can make public relations units more active, effective, and ethical in organizational decision making. They claimed that public relations practice is inherently political. Thus, networks and relationships built through practice are inherently strategic. As a result, leaders who lack professional expertise and organizational knowledge, or who are inexperienced in organizational politics and power relations, will be less effective. Therefore, one must increase his or her power and influence, "become more politically astute, employ more diverse influence resources and tactics, and exert greater political will in organizational arenas where decisions are shaped through power relations" (Berger & Reber, 2006, p. 2).

Gender and Leadership in Public Relations

The feminist perspective has been an important one in public relations research since the early 1990s as a reflection of the profession's structure. Aldoory (1998) interviewed female leaders in public relations to examine their leadership style and found that they exhibited transformational and interactive styles, grounded in a situational context. Aldoory and Toth (2004) found that practitioners strongly favored a transformational leadership style over transactional style. However, research indicated that, generally, women had fewer opportunities for leadership positions in public relations, although practitioners believed that women made better leaders due to their perceived empathy and collaborative efforts (Aldoory & Toth, 2004).

A longtime pay gap between women and men in the field is identified as the key factor for women finding it more difficult to ascend to leadership roles (L. Grunig, Toth, & Hon, 2001). Gender stereotyping is one of the key drivers. The researchers argued that issues of gender bias are essentially issues of perceptions of women created by both men and women. Although women today represent about 70% of the professional workforce, the pay gap is still an issue. This pay gap has been attributed to differences in years of professional experience, manager role enactment, participation in management decision making, income-suppressing career interruptions, and career specialization (Dozier, Sha, & Shen, 2012).

Ethical Leadership

Ethical leadership is a particular form of leadership that addresses individual traits, such as being trustworthy, inclusive, and fair as *a moral person*, and behaviors, such as punishing unethical behavior and communicating the importance of ethics as *a moral manager* (Brown, Trevino, & Harrison, 2005; Treviño, Hartman, & Brown, 2000). In encompassing behavior related to the moral person and moral leader, ethical leadership is unique in affirming both the morality of avoiding negative behaviors and the morality of aspiring the followers to engage in positive behaviors (Wiltermuth, Monin, & Chow, 2010). Limited ethical leadership research in public relations focuses on identifying the importance for public relations practitioners to address personal ethics and ethical interpersonal behaviors in developing ethical standards within organizations (Lee & Cheng, 2011). Lee and Cheng (2012) found that little ethics training and written guidelines are available in the public relations workplace and that organizational ethics initiatives are poorly communicated to employees generally.

The Behavioral Research

Public relations scholars also have examined some of the factors and types of specific behavior linked to effective leadership practice in the profession. There are several aspects or streams of contemporary leadership capabilities and behaviors (i.e., strategic decision making, individual traits, emotional leadership, and transformational leadership) being addressed and tested to identify their roles in improving the effectiveness and organization-wide influence of public relations practice (Berger et al., 2007; Jin, 2010; Meng, 2014; Meng & Berger, 2013; Meng, Berger, Gower, & Heyman, 2012; Waters, 2013; Werder & Holtzhausen, 2009, 2011).

Berger and colleagues (2007) identified a number of crucial factors and patterns in effective public relations leaders, including excellent communication and persuasion skills, interpersonal communication capabilities, and networks of internal and external relationships; a diverse portfolio of experiences; and a positive and proactive nature. Meng and Berger (2013) confirmed the integrated model of leadership in public relations by identifying six key dimensions, which include *self-dynamics, team collaboration, ethical orientation, relationship building, strategic decision-making capability*, and *communication knowledge management*. Meng (2014) further identified *organizational structure and culture* as a major environmental moderator of the leadership effectiveness in the context of communication practice.

The relationship between leadership styles and the application of public relations practice is also studied. Werder and Holtzhausen (2009, 2011) investigated how leadership styles have been presented in practice, and their findings revealed the prevalence of the transformational leadership style and the inclusive leadership style in public relations environments. Transformational leaders focus on inspiring followers through communication, whereas inclusive leaders engage in more participative practices. Waters (2013) found that the contingency theory of leaders accurately described leadership styles. Additionally, Waters also found that the use of stewardship strategies can help predict leadership orientation.

Summary

To sum up, the review of literature has suggested what leadership means in effective public relations practice. Clearly, results from previous research have confirmed that leadership has an important place in contributing to the achievement of communication effectiveness and excellence. However, the literature also indicates a need to develop further research on the role of leadership in crisis communication (Benn, Todd, & Pendleton, 2010), especially within the context of social media and empowered employees and other key groups of stakeholders. Such research is needed to provide insights into possible leadership approaches and communicative responses in a crisis. A much more strategic management perspective is needed when looking specifically at the leadership role when the power and prevalence of social media are integrated into the crisis process. Therefore, this chapter offers a strategic view on this issue from a global perspective based on a global project that specifically investigates the leadership role in today's public relations practice. This in turn will broaden the perceived leadership role in crisis responses and crisis communication.

Overview of the Global Leadership Research in Public Relations

A key challenge here is the paucity of empirical research into crisis leadership. Based on our understanding of research perspectives in public relations leadership, we now explain and present the results from a global leadership research project through which the issue of crisis management and leadership was investigated (Berger & Meng, 2014). As the largest, most comprehensive study of leadership ever conducted in public relations and communication management, the global project focuses on investigating how dynamic changes—globalization, the rise of powerful social media, empowered stakeholders, and other diverse social changes—affect organizational communications, and especially the roles, strategies, and daily practices of public relations leaders.

The project was carried out in 23 countries and regions in the years of 2011–2013. The 23 countries and regions were selected purposively to provide variations in geography, history, economic development, demographics, and sociocultural characteristics (based on House, Hanges, Javidan, Dorfman, & Gupta, 2004) and to represent a suitable context for investigating the different levels of development in the communication profession around the world. Although it is impossible to include all societies or cultures, the countries and regions investigated in this global project represent some major geographical regions in the world (i.e., Confucian Asia, South Asia, Eastern and Western Europe, North America, and Latin America). Those geographical regions reflect diverse societal cultures, powerful economies, and varying stages of development of the communication profession.

Major concepts and variables tested in the global leadership project include *critical issues in current communication practice; responsive strategies used to manage the issues; the role of excellent leadership in public relations in managing the issues; approaches in leadership development;* and *practitioners' perceptions regarding leadership and self, gender, organization, and profession.* Items used to measure the defined constructs are largely adapted from previous research in public relations, leadership development, issue management, and other critical research subjects in the field (e.g., crisis management, ethics, transparency, and employee engagement) to ensure the reliability of the measurement itself.

The most important phase in the global project is the design and administration of an global online survey of public relations practitioners in investigated countries and regions. The global online survey was implemented in nine languages, including Arabic, Chinese (both simplified and traditional), English, Estonian, German, Korean, Portuguese, Russian, and Spanish. The survey was launched in different countries from November 2011 to May 2012. During the time the survey was open, more than 10,000 public relations professionals visited the survey link and nearly 4,500 professionals worldwide completed the survey. Eventually, we were able to retain 4,483 completed online questionnaires. Because the purpose of this chapter is to discover the importance of presenting excellent leadership in effective social media and crisis communication management, we focus on presenting results that are relevant to social media and crisis communication as rated and evaluated by participants in the global study.

Insights From the Global Study

Managing Crises and Social Media Present the Biggest Challenges

The global leadership research project in public relations and communication management is intended to be an important source of assistance to public relations practitioners globally to understand the importance of learning, developing, and applying leadership skills in various situations of issues management. To be successful in dealing with or managing different issues emerging from various contexts, public relations practitioners need leadership knowledge and capabilities. Therefore, in the global online survey, we asked participants to rate 10 emerging issues in terms of their importance in affecting public relations professionals' communication practice and strategies. Across the global sample, we were able to obtain consistent results on the top three rated issues, which were (a) dealing with

TABLE 6.1 Ten Emerging Issues Rated by Public Relations Professionals Worldwide ($N = 4,483$)

Ten Emerging Issues	M	SD	Frequency
1. **Dealing with the speed and volume of information flow**	**5.88**	**1.24**	**1,029**
2. **Being prepared to deal effectively with crises that may arise**	**5.76**	**1.35**	**532**
3. **Managing the digital revolution and rise of social media**	**5.75**	**1.22**	**684**
4. Improving the measurement of communication effectiveness to demonstrate value	5.49	1.36	547
5. Improving employee engagement and commitment in the workplace	5.49	1.44	354
6. Dealing with growing demands for transparency of communications and operations	5.34	1.36	375
7. Finding, developing, and retaining highly talented communication professionals	5.25	1.59	337
8. Meeting increasing demands for corporate social responsibility	5.10	1.45	239
9. Meeting communication needs in diverse cultures and globalizing markets	4.83	1.70	274
10. Improving the image of the public relations and communication management profession	4.47	1.81	112

the speed and volume of information flow ($M = 5.88$; $n = 1,029, 23.0\%$), (b) being prepared to deal effectively with crises that may arise ($M = 5.76$; $n = 532, 11.9\%$), and (c) managing the digital revolution and rise of social media ($M = 5.75$; $n = 684, 15.3\%$). Table 6.1 lists the rating results of 10 emerging issues regarding their importance in affecting communication practice.

Not surprisingly, being prepared to deal with crises that may arise is ranked as the second most important issue by professionals in the global study. Such reality echoes findings in crisis communication research, which addresses the importance for communication leaders to function as the face of the crisis and to ensure knowledge transformation to multiple groups of stakeholders throughout the crisis management process (Hackman & Johnson, 2009). Based on the global study, 11.9% of respondents ($n = 532$) identified crisis preparedness and management as the most important issue in their organization or practice.

Respondents also indicated that they have used a variety of strategies and tactics in crisis communication and management. For example, respondents indicated that they have developed effective crisis communication plans for their organization to take actions when crises arise ($M = 5.66$). They also used an issues-management approach to constantly monitor issues in order to reduce the risk of having crises ($M = 5.11$). Relevantly, issue-scanning technologies, such as social media monitoring, have been used by respondents to track communications and identify potential problems ($M = 5.05$). Respondents also admitted that they need to put more efforts in the future in providing employees with training in crisis management procedures ($M = 4.92$) and educating stakeholders about emergency communication and responses ($M = 4.83$).

As part of affiliated consequences of the digital revolution, communication professionals are confronted with more and more information both in speed and in volume. Therefore, 15.3% of respondents ($n = 684$) in the global study indicated that managing the digital revolution and the rise of social media was the most important issue for their organization. Public relations professionals worldwide are facing the challenges and changes the digital revolution has presented in their daily communication practice. Such digital transformation affects or changes their communication practice, the strategic choices they need to make in various situations, their self-development and reflection processes, and their relationships with multiple key stakeholders.

Respondents indicated that they have been trying different strategies and tactics to manage various social media platforms. Most importantly, they said it is very important for them to revise communication strategies to make sure they integrate social media efforts ($M = 5.92$). Organizations are also trying to provide employees with training sessions on social media use ($M = 5.48$) and monitoring stakeholder communications on social media networks ($M = 5.19$). Respondents indicated that there is a great need for them to hire employees with specialized social media skills ($M = 5.01$) and to create key performance indicators (KPIs) to measure social media activities ($M = 4.65$).

What Is the Role of Public Relations Leadership in Such Situations?

Leaders evolve over time as they try to adapt to current environments and find ways to manage the situations. Therefore, a major question addressed in our global research project is: how can communication leaders apply leadership skills and capabilities to successfully manage emerging issues? In order to test the functions of leadership dimensions in issues management in this global study, we adapted the original measurement scales of all seven leadership dimensions developed by Meng and Berger (2013) and Meng (2014). We asked respondents to rate the importance of all seven leadership dimensions in helping them manage issues such as the rise of crises or social media.

The results indicated a similar and consistent pattern to further confirm the supportive functions of the seven leadership dimensions in issues management. Tables 6.2 and 6.3 display the detailed ratings on each specific leadership dimension regarding different issues. The results further confirmed that strategic

TABLE 6.2 The Role of Leadership in Managing the Digital Revolution and Rise of Social Media ($n = 684$)

Leadership Capabilities and Conditions	M	SD
Participating in your organization's strategic decision making regarding the issue	6.19	1.02
Possessing communication knowledge to develop appropriate strategies, plans, and messages	6.13	0.98
Providing a compelling vision for how communication can help the organization	6.06	1.07
Having the ability to build and manage professional work teams to address the issue	5.70	1.20
Working in an organization that supports two-way communication and shared power	5.58	1.41
Having the ability to develop coalitions in and outside the organization to deal with the issue	5.43	1.25
Possessing a strong ethical orientation and set of values to guide actions	5.28	1.48

Note. This group of respondents rated the issue of "managing the digital revolution and rise of social media" as the most important issue.

TABLE 6.3 The Role of Leadership in Dealing With Crises That May Arise ($n = 532$)

Leadership Capabilities and Conditions	M	SD
Participating in your organization's strategic decision making regarding the issue	6.44	0.90
Possessing communication knowledge to develop appropriate strategies, plans, and messages	6.30	0.93
Having the ability to build and manage professional work teams to address the issue	5.99	1.08
Providing a compelling vision for how communication can help the organization	5.87	1.21
Possessing a strong ethical orientation and set of values to guide actions	5.84	1.23
Having the ability to develop coalitions in and outside the organization to deal with the issue	5.83	1.24
Working in an organization that supports two-way communication and shared power	5.45	1.46

Note. This group of respondents rated the issue of "being prepared to deal effectively with crises that may arise" as the most important issue.

decision-making capability is the most valued leadership dimension for public relations practitioners ($M = 6.19$ for managing social media; $M = 6.44$ for managing crises). The dimension of possessing strong communication knowledge-management capability was also highly valued by respondents ($M = 6.13$ for managing social media; $M = 6.30$ for managing crises) in both situations.

The global results also reflected some variances in applying leadership dimensions to different issues. When discussing how to effectively managing crises, regression results showed three significant behavioral predictors, which include the dimensions of strategic decision making, communication knowledge management, and ethical orientation. In addition, the dimension of team collaboration was also valued when crises happened. However, results also showed three significant behavioral predictors, the dimensions of communication knowledge management, team collaboration, and strategic decision making, for the issue of social media management. Importantly, the dimension of self-dynamics (or the visionary ability) was also highly valued in managing the digital revolution and the rise of social media.

Conclusions

To sum up, results from the global study confirmed the importance of applying different leadership skills and capabilities in managing emerging issues, such as the prevalence of social media and the need to be prepared for crisis management. Although the crisis communication literature has widely addressed the importance of applying varied crisis responses, our global results confirmed that public relations leaders must possess a range of skills and capabilities and then draw from them to varying extents in issues management. Although practitioners surveyed in this study are located in different countries and societies, the common themes on the leadership roles in crisis management were identified—which have been described in detail earlier—along with a determined acceptance of leadership capabilities as crucial qualities in managing crises and social media effectively.

Although it provides an argument about taking leadership as a broad range of capabilities to learn and develop, this chapter offers insights into how public relations practitioners can use leadership skills to effectively manage crises and develop social media strategies. Such results can continue to benefit professional development in public relations leadership. We hope that readers take this chapter as an initiative for continued conversation about the growth and development of public relations leadership in effective issues and conflict management and crisis communication. As integrative, empirical, and critical research continues, we can also think of nothing more practical than learning about leadership that can facilitate public relations professionals, teams, and organizations to anticipate and respond to those emerging issues that will ensure effective communication.

References

Ahearne, M., Mathieu, J., & Rapp, A. (2005). To empower or not to empower your sales force? An empirical examination of the influence of leadership empowerment behavior on customer satisfaction and performance. *Journal of Applied Psychology, 90*, 945–955.

Aldoory, L. (1998). The language of leadership for female public relations professionals. *Journal of Public Relations Research, 10*, 73–101.

Aldoory, L., & Toth, E. (2004). Leadership and gender in public relations: Perceived effectiveness of transformational and transactional leadership styles. *Journal of Public Relations Research, 10*, 73–101.

Bass, B. M. (1990). *Bass and Stogdill's handbook of leadership: Theory, research, and managerial applications* (3rd ed.). New York: Free Press.

Benn, S., Todd, L., & Pendleton, J. (2010). Public relations leadership in corporate social responsibility. *Journal of Business Ethics, 96*, 403–423.

Berger, B. K., & Meng, J. (2010). Public relations practitioners and the leadership challenge. In R. L. Heath (Ed.), *The Sage handbook of public relations* (pp. 421–434). Thousand Oaks, CA: Sage.

Berger, B. K., & Meng, J. (Eds.). (2014). *Public relations leaders as sensemakers: A global study of leadership in public relations and communication management*. New York: Routledge.

Berger, B. K., & Reber, B. H. (2006). *Gaining influence in public relations: The role of resistance in practice*. Mahwah, NJ: Erlbaum.

Berger, B. K., Reber, B. H., & Heyman, W. C. (2007). You can't homogenize success in communication management: PR leaders take diverse paths to top. *International Journal of Strategic Communication, 1*, 53–71.

Broom, G. M., & Dozier, D. M. (1986). Advancement for public relations role models. *Public Relations Review, 12*, 37–56.

Brown, M. E., Trevino, L. K., & Harrison, D. A. (2005). Ethical leadership: A social learning perspective for construct development and testing. *Organizational Behavior and Human Decision Process, 97*, 117–134.

Cameron, G. T., Cropp, F., & Reber, B. H. (2001). Getting past platitudes: Factors limiting accommodation in public relations. *Journal of Communication Management, 5*, 242–261.

Choi, J. & Choi, Y. (2009). Behavioral dimensions of public relations leadership in organizations. *Journal of Communication Management, 13*(4), 292–309.

Conger, J. A. (1999). Charismatic and transformational leadership in organizations: An insider's perspective on these developing streams of research. *Leadership Quarterly, 10*, 145–179.

Conger, J. A., & Kanungo, R. N. (1988). The empowerment process: Integrating theory and practice. *Academy of Management Review, 3*, 471–482.

Dansereau, F., Graen, G. B., & Haga, W. (1975). A vertical dyad linkage approach to leadership in formal organizations. *Organizational Behavioral and Human Performance, 13*, 46–78.

Dozier, D. M. (1984). Program evaluation and the roles of practitioners. *Public Relations Review, 10*, 13–21.

Dozier, D. M. (1992). The organizational roles of communications and public relations practitioners. In J. E. Grunig (Ed.), *Excellence in public relations and communication management* (pp. 327–355). Hillsdale, NJ: Lawrence Erlbaum Associates.

Dozier, D. M., & Broom, G. M. (1995). Evolution of the manager role in public relations practice. *Journal of Public Relations Research, 7*, 3–26.

Dozier, D. M., Sha, B.-L., & Shen, H. (2012). Why women earn less than men: The cost of gender discrimination in U.S. public relations. *Public Relations Journal, 7*(1), 1–24.

Fiedler, F. E. (1978). The contingency model and the dynamics of the leadership process. In L. Berkowitz (Ed.), *Advances in experimental social psychology* (pp. 59–112). New York: Academic Press.

Grunig, J. E. (Ed.). (1992). *Excellence in public relations and communication management: Contributions to effective organizations.* Hillsdale, NJ: Erlbaum.

Grunig, L. A., Grunig, J. E., & Dozier, D. M. (2002). *Excellent public relations and effective organizations: A study of communication management in three countries.* Mahwah, NJ: Erlbaum.

Grunig, L. A., Toth, E. L., & Hon, L. C. (2001). *Women in public relations: How gender influences practice.* New York: Guilford.

Hackman, M. Z., & Johnson, C. E. (2009). *Leadership: A communication perspective* (5th ed.). Long Grove, IL: Waveland Press.

Heath, R. L. (2006). A rhetorical theory approach to issues management. In C. Botan & V. Hazelton (Eds.), *Public relations theory II* (pp. 63–100). Mahwah, NJ: Erlbaum.

House, R. J. (1971). A path-goal theory of leader effectiveness. *Administrative Science Quarterly, 16*, 321–339.

House, R. J., Hanges, P. J., Javidan, M., Dorfman, P. W., & Gupta, V. (Eds.). (2004). Culture, leadership, and organizations: The GLOBE study of 62 societies. Thousand Oaks, CA: Sage.

Jin, Y. (2010). Emotional leadership as a key dimension of public relations leadership: A national survey of public relations leaders. *Journal of Public Relations Research, 22*, 159–181.

Kirkman, B. L., & Rosen, B. (1999). Beyond self-management: Antecedents and consequences of team empowerment. *Academy of Management Journal, 42*, 58–74.

Lee, S., & Cheng, I. (2012). Ethics management in public relations: Practitioner conceptualizations of ethical leadership, knowledge, training and compliance. *Journal of Mass Media Ethics, 27*(2), 80–96.

Lee, S. T., & Cheng, I. (2011). Characteristics and dimensions of ethical leadership in public relations. *Journal of Public Relations Research, 23*, 46–74.

Meng, J. (2014). Unpacking the relationship between organizational culture and excellent leadership in public relations: An empirical investigation. *Journal of Communication Management, 18*(4), 363–385.

Meng, J., & Berger, B. K. (2013). An integrated model of excellent leadership in public relations: Dimensions, measurement, and validation. *Journal of Public Relations Research, 25*, 141–167.

Meng, J., Berger, B. K., Gower, K. K., & Heyman, W. C. (2012). A test of excellent leadership in public relations: Key qualities, valuable sources, and distinctive leadership perceptions. *Journal of Public Relations Research, 24*, 18–36.

Reber, B. H., & Cameron, G. T. (2003). Measuring contingencies: Using scales to measure public relations practitioner limits to accommodation. *Journalism & Mass Communication Quarterly, 80*, 431–446.

Shin, J.-H., Heath, R. L., & Lee, J. (2011). A contingency explanation of public relations practitioner leadership style: Situation and culture. *Journal of Public Relations Research, 23*, 167–190.

Stogdill, R. M. (1948). Personal factors associated with leadership: A survey of the literature. *Journal of Psychology, 25*, 35–71.

Treviño, L. K., Hartman, L. P., & Brown, M. (2000). Moral person and moral manager: How executives develop a reputation for ethical leadership. *California Management Review, 42*, 128–142.

Waller, D. J., Smith, S. R., & Warnock, J. T. (1989). Situational theory of leadership. *American Journal of Health System Pharmacy, 46*, 2335–2341.

Waters, R. D. (2013). The role of stewardship in leadership: Applying the contingency theory of leadership to relationship cultivation practices of public relations practitioners. *Journal of Communication Management, 17*, 324–340.

Werder, K. P., & Holtzhausen, D. (2009). An analysis of the influence of public relations department leadership style on public relations strategy use and effectiveness. *Journal of Public Relations Research, 21*, 404–427.

Werder, K. P., & Holtzhausen, D. (2011). Organizational structures and their relationship with communication management practices: A public relations perspective from the United States. *International Journal of Strategic Communication, 5*, 118–142.

Wiltermuth, S. S., Monin, B., & Chow, R. M. (2010). The orthogonality of praise and condemnation in moral judgment. *Social Psychological and Personality Science, 2*(4), 302–310.

Yukl, G. (1989). Managerial leadership: A review of theory and research. *Journal of Management, 15*, 251–289.

7

THE CORPORATE SOCIAL MEDIA SPOKESPERSON

Who Should Speak on Behalf of the Organization in Times of Crises?

Ratna Damayanti, Stacey Rodrigues, Samuel Chua, and Augustine Pang

Introduction

Imagine this: you are the head of corporate communications for an airline company, and you're told that an airplane had disappeared midflight and cannot be found. Immediately you start thinking about how your company needs to communicate to relevant parties in such a major crisis.

Ten years ago, you would have gathered all information possible and prepared spokespersons for that first important media conference. Today, people are consuming information differently. The spouse of a passenger on that plane is frantic, watching the news, making calls, and scanning tweets to stay updated. The reporter assigned to your media conference is digging up background information from Facebook, Instagram, and YouTube.

Preparing your company spokespersons to communicate with stakeholders during a crisis is increasingly challenging. Media training of spokespersons and supporting teams need to keep up with the changes in information demand, particularly that arising from social media.

This chapter has three important aims: (a) to identify the main tasks of corporate *social media* spokespersons; (b) to examine the traits, knowledge, and skills required of corporate *social media* spokespersons and supporting teams; and (c) to examine how public relations can assume leadership roles through *social media*.

At the end of this chapter, practitioners will be introduced to two helpful frameworks. First, the Social Media Spokesperson Task Analysis Framework will allow them to identify the knowledge and skills gaps their social media teams have and customize media training for the team to fill those gaps or hire people to fill those gaps. Second, the Social Media Task Time Line identifies the main social media activities a crisis team may need to fulfill in the first 36 hours of a crisis. This framework may serve as a foundation for organizations to develop their crisis communication plans on social media platforms, as well as a crisis simulation tool during social media training.

Survey of Literature

In times of crisis, the public's desire is to be informed, not be left in an information void (Pang, 2013), to make sense of the situation, and to decide on their actions (Coombs, 2012). Before the proliferation of new media, publics had to rely on traditional media to receive information and updates of a crisis (Liu, Jin, Briones, & Kuch, 2012). Prominent figures within an organization would deliver the organization's key statements through a media conference (Ulmer, Sellnow, & Seeger, 2007). However, online media have redefined this routine (Grunig, 2009) by allowing individuals to access information rapidly from multiple new sources such as Twitter, Facebook, blogs, and YouTube (Gonzáles-Herrero & Smith, 2008; Pang, Hassan, & Chong, 2014). Given that social media newsrooms are playing an increasing role, which opens new avenues for organizational profile, messaging, and strategic communication (Zerfass & Schramm, 2014), these platforms assume heightened importance and require greater attention of organizations (Siah, Bansal, & Pang, 2010).

Spokesperson Literature

How Are Traditional Spokespersons Chosen?

Spokespersons are important members of crisis management teams (CMTs) as they represent the organization as its "face" or "voice" during a crisis (Coombs, 2012). First, they are chosen for their functional knowledge (Crandall, Parnell, & Spillan, 2013). Second, they have relevant knowledge, skills, and traits needed to carry out specific tasks, such as working as a team executing the crisis management plan (CMP), making group decisions effectively to solve problems, and listening to stakeholders to gather real-time crisis information (Coombs, 2012). Third, spokespersons are chosen as they have the requisite knowledge, skills, and traits to gather, manage, and relay accurate crisis information to stakeholders, primarily the media (Coombs, 2012, Crandall et al., 2013). This means selecting people who have undergone media training. Fourth, spokespersons are chosen from various levels of the organizational hierarchy, from CEOs, to those with technical expertise (Crandall et al., 2013; Ulmer et al., 2007).

Which Spokesperson Should Be Deployed and When?

The default recommended spokesperson during crises is the CEO or a member of the dominant coalition (Lucero, Tan, & Pang, 2009). Those with relevant functional knowledge may also be appointed as organizational spokespersons (Coombs, 2012). The CMT must decide which spokesperson to deploy, with the following five considerations in mind.

Severity of Crisis

A severe crisis requires a CEO to step up, whereas a less severe crisis can be fronted by lower ranking organizational members (Crandall et al., 2013). If a lower ranking member is deployed as the spokesperson for a severe crisis, then stakeholders may perceive that the organization is not genuine in managing it. Conversely, if a high-ranking member is deployed for a trivial issue, it may cause undue alarm.

Type of Crisis Messages and Information

Dominant coalition members may be deployed as spokespersons to provide visible crisis leadership (Ulmer et al., 2007) and assuage stakeholders' emotional concerns (Jin, Pang, & Cameron, 2012), perhaps by providing "adjusting information"—information to help stakeholders emotionally cope with the crisis (Sturges, Carrell, Newsom, & Barrera, 2001). Non-dominant coalition members may be deployed as spokespersons when the organization needs to relay technical information in the form of "instructing information" (Sturges et al., 2001)—information telling stakeholders how to behave.

Type of Crisis

Lucero and colleagues (2009) found that CEOs should step up for the following crisis types: accidents, organizational misdeeds, workplace violence, challenges, illegal corporate behavior, and megadamage. Other spokespersons may be deployed for the remaining crisis types: strikes, rumors, product recalls, product tampering, hostile take-overs or mergers, failed mergers, and economic downturns. However, in the event in which the organization's reputation is severely threatened, the CEO should step up to be the spokesperson, regardless of the crisis type.

Timing of Information Dissemination

At the onset of a crisis, if the cause of crisis is known and the crisis is deemed severe, the CEO should step up. Otherwise, other spokespersons may be appointed. At the height of a crisis, CEOs should be the spokesperson if an unpopular stance needs to be communicated (Lucero et al., 2009).

Number of Spokespersons

Coombs (2012) suggested that organizations may have multiple spokespersons so long as the overall message is consistent. However, Barrett (2005) found that when organizations use too many spokespersons, the clarity of responses suffers. Organizations need to carefully consider the deployment of spokespersons in a crisis—one or several—in order to achieve the desired outcomes.

Corporate Social Media Spokespersons: Preparing the Source to Be Channel Ready

Earlier studies (Schultz, Utz, & Göritz, 2011; Utz, Schultz, & Glocka, 2013) proposed that social media impact how stakeholders perceive organizational crisis communication—this is termed the "channel effect." The dominant paradigm here is that the medium is more important than the message. More recently, Coombs and colleagues (2014) found that the channel has a smaller role; there is a "source effect" whereby the *information source* influences stakeholder perceptions of the crisis. Coombs and colleagues (2014) suggested that organizations should "steal thunder" from news outlets by being the first to release relevant crisis information.

What does this mean for the practitioner? If source effects are more important than channel effects, then spokespersons ought to be trained to respond in times of crises on multiple channels. Most CMPs already include traditional media training (Seeger, Sellnow, & Ulmer, 2003; Ulmer et al., 2007); however, social media training is a new realm. One should note that although traditional media training prepares spokespersons for news media, social media training has to prepare spokespersons not only to deliver organizational statements on social media platforms but also to understand the concerns raised by stakeholders, analyze the nuances in online conversations, and address the concerns in a prompt and professional manner.

Coombs's (2012) Spokesperson Media Task Analysis Framework is a good theoretical anchor for this study. The framework first identifies the tasks for crisis spokespersons and then outlines the knowledge, skills, and traits required in order to fulfill the relevant responsibilities as spokesperson. The framework can be extended to include tasks related to crisis communication via social media.

Research Questions

Publics now spend more time online during crises, especially during their onset (Liu, Austin, & Jin, 2011). Publics assign a higher credibility to news being covered on social media than on traditional news (Liu et al., 2011). Studies have shown that the use of social media by organizations in a crisis has resulted in an increase in the organization's reputation, with less boycotting by publics, and at the same time with lowering its likelihood of a secondary crisis (Schultz et al., 2011; Utz et al., 2013). However, there is a knowledge gap for spokesperson strategies for social media. Hence the question:

> **RQ1:** What strategies can organizations and their spokespersons adopt when communicating through social media during crisis?

Lucero and colleagues (2009) studied when CEOs should step up as the organizational spokesperson, but they did not address if the role extended to social media.

Siah and colleagues (2010) proposed that members of the dominant coalition should be the ones addressing stakeholders on new media, but that has not yet been empirically studied. The gap in literature led to the question:

RQ2: Who should represent an organization as its primary social media spokesperson during times of crisis?

There is scant literature on the characteristics of social media CMT members and, more specifically, how the social media spokesperson should be chosen. Traditionally, CMTs and spokespersons are recommended after a thorough task analysis and then matching this to relevant knowledge, skills, and traits needed for the spokesperson to be effective (Coombs, 2012). This analysis can be extended for social media:

RQ3: When communicating crisis on social media, what characteristics should a spokesperson have?

RQ4: How can Coombs's Spokesperson Media Task Analysis Framework be extended to include social media?

In an ideal world, a communication practitioner is either part of or has influence over the decision-making process of the organization (Bowen, 2009). Contingency theory posits that the dominant coalition will likely listen to counsel from the communication team if the team is represented from within (Pang, Cameron, & Cropp, 2006). Bowen (2009) argued for public relations practitioners to assume leadership roles in the C-suite. Her study found that assuming leadership and gaining credibility through effective crisis management is one of the most key routes to gain entry to the dominant coalition. Thus the question:

RQ5: What leadership role, if any, can public relations practitioners assume as social media spokespersons?

Method

In-depth interviews with corporate communication practitioners were conducted, as this method is useful in getting respondents to elaborate on a topic and share their opinions, values, and reasons unique to their experiences, thus providing data to generate possible theories (Brennen, 2013).

Fifteen communication practitioners from Singapore with experience in crisis communication and social media training were recruited through snowball sampling: six were from the government sector, five from private companies, and four from public relations consultancies. They had between 2 and 30 years of communication experience, with a mean of 16.4 years. All were holding senior management positions in their organizations. Eleven interviewees were responsible for the strategic direction and management of social media platforms for their organizations or their clients' organizations. Five interviewees are active users and have created a dedicated social media team for their organizations. The interviewees' experience in crisis communication for traditional media and their exposure to social media helped to determine both whether crisis communication strategies remain the same for traditional and online platforms and the requirements to select social media spokespersons.

A semistructured interview guide was drawn (Brennen, 2013) and pretested on two practitioners. After appropriate amendments to the questions, 10 interviews were conducted face to face and 5 through e-mail between October and November 2013.

Results and Discussion

From interview data, two themes emerged in answering RQ1: (a) strategies for the precrisis phase and (b) strategies during crisis.

Strategies for the Precrisis Phase

Social Media Monitoring

Coombs (2012) said that traditional environmental scanning strategies are still underdeveloped. Social media monitoring strategies, according to interviewees, are similarly underdeveloped. Monitoring can be arduous because of the sheer number of sites and comments to assess. Traditionally, organizations may already be scanning internal and external environments to identify hot issues that may escalate into crises (Crandall et al., 2013). Coombs (2012) mentioned consumer-generated media, or in this case social media, as a "reputation source" (p. 28) to check how positively or negatively people view an organization.

Interviewees said that social media monitoring helps to identify social media influencers (SMIs), such as prominent Twitter users with a large following. Such SMIs may shape how their followers perceive the organization (Pang, Tan, Lim, Kwan, & Lakhanpal, 2016). Interviewees also highlighted that the social media accounts of their own employees may be catalysts for crises. Monitoring key employees' social media accounts that are visible to public will offer insights about what your internal stakeholders say about your organization. Previously, such insights may not be possible, as "water-cooler conversations" are private. Now, disgruntled employees may tweet negative insider information that challenges the organization's reputation. If not managed, the issue may escalate. Monitoring also allows organizations to assess if social media posts have gained enough attention through viral sharing. Organizations can then determine the need to respond.

Social Media Literacy

Interviewees mentioned that spokespersons need to understand all crisis communication media to be effective. Social media can be a boon as they provide a unique opportunity for the organization to speak directly to stakeholders without any dilution of messages by a third party, such as a reporter. But interviewees cautioned a spokesperson may easily "overcommunicate or undercommunicate" on social media. Organizations should be aware of the expectations that audiences have of corporate social media profiles and set procedures for online engagement.

Establishing Social Media Presence

Individuals and organizations are still learning how to integrate social media into their operations. Interviewees suggested that organizations no longer have a choice but to have a social media presence. Asian CEOs are still found to be reticent on social media, with most choosing not to have individual social media accounts (Damayanti, Kwan, Lim, Ng, & Pang, 2014). An interviewee said the importance of social media presence is "sector specific"—it is very important for companies in some "B2C [business to consumers] sectors" to have a strong social media presence, as they tend to be more known and are on journalists' radar.

Building Relationships

Social media allow organizations to establish, build, and maintain direct relationships with external stakeholders more efficiently than traditional means allow. Pang and colleagues (2016) suggested actively engaging and building relationships with SMIs to educate them about the organization.

Strategies During Crisis

Organizations increasingly tap social media platforms to provide information to and interact directly with stakeholders. Interviewees described a post by an organization as using an "organizational voice," whereas a post by an individual is regarded as an "individual voice." Using either the individual or organizational voice, *or both*, should be deliberate, as it may lead to different outcomes. Official statements may be via the organizational voice, but an organization's spokesperson (individual voice) can also interact with publics to address their concerns on its social media platforms. This creates the perception that an organization is listening to and engaging with its stakeholders.

Literature has highlighted different types of leadership styles in behaving and communicating: authoritarian leaders are directive, and democratic leaders are mindful of input from teams, whereas laissez-faire leaders take a hands-off approach (Ulmer et al., 2007). During crises, effective leadership behavior and communication (Ulmer et al., 2007) may be dependent on leader enlightenment (Pang, Jin, & Cameron, 2010) and preparation (Crandall et al., 2013). Here, it is argued that to frame a leadership style appropriate for the crisis, the CMT may choose to employ either the individual or organizational voice or a combination of the two on social media. It is possible that using only an organizational voice conveys a laissez-faire leader, or that the crisis is not severe. Using only an individual CEO voice may convey authoritarian leadership, and that the crisis is severe. A combination of voices may convey a democratic leadership style. This study provides some insights, but these hypotheses should be empirically studied in future research.

It is also noteworthy that interviewees perceive that companies currently rely more on the organizational voice than on individual voice as a strategy. Another interviewee said, "Perhaps those with no social media presence can do social media engagement [on the organization's social media profiles]." One of the organizations studied used the Facebook chat function to link up its CEO and its stakeholders during crisis. The corporate communication practitioner's role may be that of a moderator, similar to a role played during traditional media conferences.

Choice of Corporate Social Media Spokesperson

RQ2 examined who should be the social media spokesperson. The decision for a spokesperson hinges on his or her social media literacy and presence prior to the crisis, *in addition to* the considerations used for non-social media spokespersons. Social media literacy is necessary for all potential social media spokespersons. Social media presence however, is debatable: is it necessary for all potential spokespersons—from the CEO to the CMT member with functional knowledge—to have a social media presence prior to a crisis?

Interview data suggest that high-ranking members of the dominant coalition should have a social media presence. This is akin to the visibility CEOs should have in the media's minds prior to crisis (Lucero, Kwang, & Pang, 2009). Interview data did not reveal whether technical spokespersons should have social media presence. Here, it is argued that if they have a presence, it may be used during crises, but if they do not, the organizational voice may suffice. Ultimately, which person should step up as spokesperson is the same as that for traditional media—it depends on crisis severity (Crandall et al., 2013), crisis type (Lucero et al., 2009), type of information to be relayed (adjusting or instructing information; Sturges et al., 2001), and timing (onset, height of crisis, or when crisis becomes unbearable; Lucero et al., 2009).

Toward the Spokesperson Social Media Task Analysis Framework

RQ3 examined optimal spokesperson characteristics, whereas RQ4 examined how Coombs's Spokesperson Media Task Analysis Framework can be extended to include social media. These are examined together. Interviewees highlighted four main tasks of the social media spokesperson.

Conduct Social Media Monitoring

Interviewees expressed that social media monitoring is an ongoing process, and consistent with literature, it is essential to closely observe what is being said about an organization precrisis as well as *during* the crisis (Siah et al., 2010). The organization will get ongoing snapshots of how bad the organization's reputation has been hit (Pang, 2012), which will inform the CMT of appropriate crisis communication responses at that point in time, and possibly which spokesperson(s) to deploy.

Provide Timely Updates

Siah and colleagues (2010) recommended that organizations respond to stakeholders through social media within four hours of the onset of crisis. Journalists now work around the clock and may tweet or blog a news story at any time (Robinson, 2011) and refer to personal online comments as a source of information (Bajkiewicz et al., 2011). All interviewees acknowledge the importance of delivering key crisis responses and updates with speed. It is during the crisis stage that the social media spokesperson must have the authority to deliver key organizational messages via its social media platforms in a timely manner. Time expectations may now be shorter. Interviewees suggested that an organization has within a half hour to an hour to deliver its first key message via social media, and thereafter update every hour during the crisis stage.

With the amount of user traffic that an organization's platform may experience during a crisis, some organizations have been known to shut down their social media presence as a way of dealing with the negative onslaught. However, this may backfire, as it could look like the organization is in denial about public sentiment.

Customize Key Messages for Social Media Platforms

Interviewees suggest that an organization's key messages should be consistent during crisis. However, because of the casual way in which users engage on social media platforms, conversational, informal tones work better than do formal tones. Social media facilitates dialogue during crisis, so organizations should not use social media for one-way crisis communication but for multiway conversations to build relationships with stakeholders (Ihlen & Levenshus, 2014).

Spokespersons must be aware of the amount of space in which they can deliver key messages: how do you take advantage of Twitter's 140-character microblog format to provide updates, utilize Facebook's ability to share longer posts with images, or use YouTube's video-sharing capabilities? Interviewees suggest that social media can be a platform to amplify communication hosted elsewhere: "You can shoot a video of your leadership and post it on your own channels, and amplify using social media, distribute it to the media . . . about the quality, sincerity and authenticity of the message coming from the leadership."

Take Social Media Discussions Offline

Interviewees acknowledge that social media communication should not be isolated from communication strategies on traditional media. Spokespersons need to know where stakeholders predominantly receive their information from and choose that platform to engage with or inform stakeholders. However, social media can be an incubation space for misinformation. Thus, spokespersons ought to "calm the waters while at the same time providing accurate information."

An issue may seem like a crisis when amplified on social media, but this is better described as a *paracrisis* (Coombs & Holladay, 2012). These public attacks on the organization's reputation may be aggravated by the "groundswell" of social media when information is shared virally (Li & Bernoff, 2008). Spokespersons that have carried out the first task of effectively monitoring social media will be able to judge if an incident should be addressed online or off the social media space.

Extending the Spokesperson Media Task Analysis Framework

The four task statements were matched with knowledge, skills, and traits that were evident in the interviews. The Spokesperson *Social Media* Task Analysis framework (Figure 7.1) presented in this chapter may be used to identify knowledge and skills gaps of spokespersons and the social media team supporting them.

Thereafter, customized social media training can be created to cater to individual and contextual needs. Another option is for the organization to hire employees who can fill the knowledge and skills gap of the existing team. Crisis simulations are recommended during training to improve spokespersons' efficacy (Coombs, 2012) and the crisis simulation exercise, the Social Media Task Time Line (Figure 7.2), may be used as a guide for social media activities in the first 36 hours of a crisis.

Establishing Public Relations Leadership When Crisis Hits

RQ5 examined what leadership role, if any, can public relations practitioners assume as social media spokespersons. The bane of practitioners is when their counsel is not valued (Bowen, 2009). To be deemed critical by an organization's management, a public relations practitioner must move from being a public relations "technician"—who is responsible for the execution of tasks such as writing, production of materials, and contacting the media—to a public relations "leader" (Meng, Berger, Gower, & Heyman, 2012). Strategically, a communications team may gain entry into the dominant coalition through many ways (Bowen, 2009;

Task Statement	Knowledge	Skills	Traits
Monitor social media	• Understand speed of discussion happening on social media • Understand nuances of postings	• Ability to assess sentiments of discussions or posts • Ability to identify the issue that is being discussed • Ability to assess the gravity of discussions or posts	• Meticulous • Analytical mind
Provide timely updates	• Appreciate the "round-the-clock" nature of social media • Understand that all postings are viewed by the online community • Understand that all postings may be subjected to scrutiny and ridicule • Understand that the organization should not remove negative postings on social media platforms	• Ability to post updates within an hour of the crisis • Ability to address incorrect information on social media • Ability to address the concerns of and questions from stakeholders	• Sincere, authentic • Low argumentativeness • High stress tolerance
Customize key messages for social media platforms	• Knowledge of each social media platform's capabilities (e.g. Twitter's 140-character limit and appropriate use of hashtags)	• Ability to craft messages according to each social media platform • Ability to draft key organizational messages clearly and briefly • Ability to craft consistent messages across communication platforms	• Brevity • Clarity of thought and expression
Take social media discussions offline	• Knowledge of non-social media platforms available to effectively address the issue or crisis • Knowledge of crisis versus paracrisis	• Ability to determine the seriousness of the issue • Ability to determine which platform will be most effective in engaging stakeholders involved	• Clarity of thought and expression

FIGURE 7.1 Spokesperson Social Media Task Analysis Framework

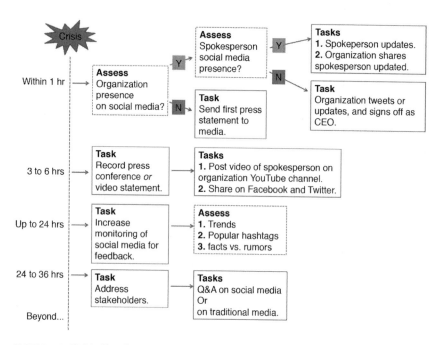

FIGURE 7.2 Crisis Simulation Exercise

Choi & Choi, 2009; Meng & Berger, 2013). The routes can be distilled into two main ideas:

1. Attributes of the communication practitioner or team: self-dynamics, communication knowledge and management, strategic decision-making capability, offering valuable analyses of issues, relationship building, team collaboration, and ethical orientation are strategic attributes to develop to gain access to the dominant coalition.
2. Situational opportunities: crises and issues high on the media agenda are two situational opportunities to show the dominant coalition the communication team's credibility to counsel the dominant coalition.

An interviewee mentioned that for CMT teams, "you can be as prepared as you like but the minute [crisis] breaks, everybody's forgotten all their training." The value of the communications team may come to the fore during crises: "To be able to orchestrate everything very quickly, it's a significant skill; and [is the] responsibility of the [corporate communications] department." Drawing from interview findings and building on Bowen's (2009) five routes for public relations practitioners to gain access to the dominant coalition, the following tactics are suggested for public relations practitioners in social media spokesperson teams to assume leadership roles:

1. Offer analyses and provide updates on issues affecting the organization's reputation being discussed, not just on mainstream media (Bowen, 2009), but also on social media.
2. Identify SMIs and devote more resources to them (Freberg et al., 2011; Pang et al., 2016). They are opinion leaders who may sway public opinion for or against your organization during crises.
3. Craft social media messages early (within the first hour) and often (update every hour).
4. Craft emotionally nuanced messages to calm internal and external publics (Jin et al., 2012). The tone of the messages can be nuanced according to feedback gathered in real time through social media (Ihlen & Levenshus, 2014).
5. Rally internal stakeholders with a clear communication strategy during crisis (Frandsen & Johansen, 2011).

Practical Implications for Social Media and Crisis Communication

Given the ever-changing landscape of communication, how could one, as a corporate communications practitioner, embrace how social media can contribute to a well-rounded CMP? The Spokesperson Social Media Task Analysis Framework and the 36-hour Social Media Task Time Line provide a basic foundation on which an organization can build its CMP. Strategically, the communications expert can coordinate efforts to make the CMP robust during peacetime. This chapter has also offered tactics for the team to show public relations leadership during crises and gain the confidence of C-suite members.

During times of calm, it's easy to go through the motions and put the ideas offered in this chapter to practice when training a CMT. It should be the intention of the team to make the aforementioned skills instinctive throughout the crisis life cycle. CMTs may customize their own 36-hour Social Media Task Time Line, taking into consideration *all* the communication channels available to the individual organization. Continually monitoring various media, sharpening the skills and knowledge of the spokesperson(s), and taking care to address the concerns of stakeholders on relevant platforms will ensure organizations stay on top of their communications strategies.

References

Bajkiewicz, T. E., Kraus, J. J. & Hong, S. Y. (2011.) The impact of newsroom changes and the rise of social media on the practice of media relations. *Public Relations Review, 37*(3), 329–331.

Barrett, M. S. (2005). Spokespersons and message control: How the CDC lost credibility during the anthrax crisis. *Qualitative Research Reports in Communication, 6*(1), 59–68.

Bowen, S. A. (2009). What communication professionals tell us regarding dominant coalition access and gaining membership. *Journal of Applied Communication Research, 37*(4), 418–443.

Brennen, B. S. (2013). *Qualitative research methods for media studies*. New York: Routledge.

Choi, J. & Choi, Y. (2009). Behavioral dimensions of public relations leadership in organizations. *Journal of Communication Management, 13*(4), 292–309.

Coombs, W. T. (2012). *Ongoing crisis communication: Planning, managing and responding* (3rd ed.). Thousand Oaks, CA: Sage Publications.

Coombs, W. T., Claeys, A. S., & Holladay, S. J. (2014, June). Social media's value in a crisis: Channel effect or stealing thunder? Paper presented at Corporate Communication International Conference, Hong Kong.

Coombs, W. T., & Holladay, J. S. (2012). The paracrisis: The challenges created by publicly managing crisis prevention. *Public Relations Review, 38*(3), 408–415.

Crandall, W. R., Parnell, J. A., & Spillan, J. E. (2013). *Crisis management: Leading in the new strategy landscape*. Thousand Oaks, CA: Sage Publications.

Damayanti, R., Kwan, T., Lim, J., Ng, C., & Pang, A. (2014, June). *Managing the CEO image: Overexposed or understated?* Paper presented to the Corporate Communications International Conference, Hong Kong.

Frandsen, F., & Johansen, W. (2011). The study of internal crisis communication: Towards an integrative framework. *Corporate Communications: An International Journal, 16*(4), 347–361.

Freberg, K., Graham, K., McGaughey, K. and Freberg, L. (2011). Who are the social media influencers? A study of public perceptions of personality. *Public Relations Review, 37*(1), 90–92.

González-Herrero, A., & Smith, S. (2008). Crisis communications management on the Web: How Internet-based technologies are changing the way public relations professionals handle business crises. *Journal of Contingencies and Crisis Management, 16*(3), 143–163.

Grunig, J. E. (2009). Paradigms of global public relations in an age of digitalisation. *PRism, 6*(2). Retrieved from http://praxis.massey.ac.nz/prism_on-line_journ.html

Ihlen, Ø., & Levenshus, A. (2014, June). *Digital dialogue: Crisis communication in social media*. Paper presented at the Corporate Communication International Conference on Corporate Communication, Hong Kong.

Jin, Y., Pang, A., & Cameron, G. T. (2012). Toward a publics-driven, emotion-based conceptualization in crisis communication: Unearthing dominant emotions in multi-staged testing of the integrated crisis mapping (ICM) model. *Journal of Public Relations Research, 24*, 266–298.

Li, C., & Bernoff, J. (2008). Groundswell: Winning in a world transformed by social technologies. Boston, MA: Harvard Business School Review Press.

Liu, B. F., Austin, L. L., & Jin, Y. (2011). How publics respond to crisis communication strategies: The interplay of information form and source. *Public Relations Review, 37*, 345–353.

Liu, B. F., Jin, Y., Briones, R., & Kuch, B. (2012). Managing turbulence in the blogosphere: Evaluating the blog-mediated crisis communication model. *Journal of Public Relations Research, 24*, 353–370.

Lucero, M., Tan, A., & Pang, A. (2009). Crisis leadership: When should the CEO step up? *Corporate Communications: An International Journal, 14(3),* 234–248.

Meng, J., & Berger, B. K. (2013). An integrated model of excellent leadership in public relations: Dimensions, measurement, and validation. *Journal of Public Relations Research*, *25*, 141–167.

Meng, J., Berger, B. K., Gower, K. K., & Heyman, W. C. (2012). A test of excellent leadership in public relations: Key qualities, valuable sources, and distinctive leadership perceptions. *Journal of Public Relations Research*, *24*(1), 18–36.

Pang, A. (2012). Towards a crisis pre-emptive image management model. *Corporate Communications: An International Journal*, *17*(3), 358–378.

Pang, A. (2013). *Social media hype in times of crises: How can organizations respond?* Paper presented at Australia and New Zealand Communication Association. Perth, Western Australia.

Pang, A., Cameron, G. T., & Cropp, F. (2006), Corporate crisis planning: Tensions, issues, and contradictions. *Journal of Communication Management*, *10*(4), 371–389.

Pang, A., Hassan, N., & Chong, A. (2014). Negotiating crisis in the social media environment: Evolution of crises online, gaining credibility offline. *Corporate Communication: An International Journal*, *19*(1), 96–118.

Pang, A., Jin, Y., & Cameron, G. T. (2010). *Contingency theory of strategic conflict management: Unearthing factors that influence ethical elocution in crisis communication.* Conference paper presented at the 13th Annual International Public Relations Research Conference, Miami, FL, March 10–13, 2010.

Pang, A., Tan., E. Y., Lim, R. S., Kwan, T. Y., & Lakhanpal, P. B. (2016). Building effective relations with social media influencers in Singapore. *Media Asia*, *43*, 56–68.

Robinson, S. (2011). Journalism as process: The labor implications of participatory content in news organizations. *Journalism & Communication Monographs*, *13*, 138–210.

Siah, J., Bansal, M., & Pang, A. (2010). New media and crises: New media—A new medium in escalating crises? *Corporate Communications: An International Journal*, *15*(2), 143–155.

Schultz, F., Utz, S., & Göritz, A. (2011). Is the medium the message? Perceptions of and reactions to crisis communication via twitter, blogs and traditional media. *Public Relations Review*, *37*, 20–27. doi: 10.1016/j.pubrev.2010.12.001

Seeger, M. W., Sellnow, T. L., & Ulmer, R. R. (2003). *Communication, organization and crisis.* Westport, CT: Quorum.

Sturges, D. L., Carrell, B., Newsom, D., & Barrera, M. (2001). Crisis communication management: The public opinion node and its relationship to environmental nimbus. *SAM Advanced Management Journal*, *56*(3), 22–27.

Ulmer, R. R., Sellnow, T. L., & Seeger, M. W. (2007). *Effective crisis communication: Moving from crisis to opportunity.* Thousand Oaks, CA: Sage.

Utz, S., Schultz, F., & Glocka, S. (2013). Crisis communication online: How medium, crisis type and emotions affected public reactions in the Fukushima Daiichi nuclear disaster. *Public Relations Review*, *39*, 40–46. doi: 10.1016/j.pubrev.2012.09.010

Zerfass, A., & Schramm, D. M. (2014). Social media newsrooms in public relations: A conceptual framework and corporate practices in three countries. *Public Relations Review*, *40*(1), 79–91.

8

EXAMINING PUBLIC RESPONSES TO SOCIAL MEDIA CRISIS COMMUNICATION STRATEGIES IN THE UNITED STATES AND CHINA

Zifei Fay Chen and Bryan H. Reber

Introduction

Crisis management and communication is a fully embraced topic in public relations research (Avery, Lariscy, Kim, & Hocke, 2010). Over the years, the theory of image restoration (Benoit, 1995, 1997, as cited in Avery et al., 2010, p. 190) and the situational crisis communication theory (SCCT; Coombs, 1995) have established two primary streams regarding studies on this topic (Avery et al., 2010). Today, with the development and increased use of social media, crisis communication has become more complicated (Coombs, 2012). Although much attention has been given to the role social media play in crisis communication, most of the studies are focused on how organizations and crisis managers should use social media to enhance crisis communication practices rather than incorporating social media and crisis communication into theoretical models. Even fewer have studied social media and crisis communication in different social and cultural contexts.

In this light, the current study examined publics' evaluation of organizational reputation, negative word-of-mouth intention, and negative online crisis-reaction intention in response to different social media crisis communication strategies and compared similarities and differences between responses in the United States and China. The goal is to increase understanding of the effects of crisis-response strategy in different social and cultural contexts and the use of social media during corporate crises in both countries.

Literature Review

Situational Crisis Communication Theory (SCCT)

With a focus on reputation management, the SCCT proposes that the appropriate crisis-response strategy should be selected based on multiple variables, such as crisis type, evidence, damage, victim status, and performance history (Coombs & Holladay, 2002).

Based on attribution theory, crises can be categorized into four types sorted by the external-internal and unintentional-intentional dimensions: faux pas, accidents, terrorism, and transgressions (Coombs, 1995, p. 455). For an accident, excuse may be considered appropriate due to the uncontrollable and unstable nature of this crisis type, but an organization's performance history, victim status, and the damage level may complicate choosing the right response strategy (Coombs, 1995; Coombs & Holladay, 2002). Mortification strategies are considered more appropriate for a major accident with true evidence (Coombs, 1995). However, accepting responsibility and mortification also means taking the risk of lawsuits and financial loss for an organization (Coombs & Holladay, 2008).

Previous empirical studies indicated mortification strategies such as apology and compensation generally lead to a more positive perception of organizational reputation (Coombs & Holladay, 2008), whereas denial of responsibility leads to a more negative impression of organizational reputation (Lee, 2004). Aside from organization reputation, the effects of crisis communication strategies were also found on other outcomes, including negative word of mouth (Coombs & Holladay, 2008) and secondary reactions such as willingness to boycott (Schultz, Utz, & Goeritz, 2011). In addition, blame shifting leads to more negative reactions compared to corrective action, bolstering, mortification, and separation (Coombs & Schmidt, 2000).

H1: Mortification strategies (apology and compensation) will generate (a) more positive evaluation of organizational reputation, (b) less negative word-of-mouth intention, and (c) less negative online crisis-reaction intention than nonmortification strategies (excuse and excuse plus ingratiation).

H2: Excuse combined with ingratiation will generate (a) more positive evaluation of organizational reputation, (b) less negative word-of-mouth intention, and (c) less negative online crisis-reaction intention than excuse alone.

Social Media and Crisis Communication

Strategies and tactics of crisis communication on social media have been examined, yet little has been studied from an international perspective. Guidelines and recommendations for the use of social media in crisis communication are provided based on extensive literature review (Veil, Buehner, & Palenchar, 2011) and in-depth case studies have been conducted, such as Domino's response to the paradoxical challenge of its hoax crisis on YouTube (Veil, Sellow, & Petrun, 2011) and Nestlé's Facebook fan page attack (Champoux, Durgree, & McGlynn, 2012) in the United States. In a different context, Utz, Schultz, and Glocka (2013) used the Fukushima Daiichi nuclear disaster as the scenario in an experiment to examine the influence of medium, crisis type, and emotions. They found crisis communication via social media may lead to a more positive reputation, less secondary crisis communication (e.g., talking about the crisis), and less secondary crisis reaction (e.g., boycotting the company) than communication via traditional media.

However, most of the studies regarding social media and crisis communication are case based and focused on practices. The only theoretical model found so far is the social-mediated crisis communication model (Liu, Austin, & Jin, 2011). Gaps also exist when it comes to the impact of media type on the effectiveness of crisis communication (Coombs & Holladay, 2009). Studies revealed media type is important in crisis communication, and social media tends to be more effective than traditional media (Schultz et al., 2011; Utz et al., 2013).

> **RQ1:** What are the publics' (a) evaluation of organizational reputation, (b) negative word-of-mouth intention, and (c) negative online crisis-reaction intention in response to different crisis communication strategies sent via social media?

Corporate Crisis Communication and Social Media in China

Crisis communication in China is different from that in Western countries. Traditional values and norms such as face saving and risk-communication avoidance play an important role (Yu & Wen, 2003) and government relationships, cover-up, and denial are frequently used (Ye & Pang, 2011).

Different effects may be found in response to the same crisis message strategy in different social-cultural contexts. Apology is oftentimes regarded as a routine and ritualistic behavior in Asian cultures and would be less in favor than more practical and specific responses such as informational instruction and compensation (Lee, 2004). However, previous research in the United States showed no significant differences among the sympathy, compensation, or apology conditions (Coombs & Holladay, 2008).

> **H3:** In China, compensation will generate (a) a more positive evaluation of organizational reputation, (b) less negative word-of-mouth intention, and (c) less negative online crisis-reaction intention than apology, whereas no such difference will be found in the United States.

Besides culture dynamics, political and media systems are also important factors to consider in crisis communication (Lyu, 2012). The social media landscape in China is different from those in the rest of the world (Luo & Jiang, 2012). Due to strong media censorship in China, Chinese citizens are not able to get access to major social media sites such as Facebook, Twitter, and YouTube (Chiu, Ip, & Silverman, 2012). Instead, they turn to domestic social networking sites such as Kaixin,

Weibo, and YouKu (Luo & Jiang, 2012). Sina Weibo is one of the most popular social media sites in China and is known as the Chinese "Twitter" (Mei, 2012).

Social media in China has drastically changed the breadth and nature of public debate (Hewitt, 2012). On Weibo, the 140 characters in Chinese can express much more than in English (Hewitt, 2012), and Weibo's inclusion of features such as threaded comments, rich media, microtopics, and a medal reward system has made it even easier to participate in online activities (Falcon, 2011). A more significant contrast is therefore assumed between the publics' response to mortification strategies and excuse on Weibo in China than on Twitter in the United States.

> **H4:** Excuse strategy sent via social media will generate (a) a more negative evaluation of organizational reputation, (b) more negative word-of-mouth intention, and (c) more negative online crisis-reaction intention in China than in the United States.

Little, if any, research has been conducted prior to this study involving social media crisis communication in the United States and in China; therefore:

> **RQ2:** What are the similarities and differences between the publics' (a) evaluation of organizational reputation, (b) negative word-of-mouth intention, and (c) negative online crisis-reaction intention in response to different crisis communication strategies via social media in the United States and China?

Method

A two (country: United States and China) by four (strategy: apology, compensation, excuse, and excuse plus ingratiation) between-subjects experiment was conducted. Four strategies used in this experiment were chosen according to the accident-decision flowchart (Coombs, 1995, p. 465). Questionnaires were designed in English and Chinese.

Population and Sample

Participants were recruited from two large universities in each country. Three hundred thirty-seven questionnaires were completed, with 176 from the United States and 161 from China.

The average age of participants in China was 20.13 (SD = 2.41). Of the participants, 37% (N = 60) were male and 62% were female (N = 99), with 1% unknown (N = 2). The average age of participants in the United States was 20 (SD = 2.67). Nineteen percent (N = 33) were male, and 81% were female (N = 143). On average, 42 (min: 37, max: 44) participants were exposed to each condition.

Stimuli

A fictional news brief in two languages and two pairs of four fictional social media crisis responses were created. The fictional crisis reported that a major airplane crash had happened and investigation of the crash indicated it was caused by engine failure. United Airlines and China Southern Airlines were chosen for this fictional crisis for several reasons. First, they are both large and well-known airlines for the experiment respondents. Second, neither of the airlines' headquarters is located in the region where the experiment took place, limiting potential bias toward a particular airline. Finally, both United Airlines and China Southern Airlines have active microblog accounts. Twitter and Sina Weibo were selected as the communication channels.

For the manipulation on crisis-response strategy, the following four messages were created. Each message was translated into Chinese for participants in China.

1. Apology: "We are very sorry, and we express our deep-felt apology to the victims and their families."
2. Compensation: "We will do all that we can to compensate the victims and their families and help them through their loss."
3. Excuse: "Investigation showed this crash was caused by engine failure. The Boeing Company should take responsibility for this incident."
4. Excuse plus ingratiation: "Flight 232/2321 crew members sacrificed their own safety for an efficient evacuation. Boeing should take responsibility for the engine failure."

Procedure

Before being exposed to the stimuli, participants were asked about their use of Twitter or Weibo and their preliminary impressions of the airlines. They were then shown the fictional news and randomly assigned to one of the crisis-response messages on the fictional Twitter or Weibo account. Following presentation of the news brief and the Twitter or Weibo message, participants answered manipulation-check items and questions about their evaluation of organizational reputation, negative word-of-mouth intention, and negative online crisis-reaction intention. At the end of the experiment, demographic information was collected. In a debriefing following completion of the experiment, participants were told no such airplane crash had happened and the scenarios were created for the purpose of research.

Dependent Measures

Participants were asked to rate items on organizational reputation, negative word of mouth, and negative online crisis reactions using 5-point Likert scales.

Organizational reputation was measured by six items. Five items were developed according to Coombs and Holladay's (2002) Organizational Reputation Scale. A sixth item, "my overall opinion of the airline company after hearing the incident," was added. Internal consistency was acceptable, α = .83.

Three items were adapted from Coombs and Holladay (2008) to measure negative word-of-mouth intention: (a) "I would encourage friends or relatives NOT to take flights with this airline company," (b) "I would say negative things about the airline company to other people," and (c) "I would recommend this airline company to someone who asked my advice." The reliability coefficient (Cronbach's alpha) for this measure was .68.

Negative online crisis-reaction intention was assessed by three items drawn from Schultz and colleagues (2011): (a) "I would retweet this message/share this Weibo," (b) "I would write negative comments about this incident online," and (c) "I would sign an online petition to boycott this airline company." The reliability coefficient (Cronbach's alpha) for this measure was .73.

Manipulation Checks

Three 5-point Likert-scaled items were used as manipulation checks: "the airline company took responsibility for the plane crash," "the airline company compensated the victims with money," and "the airline company emphasized the quality of its service." A series of one-way ANOVAs with post hoc tests showed that the manipulation of different crisis communication strategies was successful.

For the item "the airline company took responsibility for the plane crash," the ANOVA was significant, $F(3, 333)$ = 24.03, p < .001, η^2 = .18. Compensation (M = 3.12, SD = 0.91) and apology (M = 2.57, SD = 1.01) were both rated significantly higher than excuse (M = 2.00, SD = 1.01) and excuse plus ingratiation (M = 2.10, SD = 0.92). The test shows that the manipulation for mortification strategies (apology and compensation) was successful because the trait of accepting responsibility was rated higher than nonmortification strategies (excuse and excuse plus ingratiation).

The item "the airline company compensated the victims with money" also showed significant result in the ANOVA test, $F(3, 332)$ = 13.33, p < .001, η^2 = .11. Compensation (M = 3.45, SD = 0.12) was rated highest and was significantly higher than apology (M = 2.48, SD = 0.12), excuse (M = 2.70, SD = 0.12), and excuse plus ingratiation (M = 2.69, SD = 0.12). This shows that the manipulation for compensation was successful.

For the item "the airline company emphasized the quality of its service," the ANOVA was significant, $F(3, 332)$ = 23.36, p < .001, η^2 = .18. Excuse plus ingratiation (M = 3.04, SD = 0.11) was rated highest and was significantly higher than apology (M = 2.14, SD = 0.10), compensation (M = 2.47, SD = 0.10), and excuse (M = 1.86, SD = 0.10). Therefore, the manipulation of excuse plus ingratiation was successful.

Results

Effects of Crisis-Response Strategies in Combination With Countries

No significant interaction was found in a two-way MANOVA conducted to evaluate the effects of crisis-response strategies in combination with countries, $F(9, 784) = 1.30$, $\Lambda = .97$, $p = .23$, $\eta^2 = .01$. However, significant main effects were present for both crisis-response strategy, $F(9, 784) = 7.06$, $\Lambda = .83$, $p < .001$, $\eta^2 = .06$, and country, $F(3, 322) = 26.12$, $\Lambda = .80$, $p < .001$, $\eta^2 = .20$.

Main Effects of Crisis-Response Strategy

A one-way MANOVA showed significant differences among the four crisis-response strategies on the three dependent variables, $F(9, 794) = 7.15$, $\Lambda = .83$, $p < .001$, $\eta^2 = .06$.

Follow-up ANOVA tests with post hoc analyses on the dependent variables were then conducted (see Table 8.1 and Table 8.2). For the organizational reputation scale, the ANOVA was significant, $F(3, 328) = 18.95$, $p < .001$, $\eta^2 = .15$.

TABLE 8.1 Results of the Effects of Crisis-Response Strategy on Dependent Variables

Dependent Variables	df	F	P	η^2
Organizational reputation	3	18.95	.000★	.15
Negative word-of-mouth (NWOM) intention	3	3.28	.021★★	.03
Negative online crisis reaction intention	3	1.66	.175	.02

★ $p < .001$.
★★ $p < .05$

TABLE 8.2 Means and Standard Deviations of Crisis-Response Strategy on Dependent Variables

	Crisis-Response Strategies										
	Apology			Compensation			Excuse			Excuse Plus Ingratiation		
Dependent Variables	n	M	SD	n	M	SD	n	M	SD	n	M	SD
Organizational reputation	82	3.12	0.62	83	3.26	0.58	86	2.60	0.58	81	2.79	0.73
NWOM intention		3.03	0.70		3.08	0.66		3.35	0.71		3.13	0.82
Negative online crisis reaction intention		2.17	0.74		2.22	0.78		2.38	0.89		2.12	0.77

No significant difference was found between the apology group ($M = 3.12$, $SD = 0.62$) and the compensation group ($M = 3.26$, $SD = 0.58$), $p = .91$. Organizational reputation was rated more positively among the participants in the compensation group than in the excuse group ($M = 2.60$, $SD = 0.58$), $p < .001$, and the excuse plus ingratiation group ($M = 2.79$, $SD = 0.73$), $p < .001$. Similarly, participants in the apology group evaluated organizational reputation more positively than those in the excuse group, $p < .001$, and those in the excuse plus ingratiation group, $p < .01$. H1a was supported. No significant difference was found between the excuse group and the excuse plus ingratiation group, $p = .30$. H2a was not supported.

For the negative word-of-mouth intention scale, the ANOVA was significant, $F(3, 328) = 3.28$, $p = .021$, $\eta^2 = .03$. No significant difference was found between the apology group ($M = 3.03$, $SD = 0.71$) and the compensation group ($M = 3.08$, $SD = 0.66$), $p > .90$. Participants in the apology group were less likely to conduct negative word of mouth than those in the excuse group ($M = 3.35$, $SD = 0.71$), $p = .03$, but no significant difference was found between the apology group and the excuse plus ingratiation group ($M = 3.13$, $SD = 0.82$), $p > .90$. There was also no significant difference when comparing the compensation group with the excuse group, $p = .08$, or with the excuse plus ingratiation group, $p > .90$. H1b was partially supported. No significant difference was found in negative word of mouth between the excuse group and the excuse plus ingratiation group, $p = .27$. H2b was not supported.

For the negative online crisis-reaction scale, the ANOVA was not significant, $F(3, 328) = 1.66$, $p = .175$, $\eta^2 = .02$. H1c and H2c were not supported.

Country Main Effects

Follow-up ANOVA tests for countries on the dependent variables were then conducted (see Table 8.3). Results showed no significant differences between the two countries on organizational reputation, $F(1, 324) = .01$, $p = .91$, $\eta^2 < .001$, or on negative word of mouth, $F(1, 324) = 1.59$, $p = .21$, $\eta^2 = .005$. However, the ANOVA was significant on the negative online crisis reaction, $F(1, 324) = 56.20$,

TABLE 8.3 Means and Standard Deviations of Country on Dependent Variables

	Countries					
	The United States			China		
Dependent Variables	n	M	SD	n	M	SD
Organizational reputation	176	2.95	0.66	161	2.94	0.70
NWOM		3.20	0.74		3.09	0.72
Negative online crisis reaction		1.93	0.73		2.54	0.75

$p < .001, \eta^2 = .15$. Participants in China ($M = 2.54, SD = 0.75$) were more likely to conduct negative online crisis reaction than participants in the United States ($M = 1.93, SD = 0.73$).

Therefore, the compensation strategy did not generate differences in the United States and China. H3 was not supported. There were also no differences in evaluation of organizational reputation and negative word-of-mouth intention for publics in the United States and China when excuse strategy was being used. H4a and H4b were not supported. Excuse strategy did generate more likelihood to conduct negative online crisis reaction in China than in the United States. H4c was supported. However, the public in China is more likely to conduct negative online crisis reaction than the public in the United States across all strategies.

Discussion

Examining Effects of Crisis-Response Strategy Across Countries

In this study, crisis-response strategy and social-cultural context did not generate interactive effects on the three dependent measures, indicating the effects of crisis communication strategy are consistent in participants' responses across these two countries.

The dependent measure of organizational reputation produced results that further supported previous findings that mortification strategies lead to more favorable perceptions of organizational reputation than nonmortification strategies (Coombs & Holladay, 2008; Coombs & Schmidt, 2000; Lee, 2004).

There was significant difference between apology and excuse on the dependent measure of negative word-of-mouth intentions; however, no significant effects were found among other crisis-response strategies on this dependent measure. Coombs and Holladay (2008, 2009) found accommodative crisis responses and information-only responses produced similar effects on anger and negative word-of-mouth intentions. Anger serves as a driver to produce negative publicity in a crisis (Coombs & Holladay, 2007). As negative online crisis reaction, such as making negative comments online to the public and signing a boycott petition, may need even higher anger levels than negative word-of-mouth communication, it is possible that the anger level of an accident was simply not high enough to generate differences in online crisis-reaction intention among different crisis-response strategies.

Results suggest that the excuse plus ingratiation strategy was not more effective than the excuse strategy alone on all three dependent measures. Corrective action, bolstering, mortification, and separation produce the same effects on organizational reputation and potential supportive behavior, whereas only shifting blame generated less positive results (Coombs & Schmidt, 2000). Therefore, even if excuse is accompanied by ingratiation, it does not change the blame-shifting perception.

In contrast to Lee's (2004) findings, compensation strategy did not generate more positive results than apology on dependent measures in this experiment among student participants from China. Even within Asian cultures, the social-cultural contexts may differ due to different political and media systems (Lyu, 2012). Facing similar crisis events, two corporations in mainland China and Taiwan selected different response strategies and used them in different sequences (Lyu, 2012). As crisis management in mainland China tends to focus more on government relationships, cover-ups, and denial (Ye & Pang, 2011), the apology strategy in this experiment may be seen as an act from the airline that showcases its willingness to take responsibility and an openness to communicate with the public. It was therefore as well received as the compensation strategy by the participants from China in this study.

Examining Effects of Different Contexts in the United States and China

Results indicated the participants from the Chinese university tend to have higher negative online crisis-reaction intentions than participants from the U.S. university across all crisis-response strategy conditions. Negative online crisis reaction is usually associated with the level of anger. However, because there was no significant difference in negative word-of-mouth intentions, which is also triggered by anger (Coombs & Holladay, 2007), between participants from the two countries, it is unlikely that the varying anger levels is the cause for the difference. There are three possible explanations for the different negative online crisis-reaction intentions among participants from the two countries.

First, social media in China have encouraged the public's self-expression online in a society where people are not used to expressing their personal opinions offline. As such, Chinese people tend to have a stronger reaction online than does the public in the United States, where self-expression is encouraged both online and offline. "Chinese people are socialized to remain silent" because they believe "trouble is born out of the words you speak" (Yu & Wen, 2003, p. 54). Social media created a platform for Chinese people to express themselves freely. Without enough space to express their anger in the offline world, Chinese people may seek to vent all of their anger through social media, where they do not have to worry about being too expressive. Therefore, compared with people from the United States, people in China tend to have stronger crisis reactions online, and participants' online crisis reactions in this study supported this tendency.

Second, although Weibo is considered the Chinese equivalent of Twitter, there are still distinctive differences in their features. Weibo has eight features that are not embodied in Twitter: threaded comments, rich media, microtopics, trends categorization, verified accounts and the hall of celebrity, a medal reward system, more style templates, and Weibo events (Falcon, 2011). These features have made it easier for users to engage in conversations and track progress (Falcon, 2011). Moreover, although Twitter and Weibo both have restricted the content length to 140 characters per post, one post can contain much more information in Chinese than in English. In Chinese, a word usually only consists of two to four characters, with two-character words being used the most often, whereas in English, words usually consist of many more characters.

In addition, the "rumor-driven" behavior among Chinese social media users (Luo & Jiang, 2012) may also contribute to this finding. Chinese online users' tendency to "follow the crowd" (Luo & Jiang, 2012) makes it possible to generate more online crisis reaction when a negative comment starts a conversation.

Theoretical and Practical Implications

The findings of this study provide meaningful theoretical and practical implications for social media and crisis communication in different social-cultural contexts. Theoretically, by examining the effects of different social media crisis-response strategies among college student samples drawn from two different countries, this study provided empirical evidence for SCCT-recommended strategies on social media in different social-cultural contexts. It also incorporated the use of social media into SCCT with an international perspective.

Practically, the findings provide implications for public relations professionals to make more informed decisions when choosing the most effective social media crisis-response strategy in the United States and China. First of all, the empirical evidence from this study suggests that the SCCT-recommended strategies are effective among college student participants in both the United States and China during a major corporate accident crisis like a plane crash. In a severe accident with true evidence, organizations need to demonstrate the willingness to take responsibility and express concerns for the victims in their crisis response on social media. Shifting the blame generally leads to a more negative evaluation of the organization's reputation, especially in the social sphere. Second, specific social-cultural contexts should be taken into consideration when communicating during corporate crisis events on social media. The findings indicate that college students in China may have more negative online crisis-reaction intention than those in the United States. This also indicates that Chinese Internet users may be the driving forces in future grassroots campaigns. Choosing the appropriate response strategy on social media, in this regard, is especially important for crisis communication in China. Organizations need to be aware of the negative consequences online during crises and establish credibility and trust on social media with the public in their everyday communication. They need to conduct environmental scanning on social media proactively, build two-way dialogues with the public, and respond with the appropriate messages should a crisis occur.

Limitations and Future Research

Although this study provides meaningful implications for social media and crisis communication, there are several limitations. First, this research only covered one crisis type. An accident is an unintentional action caused by internal factors.

Intentional crisis conditions usually generate a higher volume of anger than unintentional crisis conditions (Coombs & Holladay, 2002; Utz et al., 2013). Future research with intentional crisis conditions can further test the effects on reputation, negative word-of-mouth intention, and negative online crisis-reaction intention. Second, this study did not take the organization's performance history into consideration. Future research may manipulate the organization's performance history and crisis-response strategy to further examine the applicability of SCCT in different cultural settings. Third, findings cannot be fully generalized without a broader spectrum of participants. Future research should cast a net for a more diversified sample or even representative sample. Finally, the cross-cultural implications in this study can only apply to the United States and mainland China. Empirical evidence from more countries is needed to provide a broader international perspective.

References

Avery, E. J., Lariscy, R. W., Kim, S., & Hocke, T. (2010). A quantitative review of crisis communication research in public relations from 1991 to 2009. *Public Relations Review*, *36*, 190–192.

Benoit, W. L. (1995). *Accounts, excuses, and apologies: A theory of image restoration*. Albany, NY: State University of New York Press.

Benoit, W. L. (1997). Image repair discourse and crisis communication. *Public Relations Review*, *23*(2), 177–180.

Champoux, V., Durgree, J., & McGlynn, L. (2012). Corporate Facebook pages: When "fans" attack. *Journal of Business Strategy*, *33*(2), 22–30.

Chiu, C., Ip, C., & Silverman, A. (2012, May). Understanding social media in China. Retrieved from http://www.mckinseyquarterly.com/Understanding_social_media_in_China_2961

Coombs, W. T. (1995). Choosing the right words: The development of guidelines for the selection of the "appropriate" crisis-response strategies. *Management Communication Quarterly*, *8*(4), 447–476.

Coombs, W. T. (2012). *Ongoing crisis communication: Planning, managing, and responding* (3rd ed.). Thousand Oaks, CA: Sage.

Coombs, W. T., & Holladay, S. J. (2002). Helping crisis managers protect reputational assets: Initial tests of the situational crisis communication theory. *Management Communication Quarterly*, *16*, 165–186.

Coombs, W. T., & Holladay, S. J. (2007). The negative communication dynamic: Exploring the impact of stakeholder affect on behavioral intention. *Journal of Communication Management*, *11*(4), 300–312.

Coombs, W. T., & Holladay, S. J. (2008). Comparing apology to equivalent crisis response strategies: Clarifying apology's role and value in crisis communication. *Public Relations Review*, *34*, 252–257.

Coombs, W. T., & Holladay, S. J. (2009). Further exploration of post-crisis communication: Effects of media and response strategies on perceptions and intentions. *Public Relations Review*, *35*, 1–6.

Coombs, W. T., & Schmidt, L. (2000). An empirical analysis of image restoration: Texaco's racism crisis. *Journal of Public Relations Research*, *12*, 163–178.

Falcon, A. (2011). Twitter vs. Weibo: 8 things Twitter can learn from the latter. Retrieved from http://www.hongkiat.com/blog/things-twitter-can-learn-from-sina-weibo/

Hewitt, D. (2012, July 31). Weibo brings change to China. *BBC News*. Retrieved from http://www.bbc.co.uk/news/magazine-18887804

Lee, B. K. (2004). Audience-oriented approach to crisis communication: A study of Hong Kong consumer's evaluation of an organizational crisis. *Communication Research, 31*(5), 600–618.

Liu, B. F., Austin, L., & Jin, Y. (2011). How publics respond to crisis communication strategies: The interplay of information form and source. *Public Relations Review, 37*, 345–353.

Luo, Y., & Jiang, H. (2012). A dialogue with social media experts: Measurement and challenges of social media use in Chinese public relations practice. *Global Media Journal—Canadian Edition, 5*(2), 57–74.

Lyu, J. C. (2012). A comparative study of crisis communication strategies between Mainland China and Taiwan: The melamine-tainted milk powder crisis in the Chinese context. *Public Relations Review, 38*(5), 779–791.

Mei, Y. (2012, July 2). 5 Chinese social networks you need to watch. Retrieved from http://mashable.com/2012/07/02/china-social-networks/

Schultz, F., Utz, S., & Goeritz, A. (2011). Is the medium the message? Perceptions of and reactions to crisis communication via Twitter, blogs and traditional media. *Public Relations Review, 37*, 20–27.

Utz, S., Schultz, F., & Glocka, S. (2013). Crisis communication online: How medium, crisis type and emotion affected public reactions in the Fukushima Daiichi nuclear disaster. *Public Relations Review, 39*(1), 40–46.

Veil, S. R., Buehner, T., & Palenchar, M. J. (2011). A work-in-process literature review: Incorporating social media in risk and crisis communication. *Journal of Contingencies and Crisis Management, 19*(2), 110–122.

Veil, S. R., Sellow, T. L., & Petrun, E. L. (2011). Hoaxes and the paradoxical challenges of restoring legitimacy: Domino's response to its YouTube crisis. *Management Communication Quarterly, 26*(2), 322–345.

Ye, L., & Pang, A. (2011). Examining the Chinese approach to crisis management: Cover-ups, saving face, and taking the "upper level line." *Journal of Marketing Channels, 18*(4), 247–278.

Yu, T.-H., & Wen, W.-C. (2003). Crisis communication in Chinese culture: A case study in Taiwan. *Asian Journal of Communication, 13*(2), 50–64.

SECTION III-B

Foundations and Frameworks

Audience-Oriented Approaches and Considerations

9

TOWARD MORE AUDIENCE-ORIENTED APPROACHES TO CRISIS COMMUNICATION AND SOCIAL MEDIA RESEARCH

Julia Daisy Fraustino and Brooke Fisher Liu

Since the launch of sites such as Facebook in 2004, Twitter in 2006, and Instagram in 2010, social media have altered the pace and landscape of crisis communication. People post thousands of tweets per second as crises unfold, for example, and now often obtain crisis news and updates from family and friends online before professional news media report it. Social media have opened up new possibilities for crises as well. Indeed, people use social media for more than crisis information seeking or sharing. In the context of disasters, they increasingly expect emergency managers to constantly monitor and respond to social media posts, often demanding immediate action. However, emergency responders have yet to fully catch up with the demand, still primarily using social media for one-way information pushing rather than responding to and conversing with their publics (Su, Wardell, & Thorkildsen, 2013). And when expectations are not met, individuals can now turn to social media to form groups that fill informational and material voids. Grassroots communities may rise to take control of the crisis narrative and fulfill renewal-based and resilience-related needs during the perceived absence of adequate organizational crisis responses, as was evident following Hurricane Katrina (Procopio & Procopio, 2007) and in the Penn State Sandusky child abuse crisis in 2011, as well as during a chemical spill that contaminated municipal water supplies in West Virginia's Elk River in 2014 (Fraustino, 2014).

Thus, crisis communication and management research that builds theory and enhances practical understanding of the flow of crisis information, especially on social media, is important for understanding the new crisis communication landscape. Much research in this realm, however, focuses on how single organizations can manage messages during crises to mitigate reputational harm (Heath, 2010) rather than fully exploring multivocal responses from diverse social actors, hallmarks of both social media and modern conceptions of public relations

(Sommerfeldt, 2013). Put another way, how and why audiences think, feel, and act surrounding crisis information is subjugated under dominant organization-oriented research that focuses on image and legitimacy concerns and has yet to fully incorporate social media (Avery, Lariscy, Kim, & Hocke, 2010; Heath, 2010). Given these critiques and as an extension of the call for future research to focus on cocreational approaches incorporating social media, this chapter synthesizes literature in the domain of publics-oriented approaches to crisis communication, underscoring social media incorporation (or lack thereof). It first defines baseline terms and contrasts organizational (cf. managerial) and audience (cf. publics) perspectives before categorizing perspectives in the literature. It concludes with recommendations for future research.

Key Terms

Reviewing more than 20 crisis definitions, Heath and Millar (2004) identified that in general, crises (a) require organizational efforts beyond what is normal; (b) cause stakeholder stress; (c) violate laws, ethics, or expectations; and (d) originate from a major organizational mistake or misdeed, potentially causing a turning point. Such overlapping conceptualizations share two common themes: locus of control and accountability. Most crisis definitions encompass at least some aspect of "whether the organization knew, appreciated, planned, and appropriately enacted sufficient control over operations to prevent, mitigate, respond, and learn from a crisis" (p. 3).

These notions hint at or overtly exhibit an emphasis on the organization, more particularly on its reputation. Organizational reputation has often been a primary concern in crisis management research, as many have noted (e.g., Coombs, 2015; Heath, 2010; Liu & Fraustino, 2014). As Coombs (2015) defined, a *crisis* "is the perception of an unpredictable event that threatens important expectancies of *stakeholders* . . . and can seriously impact an *organization's* performance and generate negative outcomes" (Coombs, 2015, p. 3, emphasis added). Accordingly, it is not surprising that in dominant crisis theories (e.g., Benoit, 1997; Coombs, 2007), organizational image and legitimacy are often primary concerns, to the extent that crisis scholars have criticized this literature for its "managerial bias" (Heath, 2010, p. 7).

Crises are similar to but can be distinguished from risks, issues, and disasters. Namely, crises are organization-based adverse events (or perceptions of such events), whereas disasters are community-based adverse events. That is, disasters may be considered community-centric, such as when natural (e.g., hurricanes) or person-made (e.g., bombings) events overcome a community's ability to adequately respond and protect itself. Coombs (2015) explained that "disasters are events that are sudden, seriously disrupt routines of systems, require new courses of action to cope with the disruption, and pose a danger to values and social goals" (p. 3). Risks, however, are possible hazards that hold the potential to manifest into crises, and issues are contested ideas or policies that can prompt or sustain crises

(Coombs, 2015; Heath, 2010). That is, risks and issues can evolve into organizational crises, and disasters can spawn organizational crises when stakeholders or publics shift attention to how the organization (mis)handled disaster-related decisions. Thus, these terms can be understood as conceptually distinct.

Publics, Stakeholders, and Audiences

Just as social media have altered the way organizations communicate about crises and disasters, they have changed how stakeholders and publics seek and share crisis information and assistance. There are similarities among audiences, stakeholders, and publics, yet it can be argued that each is conceptually distinct. Audiences are generally understood most broadly—they are message receivers (Rawlins, 2006). Stakeholders, however, are more closely linked to management orientations, as they are defined in terms of their relationship to the organization (Rawlins, 2006). Namely, stakeholders are "any group that can be affected by the behavior of an organization" (Coombs, 2007, p. 164) or that, on the other hand, can impact an organization's ability to achieve its goals. Publics can be understood more autonomously than in relation to traditional market-based organizations (Sommerfeldt, 2013)—that is, as groups that perceive a problem and organize to solve it (Grunig, 1997).

Having created a working vocabulary of essential terms, it is now possible to compare and contrast management-oriented and audience-oriented approaches to crisis communication.

Management-Oriented Versus Audience-Oriented Crisis Communication Perspectives

Crisis communication, although a distinct and interdisciplinary scholarly area, is often approached from public relations standpoints and is among the most popular areas of public relations scholarship. Crises spur uncertainty (Heath, 2010; Palenchar, 2010) and can prompt a diverse host of organizational and individual repercussions ranging from reputational damage to legal action to personal injuries (Coombs, 2015). It makes sense, then, that scholars seek to find ways to ethically and effectively navigate such negative events—and that practitioners have noted that effectively managing a crisis often leads to their increased standing in the organization (Liu & Pompper, 2012). Thus, crisis scholars must reflect on how and to what ends crisis is studied to shape meaningful future research and guide ethical and effective practice.

As noted previously, dominant crisis communication theories focus on organizational image and reputation concerns to the minimization of publics-oriented concerns. Perhaps this organizational orientation to crisis literature stems in part from the tradition of public relation's strategic management camp, which defines public relations as "a unique management function that helps an organization interact with the social and political components of its environment" in order to fulfill organizational goals (Grunig, Grunig, & Dozier, 2006, p. 55). In accordance with this perspective, early crisis research has concerned itself with categorizing how audiences, stakeholders, and publics might react to various crisis types and organizational responses so that the organization could take control and frame the crisis story so as to best prevent tarnishing its image (e.g., Benoit, 1997). Such organization-focused perspectives may be considered crisis managerial-oriented perspectives.

Although scholars have sought to enrich understanding of the multifaceted roles of public relations beyond contributing to for-profit bottom lines, organizational strategic management perspectives rooted in market-based concerns have made room for cocreational perspectives (Botan & Taylor, 2004). Such perspectives view the function of public relations as facilitating shared meaning between organizations and publics or more broadly between organizations and message recipients. Accordingly, one contemporary definition of public relations places it as the meaning-making and relationship-building function by social actors (Sommerfeldt, 2013). Given these ideas, audience-oriented approaches to crisis communication, then, can be considered those that genuinely incorporate message receivers' thoughts, feelings, and behaviors into organizational decision making and communication. That is, instead of organizations solely attempting to persuade in ways that reflect the image-related concerns of the organization above and beyond care for or impact on audiences, audience-oriented approaches respect the needs of the organization (including image-related needs) while at the same time considering the well-being and interests of those receiving crisis information. Managerial and audience approaches are not mutually exclusive. With this in mind, the chapter will now summarize literature that takes on various levels of such audience-oriented approaches.

Conceptualizing Audience-Based Approaches to Crisis Communication

As Sellnow and Seeger (2013) asserted, "Arguably, theory is the most important tool researchers have for building broader understanding of phenomena" (p. 15). Consequently, in the present context, theory promotes understanding of how crises "develop, what role they play and how they can be managed" (p. 23). In that vein, this synthesis of existing theories and emerging frameworks (i.e., models or related research perspectives) can help guide the important path toward theory building. Of course, a couple of caveats are worth noting. Namely, these research perspectives could be grouped differently according to other characteristics, and this discussion is not exhaustive of all the perspectives available in crisis scholarship.

Organization-Public Relationships and Responses Approaches

Organization-public relationships and responses approaches to crisis communication seek to uncover how organizations can build relationships with publics to increase understanding of effective crisis messages that minimize potential negative responses. Although at first blush this might appear managerial, these approaches are also audience oriented because they take into consideration how audiences feel and think about the crisis when crafting organizations' communicative responses. Despite these advances in incorporating an audience orientation, these stances might be critiqued for still being too organization oriented, particularly in their measured outcomes (e.g., tarnished images). Such perspectives include situational crisis communication theory (SCCT) and the networked crisis communication (NCC) model.

Situational Crisis Communication Theory (SCCT)

SCCT gives guidance about messaging strategy to organizations experiencing crises (Coombs, 2007, 2015). SCCT dictates that during crises, first and foremost organizations must fulfill their ethical obligation to care for and protect their stakeholders. They do this by giving stakeholders (a) *instructing information*, related to physical coping, and (b) *adjusting information*, related to psychological coping. The organization then turns to mending its reputation through implementing strategic message strategies that assume the amount of accommodation likely required by audiences, dominantly based on their levels of attributed crisis responsibility. Strategies include deny, diminish, rebuild, or reinforce (Coombs, 2015). Crisis types may fall into one of three categories also with varying levels of responsibility assigned and recommended messaging in response.

SCCT takes into consideration the ethical imperative first to protect those who might be harmed, reflecting care for audiences. Then the theory turns to framing crisis narratives in ways that will mitigate harmful effects on organizational reputation. Perhaps adding additional outcome variables to this theory that are more reflective of audience concerns rather than solely organizational concerns could strengthen the theory from a cocreational or audience orientation. The theory has begun to be examined in light of new and social media, but these examinations are sparse and much more work in this arena remains.

Networked Crisis Communication (NCC) Model

Utz, Schultz, and Glocka's (2013) NCC model "challenges classical crisis communication theories by showing that the medium used affects the impact of crisis communication" (p. 41). The model posits crises are "social constructions" influenced by "organization-driven sense-giving processes" and "individuals' sense-making processes" (Utz et al., 2013, p. 41). The model attempts to better illuminate the many-to-many model of communication that social media can afford, reflecting one of the few development efforts that espouses a cocreational perspective and fully considers social media. Yet, again, the minimal research developing this model has ultimately examined how the form and source of the message impacts audience responses that could be negative for the organization (as opposed to constructive for both the organization and the audience), such as perceived reputation or intentions to boycott (Schultz, Utz, & Göritz, 2011; Utz et al., 2013). Testing the model in ways that can expand examined outcomes could tip the NCC model further into the audience-oriented arena.

Understanding and Segmenting Audience Approaches

The understanding and segmenting audience approaches to crisis communication consider a wide array of audience attributes that allow an organization to more appropriately and effectively target communication where it is needed. This approach seeks to uncover enduring and situational characteristics of key audiences, which may allow an organization to ensure its communication contains the content that will be most helpful to and best received by key groups. But, again, this approach may be criticized for being used to allow organizations to silence rather than empower its audiences. This category could include situational theory of publics (STP) and situational theory of problem solving; audience and demographics perspectives; and cultures, values, and norms perspectives.

Situational Theory of Publics (STP)

STP is a general public relations theory that segments publics to predict their most likely attitudes and behaviors based on their levels of three independent variables: (a) problem recognition, (b) constraint recognition, and (c) level of involvement (Grunig, 1997). These three variables are posited to influence two dependent variables: (a) information seeking and (b) information processing. Although STP is extensively applied throughout public relations scholarship, limited research has tested the theory in crisis communication contexts, and even less in the new media environment (Avery et al., 2010). Relatedly, situational theory of problem solving (Kim & Grunig, 2011), which is based on STP ideas but does not replace STP, has not yet been applied to crisis contexts but is another similar example that could fit in this category of an audience-based crisis communication approach that bears potential for future research.

Audience Demographics Perspectives

This and the next set of perspectives attempt to engage audience orientations, so they belong here, but they do not yet have frameworks, models, or other cohesive structures to guide examinations. Thus, this and the next category will be briefly covered with an eye toward building future research rather than reviewing the past.

Audience demographics perspectives explore the role of individuals' relatively enduring (rather than situational) characteristics, such as race, ethnicity, gender, sex, socioeconomic status, and education level, in understanding how audiences seek, share, and interpret crisis information (e.g., Spence, Lachlan, & Griffin, 2007). Oftentimes investigations in this area are tacked on to larger studies looking at other variables and treated as secondary, but these characteristics can alone contribute to better understanding how and where to reach key audiences with potentially life altering messages. Research is beginning to show, for example, that gender is associated with varying levels of intentions to seek crisis and disaster information, to take a variety of protective actions, and to help others protect themselves (Spence et al., 2007). Some demographic information has begun to be collected regarding social media use more generally, but more concentrated effort on this topic is needed in crisis communication.

Cultures, Values, and Norms Perspectives

Again, this is an area with little research in crisis communication, but it is one warranting development. In addition to the managerial bias, crisis communication literature has also been critiqued for its Western bias (Heath, 2010; Liu & Fraustino, 2014). However, it certainly stands to reason that people's cultural backgrounds, moral values, and the presiding social norms in which they operate can influence the way they seek, share, and interpret crisis information. Some have conducted critical analysis of such ideas and called for greater critical examination of such features from others as well (e.g., Falkheimer & Heide, 2006), but a thorough explication of these concepts and their application to theory building in crisis is lacking, especially including social media.

Publics' Emotions and Coping Approaches

Publics' emotions and coping approaches to crisis communication research are audience oriented because they probe audience characteristics for inclusion in organizational choices. Yet again, these, too, could be critiqued for being used primarily to leverage organizational advantages rather than to understand and prioritize audience well-being. This grouping includes the integrated crisis mapping (ICM) model and discrete crisis-related affect perspectives.

Integrated Crisis Mapping (ICM) Model

The ICM model (Jin, Pang, & Cameron, 2010) provides an examination of affect from a "publics-based, emotion-driven perspective" (Jin et al., 2010, p. 428). This model maps crises onto two continua, the organization's engagement with the crisis (high to low) and the primary public(s)' coping strategy (conative to cognitive). Its research has demonstrated that audiences' emotions provoke varied communication requirements. Although it acknowledges the value of situation-based response strategies (cf. SCCT), this model asserts that a more systemic approach would shape crisis responses based on emotion and filling publics' emotional needs, reflecting a highly audience-oriented approach to crisis communication. As this model is still young, more research is needed to flesh out the various emotions and map them onto various crisis types, particularly integrating social media.

Discrete Crisis-Related Affect Perspectives

Similar to the ICM model, these perspectives examine affect in terms of discrete crisis-related emotions (Jin, 2010; Jin, Liu, Anagondahalli, & Austin, 2014; Liu, Fraustino, & Jin, 2015). Some such studies tend to investigate emotions in terms of negative reactions audiences might have to crisis messages, presumably to avoid anger directed toward the organization and the host of negative cognitive and behavioral results that follow (Coombs, 2007). Yet there are alternate venues research could take to more fully understand a host of audiences' emotions, their antecedents, and their outcomes. For example, work could be done to unpack how organizations can contribute to social-mediated conversations in ways that facilitate emotional support.

Two-Way and Cocreational Approaches

Finally, the two-way and cocreational approaches reflect perhaps the most audience-oriented approaches of the categories, at least in their current applications. This category is composed of theories and models such as discourse of renewal theory, dialogic communication theory, and the social-mediated crisis communication model.

Discourse of Renewal Theory

Discourse of renewal theory explores how organizational rhetoric can prompt renewal (Sellnow & Seeger, 2013). Renewal, as described by two of the theory's dominant proponents in public relations, is understood as "a development process intended to move organizations to 'higher stages progressively and to preclude a decline toward a lower stage' " (Sellnow & Seeger, 2013, p. 96). It posits that organizational leaders with good character and natural urges to rebuild and grow after crises can engage in renewal-based communicative behavior when crises occur, ultimately resulting in strengthened survival for the organization and its publics. This is to say that a leader during a crisis will prompt renewal by engaging discourse in ways that indicate (a) provisional rather than strategic communication; (b) prospective rather than retrospective orientation; (c) capitalizing on learning opportunities presented by the crisis; and (d) vocal, ethical leadership. Discourse of renewal theory has not yet fully incorporated social media, despite the relevance and ability to advance explanatory and predictive power. For instance, publics may use social media to launch renewal or resilience discourse in the absence of an ethical organizational leader; conversely, rumors and misinformation spreading quickly via social media could potentially thwart organizational renewal discourse efforts.

Dialogic Communication Theory and Cocreational Framework

While reviewing the state of public relations research more than a decade ago, Botan and Taylor (2004) identified (a) a functional perspective and (b) a cocreational perspective. Whereas functional perspectives focus on publics and communication as organizational tools to leverage toward advancing positive outcomes for the organization, cocreational perspectives instead widely view publics and communication as the means for achieving shared meaning and mutual goals. That is, as noted previously, in the cocreational perspective, mutually beneficial relationships take precedence over organizational goal attainment. Through the cocreational framework, thus, "publics are not instrumentalized but instead are partners in the meaning-making process" (Botan & Taylor, 2004, p. 652), a position echoed by the spirit of audience-oriented approaches supported herein.

Fitting the cocreational framework, dialogic communication theory asserts that cocreation of meaning involves conversational exchanges in which one orients oneself to the other rather than concerning oneself with closed-off and aggressive persuasive attempts. As such, dialogic communication has been studied from points of view ranging from activist groups to Fortune 500 companies. Applying principles of open and other-oriented, two-way dialogic communication to websites, Kent and Taylor (2001) offered five principles that organizations could use to enhance their online responses to publics: (a) dialogic loops, (b) ease of interface, (c) conservation of visitors, (d) generation of return visits, and (e) providing information relevant for a variety of publics. Researchers have begun to engage how organizations might implement dialogic principles using social media, but this approach, too, has yet to take hold in crisis communication. As such, this theory provides many potentially fruitful avenues for future researchers to pursue.

Social-Mediated Crisis Communication (SMCC) Model

The SMCC model consists of two parts (e.g., Liu et al., 2015; Liu & Pompper, 2012). The first aims to explain and predict how crisis-related information flows among various actors before, during, and after crises via traditional media, social media, and word-of-mouth communication. Through mapping a comprehensive understanding of how organizations and audiences cocreate meaning surrounding the crisis, considering a multitude of factors that can impact the creation and interpretations of those meanings, the second step modifies SCCT to help organizations communicate with the most effective message strategies.

Whereas original SMCC studies took more management-oriented approaches to the examined outcomes in the second step of the model (i.e., reputational concerns), recent endeavors have begun to add additional audience-oriented considerations, such as taking protective actions or giving helpful information to others (Liu & Fraustino, 2014). Further, this is an example of one of the few perspectives in crisis communication that was created with the attempt to fully account for the new media environment. However, this work is less than a decade old and has yet to be adopted by more than a few key researchers, so as with all crisis research, much work remains to be done in this realm.

In Summary

Recent crisis scholarship has attempted to more fully incorporate publics' and audiences' perspectives into a dominantly management-focused body of literature. There have been fewer attempts to incorporate social media, but these, too, appear on the rise. Such areas of scholarship are promising and important for building theory and providing evidence-based guidelines to practitioners for ethical and effective crisis communication efforts. But there are perhaps more gaps than answers; key gaps are briefly discussed here.

First, audience-oriented approaches to crisis communication have at their core ethical intentions. They reflect an outward orientation of care for others rather than a myopic focus on self-preservation. Thus, it is surprising that explicit treatment of crisis communication ethics is minimal (e.g., Huang & Su, 2008). As growth of social media opens up new ethical concerns, such as privacy and information accuracy, crisis theories will need not only to adapt to more explicitly contend with ethics related to current theoretical constructs but also to expand to contend with ethics related to new media.

Second, crisis literature needs to turn its attention to adding multiplicity in its outcome measures. That is, even when gathering and considering information about and from stakeholders, publics, and audiences in addition to organizational concerns, crisis research ultimately tends to revert to studying these groups with the ultimate end measures being how responses will impact organizational goals and longevity (e.g., SCCT and NCC). For example, testing could reveal tensions between organizational and audience interests that a truly audience-oriented approach would more seriously consider, such as tensions between message approaches that limit organizational responsibility but also limit the likelihood of publics' taking recommended protective actions (Liu et al., 2015).

Third, although crisis researchers have taken strides to help theory advance along with the rapidly changing new media realities (e.g., SMCC and NCC), more work needs to be done in this arena. Emerging research and anecdotal evidence is beginning to show how social media may increase a variety of actors' access to crisis information-seeking and sharing capabilities, including the ability to quickly form groups around issues and take control of the crisis narrative and influence shared meaning. Further, social media have contributed to a globalized environment; incorporating a better understanding of culture, values, and norms into existing theories and crafting new theories to account for these important concepts is paramount. Crisis theory must adapt and grow to reflect the multivocality and global nature of crisis communication, especially social-mediated crisis communication.

Finally, future research should further investigate how people plan for, respond to, and recover from crises completely independent of or in the absence of rapid organizational responses. For example, communities may self-organize on social media in response to disasters because governments are not directly, adequately, or timely meeting people's information and recovery needs or expectations (Janoske, 2014; Procopio & Procopio, 2007).

As Liu and Fraustino (2014) proposed, "Ultimately, public relations researchers need to ask ourselves a fundamental question: What is the goal of our scholarship?" (p. 3). In taking this question to heart, work will expand to provide actionable guidance on how social media can optimally contribute to effective and ethical organization-public and public-public crisis communication and actions.

References

Avery, E. J., Lariscy, R. W., Kim, S., & Hocke, T. (2010). A quantitative review of crisis communication research in public relations from 1991 to 2009. *Public Relations Review, 36*(2), 190–192.

Benoit, W. L. (1997). Image repair discourse and crisis communication. *Public Relations Review, 23*(2), 177–186.

Botan, C., & Taylor, M. (2004). Public relations: State of the field. *Journal of Communication, 54*(4), 645–661.

Coombs, W. T. (2007). Protecting organization reputations during a crisis: The development and application of situational crisis communication theory. *Corporate Reputation Review, 10*(3), 163–176.

Coombs, W. T. (2015). *Ongoing crisis communication: Planning, managing, and responding* (4th ed.). Thousand Oaks, CA: Sage.

Falkheimer, J., & Heide, M. (2006). Multicultural crisis communication: Towards a social constructionist perspective. *Journal of Contingencies and Crisis Management, 14*(4), 180–189.

Fraustino, J. D. (2014). *Beyond the CEO: Discourse of renewal, social media, and crisis resilience.* Paper presented at the annual meeting of the Pennsylvania Communication Association, Pittsburgh, PA.

Grunig, J. E. (1997). A situational theory of publics: Conceptual history, recent challenges and new research. In D. Moss, T. MacManus, & D. Verčič (Eds.), *Public relations research: An international perspective* (pp. 3–48). London: International Thomson Business.

Grunig, J. E., Grunig, L. A., & Dozier, D. M. (2006). The excellence theory. In C. H. Botan & V. Hazelton (Eds.), *Public relations theory II* (pp. 21–62). Mahwah, NJ: Lawrence Erlbaum Associates.

Heath, R. L. (2010). Crisis communication: Defining the beast and de-marginalizing key publics. In W. T. Coombs & S. Holladay (Eds.), *The handbook of crisis communication* (pp. 1–13). Malden, MA: Wiley-Blackwell.

Heath, R. L., & Millar, D. P. (2004). A rhetorical approach to crisis communication: Management, communication process, and strategic responses. In D. P. Millar & R. L. Heath (Eds.), *Responding to crisis: A rhetorical approach to crisis communication* (pp. 1–17). Mahwah, NJ: Lawrence Erlbaum Associates.

Huang, Y.-H., & Su, S.-H. (2008). Public relations autonomy, legal dominance, and strategic orientation as predictors of crisis communicative strategies. *Journal of Business Ethics, 86*, 29–41.

Janoske, M. (2014). *Building online communities after crises: Two case studies* (Unpublished doctoral dissertation). University of Maryland, College Park, MD.

Jin, Y. (2010). Making sense sensibly in crisis communication: How publics' crisis appraisals influence their negative emotions, coping strategy preferences, and crisis response acceptance. *Communication Research, 37*(4), 522–552.

Jin, Y., Liu, B. F., Anagondahalli, D., & Austin, L. (2014). Scale development for measuring publics' emotions in organizational crises. *Public Relations Review, 40*(3), 509–518.

Jin, Y., Pang, A., & Cameron, G. T. (2010). The role of emotions in crisis responses: Inaugural test of the integrated crisis mapping (ICM) model. *Corporate Communications: An International Journal, 15*(4), 428–452.

Kent, M. L., & Taylor, M. (2001). Toward a dialogic theory of public relations. *Public Relations Review, 28*(1), 21–37.

Kim, J.-N., & Grunig, J. E. (2011). Problem solving and communicative action: A situational theory of problem-solving. *Journal of Communication, 61*, 120–149.

Liu, B. F., & Fraustino, J. D. (2014). Beyond image repair: Suggestions for crisis communication theory development. *Public Relations Review*. Retrieved from http://dx.doi.org/10.1016/j.pubrev.2014.04.004

Liu, B. F., Fraustino, J. D., & Jin, Y. (2015). Social media use during disasters: How information form and source influence intended behavioral responses. *Communication Research*. Retrieved from http://crx.sagepub.com/content/early/2015/01/12/0093650214565917.abstract

Liu, B. F., & Pompper, D. (2012). The crisis with no name: Defining the interplay of culture, ethnicity, and race on organizational issues and media outcomes. *Journal of Applied Communication Research, 40*(2), 127–146.

Palenchar, M. (2010). Historical trends of risk and crisis communication. In R. L. Heath & D. O'Hair (Eds.), *Handbook of risk and crisis communication* (pp. 31–52). New York: Routledge.

Procopio, C. H., & Procopio, S. T. (2007). Do you know what it means to miss New Orleans? Internet communication, geographic community, and social capital in crisis. *Journal of Applied Communication Research, 35*(1), 67–87.

Rawlins, B. L. (2006). *Prioritizing stakeholders for public relations*. Gainesville, FL: Institute for Public Relations. Retrieved from http://www.instituteforpr.org/wpcontent/uploads/2006_stakeholders-1.pdf

Schultz, F., Utz, S., & Göritz, A. (2011). Is the medium the message? Perceptions of and reactions to crisis communication via Twitter, blogs and traditional media. *Public Relations Review, 37*(1), 20–27.

Sellnow, T. L., & Seeger, M. W. (2013). *Theorizing crisis communication*. Oxford, UK: Wiley-Blackwell.

Sommerfeldt, E. J. (2013). The civility of social capital: Public relations in the public sphere, civil society, and democracy. *Public Relations Review, 39*, 280–289.

Spence, P. R., Lachlan, K. A., & Griffin, D. R. (2007). Crisis communication, race, and natural disasters. *Journal of Black Studies, 37*(4), 539–554.

Su, Y. S., Wardell, C., & Thorkildsen, Z. (2013, June). Social media in the emergency management field: 2012 survey results. *CNA*. Retrieved from http://www.cna.org/sites/default/files/research/SocialMedia_EmergencyManagement.pdf

Utz, S., Schultz, F., & Glocka, S. (2013). Crisis communication online: How medium, crisis type and emotions affected public reactions in the Fukushima Daiichi nuclear disaster. *Public Relations Review, 39*(1), 40–46.

10

SOCIAL MEDIA, HASHTAG HIJACKING, AND THE EVOLUTION OF AN ACTIVIST GROUP STRATEGY

Nathan Gilkerson and Kati Tusinski Berg

What Is Hashtag Hijacking?

An attention grabbing and dramatic moniker, which has quickly become a favorite of the news media, the term *hashtag hijacking* typically refers to a situation in which a *hashtag* (#), a tool widely used for designating and organizing online conversations on social media sites, becomes commandeered by others in the community and is then instead used to mock, satirize, or negatively critique the original hashtag sponsor. The popular social media platform Twitter is most closely associated with the use of hashtags, but most online communities today commonly use the content-organizing method.

Hashtag campaigns have been around in some form since the initial widespread adoption of social media, but the trend of strategically "hijacking" social media hashtags is relatively new. The first widely publicized example came in January of 2012, when the global fast-food giant McDonald's launched a promotional campaign on Twitter using the hashtag "#McDStories," with the intent of inspiring customers and fans of the brand to post cheerful anecdotes about personal experiences at the restaurant and positive memories associated with the food. In an effort to increase awareness of the campaign, McDonald's paid Twitter to boost visibility of the hashtag through its "promoted trends" offering, in which the social network gives visual prominence on users' screens to a limited number of corporate-sponsored hashtags.

Within a matter of hours of launching the promotion, McDonald's "pulled" formal sponsorship of the Twitter campaign due to the prevalence of overtly negative, sarcastic, and inappropriate responses tweeted by the platform's users incorporating the hashtag. Despite, or perhaps because of, the company's quick decision to cancel the campaign, major news organizations capitalized on the opportunity to cover the embarrassing event for one of the world's most well-known and iconic brands, with many articles including examples of particularly harsh or humorous individual tweets:

> Dude, I used to work at McDonald's. The #McDStories I could tell would raise your hair. (via Twitter)
>
> My brother finding a fake fingernail in his fries #McDStories (via Twitter)
>
> One time I walked into McDonalds and I could smell Type 2 diabetes floating in the air and I threw up. #McDStories (via Twitter)
>
> These #McDStories never get old, kinda like a box of McDonald's 10 piece Chicken McNuggets left in the sun for a week (via the *LA Times*; Hill, 2012)
>
> #McDStories I lost 50lbs in 6 months after I quit working and eating at McDonald's (via *The Daily Mail*; Hill, 2012)

Although obviously wanting to minimize the publicity of such disparaging tweets and snarky horror stories from customers, the social media team at McDonald's "discovered that crowd-sourced campaigns are hard to control" (Hill, 2012) and that little could be done to stop the negative online phenomenon linked to its brand. Instead, McDonald's and the #McDStories incident have become a textbook example used in public relations courses and a cautionary tale among strategic communication professionals coordinating social media campaigns.

In the short time since this bellwether moment in social media history, the coordinated hashtag hijack has become a viable and effective strategic tool used by individuals and activist groups to publicly shame companies, to pressure organizations to action, and to help get their own messages amplified and heard by the general public. Following a brief review of academic literature of the relevant scholarship related to this phenomenon, several additional and more recent examples are discussed—all of which help to illustrate the *evolution* and growing sophistication of hashtag hijacking as an activist strategy. Finally, the implications of this evolving use of social media hashtags as a strategic communication tool, for both academic scholars and professional practitioners of public relations, will be discussed, along with a brief summary of practical advice to help organizations avoid becoming the victim of hashtag hijacking.

Literature Review

Social Media and Public Relations

As of January 2014, the Pew Internet Project reported that 74% of American adults who are online use social networking sites and 19% of those online adults use Twitter (Social Networking Fact Sheet, 2014). And according to the *Social, Digital & Mobile Worldwide* report conducted by We Are Social, social channels continue to show strong growth with top social networks adding more than 135 million new users in 2013 (Kemp, 2014). Although Facebook topped the list with 1.2 billion users globally, Twitter had 232 million active users as of January 2014 (Kemp, 2014). Not only are individuals gravitating toward social media but so are brands, including small, local boutiques, nonprofit organizations, and global Fortune 500 brands. The trend toward using social media as a public relations strategy continues to be embraced by brands looking to engage with a variety of stakeholders (Hird, 2011; McCorkindale, 2010). Today, nearly every major brand is on Twitter and many publications like *AdWeek*, *Time*, and *Business Insider* rank the best brands for users to follow.

Yet, research indicates that although public relations practitioners are doing a better job of taking advantage of the dialogic opportunities on Twitter, there is still room for improvement when trying to establish dialogue with stakeholders (Lee, Gil de Zúñiga, Coleman, & Johnson, 2014). For example, Phillips (2009) suggests that most communication programs utilize digital media that are one-way and asymmetrical. Grunig (2009), on the other hand, argued, "many organizations are now developing two-way, interactive, and dialogical communication programs through digital media, especially using blogs and microblogs such as Twitter" (p. 13). Phillips (2009) also limited the potential of both public relations and social media by describing them as sources of information exchange rather than focusing on their ability to build relationships and engage with stakeholders. In contrast, Solis (2014) emphasized relationships as the epicenter of social networking, stating, "at its very core, social media is not about technology, it's about people" (p. xv).

Practitioners most often focus on the positive outcomes of social media (e.g., interactivity, engagement, transparency) because a key aspect of contemporary public relations is open conversations with stakeholders (Coombs & Holladay, 2010), yet—as scholars have noted—because "what you say and what people hear can in fact create two or more different outcomes" (Solis, 2014, p. xvi), practitioners also need to be prepared to deal with potential fallout from online engagement. One example of such fallout is the hijacked hashtag.

Symmetrical Model of Public Relations

One of the most prominent themes in public relations scholarship and commentary over the past several decades has focused on the support for or challenge of James Grunig's (1989) symmetrical model of public relations as the most ethical way to conduct public relations (Cancel, Mitrook, & Cameron, 1999; Kent & Taylor, 2002; Pieczka, 1997; Stoker & Tusinski, 2006; Van der Meiden, 1993). Taylor, Kent, and White (2001) note, "Alternative frameworks have slowly emerged, however, that are pushing the field in a new direction and raising critical questions about past assumptions" (p. 265). One of the frameworks to have emerged during this time is the relational approach to public relations. This approach situates relationship building as the central public relations activity rather than the conventional focus on public relations as a management function. Not only has it gained quite a bit of momentum, but its growth in the public relations literature over the last dozen or so years has been impressive. The bulk of this research demonstrates that effective relationship management matters for the overall success of an organization. Ledingham (2003) noted,

> Research demonstrates that programs designed to generate mutual understanding and benefit—the desired outcome of management of organization-public relationships—can contribute to attainment of an organization's social, economic, and political goals when those programs focus on the common wants, needs, and expectations of organizations and interacting publics.
>
> *(pp. 193–194)*

Thus, it is imperative that organizations understand how to effectively cultivate, build, and maintain relationships with a variety of stakeholders. As such, public relations professionals often bear the responsibility of communicating and negotiating with strategic stakeholders, including activist groups. L. Grunig (1992) suggested, "Whether they are called pressure groups, special interest groups, grassroots opposition, social movements, or issue groups . . . they all allude to collections of individuals organized to exert pressure on an organization on behalf of a cause" (p. 504). As an external force, activists are most often viewed as problematic for organizations.

Activist Groups

White (2012) noted, "Earlier studies in the public relations literature look at activists from the point of view of the organization being 'acted' on in order to discover how organizations 'respond' to activism" (p. 77). An *activist public* is defined as "a group of two or more individuals who organize in order to influence another public or publics through action that may include education, compromise, persuasion, pressure tactics or force" (Grunig, Grunig, & Dozier, 2002, p. 446). By joining together and making noise in society, activist groups seek to put pressure on organizations. Although many public relations scholars recognize the negative impact activist groups can have on an organization (Grunig, 1992; Grunig et al., 2002; Jones, 1978; Mintzberg, 1983), others contend that such pressure can push organizations toward excellence (Grunig et al., 2002) and serve as a source of rejuvenation (Gollner, 1984). Thus, activist organizations are important to the study of public relations, particularly as they relate to the changing digital landscape of the practice.

Taylor and colleagues (2001) suggested that activist organizations have unique communication and relationship-building needs. They also noted that the Internet is one way that activist organizations can better serve their publics, extend their reach, and coordinate efforts with other like-minded groups. Specifically, activist groups can use the Internet to build relationships with publics by fostering dia-logic communication. Coombs (1998) acknowledged the potential of the Internet as an equalizer for activist organizations because it offers a "low-cost, direct, con-trollable communication channel" (p. 299) "that can magnify their efforts and create linkages with other like-minded stakeholders" (Taylor, Kent, & White, 2001, p. 264). Likewise, Chadwick and Howard (2009) explained that the Internet has been an effective platform for social and political activism because social net-working sites have attracted more people worldwide to join in public debates on different political or societal issues. The significant growth of social media channels in today's societies has made them powerful tools of social and political activism (Segerberg & Bennett, 2011). From a public relations perspective, Bortree and Seltzer (2009) contended, "Social networking sites provide organizations with a space to interact with key publics and to allow users to engage with one another on topics of mutual interest; this should provide the ideal conditions necessary for stimulating dialogic communication" (p. 317). At the same time, social network-ing sites have also become the space in which today's organizations find themselves addressing and managing issues in a very public manner.

Issues Management and Crisis Communication

Lyon and Cameron (2004) noted that facing unfavorable coverage is inevitable for most organizations, yet how organizations *respond* to such coverage is imperative from an issues management perspective. Issues management, a dominant paradigm of research and practice in public relations, includes "the identification, monitoring, and analysis of trends in key publics' opinions" (Heath, 1997, p. 6). Yet, the stakes are even higher when the issue is being played out on social media because bad news travels much faster, the audience is much broader, and the issue can persist much longer (Rahmati, 2014). According to Coombs and Holladay (2010), trust and trans-parency are increasingly important for organizations in order to build relationships and create support. When an organization faces an issue on social media, this focus on transparency is elevated due to the interactivity of the medium and the ability of the audience to determine the length and severity of the issue. Grunig (2009) favored two-way communication and highlights the significance of social media on dialogic communication because it allows for not only management of the issue but also engagement with the audience throughout the issue. Practitioners need to be prepared to deal with issues occurring on social media because, as marketing experts have noted, "if your brand is not out there telling your story, someone else will be . . . and it will likely be the wrong story" (Rahmati, 2014, para. 8). Therefore, all organizations that are active on social platforms must plan, monitor, assess, engage, and review so they are prepared for issues. Rahmati (2014) explains, "We used to live in a world where the producers of content determined the channels of distribution. But now we live in a world where the consumers of content are the ones determin-ing the channels of distribution and consumption" (para. 15).

The Evolution of a Strategy

#AskJPM

Despite the instructive forewarning offered to communication planners through the #McDStories mishap, headlines of the past two years have frequently reported similar hashtag-linked social media missteps by major companies and high-profile organizations alike. One of the most prominent examples came in November of 2013, when JPMorgan Chase, the largest bank in the United States, scheduled a "Q&A" session with one of its top executives on Twitter. Promoted as an opportunity for members of the financial community and general public to ask the executive questions about "leadership and life" in an open, online forum, the bank announced that it was soliciting inquiries for the session through a designated hashtag, #AskJPM. The timing of the promotion, however, was problematic. Along with still-lingering public anger toward the finance industry following the 2007 recession, JPMorgan had also just recently been in the news regarding the announcement of a $13 billion settlement with the U.S. government related to illegal actions surrounding the sale of mortgage-backed securities. The #AskJPM hashtag quickly began trending with thousands of negative Twitter responses, which one news article described as overwhelmingly "harsh criticism and outright nastiness" directed toward the bank and its leaders (Eha, 2013). Critical responses to the bank's ill-conceived hashtag, as reported by *Public Relations Strategist* (Swann, 2014), ranged from tweets that were simple and woeful ("Can I have my house back? #AskJPM") to sarcastic, vitriolic, and accusatory ("Did you have a specific number of people's lives you need to ruin before you considered your business model a success? #AskJPM").

Similar to the earlier McDonald's example, JPMorgan quickly announced it was canceling the online Q&A event and no longer officially sponsoring the hashtag. News headlines of the social media "debacle," however, continued to draw attention to the bank's embarrassing strategic mistake, and Twitter users happily helped feed the frenzy through what seemed to be a spontaneous online competition to post the snarkiest and most entertaining tweets using the hashtag (Kopecki, 2013).

It is evident that by late 2013 a somewhat predictable process was unfolding, within both the online community's response to the situation, and the news media's subsequent coverage, and amplification, of the event itself. Articles covering JPMorgan Chase's blunder often referenced the earlier #McDStories hashtag incident, with some seeming to adopt an almost gleeful tone in announcing the *latest* social media gaffe, with headlines such as "#AskJPM: A Twitter Fail for the Ages" (Taibbi, 2013), and "Best #AskJPM Questions" (Lindsey, 2013). A media template of sorts had been formed for covering moments when companies and organizations encountered unexpected, and especially self-induced, public backlash via social media platforms. It could also be argued that in recent years many members of online communities, in particular Twitter users, have become accustomed to encountering the semiregular corporate social media mishap—and rushing in to join and helping to contribute to the mortification of an organization have become a form of entertainment or online sport for many individuals.

Thus, what has become known today as the phenomenon of "hashtag hijacking" often thrives at least partially because of a mixed dynamic of what could be considered a form of social media schadenfreude—and the news media's natural interest, driven by a motivation for increased readership, to aggressively cover major companies' embarrassing and often entertaining moments of failed marketing strategy. Some have argued that coverage of hashtag hijacking scenarios can become blown out of proportion by the news media. In reaction to a *Forbes* piece about #McDStories, Rick Wion, then director of social media at McDonald's USA, posted a lengthy response to the article's "Comments" section. Wion argued the *Forbes* article lacked perspective on the entirety of McDonald's full volume of social media activity, and noted that the #McDStories related "tweets" accounted for only a tiny percentage of the company's overall daily Web traffic. Furthermore, he argued, it is very easy for members of the news media to "cherry pick" the most negative online posts, which can then be used to paint an unfair and inaccurate picture of public sentiment. Wion wrote:

> Bottom line—the negative chatter wasn't as much as today's headlines have lead [*sic*] people to believe. This happened almost a week ago and the hashtag is only living on because many media outlets are using the chance to push a provocative and tweetable headline. Part of being in social media is knowing that you can't control the message 100 percent of the time. As Twitter continues to evolve its platform and engagement opportunities, we're learning from our experiences.

Along with noting the inherent lack of message control within social media platforms, which speaks to the public relations theoretical notion of two-way symmetrical communication, Wion's comments insinuated that some in the news media might have overemphasized and thus exploited the McDonald's hashtag situation for their own benefit. Additionally, Wion stressed that the organization was "learning" from its use of social media as a strategic tool. Akin to this message, in reaction to the barrage of negative responses generated by its #AskJPM promotion, the JPMorgan Chase bank Twitter account attempted to convey a light-hearted and self-deprecating tone in publicly conceding failure, announcing the company's decision to abandon the promotion by tweeting the succinct and conciliatory message, "#Badidea! Back to the drawing board," in regards to the canceled Q&A event.

In both the #AskJPM and #McDStories incidents, the power of social media's ability to facilitate and organize a unified response becomes evident. Certainly, the traditional mass media also play a key role in the prototypical hashtag hijack—instantly turning a relatively minor situation, occurring in a niche online community, into one that is blared from the headlines and discussed on the evening news. Arguably the groundswell of negative response to both the JPMorgan Chase and McDonald's examples was largely uncoordinated and "organic" in nature. Nothing reported about either situation discussed a significant role played by activists or activist organizations, and instead of an organized and coordinated effort with a clear intent to pressure or persuade the companies, both instances appeared largely driven by individuals who lacked a significant motive or unified front. More recent examples, however, show a *shift* in the use of hashtag hijackings, to that of a more deliberate and intentional communication strategy, often now employed by organized or semiorganized activist organizations.

#CheersToSochi

In late January 2014, during the lead-up to the Winter Olympic Games being held in Sochi, Russia, McDonald's announced another social media campaign, this time intended to promote the international sporting event and highlight its role as a top corporate sponsor. On January 21, the company launched the new campaign by posting the following message on its Twitter account: "We're kicking off a way to send your well wishes to any Olympian today. Are you ready to send your #CheersToSochi?" In the preceding months, however, the Sochi games had become highly controversial, especially among gay rights activists due to Russia's antigay propaganda laws and the host country's harsh treatment of gay citizens. Additionally, the week before, international news media had reported on statements made by Russian president Vladimir Putin intimating that he viewed homosexuals as potential pedophiles and a risk to the country's young people (Lally, 2014). The #CheersToSochi hashtag quickly became a lightning rod for lesbian, gay, bisexual, and transgender (LGBT) activists to focus their anger and express their displeasure with McDonald's and other major corporate sponsors of the games. *The New York Times* reported on the social media–based protests, printing a tweet from author and gay activist Dan Savage in response to the McDonald's promotion, which read, "Hey, @McDonalds: You're sending #CheersToSochi while goons wearing Olympic uniforms assault LGBT people" (Elliott, 2014).

Noting that previous activism by the Human Rights Campaign had condemned Russia's antigay laws and "warned" the largest corporate Olympic sponsors against continued support for the Sochi games, *The Huffington Post* also devoted significant coverage to the controversy. In one column, the site published a screen grab of a Twitter post from another outspoken gay rights activist, author and media personality Mike Signorile, appropriating the McDonald's hashtag and shaming the company for its actions (Wooledge, 2014). The same piece also referenced enthusiastic support for the coordinated hijacking effort from John Becker, an author with The Bilerico Project, an online organization that describes itself as "the web's largest LGBTQ group blog with dozens of lesbian, gay, bisexual, transgender, queer, and genderqueer contributors" (*The Bilerico Project*, 2007). Providing his own Twitter post as an example, which succinctly stated, "I thought about visiting the #Sochi Olympics, but I'm fatally allergic to McHateCrimes. #CheersTo-Sochi #LGBT," Becker encouraged readers of the blog to retweet and "favorite" the appropriated messages and to create their own versions of tweets using the #CheersToSochi hashtag (Becker, 2014).

The backlash from the gay rights activist community quickly spread to the other high-profile Olympic Games sponsors, with protestors incorporating the now sarcastic #CheersToSochi hashtag into dozens of posts targeting the social media accounts of Visa, Coca-Cola, and Proctor & Gamble—all of which were then covered and thus also amplified by traditional media outlets including *The New York Times*. Activists also appropriated the well-known advertising imagery and slogans of their targets, posting mock advertisements and other visuals to convey their anger toward the corporate sponsors. McDonald's eventually released a formal statement on its website responding to the controversy, describing the #CheersToSochi campaign as intended only to "send Olympic athletes and teams messages of good luck" (Elliott, 2014). Directly addressing the issue of gay rights, the McDonald's statement read,

> We are aware that some activists are targeting Olympic sponsors to voice their concerns regarding the Russia LGBT legislation . . . McDonald's supports human rights, the spirit of the Olympics and all the athletes who've worked so hard to compete in the Games. We believe the Olympic Games should be open to all, free of discrimination, and that applies to spectators, officials, media and athletes.

As is evident from the aforementioned statement, the LGBT activist community was successful in its social media protest strategy in not only gaining the attention of one of the largest companies affiliated with the Olympic Games but also prompting the organization to publicly declare support for its cause.

#myNYPD

In the months following the #CheersToSochi episode, several other high-profile examples of activist appropriation of hashtag campaigns occurred. The most widely reported instance transpired when, on April 22, 2014, the New York City police department initiated an effort intended to strengthen public support for the organization through a designated hashtag, #myNYPD. The department prompted Twitter users to participate in the campaign by posting the seemingly innocuous request, "Do you have a photo w/ a member of the NYPD? Tweet us & tag it #myNYPD. It may be featured on our Facebook," accompanied by a sample photo showing a smiling citizen standing next to a patrol car flanked by two friendly looking NYPD officers.

As a multitude of news stories reported, perhaps predictably, the hashtag was almost immediately hijacked with dozens of users posting photos and video clips depicting alleged instances of police brutality, many occurring during the recent Occupy Wall Street protests. One of the leaders of the Occupy Wall Street movement, political activist Justin Wedes, posted a photo showing himself being pushed face first against the sidewalk by a New York City police officer. In another message posted by the @OccupyWallStNYC Twitter account, which has more than 179,000 followers, a tweet included a dramatic photo of an officer brandishing a police baton and lunging toward a protester and sarcastically read, "Here the #NYPD engages with its community members, changing hearts and minds one baton at a time. #myNYPD" (Phillip, 2014). Within a day of the launch of the NYPD hashtag, protest tweets and photos from the Occupy Wall Street activist community had received thousands of retweets, and numerous news outlets declared the social media effort an ill-conceived public relations disaster (Berman, 2014).

The backlash also quickly spread beyond the New York area, as ABC News reported police brutality activist groups from across the country had rapidly co-opted the hashtag strategy and were creating their own similar, localized, hashtag-driven protests (i.e., #myLAPD), targeting police departments in major cities including Los Angeles, San Francisco, Oakland, Denver, Seattle, and Austin (Fields, 2014). When questioned about the negative response to the hashtag campaign, the New York City police commissioner claimed to not be overly concerned about the hostile criticism, arguing instead that the department welcomed the attention and intended to maintain the Twitter effort as an opportunity to reach out to the community and "gauge public opinion" (Berman, 2014). Six months after its launch, the #NYPD hashtag continued to be actively utilized on Twitter, with the moniker seemingly most often used as a catch-all designation assigned to random complaints and other negative commentary related to the New York City police department.

#askChevron

The most significant recent development in the evolution of hijacked hashtags used for the purposes of political activism came in late May 2014, when the hashtag #AskChevron began trending on Twitter. Although many users initially assumed the hashtag had been sponsored by the global oil giant, and that the barrage of negative comments generated about Chevron and its business operations was just evidence of yet another ill-conceived social media promotion put forth by a naïve and tone deaf corporate marketing department, the hashtag was in fact conceived of and sponsored by the environmental activist group Toxic Effect (Bradley, 2014). Anticipating that many Twitter users, whether or not they knew the true sponsor of the hashtag, would quickly jump on the social media bandwagon and use the hashtag to harshly critique and admonish Chevron—and that news outlets would also follow past patterns of eagerly covering the hashtag-driven protest—Toxic

Effect successfully grabbed headlines and generated "its fair share of desired negative responses" focused on allegations of wrongdoing and pollution caused by the oil company (Bradley, 2014).

The Ecuador-based environmental group had strategically timed the online protest to coincide with Chevron's annual shareholder meeting that was taking place in Midland, Texas, and ensured that the hashtag would be seen and garner attention by reportedly paying Twitter's hefty $200,000-per-day "promoted trend" fee to boost its ranking and visibility (Johnson, 2014; Smith, 2014). Despite the fact that Chevron had done nothing to instigate the situation, many news outlets covered the story as yet another social media "hijacking" event, with many articles including multiple examples of tweets criticizing the company (i.e., "When will you pay for the damage in the Ecuadorian amazon!? #AskChevron")—and some focusing on the "brilliant" attention-grabbing protest strategy employed by Toxic Effect (Abrams, 2014). Along with the #AskChevron hashtag, the environmental group also simultaneously sponsored a second hashtag, #WeThePeople, which provided the organization with an additional venue to leverage the online attention and promote its message to both news media and individual users alike.

Described as a "brandjacking" event by several business media articles, the #AskChevron example illustrates the latest evolution in the use of hashtags, and "manufactured" or "engineered" social media controversy, intended to further a strategic protest objective. Although the oil company initially ignored the Twitter-based campaign, Morgan Crinklaw, a Chevron spokesperson, was later quoted in *AdWeek* criticizing the efforts of Toxic Effect and dismissing the online campaign as artificial and insignificant:

> We view it as nothing more than inconsequential noise, and we know that it is not a result of any organic advocacy . . . This is all manufactured, it's all paid for, and it's all a stunt. So we are continuing to promote the positive impact that our company has on the places where we do business, and we are continuing to focus on exposing these groups for who they really are.
>
> *(Johnson, 2014, para. 4)*

Although the organization was dismissive toward the event after the fact, the incident likely garnered the attention of both Chevron executives and shareholders during a pivotal time for the company—and, it can be assumed, the environmental protesters behind Toxic Effect likely claimed a messaging and publicity victory for their cause.

Implications for Theory and Practice

From a practical perspective, public relations practitioners need to be prepared to deal with issues on social media that may compromise the reputation of their brands because "even the smallest issue has the potential to turn into a complete firestorm on social," especially when the controversy shifts from digital media to traditional media outlets (Rahmati, 2014, para. 7). More importantly, practitioners should critically reflect on the potential unintended consequences of strategically planning a hashtag campaign while also proactively monitoring social media sites for possible backlash from activist groups. Environmental scanning is more important than ever when actively engaging with audiences via social media platforms. Additionally, organizations need to have an active social media crisis communication plan in place so they can strategically respond to an issue without delay. Although the benefits of social media align with the broader goal of two-way symmetrical public relations, practitioners need to be aware of and prepared to deal with the potential downfalls.

Although social media ultimately remains a powerful and largely beneficial tool for practitioners, today's organizations do face an increasingly complex and at times perilous online landscape in which to communicate with their various publics. In its coverage of the #AskChevron incident, *Inc. Magazine* noted the "precarious position" brands face with the growing sophistication of online activists and stressed that companies should actively prepare for the possibility of being "brandjacked" with a paid ad on social media (Kerpen, 2014). A similarly ominous message appeared in a *PR Week* article, which warned social media brand managers, "You can be brandjacked without even initiating the conversation" (Wilson, 2014). Although perhaps worrisome, most companies and organizations likely have little to fear—unlike McDonald's, the NYPD, and Chevron, for example—as most are not high-profile brands engaged in controversial industries and are therefore much less likely to become targets for online protestors.

For practitioners considering the possible benefits of a hashtag-driven promotion, a number of public relations educators and social media marketing experts have offered some general advice. Writing for *The Public Relations Strategist*, a publication of the Public Relations Society of America (PRSA), Professor Patricia Swann noted that organizations interested in adopting hashtag initiatives should focus on engaging people online, having honest and sincere conversations with users, and building meaningful relationship with key stakeholders (Swann, 2014). Writing about how organizations can avoid having their hashtag hijacked, an article appearing in *MediaBistro* similarly stresses the need for social media practitioners to "talk to people on Twitter as a person, not as a corporate entity" and warns organizations with mixed reputations to approach hashtag campaigns with caution (Dugan, 2012). Finally, advice on hashtag-driven promotions from Sprout Social urges organizations, first, to carefully "consider every single way the hashtag could be twisted into something inappropriate, critical or even damaging" before implementing a campaign, to steer clear of controversial topics, and, perhaps most importantly, to avoid crafting hashtags that are vague or open ended, which can easily serve as an invitation for sarcasm or misappropriation (BeDell, 2012).

References

Abrams, L. (2014, May 28). The best of #AskChevron: Protestors engineer a brilliant P.R. disaster. *Salon.com*. Retrieved from http://www.salon.com/

Becker, J. (2014). LGBT advocates hijack #CheersToSochi campaign. *LGBTQ Nation*. Retrieved from http://bilerico.lgbtqnation.com/2014/01/lgbt_advocates_hijack_mcdonalds_cheerstosochi_camp.php

BeDell, C. (2012, December 27). 4 Strategies for avoiding Twitter hashtag hijackings. *SproutSocial.com*. Retrieved from http://sproutsocial.com/insights/

Berman, M. (2014, April 23). NYPD commissioner welcomes attention from disastrous #myNYPD hashtag. *The Washington Post*. Retrieved from https://www.washingtonpost.com/news/post-nation/wp/2014/04/23/nypd-commissioner-welcomes-attention-from-disastrous-mynypd-hashtag/?utm_term=.cc8c7eeef533

The Bilerco Project. (2007). About us. Retrieved from http://bilerico.lgbtqnation.com/about

Bortree, D. S., & Seltzer, T. (2009). Dialogic strategies and outcomes: An analysis of environmental advocacy groups' Facebook profiles. *Public Relations Review, 35*(3), 317–319.

Bradley, D. (2014, May 28). Environmental group tees up anti-Chevron tweets with #AskChevron hashtag. *PR Week*. Retrieved from http://www.prweek.com/

Cancel, A. E., Mitrook, M. A., & Cameron, G. T. (1999). Testing the contingency theory of accommodation in public relations. *Public Relations Review, 25*, 171–197.

Chadwick, A., & Howard, P. N. (Eds.). (2009). *Routledge handbook of Internet politics*. New York: Routledge.

Coombs, W. T. (1998). The Internet as potential equalizer: New leverage for confronting social irresponsibility. *Public Relations Review, 24*(3), 289–304.

Coombs, W. T., & Holladay, S. J. (2010). *PR strategy and application: Managing influence*. West Sussex: Wiley-Blackwell.

Dugan, L. (2012, March 27). How not to get your hashtag hijacked (Like McDonald's Did). *MediaBistro.com*. Retrieved from http://www.mediabistro.com/

Eha, B. P. (2013). Like McDonald's before it, JPMorgan suffers a hashtag hijacking on Twitter. *Entrepreneur*. Retrieved from https://www.entrepreneur.com/article/229939

Elliott, S. (2014). Activists try to hijack promotions by sponsors of Sochi Olympics. *New York Times*. Retrieved from https://www.nytimes.com/2014/01/28/business/media/activists-try-to-hijack-promotions-by-sponsors-of-sochi-olympics.html?_r=0

Fields, L. (2014, April 24). #MyNYPD Twitter campaign spawns hashtags across the country. *ABC News*. Retrieved from http://abcnews.go.com

Gollner, A. (1984). Interdependence and its impact on public relations/public affairs. *Tips & Tactics (supplement of PR Reporter), 22*(14), 1–2.

Grunig, J. E. (1989). Symmetrical presuppositions as a framework for public relations theory. In C. Botan & V. T. Hazelton (Eds.), *Public relations theory* (pp. 17–44). Hillsdale, NJ: Lawrence Erlbaum Associates.

Grunig, J. E. (2009). Paradigms of global public relations in an age of digitalization. *PRism, 6*(2). Retrieved from http://www.prismjournal.org/

Grunig, L. A. (1992). Activism: How it limits the effectiveness of organizations and how excellent public relations departments respond. In J. Grunig (Ed.), *Excellence in public relations and communication management* (pp. 503–530). Hillsdale, NJ: Lawrence Erlbaum Associates.

Grunig, L. A., Grunig, J. E., & Dozier, D. M. (2002). *Excellent public relations and effective organizations: A study of communication management in three countries*. Mahwah, NJ: Lawrence Erlbaum.

Heath, R. L. (1997). *Strategic issues management: Organizations and public policy challenges.* Thousand Oaks, CA: Sage.

Hill, L. (2012, January). #McDStories: When a hashtag becomes a bashtag. *Forbes.* Retrieved from https://www.forbes.com/sites/kashmirhill/2012/01/24/mcdstories-when-a-hashtag-becomes-a-bashtag/#582fec37ed25

Hird, J. (2011). 20+ Mind blowing social media statistics: One year later. Retrieved from https://econsultancy.com/

Johnson, L. (2014, June 5). Chevron thinks Ecuador is conspiring against it on Twitter Energy giant speaks out about #AskChevron. *AdWeek.* Retrieved from http://www.adweek.com/

Jones, B. L. (1978). Issue management by objective: The new frontier for business. *Enterprise, 23,* 19–21.

Kemp, S. (2014, January 9). Social, digital, and mobile worldwide 2014. Retrieved from http://wearesocial.net/blog/2014/01/social-digital-mobile-worldwide-2014/

Kent, M. L., & Taylor, M. (2002). Toward a dialogic theory of public relations. *Public Relations Review, 28,* 21–37.

Kerpen, C. (2014, May 28). What #AskChevron means for Twitter, Activists, and Brands. *Inc. Magazine.* Retrieved from http://www.inc.com/

Kopecki, D. (2013, November 14). JPMorgan's #AskJPM Twitter hashtag backfires against bank. *Bloomberg News.* Retrieved from http://www.bloomberg.com

Lally, K. (2014). Putin: Gay people will be safe at Olympics if they "leave kids alone." *Washington Post.* Retrieved from https://www.washingtonpost.com/world/putin-gays-will-be-safe-at-olympics-if-they-leave-kids-alone/2014/01/17/e6f8c47e-7f7d-11e3-95c6-0a7aa80874bc_story.html?hpid=z4&utm_term=.3a70de7b97d0

Ledingham, J. A. (2003). Explicating relationship management as a general theory of public relations. *Journal of Public Relations Research, 15,* 181–198.

Lee, A. M., Gil de Zúñiga, H., Coleman, R., & Johnson, T. J. (2014). The Dialogic potential of social media: Assessing the ethical reasoning of companies' public relations on Facebook and Twitter. In M. W. DiStaso & D. S. Bortree (Eds.), *Ethical practice of social media in public relations* (pp. 157–175). New York: Routledge.

Lindsey, E. (2013, November 13). Best #AskJPM questions. *Marketplace World.* Retrieved from http://www.marketplace.org/

Lyon, L., & Cameron, G. T. (2004). A relational approach examining the interplay of prior reputation and immediate response to a crisis. *Journal of Public Relations Research, 16*(3), 213–241.

McCorkindale, T. (2010). Can you see the writing on my wall? *Public Relations Journal, 4*(2). Retrieved from http://www.prsa.org/intelligence/prjournal/documents/2010mccorkindale.pdf

Mintzberg, H. (1983). *Power in and around organizations.* Englewood Cliffs, NJ: Prentice Hall.

Phillip, A. (2014, April 22). Well, the #MyNYPD hashtag sure backfired quickly. *The Washington Post.* Retrieved from http://www.washingtonpost.com/

Phillips, D. (2009, January 9). A Grunigian view of model PR. *Leverwealth.* Retrieved from http://leverwealth.blogspot.com/2002/01/grunigian-view-of-modernpr.html?discus_reply=5552359#comment-5552359

Pieczka, M. (1997). Understanding in public relations. *Australian Journal of Communication, 24*(2), 65–79.

Rahmati, R. (2014, July 29). Bad news travels fast in social: A framework for social issues management. *Spredfast*. Retrieved from http://www.spredfast.com/social-marketing-blog/bad-news-travels-fast-social-framework-social-issues-management

Segerberg, A., & Bennett, W. L. (2011). Digital media and the personalization of collective action: Social technology and the organization of protests against the global economic crisis. *Information, Communication & Society, 14*(6), 770–799. doi: 10.1080/1369118X.2011.579141

Smith, H. (2014, May 30). #AskChevron: The hashtag that roared (and paid). *Grist.org*. Retrieved from http://grist.org/

Social Networking Fact Sheet. (2014). Retrieved October 17, 2014, from www.pewinternet.org/fact-sheets/social-networking-fact-sheet

Solis, B. (2014). Social media is lost without a social compass. In M. W. DiStaso & D. S. Bortree (Eds.), *Ethical practice of social media in public relations* (pp. xv–xxiv). New York: Routledge.

Stoker, K., & Tusinski, K. (2006). Reconsidering public relations' infatuation with dialogue: Why engagement and reconciliation can be more ethical than symmetry and reciprocity. *Journal of Mass Media Ethics, 21*(2/3), 156–176.

Swann, P. (2014, July 15). NYPD blues: When a hashtag becomes a bashtag. *The Public Relations Strategist*. Retrieved from http://www.prsa.org/Intelligence/TheStrategist/

Taibbi, M. (2013, November 15). #AskJPM: A Twitter fail for the ages—Chase's Twitter gambit devolves into all-time PR fiasco. *Rolling Stone*. Retrieved from http://www.rollingstone.com/

Taylor, M., Kent, M. L., & White, W. J. (2001). How activist organizations are using the Internet to build relationships. *Public Relations Review, 27*, 263–184.

Van der Meiden, A. (1993). Public relations and "other" modalities of professional communication: Asymmetric presuppositions for a new theoretical discussion. *International Public Relations Review, 16*(3), 8–11.

White, C. (2012). Activist efforts of the center for media and democracy to affect FCC policy for video news releases. *Public Relations Review, 38*, 76–82.

Wilson, M. (2014, May 29). Chevron gets brandjacked without writing a word. *PR Daily*. Retrieved from http://www.prdaily.com

Wooledge, S. (2014, January 23). McDonald's #CheersToSochi campaign meets with LGBT backlash. *The Huffington Post*. Retrieved from http://www.huffingtonpost.com

SECTION III-C
Foundations and Frameworks

Characteristics and Types of Social Media

11

SOCIAL MEDIA'S VALUE IN A CRISIS

Channel Effect or Stealing Thunder?

W. Timothy Coombs, An-Sofie Claeys, and Sherry Holladay

As an applied area of research, crisis communication frequently finds itself trying to understand changes in the practice. This is another way of saying the practice evolves faster than the research and theory seeking to explain and to improve it. For crisis communication, the application of social media to crisis communication is the most dramatic evolution of the practice in need of greater understanding. Researchers have just begun to explore the ways social media are affecting crisis communication. Researchers are analyzing and theorizing about how organizations use social media during a crisis (e.g., Freberg, 2012; Liu, Austin, & Jin, 2011; Veil, Sellnow, & Petrun, 2012), the effects of stakeholder use of social media during a crisis (Valentini & Romenti, 2011), the utility of social media as an evaluative tool for crisis communication efforts (e.g., Coombs & Holladay, 2014), and the idea that social media creates a channel effect in crisis communication. Social media as a channel effect posits that simple use of a social media channel alters how people perceive and react to crisis communication messages (e.g., Utz, Schultz, & Glocka, 2013). What we have is a manifestation of Marshall McLuhan's (1967) idea of the medium as the message. A channel effect would be a critical piece of information for crisis managers if the tentative findings generate further validation. However, there is a need for additional research.

The initial findings on the social media channel effect in crisis communication are designated as tentative and in need of further evaluation due to the design of the initial studies. There are plausible alternative hypotheses to the interpretation of this data (Utz et al., 2013). The design and materials used in the study do not rule out stealing thunder as an explanation of the findings. With stealing thunder, an organization experiences fewer negative outcomes, such as less reputational damage, from a crisis when the organization is the first to release information about the crisis. In other words, a crisis inflicts less damage if stakeholders first hear about the crisis from the organization rather than from some other source, such as the news media (Arpan & Pompper, 2003; Claeys & Cauberghe, 2012). When social media are used to convey the message, another interpretation of the results could be stealing thunder. The organization can be perceived to be the first to release the crisis information when an organizational tweet or Facebook post is used as stimuli in an experiment. Effects generated by the organizational tweet or Facebook post could be a result of the channel or from stealing thunder. The point is, the effects from the "social media" might be a function of stealing thunder rather than a channel effect. This is an important question that needs to be addressed.

This pilot study attempts to ascertain if previously reported social media effects were a channel effect or a stealing-thunder effect. The chapter begins by refining the rationale for the study and articulating the hypotheses. The next section presents the design and methodology, followed by the results. The final section provides a discussion of the results and implications for theory and practice.

Literature Review: Social Media's Channel Effect on Crisis Communication

As noted in the introduction, there is a growing body of crisis communication research that considers social media as a critical variable or context. For this study, we narrow the focus to research that argues for a channel effect. Social media compose a broad category of communication channels that allow users to generate the content (Kaplan & Haenlein, 2010). The channel effects research argues that simply using a social media channel alters how people perceive and react to the crisis messages (Utz et al., 2013). This section reviews a specific line of social media channel research and its potential connection to stealing thunder.

Social Media Channel Effects

In 2011, Schultz, Utz, and Göritz published an article titled "Is the Medium the Message? Perceptions of and Reactions to Crisis Communication via Twitter, Blogs, and Traditional Media." Though studying three different crisis-response strategies using an experimental study, Schultz, Utz, and Göritz (2011) concentrated on the effects of different media types on reputation, secondary crisis reactions, and secondary crisis communication. The study employed three media types: online newspapers, Twitter, and blogs. Because participants could click a link in the tweet that connected them to the blog, a Twitter plus blog media type emerged, too. The crisis situation was a problem with spark plugs in Mercedes Benz automobiles. There were three dependent variables: organizational reputation, secondary crisis communication, and secondary crisis reactions. Secondary crisis communication included sharing the message with others, telling friends about the incident, and leaving a reaction online. Secondary crisis reactions included signing an online petition and saying negative things about the organization and product. The study found a main effect for media on reputation and secondary crisis reactions but not for secondary crisis communication. The reputation scores in the Twitter plus blog condition were higher and significantly different from the blog- and Twitter-only conditions. The Twitter plus blog and Twitter-only conditions reported fewer secondary crisis reactions (negative word of mouth and boycott) than the blog posting or newspaper conditions. The results lead to the conclusion "the media turned out to be more important than the message" (Schultz et al., 2011, p. 26). This was the initial and preliminary study of a channel effect for social media in crisis communication.

In 2013, Utz and colleagues (2013) published a second study that examined the channel effect of social media. The crisis situation was the Fukushima nuclear reactor disaster. This study utilized three channels: Twitter, Facebook, and an online newspaper. The dependent variables were reputation, secondary crisis reaction, and secondary crisis communication. The three following hypotheses were tested:

H1: Crisis communication via Twitter and Facebook leads to higher post-crisis reputations than crisis communication via newspaper.

H2: Crisis communication via Twitter and Facebook leads to fewer secondary crisis reactions than crisis communication via newspaper.

H3: Crisis communication via newspaper leads to more secondary crisis communication than crisis communication via Twitter and Facebook.

The perceived credibility of the various media was assessed as well. Utz and colleagues (2013) included an analysis of crisis type and the study of anger as mediators but that is not relevant to current study in this chapter.

The analyses by Utz and colleagues (2013) found support for the effect of media type on reputation, as the respondents rated the organizational reputation higher in the Twitter and Facebook conditions than in the online newspaper condition. Media type had a marginally significant effect on secondary crisis reactions. The newspaper condition had a stronger secondary crisis reaction than the Facebook condition. Media type had a marginally significant effect on secondary crisis communication. Respondents were more likely to engage in secondary crisis communication in the newspaper condition than the Twitter condition. The online newspaper was found to be the most credible source of information. The results led to the following conclusions: "Although crisis communication via social media is better for an organization's reputation and reduces unfavorable secondary crisis reactions, crisis communication via traditional media still plays an important role because journalists are credible gatekeepers" (Utz et al., 2013, p. 46).

Stealing Thunder: A Plausible Alternative Hypothesis

A well-documented effect in crisis communication is stealing thunder (e.g., Arpan & Pompper, 2003). Stealing thunder is when the organization is the first source to disclose the existence of a crisis. The opposite of stealing thunder is when the news media or some other source is the first to report on the existence of the crisis. Research consistently finds that all else being equal, an organization suffers less damage from a crisis when the organization is the first to report the crisis, as opposed to some other source, typically the news media, being the first to report the crisis (Arpan & Roskos-Ewoldsen, 2005; Claeys, Cauberghe, & Leysen, 2013). When the organization steals thunder, the crisis does less damage to the organization. We posit that stealing thunder may be the reason for the reported social media channel effects in earlier studies.

In the two social media channel-effects studies, the social media channels were operated by the organization. The blog, Twitter, or Facebook conditions (the social media channels) all present the organization as the source of the crisis information—the organization is the first to report the existence of a crisis. Hence, the benefits attributed to the channel might actually be the result of stealing thunder. What is needed is a comparison of channels where the source is held constant. We examined the following revised hypotheses utilized by Utz and colleagues (2013) and added crisis responsibility as a dependent variable. Crisis responsibility was added because its assessment has implications for how people react to crises (e.g., Coombs, 2007). (We did not use the secondary crisis communication variable. This was because the original did not differentiate between positive and negative comments, just if a comment was made. Hence, it is difficult to judge the actual implications from this variable):

H1: When the source is held constant, crisis communication via Twitter and Facebook is associated with higher reputation scores than crisis communication via newspaper.

H2: When the source is held constant, crisis communication via Twitter and Facebook is associated with lower attributions of crisis responsibility than crisis communication via newspaper.

H3: When the source is held constant, crisis communication via Twitter and Facebook is associated with fewer secondary crisis reactions than crisis communication via newspaper.

To determine if stealing thunder is a possible explanation, sources must be compared across social media channels. We must also consider if there is an interaction effect between channel and source.

H4: Respondents in the stealing-thunder condition will hold more positive organizational reputations than respondents in the news media condition.

H5: Respondents in the stealing-thunder condition will perceive less crisis responsibility reputations than respondents in the news media condition.

H6: Respondents in the stealing-thunder condition will report weaker secondary crisis reactions than those in the news media condition.

RQ1: Is there any interaction effect between channel and source for organizational reputation, crisis responsibility, or secondary crisis reaction?

Methods

Participants

The participants were recruited using the SurveyMonkey Audience database. Through SurveyMonkey, we could specify the respondent had to be 18 years old or older, speak English, and use Facebook. Participants were 55% female (n = 83) and 45% male (n = 69). The age distribution was 24% 18–29 years old (n = 38), 29% 30–44 years old (n = 44), 26% 45–60 years old (n = 40), and 30% over 60 years old (n = 30).

Design

The study's design was three (channel) by two (source) incomplete factorial design. The channels are Facebook, Twitter, and online news story. The source is CNN (a media outlet) or Taylor Farms (the organization in crisis). An incomplete factorial design is used when a fully crossed factorial design is not necessary (Trochim, 2006). In our study, it makes no sense to have a news story from Taylor Farms because it is not a media outlet. There are a total of five rather than six conditions because a Taylor Farms online news story was unnecessary.

Materials

Five different messages were created for the five conditions. Each condition reported that there had been a recall of certain Taylor Farms products due to food contamination. The messages were taken from an actual 2010 case involving a recall by Taylor Farms to preserve ecological validity of the stimuli. The two Facebook posts and the online news story used the same text. The two Twitter messages used the same text as well. The message was condensed to 140 characters to fit the Twitter format.

Organizational reputation (Cronbach's alpha = .87) and crisis responsibility (Cronbach's alpha = .87) were measured using 5-item scales from Coombs and Holladay (2002). Secondary crisis reaction (Cronbach's alpha = .93) was measured using three items from Utz and colleagues (2013). Anger was measured because of its close relationship with secondary crisis reactions (Utz et al., 2013). Anger was assessed (Cronbach's alpha = .93) with items asking the degree to which respondents felt the following emotions when reading the information (anger, irritation, and annoyance). Respondents rated the credibility of each channel on a scale that ranged from "not credible at all" to "very credible." Credibility of the message (Cronbach's alpha = .80) was assessed using three items: the message was convincing, the message was believable, and the message was unbiased. All of the items used a 7-point scale. Two manipulation checks were used to determine if respondents could recall the source of the message and the channel through which the message was delivered. Respondents were excluded from the analysis if they failed to recall either the proper source (3% answered incorrectly) or the channel (3% answered incorrectly) in their condition. A total of nine respondents were removed because of their responses to the manipulation check resulting in a final total of 141 respondents.

Procedures

The survey was designed and placed on the SurveyMonkey website. After selecting the criteria for the population, SurveyMonkey send a recruitment message to potential respondents. When respondents began the survey, they were randomly assigned to one of the five message conditions. The survey took about 15 to 20 minutes to complete.

Results

A one-way MANOVA was used to test H1–H3. The results revealed a significant effect for channel and crisis responsibility, $F(2, 2.72) = 4.94$, $p = .01$, $\eta^2 = .13$, power = .79. The follow-up analysis found a significant difference between only Twitter ($M = 4.91$, $SD = 1.22$) and Facebook ($M = 5.96$, $SD = 1.07$), not between the social media channels and the online news story. There was no significant effect for channel with reputation ($p = .06$) or secondary crisis reaction ($p = .87$). The analyses do not support H1–H3 and the idea that there is a channel effect for social media in crisis communication.

A MANOVA was used to test R1 to determine if there were any interaction effects between channel and source and to test H4–H6 for stealing thunder (source effect). There was no significant interaction effect between source and channel for reputation ($p = .98$), crisis responsibility ($p = .18$), or secondary crisis reaction ($p = .99$). The analysis revealed a significant main effect for source with both reputation, $F(1, 5.18) = 3.82$, $p = .053$, $\eta^2 = .03$, power = .49, and crisis responsibility, $F(1, 12.69) = 7.83$, $p = .006$, $\eta^2 = .07$, power = .79, but not for secondary crisis reaction ($p = .83$). For reputation, the news media source conditions were associated with a lower evaluation of organizational reputation ($M = 4.65$, $SD = 1.25$) than the organization source conditions ($M = 5.05$, $SD = 1.06$) and higher attributions of crisis responsibility ($M = 5.46$, $SD = 1.27$) than the organization source conditions ($M = 4.67$, $SD = 1.38$). The results support H4 and H5 but not H6.

A series of *t*-tests were conducted to explore further for any differences between the news organization and organizational social media messages. Respondents in the CNN Facebook page condition (M = 5.96, SD = 1.07) reported higher attributions of crisis responsibility than respondents in the Taylor Farms Facebook condition (M = 4.89, SD = 1.14), $t(49)$ = 3.48, p = .001. There was no significant difference between the CNN Facebook and Taylor Farms Facebook conditions for reputation (p = .13). There was no significant difference between the CNN Twitter and Taylor Farms Twitter conditions for reputation (p = .23) or crisis responsibility (p = .31). The *t*-test results provide partial support for the stealing-thunder effect. Overall, the results suggest stealing thunder is a viable interpretation of the data.

Some additional analyses were run to provide greater context for interpreting the results. Anger was found to be strongly correlated (r = −.48, p < .001) with secondary crisis reactions, consistent with the study by Utz and colleagues (2013). Also, anger was low across all five conditions ranging from 2.56 to 3.03 on a 7-point scale. The crisis scenario used in this study seemed to generate very little anger. As with Utz and colleagues (2013), the online news story was rated as a more credible source (M = 4.51, SD = 1.43) than Facebook (M = 3.45, SD = 1.61) or Twitter (M = 3.23, SD = 1.61).

Discussion

The driving force behind this study was to explore the reported channel effect for social media in crisis communication. Studies have reported that social media channels alter how people react to crisis communication. More precisely, people view the same crisis communication differently when it is delivered via social media than by traditional or other digital media (e.g., Utz et al., 2013). One concern about these early social media channel-effects studies is that stealing thunder (a source effect) serves as a plausible alternative hypothesis to the social media channel effects. The social media channels used in the study were from the organization in crisis and the data are consistent with stealing-thunder results. The current study sought to control for source effects and determine if social media channel effects, stealing thunder, or some combination of the two were the best explanatory framework for the findings.

When the source was the same across identical crisis communication messages using Twitter, Facebook, and an online news story, no source effect was detected from the social media channels. However, the data did reveal a slight source effect (stealing thunder) and no interaction effect between channel and source. Generally, respondents viewed an organization's reputation more favorably and attributed less crisis responsibility when the source was the organization rather than a news media outlet. At least for this study, stealing thunder proved to be a more viable explanation of the variance in the data than a social media source effect.

Limitations

As with the early social media channel-effect studies, this study is exploratory. It used a sample of under 140 subjects and utilized only one crisis type. The product-harm crisis generated moderate amounts of crisis responsibility and low levels of anger. That lack of anger could explain the failure to find any source or channel differences for secondary crisis reactions. Anger is key element in generating secondary crisis reactions. Perhaps a management-misconduct crisis that generates strong attributions of crisis responsibility and anger might generate different results. Moreover, the power was rather low in the MANOVA analysis due to utilizing only 140 respondents. Additional research is necessary to clarify the actual conditions when a social media channel effect might emerge.

Conclusion

For this study, stealing thunder (source effect) is a more appropriate interpretation of the data than a social media channel effect. Unlike previous research using social media channels, this study was designed to examine the possible effects of stealing thunder as another possible explanation of the results from the use of social media in crisis communication. By controlling for message source, the analyses could determine if source (stealing thunder) or channel (social media channel effect) was the best explanation for the variance. The results of the data analysis found support for a source effect (stealing thunder) and found virtually no support for a channel effect (social media channel effect). The results of this study suggest a modification to the recommendations that social media channels will serve to protect organizational reputations and lessen secondary crisis reactions. Such benefits are likely to accrue only when the organization is the source of the crisis communication. We concur that there are advantages to organizations using their social media channels to report a crisis. It is better that stakeholders learn about the crisis via an organization's social media that from another source. We would argue than the benefits found in the earlier social media channel-effects study are more likely due to stealing thunder than to the nature of the medium. Additional research is required to determine if the supposed social media channel effect is simply a result of stealing thunder or the precise circumstances under which a social media channel effect is found.

References

Arpan, L. M., & Pompper, D. (2003). Stormy weather: Testing "stealing thunder" as a crisis communication strategy to improve communication flow between organizations and journalists. *Public Relations Review, 29,* 291–308.

Arpan, L. M., & Roskos-Ewoldsen, D. R. (2005). Stealing thunder: Analysis of the effects of proactive disclosure of crisis information. *Public Relations Review, 31*(3), 425–433.

Claeys, A. S., & Cauberghe, V. (2012). Crisis response and crisis timing strategies: Two sides of the same coin. *Public Relations Review, 38*(1), 83–88.

Claeys, A. S., Cauberghe, V., & Leysen, J. (2013). Implications of stealing thunder for the impact of expressing emotions in organizational crisis communication. *Journal of Applied Communication Research, 41*(3), 293–308.

Coombs, W. T. (2007). Protecting organization reputations during a crisis: The development and application of situational crisis communication theory. *Corporate Reputation Review, 10*(3), 163–176.

Coombs, W. T., & Holladay, S. J. (2002). Helping crisis managers protect reputational assets: Initial tests of the situational crisis communication theory. *Management Communication Quarterly, 16*(2), 165–186.

Coombs, W. T., & Holladay, S. J. (2014). How publics react to crisis communication efforts: Comparing crisis response reactions across sub-arenas. *Journal of Communication Management, 18*(1), 40–57.

Freberg, K. (2012). Intention to comply with crisis messages communicated via social media. *Public Relations Review, 38*(3), 416–421.

Kaplan, A. M., & Haenlein, M. (2010). Users of the world, unite! The challenges and opportunities of social media. *Business Horizons, 53*(1), 59–68.

Liu, B. F., Austin, L., & Jin, Y. (2011). How publics respond to crisis communication strategies: The interplay of information form and source. *Public Relations Review, 37*(4), 345–353.

McLuhan, M. & Fiore, Q. (1967). *The medium is the massage: An inventory of effects*. New York: Bantam Books.

Schultz, F., Utz, S., & Göritz, A. (2011). Is the medium the message? Perceptions of and reactions to crisis communication via Twitter, blogs and traditional media. *Public Relations Review, 37*(1), 20–27.

Trochim, W. M. (2006). Factoral designs. Retrieved from http://www.socialresearchmethods.net/kb/expfact.php

Utz, S., Schultz, F., & Glocka, S. (2013). Crisis communication online: How medium, crisis type and emotions affected public reactions in the Fukushima Daiichi nuclear disaster. *Public Relations Review, 39*(1), 40–46.

Valentini, C., & Romenti, S. (2011). Blogging about crises: The role of online conversations in framing Alitalia's performance during its crisis. *Journal of Communication Management, 15*(4), 298–313.

Veil, S. R., Sellnow, T. L., & Petrun, E. L. (2012). Hoaxes and the paradoxical challenges of restoring legitimacy dominos' response to its YouTube crisis. *Management Communication Quarterly, 26*(2), 322–345.

12

THE WORLD'S ALL ATWITTER

Image Repair Discourse on Social Media

Mark Glantz and William L. Benoit

Since its launch in 2006, much has been made of the ways in which Twitter is different from other social media platforms. All messages (tweets) posted on Twitter are limited to 140 characters. This limitation certainly restricts the amount of content a user can fit into one post (Miller, 2011) but also increases the speed at which information is sent and received (Lovejoy, Waters, & Saxton, 2012). Levinson (2012) has observed that Twitter allows users to "follow" organizations and individuals that might not follow them in return. This one-way relationship represents a stark difference from Facebook's more reciprocal, "friendship" model of connecting users. Ultimately, Twitter is designed not only to build and maintain relationships but also to share information (Acar & Muraki, 2011). According to Lunden (2012, July 13), Twitter boasts over 500 million registered accounts. This enormous user base, coupled with journalists' willingness to regard tweets as newsworthy (Fitzgerald, 2013), ensures that high-profile individuals and organizations can find large audiences for their messages.

Image repair tweets are an increasingly common form of Twitter message. Before presenting examples of image-repair tweets and examining the nature of image-repair strategies on Twitter, this chapter presents a brief discussion of the theories that inform this analysis.

Theory of Image-Repair Discourse

Benoit's (1995a, 2014) theory of image-repair discourse (built on the work of Burke, 1969; Goffman, 1963; Scott & Lyman, 1968; and Ware & Linkugel, 1973) outlines the conditions under which those who are accused of wrongdoing come to feel pressure to repair their public image. First, the accused party must be perceived as responsible for an action. Second, the act of which the party is accused must be regarded as offensive. Under these circumstances, accused parties typically resort to some combination of 14 potential image-repair strategies.

Accused parties often decide to deny wrongdoing. This can be achieved through *simple denial* or through *shifting the blame* to the "real" culprit. Four image-repair strategies are designed to evade responsibility: claiming *provocation*, using *defeasibility*, claiming the act was an *accident*, and arguing that the accused party had *good intentions*. Six strategies allow the accused to try to reduce the offensiveness of an act. These include *bolstering* one's good traits; *minimizing* the seriousness of the act; *differentiating* the act from other, even less desirable acts; using *transcendence* to discuss more important considerations; *attacking the accuser*; and reimbursing victims of the act through *compensation*. Accused parties can also use *corrective action* to solve or prevent recurrence of the problem or act in question. Finally, accused parties can resort to *mortification* by claiming responsibility for a wrongful act and issuing an apology.

These strategies have been documented in the image-repair rhetoric of politicians (Benoit, 2006; Davis, 2013), corporations (Benoit, 1995b; Benoit & Brinson, 1994), celebrities (Benoit, 1997; Oles, 2010), and athletes (Brazeal, 2008; Glantz, 2010). Typically, these studies analyze messages from speeches, press releases, press conferences, and various other media appearances. Few scholarly articles focus on individuals or organizations that have used social media in their image-repair efforts. Moody (2011) examined how Jon Gosselin, costar of the popular reality program, *Jon & Kate Plus 8*, used Twitter to attack his accusers, bolster his reputation, and apologize for his actions (mortification) in the wake of his messy divorce from his wife, Kate. Muralidharan, Dillistone, and Shin (2011) found that after BP's oil rig exploded and polluted the Gulf of Mexico, the corporation used corrective action, compensation, mortification, and simple denial strategies in messages posted to Twitter and other social media sites. Finally, when basketball star Gilbert Arenas was suspended from the NBA and charged with carrying unlicensed firearms, he used Twitter in an attempt to reduce the offensiveness of his act (Sheckels, 2013).

Image Repair on Twitter

Image repair messages can be identified in three different forms of Twitter discourse—tweets, retweets, and replies. The following paragraphs explore multiple examples of each.

In some situations, 140 characters is sufficient opportunity for an image-repair message. When *The Sunday Times* came under scrutiny for publishing a Gerald Scarfe editorial cartoon that many readers and critics perceived as anti-Semitic, owner Rupert Murdoch issued the following tweet: "Gerald Scarfe has never reflected the opinions of *The Sunday Times*. Nevertheless, we owe major apology for grotesque, offensive cartoon." Although Murdoch's language is terse, his message is complete enough to feature two distinct image-repair strategies. In the first sentence, Murdoch shifts blame for the offensive cartoon to its illustrator, Gerald

FIGURE 12.1 Rupert Murdoch's Twitter Message

Scarfe (see Figure 12.1). In the second sentence, Murdoch uses mortification to acknowledge, and apologize for, Scarfe's offensive cartoon, which was published in *The Sunday Times*.

The Los Angeles Kings hockey team provided a similar example of an organization that managed to fit the entirety of their image-repair discourse into a single tweet. The organization had to resort to crisis communication when local radio host and guest tweeter, Kevin Ryder, used the official LA Kings Twitter handle to send an offensive tweet about some on-the-ice action. The offensive tweet said, "Galiardi gets a penalty for running over Quick. Power play Kings. Kopitar just got sexually assaulted in front of Niemi.—@TheKevinRyder." First, the organization deleted the tweet. Next, the Kings tweeted the following message: "We apologize for the tweets that came from a guest of our organization. They were inappropriate and do not reflect the LA Kings." By acknowledging that the tweets about sexual assault were "inappropriate" and issuing an apology, the Kings used mortification. By reminding audiences that the offensive tweet came from a guest of their organization, they shifted the blame. The organization incorporated two distinct image-repair strategies in fewer than 140 characters.

For some image-repair rhetors, however, 140 characters is just not enough. When San Francisco 49ers quarterback Colin Kaepernick was named as a suspect in a sexual assault investigation, he spread his image-repair efforts across three separate tweets, sent in quick succession. He numbered the tweets so that his overall message was more intelligible and could be recognized as a comprehensive set. This gave him enough space to deny the charges against him and attack the celebrity news website that had been circulating information about the investigation.

> (1/3) The charges made in the TMZ story and other stories I've seen are completely wrong. They make things up about me that never happened.
>
> (2/3) I take great pride in who I am and what I do, but I guess sometimes you have to deal with someone who makes things up.
>
> (3/3) I want to thank all of the people who have shared their encouraging sentiments. I assure you that your faith is not misplaced.

FIGURE 12.2 Julianne Hough's Twitter Message

Kaepernick's tweets incorporate three complementary image-repair strategies. He used simple denial when he noted that the charges against him were "completely wrong." He also attacked his accuser, the gossip news agency TMZ, when he claimed that the group fabricated the details of their story (this also reinforces denial). Finally, he bolstered his image by noting that he took "great pride" in his identity and by alluding to all the support he has received. Kaepernick's method of circumventing the Twitter's character limits was simple but effective.

Another way an accused party can work around Twitter's character constraints is to tweet a link to a third-party website that hosts the bulk of the image-repair message. Actress Julianne Hough used this tactic after photographs of her wearing blackface surfaced online. More specifically, the white actress alienated fans by dressing up as Suzanne "Crazy Eyes" Warren, a black character from HBO's prison comedy drama *Orange Is the New Black*, for Halloween. In an effort to repair her reputation, she tweeted, "I am a huge fan of the show Orange is the new black, actress Uzo Aduba, and the character she has created. (cont) tl.gd/n_irqfec1" The random string of letters and numbers at the end of her tweet was a hyperlink (see Figure 12.2). Although this message proclaims Hough's appreciation for the television program *Orange Is the New Black*, it is otherwise an incomplete image-repair message. To read the rest of her message, users had to click on the hyperlinked blue text, which took them to a longer message housed at TwitLonger.com (see Figure 12.3). The TwitLonger message said, "I am a huge fan of the show Orange is the New black, actress Uzo Aduba, and the character she has created. It certainly was never my intention to be disrespectful or demeaning to anyone in any way. I realize my costume hurt and offended people and I truly apologize."

Hough's longer message continued in the vein of a good-intentions defense by claiming she is a fan of *Orange Is the New Black* and she never meant to be disrespectful or demeaning. She also used mortification to take responsibility for her actions, acknowledge that she hurt people, and apologize. Ultimately, this new media communication tactic takes advantage of the large audience and sense of immediacy that Twitter offers, while still benefiting from the space affordances of other media forms.

Notably, the URL in Hough's initial tweet is exceptionally short. This is part of a trend in which content providers and third-party applications have found

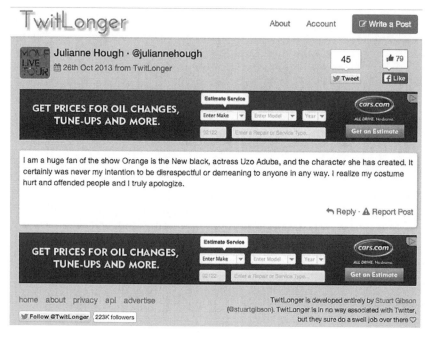

FIGURE 12.3 Julianne Hough's TwitLonger Message

ways to condense external links as much as possible so that users can fit them into Twitter messages. It is also worth noting the prominence and placement of TwitLonger's banner ads. For a small fee, TwitLonger also offers an ad-free service. Clearly, the appeal of TwitLonger is a user-friendly design that makes it easy for social media users to extend their tweets. For those Twitter users who are just slightly more computer literate, tweeting a link to a personal blog or website might be a similarly appealing option.

Retweets are a key feature of Twitter that can be used to help repair an accused party's image. Retweets are essentially repostings or forwards of tweets from other users. Typically, users retweet messages that they think deserve an even greater audience—something important, insightful, or humorous. When it comes to image-repair efforts, accused parties use retweets to strengthen their persuasive defense.

In spring 2014, Dallas Mavericks owner Mark Cuban gave an interview to *Inc. Magazine* in which he made several comments that were interpreted as racist. Cuban relied primarily on his subsequent media appearances to clarify, elaborate, and defend his initial remarks. However, he used Twitter to retweet supportive comments from fans and observers. For instance, he retweeted a Nebraska radio host named Mike Welch (@RealMikeWelch), who wrote, "Just heard the full @mcuban interview. It's about recognizing internal prejudices to overcome them. What @JPCavan did is disgraceful." This sort of retweeting ought to be regarded

FIGURE 12.4 Mark Cuban's Retweet of Mike Welch's Message

as an instance of third-party image repair (Benoit, 2014), in which another person or organization helps defend the accused. This statement not only bolsters Cuban but also attacks an outspoken accuser, sports blogger Jim Cavan, for unfairly criticizing Cuban. Rather than producing his own messages, Cuban let other people's words speak for him (see Figure 12.4).

Hall of Fame football player Deion Sanders also used retweets to complement his other image-repair strategies. In summer 2014, the state of Texas moved to shut down Sanders's Prime Prep Academy charter school. The state alleged that the organization misused federal funds and violated University Interscholastic League rules. Sanders used several tweets to shift blame for poor management to the school's cofounder, D. L. Wallace, but relied on retweets to bolster his own good works at Prime Prep. For instance, he retweeted a testimonial from Lisa Perkins, the mother of a Prime Prep Academy student who benefited academically from the program. She placed Sanders's Twitter handle at the beginning of her message to ensure that Sanders would see the message. Perkins wrote, "@DeionSanders my white son attends PP, great grades & test scores, my husband is a lawyer too . . . not what you think of PP is it? Love PP!" This message attempts to reduce the offensiveness of the charges against Sanders and his academy by highlighting a positive accomplishment. Sanders also reproduced a message from the online sports and hip-hop video site, Hip Hop Nonstop. The original message praised not only the school but also Sanders in particular, arguing, "Keep doing what u do @Deion Sanders u go hard for the kids. I'm a witness to it! U can be anywhere in the world, but you ur with the #KIDS." Supportive comments such as this bolstered Deion Sanders's positive traits. When Sanders retweeted them, they reached an even greater audience.

Twitter's "reply" feature allows for even more image-repair possibilities. A reply is a direct response to another user's tweet. Although replies often take the form of witty rejoinders or encouraging words, they are used much differently when put to the task of image repair. Replies let accused parties directly address tweets that attack them.

Actor Jason Priestley made use of Twitter replies when celebrity news groups began to speculate about the content of his book, *Jason Priestly: A Memoir*. Specifically, the celebrity rumor mill accused Priestly of disparaging his former *90210* costars. A Canadian website's (Canoe.ca) business arm tweeted, "@JasonPriestley unloads on @DohertyShannen in new memoir" and included a link to their website, as well as photos of both Priestley and Doherty. The inclusion of both celebrities' Twitter handles ensured that Priestley and Shannen Doherty would eventually see the tweet. Figure 12.5 shows Priestley's simple denial of Canoe's charges ("I do not 'unload' on Shannen in my memoir"). Notably, Doherty's own response to the message was actually posted before Priestley's.

Priestley also replied directly to messages from another costar, Kelly Reaves, after she weighed in on the rumors that Priestley's memoir would attack former castmate Tori Spelling and her husband, Dean McDermott. Priestley wrote, "@KellyLReeves @torianddean Regardless, I said nothing negative about Tori . . . Not even Dean . . . Just the way their actions made me feel." Here, Priestley uses simple denial and differentiation. Fittingly, the Twitter interactions between these celebrities resemble exactly the sort of melodrama that characterized *90210*. Still, Priestley's replies to the accusations against him were helpful for quickly disseminating image-repair strategies and perhaps stopping the spread of negative press.

For some accused parties, to reply directly to an attack on Twitter is to risk a lengthy, perhaps even messy argument. Recall the previously mentioned

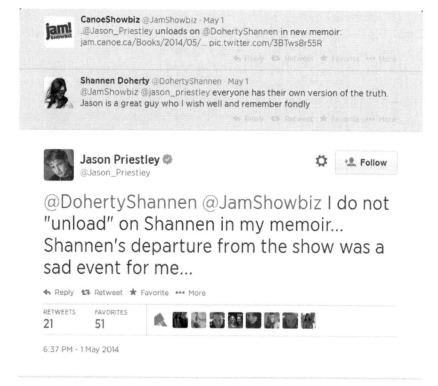

FIGURE 12.5 Jason Priestley's Reply to CanoeShowbiz and Shannen Doherty

example of Mark Cuban's allegedly racist comments during an interview with *Inc.* When ESPN personality Bomani Jones used Twitter to publicly admonish Cuban for his remarks, Cuban defended himself directly to Jones. The two men then proceeded to reply to one another on Twitter for over an hour. Jones attempted to highlight the racial undertones of Cuban's interview statements about being fearful of people who have tattoos and who wear hooded sweatshirts. Cuban's replies alternated between attempting to clarify his own remarks and trying to attack his accuser. All told, the medium further complicated an already difficult to discuss topic. Both Cuban and Jones could be criticized for being petty and dealing in trivialities. In a media appearance later that day, Jones clarified that he did not think Cuban was a racist and observed that a Twitter argument was probably "not the most efficient way" to communicate. A small portion of the initial exchange between Cuban and Jones is provided by Figure 12.6.

FIGURE 12.6 An Excerpt of the Twitter Exchange Between Mark Cuban and Bowmani Jones

The image-repair discourse analyzed here ranges from simple and straight-forward (Murdoch, the LA Kings) to relatively complex and difficult to follow (Priestley, Cuban). Like any other communication platform, Twitter is used and *mis*used in efforts to repair an individual or organization's reputation. The following section further examines the advantages and disadvantages of Twitter as an image-repair medium.

Implications

The diverse case studies presented here suggest many advantages and disadvantages of using Twitter as an image-repair medium. Moreover, the rise of social media as a tool for repairing one's image suggests a number of implications for scholars.

One clear advantage of Twitter, compared to other image-repair media, is its immediacy. Twitter affords its users the opportunity to craft and send messages the moment their image is threatened. More traditional image-repair forums, such as press conferences and press releases, require much more time and effort to construct. Of course, if there is a downside to the ease and speed with which accused parties can send messages via Twitter, it is that accused parties may risk sending inappropriate, or poorly crafted, messages in the heat of the moment, without thoroughly considering their situation and their message options. Mark Cuban's decision to engage in a lengthy back-and-forth with ESPN commentator Bowmani Jones is an example of such behavior.

Another advantage of Twitter in image repair stems from the fact that tweets are, by definition, short messages (even though sometimes image repair is spread over more than one tweet). This means that they are relatively easy for the audience to process. Compare a short tweet (or even a few short tweets) with a lengthy speech or press conference. Tweets require less time and effort for audiences to receive.

Twitter also offers a great deal of control over users' messages. Just like a press release, careful communicators can assemble precisely the message they want, free from the reach of prodding reporters and journalists. Twitter allows accused parties to speak directly to their stakeholders without the filter of media organizations. Athletes and media personalities such as Deion Sanders are wise to use Twitter for their image-repair messages because it helps them communicate directly with the fans that have supported them in the past and are likely to support them in times of adversity.

Twitter is important because of the way it works to connect rhetors with audiences. Tweets reach those individuals who are interested in the rhetor—who have taken action to be included on the rhetor's Twitter feed. Tweets may not reach all of a rhetor's intended audience, but they can be assured of reaching many of those who are most interested in the rhetor.

Furthermore, Twitter messages are reproducible. It takes only a couple of clicks for an accused party's followers to retweet image-repair messages or for online news agencies to embed those tweets in their websites. These retweets and embedded tweets necessarily reproduce messages exactly as the accused party intended them. The instantly reproducible nature of tweets guarantees accused parties an audience much larger than their own list of followers. Almost every instance of image repair discussed in this chapter was discussed in Internet news articles that included the original text of the accused party's tweets.

Twitter is multimodal. Users can post text, images, small videos, and links to other websites, as was illustrated previously. Such microcontent is theoretically invaluable as a potential source of supporting evidence for an individual's image-repair strategies. Although Julianne Hough's strategies for persuasive defense are illustrative of the use of links in tweets, the other rhetors examined here chose not to use any supporting images or videos. Still, Twitter offers communicators many options beyond a simple 140 characters of text.

Twitter provides public figures, as well as everyday citizens, with the tools for sharing messages with large audiences at almost no cost. It takes no special knowledge or effort to tweet. Therefore, Twitter may be celebrated for its democratization of communication and its capacity to empower those without means or influence. This is important because contrary to some of the examples provided here, not everybody with a tarnished image to restore is a wealthy organization, athlete, or celebrity with a powerful pulpit from which to express their ideas.

The most glaring disadvantage of Twitter as an image-repair medium is its 140-character limit. Some users, such as Rupert Murdoch or the LA Kings, simply found a way to fit their message into those 140 characters. Straightforward denials and apologies may work well on Twitter, but more nuanced image-repair strategies may not. However, Colin Kaepernick's image-repair efforts demonstrate how Twitter users can efficiently circumvent the 140-character restriction just by spreading their messages over several tweets. Similarly, Julianne Hough's use of TwitLonger suggests that Twitter's character limits are often a mere technicality.

Notably, this chapter has relied primarily on messages from athletes and celebrities to demonstrate how Twitter is used as an image-repair medium. Few high-ranking political officials have used Twitter to defend themselves. Individuals and organizations that are respected for their seriousness, their professionalism, and their good judgment continue to choose more traditional or proven methods for image repair: press releases, press conferences, talk show appearances, and so forth. However, we expect that Twitter will be used more frequently by politicians in the future. Muralidharan and colleagues (2011) found that BP used Twitter as part of its image-repair effort.

In addition to democratizing communication, Twitter also de-professionalizes communication. Social media give communicators the ability to quickly craft and send messages on their own, regardless of their communication skills, abilities, and experiences. Twitter encourages a do-it-yourself attitude that may not be wise in all image-repair situations. Accused parties need to know when to consult with strategic communication professionals, so as not to risk exasperating already difficult circumstances.

References

Acar, A., & Muraki, Y. (2011). Twitter for crisis communication: Lessons learned from Japan's tsunami disaster. *International Journal of Web Based Communities, 7,* 392–402. doi: 10.1504/IJWBC.2011.041206

Benoit, W. L. (1995a). *Accounts, excuses, and apologies: A theory of image restoration discourse.* Albany, NY: State University of New York Press.

Benoit, W. L. (1995b). Sears' repair of its auto repair image: Image restoration discourse in the corporate sector. *Communication Studies, 46,* 89–109. doi: 10.1080/10510979509368441

Benoit, W. L. (1997). Hugh Grant's image restoration discourse: An actor apologizes. *Communication Quarterly, 45,* 251–267. doi: 10.1080/01463379709370064

Benoit, W. L. (2006). President Bush's image repair effort on meet the press: The complexities of defeasibility. *Journal of Applied Communication Research, 34,* 285–306. doi: 10.1080/00909880600771635

Benoit, W. L. (2014). *Accounts, excuses, and apologies: A theory of image restoration strategies* (2nd ed.). Albany, NY: State University of New York.

Benoit, W. L., & Brinson, S. L. (1994). AT&T: Apologies are not enough. *Communication Quarterly, 42,* 75–88. doi: 10.1080/01463379409369915

Brazeal, L. M. (2008). The image repair strategies of Terrell Owens. *Public Relations Review, 34,* 145–150. doi: 10.1016/j.pubrev.2008.03.021

Burke, K. (1969). *A rhetoric of motives.* Berkeley: University of California Press.

Davis, C. B. (2013). An inconvenient vote: Hillary Clinton's Iraq war image repair debate strategies and their implications for representative democracy. *Public Relations Review, 39,* 315–319. doi: 10.1016/j.pubrev.2013.07.008

Fitzgerald, A. (2013, October 18). Verifying Tweets when news breaks: Q&A with the NYT's Jennifer Preston. *The Twitter Media Blog.* https://blog.twitter.com/2013/verifying-tweets-when-news-breaks-qa-with-the-nyts-jennifer-preston-0

Glantz, M. (2010). The Floyd Landis doping scandal: Implications for image repair discourse. *Public Relations Review, 36,* 157–163. doi: 10.1016/j.pubrev.2009.09.002

Goffman, E. (1963). *Stigma.* London: Penguin.

Levinson, P. (2012). *New new media* (2nd ed.). London: Penguin.

Lovejoy, K., Waters, R. D., & Saxton, G. D. (2012). Engaging stakeholders through Twitter: How nonprofit organizations are getting more out of 140 characters or less. *Public Relations Review, 38,* 313–318. doi: 10.1016/j.pubrev.2012.01.005

Lunden, I. (2012, July 31). Twitter may have 500+ Users but only 170M active, 75% on Twitter's own clients. *TechCrunch.* Retrieved from http://techcrunch.com/2012/07/31/twitter-may-have-500m-users-but-only-170m-are-active-75-on-twitters-own-clients/

Miller, V. (2011). *Understanding digital culture.* Thousand Oaks, CA: Sage.

Moody, M. (2011). Jon and Kate Plus 8: A case study of social media and image repair tactics. *Public Relations Review, 37,* 405–414. doi: 10.1016/j.pubrev.2011.06.004

Muralidharan, S., Dillistone, K., & Shin, J.-H. (2011). The gulf coast oil spill: Extending the theory of image restoration discourse to the realm of social media and beyond petroleum. *Public Relations Review, 37,* 226–232. doi: 10.1016/j.pubrev.2011.04.006

Oles, D. L. (2010). Deny, delay, apologize: The Oprah Winfrey image-defense playbook. *Northwest Journal of Communication, 39,* 37–63. Retrieved from http://www.northwest-comm.org/?page_id=14

Scott, M. B., & Lyman, S. M. (1968). Accounts. *American Sociological Review, 33,* 46–62. Retrieved from http://www.asanet.org/journals/asr/american_sociological_review.cfm

Sheckels, T. F. (2013). The failed comedy of NBA's Gilbert Arenas: Image restoration in context. In J. R. Blaney, L. R. Lippert, & J. S. Smith (Eds.), *Repairing the athlete's image: Studies in sports image repair* (pp. 169–185). Lanham, MD: Lexington.

Ware, B., & Linkugel, W. (1973). They spoke in defense of themselves: On the generic criticism of apologia. *Quarterly Journal of Speech, 59,* 273–283. doi: 10.1080/00335637309383176

13

AUGMENTED REALITY, WEARABLE TECHNOLOGY, AND GAMIFICATION

Mobile Media and Crisis Communication Emerging Specializations

Karen Freberg and Michael J. Palenchar

Introduction

Mobile technologies integrated with social media applications are transforming the study and application of crisis communication, as well as transforming how risk bearers manage and share crisis experiences. The rise in adoption of mobile technologies helps create a fusion of digital and real-world crisis communication practices, and crisis communication experts have viewed this growth both positively and negatively. Interest in understanding the role of emerging technologies for crisis and emergency responders continues to increase, and according to Palen and colleagues (2010), the present focus is to find a balance between the knowledge and narratives shared within the digital community and the ability to initiate a response that is localized, immediate, and socially distributed across various social media sites. In addition, the current landscape of the mobile and social media sphere has allowed individuals and organizations the power to ignite conversations involving daily activities and normal business practices or advocate and empower their communities in a time of crisis (Westlund & Ghersetti, 2014).

With that in mind, the purpose of this chapter is to extend the existing crisis and risk literature within emerging mobile media and technologies (Palenchar & Freberg, 2011) to include augmented-reality (AR) applications, wearable technologies, and the implementation of gamification principles within crisis communication. In addition, practical implications will be discussed focusing on building trust through engagement and collaborative decision making, transparency versus privacy, and acknowledging and embracing uncertainty during a crisis event in an effort to address the ever-changing and eclectic implications these emerging mobile tools and specializations bring forth for both those who bear risk during a crisis and crisis communicators. By marrying literature and examples of new mobile media specializations, crisis communication professionals can strategically incorporate these issues with best practices while also embracing emerging specializations to better manage a crisis.

Review of Literature

Rise of Mobile Technologies Within Crisis Communication

The use of mobile technologies within crisis and risk communications is not a new phenomenon. Mobile messages and other forms of mobile technologies have been implemented in various crisis and disaster situations over the years, allowing emergency management professionals to send out real-time updates and alerts about their location and work environments (Bean et al., 2015). Mobile technologies have experienced an evolution and truly have changed during the past couple of decades from primarily a mobile telephone to a complex communication and information technology platform.

The integration between mobile phones and social media has risen over the past few years as well. According to the Pew Research Internet Project Mobile and Social Media Report (2015) nearly half (49%) of smartphone owners aged 18–29 use messaging apps to create content and communicate through various applications. Social media applications such as WhatsApp, Snapchat, and Kik are just a few of the more popular apps among not only this age cohort but also others as well. Specifically for crisis communicators and first responders, new software and mobile hardware are being created to enhance public safety based on being user friendly, mobile on location, and interoperability (Howard, 2014)

These mobile devices equipped with social media applications have allowed crisis communicators and risk bearers the opportunity to create, curate, and disseminate information and engage in coconstructed dialogue during a crisis (see Veil, Buehner, & Palenchar, 2011, for a thorough review of the emerging media opportunities and challenges for crisis communication professionals). For example, mobile communication technologies have been incorporated into crisis communication practices during various natural disasters and emergency situations, such as wildfires (Sutton, Palen, & Shklovski, 2008), terrorist attacks (Gordon, 2007), and school shootings (Vieweg, Palen, Liu, Hughes, & Sutton, 2008). In addition, mobile communication technologies have been used for fundraising related to crisis events, such as the Text for Haiti campaign (Weberling & Waters, 2012).

Mobile technologies like smartphones and wearable devices continue to be adapted in various aspects of society. Technology experts shared with Pew Research (Anderson & Rainie, 2014) about how the line between humans and machines (e.g., mobile devices like smartphones and wearable technologies) is blending together more than ever before. A wearable technology, like Google Glass, Snapchat Spectacles, and some smart watches, in particular, allows its users to instantaneously receive personalized information and content.

Mobile devices not only enhance the communication individuals have with their personal contacts but also forge connections with an entire online virtual community (Palen, 2002). In many-to-many message exchanges, the mobile device is used to connect groups of people using mobile Internet capabilities and social networking sites like Facebook, microblogs like Twitter, photo-sharing social-networking sites like Instagram and Snapchat, and video-sharing sites like YouTube and Vimeo.

By doing so, users contribute directly to the available media by providing eye-witness perspectives through video, photos, or texted accounts of an event, often bypassing the professional reporters on the scene and providing unfiltered views of what is happening in the world in real time (Gordon, 2007). These new mobile forms of technology "provide a broad, multi-faceted and interactive connection with the outside world. In fact, the very promise of being informed and con-nected seems to motivate high rates of communication technology adoption and appropriation in times of disaster," (Shklovski, Palen, & Sutton, 2008, p. 6).

According to Shklovski and colleagues (2008), mobile communication channels also serve as a valuable resource for the community during a crisis by contribut-ing to a sense of normalcy, delivering information, and helping to pass the time. Mobile devices help to reduce fear and anxiety by allowing people the means to obtain the information they need (2008), as well as contact with others experienc-ing the crisis or concerned about their health and safety.

From recording on-the-ground footage of the tsunami in Southeast Asia in 2004, to uploading radiation updates and information during the Japanese tsu-nami in 2011, to the firsthand experiences of war victims in Ukraine and the Middle East in 2014, mobile technologies have been a formidable communication platform and transformed sharing textual and visual information with the global community. For example, the 7.0-magnitude earthquake that hit Haiti in 2010 left millions of people without basic necessities, such as food, water, and shelter. The country's communications infrastructure was so devastated that it left people almost completely isolated from the rest of the world (Coyle & Meier, 2009). According to Bulkely (2010), mobile phones were used to communicate first aid information and to provide information about where to go for shelter, food, water, and other immediate needs. The Haiti earthquake disaster, according to Bulkely, highlighted a more mature use of short message service (SMS) text messages to communicate first response aid to individuals needing immediate medical atten-tion or who were trapped under buildings and other fallen structures.

New Media Specializations Within Crisis Communication

Crisis communicators have an obligation to their colleagues, as well as to the impacted risk bearers in a crisis situation, to use the most effective communication channels when disseminating their messages. A thorough examination of academic literature, industry white papers, and trade publications was conducted on mobile

media, AR, and gamification related to crisis communication. Two separate literature searches were performed. The first search pulled all research according to the
keywords "augmented reality," "risk," "crisis," "crisis communication," "mobile
technology," and "wearable technologies." The second search was conducted just
before completion of the analysis for "crisis communication" and "mobile media"
to confirm the most recent, relevant research was included. The purpose was not
to count or even include all information or every article but instead to provide
examples of how mobile media can be used to improve communication in crisis
management and extend base knowledge of research in this area.

Augmented Reality (AR) and Wearable Technologies

Two distinct areas involving emerging mobile and experiential media will have
direct implications on crisis planning, risk-communication safety exercises (Stubbe,
van Emmerik, & Kerstholt, 2015), simulation workshops, crisis and emergency
response teams, and postcrisis recovery protocols. AR has allowed programmers
and users to be able to create real and virtual elements that allow the individual
user to be interactive with the technology in real time (Azuma, 1997). AR is quite
different from virtual reality because AR is "a view of physical, real world, but
supplements it with layers of digital elements," (Hofmann & Mosemghvdlishvili,
2014, p. 266).

Walker, Giddings, and Armstrong (2011) advocated the use of new emerging
technology such as AR and visualization simulation training for crisis communicators for a variety of reasons. Crisis communicators can use real-time crisis
information captured from previous situations for the organization or others in
the same industry (e.g., military, chemical plants, government) to provide a real-
world simulation into their training and education. Certain characteristics of the
scenario need to be incorporated within the AR application technology for the
crisis communicator, such as time setting, level of detail and information, knowledge of the situation, and current status in the environment (Walker et al., 2011).

AR and gamification also come together in this new evolution for new media
and mobile technology practices within crisis communications. Teaching, training, and experimentation within these various crisis scenarios and situations can
unveil current issues or challenges that need to be addressed through more education and training, as well as exploring new potential issues to address with the
technology (Walker et al., 2011).

One emerging form of wearable technology that is being used was Google
Glass, which was discontinued in January 2015. Google Glass was considered to
be a form of wearable mobile technology: a personalized computer the user wears
as a pair of everyday glasses. Google Glass allowed users to update social media,
take pictures, and record their own point-of-view experience. Google Glass was
incorporated in emerging management services, hospitals, classrooms, and even
the police. However, there are still several challenges and issues with wearable

technologies like Google Glass facing not only crisis communicators but also all consumers. Two that Hong (2013) mentioned when it comes to wearable technologies like Google Glass were a lack of experience and too-high expectations of audiences. Roesner, Kohno, and Molnar (2014) also add the issue of security, and recent hacking attempts on Google Glass users raises another red flag toward this young, emerging form of wearable technology.

Gamification

Deterding, Sicard, Nacke, O'Hara, and Dixon (2011) conceptualized gamification as the "use of video game elements in non-gaming systems to improve user experience (UX) and user engagement" (p. 1). With the advancement of technology through various mobile devices, society is becoming more intrigued with the concept of engaging in activities similar to the gaming experience in other social contexts (Fitz-Walter & Tjondronegoro, 2011). Gamification practices can be applied to various situations and contexts to build social communities within a game setting. Encouraging users to create and generate content to facilitate collaboration and curation of information is one way to incorporate gamification principles for an organization (Deterding et al., 2011).

Research is just beginning on gamification and crisis communications. One example of gamification principles being implemented for emergency situations and preparedness is SF Heroes, which was created by the San Francisco Department of Emergency Management in partnership with two companies specializing in gamification technologies and platforms. This mobile application was created for residents so they feel prepared in case of an emergency situation, as well as to be a one-stop shop of information and updates through new media technologies. Some of the features of the application include opportunities to check in at various locations in the city, test knowledge and skills related to emergency preparedness, keep track of emergency contacts, and create checklists before a crisis event occurs.

Within crisis communications, there are many ways gamification principles could improve the training aspect for crisis communicators. Gaming principles incorporated with new media technologies can help by testing crisis communicators' decision making, response planning, and response time during a crisis and by providing an evaluation of performance before, during, and after the crisis (Walker et al., 2011). Gaming has also been examined in the use of diplomatic crises and the tone of messages sent between adversaries, finding that "hostile communications precipitate higher amounts of weapons purchasing and lower allotments of money to industrial production," (McDermott, Cowden, & Rosen, 2008, p. 151).

Gamification-inspired crisis training also provides feedback to the organization, agency, and business about how effective their crisis team would be in a given situation, which would provide them with the evidence they would need to adapt and reassess their team members. Because this technology is coordinated with mobile devices, crisis communicators can bring their training on the go. Gamification within mobile technologies for crisis and risk-communication professionals can open a window of opportunity, as well raise some challenges. Lack of education and training with the technology, an overwhelming amount of data creating an overload on bandwidth, and cyber security threats and risks (e.g., hacks) toward these mobile applications incorporating gamification principles need to be taken into consideration.

Practical Implications for Social Media and Crisis Communication

In times of crisis, risk bearers and other stakeholders are likely to turn to one or more individuals or organizations for answers, as well as likely to participate in the information- and experience-sharing process via social media through mobile technologies. With that in mind, and building from the previous literature about AR applications, wearable technologies, and gamification principles related to better managing a crisis event from both a crisis communicator's perspective and risk bearers' experiences, the following is a discussion of the practical implications for social media and crisis communication focusing on three ethical and strategic best practices, including (a) building trust through community outreach and collaborative decision making, (b) transparency versus privacy, and (c) acknowledging and embracing uncertainty as important requirements for good organizations communicating well—keys for risk communication if it is to legitimate the core functions of the crisis-generating organization and risk arbiters while adding value to society.

Building Trust Through Engagement and Collaborative Decision Making

Palenchar and Heath (2007) argued that building trust is a long-term commitment on behalf of risk-generating organizations, and from their 10-year review of risk and crisis communication literature discovered that

> organizations that work to build trust over time through community outreach and collaborative decision making help to demonstrate their efforts to achieve reasonable levels of health and safety and such levels need to withstand the knowledgeable skepticism of risk bearers and communicate in ways that increase rather than decrease their security.
>
> *(p. 125)*

One way to build trust and withstand knowledge skepticism is through engagement and collaborative decision making via AR applications and mobile, including wearable, technologies. *Engagement* from a social media perspective has been defined as "some action beyond exposure, and implies an interaction between two or more parties . . . that typically occurs in response to content on an owned channel," (The Conclave, 2013, p. 6).

During a crisis situation, a crisis communicator can explore the various abilities of individuals on the ground to be able to take on specific tasks in updating the digital community online (Starbird & Palen, 2011). According to Jaeger and colleagues (2007), the combination of mobile media technologies and remote entrée to the online community via those devices creates a gateway to handle a disaster more effectively for emergency managers and crisis communication professionals.

With these new forms of mobile technologies, crisis communication professionals in crisis situations have immediate remote access to information, along with the ability to communicate with their home base or others on-site (Chan, Killeen, & Griswold, 2004). Having information available visually through AR applications, which allow a person to see what others are posting, sharing, and uploading to a designated centralized location, is just one of the many benefits for crisis communication professionals.

Having a centralized place online or access through a centralized platform on a mobile device for community members to contribute information in various formats can be beneficial, but there are other issues that need to be explored further as this form of technology becomes more mainstream in crisis communications. Official agencies and crisis communication professionals need to be vigilant in evaluating the information being shared, listening to the overall tone of the dialogue emerging through the online community, and making sure that the communication dialogue between first emergency responders and other community networks is consistently maintained.

Even though these new specializations are being discussed and experimented with in various disciplines and professions, this does not mean that everyone involved in the crisis communications or the stakeholders within specific community know or understand these forms of technologies. Lack of education and training along with the limited amount of mobile technology resources available are other potential challenges and risks that may plague crisis communication professionals in this new area. Finally, audience age segmentation, based on an understanding of how each age cohort is using mobile technologies to share, create, and redistribute information during a crisis situation is an important component in crisis research and application (Freberg, 2012).

Transparency Versus Privacy

Part of trust building is also working to maintain the privacy of those who bear risk during a crisis event while being transparent about how an organization manages and communicates about a crisis event. Transparency from a public relations perspective, according to McCorkindale and DiStaso (2014), rests on three basic tenets: being open and honest, reporting the good and bad, and providing information in a timely manner. Transparency in the social media world is not solely about sharing more information but rather about being part of the online communication and an active participant in distributing and creating new knowledge collaboratively with those who bear the risk during a crisis event, their families and friends, and other stakeholders and concerned citizens, backpack journalists, and traditional media, who are sharing their on-time experiences.

For example, mobile, wearable technology like Google Glass enables organizations to communicate instantly and continually with a myriad of stakeholders from the scene of the crisis, often filling a professional information void of content, including video, of the crisis event. According to Gower (2006), the Internet has both shaped the expectation of transparency and provided the facility to be transparent.

Thinking about transparency and social and mobile media during a crisis also requires practitioners to consider privacy issues. According to Belmas (2013), privacy has perhaps topped the list of concerns of the public in regard to social media law, with primary concerns about data privacy and how personal data, gathered online, are used and sometimes abused. For example, Hong (2013) pointed out that a major issue with Google Glass was the understanding of mitigating privacy issues with their audiences.

It is important to remember that what is being shared by either risk bearers or crisis communicators during a crisis via social and mobile media, or images used during gamification training based on real-world scenarios, often includes digital content that was captured and shared from a large and undefined group of people without an appropriate understanding of their privacy concerns. Crisis communication and social media policies need to be reviewed in this context. For example, many organizational policies require approval from clients or customers to quote them or use their information on social media.

According to Watson and Finn (2013),

> As new media and social networking technologies and applications are increasingly deployed in crisis situations, users are often not given enough information about how their personal data is being used by service providers, social media companies and technology companies. This implicates data protection principles such as transparency and consent, creating an information asymmetry.
>
> *(p. 418)*

In this "information asymmetry," users know very little about what information is collected and how it's being used during a crisis.

Another challenge Watson and Finn (2013) discussed in their work was if users depended on the information but had some concerns about what information these platforms or other brands were collecting about them. The terms of service agreements for certain platforms have significantly changed, which has resulted in a heightened awareness of the security of individual's privacy. This is aligned with privacy concerns on social media among individuals, raising the need to still have other additional channels with crisis information readily available and accessible to everyone.

Acknowledging and Embracing Uncertainty During a Crisis Event

The very nature of risk prohibits absolute definitions and knowledge (Palenchar & Heath, 2007). According to Berger and Calabrese (1975) and their uncertainty reduction theory, uncertainty motivates information seeking because uncertainty is a difficult state to remain in and is uncomfortable. Using that principle, uncertainty reduction theory explains the human incentive to seek information. Risk bearers and other stakeholders during a crisis want information to reduce their uncertainties. They can also create, curate, and generate risk information on their mobile devices while the crisis is being experienced—sometimes by those in the middle of the crisis—and can use this specialized media content as an incentive for constantly seeking better answers to the questions raised.

In addition to the uncertainty, this direct and real-time digital communication has compressed the time organizations have to respond to a crisis event, and it has allowed individuals to be able to create and curate information to just one person or to a mass audience group through this new communication platform in real time, breaking the barriers in both time and location (Alt et al., 2010). According to Veil and colleagues (2011), "the direct and real-time nature of social media and the dynamically personal touch through photo and video sharing, chatting, and conversation, makes it an ideal supplemental touch point between stakeholders and crisis communicators" (p. 116).

Still, organizations need to provide timely information as it becomes available. Wright and Hinson (2009, 2014) noted that social media are ideal to incorporate changes or corrections to the original content of a message, whereas Johnson (2009) discussed how microblogging services are "an excellent way to send out a brief, crisp message that will satiate whoever may be waiting for an answer, even though it may not illustrate the whole picture" (p. 24).

Crisis communication professionals would not be the only ones benefiting from these new specializations within mobile technologies. Individual community members and potential risk bearers would benefit for the access to real-time information and updates that would allow them to get a sense of normalcy and a reduction of uncertainty until the crisis subsides (Shklovski et al., 2008). In addition to having access to real-time information about a crisis, potential risk bearers would also have the power to create, collaborate, and help others, leading to a sense of perceived control and increased self-efficacy over their actions during highly tense crisis situations.

One final point is that uncertainty can demonstrate disagreements among how risk bearers and the risk-generating organizations, and other risk arbiters, see a solution to the crisis. The online disagreement is often problematic for the risk-generating organization, but much could be learned from this process. Communications can be a way to bring people closer to agreement by exposing the disagreement lying in between. Organizational communication scholars often point to the ways tension is actually the "stuff of organizing," and analyzing these tensions can lead to a better "understanding of organizational processes, particularly those processes that structure . . . organizations," (Trethewey, 1999, p. 142).

Conclusion

As technology increases and mobile technologies become integrated into daily social and business communication practices, these emerging tools and specializations need to become a focus of discussion and research within mobile media communications and crisis communications research. Yet although these emerging specializations are important, it does not replace the theoretical and historical foundation of crisis communication practices, which includes transmitting risk messages to the public, engaging risk bearers during a crisis, or disseminating messages to the media about updates during a crisis situation. Instead, they should be incorporated into these practices because these specializations can add many opportunities to evolve the crisis communication field. Challenges such as facing a rapidly evolving communication medium, the 24/7 pace of communication via digital platforms, and risks associated with the lack of understanding or time to formulate policies can raise concerns among organizations about incorporating mobile media into their crisis communication practices. Yet, crisis communicators can address these challenges with decisions based on solid theoretical foundations and evidence from applied research.

References

Alt, F., Shirazi, A. S., Shmidt, A., Kramer, U., & Nawazm, Z. (2010). *Location-based crowdsourcing: Extending crowdsourcing to the real world.* Paper presented at NordiCHI 2010 Conference, Reykjavik, Iceland, October 16–20, 2010.

Anderson, J., & Rainie, L. (2014, May 14). *The Internet of things will thrive by 2025.* Retrieved from http://www.pewinternet.org/2014/05/14/internet-of-things/

Azuma, R. T. (1997). A survey of augmented reality. *Presence: Teleoperators and Virtual Environments, 6*(4), 355–385.

Bean, H., Suttonm, J., Liu, B. F., Madden, S., Wood, M. M., & Mileti, D. S. (2015). The study of mobile public warning messages: A research review and agenda. *Review of Communication, 15*(1), 60–80.

Belmas, G. I. (2013). Legal issues in social media. In H. N. Al-Deen & J. A. Hendricks (Eds.), *Social media and strategic communications* (pp. 218–233). New York: Palgrave Macmillan.

Berger, C. R., & Calabrese, R. J. (1975). Some explorations in initial interaction and beyond: Toward a developmental theory of interpersonal communication. *Human Communication Research, 1*(2), 99–112.

Bulkely, K. (2010, June 18). Mobile technology takes centre stage in disaster relief. Retrieved from http://www.guardian.co.uk/activate/mobile-technology-disaster-relief

Chan, T. C., Killeen, J., & Griswold, W. (2004). Information technology and emergency medical care during disasters. *Academy of Emergency Medicine, 11*(11), 1229–1236.

The Conclave. (2013, June). Complete social media measurement standards June 2013. Retrieved from http://www.smmstandards.com/wp-content/uploads/2013/06/Complete-standards-document4.pdf

Coyle, D., & Meier, P. (2009). New technologies in emergencies and conflicts report: The role of information and social networks. Washington, DC: United Nations Foundation-Vodafone Foundation Partnership. Retrieved from http://www.unfoundation.org/news-and-media/publications-and-speeches/new-technologies-emergencies-conflicts.html

Deterding, S., Sicart, M., Nacke, L., O'Hara, K., & Dixon, D. (2011, May). *Gamification: Using game design elements in non-gaming contexts.* Proceedings of the International Conference on Human Factors in Computing Systems, Vancouver, BC, Canada, 2425–2428.

Fitz-Walter, Z., & Tjondronegoro, D. (2011, September). *Exploring the opportunities and challenges of using mobile sensing for gamification.* ACM International Conference on Ubiquitous Computing, Beijing, China. Retrieved from http://research.microsoft.com/en-us/um/beijing/events/ms_ubicomp11/papers/fitzwalter.pdf

Freberg, K. (2012). Intention to comply with crisis messages communicated via social media. *Public Relations Review, 38*(3), 416–421. doi: 10.1016/j.pubrev.2012.01.008

Gordon, J. (2007). The mobile phone and the public sphere: Mobile phone usage in three critical situations. *Convergence, 13*(3), 307–319.

Gower, K. K. (2006). Truth and transparency. In K. Fitzpatrick & C. Bronstein (Eds.), *Ethics in public relations: Responsible advocacy* (pp. 89–105). Thousand Oaks, CA: Sage.

Hofmann, S., & Mosemghvdlishvili, L. (2014). Perceiving spaces through digital augmentation: An exploratory study of navigational augmented reality apps. *Mobile Media & Communication, 2*(3), 265–280.

Hong, J. (2013, November). Considering privacy issues in the context of google glass. *Communication of the ACM, 56*(11), 1–2.

Howard, C. E. (2014, May). Advanced technologies for enhancing public safety. *Military & Aerospace Electronics, 25*(5), 24–29.

Jaeger, P. T., Shneiderman, B., Fleischmann, K. R., Preece, J., Qu, Y., & Wu, P. F. (2007). Community response grids: E-government, social networks, and effective emergency management. *Telecommunications Policy, 31*, 592–604.

Johnson, C. (2009). Social media in a crisis: Blog and tweet your way back to success. *Public Relations Strategist, 15*(2), 23–24.

McCorkindale, T., & DiStaso, M. W. (2014). The state of social media research: Where are we now, where we were and what it means for public relations. *Research Journal of the Institute for Public Relations, 1*(1), 1–17.

McDermott, R., Cowden, J. A., & Rosen, S. (2008). The role of hostile communications in a crisis simulation game. *Peace & Conflict, 14*(2), 151–168.

Palen, L. (2002). Mobile telephony in a connected life. *Communications of the ACM, 45*(3), 78–82.

Palen, L., Anderson, K. M., Mark, G., Martin, J., Sicker, D., Palmer, M., & Grunwald, D. (2010, April). *A vision for technology-mediated support for public participation and assistance in mass emergencies and disasters.* Proceedings of ACM-BCS Visions of Computer Science (pp. 1–12), Edinburgh, UK.

Palenchar, M. J., & Freberg, K. (2011, May). *Conceptualizing social media and mobile technologies in risk and crisis communication practices.* Paper presented at the meeting of the International Communication Association, Boston, MA.

Palenchar, M. J., & Heath, R. L. (2007). Strategic risk communication: Adding value to society. *Public Relations Review, 33,* 120–129.

Pew Research Internet Project. (2015, August 19). Mobile media and social media 2015. Retrieved from http://www.pewinternet.org/2015/08/19/mobile-messaging-and-social-media-2015/

Roesner, F., Kohno, T., & Molnar, D. (2014, April). Security and privacy for augmented reality systems. *Communications of the ACM, 57*(4), 88–96.

Shklovski, I., Palen, L., & Sutton, J. (2008). *Finding community through information and communication technology in disaster events.* Paper presented at the ACM Proceedings of Computer Supported Cooperative Work Conference, San Diego, CA.

Starbird, K., & Palen, L. (2011). *"Voluntweeters": Self-organizing by digital volunteers in times of crisis.* ACM 2011 Conference on Computer Human Interaction, Vancouver, BC, Canada.

Stubbe, H. E., van Emmerik, M. L., & Kerstholt, J. H. (2015). Helping behavior in a virtual crisis situation: Effects of safety awareness and crisis communication. *Journal of Risk Research, 20,* 433–444.

Sutton, J., Palen, L., & Shklovski, I. (2008, May). *Backchannels on the front lines: Emergent use of social media in the 2007 Southern California Fires.* Proceedings of the Information Systems for Crisis Response and Management Conference, Washington, DC.

Trethewey, A. (1999). Isn't it ironic: Using irony to explore the contradictions of organizational life. *Western Journal of Communication, 63*(2), 140–167.

Veil, S., Buehner, T., & Palenchar, M. J. (2011). A work-in-process literature review: Incorporating social media in risk and crisis communication. *Journal of Contingencies and Crisis Management, 19*(2), 110–122.

Vieweg, S., Palen, L., Liu, S., Hughes, A., & Sutton, J. (2008, May). *Collective intelligence in disaster: An examination of the phenomenon in the aftermath of the 2007 Virginia Tech Shootings.* Proceedings of the Information Systems for Crisis Response and Management Conference, Washington, DC.

Walker, W. E., Giddings, J., & Armstrong, S. (2011). Training and learning for crisis management using a virtual simulation/gaming environment. *Cognition, Technology and Work, 13*(3), 163–173.

Watson, J., & Finn, R. L. (2013, May). *Privacy and ethical implications of the use of social media during a volcanic eruption: Some initial thoughts.* Proceedings of the Information Systems for Crisis Response and Management Conference (ISCRAM), Baden-Baden, Germany.

Weberling, B., & Waters, R. D. (2012). Gauging the public's preparedness for mobile public relations: The "Text for Haiti" campaign. *Public Relations Review, 38*(1), 51–55.

Westlund, O., & Ghersetti, M. (2014). Modelling news media us: Positing and applying the MC/GC model to the analysis of media use in everyday life and crisis situations. *Journalism Studies, 16*(2), 133–151.

Wright, D. K., & Hinson, M. D. (2009). Examining how public relations practitioners actually are using social media. *Public Relations Journal, 3*(3), 2–32.

Wright, D. K., & Hinson, M. D. (2014). An updated examination of social and emerging media use in public relations practice: A longitudinal analysis between 2006 and 2014. *Public Relations Journal, 8*(2), 1–35.

SECTION IV
Areas of Application

SECTION IV-A

Areas of Application

Corporate

14

USING TWITTER FOR CRISIS COMMUNICATION

A Content Analysis of Fortune 500 Companies

Michael North, Cong Li, Jiangmeng Liu, and Yi Grace Ji

Thirty-two people lost their lives when the Costa Concordia struck the Italian coastline in 2012 (Gantt, 2013). The incident caused Carnival Cruise Lines' stock price to plummet 14% by the next trading day and for CEO Micky Arison to lose nearly $500 million in net worth (Gantt, 2013). The loss in corporate reputation was also substantial, as Arison and Carnival committed several public relations blunders in the following days. For instance, Arison eschewed traveling to Italy to oversee the cleanup, avoided the media, and communicated as the voice of Carnival through a series of tweets from his personal account (Booton, 2012), such as "I am deeply saddened by reports of more deaths following the grounding of #Concordia," and "I won't be as active on Twitter for the next while. Helping our @costacruises team manage this crisis is my priority right now. Thnx" (Gantt, 2013, pp. 28–29).

Unsurprisingly, these tweets were not well received by a public wanting information, contrition, and a promise of restitution (Camp, 2012), but Carnival was not wrong to use social media during a time of crisis. Social media use actually increases during a crisis as users assign a high level of credibility to social media (Austin, Liu, & Jin, 2012). Because Twitter is perceived as a credible medium with an increasing number of users, companies use tweets for special promotions, company news, and as a customer service forum. The latter generates a considerable volume of tweets between companies and followers. Whereas day-to-day incidents pale in comparison to the likes of the Costa Concordia ordeal, public criticism on social media necessitates a response from the offending company. This research content analyzes more than 9,000 tweets from Fortune 500 companies between 2009 and 2013, focusing on crisis situations and company responses. This study also examines the relationship between the companies' crisis tweets and responses in the form of replies, retweets, and likes.[1]

Literature Review

Crisis and Situational Crisis Communication Theory (SCCT)

Coombs (2007) defined an *organizational crisis* as a "sudden and unexpected event that threatens to disrupt an organization's operations and poses both a financial and a reputational threat" (p. 164). Of lesser impact is an organizational issue, which includes minor conflicts and disagreements that have the potential to cast the organization in a negative light (Heath & Palenchar, 2009). Be it an insignificant issue or a major crisis, the common themes are that these events are unpredictable and have the potential to damage an organization's reputation due to prominence in the media and lingering negativity (Meer & Verhoeven, 2014).

Kim (2014) presented two distinct approaches for studying crises: the event approach and the process approach. Specifically, the event approach presents the crisis event as a marker so any subsequent messages are characterized as postcrisis communication (Kim, 2014). The process approach is not as strict in categorizing what is and what is not postcrisis communication due to the fluid nature of crisis events (Kim, 2014). Regardless of the approach, crisis communication research focuses on organizations' responses with the mind-set to avoid criticism or additional negativity, but Olsson (2014) argued that a crisis situation, when handled adroitly, is an opportunity for the organization to strengthen its reputation and solidify relationships with its stakeholders.

Coombs (2007) developed the situational crisis communication theory (SCCT) to guide organizations through adverse situations by categorizing various crises into hierarchical clusters and presenting the appropriate responses designed to preserve reputation. Coombs (2007) instructs crisis managers to attend to any victims before employing SCCT to repair reputational damage. This concern stems from people attributing responsibility when they are wronged and their willingness to do so with emotion and sometimes anger (Coombs, 2007). Based on the level of attribution assigned, Coombs (2007) begins with the victim cluster, which has the lowest level of attribution and includes events such as natural disasters, product tampering, and rumor, meaning the organization is victimized as well. Next, the accidental cluster places a moderate level of responsibility on the organization and includes events such as technical errors, accidents, and challenges. These events are "unintentional or uncontrollable" (Coombs, 2007, p. 167). Last, events such as human-error accidents, harmful products, and organizational misdeeds are categorized within the preventable cluster, which has the highest level of attribution because these events are either negligent or purposeful (Coombs, 2007).

Crisis managers have three primary strategies to respond to the aforementioned clusters. First, organizations can use the deny response, which employs tactics such as attacking the accuser, scapegoating, or denying the crisis (Coombs, 2007). A deny strategy is designed to distance the organization from the crisis, but the strategy is only successful if the organization is not at fault (Coombs,

2007). Organizations often use the deny strategy, but studies have shown that this strategy is rarely successful (Meer, 2014). Second, the diminish response features strategies such as making excuses or providing justification to minimize responsibility (Coombs, 2007). With the diminish response, the organization admits there is a crisis but that the situation is not severe or that the organization's role is inconsequential (Coombs, 2007). Last, the rebuild response uses compensation or apologies to admit fault (Coombs, 2007). When an organization is at fault, an accommodative strategy featuring apologies and compensation is recommended and, when an organization is blameless, a diminish or even a deny strategy is suggested (Utz, Schultz, & Glocka, 2013).

How Businesses Should Respond to a Crisis

The SCCT is a guide to follow, but additional conditions must be taken into account. For instance, a history of shady business practices or negligence can negatively influence future attributions of responsibility (Ki & Brown, 2013). Even if an organization selects the proper crisis response, the efforts could be for naught simply because of a poor existing reputation. Conversely, an organization that has established a positive dialogue with its stakeholders or has demonstrated a pattern of admirable behavior will receive more forgiveness (Ki & Brown, 2013). This positive reputation can aid an organization when attempting a deny response (Meer, 2014).

Even when taking into account organizational history, the most effective response strategy incorporates the use of apology, restitution, and a promise to change (Kim, Avery, & Lariscy, 2009). The denial strategy is the least effective, but even the diminish strategy provides little value when compared to the rebuild strategy (Meer & Verhoeven, 2014). Although many crisis managers provide an abundance of information, the best strategy incorporates sympathy while focusing on the victims (Schultz, Utz, & Goritz, 2011), drawing from the principles of the rebuild strategy.

Due to the high stakes of crisis communication and the potential fallout from a poorly executed response, those in crisis management develop plans in advance. This has led to a substantial amount of organizational crisis communication to be perceived as top-down with nonexistent dialogue with stakeholders (Falkheimer & Heide, 2010). Too much generic, top-down communication can upset stakeholders, and one of the tasks of crisis managers is to reduce uncertainty. Coupled with the fact that stakeholders value frequent updates directly from a source close to the crisis (Olsson, 2014), it becomes clear that social media are perfect tools for crisis managers to cultivate positive, dialogic relationships designed to reduce uncertainty on a per-minute basis.

Social Media and Twitter

From 2007 to 2010, social media use increased 230% in the United States, leading to two thirds of Americans belonging to at least one social networking site (Liu,

Jin, & Austin, 2013). Facebook boasts upward of a billion users, Twitter claims almost 600 million, and Google+ has more than 400 million (Bennett, 2014). Social media's substantial user numbers have attracted businesses searching for a direct line to customers. Importantly, organizations can not only create a one-to-many message to stakeholders but also engage in one-to-one communication with individuals during a crisis due to the dialogic nature of social media (Utz et al., 2013).

Although organizations believe social media are useful tools to reach stakeholders, social media are only valuable if users believe the organizations' messages to be legitimate. Research has shown that social media usage actually increases during a crisis (Austin et al., 2012), largely due to the perceived credibility of social media and the explicit access it affords (Procopio & Procopio, 2007). Credibility stems not only from the fact that the social media messages originate from the organization but also because the messages "cater to those who want information in real time" (Westerman, Spence, & Der Heide, 2014, p. 174). Those active on social media, and they number more than a billion, no longer passively wait for traditional media to report but aggressively seek information (Brown & Billings, 2013).

Perhaps because of its simplicity, Twitter is seen as a reliable tool for crisis managers to quickly send short messages to thousands of followers who can then forward the message throughout the Twittersphere. Developed in San Francisco in 2006, Twitter usage increased rapidly and there are now millions of users generating 5,700 tweets per second (Ahmad, 2013). Twitter provides an unparalleled one-to-many opportunity offering a simple means to disseminate information, and coupled with almost nonexistent entrance barriers, Twitter is one of the top 10 most visited websites on the Internet (Fitzgerald, 2012).

Based on the statistics, it is not surprising that Twitter is a preferred means for communicating with stakeholders during a crisis (Jin, Liu, & Austin, 2014). The rapid developments and unpredictability of crises have influenced stakeholders to access Twitter "to share information, react to the situation, and rally support" (Westerman et al., 2014, p. 179). Research supports the notion that this relationship is worthwhile, as Schultz and colleagues (2011) found that reactions to crisis communication on Twitter were more positive than with the traditional media. Those who read the tweets in Schultz's study were less likely to boycott or spread negative information than those who received information through traditional media. Last, a pure information response on Twitter was more successful than a rebuild strategy (Schultz et al., 2011), perhaps due to the 140-character limit, meaning Twitter may distance organizations from a crisis more successfully than traditional media.

How Companies Use Different Social Media During a Crisis

Each social media site offers a different opportunity and has a unique effect on the audience. When users post content on YouTube relating to an organization, the organization tends to take a back seat to the user as YouTube's foundation is self-promotion (Smith, Fischer, & Yongjian, 2012). Organizations open themselves to negativity on YouTube as the tone within the comments section can be harsh (Smith et al., 2012). Facebook has less of a problem with self-promotion and is a better forum for comments than YouTube but requires some effort from organizations to maintain a dialogue (Smith et al., 2012). Twitter is the least likely to be interpreted as self-promotional, and it is the most conversational of the main social media sites (Smith et al., 2012). With the sheer number of users, the Twitter universe can resemble a cluttered collection of informational tidbits, but the website is more than just ambient noise featuring "greetings, weather, small talk, emotion, and meta-commentary" (Schandorf, 2013, p. 334); it is a medium for people to gratify a need to connect and belong to a group (Chen, 2011). A typical tweet includes a hyperlink and a brief opinion of the content brought about by clicking on the link (Schandorf, 2013), leading many to characterize Twitter as water-cooler talk where users discuss the news of the day. The public has shifted from being an "empty receptacle waiting for news" to an active participator in the information-dissemination process through Twitter (Hermida, 2010). Because of this, Smith and colleagues (2012) caution that nondialogic organizations risk turning away users by ignoring tweets, but dialogic organizations "bask in positive sentiment and respond to negative posts" (p. 111).

On a practical level, Diers's study examined BP's handling of the oil spill in the Gulf of Mexico. BP's crisis management team used both Facebook and Twitter along with press releases to repair the company's image. Facebook became a forum for complaints, and Twitter was a means to disseminate information (Diers & Donohue, 2013). Online comments, which tend to be negative, appeared on Facebook (Diers & Donohue, 2013), perhaps due to the lack of a character limit. BP used Twitter to call attention to its progress and "to promote its corporate identity, and defend criticisms of the corrective work it was doing" (Diers & Donohue, 2013, p. 262). Twitter was referred to as a "work horse" for BP because the organization maintains a level of control not found in other social media due to the character limit of replies (Diers & Donohue, 2013).

This study examined Fortune 500 companies' use of Twitter in crisis situations using the SCCT crisis clusters and response strategies as a framework. A content analysis of more than 9,000 individual tweets was conducted to reveal which clusters and response strategies generated the most engagement in the form of replies, retweets, and likes along with recommendations for crisis managers when using Twitter. With this in mind, the following research questions were posed:

RQ1a: Do Fortune 500 companies use Twitter for crisis communication?
RQ1b: How often do Fortune 500 companies tweet about a crisis?
RQ2a: What is the preferred response strategy of Fortune 500 companies on Twitter for crisis communication?

RQ2b: What crisis-response strategy from Fortune 500 companies will engage the public the most on Twitter?

RQ3: What impact does crisis type have on generating replies, retweets, and likes in crisis situations concerning Fortune 500 crisis tweets?

Method

Fortune 500 companies were analyzed in this study (based on the 2013 ranking) because these companies are deemed the most successful in the United States. The Twitter pages selected were either verified, dealt with the main news of the company, or were clearly the most engaged with the most followers and thus assumed to be the main Twitter page. Tweets from each company with an account were collected from one randomly selected day each month from 2009 to 2013, yielding a potential total of 60 tweets for each company. If there were multiple tweets on the selected day, another random number was selected to narrow the selection to just one tweet. Twitter does limit how many past tweets are visible to users, thereby limiting the number of tweets collected for some highly engaged companies. A screenshot was taken of each tweet collected, and the number of replies, retweets, and likes was recorded. If the tweet had replies, screenshots of the two most recent replies were collected. This was done for each company until no more tweets were visible or until January 2009.

Based on Coombs's SCCT, the subject matter of the tweet was coded for no crisis present, victim cluster, accidental cluster, and preventable cluster. Tweets with a crisis present were further coded for response strategy, which included deny, diminish, and rebuild. Last, each tweet's replies were coded for valence, which included positive (compliment), negative (complaint), and neutral (question, self-promotion, and neutral feedback or opinion). Two graduate students at a southern American university served as the coders for this project. In a pretest, they independently coded five randomly selected companies' tweets and their coding appeared to be reliable (Cohen's κ ranged from 0.74 to 1.00). The discrepancies between the two coders were resolved by a later discussion. The remaining sample tweets were evenly divided and coded by each coder.

Results

Sampling procedures yielded a total of 9,122 tweets. Three fourths of the tweets included a hyperlink. Only 6% of the tweets included a picture, and less than 3% included a video. Almost 70% of the tweets did not use an @ mention and nearly two thirds did not include a hashtag.

Addressing RQ1a revealed that 36 of the 420 companies with Twitter accounts (8.6%) conducted crisis communication in the tweets analyzed from 2009 to 2013. Based on industry classification, utility and power composed 26%, food production was 12%, and insurance companies made 10.9% of the crisis tweets in this study. Of the 9,122 tweets within the sample, only 92 were coded as crisis communication (1.0%).

The RQ2a addressed crisis type and crisis response. Of the 92 tweets coded as having crisis subject matter, 71.7% were in the accidental cluster, 22.8% were in the victim cluster, and 5.5% were in the preventable cluster. The rebuild response strategy was the most common at 84.8%, followed by the diminish strategy at 9.8% and the deny strategy at 5.4%.

A series of one-way ANOVA tests was conducted to answer the RQ2b to learn which crisis-response strategy generated the most engagement in the form of replies, retweets, and likes. The effect of crisis response on replies was found to be significant, $F(2, 89) = 8.91, p < .001$, along with retweets, $F(2, 89) = 12.33, p < .001$, and likes, $F(2, 89) = 14.09, p < .001$. Post hoc analyses using the LSD method revealed that the deny response generated significantly more replies ($M = 5.00, SD = 7.68$) than diminish ($M = 1.56, SD = 4.30$) and rebuild ($M = 0.54, SD = 1.17$). The deny response generated significantly more retweets ($M = 145.20, SD = 290.74$) than diminish ($M = 3.22, SD = 8.60$) and rebuild ($M = 2.37, SD = 10.83$). Last, the deny response also generated significantly more likes ($M = 81.80, SD = 156.96$) than diminish ($M = 1.22, SD = 3.31$) and rebuild ($M = 0.37, SD = 1.51$; see Table 14.1).

To answer RQ3, a series of one-way ANOVA tests was conducted, but crisis cluster type did not have a significant effect on replies, retweets, or likes. However, the effects on retweets and likes were close to significance ($p = .07$ and $p = .10$,

TABLE 14.1 Effect of Crisis-Response Strategy on Replies, Retweets, and Likes

	Response Strategy	*N*	*M*	*SD*
Replies	Deny	5	5.00	7.68
	Diminish	9	1.56	4.30
	Rebuild	78	0.54	1.17
	Total	**92**	**0.88**	**2.54**
Retweets	Deny	5	145.20	290.74
	Diminish	9	3.22	8.60
	Rebuild	78	2.37	10.83
	Total	**92**	**10.22**	**69.86**
Likes	Deny	5	81.80	156.96
	Diminish	9	1.22	3.31
	Rebuild	78	0.37	1.51
	Total	**92**	**4.88**	**37.81**

respectively). A post hoc analysis using the LSD method revealed that the victim cluster generated significantly more retweets (M = 40.67, SD = 144.17) than the accidental cluster (M = 0.50, SD = 3.20). The victim cluster generated significantly more likes (M = 20.43, SD = 78.54) than the accidental cluster (M = 0.21, SD = 1.25). No other significant difference was detected.

To analyze replies, a t-test was conducted between tweets with a crisis and tweets without a crisis. Tweets with a crisis generated significantly more replies (M = 0.88, SD = 2.54) than tweets without a crisis (M = 0.43, SD = 2.14), $t(9,075)$ = 2.01, p < .05 (two-tailed; see Table 14.2). However, crisis tweets did not significantly generate more retweets or likes than noncrisis tweets. Going further, the valence of each reply in our sample was recoded as positive being +1, neutral being 0, and negative being −1. The valence of two replies of each tweet was averaged. A t-test revealed that replies to crisis tweets were significantly more negative (M = -.25, SD = 0.43) than replies to noncrisis tweets (M = 0.12, SD = 0.42), $t(1,110)$ = 4.43, p < .001 (two-tailed; see Table 14.3). To test the effect of crisis-response strategy on reply valence, an ANOVA test was conducted. The results were not statistically significant, $F(2, 23)$ = .06, p = .94. Average valence of two replies did not differ across different crisis-response strategies (see Table 14.4).

TABLE 14.2 Effect of Crisis on Number of Replies

		N	M	SD
Reply	No crisis	8,985	0.43	2.14
	Crisis present	92	0.88	2.54

TABLE 14.3 Effect of Crisis on Reply Valence

		N	M	SD
Reply valence	No crisis	1,086	0.12	0.42
	Crisis present	26	−0.25	0.43

TABLE 14.4 Effect of Crisis-Response Strategy on Reply Valence

	Response Strategy	N	M	SD
Reply valence	Deny	3	−0.17	0.29
	Diminish	2	−0.25	0.35
	Rebuild	21	−0.26	0.46

Discussion

With social media growing in popularity and with users turning to Facebook and Twitter during a crisis for credible information, it is no surprise that companies' public relations teams adopted social media. The speed of the messages and audience size is attractive, but this study demonstrates that Fortune 500 companies favor top-down announcements over dialogue. The companies rarely directed tweets at specific users, or even used hashtags, which are designed to increase a tweet's visibility. Instead, companies tweeted messages only followers could see in much the same way companies used to mail newsletters to specific addresses on a list. Building goodwill with stakeholders before a potential crisis is essential to softening the blow (Coombs, 2007; Ki & Brown, 2013), so tweeting at less-than-maximum dialogic potential decreases a company's chances at engaging the public. Crisis tweets are only effective with large audiences, but they probably are not reaching full audience potential.

Companies that are engaging in crisis communication are using the rebuild strategy far more often than the diminish and deny strategies. Coombs (2007) recommends accommodative responses, such as compensation and apologies, and Meer (2014) argued that the denial response is the least effective. The Fortune 500 companies in this study may have been searching for goodwill by apologizing, but another explanation could be the nature of the crises in the sample. Almost three fourths of the crisis tweets fell into the accidental cluster, meaning the company was at fault so a rebuild strategy was appropriate. However, when examining engagement, the deny strategy generated significantly more replies, retweets, and likes than the diminish or rebuild strategies. It is conceivable that users were closely following the crisis, and because the company employed a potentially contentious deny strategy, any tweet from the company would receive a substantial amount of engagement. The companies' apologies were often to individual users, and these tweets do not often "go viral." However, denials aimed at a large audience would have a greater chance to generate replies, retweets, and likes. A crisis manager should only use a deny strategy when absolutely necessary (Meer, 2014), and only when the company is not at fault, because this strategy could potentially generate unwanted attention that spreads like wildfire. Researchers at Sysomos (2010) found that less than 2% of tweets generated three levels of replies, meaning a quick rebuild response, when warranted, can potentially limit the number of negative replies.

Even though the results concerning crisis strategy valence were not significant in this study, the results still necessitate a brief discussion. The deny strategy averaged the least amount of negativity within company tweets. The diminish and rebuild strategies both averaged more negativity. This is perhaps due to the company attempting to distance itself from the negative situation when denying culpability. Both the diminish and rebuild strategies most likely require the company to mention the crisis while addressing the situation, leading to the increased average levels of negativity within company tweets. Whereas a deny strategy may lead to a more positive overall tone, denials tend to generate more attention in the form of replies, retweets, and likes.

Curtailing replies should be a priority for crisis managers. Both the victim and the accidental crisis clusters displayed a slight effect on retweets and likes in this study. These clusters, although still adverse, are mild to moderate threats to an organization's reputation. A message responding to a victim or accidental cluster will most likely be a rebuild response, which could generate positivity in the form of likes and retweets. Likes implying positivity and retweets appear on a user's Twitter feed as if they originated from the user, so it makes sense that both of these functions trend positively. Conversely, crisis situations generate more replies than noncrisis situations and these crisis replies are significantly more negative than ordinary replies in the sample. Brown and Billings (2013) remarked that online audiences are no longer passive, and these motivated users will seek a forum to vent frustrations. Facebook was used as a complaint box during the BP oil spill (Diers & Donohue, 2013), and, with increased usage, perhaps the reply function on Twitter is being used to air grievances. The effort to type a reply is far greater than clicking "Retweet" or "Like" so the motivation behind a reply has to be somewhat intense. Crisis managers should work for likes and retweets to control the message because replies tend to be negative and they cede control of the message to users. With that being said, social media teams should examine likes closely because some users "hate-like" to sarcastically mock a mistake or to somewhat anonymously support a controversial view (Rosman, 2013). Favoriting is the "primary way for users to signal agreement, acknowledgement, laughter, support, and occasionally (and perversely) utter hatred" (Newton, 2015), so it behooves social media managers to parse every engagement indicator to understand the honest reaction from users. Still, a large volume of retweets and likes is generally positive.

Conclusion

Although unpredictable and low in probability, a crisis is nonetheless high stakes for an organization. Speed and sincerity are still vital and perhaps more so now with the rapidity and permanence—thanks to screenshots—of social media. Although a crisis can be destructive, the situation poses an opportunity to strengthen relationships with stakeholders and improve reputation, if handled well. If mistakes are made, the damage can be long lasting, like in the case with Carnival, or seem weak, and reactive like with BP, which created a Twitter account only after the oil spill in the gulf.

Notes

1 At the time of this research, what are now called "likes" by Twitter were referred to as "favorites."

References

Ahmad, I. (2013, October 24). 30+ of the most amazing Twitter statistics [Infographic]. *Socialmedia Today*. Retrieved from http://socialmediatoday.com/irfan-ahmad/1854311/twitter-statistics-IPO-infographic

Austin, L., Liu, B. F., & Jin, Y. (2012). How audiences seek out crisis information: Exploring the social-mediated crisis communication model. *Journal of Applied Communication Research, 40*(2), 1–20.

Bennett, S. (2014, January 20). Pinterest, Twitter, Facebook, Instagram, Google+, LinkedIn—social media stats 2014 [INFOGRAPHIC]. *AllTwitter*. Retrieved from http://www.mediabistro.com/alltwitter/social-media-stats-2014_b54243

Booton, J. (2012). Carnival fails crisis 101 in Costa response. *Fox Business*. Retrieved from http://www.foxbusiness.com/travel/2012/01/26/experts-say-carnival-should-have-learned-from-wendys-fedex-post-crisis

Brown, N., & Billings, A. (2013). Sports fans as crisis communicators on social media websites. *Public Relations Review, 39*, 74–81.

Camp, S. V. (2012). PR lessons to be learned from the Costa Concordia tragedy. *PR News*. Retrieved from http://www.prnewsonline.com/featured/2012/01/23/pr-lessons-to-be-learned-from-the-costa-concordia-tragedy

Chen, G. M. (2011). Tweet this: A uses and gratifications perspective on how active Twitter use gratifies a need to connect with others. *Computers in Human Behavior, 27*, 755–762.

Coombs, W. (2007). Protecting organization reputations during a crisis: The development and application of situational crisis communication theory. *Corporate Reputation Review, 10*(3), 163–176.

Diers, A., & Donohue, J. (2013). Synchronizing crisis responses after a transgression. *Journal of Communication Management, 17*(3), 252–269.

Falkheimer, J., & Heide, M. (2010). Crisis communicators in change: From plans to improvisations. In W. T. Coombs & S. J. Holladay (Eds.), *The handbook of crisis communication* (pp. 511–526). Oxford: Wiley-Blackwell.

Fitzgerald, B. (2012). Most popular sites 2012: Alexa ranks the 500 most-visited websites. Retrieved from http://www.huffingtonpost.com/2012/08/09/most-popular-sites-2012-alexa_n_1761365.html

Gantt, J. (2013). Carnival corporation: The Costa Concordia crisis. *Arthur W. Page Society*. Retrieved from http://www.awpagesociety.com/wp-content/uploads/2013/03/Carnival-Corporation-Case-A-and-B.pdf

Heath, R. L., & Palenchar, M. J. (2009). *Strategic issues management: Organizations and public policy changes* (2nd ed.). Thousand Oaks, CA: Sage.

Hermida, A. (2010). From TV to Twitter: How ambient news became ambient journalism. *Media-Culture Journal, 13*(2).). Retrieved from http://journal.media-culture.org.au/index.php/mcjournal/article/view/220

Jin, Y., Liu, B. F., & Austin, L. (2014). Examining the role of social media in effective crisis management: The effects of crisis origin, information form, and source on publics' crisis responses. *Communication Research, 41*, 74–94.

Ki, E., & Brown, K. (2013). The effects of crisis response strategies on relationship quality outcomes. *Journal of Business Communications, 50*(4), 403–420.

Kim, S. (2014). The role of prior expectancies and relational satisfaction in crisis. *Journalism & Mass Communication Quarterly, 9*(1), 139–158.

Kim, S., Avery, E. J., & Lariscy, R. W. (2009). Are crisis communicators practicing what we preach? An evaluation of crisis response strategy analyzed in public relations research from 1991 to 2009. *Public Relations Review*, *35*, 446–448.

Liu, B., Jin, Y., & Austin, L. (2013). The tendency to tell: Understanding publics' communicative responses to crisis information form and source. *Journal of Public Relations Research*, *25*, 51–67.

Meer, T. v. der. (2014). Organizational crisis-denial strategy: The effect of denial on public framing. *Public Relations Review*, *40*, 537–539.

Meer, T. v. der, & Verhoeven, J. (2014). Emotional crisis communication. *Public Relations Review*, *40*, 526–536.

Newton, C. (2015). Twitter officially kills off favorites and replaces them with likes. Retrieved from http://www.theverge.com/2015/11/3/9661180/twitter-vine-avorite-fav-likes-hearts

Olsson, E. (2014). Crisis communication in public organizations: Dimensions of crisis communication revisited. *Journal of Contingencies & Crisis Management*, *22*, 113–125.

Procopio, C. H., & Procopio, S. T. (2007). Do you know what it means to miss New Orleans? Internet communication, geographic community, and social capital in crisis. *Journal of Applied Communication Research*, *35*(1), 67–87.

Rosman, K. (2013). On Twitter, more "favoriting." Retrieved from http://www.wsj.com/articles/SB10001424127887324564704578626070775502176

Schandorf, M. (2013). Mediated gesture: Paralinguistic communication and phatic text. *Convergence: The International Journal of Research into New Media Technologies*, *19*(3), 319–344.

Schultz, F., Utz, S., & Goritz, A. (2011). Is the medium the message? Perceptions of and reactions to crisis communication via Twitter, blogs and traditional media. *Public Relations Review*, *37*, 20–27.

Smith, A., Fischer, E., & Yongjian, C. (2012). How does brand-related user-generated content differ across YouTube, Facebook, and Twitter? *Journal of Interactive Marketing*, *26*, 102–113.

Sysomos Career. (2010). Twitter conversation statistics. Retrieved from http://www.sysomos.com/insidetwitter/engagement

Utz, S., Schultz, F., & Glocka, S. (2013). Crisis communication online: How medium, crisis type and emotions affected public reactions in the Fukushima Daiichi nuclear disaster. *Public Relations Review*, *39*, 40–46.

Westerman, D., Spence, P., & Der Heide, B. V. (2014). Social media as information source: Recency of updates and credibility of information. *Journal of Computer-Mediated Communication*, *19*, 171–183.

15

A STUDY OF MALAYSIA AIRLINES' MISSING FLIGHT CRISIS

News Frames, Crisis Emotions, Negative Behavioral Intentions, Corporate Reputation, and Country Image

Jueman (Mandy) Zhang, Yi Wang, Yue Wu, Xiuli Wang, and Ross Buck

News media and social media are external sources to monitor warning signs of a crisis (Coombs, 2014). News frames can induce negative emotions (Kim & Cameron, 2011), which can lead to negative behavioral intentions (Coombs, 2007, 2014). Prior research of news framing in crisis communication has focused on typology and effects of news frames (An & Gower, 2009; Cho & Gower, 2006). Little is known about the emotional effects of news frames that coexist in a news story (An & Gower, 2009; Semetko & Valkenburg, 2000), especially when the news story is disseminated on social media. The emerging model of social-mediated crisis communication (SMCC), posited by Jin, Liu, and Austin (2014), asserted the importance of dealing with negative emotions on social media. In our study of Malaysia Airlines' missing flight crisis, we examined how the salience and order of two news frames (the investigation frame and the victims frame) in one news video, which was disseminated on social media, affected viewer emotions, and how the news-evoked emotions affected reposting intention, negative behavioral intentions, corporate reputation, and country image. The findings provide implications for how to provide effective organizational crisis responses.

Literature Review

News Media and Social Media as Sources of Warning Signs

Malaysia Airlines received widespread criticism from news media ("Commentary: Information-sharing," 2014; Tilley, 2014) and the Internet (Li, 2014) for mishandling the incident of MH370, which went missing en route from Kuala Lumpur to Beijing on March 8, 2014. The unprecedented search for the plane—with two thirds of the 239 people on board from China—involved 26 countries. The airline and Malaysian officials provided delayed, ambiguous, inaccurate, and even contradictory information, which misguided the initial search from the flight path to the South China Sea and the Straits of Malacca, wasting valuable time ("Commentary: Information-sharing," 2014; Tilley, 2014). Meanwhile, transnational investigative journalism played a vital role in seeking the truth. CNN saw a double-digit increase in viewership (Zara, 2014). People flooded onto the Internet to get information and express opinions. A search by the hashtag #马航飞机失联# (#the missing Malaysia Airline flight#) resulted in 3.79 million discussions and 35.49 million views on Sina Weibo (referred to as Weibo hereafter), the Twitter-like Chinese microblog, as of September 2014. Weibo is prevalent in China, with 87.67% of Chinese citizens as users, according to the Data Center of China Internet (DCCI, 2012).

The Internet serves as an external source for online information from traditional media and information unique to social media (Coombs, 2014). The presence of traditional media on social media makes social media such as microblogs a platform where mass communication and interpersonal communication converge. The sharing features on social media allow information to spread quickly. Interpersonal communication via social media can be powerful in distributing word-of-mouth (WOM) information (Laczniak, DeCarlo, & Ramaswami, 2001).

Effects of News Frame on Audience Emotions

Coombs's (2007) situational crisis communication theory (SCCT) identified three types of corporate crises—victim, accidental, and preventable—based on attribution of crisis responsibility. Although Malaysia Airlines was criticized for mishandling the MH370 crisis, there was uncertainty about crisis type (Coombs, 2007) and crisis origin (Jin et al., 2014), which made the classic typology of organization crises blurry. Content analysis has revealed five primary news frames of corporate crises: attribution of responsibility, economic, human interest, conflict, and morality (An & Gower, 2009). Much of the media coverage of MH370 focused on the investigation, which reflected conflicts among different parties (An & Gower, 2009) and at different stages. A survey by the Pew Research Center (2014) showed that 81% of respondents thought the investigation received the right amount or too much coverage. Some media coverage focused on the victims from a human-interest approach, which "brings a human face or an emotional angle" to the news (Semetko & Valkenburg, 2000, p. 95). The nature of an incident and its media worthiness have been shown to affect the salience of the victims (Fominaya & Barberet, 2011). In a transnational crisis, families of the victims of the MH370 incident received great media attention.

News frames have also been shown to affect emotions (Kim & Cameron, 2011). Among six clusters of emotions, reduced from 135 emotion words, love, joy, and surprise are positive emotions, whereas, anger, sadness, and fear are negative ones (Shaver, Schwartz, Kirson, & O'Connor, 1987). Out of them, love, joy, anger, and fear, emerged in Buck, Anderson, Chaudhuri, and Ray's (2004) typology of 18 emotions of persuasion, assessed from a rational-affective approach. Primary negative crisis emotions include anger, anxiety, sadness, flight, and shame (Jin et al., 2014; Jin, Pang, & Cameron, 2007, 2010). We predicted that the relative salience of the investigation frame over the victim frame in a news video about the MH370 incident would affect viewer emotions as follows:

H1: A news video with a salient investigation frame and a weak victim frame will induce stronger positive and weaker negative emotions than one with a salient victim frame and a weak investigation frame.

The way a news story is structured can affect information processing. Previous research has shown that readers exert more attentional effort when reading news using the inverted pyramid style, which presents information in the descending order of importance, than when reading news using the narrative style, which usually starts with a personal story (Wise, Bolls, Myers, & Sternadori, 2009). However, little is known about the effects of frame order on emotions. Thus we raised the following research question:

RQ1: How will the order of the frames in a news video affect viewer emotions?

News-Evoked Emotions, Reposting Intention, and Negative Behavioral Intentions

Weibo users, who can be interconnected without real-life social ties, can publish short posts, each with up to 140 Chinese characters. Weibo interactive features include repost, favorite, and comment. Malaysia Airlines launched its Weibo account (www.weibo.com/malaysiaairlines) on March 9, 2014. Through March 24, when it announced the possible crash of the plane in the Indian Ocean, it published 17 posts, 14 of which were media statements in both English and Chinese, and in comparison, received 10,213 likes, 17,510 reposts, and 37,928 comments. Reposting prevails on Weibo (Yu, Asur, & Huberman, 2012). An average microblog user in China posts 2.13 messages and reposts 3.12 messages every day (DCCI, 2012). Berger and Milkman (2013) suggested that high-arousal negative emotions such as anger and anxiety facilitated content sharing. Thus we predicted the following:

> **H2:** Anger and anxiety evoked by the news video will be positively associated with the intention to repost the news video.

Negative word of mouth (NWOM) is defined as interpersonal communication denigrating an organization or product (Richins, 1984). The SCCT (Coombs, 2007) postulates that negative crisis emotions such as anger are positively related to the likelihood of engaging in NWOM and negatively related to behavioral intentions in support of the organization. Not only did people criticize Malaysia Airlines for mishandling the crisis, but several online travel agencies in China boycotted the airline (Li, 2014). Thus we formed the following hypothesis and research question:

> **H3:** Anger evoked by news videos will be positively associated with offline NWOM and online negative behavioral intentions.
>
> **RQ2:** How will other news-evoked emotions be associated with offline NWOM and online negative behavioral intentions?

Emotions, Company Reputation, and Country Image

Media and public criticism amplified by social media can lead to reputation damage, negative behavior, and financial problems (Coombs, 2014). Reputation is affected by the expectation gap between what a company does and what the public expects (Coombs, 2014). Malaysia Airlines' first response came five hours after it lost contact with the flight. Subsequent misinformation, which misguided the initial search, worsened its credibility (Tilley, 2014). The negative emotions deepened its ongoing financial plight, and the airline saw a 60% drop in sales in China and lost 40% of its market value as of May 2014 ("Malaysia Airlines losses," 2014). Further affected by the crash of its Flight 17 in eastern Ukraine in July, Malaysia Airlines announced in August 2014 its removal from the Malaysian stock exchange and an overhaul including the launch of a new company. The state investor Khazanah National, the majority shareholder that owned 69% of the airline, announced taking 100% ownership by buying out small shareholders (Ng & Chan, 2014). Considering that the airline is government owned, and that Malaysian officials provided misinformation, we wondered if the crisis would affect the country's image. We put forward the following hypothesis and research question:

> **H4:** News-evoked negative emotions will be negatively associated with corporate reputation.
>
> **RQ3:** How will news-evoked negative emotions relate to the country image of Malaysia?

Knowledge of the crisis emotions and the effects of the emotions on the examined dependent variables may provide implications of how to provide effective organizational crisis responses (Coombs & Holladay, 2005; Jin, 2010).

Method

Participants

A total of 90 Weibo users participated in the study. This sample had 42 males (46.7%) and 48 females (53.3%). On average, the participants were 26.85 years old ($SD = 7.61$).

Design

The study consisted of two parts. The first part was an experiment with a two (frame salience) by two (frame order) between-subjects design. Each participant was randomly assigned to watch one of four news videos: one with a salient investigation frame followed by a weak victim frame (SI-WV; 20 participants), one with a weak victim frame followed by a salient investigation frame (WV-SI; 22 participants), one with a salient victim frame followed by a weak investigation frame (SV-WI; 22 participants), and one with a weak investigation frame followed by a salient victim frame (WI-SV; 26 participants). After watching the video, participants reported their emotions. The second part was a survey. Participants answered questions about reposting intention, negative behavior intentions, corporate reputation, country image, and demographics.

Stimuli

We produced stimuli videos by editing news videos from CNN.com. Each video was 3 minutes and 10 seconds long. The two videos contained a salient investigation frame (2 minutes and 40 seconds long) and a weak victim frame (40 seconds long). The other two videos contained a weak investigation frame and a salient victim frame. The salient and weak versions of the same frame addressed the same key points. The investigation frame focused on two topics: (a) key moments of the flight and (b) whether there was an act of terrorism. The victim frame focused on one topic: the victims' families. The salient version contained more detailed information than the weak version of the same frame. All the videos were titled, "The mystery of Malaysian Airlines Flight 370," started with a short opening titled, "What do we know?" and ended with a short ending titled, "An unprecedented missing aircraft mystery." Videos were in English, and Chinese subtitles were added. CNN is unavailable in China, and participants rated on a 7-point Likert scale how novel, deviant, important, interesting, recent, and useful the news video was ($\alpha = .92$). Responses were averaged into an index, showing a moderate level of news value ($M = 4.02, SD = 1.37$).

Procedure

We published on Weibo a post with a video link on March 21, inviting its users to participate in the study. We also sent our post to popular account owners asking for reposting. The video played automatically with a click, which mimicked the real experience of reading a Weibo post with a video attached. After watching the video, participants answered questions about their emotions, their reposting intention, their negative behavioral intentions, corporate reputation, country image, and demographics. The questionnaire was worded in Chinese. To guarantee the news value of the stimuli videos, data were collected until Malaysia Airlines announced the possible crash of the plane in the south Indian Ocean and the switch of the search on March 24 (Malaysia Airlines, 2014). Qualtrics (www.qualtrics.com/) was used to control random assignment, present news videos and the questionnaire, and collect data. Participation was voluntary.

Measures

Except where noted, 7-point Likert scales were used.

Manipulation Check

Participants rated on two semantic differential scales: uninformative-informative and negative-positive (reverse-scored item).

News-Evoked Emotions

After watching the news video, participants rated how they felt on 20 emotion items (*not at all* to *very much*), adapted from the Communication via Analytic and Syncretic Cognition Scale (Buck et al., 2004). We added several emotion items, such as doubt and hope.

Intention to Repost

Participants responded the extent to which they would like to repost the news video on Weibo (*not at all* to *very much*).

Offline NWOM

Participants rated three statements (*strongly disagree* to *strongly agree*) adapted from Coombs and Holladay (2008), such as "I would encourage friends or relatives NOT to take flights with Malaysian Airlines." Responses were averaged into an index ($\alpha = .80$).

Online Negative Behavioral Intentions

Participants rated two items (*strongly disagree* to *strongly agree*) adapted from Schultz, Utz, and Göritz (2011): (a) "I would write negative comments about Malaysian Airlines on Weibo," and (b) "I would sign an online petition to boycott Malaysia

Airlines." They were not combined into an index as the former emphasized communication and the latter addressed action (Schultz et al., 2011).

Corporate Reputation

Participants rated five items (*strongly disagree* to *strongly agree*) adapted from Coombs and Holladay (2002), such as "Malaysia Airlines is concerned with the well-being of its publics." Responses were averaged into an index ($\alpha = .74$).

Country Image

Participants rated eight items (*strongly disagree* to *strongly agree*) used by Wang, Li, Barnes, and Ahn (2012), such as "friendly toward us" and "cooperative with us." Responses were averaged into an index ($\alpha = .93$).

Control Variables

Participants reported perceived credibility level of CNN by rating five semantic differential items used by Lee and Sundar (2013): undependable-dependable, dishonest-honest, unreliable-reliable, insincere-sincere, and untrustworthy-trustworthy ($\alpha = .98$). Participants reported their Weibo interactivity by responding how frequently (*not at all* to *very frequently*) they repost and comment on Weibo. Responses were averaged into an index ($\alpha = .74$).

Demographics

Participants reported age and sex.

Data Analysis

Factor analysis was used to reduce news-evoked emotions. ANOVA was used to investigate the effects of the salience and order of the news frames on emotions. Hierarchical multiple regression was used to examine the relationships between emotions and dependent variables. Weibo interactivity and perceived source credibility were included as covariates for regression analyses to remove possible confounding effects (Lee & Sundar, 2013).

Results

Manipulation Check

Participants rated the news videos with an SI frame and a WV frame as more informative ($M = 5.10$, $SD = 1.85$) than the videos with a WI frame and an SV frame ($M = 3.53$, $SD = 1.58$), $F(1, 88) = 18.71$, $p < .001$. They also rated the former less negative ($M = 3.78, SD = 1.39$) than the latter ($M = 4.60, SD = 1.31$), $F(1, 88) = 8.14, p < .01$. Manipulation worked.

News-Evoked Emotions

Principal component factor analysis with varimax rotation was performed, which extracted five emotion dimensions out of the 20 emotion items (see Table 15.1). Items loaded on each dimension were averaged into indices. Doubt ($M = 4.35$, $SD = 1.81, \alpha = .83$) was the strongest emotion, followed by sympathy ($M = 4.16$, $SD = 1.45, \alpha = .85$), anxiety ($M = 3.42, SD = 1.63, \alpha = .86$), anger ($M = 2.45, SD = 1.32, \alpha = .87$), and hope ($M = 2.41, SD = 1.00, \alpha = .68$).

TABLE 15.1 Factor Analysis (Principal Components Analysis and Varimax Rotation) of News-Evoked Sentiments

Variables	Factor 1 Anger	Factor 2 Anxiety	Factor 3 Sympathy	Factor 4 Hope	Factor 5 Doubt
Hostile	**.86**	.11	−.05	.003	−.06
Insulted	**.84**	.10	−.02	.11	.09
scornful	**.80**	.14	−.04	−.12	.04
Angry	**.70**	.35	.001	.01	−.13
Sad	.06	**.84**	−.003	−.01	−.17
Afraid	.17	**.83**	.06	.05	.07
Uneasy	.17	**.81**	−.15	−.04	−.11
Nervous	.27	**.80**	.14	.07	.15
Helpless	.49	**.49**	.18	−.04	.04
Sympathetic	−.06	−.07	**.90**	−.05	.15
Compassionate	.01	.00	**.83**	.04	.27
Caring	−.12	.12	**.76**	.38	−.05
Loving	.01	.09	**.67**	.45	−.07
Trustful	−.13	.09	.09	**.72**	−.15
Hopeful	−.11	−.02	.12	**.69**	.23
Happy	.33	−.19	.003	**.68**	−.14
Surprised	.04	−.07	.09	**.63**	.36
Excited	.16	**.15**	.14	**.47**	.16
Doubtful	.05	**−.03**	.14	−.001	**.89**
Frustrated	.03	**−.03**	.11	.23	**.86**
Eigenvalues	4.81	3.77	2.29	1.77	1.45
% of variance accounted for	22.92	17.93	10.91	8.43	6.92

Effects of News Frame on Emotions

H1 predicted that videos with an SI frame and a WV frame would lead to weaker negative emotions and stronger positive emotions than videos with a WI frame and an SV frame. Controlling for demographics and perceived source credibility, the former led to stronger hope ($M = 2.71$, $SD = 1.01$) than the latter ($M = 2.15$, $SD = 0.93$), $F(1, 85) = 5.32$, $p = .02$, $\eta_p^2 = .059$. Frame salience did not affect other emotions. H1 was supported in terms of hope. Tukey's post hoc comparisons revealed that the SI-WV video elicited stronger hope ($M = 2.82$, $SD = 0.85$) than the WI-SV video ($M = 1.98$, $SD = 0.88$), $M_D = .84$, $p = .02$. RQ1 asked about the effects of frame order on emotions. There was no effect.

Effects of News-Evoked Emotions on Reposting Intention

H2 predicted that anger and anxiety would be positively associated with the intention to repost the news video. As shown in Table 15.2, there was a positive relationship between anxiety and the intention to repost the video. H2 was partially supported.

Effects of News-Evoked Emotions on Negative Behavioral Intentions

H3 predicted that anger would be positively associated with negative behavioral intentions. RQ2 asked how other news-evoked emotions would be associated with negative behavioral intentions. As Table 15.2 shows, after controlling for demographics, perceived news source credibility, and Weibo interactivity, there was a positive relationship between anger and offline NWOM and a positive relationship between doubt and offline NWOM. The β for anger was larger than that for doubt, indicating the stronger influence of anger than doubt in offline NWOM. However, anger was not related to online negative behavioral intentions. H3 was partially supported. It is worth mentioning that anger was just a little shy of the significance level ($p = .06$) to be related with the intention to write negative comments on Weibo, and that Weibo interactivity was positively related to it.

Effects of News-Evoked Emotions on Corporate Reputation and Country Image

H4 predicted news-evoked negative emotions would be negatively associated with corporate reputation. RQ3 asked about how negative emotions would be associated with country image. As Table 15.3 shows, after controlling for demographics and perceived source credibility, anger was negatively associated with corporate reputation. Perceived source credibility was close to the significance level ($p = .10$) to be negatively related with corporate reputation. No negative emotions were correlated with country image.

TABLE 15.2 Hierarchical Regression Analyses of Demographic Variables, Perceived Source Credibility, Weibo Interactivity, and Video-Evoked Emotions on Intentions to Repost the News Video, Offline NWOM, and Online Negative Behavioral Intentions

Blocks of independent variables	Intention to repost the news video	Offline NWOM	Intention to write negative comments about the airline on Weibo	Intention to sign an online petition to boycott the airline
Demographic variables				
Sex	$\beta = .05$, $p = .66$	$\beta = -.16$, $p = .18$	$\beta = -.16$, $p = .18$	$\beta = -.17$, $p = .16$
Age	$\beta = .12$, $p = .29$	$\beta = -.03$, $p = .79$	$\beta = .09$, $p = .43$	$\beta = .11$, $p = .34$
R^2 change	.01	.002	.02	.02
Perceived source credibility	$\beta = .13$, $p = .20$	$\beta = .03$, $p = .80$	$\beta = -.16$, $p = .15$	$\beta = -.02$, $p = .85$
R^2 change	.03	.01	.03	.001
Weibo interactivity	$\beta = -.02$, $p = .85$	$\beta = -.01$, $p = .92$	$\boldsymbol{\beta = .28}$, $\boldsymbol{p = .02}$	$\beta = .05$, $p = .64$
R^2 change	.01	.000	.07	.02
News-evoked sentiments				
Doubt	$\beta = .10$, $p = .39$	$\boldsymbol{\beta = -.26}$, $\boldsymbol{p = .04}$	$\beta = -.18$, $p = .15$	$\beta = -.12$, $p = .34$
Sympathy	$\beta = .03$, $p = .85$	$\beta = .20$, $p = .13$	$\beta = .10$, $p = .48$	$\beta = -.06$, $p = .66$
Anxiety	$\boldsymbol{\beta = .35}$, $\boldsymbol{p = .02}$	$\beta = .11$, $p = .47$	$\beta = .12$, $p = .44$	$\beta = .21$, $p = .19$
Anger	$\beta = .03$, $p = .81$	$\boldsymbol{\beta = .34}$, $\boldsymbol{p = .01}$	$\beta = .06$, $p = .63$	$\beta = .25$, $p = .06$
Hope	$\beta = .16$, $p = .16$	$\beta = -.23$, $p = .06$	$\beta = -.04$, $p = .76$	$\beta = .59$, $p = .56$
R^2 change	.23	.19	.04	.11
Total R^2	.27	.20	.17	.15
Adjusted total R^2	.18	.10	.07	.05
Model significance	**.003**	**.04**	.10	.17

TABLE 15.3 Hierarchical Regression Analysis of Demographic Variables, Perceived Source Credibility, and Video-Evoked Emotions on Corporate Reputation and Country Image

Blocks of Independent Variables	Corporate Reputation	Country Image
Demographic variables		
Sex	$\beta = .04, p = .71$	$\beta = .16, p = .19$
Age	$\beta = -.03, p = .82$	$\beta = -.01, p = .93$
R^2 change	.001	.01
Perceived source credibility	$\beta = -.18, p = .10$	$\beta = .04, p = .76$
R^2 change	.02	.004
Weibo interactivity	$\beta = -.003, p = .98$	$\beta = .10, p = .40$
R^2 change	.003	.003
News-evoked sentiments		
Doubt	$\beta = .07, p = .59$	$\beta = -.02, p = .90$
Sympathy	$\beta = .03, p = .80$	$\beta = .19, p = .19$
Anxiety	$\beta = -.04, p = .81$	$\beta = -.18, p = .28$
Anger	$\boldsymbol{\beta = -.38, p = .004}$	$\beta = -.05, p = .73$
Hope	$\beta = .21, p = .08$	$\beta = .19, p = .15$
R^2 change	.15	.07
Total R^2	.17	.08
Adjusted total R^2	.07	−.02
Model significance	.09	.63

Discussion

This study examined how the salience and order of two frames (the investigation frame and about the victims frame) in a news video about the Malaysia Airlines missing plane affected emotions, and how news-evoked emotions affected reposting intention, negative reaction intention, corporate reputation, and country image. The findings may provide implications of how to provide effective organizational crisis responses.

News-Evoked Emotions, Anxiety, and Reposting Intention

The news videos evoked five emotions, with doubt as the strongest one, followed by sympathy, anxiety, anger, and hope. Sympathy, anxiety, and anger are crisis emotions commonly found in previous studies (e.g., Coombs, 2007, 2014; Jin et al., 2014; Jin et al., 2007, 2010). Doubt and hope were unique to the MH370 crisis, probably due to the uncertainty of crisis type (Coombs, 2007) and crisis origin (Jin et al., 2014). Frame salience only affected hope. News videos with an SI frame and a WV frame resulted in stronger hope than news videos with an SV frame and a WI frame. When frame order was considered, the SI-WV video led to the strongest hope, whereas the WI-SV video led to the weakest hope, and the difference was significant. It seems that an emphasis on the coverage of the investigation in terms of information amount and placement order yielded the strongest hope. Anxiety motivated the intention to repost the news video, which suggests that people tend to depend more on the news media during a crisis of high uncertainty.

Anger, Doubt, and Implications for Organizational Crisis Responses

Among the five emotions, anger was negatively associated with NWOM and corporate reputation. Also, the relationship between anger and the intention to sign an online petition to boycott the airline was just a little shy of the significance level. The findings were consistent with prior research, which suggested the effects of anger on NWOM and negative behavioral intentions (Coombs, 2007). It is worth noting that anger did not differ by the salience and order of the two frames, which implies that anger derived from media coverage of the investigation and that of the victims. It would be helpful for Malaysia Airlines to find out the origins of anger and prioritize crisis responses to address this emotion (Coombs & Holladay, 2005). Jin (2010) found out that in a crisis when people perceived low predictability of what would happen next, they were more likely to report more anger when they perceived a low ability to influence the situation. Thus, to control anger, Malaysia Airlines may employ strategies that can increase people's influence. As this is a transnational crisis that mainly affects China, the airline can use social media in China as a channel to respond to people's criticisms and questions. It started an account on Weibo, but its passive status made the account no different from a regular website. Also, the airline can make more use of online resources to provide people with opportunities to help. For example, the airline can initiate an online crowdsourcing search and even crowdfund research to address people's concerns. Considering the positive relationship between doubt and offline NWOM, the airline can provide more information about the investigation.

Control Variables and Implications for Organizational Crisis Responses

The negative relationship between perceived source credibility and company reputation was close to the significance level ($p = .10$). This implies that the airline should pay more attention to credible news sources when looking for origins of anger in the media coverage. Weibo interactivity was related to the intention to write negative comments about the airline on Weibo. This suggests the importance of targeting organizational crisis responses to active Weibo users.

Limitations and Future Study

The study is limited by its sample size. Three days after we posted the stimuli videos and started the data collection, the search for the missing plane switched to the south Indian Ocean. As such major progress made our stimuli videos of less news value, we stopped data collection at that point. We found no impact of frame salience and frame order on anger, which suggests that anger derived from the news coverage of the investigation and that of the victims. A comparison between what the media reported and what the airline released, as well as the timing of the reportage from both sides, would provide empirical evidence of why the airline's crisis strategies failed. Further research can also validate the organizational crisis responses recommended in the study.

References

An, S., & Gower, K. K. (2009). How do the news media frame crises? A content analysis of crisis news coverage. *Public Relations Review, 35*(2), 107–112. doi: 10.1016/j.pubrev.2009.01.010

Berger, J., & Milkman, K. (2013). Emotion and virality: What makes online content go viral? *GfK Marketing Intelligence Review, 5*(1), 18–24. Retrieved from http://www.gfkmir.com/issues/previous-issues/vol-5-no-1-2013/art3-no1-2013.html

Buck, R., Anderson, E., Chaudhuri, A., & Ray, I. (2004). Emotion and reason in persuasion: Applying the ARI model and the CASC Scale. *Journal of Business Research, 57*(6), 647–656. doi: 10.1016/S0148-2963(02)00308-9

Cho, S. H., & Gower, K. K. (2006). Framing effect on the public's response to crisis: Human interest frame and crisis type influencing responsibility and blame. *Public Relations Review, 32*(4), 420–422. doi: 10.1016/j.pubrev.2006.09.011

Commentary: Information-sharing vital to MH370 search mission. (2014, March 18). *Xinhua news agency*. Retrieved from http://news.xinhuanet.com/english/indepth/2014-03/18/c_133195943.htm

Coombs, W. T. (2007). Protecting organization reputations during a crisis: The development and application of situational crisis communication theory. *Corporate Reputation Review, 10*(3), 163–176. doi: 10.1057/palgrave.crr.1550049

Coombs, W. T. (2014). *Ongoing crisis communication* (4th ed.). Los Angeles, CA: Sage.

Coombs, W. T., & Holladay, S. J. (2002). Helping crisis managers protect reputational assets: Initial tests of the situational crisis communication theory. *Management Communication Quarterly, 16*(2), 165–186. doi: 10.1177/089331802237233

Coombs, W. T., & Holladay, S. J. (2005). An exploratory study of stakeholder emotions: Affect and crises. In N. M. Ashkanasy, W. J. Zerbe, & C. E. J. Härtel (Eds.), *The effect of affect in organizational settings (research on emotion in organizations, Volume 1)* (pp. 263–280). London: Emerald Group Publishing. doi: S1746-9791(05)01111-9

Coombs, W. T., & Holladay, S. J. (2008). Comparing apology to equivalent crisis response strategies: Clarifying apology's role and value in crisis communication. *Public Relations Review, 34*(3), 252–257. doi: 10.1016/j.pubrev.2008.04.001

Data Center of China Internet (DCCI). (2012). Bluebook of China Microblog. Retrieved from http://doc.mbalib.com/view/09f60d450e5b15218899909cd809d49e.html

Fominaya, C. F., & Barberet, R. (2011). Defining the victims of terrorism: Competing frames around victim compensation and commemoration post-9/11 New York City and 3/11 Madrid. In A. Karatzogianni (Ed.), *Violence and war in culture and the media: Five disciplinary lenses* (pp. 113–130). New York: Routledge.

Jin, Y. (2010). Making sense sensibly in crisis communication: How publics' crisis appraisals influence their negative emotions, coping strategy preferences, and crisis response acceptance. *Communication Research, 37*(4), 522–552. doi: 10.1177/0093650210368256

Jin, Y., Liu, B. F., & Austin, L. L. (2014). Examining the role of social media in effective crisis management: The effects of crisis origin, information form, and source on publics' crisis responses. *Communication Research, 41*(1), 74–94. doi: 10.1177/0093650211423918

Jin, Y., Pang, A., & Cameron, G. T. (2007). Integrated crisis mapping: Towards a publics-based, emotion driven conceptualization in crisis communication. *Sphera Publica, 7,* 81–96.

Jin, Y., Pang, A., & Cameron, G. T. (2010). The role of emotions in crisis responses: Inaugural test of the integrated crisis mapping (ICM) model. *Corporate Communications: An International Journal, 15*(4), 428–452. doi: 10.1108/13563281011085529

Kim, H. J., & Cameron, G. T. (2011). Emotions matter in crisis: The role of anger and sadness in the publics' response to crisis news framing and corporate crisis response. *Communication Research, 38*(6), 826–855. doi: 10.1177/0093650210385813

Laczniak, R. N., DeCarlo, T. E., & Ramaswami, S. N. (2001). Consumers' responses to negative word-of-mouth communication: An attribution theory perspective. *Journal of Consumer Psychology, 11*(1), 57–73. doi: 10.1207/S15327663JCP1101_5

Lee, J. Y., & Sundar, S. S. (2013). To tweet or to retweet? That is the question for health professionals on Twitter. *Health Communication, 28*(5), 509–524. doi: 10.1080/10410236.2012.700391

Li, A. (2014, March 28). Chinese online travel agencies ban Malaysia Airlines ticket sales. *South China Morning Post.* Retrieved from http://www.scmp.com/news/china-insider/article/1459124/chinese-online-travel-agencies-ban-malaysia-airlines-ticket-sales

Malaysia Airlines. (2014). Latest media statements & information on MH370. Retrieved from http://www.malaysiaairlines.com/my/en/site/mh370.html

Malaysia Airlines losses worsen on MH370 disappearance. (2014, May 16). *BBC.* Retrieved from http://www.bbc.com/news/business-27435455

Ng, E., & Chan, K. (2014, August 29). Malaysia Airlines to cut 6,000 staff in overhaul. *Associated Press.* Retrieved from http://bigstory.ap.org/article/malaysia-airlines-cut-6000-staff-overhaul

Pew Research Center. (2014, March). Nearly half of public says "right amount" of Malaysian Jet coverage. Retrieved from http://www.people-press.org/2014/03/24/nearly-half-of-public-says-right-amount-of-malaysian-jet-coverage/

Richins, M. L. (1984). Word of mouth communication as negative information. *Advances in Consumer Research, 11*(1), 697–702.

Schultz, F., Utz, S., & Göritz, A. (2011). Is the medium the message? Perceptions of and reactions to crisis communication via Twitter, blogs and traditional media. *Public Relations Review, 3*(1), 20–27. doi: 10.1016/j.pubrev.2010.12.001

Semetko, H. A., & Valkenburg, P. M. (2000). Framing European politics: A content analysis of press and television news. *Journal of Communication, 50*(2), 93–109. doi: 10.1093/joc/50.2.93

Shaver, P., Schwartz, J., Kirson, D., & O'Connor, C. (1987). Emotion knowledge: Further exploration of a prototype approach. *Journal of Personality and Social Psychology, 52*(6), 1061–1086. doi: 10.1037/0022-3514.52.6.1061

Tilley, J. (2014, March 21). Analysis: Malaysia Airlines' mishandled response to the MH370 crisis. *PR Week.* Retrieved from http://www.prweek.com/article/1286333/analysis-malaysia-airlines-mishandled-response-mh370-crisis

Wang, C. L., Li, D., Barnes, B. R., & Ahn, J. (2012). Country image, product image and consumer purchase intention: Evidence from an emerging economy. *International Business Review, 21*(6), 1041–1051. doi: 10.1016/j.ibusrev.2011.11.010

Wise, K., Bolls, P., Myers, J., & Sternadori, M. (2009). When words collide online: How writing style and video intensity affect cognitive processing of online news. *Journal of Broadcasting & Electronic Media, 53*(4), 532–546. doi: 10.1080/08838150903333023

Yu, L. L., Asur, S., & Huberman, B. A. (2012). *Artificial inflation: The real story of trends and trend-setters in Sina Weibo.* Proceedings from the 2012 IEEE International Conference on Social Computing (pp. 514–519). Amsterdam, The Netherlands: IEEE International

Zara, C. (2014, March 27). Cable news ratings: MH370 obsession boosts CNN and Fox News, while Al Jazeera America avoids indulgent coverage. *International Business Times.* Retrieved from http://www.ibtimes.com/cable-news-ratings-mh370-obsession-boosts-cnn-fox-news-while-al-jazeera-america-avoids-indulgent

SECTION IV-B

Areas of Application

Nonprofit

16

NONPROFIT ORGANIZATIONS' USE OF SOCIAL MEDIA IN CRISIS COMMUNICATION

Melony Shemberger

Introduction

When social networking sites such as MySpace and Facebook began allowing organizations to open accounts, create profiles, and become active members, organizations quickly embedded the practice into their communication plans and public relations efforts. For-profits especially have used social media to launch their products and build support for their brand. Nonprofit organizations also have been using social media for a variety of functions, including fundraising and community interaction.

Nonprofits are attracted to social media more than to traditional communication venues such as newspapers, television, and radio. Websites also might be included on this list. Prior studies (e.g., Kent, Taylor, & White, 2003; Saxton, Guo, & Brown, 2007) have shown that nonprofit organizations have not been able to use websites as strategic, interactive stakeholder engagement tools, perhaps due to a lack of knowledge or staff. Consequently, newer social media applications present communication opportunities—for example, quicker message dissemination, audience interaction, and immediate updates—that differ dramatically from organizationally supported websites (Lovejoy & Saxton, 2012).

In times of trouble, nonprofits are turning to social media to connect more immediately and closely with their audience. Social networking sites are the new crisis paradigm for nonprofits to reevaluate how they approach relationship development with their audience. For nonprofits especially, effective crisis management is vital. When a crisis does occur, social media can offer monitoring and communication solutions to disseminate information at a more rapid rate than most traditional media. This has been evident in the aftermath of the Boston Marathon bombings, as well as other highly visible crisis incidents involving nonprofits. These are explored later in this chapter.

Literature Review

The Internet revolutionized how both individuals and organizations communicate. Information from around the world became available on demand and provided the ability to connect with others around the globe with the advent of websites. Nonprofits, however, are finding they need interactivity that websites—characterized mostly as one-way, static communication—cannot provide. Social media applications, such as Facebook and Twitter, have changed the way the Internet is used. This section documents the process of how nonprofits have come to use and rely on social media and discusses the popularity that Twitter especially has had among the nonprofit sector.

Nonprofit organizations' use of social media as a crisis communication tool can be connected to the rise of technological advances, transforming how nonprofit leaders interact with and disseminate information to their audience and communities in a crisis situation. The evolution of the mobile phone, as well as other mobile technologies such as tablets, computers, Internet access, social media, and digital video equipment, has reshaped the communication network for nonprofit organizations.

Nonprofit organizations use social media to streamline their management functions, interact with volunteers and donors, and educate others about their programs and services (Waters, 2009). Although these kinds of messages are simple, the demands for organizations to be open and transparent on social networking sites have escalated, prompting nonprofits to achieve credibility and full disclosure in their online communication activities, including social media. For example, a nonprofit organization should use hyperlinks to connect to its website and provide logos and visual cues to establish the connection (Kelleher, 2006).

The adoption of social media appears to have created new paradigms of public engagement (Lovejoy & Saxton, 2012). Nearly every kind of organization—for-profit, government, civic, education, and nonprofit—uses a social networking site to inform, promote, or build customer or client relationships. Several studies (e.g., Kang & Norton, 2004; Kent et al., 2003; Lovejoy & Saxton, 2012; Waters, 2007) have confirmed these are the main reasons why organizations use social media. Information sharing might be the greatest reason. In their content analysis of 2,437 tweets made in a two-week period by 73 nonprofit organizations, Lovejoy and Saxton (2012) classified three functions of Twitter on a nonprofit-organizational level: information, community, and action. According to the results from the study, most messages, 59%, were classified as informational. The finding is consistent with prior research (Greenberg & MacAulay, 2009; Jansen, Zhang, Sobel, & Chowdury, 2009).

The strong adoption of social media does not mean that online technology has replaced the more traditional communication technologies in the workplace; rather, the use of digital tools is growing. In a 2009 survey, 17 workplace communication technologies were regarded as "mandatory" by 50% or more of respondents. Ten of those were computer mediated, including e-mail, the Internet, collaboration software, wikis, and Web teleconferencing (D'Urso & Pierce, 2009). Interactions between nonprofit organizations and shareholder interactions have become more critical to organizational performance (Lovejoy & Saxton, 2012).

Twitter appears to be the favorite social media outlet. Although Facebook has a larger range of functionality, Facebook statuses and tweets are so similar that many users, including nonprofits, send the same messages simultaneously on both sites. However, large charitable organizations are more likely than smaller organizations to have a significant presence on Twitter (Lovejoy & Saxton, 2012). This might be due to smaller organizations lacking the resources or time to provide attention to social media. No matter their size, however, nonprofits collectively have embraced Twitter, so much so that the social media tool has become a standard practice among them. These organizations prefer Twitter over Facebook and other social media that might offer a richer experience (Lovejoy & Saxton, 2012), but it is unclear as to why. As of now, there is no theory to help explain this adoption. Some theories have been discussed as possible explanations. For example, the media-richness theory (Daft & Lengel, 1986) orders communication technologies according to their ability to facilitate shared meaning. Other theories, such as critical mass (Markus, 1987) and social and institutional forces (Zorn, Flanagin, & Shoham, 2011), explain why organizations use Twitter but are unable to show why this particular venue is chosen over the others. As such, theories to explain the benefits of Twitter for organizational communication have yet to exist.

Studies (Hughes & Palen, 2009; Smith, 2010) have shown how Twitter can serve as a valuable communication and information-sharing resource during emergency relief efforts. Because information is a powerful tool during crises (Macias, Hilyard, & Freimuth, 2009), crisis communication messages can be classified as part of the information function of social media. It involves a one-way interaction, the exchange of information from the organization to the public (Lovejoy & Saxton, 2012). These messages are not designed to build a community or employ action, although such results could occur. The case studies explored next highlight the information function, although some of the messages also demonstrate a call to action.

Case Studies: Social Media Use in Action

Social media and digital advancements in technology have become critical components of emergency preparedness, response, and recovery (Homeland Security Science and Technology, 2013). Whereas nonprofit organizations are increasingly experimenting with social media before deciding whether to implement it into their crisis communication plan, some have embraced the technology with full throttle. Three nonprofit organizations that recently experienced crisis situations are featured in this section as case studies to help demonstrate how social media were used during a crisis. These were selected based on the timeliness of the crisis events. Plus, each organization's use of social media technology was a factor. Each case provides background information of the crisis event and explains the results or implications of their social media use.

Boston Athletic Association and the April 2013 Boston Marathon Bombings

More than 5,600 runners were not able to cross the finish line at the 117th Boston Marathon. At 2:49:43 p.m. Eastern time, April 15, 2013, right when the race clock approached the 4-hour, 10-minute mark, a bomb detonated on Boylston Street near the finish line. Thirteen seconds later, 550 feet from the first, a second bomb exploded. Three people were killed, including an eight-year-old boy, and more than 260 people—some whose limbs were severed—were injured.

As the events surrounding the Boston Marathon bombings unfolded, social media supplied timely information for many people. A quarter of Americans received information about the devastating explosions on social networking sites such as Facebook and Twitter, according to an April 2013 report from the Pew Research Center (Petrecca, 2013). The sites offered a convenient way to get news, especially because many users are constantly on them.

Many runners who carried their smartphones with them on the course had already learned about the bombs and knew the finish line had been suspended. As social media sites began to post graphic images and video from the explosions, the Boston Athletic Association (BAA) launched its communication plan to keep runners and their families informed.

Twitter and Facebook enabled the BAA to communicate directly with runners and the public. Race officials had to relocate the bag pickup and family meeting areas, while working to determine if there would be a postrace party for the finishers. Most likely, this kind of information would not have been broadcast on mainstream media, such as radio and television. Trying to relay this information through volunteers would have been cumbersome and time-consuming, not to mention messages would have been distorted through all the various transfers.

After the bombings occurred, the BAA race organizers gathered as much information as it could from reliable sources and disseminated simple messages via the organization's Facebook and Twitter accounts. See Box 16.1 to view some of the messages that the BAA sent throughout the day after the bomb explosions.

BOX 16.1 BOSTON MARATHON SOCIAL MEDIA MESSAGES SENT BY THE BAA MOMENTS AFTER THE BOMBINGS ON APRIL 15, 2013

There were two bombs that exploded near the finish line in today's Boston Marathon. We are working with law enforcement to understand what exactly has happened.

The Family Meeting Area has been moved to Boston Common. Runners are being directed there to meet friends and family. City of Boston assets have been deployed to assist runners at the Common.

Streets within the Back Bay, including those of our post-race area remain under lock down. If you're a runner in today's race unable to retrieve your bag from a baggage bus in Back Bay, you will not be able to retrieve your bag today. It will remain in our secure possession and we will provide you more information as it becomes available.

Baggage Update

For runners looking to claim their bags—baggage claim is now open on Berkeley Street between Boylston Street and St. James Avenue. All unclaimed bags will remain secure. Stay posted for further details. Thank you for your patience.

Family meeting area—Boston Common. baggage claim is now open on Berkeley Street between Boylston Street and St. James Avenue.

Tonight's Post-Race Party has been cancelled.

Busses from Boston to Hopkinton are running. They are picking up on Stuart Street between Clarendon and Dartmouth.

Correction on baggage claim: Runner's bags can now be picked up on Berkeley Street, between St. James and Boylston. There are no bags at 101 Arlington Street.

The BAA's social media messages were brief, clear, honest, and timely, making social media a tool for collaboration. The organization first acknowledged a problem and then began the task of informing its audience after working with law enforcement and city employees.

A key feature of social media is the ability to facilitate group action. The messages were well received by the intended audience—runners and their families. Thousands of social media users also commented on BAA's Facebook posts or replied to the Twitter posts, but in a crisis situation, it might not be possible to respond to comments. It is more important for an organization to disseminate timely and accurate information rather than to try to maintain fan or follower interaction. However, if followers are asking similar questions or relaying concerns, it might be necessary for the organization to post updated information that would offer answers.

The Salvation Army and the May 2013 Tornado in Oklahoma

A series of deadly tornadoes in May 2013 ravaged central Oklahoma—claiming the lives of 49 people, injuring others, and causing more than $2 billion in property damage. On May 19, the first storm—with tornado strengths of EF3 and EF4—struck Cleveland, Lincoln, Oklahoma, and Pottawatomie counties. The next day, an EF5 tornado struck Cleveland and Oklahoma counties, as well as Grady and McClain counties. The third storm, the widest tornado in recorded history, struck on Canadian County on May 31.

When the Salvation Army of Arkansas and Oklahoma learned of the approaching storms, the agency took to Twitter, its handle @SalArmyAOK, beginning May 17 to warn residents of the developing weather: "This weekend could see some severe weather! Does your family know what the plan is in case of an emergency? Talk it over tonight!"

Then on May 19, the agency tracked the first storm and tweeted a number of messages: "Major storms in Oklahoma City/Edmond. Please let us know if you or anyone you know needs assistance. We are praying for you all," "Luther! Get in your shelters right now!" and "We are here to brave the storms with you. If you were affected by today's storms, please let us know how we can help!" On May 20, the Salvation Army used Twitter to express how the agency was helping tornado victims and to keep everyone updated on the current situation. Some of the tweets also asked followers to donate money to help recovery and relief efforts (see Box 16.2).

BOX 16.2 TWEETS BY THE SALVATION ARMY ON MAY 20, 2013, IN RESPONSE TO THE TORNADO IN OKLAHOMA

We've been responding through the night & we won't rest until our neighbors are cared for! Will you help us respond?

This event is not over. We are still tracking storms in Oklahoma right now. Stay alert, Oklahoma!

Text STORM to 80888 to donate $10 to the recovery and relief efforts in #Moore, Oklahoma.

If we haven't said it yet, we are overwhelmed by your support. Thank you so much!

Messages on the Salvation Army of Arkansas and Oklahoma's Facebook page were not posted as frequently as they were on Twitter, but the agency posted some of the same ones. In the hours and days after the devastations, the Salvation Army tweeted photos showing devastation and officials surveying the damage, victims hugging, and prayer circles. In addition, as donations poured in to the Salvation Army's command center, photos were shared.

According to a May 2, 2014 press release posted on its website, the Salvation Army raised $18.2 million from the public, corporate donors, and philanthropic organizations for response and recovery efforts (The Salvation Army, 2014). Of that total, the Salvation Army spent $2.4 million—more than 13%—on response operations, including the deployment of 28 mobile kitchens and the opening of a 100,000-square-foot distribution center. During response operations, the Salvation Army provided 389,037 meals, drinks, and snacks; 28,891 hours of employee and volunteer service; emotional and spiritual care to 14,728 individuals; and emergency financial aid to 3,681 families (31,208 individuals), with assistance such as gift cards, vouchers to Family Thrift Stores, and referrals for a variety of services. All the while, the Salvation Army continued to operate its regular programs and services, providing meals, emergency shelter, clothing, and energy assistance to residents in need who were not affected by the disasters.

The American Red Cross and Hurricane Sandy, October 2012

The American Red Cross has been helping disaster victims since 1881, but the organization recently has embraced Twitter as part of its crisis communication strategy. A prominent example of the agency's social media involvement was Hurricane Sandy, which made landfall on the East Coast on October 29, 2012. More than 3,200 people spent the night in 112 Red Cross shelters in nine states—New Jersey, New York, Pennsylvania, Connecticut, Rhode Island, Maryland, Delaware, Virginia, and Massachusetts.

The prior week, the Red Cross shared information on social media instructing residents to take simple steps to prepare for the superstorm. The agency urged people to secure shutters and homes, stock up on emergency and medical supplies, make sure generators worked, and find possible safe haven if in flood-prone areas: "If you need a safe place to stay, shelter info avail. in #Hurricane app . . . #Sandy."

The hashtag #Sandy was typed more than 4 million times by hundreds of thousands of users. In addition to #Sandy, the hashtag #hurricane was used. The Red Cross not only posted its own tweets but also retweeted posts from other organizations such as the Federal Emergency Management Agency and the Weather Channel to help spread important messages.

At the height of the storm, the Red Cross's social media command center in Washington, DC, processed 27,000 pieces of social data per hour (American Red Cross, 2013). In November 2012, it touched 2.5 million pieces of social data mentioning the Red Cross or storm aid (Prosinski, 2014). Of these messages, 229 were sent to mass care teams, and 88 resulted in responders shifting the focus of on-ground operations (American Red Cross, 2013).

In addition, social media can be used to encourage donations and collect funding and support. The Red Cross used social media to encourage collective action toward more funding during emergencies (Wendling, Radisch, & Jacobzone, 2013). The Red Cross's audience also helped through social media by calling or posting tweets to the Red Cross on ways to aid victims. Audience interaction was key to the Red Cross's social media operation.

The Red Cross extended its digital presence with its free hurricane app, which had more than 400,000 downloads in October. The app, promoted through social media and traditional media, gave real-time hurricane safety information at users' fingertips. Users also accessed the app to receive weather alerts and get information on Red Cross shelters. The app also featured a tool kit with a flashlight, strobe light, and alarm, and the one-touch "I'm Safe" button allowed individuals use social media outlets to tell family and friends they were well.

Practical Guidelines and Tips

Each of the three case studies showed that social media are highly viable digital tools to disseminate emergency messages. In addition, the concepts of developing relationships and fundraising were evident. Of course, social media use in the three case studies was handled by large organizations that have resources available to oversee the social media function. However, any organization, agency, or unit can incorporate Twitter, Facebook, or other social media tools into a crisis communication plan.

Using social media to educate the public regarding risks, encourage support of an organization or cause, and establish an online venue for open dialogue are all approaches to incorporating social media in crisis communication plans. However, the challenges in the use of social media in risk and crisis communication must be considered and taken into account when developing social media strategies (Wendling et al., 2013). Social media use in crisis communication must be handled with care. Financial issues, legal issues, political issues, and security concerns should be at the forefront when developing the use of social media in emergencies.

The following guidelines offer checklists and tips to help nonprofit organization leaders answer some of these core questions: How will the organization keep people updated on what is happening, when it is happening? What hashtags can be used to help connect people to timely information? What easy ways can people access to donate and pitch in at any given moment?

Best Practices: Using Social Media in a Crisis

For social media to work in a crisis communication plan, organizations need to understand how social media can help leverage situations. Here are some guidelines, presented in a prioritized manner, to follow when considering the inclusion of social media:

1. Look through the crisis communication plan for ways to use social media as an effective communication channel to employees, key third parties, customers, and stakeholders.
2. Decide which social media networks will be most useful for crisis communication. Many organizations use Facebook, Twitter, Google+, Pinterest, and others as part of their marketing tactics. Most organizations have found that Facebook and Twitter work best to disseminate messages in times of a crisis or emergency.
3. Select one or two social media networks that personnel are most comfortable using. Having more than two networks is possible; however, because time is of the essence in crisis communication, the ability to access a social media account and send a message is crucial.
4. Make sure that all involved in the social media component of the crisis communication plan are trained to handle the technology (e.g., social media apps on smartphones, tablets) and manage messages relevant to the audience and situation. Although interaction between the organization and audience might be limited during a crisis because of the immediacy factor in posting messages, it is helpful for an employee to monitor comments posted by the public to gauge concerns.
5. Consider the more likely crisis and risk scenarios to determine if social media could be used to facilitate crisis identification, internal and external communications, and recovery coordination efforts.
6. Avoid information overload when sending messages during an emergency. During a crisis, the number of information exchanges through social media can be so high that it becomes impossible to have a clear picture of what is happening.
7. Choose a hashtag that is simple and does not confuse an audience. Have others to review it for feedback and modification.
8. Keep in touch with those population segments not familiar with social media. The elderly, the disabled, people who do not speak the local language, and other groups might not be able to access the data provided by social media. Traditional media, primarily television and radio, are still vital, so press releases or press conferences can be methods of transferring information to news media, which then can disseminate it to the public.
9. Assess the impact of social media after the crisis communication event has minimized or dissolved. Because people follow social media differently and for various reasons, nonprofit organizations might consider conducting surveys of the populations they serve for a clearer look at the effectiveness of their social media efforts.

Social media can enable any organization to identify and respond to crisis events. When a crisis does occur, social media can offer monitoring and communication solutions to disseminate information at a more rapid rate than most traditional media. Used strategically and as part of an overall communication mix, social media can add depth, breadth, and speed to crisis communication efforts.

Conclusion

The use of social media in crisis communication remains in its infancy (Wendling et al., 2013). As communication technology diversifies, social media use will increase in times of crises to send warnings, issue updates, and conduct awareness. For some nonprofit organizations, social media seem to be more effective dialogic communication tools than a website or other traditional methods. This does not mean that traditional news media, such as television and radio, and other technology, including sirens, should be replaced or discontinued. Rather, these tactics must have a strong presence in the crisis communication plan. In fact, some of these tools, such as sirens, can work with social media, so any possible interaction with social media merits attention.

Nevertheless, Facebook and Twitter, as well as a host of other sophisticated social media applications, have enabled nonprofits to implement them in their crisis communication plans and use them at critical moments quickly. The three case studies illustrated this. Plus, social media communication is more individual and less massive, giving a nonprofit's message the potential for a greater impact on behavioral changes (Wendling et al., 2013).

Preparation is key. Nonprofits need to think about how social media can fit into their crisis communication plan, in much the same way they might already use the tools to build relationships or raise money. Although the decision to add social media to the crisis communication mix must be made according to the means and resources available to a nonprofit organization, not doing anything is no longer an option.

References

American Red Cross. (2012). Thousands look to Red Cross for shelter from Sandy. *Press release*. Retrieved from http://www.redcross.org/news/press-release/Thousands-Look-to-Red-Cross-For-Shelter-from-Sandy

American Red Cross. (2013). FirstToSee: Leveraging social media for emergency response. Retrieved from http://first2see.org/wp-content/uploads/2013/05/FirstToSee-System-White-Paper-Final-06212013.pdf

Daft, R. L., & Lengel, R. H. (1986). Organizational information requirements, media richness, and structural determinants. *Management Science, 32*, 554–571.

D'Urso, S. C., & Pierce, K. M. (2009). Connected to the organization: A survey of communication technologies in the modern organizational landscape. *Communication Research Reports, 26*, 75–81.

Greenberg, J., & MacAulay, M. (2009). NPO 2.0? Exploring the Web presence of environmental nonprofit organizations in Canada. *Global Media Journal-Canadian Edition, 2*, 63–88.

Homeland Security Science and Technology. (2013). Lessons learned: Social media and Hurricane Sandy. Retrieved from http://www.ghinternational.com/docs/DHS_VSMWG_Lessons_Learned_Social_Media_and_Hurricane_Sandy_Formatted_June_2013_FINAL.pdf

Hughes, A. L., & Palen, L. (2009). Twitter adoption and use in mass convergence and emergency events. *International Journal of Emergency Management, 6,* 248–260.

Jansen, B., Zhang, M., Sobel, K., & Chowdury, A. (2009). Twitter power: Tweets as electronic word of mouth. *JASIST, 60,* 2169–2188.

Kang, S., & Norton, H. E. (2004). Nonprofit organizations' use of the World Wide Web: Are they sufficiently fulfilling organizational goals? *Public Relations Review, 30,* 279–284.

Kelleher, T. (2006). *Public relations online: Lasting concepts for changing media.* Thousand Oaks, CA: Sage.

Kent, M. L., Taylor, M., & White, W. J. (2003). The relationship between Web site design and organizational responsiveness to stakeholders. *Public Relations Review, 29,* 63–77.

Lovejoy, K., & Saxton, G. D. (2012). Information, community, and action: How nonprofit organizations use social media. *Journal of Computer-Mediated Communication, 17*(3), 337–353. Retrieved from http://ssrn.com/abstract=2039815

Macias, W., Hilyard, K., & Freimuth, V. (2009). Blog functions as risk and crisis communication during Hurricane Katrina. *Journal of Computer-Mediated Communication, 15,* 1–31.

Markus, M. L. (1987). Toward a "critical mass" theory of interactive media: Universal access, interdependence and diffusion. *Communication Research, 14,* 491–511.

Petrecca, L. (2013, April 23). After bombings, social media informs (and misinforms). *USA Today.* Retrieved from http://www.usatoday.com/story/news/2013/04/23/social-media-boston-marathon-bombings/2106701/

Prosinski, S. (2014). Red Cross offers key lessons in crisis communications. Retrieved from http://www.prdaily.com/Main/Articles/Red_Cross_offers_key_lessons_in_crisis_communicati_15887.aspx#

The Salvation Army. (2014). Salvation Army marks one-year anniversary of 2013 central Oklahoma tornadoes [Press release]. Retrieved from http://www.salvationarmyusa.org/usn/news/Salvation_Army_Marks_One_Year_Anniversary_of_2013_Central_Oklahoma_Tornadoes

Saxton, G. D., Guo, C., & Brown, W. (2007). New dimensions of nonprofit responsiveness: The application and promise of Internet-based technologies. *Public Performance and Management Review, 31,* 144–173.

Smith, B. G. (2010). Socially distributing public relations: Twitter, Haiti, and interactivity in social media. *Public Relations Review, 36,* 329–335.

Waters, R. D. (2007). Nonprofit organizations' use of the Internet: A content analysis of communication trends on the Internet sites of the organizations on the Philanthropy 400. *Nonprofit Management & Leadership, 18,* 59–76.

Waters, R. D. (2009). The use of social media by nonprofit organizations: An examination from the diffusion of innovations perspective. In T. Dumova & R. Fiordo (Eds.), *Handbook of research on social interaction technologies and collaboration software: Concepts and trends* (pp. 473–485). Hershey, PA: IGI Publishing.

Wendling, C., Radisch, J., & Jacobzone, S. (2013). The use of social media in risk and crisis communication. *OECD Working Papers on Public Governance, No. 25.* OECD Publishing. http://dx.doi.org/10.1787/5k3v01fskp9s-en

Zorn, T. E., Flanagin, A. J., & Shoham, M. D. (2011). Institutional and noninstitutional influences on information and communication technology adoption and use among nonprofit organizations. *Human Communication Research, 37,* 1–33.

17

WORLD VISION'S LACK OF VISION

A Case Study of the 2014 Gay Hiring Crisis

Nance McCown

In March 2014, World Vision, a Christian humanitarian nonprofit organization (NPO) offering aid to children, families, and communities in more than 100 countries, jumped feetfirst into one of Christianity's most hotly debated issues of the 21st century: homosexuality. Within just two days' time, the NPO first announced and then reversed its decision to hire employees involved in legal, same-sex marriages, creating a firestorm of social media response, particularly on Twitter and in the blogosphere. Unfortunately, World Vision seemed ill prepared for both the initial response and the aftermath, violating even the most basic principles of appropriate social media usage and public relations best practice.

This chapter explores the interplay of nonprofit social media usage with crisis communication theories and models through an examination of World Vision's crisis preparation, response, and postcrisis discourse and actions.

Relevant Literature

Prior to delving into the World Vision case itself, some background understanding of NPOs, social media usage, and crisis communication theory provides context.

Impact of Use of Social Media on NPOs

Since social media's inception, NPOs have recognized their communicative value in engaging publics. As Breakenridge notes, social media as a public relations tool allow organizations to "hear first hand customer comments, concerns, and insights into what influences their thinking and decision-making" (2008, p. 257). Specifically, those NPOs relying most heavily on public donations are most likely to engage in social media use (Nah & Saxton, 2013). But exactly what sort of engagement do they employ?

Although NPOs often include social media in their strategic and tactical campaigns, most continue to use these online communication channels primarily as information-dissemination tools. Frequently, they employ one-way communication strategies—the public information model of public relations (Grunig & Hunt, 1984)—rather than taking full advantage of social media's dialogic nature and two-way symmetrical relationship-building possibilities (Cho, Schweickart, & Haase, 2014; Curtis et al., 2010; Lovejoy & Saxton, 2012; Waters & Jamal, 2011). In recent years, several studies have explored NPO usage of prominent social media channels.

Not surprisingly, publics respond positively to a variety of NPO Facebook status update types (information sharing, promotion and mobilization, and community building) but are "more likely to engage with organizations when they use community-building updates" (Saxton & Waters, 2014). Similarly, publics more frequently engage (i.e., comment on posts) when NPOs employ two-way symmetrical (Grunig & Hunt, 1984) Facebook communication strategies because those messages more successfully foster dialogue (Cho et al, 2014). However, two-way asymmetrical posts, despite their intention to encourage conversation through public-opinion sharing or response, do not result in public engagement, possibly due to the fact that "publics are savvy enough to distinguish between whether organizations are trying to build a relationship with them and taking advantage of the social relationship opportunities afforded on Facebook" (Cho et al, 2014, p. 567).

Turning to Twitter, trends remain the same. For example, NPOs most often used Twitter to adopt the one-way public information model of public relations (Grunig & Hunt, 1984), and when they tweeted using two-way communication, it was more often asymmetrical in nature, such as invitations for public participation in surveys or polls or public support through volunteerism or donations. "Rather than capitalizing on the interactive nature and dialogic capabilities of the social media service, nonprofit organizations are primarily using Twitter as a means of sharing information instead of relationship building" (Waters & Jamal, 2011, p. 323). However, some researchers posit that although public relations research has long suggested that dialogic communication "is the pinnacle of organizational communication . . . it may be that dialogue is simply one essential piece of the communication puzzle, and that information may always be the 'base' form of communication" (Lovejoy & Saxton, 2012, p. 349). Thus, the presently lopsided, one-way communication prevalence of NPOs' informational tweets should not be surprising.

In recent years, NPOs have incorporated blogs into the mainstream of their social media efforts. The American Red Cross, for example, uses blogs to foster stakeholder conversations and deliver to-the-moment updates (Briones, Kuch, Liu, & Jin, 2011). In addition, publics see NPOs' blogs as more credible, transparent, and inviting of dialogue than other social media channels (Sweetser, Porter, Chung, & Kim, 2008). For both organizational blogs and independently written blogs about NPO-related topics, nonprofits should monitor blog conversations closely to "listen, observe, participate (with appropriate reactions), and answer questions" (Solis & Breakenridge, 2010, p. 237).

Religious NPOs and Social Media

Because of World Vision's status as a faith-based nonprofit, research in this particular realm provides helpful background. However, relatively few studies have delved specifically into the area of religious NPOs' use of social media. Most often, scholars researching social media have not broken down their findings into NPO categories (i.e., health care, arts and education, religious). Exceptions include Malvini (2009) and Mano (2014). First, the more nonprofits use Internet communication (including social media), the more their publics engage in online donations; also, an individual's "faith has no effect on the level of online monetary contributions, but increases the offline level" (Mano, 2014, p. 290). Second, a religious health care NPO used a variety of communication channels (print, online, and face to face) to emphasize its spiritual mission; study results demonstrated mission communication primarily through the website and company intranet, with little reference to social media (Malvini, 2009).

Crisis Communication and Social Media

Beyond general social media usage, background regarding crisis communication and social media strategies provides critical foundation for the World Vision case study analysis. Several key theories and practical principles lend insight and offer best practices for use of social media in crisis communication engagement.

Early communication-based approaches to crises still relevant to this case study include corporate apologia (particularly Hearit, 1995, 2006) and image restoration theory (IRT; Benoit, 1995). In corporate apologia, organizations attempt to restore their "social legitimacy" through apology, thereby protecting their reputations. Of note, organizations use the act-essence dissociation strategy to recognize responsibility in the crisis but ask for publics' forgiveness for the isolated incident (Hearit, 1995). IRT strategies include denial, evading responsibility (specifically through noting good intentions of the organization), reducing offensiveness (especially bolstering through highlighting past successes), taking corrective action (to return to precrisis status), and implementing mortification (admission of guilt, expression of concern, and asking for forgiveness; Benoit, 1995).

Sharing some similarities with apologia and IRT, situational crisis communication theory (SCCT) links potential crisis responses with an organization's crisis responsibility. When used appropriately, the four response postures—denial, diminishment (particularly excusing by noting no intent to harm), rebuilding (particularly apologizing), and bolstering (reminding publics of past successes)—help with organizational reputation repair (Coombs, 1999, 2009, 2014, 2015). Several studies have analyzed NPOs' usage of SCCT strategies. Notably, an experiment testing SCCT in nonprofit scenarios found "if a nonprofit organization responds correctly to a crisis, then it has a greater likelihood of preserving the public's favor and sustaining the public's engagement in the future" (Sisco, 2012a, p. 13). In another study, Sisco (2012b) determined that now-defunct NPO Association of Community Organizations for Reform Now (ACORN) did not apply SCCT strategies appropriately, which may have contributed significantly to its demise.

In addition to SCCT strategies, Coombs suggests "four basic rules when using online crisis communication channels: (1) be present, (2) be where the action is, (3) be there before the crisis, and (4) be polite" (2015, p. 28). Coombs also notes that organizations should continue to use social media to provide updates and follow-up information postcrisis.

However, complex social media and online channels display complex communication patterns, often muddying organization-publics engagement during crises. Organizations may share information and even invite publics' engagement through Facebook, Twitter, organizational blogs, and other social media channels, but online third parties (whether bloggers, news sites, or even individuals) add to the complexity. To better explain this web of communication interaction, the social-mediated crisis communication (SMCC) model provides additional framework for the World Vision case study. The model suggests that during crises, publics use social media for three purposes: to determine relevance of issues, to seek and share information, and to find emotional support or space for emotional venting (Jin & Liu, 2010). Beyond that, the two-part model (Jin & Liu, 2010; Liu, Jin, Briones, & Kuch, 2012) first details crisis information source and form. In addition to the organization itself, other entities serve as crisis information sources: influential social media creators (individuals or other organizations), social media followers (consumers of the creators' information), and social media inactives (indirect consumers, either individuals or traditional media, accessing crisis information through relationships with social media creators or followers). Regarding crisis information form, the authors explain three transmission options: traditional media, social media, and offline, word-of-mouth communication (Liu et. al, 2012). Applying the SMCC model, organizational crisis managers may choose the most appropriate means of crisis communication by understanding publics' potential acceptance of the response strategies based on crisis information source and form.

Testing the SMCC model, researchers connected SMCC to Coombs's SCCT (1999, 2009, 2014, 2015), with findings demonstrating the clear need for crisis managers to tie crisis information source and form during crisis response. (For a more complete explanation, see Liu, Austin, & Jin, 2011.) Specific to the World Vision case study, the model found publics more likely to accept certain types of organizational crisis responses when learned through the following sources:

- defensive or evasive responses: directly from the organization in crisis via traditional media;

- supportive responses: from a third party via traditional media; and
- accommodative responses: directly from the organization in crisis via word of mouth (Liu et al., 2011).

One final testing of the SMCC model revealed that publics preferred traditional media over social media when seeking information during a crisis (Austin, Liu, & Jin, 2012), likely because of traditional media's perceived credibility over social media. In that study, publics did not use blogs or Twitter during the crisis, although they did use Facebook and text messages. In contrast, previous research (Bates & Callison, 2008) noted publics' perception of social media credibility was higher during crises, particularly for those already highly engaged with social media.

Crisis Communication Application: World Vision

On March 24, 2014, World Vision president Richard Stearns gave an exclusive interview with popular Christian publication *Christianity Today* (*CT*) announcing the organization's decision to hire employees involved in legal, same-sex marriages (Gracey & Weber, 2014a). With staffers hailing from more than 50 Christian denominations—many of which authorize same-sex marriage—World Vision continued its long-standing practice of deferring theological issues to individual churches (Gracey & Weber, 2014a). Citing a desire to create an equality-based employment policy "more consistent with our practice on other divisive issues," Stearns added that the organization's decision was not a rejection of the traditional definition of marriage nor an endorsement of same-sex marriage (Gracey & Weber, 2014a). Public response was swift, immediate, and viral as social media, blogs, and online news sites hosted heated discussions, appeals to scriptures, and vitriolic arguments. Why the buzz? As a Christian organization with a large evangelical donor base, World Vision had stepped, albeit after 10 years of decision-making prayer by its board (Portella, 2014), straight into one of the Christian church's most divisive issues: homosexuality and gay marriage.

The response from all sides—gay and straight, professing Christians and atheists, prominent evangelical leaders and notable bloggers? Multifaceted and loud, at least in terms of social media volume. A sampling of posts included the following:

- The #worldvision problem is a perfect example of why people outside the church thnk [*sic*] Christians are idiots ("Pilar," Twitter, 11:24 p.m., March 24, 2014).
- Hey #WorldVision—"It is far more important to be divided by truth than be united by error."—John MacArthur #fb ("Dan," Twitter, 9:46 p.m., March 24, 2014).
- Proud to be unlikeing [*sic*] you today and canceling my world vision child sponsorship. I'll continue to support Christian organizations that follow my personal beliefs . . . just like everyone else is entitled to do ("Amy," Facebook, March 24, 2014).

- My view is that as Christians, we should be willing to partner with anyone wanting to advance our call to help the poor. You have 13 sexual partners each week but you want to help me build a school in Haiti? Alright. Get your work shoes on (Howerton, Rage Against the Minivan blog, 2014).

Basic crisis communication principles (i.e., Coombs, 1999, 2015; Fearn-Banks, 2007) promote proactive thinking and planning regarding an organization's potential crisis situations. Yet research has revealed NPOs as woefully unprepared for crisis communication, even when they have experienced past crises (Schwarz & Pforr, 2011). World Vision is no different, appearing to have lacked any communication plans regarding handling responses related to its announcement. In fact, in his initial *CT* interview, Stearns simply appealed to sponsor goodwill and desire for unity:

> I don't want to predict the reaction we will get. I think we've got a very persuasive series of reasons for why we're doing this, and it's my hope that all of our donors and partners will understand it, and will agree with our exhortation to unite around what unites us. But we do know this is an emotional issue in the American church. I'm hoping not to lose supporters over the change. We're hoping that they understand that what we've done is focused on church unity and our mission. (Gracey & Weber, 2014b)

Measured against crisis communication best practices, World Vision's lack of contingency planning for the debacle that ensued fell short, particularly given the organization's historically well-developed communication program. After all, the organization was already (and continues to be) "there [in the social media space] before the crisis" (Coombs, 2015, p. 28). Portella sums up effectively, "The most shocking thing . . . is that World Vision—an organization with sophisticated donor relations and communication teams—seems to have been caught completely off-guard" (n.p., 2014).

Publics shared this perspective. World Vision's lack of common sense in its communication approach was equally reprehensible, in part because publics felt excluded in the decision-making process and rightly recognized the organization's communication naïveté, even when the organization did not. Prominent blogger Jen Hatmaker noted,

> I would have preferred Stearns admit that they absolutely know they will lose some supporters and weighed that cost soberly, they have X amount in the bank to cover the initial losses so the shortfall doesn't get passed down to the least culpable here—the kids—and offer a gracious way out. To change a policy that knowingly offends the majority of his base without acknowledging their established theology or making any concessions for their conscience was unfair and passive aggressive. (Hatmaker, 2014)

Within days of World Vision's initial announcement, more than 10,000 children had lost their supporters (Weiseth, 2014), leaving the organization reeling from this unanticipated stakeholder backlash. And less than 48 hours after its initial decision, World Vision reversed its policy, apologized for creating further division among Christians, asked for forgiveness, and cited significant financial losses and a desire to put the children it serves first (See Figure 17.1).

In a letter published by *CT* appealing to both stakeholder goodwill and the organization's past good works, Stearns noted,

> Rather than creating more unity [among Christians], we created more division, and that was not the intent. Our board acknowledged that the policy change we made was a mistake . . . and we believe that [World Vision supporters] helped us to see that with more clarity . . . and we're asking you to forgive us for that mistake. (Gracey & Weber, 2014b)

Stearns also stated, "We did inadequate consultation with supporters and others. If I could have a do-over on one thing, I would have had much more consultation with Christian leaders" (Gracey & Weber, 2014b).

How does World Vision's crisis response mesh with crisis communication theory and principles? A closer review of World Vision's decision reversal and apology letter (see Figure 17.1) reveals a number of theory-practice connections. First, following apologia's act-essence dissociation strategy (Hearit, 1995, 2006), World Vision admitted responsibility for the crisis and appealed to its supporters for forgiveness (paragraph 1, sentence 2; paragraph 2, sentence 3). Second, the organization enacted several IRT strategies (Benoit, 1995), including evading responsibility by noting its good intentions (paragraph 3, sentence 1); reducing offensiveness through bolstering tactics, such as pointing out the many children it has helped in the past (paragraph 6, mission statement); taking corrective action to reverse its decision (paragraph 1); and implementing mortification by taking responsibility, expressing concern, and asking for forgiveness (paragraphs 1–4). Third, SCCT (Coombs, 1999, 2009, 2014, 2015) also helps to explain some of World Vision's responses, most notably diminishment (excusing itself by noting no intent to harm; paragraph 4, sentence 2), rebuilding through apology (paragraph 1, sentence 2; paragraph 2, sentence 3), and as mentioned with IRT, bolstering through appeals to past successes (paragraph 6, mission statement). Theoretically, these strategies should have helped World Vision preserve public favor and sustain (or, in this case, regain) public engagement and support (Sisco, 2012a). However, as with World Vision's initial announcement, publics' responses to its decision reversal were rampant, emotional, and mixed, as evidenced by these samples:

- I applaud World Vision for reversing its poor decision and returning to biblical standards. It is, after all, a Christian organization. As such, it is morally

World Vision U.S. Board Reverses Decision

Dear Friends,

Today, the World Vision U.S. board publicly reversed its recent decision to change our employment conduct policy. The board acknowledged they made a mistake and chose to revert to our longstanding conduct policy requiring sexual abstinence for all single employees and faithfulness within the Biblical covenant of marriage between a man and a woman.

We are writing to you our trusted partners and Christian leaders who have come to us in the spirit of Matthew 18 to express your concern in love and conviction. You share our desire to come together in the Body of Christ around our mission to serve the poorest of the poor. We have listened to you and want to say thank you and to humbly ask for your forgiveness.

In our board's effort to unite around the church's shared mission to serve the poor in the name of Christ, we failed to be consistent with World Vision U.S.'s commitment to the traditional understanding of Biblical marriage and our own Statement of Faith, which says, *"We believe the Bible to be the inspired, the only infallible, authoritative Word of God."* And we also failed to seek enough counsel from our own Christian partners. As a result, we made a change to our conduct policy that was not consistent with our Statement of Faith and our commitment to the sanctity of marriage.

We are brokenhearted over the pain and confusion we have caused many of our friends, who saw this decision as a reversal of our strong commitment to Biblical authority. We ask that you understand that this was never the board's intent. We are asking for your continued support. We commit to you that we will continue to listen to the wise counsel of Christian brothers and sisters, and we will reach out to key partners in the weeks ahead.

While World Vision U.S. stands firmly on the biblical view of marriage, we strongly affirm that all people, regardless of their sexual orientation, are created by God and are to be loved and treated with dignity and respect.

Please know that World Vision continues to serve all people in our ministry around the world. We pray that you will continue to join with us in our mission to be *"an international partnership of Christians whose mission is to follow our Lord and Savior Jesus Christ in working with the poor and oppressed to promote human transformation, seek justice, and bear witness to the good news of the Kingdom of God."*

Sincerely in Christ,

Richard Stearns, President

Jim Beré, Chairman of the World Vision U.S. Board

FIGURE 17.1 World Vision's Decision Reversal and Apology Letter

obligated to hold to God's standards, despite any politically correct pressure to the contrary ("Marla," Facebook, March 26, 2014).

- I sponsored a child because of [World Vision's] original decision . . . As a gay man, I am once again disappointed by the actions of some evangelical Christians. I have learned not to expect much from conservative Christianity and tend to give conservative Christians a wide berth. I want to reconcile. I am a graduate of Azusa Pacific University and remain a committed, Episcopalian, Christian. But I often feel like Charlie Brown when he tries to kick Lucy's football when engaging evangelical Christians and this is no exception. However, none of this is the fault of the child I sponsored. I'm not going to unsponsor because they reversed their decision. It's ultimately about the child's welfare ("Dan," in Evans, 2014).

Applying the SMCC model to the World Vision crisis is both easy and difficult. Clearly, publics used social media to determine issue relevance, seek and share information, and gain emotional support or participate in emotional venting (Jin & Liu, 2010). In addition, the rapid interplay and spread of the crisis information through influential social media creators, social media followers, and social media inactives offers support for the SMCC model (Jin & Liu, 2010; Liu et.al, 2012), as well as for prior research (regarding social media usage during crises, Bates & Callison, 2008). However, the speed with which the crisis escalated—within literally hours—and the difficulty of determining exact sources for users' first engagement with the crisis information muddy the crisis communication analysis. Although World Vision may have rightly matched its initial announcement to (online) traditional media (Austin et al., 2012) through the *CT* interview and article, its response letter reversing its decision is no longer to be found anywhere other than through a follow-up *CT* article, in direct opposition to research findings suggesting accommodative responses should come directly from the organization in crisis via word of mouth (Liu et al., 2011).

Moreover, within days of the crisis' escalation, World Vision deleted all references to the hiring policy change and reversal from all of its social media sites, including Facebook, Twitter, and its organizational blog, as well as its website. It's as though the organization is both denying the crisis ever took place and denying its publics the opportunity for continued engagement through the social media sphere. This practice obviously violates not only suggested best crisis communication practices set forth in the SMCC model (Liu et al., 2012) but also the coveted organizational transparency and engagement urged by best public relations and social media practices in general.

Current Status and Lessons Learned

Although the organization may have only fallen two spots—from 10 to 12—on the Forbes list of top U.S. charities (Barrett, 2013; The 100 largest U.S. charities, 2016),

World Vision did fall to number 26 (down from number 8 in 2009) on the Chronicle of Philanthropy's 2014 rankings of the 400 U.S. "charities collecting the most from private sources" (Hall, 2014); in 2016, the organization had regained a small bit of ground, coming in at 21 on the list (Philanthropy 400, 2016). Additionally, despite an overall drop in growth rate, the nonprofit reported "no decline in overall donations" in the first year following the hiring crisis (Bailey, 2014). The organization's board has undergone change as well, with the resignation of one member and term endings of several others; new board members and the new chair all hail from prominent evangelical organizations (Bailey, 2014), indicating the organization's continued accommodative response. Also, to strengthen connections with Evangelical leaders, World Vision created a Ministry Advisory Council as well as a peer advisory council for Stearns (Charisma, 2015), further demonstrating its desire for better understanding its publics.

Overall, World Vision's crisis communication and limited postcrisis discourse reveal a naïve knowledge of stakeholder values; a simplistic view of a complex issue; and a blatant disregard for public relations, social media, and crisis communication best practices. Moreover, the nonprofit's "head-in-the-sand" approach to crisis anticipation and continued risk for crisis recurrence demonstrate a need for thorough crisis planning and serve as prodromes to similar organizations. Refusal to engage its publics online and failure to remain committed to transparency reveal World Vision's lack of vision and may undermine future efforts the NPO may put forth to foster meaningful, dialogic conversation on any topic, not just the gay hiring issue.

References

The 100 largest U.S. charities (2016). Retrieved April 24, 2017, from https://www.forbes.com/top-charities/list/#tab:rank

Austin, L., Liu, B. F., & Jin, Y. (2012). How audiences seek out crisis information: Exploring the social-mediated crisis communication model. *Journal of Applied Communication Research*, *40*(2), 188–207.

Bailey, S. P. (2014). World Vision, recovering from gay policy shift, tries to shore up its evangelical base. *Religion News Service*. Retrieved from http://www.religionnews.com/2014/06/26/world-vision-recovering-from-gay-policy- shift-tries-to-shore-up-its-evangelical-base/ Retrieved 12.19.14

Barrett, W. P. (2013). The largest U.S. charities for 2013. *Forbes*. Retrieved 28 December, 2014 from www.forbes.com/sites/williampbarrett/2013/11/25/the-largest-u-s-charities-for-2013/

Bates, L., & Callison, C. (2008, August). *Effect of company affiliation on credibility in the blogosphere*. Paper presented at the Association for Education in Journalism and Mass Communication Conference, Chicago, IL.

Benoit, W. L. (1995). *Accounts, excuses, and apologies: A theory of image restoration*. Albany, NY: State University of New York Press.

Breakenridge, D. (2008). *PR 2.0: New media, new tools, new audiences*. Upper Saddle River, NJ: Pearson.

Briones, R. L., Kuch, B., Liu, B. F., & Jin, Y. (2011). Keeping up with the digital age: How the American Red Cross uses social media to build relationships. *Public Relations Review*, *37*(1), 37–43.

Cho, M., Schweickart, T., & Hasse, A. (2014). Public engagement with nonprofit organizations on Facebook. *Public Relations Review*, *40*, 565–567.

Coombs, W. T. (1999). *Ongoing crisis communication: Planning, managing, and responding* (1st ed.). Thousand Oaks, CA: Sage.

Coombs, W. T. (2009). Conceptualizing crisis communication. In R. L. Heath & H. D. O'Hair (Eds.), *Handbook of risk and crisis communication* (pp. 100–119). New York: Routledge.

Coombs, W. T. (2014). *Applied crisis communication and crisis management: Cases and exercises.* Thousand Oaks, CA: Sage.

Coombs, W. T. (2015). *Ongoing crisis communication: Planning, managing, responding* (4th ed.). Thousand Oaks, CA: Sage.

Curtis, L., Edwards, C., Fraser, K. L., Gudelsky, S., Holmquist, J., Thornton, K., & Sweetser, K. D. (2010). Adoption of social media for public relations by nonprofit organizations. *Public Relations Review*, *36*, 90–92.

Evans, R. H. (2014). World Vision update. *Rachel Held Evans blog*. Retrieved December 19, 2014, from http://rachelheldevans.com/blog/world-vision-update

Fearn-Banks, K. (2007). *Crisis communications: A casebook approach.* Mahwah, NJ: Erlbaum.

Gracey, C., & Weber, J. (2014a). World Vision: Why we're hiring gay Christians in same-sex marriages. *Christianity Today*. Retrieved December 19, 2014, from http://www.christianitytoday.com/ct/2014/march-web-only/world-vision-why-hiring-gay-christians-same-sex-marriage.html

Gracey, C., & Weber, J. (2014b). World Vision reverses decision to hire Christians in same-sex marriages. *Christianity Today*. Retrieved 19 December, 2014 from www.christianitytoday.com/ct/2014/march-web-only/world-vision-reverses-decision-gay-same-sex-marriage.html

Grunig, J. E., & Hunt, T. (1984). *Managing public relations.* New York: Holt, Rinehart, and Winston.

Hall, H. (2014). Shaking up the Ranks of America's Big Charities. *Chronicle of Philanthropy*. Retrieved 28 December, 2014 from http://philanthropy.com/article/Shaking-Up-the-Ranks-of/149479/

Hatmaker, J. (2014, March 25). World Vision, gay marriage, and a different way through. *Jen Hatmaker blog*. Retrieved 19 December, 2014 from http://jenhatmaker.com/blog/2014/03/25/world-vision-gay-marriage-and-a-different-way-through

Hearit, K. M. (1995). "Mistakes were made": Organizations, apologia, and crises of social legitimacy. *Communication Studies*, *46*, 1–17.

Hearit, K. M. (2006). *Crisis management by apology: Corporate response to allegations of wrongdoing.* Mahwah, NJ: Erlbaum.

Howerton, K. (2014, March 24). On World Vision, gay marriage, and taking a standing on the backs of starving children. *Rage against the minivan blog*. Retrieved 19 December, 2014 from www.rageagainsttheminivan.com/2014/03/on-world-vision-gay-marriage-and-taking.html

Jin, Y., & Liu, B. F. (2010). The blog-mediated crisis communication model: Recommendations for responding to influential external blogs. *Journal of Public Relations Research*, *22*, 429–455.

Liu, B. F., Austin, L., & Jin, Y. (2011). How publics respond to crisis communication strategies: The interplay of information form and source. *Public Relations Review, 37,* 345–353.

Liu, B. F., Jin, Y., Briones, R. L., & Kuch, B. (2012). Managing turbulence online: Evaluating the blog-mediated crisis communication model with the American Red Cross. *Journal of Public Relations Research, 24,* 353–370.

Lovejoy, K., & Saxton, G. D. (2012). Information, community, and action: How nonprofit organizations use social media. *Journal of Computer-Mediated Communication, 17*(3), 337–353.

Malvini, S. (2009, November). *In print, online, and in your face: Conceptualizing and communicating spiritual mission in a religious non-profit health care organization.* Paper presented at the annual meeting of the NCA 95th Annual Convention, Chicago. Retrieved 19 December, 2014 from http://citation.allacademic.com/meta/p365760_index.html

Mano, R. S. (2014). Social media, social causes, giving behavior, and money contributions. *Computers in Human Behavior, 31,* 287–293.

Nah, S., & Saxton, G. D. (2013). Modeling the adoption and use of social media by nonprofit organizations. *New Media & Society, 15,* 294–313.

Philanthropy 400. (2016). Chronicle of Philanthropy. Retrieved April 24, 2017, from https://www.philanthropy.com/interactive/philanthropy-400#id=table_2016

Portella, J. (2014). World Vision's flip-flop on hiring married gays shows a stunning lack of foresight. *The Chronicle of Philanthropy.* Retrieved 19 December, 2014 from http://philanthropy.com/article/World-Vision-s-Flip-Flop-on/145645/

Saxton, G. D., & Waters, R. D. (2014). What do stakeholders like on Facebook? Examining public reactions to nonprofit organization's informational, promotional, and community-building messages. *Journal of Public Relations Research, 26,* 280–299.

Schwarz, A., & Pforr, F. (2011). The crisis communication preparedness of nonprofit organizations: The case of German interest groups. *Public Relations Review, 37,* 68–70.

Sisco, H. F. (2012a). Nonprofit in crisis: An examination of the applicability of Situational Crisis Communication Theory. *Journal of Public Relations Research, 24,* 1–17.

Sisco, H. F. (2012b). The ACORN story: An analysis of crisis response strategies in a nonprofit organization. *Public Relations Review, 38,* 89–96.

Solis, B., & Breakenridge, D. (2010). *Putting the public back in public relations: How social media is reinventing the aging business of PR.* Upper Saddle River, NJ: Pearson.

Sweetser, K. D., Porter, L., Chung, D., & Kim, E. (2008). Credibility and the use of blogs in the communication industry. *Journalism & Mass Communication Quarterly, 85*(1), 169–185.

Waters, R. D., & Jamal, J. Y. (2011). Tweet, tweet, tweet: A content analysis of nonprofit organizations' Twitter updates. *Public Relations Review, 37,* 321–324.

Weiseth, N. (2014). Ten thousand kids. *Nish Weiseth blog.* Retrieved 19 December, 2014 from http://nishweiseth.com/blog/2014/4/ten-thousand-kids

World Vision on the 'same-sex unions' controversy. (2015). *Charisma Magazine.* Retrieved 24 April, 2017, from http://www.charismamag.com/life/culture/22543-world-vision-on-the-same-sex-unions-controversy

SECTION IV-C
Areas of Application

Health

18

WHEN A PANDEMIC STRIKES

Toward the Social Media Pandemic Communication Model

Rachael Song-Qi Lim, Elizabeth Yingzhi Tan,
Eric Wei Lim, Norshima Bte Abdul Aziz, and Augustine
Pang

The rapidity at which epidemics have surfaced in recent years at various levels of severity calls for communications guidelines that allow greater flexibility and reactivity so that measures can be implemented to control the disease at its onset (Usman, 2014). As the World Health Organization (WHO) argued, "national and local government authorities [need to] provide information to the public in an understandable, timely, transparent and coordinated manner before, during and after a health emergency" (WHO, 2013, p. 15).

The proliferation of social media platforms since 2006 has revolutionized communication. Crisis scholars have suggested that in a pandemic, organizations should react proactively, utilizing official organizational social media channels to establish information authority and accessibility (Jin, Liu, & Austin, 2014). More than tools for information dissemination, the networking offered by social media channels can link relevant organizations together to share and promote pandemic-related online content (Pan American Health Association [PAHO], 2009).

This study draws insights from the health belief model and crisis communication literature to develop the social media pandemic communication (SMPC) model. It is significant on two fronts. First, it offers practitioners a practicable guide to the types of information published on social media (i.e., whether instructing, adjusting, or internalizing; Sturges, 1994), which are most effective at each of the four phases of the WHO's continuum of pandemic phases. Second, the proposed SMPC model can be considered as part of pandemic outbreak-preparedness efforts. It is useful and applicable as it allows public and private health care organizations to better strategize their public communication efforts to meet increasing public expectations for timely and accurate information during a pandemic.

Background

More than 7,820 deaths worldwide have been attributed to the 2009 H1N1 pandemic, affecting more than 207 countries and overseas territories or communities (WHO, 2009). Prior to 2009, social media were hardly used for public communication during pandemics. To test its rigor, we apply the SMPC model to the 2009 H1N1 pandemic, as the event was heralded as a benchmark for the effective use of social media to respond to crisis (Liu & Kim, 2011). Chew and Eysenbach (2010) argued that "H1N1 marks the first instance in which a global pandemic has occurred in the age of Web 2.0 and presents a unique opportunity to investigate the potential role of these technologies in public health emergencies" (p. 2).

Literature Review

Pandemic Influenza Risk Management

After the 2009 H1N1 pandemic, the WHO produced Pandemic Influenza Risk Management to consolidate the lessons learned and streamline communication to the public. The WHO mapped out a continuum of four pandemic phases: (a) the interpandemic phase, or the period between influenza pandemics; (b) the alert phase, where influenza caused by a new subtype has been identified in humans; (c) the pandemic phase, which is the global spread of human influenza caused by a new subtype; and (d) the transition phase, marked by recovery measures as the assessed global risk reduces and countries reduce their response activities and move toward recovery actions.

Supporting this was a framework that proposed the communication strategies to implement at each pandemic phase. Its intent was to encourage behavioral interventions to reduce the transmission and impact of the virus (WHO, 2009). The framework lacks messages specific to social media at each phase of the pandemic (Covello, n.d.). This study aims to address the gap.

Role of Social Media in Health Crisis Communication

Communication strategy should not only include the collection, development, and distribution of information in a timely manner to help people take action during an outbreak or to prevent illness but also take into account behavioral aspects of how people react and act on advice and information they receive (McNab, 2009). Social media are argued to be one key public engagement platform as they offer "unlimited possibilities of connection with stakeholders" (Siah, Bansal, & Pang, 2010, p. 143), provide myriad ways to reach different segments of the population, bring together a "huge network of potential communicators to heed and help spread public health emergency messages" (Currie, 2009), and provide a "rich source" of opinions and experiences (Chew & Eysenbach, 2010, p. 12).

Health-Related Decision Making

Durham, Casman, and Albert (2012) examined the six factors in the health belief model that determined an individual's decision to adopt a health-promoting behavior in an epidemic. There was a significant decrease in perceived susceptibility of contracting the virus in the later months of the epidemic, though the perceived severity, perceived benefits, and perceived barriers of protective behaviors did not change. To address this dissonance, the authors suggested that the cognitive, numerical representations of risk be translated into a more vivid, self-related, and affect-related form of risk perception, such as perceived threat, risk, and worry, as "it was much likely to trigger preventive intentions and behaviors" (Reuter & Renner, 2011, p. 8). What is required is identifying "the conditions under which each of the types of interventions is most likely to be effective" (Heaney & Israel, 2002, p. 199) and addressing the question of "who should provide what to whom, and when" (p. 207) on social media.

Crisis Communication in Times of Pandemics

The objective of communication in a pandemic is to control the spread of a highly infectious disease and to present facts of the situation to maintain public confidence (PAHO, 2009). Sturges (1994) suggested three categories of information content as a crisis progresses through its life cycle: (a) instructing information, which informs people affected by the crisis of how they should physically react to the crisis; (b) adjusting information, which informs people of how to cope psychologically given the magnitude of the crisis situation; and (c) internalizing information, which is information that people can use to help formulate an image about the organization.

Prior to a crisis situation or during a crisis buildup, messages should emphasize internalizing information to precondition the audience to the organization's leadership position related to a crisis situation. As buildup continues and a crisis is deemed imminent, message emphasis should shift to instruction to prepare publics to respond with specific actions to a crisis. At the crisis breakout stage, the emphasis remains on instruction especially "as the need to induce immediate behavior responses among audience members increases dramatically" (p. 309). As the immediate effects of the crisis breakout subside, emphasis may shift to adjusting information.

Development of the Social Media Pandemic Communication Model

The conceptualized SMPC model (see Figure 18.1) is aimed toward identifying the types of message themes and social media content to focus on at each of the WHO's continuum of pandemic phases. The WHO's Pandemic Risk Management Interim Guidance is integrated with the variables that determine an individual's decision to adopt a health-promoting behavior as posited in the health belief model (see Table 18.1) and Sturges's recommendations on the message characteristics that should be the focus at each phase of the pandemic.

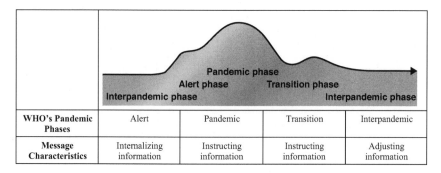

WHO's Pandemic Phases	Alert	Pandemic	Transition	Interpandemic
Message Characteristics	Internalizing information	Instructing information	Instructing information	Adjusting information

FIGURE 18.1 Conceptualized Social Media Pandemic Communication Model
The model aims to identify the types of message themes and social media content to focus on at each of the WHO's continuum of pandemic phases.

TABLE 18.1 Description of Variables That Determine an Individual's Decision to Adopt a Health-Promoting Behavior as Posited in the Health Belief Model

Variables	Description of Variables
Perceived severity of H1N1 pandemic	Define population(s) at risk and risk levels, personalize risk based on a person's characteristics or behavior, and make perceived susceptibility more consistent with individual's actual risk.
Perceived susceptibility	Specify consequences of risks and conditions.
Perceived benefits in adopting recommended behavior	Define action to take (how, where, when) and clarify the positive effects to be expected.
Addressing perceived barriers to adopting the protective behavior	Identify and reduce perceived barriers through reassurance, correction of misinformation, incentives, and assistance.
Cues to action	Provide how-to information, promote awareness, and use appropriate reminder systems.
Self-efficacy	Provide training and guidance in performing recommended action, use progressive goal setting, give verbal reinforcement, demonstrate desired behaviors, and reduce anxiety.

To understand the applicability of our model, we asked the following questions:

1. What was the role of social media in each phase of the pandemic?
2. What was the recommended instructing, adjusting, and internalizing information that health care institutions and governments used at each phase of the H1N1 pandemic?
3. How relevant is the SMPC model in engendering effective communication in a pandemic?

Method

Data Collection

Our case study focused on the spread of the H1N1 pandemic in the United States. The 2009 H1N1 pandemic was the first pandemic that broke out after the proliferation of social media, which provides a premise for its uniqueness as a case study. This allows for examination of the unique decision-making rationale and responses of health communicators when using a new medium—that is, social media (Gummesson, 2000). Using a real-life example like the 2009 H1N1 pandemic can also contribute to theory building and development (Yin, 2012).

The team sampled content related to H1N1 posted on Facebook, YouTube, and Twitter by the Centers for Disease Control and Prevention (CDC) and the U.S. Department of Health and Human Services (HHS). These accounts were the CDC Facebook page; Twitter accounts @CDC_eHealth (n.d.), @CDCemergency (n.d.), @CDCFlu (n.d.), @CDCGov (n.d.), @FluGov (n.d.), and @HHSGov (n.d.); as well as YouTube accounts for HHS (n.d.) and CDC (n.d.). All relevant posts, with keywords such as "H1N1" and "pandemic," were considered. For example, the research team searched for relevant tweets with the hashtag #H1N1 within the Twitter accounts (e.g., @FluGov). Retweets by other users were excluded.

Analysis of the social media content was conducted against the backdrop of the larger context of the studied H1N1 pandemic and related episodes in the United States. The data-sampling period starts from April 2009, when CDC recorded that the 2009 H1N1 was first detected in the United States (CDC, 2009, April 30). The U.S. public health emergency for the H1N1 influenza expired on June 23, 2010 (CDC, 2010; CDC, June 16, 2010). To consider the postpandemic response of the organizations, we sampled social media content postexpiration of the U.S. public health emergency. Hence the data-sampling period starts from April 2009 and ends on December 2010.

Based on the WHO's description of the continuum of four pandemic influenza phases, the four periods we analyzed were:

1. Alert phase, April 15–28, 2009. Infection with a new influenza A virus was first detected in the U.S. in a 10-year-old patient in California on April 15, 2009 (CDC, 2009, April 24).
2. Pandemic phase, April 29, 2009–April 30, 2010. The CDC organized 60 H1N1-related press briefings and tele-briefings for more than 35,000 participants, signifying a proactive approach to communication with stakeholders. The last CDC H1N1 media briefing was held in April 2010.
3. Transition phase, May 1, 2010–June 23, 2010. The U.S. public health emergency for the H1N1 Influenza expired on June 23, 2010.
4. Interpandemic phase, June 24, 2010–December 31, 2010. To examine a period between influenza pandemics, December 2010 was selected as the last data point to study postpandemic responses of organizations after the expiration of the U.S. public health emergency.

Data Analysis

A total of 553 posts on Twitter, Facebook, and YouTube were analyzed across the four phases. Posts were coded against the six variables that determined an individual's decision to adopt a health-promoting behavior as posited in the health belief model. They are perceived severity of the pandemic, perceived susceptibility, perceived benefits in adopting the recommended behavior, addressing perceived barriers to adopting the protective behavior, cues to action, and self-efficacy. These are matched against Sturges's (1994) three message characteristics: instructing, adjusting, or internalizing information. A codebook and coding form were designed to assist the analysis and evaluation of the message parameters of the social media content. Descriptions of variables were clearly elucidated in the codebook to aid the coding team, comprising two coders, in identifying the presence and absence of variables within the posts. The Cronbach's α value was between 0.774 and 0.954.

Results

Role of Social Media at Each Pandemic Phase

The first research question examined the role of social media in each phase of the pandemic.

Alert Phase

As health authorities assessed the possibility of the virus developing to a new pandemic strain, they had to consider the information to present so that the public was *prepared to take appropriate actions based on what could happen* to protect themselves and others. Given the quick lead-up from reports of the new virus to the declaration of the start of the 2009 U.S. H1N1 pandemic, content volume posted during this period was low (see Table 18.2).

TABLE 18.2 Number of H1N1-Related Social Media Posts by the HHS and CDC During the Four Pandemic Influenza Phases

Organization	Alert	Pandemic	Transition	Interpandemic	Total
		Number of H1N1-Related Posts During Phase			
HHS	0	1,229 (345 sampled)	17 (5 sampled)	14 (5 sampled)	1,260
CDC	4	165	0	20	189
Frequency (*n* of posts/*n* of days)	0.27	3.8	0.31	0.18	
Number of posts sampled	4	510	5	34	553

Pandemic Phase

As the emphasis was on enacting responses that would *reduce the transmission of the virus and mortality, counter panic, and dispel rumors*, dissemination of protective health behavior and coping messages for individuals and their families was paramount. In line with the WHO's recommendation to ensure the "widest possible dissemination of information" (WHO, 2013, p. 29), HHS and CDC leveraged Facebook, Twitter, and YouTube to deliver their messages. As information had to be consistent and up to date, 96.2% of the total 1,449 H1N1 posts collected from the surveyed accounts were posted during this phase.

Transition Phase

During this phase, authorities should *communicate that subsequent waves are possible and that the virus will revert to a seasonal strain* (WHO, 2013). Messages sent during this phase were related to the infection status updates, news on a possible new season of H1N1 flu, review of flu policies, WHO updates on international pandemic status, and updated guidance on infection control measures for influenza in health care settings.

Interpandemic Phase

Some recovery actions recommended for the transition phase were enacted during the interpandemic phase, where CDC and HHS *reviewed the preparedness, surveillance, vaccine development, and risk communication by the different agencies and partners and made recommendations in preparation for similar events.*

Risk-Communication Messages at Different Phases

The second research question examined the recommended instructing, adjusting, and internalizing information that health care institutions and governments used at each phase of the H1N1 pandemic.

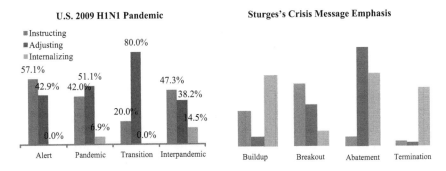

FIGURE 18.2 Breakdown of Risk-Communication Messages at Each Phase of the U.S. H1N1 Pandemic vis-à-vis Sturges's Crisis Message Emphasis at Each Crisis Stage (1994)

In line with the communication imperative for the alert phase, a mix of instructing (57.1%) and adjusting information (42.9%) was delivered to prepare the public to take appropriate physical and psychological actions in the event of a pandemic outbreak.

More than half of the posts sampled from the pandemic phase were adjusting information (51.1%) to help people cope psychologically with the crisis with instructing information (42%) on physical protection following behind. U.S. health authorities also addressed specific episodes that emerged during this phase. When vaccination was strongly promoted, CDC and HHS took to different platforms to manage public expectations of efficacy, supply adequacy, and vaccine safety especially for pregnant women and children (Hartocollis, 2009; Steinhauer, 2009).

@FluGov was the only account that continued to post updates during the transition and interpandemic phases. Based on selected tweets analyzed, 80% of the messages were adjusting information, such as status updates and efficacy of recommended preventive measures, and 20% were instructing information on measures, such as vaccination.

During the interpandemic phase, instructing information (47.3%; e.g., vaccination, antiviral drugs, and sneezing into the elbow) and adjusting information (38.2%; e.g., where to get vaccinated) continued to be heavily featured. Internalizing information (14.5%) had increased prominence compared to other phases (none were recorded within the sample we extracted for the alert and transition phases, and 6.9% in the pandemic phase). Content on review of lessons learned and revised actions were communicated. By continuing to disseminate relevant information pertaining to the pandemic, HHS and CDC reinforced their role as leading authorities for future health care crises.

Compared to Sturges's (1994) analysis of risk-communication messages during corporate crises, the composition of risk-communication messages during a pandemic crisis differed. During this pandemic, instructing and adjusting information complemented each other across most of the phases. At the alert and pandemic phases, both instructing and adjusting message types worked hand in hand to address and manage stakeholder emotions. Internalizing information took a backseat as public health took precedence over the reputation of affected organizations.

Application of the SMPC Model

The third research question assesses the relevance of the SMPC model in engendering effective communication in a pandemic.

The individual, being the first level of intervention, was the key target of social media communication messages during the H1N1 pandemic. Table 18.3 presents the composition of individual health behavior messages analyzed in this study. The majority of the messages focused on the key concepts of self-efficacy and cues to action, which overlapped with instructing information of preventive measures and adjusting information of status updates and coping handlers.

TABLE 18.3 Percentage of H1N1-Related Social Media Posts With Individual Health Behavior During the Four Pandemic Influenza Phases

	Individual Health Behavior					
Phases	*Perceived Susceptibility*	*Perceived Severity*	*Perceived Benefits*	*Perceived Barriers*	*Cues to Action*	*Self-Efficacy*
Total	8.30%	8.03%	21.2%	6.5%	26.3%	29.7%

A critical review of health behavior studies identified *perceived barriers* as the most significant single predictor across all studies (Becker, 1974; Champion & Skinner, 2008). Perceived barriers need to be addressed first as these set the stage for public receptivity of self-efficacy measures and cues to action at the height of the pandemic. One way communicators could do so is to address the tangible and psychological costs of the advised action, such as vaccination risk.

The SMPC model was revised based on the findings. Sturges (1994) argued for a dominant message characteristic at each phase of a crisis. We suggested that message characteristics *complement* one another at each phase of the pandemic. In addition, we added and ranked the message themes to focus on at each phase of the pandemic. Our study found that message themes are ranked similarly at the

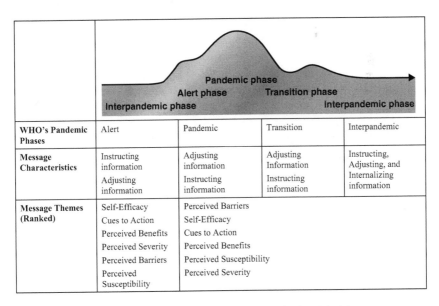

FIGURE 18.3 Revised Social Media Pandemic Communication Model
The model posits the message characteristics and themes to focus on at each of the WHO's continuum of pandemic phases based on social media content published by the HHS and CDC during the 2009 H1N1 pandemic.

pandemic, transition, and interpandemic phases. In a heightened pandemic threat situation, the possibility of multiple pandemic "peaks" would require the same message themes to be reinforced to ensure continued public vigilance.

Discussion

Alert and Pandemic Phases

Both the CDC and HHS used several social media platforms to communicate instructing and adjusting information to enable the public to take appropriate action when the pandemic reached its peak. YouTube videos were used to instruct the public on preventive health care measures, which was important to increase preparedness and reduce panic during the next phase. However, there was a notable absence of interactive elements in their approach.

Transition and Interpandemic Phases

At this postcrisis and postrecovery stage, the interest in the pandemic may be decreasing with a sense of relief that the episode is drawing to a close. This is the stage that health care communications should seize to take stock, share lessons learned, and pay tribute to all partners who have contributed to the fight against the pandemic. The type of messages at this point is one of adjusting and internalizing information; they ride on the new reputation built during the crisis to ensure that the public continues to support the organization. This is a critical move to resolve and address any misconceptions or rumors that the public had formed against the health care organizations during the pandemic. This internalizing information will form the basis for long-term judgments about organizations involved in the crisis (Sturges, Carrell, Newsom, & Barrera, 1994).

Practical Implications for Social Media and Crisis Communication

Some key takeaways from the application of the SMPC model on the H1N1 pandemic are provided next. Organizations can prioritize key tasks:

1. Always keep the public at the forefront of policy decisions and communication efforts: Doing this is vital to reinforcing the publics' understanding of their important roles during the pandemic as partners to health care organizations. This will increase publics' trust in health care organizations for subsequent pandemic episodes.
2. Always acknowledge, instead of stonewall, issues that have happened during the pandemic: Acknowledging issues that occurred during the pandemic demonstrates the organization's accountability for certain decisions, actions,

and delays. This also serves as a good opportunity to explain the rationale for future plans.

3. Pay tribute to people who drive the pandemic efforts: This is to honor health care workers who played an indispensable role in the containment of the pandemic and those who made sacrifices in their line of duty.

Although the SMPC model suggests message characteristics and themes to focus on at each phase of the health crisis, social media *platforms* can be leveraged to a further extent to deepen message receptivity and induce behavioral change among the target audience. The medium can be as important, if not more so, than the message (Schultz, Utz, & Goritz, 2011), and optimizing the strengths of social media platforms is critical while ensuring message consistency (Damayanti, Rodrigues, Chua, & Pang, 2014).

At the implementation levels, practitioners can consider using YouTube videos not only as an instructional tool for care instructions but also as one of the feedback channels for audiences to better interact with the health care organization. Intention to comply with the message seems to be greater when it originates from an organizational source than when it originates from a user-generated source (Freberg, 2012), especially in scenarios where information is not confirmed or in an information vacuum (Pang, 2013). This is particularly relevant in a pandemic, where "even with the current state of science, it's impossible to predict which flu virus will become a danger to humans and to what degree" (Roos, 2014). Doing so will also allow the health care organizations to identify and address information gaps.

Organizations could also consider engaging netizens, cultivating online champions or social media creators (Liu, Jin, Briones, & Kuch, 2012) and social media influencers to help spread the word on preventive measures. Online champions are those receiving the official, organizationally sanctioned crisis message who become crisis communicators when they communicate their reactions of support to the organization's message (Coombs & Holladay, 2013). The trust cultivated in such relationships has a cascading effect on the target audience and would better prepare them to respond to the crisis.

Heightened public interest in a crisis warrants frequent and regular updates and engagement of stakeholders. This is especially critical on social media, or the *rhetorical arena*, defined as the space where numerous crisis actors talk about the crisis and respond to talk about the crisis (Coombs & Holladay, 2013). Here, distortions, rumors, untruths, and misinformation can abound; Freberg's (2012) study found that "publics very quickly blur any distinctions between 'we think we might have a problem' and 'we know we have a problem' and intend to behave similarly in response to both types of message" (p. 420). The possibility that unconfirmed information will carry the same weight as official, confirmed information may leave organizations quite vulnerable to rumor and misunderstanding.

One way to mitigate this is for organizations to decide on a consistent use of the appropriate organizational spokesperson—pitched at the right level of authority—who will front information dissemination. This is crucial, as how credible the spokesperson appears to be impacts the extent to which publics follow the instructions shared. Spokespeople must also be meticulous and understand the nuances of social media posts (Damayanti et al., 2014) given the speed at which a misconstrued post could go viral. In the event of rumor mongering or online arguments, spokespeople must be able to react quickly to quell misinformation or untruths with useful and accurate information to maintain organizational credibility. To minimize these occurrences, organizations must tailor information dissemination in ways their target audience segments understand (Freberg, 2012). Choice of language in addressing the public to disseminate information must be easily understood by the masses. In addition, information can and should be replicated on various platforms to ensure consistency of messages (Coombs & Holladay, 2013).

In a pandemic crisis where the situation is constantly evolving, dynamic responses via social media can provide the stability and consistency needed to restore calm. The SMPC model is the first step toward enabling communication practitioners to do so.

Limitations and Future Research

There are a number of limitations to the study. For more nuanced findings, future similar studies will benefit from a larger sample size. A larger sample size could yield even more valuable recommendations for practitioners. Also, the study was limited to the H1N1 pandemic outbreak in the United States and did not examine the strategies that other health care agencies such as the WHO undertook. Future research could look at the use of social media in other countries to compare and contrast practices and to extract best practices.

The sociocultural, economic, and political conditions of the countries may also contribute to the extent of use of social media. Countries that do not have high Internet bandwidths or pervasive social media usage and have diverse sociocultural backgrounds may vary in their approach in disseminating information to the public.

Future studies could also consider evaluating the effectiveness of the framework from the users' perspectives. Currently, the framework is theoretical in nature and requires further testing. This can only be carried out when the next pandemic outbreak occurs. Another possibility of future study could examine the question of the most effective spokesperson or spokespeople at the different stages of the pandemic.

References

Becker, M. H. (1974). The health belief model and personal health behavior. *Health Education Monographs, 2*, 324–473.

CDC. (2009, April 24). Swine influenza a (H1N1) infection in two children—Southern California, March—April 2009. *Morbidity and Mortality Weekly Report.* Retrieved 27 March, 2014 from www.cdc.gov/mmwr/preview/mmwrhtml/mm5815a5.htm

CDC. (2009, April 30). Outbreak of swine-origin influenza a (H1N1) virus infection—Mexico, March—April 2009. *Morbidity and Mortality Weekly Report.* Retrieved 27 March, 2014 from www.cdc.gov/mmwR/preview/mmwrhtml/mm58d0430a2.htm

CDC. (2010). Situation update. *2009 H1N1 Flu.* Retrieved 27 March, 2014 from www.cdc.gov/h1n1flu/

CDC. (2010, June 16). The 2009 H1N1 Pandemic: Summary highlights, April 2009-April 2010. *H1N1 Flu.* Retrieved 27 March, 2014 from www.cdc.gov/h1n1flu/cdcresponse.htm

CDC. (n.d.). The Centers for Disease Control and Prevention (CDC). *YouTube.* Retrieved 27 March, 2014 from www.youtube.com.sg/user/CDCStreamingHealth

CDC_eHealth. (n.d.). @CDC_eHealth. *Twitter.* Retrieved from https://twitter.com/CDC_eHealth

CDCemergency. (n.d.). @CDCemergency. *Twitter.* Retrieved from https://twitter.com/CDCemergency

CDCFlu. (n.d.). @CDCFlu. *Twitter.* Retrieved from https://twitter.com/CDCFlu

CDCGov. (n.d.). @CDCGov. *Twitter.* Retrieved from https://twitter.com/CDCGov

Champion, V. L., & Skinner, C. S. (2008). The health belief model. *Health Behavior and Health Education: Theory, Research, and Practice, 4,* 45–65.

Chew, C., & Eysenbach, G. (2010). Pandemics in the age of Twitter: Content analysis of tweets during the 2009 H1N1 outbreak. *PLoS ONE, 5*(11), 1–13.

Coombs, W. T., & Holladay, S. J. (2013). How publics react to crisis communication efforts. *Journal of Communication Management, 18*(1), 40–57.

Covello, V. (n.d.). H1N1 risk and crisis communications: Successes and challenges. [PowerPoint slides]. Retrieved from http://www.cdc.gov/about/grand-rounds/archives/2010/download/09-September/Covello_Risk_Comm_Presentation.ppt

Currie, D. (2009, August). Public health leaders using social media to convey emergencies. *The Nation's Health, 39*(6), 1–10.

Damayanti, R., Rodrigues, S. A., Chua, S., & Pang, A. (2014, June). *Corporate social media spokesperson: Who should speak on behalf of the organization in times of crises?* Proceedings of the 12th Conference on Corporate Communication (pp. 139–153). Hong Kong: CCI.

Durham, D. P., Casman, E. A., & Albert, S. M. (2012). Deriving behavior model parameters from survey data: Self-protective behavior adoption during the 2009–2010 Influenza A (H1N1) pandemic. *Risk Analysis, 32*(12), 2020–2031.

FluGov. (n.d.). @FluGov. *Twitter.* Retrieved from https://twitter.com/FluGov

Freberg, K. (2012). Intention to comply with crisis messages communicated via social media. *Public Relations Review, 38*(3), 416–421.

Gummesson, E. (2000). *Qualitative methods in management research.* Thousand Oaks, CA: Sage.

Hartocollis, A. (2009, October 5). Swine Flu Vaccine Reaches an Anxious Nation. *New York Times.* Retrieved 19 April, 2014 from www.nytimes.com/2009/10/06/nyregion/06vaccine.html?_r=0

Heaney, C. A., & Israel, B. A. (2002). Social networks and social support. *Health Behavior and Health Education: Theory, Research, and Practice, 3,* 185–209.

HHS. (n.d.). USGOVHHS. *YouTube.* Retrieved 27 March, 2014 from www.youtube.com/user/USGOVHHS

HHSGov. (n.d.). @HHSGov. *Twitter.* Retrieved from https://twitter.com/HHSGov

Jin, Y., Liu, B. F., & Austin, L. L. (2014). Examining the role of social media in effective crisis management: The effects of crisis origin, information form, and source on publics' crisis responses. *Communication Research, 41*(1), 74–94.

Liu, B. F., Jin, Y., Briones, R., & Kuch, B. (2012). Managing turbulence in the blogosphere: Evaluating the blog-mediated crisis communication model with the American Red Cross. *Journal of Public Relations Research, 24*(4), 353–370.

Liu, B. F., & Kim, S. (2011). How organisations framed the 2009 H1N1 pandemic via social and traditional media: Implications for US health communicators. *Public Relations Review, 37*, 233–244.

McNab, C. (2009). What social media offers to health professionals and citizens. *Bulletin of the World Health Organisation, 87*(8), 566–566.

PAHO. (2009, April). *Creating a communication strategy for pandemic influenza.* Washington, DC: Pan American Health Organization/World Health Organization.

Pang, A. (2013). Dealing with external stakeholders during the crisis: Managing the information vacuum. In A. J. DuBrin (Ed.), *Handbook of research on crisis leadership in organizations* (pp. 209–229). Northampton, MA: Edward Elgar.

Reuter, T., & Renner, B. (2011). Who takes precautionary action in the face of the new H1N1 influenza? Prediction of who collects a free hand sanitizer using a health behavior model. *PLoS ONE, 6*(7), e22130.

Roos, R. (2014). Fineberg: 5 years after H1N1, world still not ready for pandemic. Retrieved 19 April, 2014 from www.cidrap.umn.edu/

Schultz, F., Utz, S., & Goritz, A. (2011). Is the medium the message? Perceptions of and reactions to crisis communication via Twitter, blogs and traditional media. *Public Relations Review, 37*(1), 20–27.

Siah, J. S. A., Bansal, N., & Pang, A. (2010). New media: A new medium in escalating crises? *Corporate Communications: An International Journal, 15*(2), 143–155.

Steinhauer, J. (2009, October 15). Swine flu shots revive a debate about vaccines. *New York Times.* Retrieved 19 April, 2014 from www.nytimes.com/2009/10/16/health/16vaccine.html

Sturges, D. L. (1994). Communicating through crisis: A strategy for organisational survival. *Management Communication Quarterly, 7*(3), 297–316.

Sturges, D. L., Carrell, B. Jr., Newsom, D., & Barrera, M. (1994). Crisis communication: Knowing how is good; knowing why is essential. In M. B. Goodman (Ed.), Corporate communication: Theory and practice (pp. 339–353). Albany, NY: State University of New York Press.

Usman, A. (2014, April 8). Epidemic concerns: Hospitals get guidelines to control swine flu. *The Express Tribune.* Retrieved from http://tribune.com.pk/story/692685/epidemic-concerns-hospitals-get-guidelines-to-control-swine-flu/

WHO. (2009, June 11). World now at the start of 2009 influenza pandemic. *Media Center.* Retrieved 27 March 2014 from www.who.int/mediacentre/news/statements/2009/h1n1_pandemic_phase6_20090611/en/

WHO. (2009). Behavioral interventions for reducing the transmission and impact of influenza A (H1N1) virus: A framework for communication strategies. Retrieved from http://www.who.int/csr/resources/publications/swineflu/framework/en/

WHO. (2013). Pandemic influenza risk management: WHO interim guidance. Retrieved from http://www.who.int/influenza/preparedness/pandemic/influenza_risk_management/en/

Yin, R. K. (2012). *Case study research: Design and methods* (Vol. 5). Thousand Oaks, CA: Sage.

19

HEALTH MISINFORMATION VIA SOCIAL MEDIA

The Case of Vaccine Safety on Pinterest

Jeanine Guidry and Marcus Messner

Introduction

Vaccination is an effective public health measure that has been instrumental in greatly reducing morbidity and mortality due to infectious diseases (Ołpiński, 2012). However, the past 20 years have seen a renewed growth of a persistent antivaccination movement fueled by unsubstantiated reports that both the measles, mumps, and rubella (MMR) vaccine and the diphtheria, tetanus, and pertussis (DTP) vaccine cause autism. Vaccine rejection can be dangerous and sometimes even deadly. Researchers estimate that MMR vaccine rejection has contributed to increased illnesses and deaths (Kitta, 2012, p. 2; Love, Himelboim, Holton, & Stewart, 2013).

However, the social amplification of risk model states that *risk events*, defined as actual or presumed accidents or incidents, will be irrelevant or localized in their impact unless they are communicated (Kasperson et al., 1988). Several studies on vaccine portrayal on social media have been carried out in the past 10 years, and most show an increasingly negative portrayal of vaccines on various social media platforms including Pinterest (Briones, Nan, Madden, & Waks, 2012; Guidry, Carlyle, Messner, & Jin, 2015). Given the significant public health impact of vaccines, this study focuses on how Pinterest users talk about the MMR vaccine and the DTP vaccine, as well as how influential pediatric health organizations approach these vaccine discussions.

Literature Review

Vaccines and Controversies

Over the past 30 years, two prominent vaccine controversies have formed the foundation of the recent antivaccination movement. In April 1983, an NBC affiliate aired a documentary that claimed that the DTP vaccine (also called DPT and, in its newer versions, TDaP) was dangerous and could cause brain damage in children (Allen, 2007, pp. 251–252).

A second high-profile controversy centered on the MMR vaccine. Measles is a highly infectious viral disease that, up until the introduction of the MMR vaccination, caused 48,000 hospitalizations and 500 deaths annually in the United States (Poland, 2011; Poland & Jacobson, 1994; Sugerman et al., 2010). In 1998, Andrew Wakefield, a British physician, published a study in *The Lancet* that described 12 children with a new form of bowel disease, as well as symptoms of autism (Wakefield et al., 1998). Wakefield claimed that the children's symptoms developed soon after they received the MMR vaccination. He then proposed a hypothesis linking the MMR vaccine and brain damage that leads to autism (Kitta, 2012, pp. 68–69; Offit & Coffin, 2003), but this was rejected by several epidemiological studies (Smith, Chu, & Barker, 2004; Taylor et al., 1999). Nevertheless, awareness and perceived safety of the MMR vaccine fell (Boyce, 2007, pp. 9–10), even when this study was retracted by *The Lancet* (Godlee, Smith, & Marcovitch, 2011). Despite this retraction, Wakefield's conclusions are still widely circulating and form the basis of the current antivaccine movement.

The Internet and Social Media

Antivaccination messages are more common on the Internet than in print or broadcast media (Kata, 2012) and antivaccination websites appear more often in top Google search results (Davies, Chapman, & Leask, 2002). Both dynamics result in widespread exposure to antivaccination sentiment and a greater potential for individuals to be influenced by such messaging. Few studies have been carried out focusing on vaccination representation on social media platforms, and the results have been mixed. A study of YouTube video clips found that 74.7% of the clips showed the HPV vaccine in a positive light (Ache & Wallace, 2008). Keelan, Pavri-Garcia, Tomlinson, and Wilson (2007), in an earlier study, focused on general vaccination-themed studies on the YouTube platform and found that the negative videos in their study received more ratings and more likes. A study among MySpace blog posts, again focusing on the HPV vaccine, found a similar ratio positive versus negative representations (Keelan, Pavri, Balakrishnan, & Wilson, 2010). Briones and colleagues (2012) found that most HPV-vaccine-focused videos on YouTube were negative in tone, and that negative HPV vaccine videos were liked more often. A recent study on vaccines and the way they are portrayed on Pinterest found that almost 75% of pins mentioning any type of vaccine were antivaccine in nature (Guidry et al., 2015).

Visual Communication and Social Media

The aforementioned studies address more established social media platforms like YouTube and Twitter. Pinterest is a newer visual social media platform that has not received much academic attention. Launched in March 2010, it quickly grew to more than 100 million users by the middle of 2015 (Pinterest, 2015). Pinterest allows people to collect ideas and information for different projects and interests. Users create collections ("boards") of visual bookmarks ("pins") to file ideas, articles, photos, and quotes. Pins and boards are easily shared through "repinning," Pinterest's equivalent of Twitter retweet function.

When users engage with friends on social media sites, they report enjoying the pictures the most (ROI Research, 2012). Pictures seem to play an especially significant role in communication of health topics. Pictures that are closely linked to text, when compared to text alone, markedly increase attention to and recall of health education information (Houts, Doak, Doak, & Loscalzo, 2006). Depending on the emotional response to the pictures, adherence to desired health behaviors can increase or decrease (Houts et al., 2006). In a study on the effect of images on women's comprehension of cervical cancer prevention information, Michielutte and colleagues (1992) found that brochures with pictures were not only rated more positively than those with text alone but also comprehended at a higher rate. Mansoor and Dowse (2003), in a study on the effects of pictograms on understanding medication information, found that pictures and text together yielded almost double the correct retention rate of medication dosage information.

Audiences receive messages from both text and images, and evidence from the area of cognitive psychology suggests that textual and visual elements are processed differently. Corner, Richardson, and Fenton (1990) posit that images can exert "positioning" influence on a viewer, which may be resistant to subsequent commentaries that challenge the feelings they produce.

A recent study found that users who have both Twitter and Pinterest accounts tend to post items first on the more visual of the two platforms: Pinterest (Ottoni et al., 2014). The first research question of this study, therefore, attempts to analyze the types of visuals that are posted on Pinterest in the context of vaccinations.

RQ1:   What types of visuals are used to represent the MMR and DTP vaccines on Pinterest?

Crisis Communications

Because researchers are primarily looking at negative vaccination portrayals on Pinterest, the crisis in this case is the perceived crisis (by members of the public) of harmful side effects of vaccines. Most crisis communication theories focus on the organization's communications in dealing with a crisis. In this case, the study primarily focuses on the publics' communications and attribution of responsibility for the perceived crisis of harmful vaccine side effects.

The Social-Mediated Crisis Communication (SMCC) Model

The social-mediated crisis communication (SMCC) model is a revised model of the blog-mediated crisis communication (BMCC) model, which serves as a road map for organizations to decide if and how to respond to influential blogs before, during, and after a crisis (Jin & Liu, 2010). The SMCC, through this adaptation, reflects the concept that crises can be sparked and spread online through a variety of social media platforms (Jin, Liu, & Austin, 2014). In addition, the SMCC added five considerations to the original blog-based model: crisis origin, crisis type, infrastructure, message content, and message form. This study will focus on crisis origin and crisis type. Crisis origin addresses whether the crisis was initiated from an internal organizational perspective or from an issue external to the organization (Jin et al., 2014). Crisis type is based on two additional theories: attribution theory and situational crisis communication theory (SCCT).

Attribution Theory and Situational Crisis Communication Theory (SCCT)

Attribution theory states that people particularly need to assign responsibility for events, particularly for negative and unexpected ones (Coombs, 2007a, 2007b). SCCT is informed by attribution theory and deals with determining the initial crisis responsibility attached to a crisis (Coombs, 2007b). SCCT research has identified three crisis clusters based on attributions of initial crisis responsibility by crisis type: the victim cluster (the organization is viewed as a victim of the crisis), the accidental cluster (the crisis is considered unintentional or uncontrollable by the organization), and the intentional cluster (the organization is believed to have purposefully created the incident that caused the crisis; Coombs, 2007a). Because this study deals with a perceived crisis of vaccine-adverse events, it is important to determine what type of blame is placed on organizations responsible for vaccines and vaccinations. As such, the following research questions are posed:

> **RQ2:** How do the posters of anti-MMR and anti-DTP vaccine pins attribute crisis responsibility by crisis cluster on Pinterest?
>
> **RQ3:** What do the posters of anti-MMR and anti-DTP vaccine pins determine to be the origin of the perceived vaccine side effect crisis?

Two-Way Communication on Social Media

Although social media in many ways provide a new way to relay crisis and risk information, as well as facilitate a two-way dialogue between organizations and their publics, many organizations have been slow to actively adopt the platforms and often use social media primarily as a one-way megaphone. During the recent H1N1 flu outbreak, a study by Tirkkonen and Luoma-aho (2011) found that the lack of authorities' early input on social media provided an opportunity for hostile and distorted comments by the public. Considering the presence of antivaccine sentiment online and on social media, it is important to know if organizations responsible for distributing and administering these vaccines (e.g., pediatric clinics and large health organizations) address vaccine concerns on the same channels. In addition, it is of interest to find out if these types of medical organizations respond to any of the antivaccine messages found on Pinterest, because two-way communication and cocreation of content are the strengths of social media (Bortree & Seltzer, 2009; Rybalko & Seltzer, 2010).

> **RQ4:** How do health and medical organizations that are responsible for distributing and administering vaccines address vaccine information on Pinterest?

Framing

Narrative Versus Statistical

Narratives are story-like, coherent prose pieces that describe a personally experienced event from a first- or third-person perspective, whereas statistical information presents incidence rates of vaccine-adverse events, or of vaccine-preventable diseases, depending on the viewpoint of the author (C. Betsch, Ulshofer, Renkewitz, & Betsch, 2011). Narrative information about alleged vaccine-adverse events is widely available online, and this type of information increases the risk perception of vaccines and tends to decrease vaccination intentions (C. Betsch, Renkewitz, Betsch, & Ulshöfer, 2010). Narratives appeared to have a stronger influence than statistical risk information on vaccination intent (C. Betsch et al., 2011). Risk theoretically consists of two variables: the perceived probability of an event and the perceived expected severity of the event (C. Betsch et al., 2011). Confirming earlier studies, the previously mentioned study of vaccines on Pinterest found that antivaccine pins used more narrative information than statistical information (Guidry et al., 2015). This study therefore hypothesizes the following:

> **H1:**   Pinterest will contain more pins focusing on narrative MMR and DTP vaccination information than on statistical representations.

Positive Versus Negative

The tonality of content can be framed negatively or positively as demonstrated by existing research studies on online and social media content (DiStaso & Messner, 2010; DiStaso, Messner, & Stacks, 2007). As previously mentioned, in a study on the portrayal of the HPV vaccine on video-sharing platform YouTube, videos with a negative stance toward the HPV vaccine were liked more often by viewers than positive or neutral videos (Briones et al., 2012). However, in a recent study on the general representation of vaccines (including the MMR and DTP vaccines) on Pinterest, Guidry found that pins with a provaccine stance elicited more engagement in the form of repins, likes, and comments than antivaccine pins. This study therefore hypothesizes the following:

H2: Pinterest pins focused on anti–MMR and anti–DTP vaccination information will elicit less engagement than pins focused on provaccination information.

Methods

This study examined information relating to childhood vaccinations and vaccines on the social media platform Pinterest. Two separate quantitative content analyses were conducted: one focused on 788 pins specifically addressing the MMR and DTP vaccines posted by Pinterest users with a variety of vaccine-related hashtags, and one analyzing 933 pins published by 10 child-health-focused organizations' Pinterest accounts. Coding protocols for both sets of pins were developed, tested, and implemented for the coding process.

First Content Analysis: Hashtag-Based Postings

For the first content analysis, this study, drawing upon the existing literature, identified the following keywords to select the pins for the sample: "MMR vaccine," "measles vaccine," "mumps vaccine," "rubella vaccine," "DTP vaccine," "DPT vaccine," "diphtheria vaccine," "tetanus vaccine," "pertussis vaccine," and "whooping cough vaccine" (Ache & Wallace, 2008; Briones et al., 2012; Keelan et al., 2007; Love et al., 2013). On August 19, 20, and 21, 2014, each fifth pin for each keyword search was selected by scrolling down the page with search results and any links to connected websites noted, reaching a total of 200 pins per keyword for a total of 800 pins in the sample. Between collecting the sample and coding the sample, 12 pins were deleted from Pinterest by the authors of the pins; therefore, the final sample consisted of 788 pins.

For the first content analysis, the pins were coded for a series of typical Pinterest characteristics, including time frame of the post, poster identity, whether the pin originally was a repin, number of repins, number of likes, number of comments, links to other websites, how many types of engagement were present for each pin, and how many times the pin had been engaged between the three types of engagement.

In addition to these characteristics, the pins were coded for the following content-related variables: type of image, stance or tonality of image, caption, website to which the pin pointed, and story type. All pins were coded for the following dichotomous variables: presence of conspiracy theories, questions of civil liberties, and crisis origin (referring to whether the crisis was initiated from an issue internal or external to the organization). Finally, crisis responsibility was coded for three different clusters: victim (the organization is perceived as a victim of the crisis), accidental (the crisis is considered as unintentional or as uncontrollable by the organization), and intentional (the organization is believed to have intentionally created the incidence that caused the crisis; Coombs, 2007a; Jin et al., 2014).

Second Content Analysis: Pediatric Health Organizations

For the second content analysis, this study selected the Pinterest accounts of 10 influential organizations in the area of pediatric health. Included were two national organizations (the Centers for Disease Control and Prevention [CDC] and Healthychildren.org, the official parenting website for the American Academy of Pediatrics), as well as eight general pediatric clinics (Pediatric Wellness Wall, Way to Grow Pediatrics, Family First Pediatrics, ABC Pediatrics, SW Pediatrics, Northeast Cincinnati Pediatrics, Patterson & Tedford Pediatrics, and ABC Pediatrics of Dunn, NC). The eight general pediatric clinics' accounts were decided by choosing each 10th organization after a search for "general pediatric office" among pinners' handles on Pinterest. The sample was created by randomly selecting 10% of the pins for each account, and each of the resulting 933 pins was coded on the presence or absence of vaccines as a pin topic.

Intercoder Reliability

Two coders were trained to establish intercoder reliability. The first coder coded all of the posts in the first sample ($n = 788$) and in the second sample ($N = 933$), whereas the second coder coded approximately 10% of the posts ($n = 80$) in the first sample, as well as the second sample ($N = 100$). After pretesting and subsequent changes to the coding protocol, the intercoder reliability test with the ReCal statistical program showed an overall Scott's (Scott, 1955) coefficient of 0.84. Coefficients for individual categories varied from 0.77 to 1.00.[1]

Results

This study focused on the portrayal of the MMR and DTP childhood vaccines on Pinterest, and studied 788 pins that mentioned these vaccines as well as 933 pins posted by 10 organizations that are influential in the area of pediatric health. Repinning was by far the most popular form of interaction: 85.8% ($n = 676$) of the pins in this sample were repinned at least once, whereas 14.2% ($n = 112$) were not. In contrast, 56.5% ($n = 445$) of the pins received at least one "like," whereas 43.5% ($n = 343$) did not. Only 15.2% ($n = 121$) of the pins attracted at least one comment, whereas 84.6% ($n = 667$) did not. The mean number of repins was 17.03, the mean number of likes 3.12, and the mean number of comments 1.10. The research questions and hypotheses will be addressed individually in the following parts:

RQ1: What types of visuals are used to represent the MMR and DTP vaccines on Pinterest?

The findings of this study show that of the 788 visuals pinned, a majority, 56.5% (n = 445), of pins were primarily image based, meaning little or no text was included in the actual image. Of these, 11.4% (n = 90) were primarily text based, 22.2% (n = 175) were a mix of image and text, 3.9% (n = 31) consisted of infographics, 3.9% (n = 31) belonged to a video, and the remaining 2.0% (n = 10) were tables or charts.

Of the 145 provaccine visuals pinned, the majority, 57.5% (n = 84), were primarily image based, 5.5% (n = 8) were primarily text based, 19.3% (n = 28) were a mix of image and text, 15.2% (n = 22) consisted of infographics, 1.4% (n = 2) belonged to a video, and 0.7% (n = 1) were tables or charts. Of the 593 antivaccine visuals pinned, the majority, 54.8% (n = 325), were primarily image based, 13.2% (n=78) were primarily text based, 23.3% (n = 138) were a mix of image and text, 1.5% (n = 9) consisted of infographics, 4.9% (n = 29) belonged to a video, and 2.4% (n = 14) were tables or charts.

RQ2: How do the posters of anti-MMR and anti-DTP vaccine pins attribute crisis responsibility by crisis cluster on Pinterest?

In 82.5% (n = 489) of the anti-MMR and anti-DTP pins (hereafter referred to as antivaccine pins), pinners determined the alleged crisis to be of an intentional type: the organization referenced (the government, the CDC, pharmaceutical companies, medical practices) was believed to have purposely created the event that caused the crisis. In addition, 54.2% of all pins in the sample and 69.6% of the antivaccine pins mention conspiracy theories, such as pharmaceutical companies intentionally creating vaccines to fail.

RQ3: What do the posters of anti-MMR and anti-DTP vaccine pins determine to be the origin of the perceived vaccine side effect crisis?

In 82.5% (n = 489) of the antivaccine pins, pinners determined the responsibility for the alleged crisis to be from an internal organizational perspective as opposed to an issue external to the organization.

RQ4: How do health and medical organizations that are responsible for distributing and administering vaccines address vaccine information on Pinterest?

In the first, keyword-based content analysis, this study found that no health or medical organizations responded to any of the antivaccine pins (N = 593) in this sample. In the second organization-based content analysis, the results showed that, of the 933 pins by health organizations, only 0.9% ($N = 9$) were focused on vaccines and vaccinations. Of these nine pins, only 0.22% ($n = 2$) mentioned either the MMR or the DTP vaccine—the rest addressed vaccines in general. Regarding visual type, 0.44% ($n = 4$) consisted primarily of an image, whereas 0.22% ($n = 2$) utilized an infographic and another 0.22% ($n = 2$) consisted of primarily text. The remaining pin was a mix of image and text. Finally, 0.22% ($n = 2$) of the nine pins used narrative information, 0.22% ($n = 2$) used statistical information, and 0.56% ($n = 5$) did not use either.

H1: Pinterest will contain more pins focusing on narrative MMR and DTP vaccination information than on statistical representations.

Of all 788 pins, 25.1% ($n = 198$) used narrative information, whereas 45.4% ($n = 358$) used primarily statistical information to communicate; 29.4% ($n = 232$) did not use either. Provaccine pins used more statistical information (55.9%, $n = 81$) than narrative information (27.6%, $n = 40$). Antivaccine pins also used more statistical information (44.9%, $n = 266$) than narrative information (25.1%, $n = 149$). HI is therefore not supported: whereas not all pins in this study used this manner of framing, the pins that did used statistical framing more frequently. In addition, both provaccine pins and antivaccine pins used more statistical information than narrative information.

H2: Pinterest pins focused on anti-MMR and anti-DTP vaccination information will elicit less engagement than pins focused on provaccination information.

The mean of the third of the fourth engagement variables (repins, likes, and total engagement) was lower for the antivaccine pins than for the provaccine pins. The mean number of repins for antivaccination pins was 16.04, whereas the mean number of repins for provaccination pins was 18.50. The mean number of likes for antivaccination pins was 2.76, whereas the mean number of likes for provaccination pins was 4.58. However, the mean number of comments for antivaccination pins was 1.27, whereas the mean number of comments for provaccination pins was 0.72. Finally, the mean number of total engagement (the sum of the number of repins, likes, and comments per pin) for antivaccination pins was 20.09, whereas the mean number of total engagement for provaccination pins was 23.80, which is not a significant difference ($t = 0.42$ (157.59), $p = 0.674$). Thus, H2 is not supported: in this study, contrary to earlier studies in the field, there is no difference in total engagement between provaccination pins and antivaccination pins.

Discussion and Practical Implications

This study focused on the portrayal of two common childhood vaccines—the MMR vaccine and the DTP vaccine—on the social media platform Pinterest. Two quantitative content analyses of keyword-based pins and pins posted by pediatric health organizations showed that the majority of pins, as was the case in a previous study, had an antivaccine stance (Guidry et al., 2015). This is a concerning result considering the role these vaccines play in preventing often serious infectious diseases like the measles, tetanus, and pertussis (whooping cough).

Two interesting findings are related to the level of engagement the keyword-based pins elicit: in contrast to earlier studies (Briones et al., 2012; Guidry et al., 2015), there was no difference in engagement level between provaccine posts and antivaccine posts. However, the level of engagement was higher than in the previous Pinterest study focused on vaccines, perhaps because this study deals with two childhood-specific vaccines and Pinterest has a majority of moms among its users (Guidry et al., 2015).

Surprisingly, both pro- and antivaccine pins used more statistically framed information in the pins included in this sample. This is surprising because in previous studies antivaccine posts were more likely to use narrative information. Still, several studies have noted that narrative information focused on adverse vaccination events will decrease vaccination intentions, as well as narratives having an overall stronger influence than statistical information (C. Betsch et al., 2011). Public health professionals and health educators should consider including narrative information when they address vaccine safety.

Using both the SMCC model and attribution theory, the results of this study show that many antivaccine pinners attribute blame for alleged vaccine-adverse events to the organizations and groups who distribute and manufacture childhood vaccines (such as the CDC, the pharmaceutical industry, and medical professionals) and believe they (the pinners) are intentionally being misled regarding the safety and effectiveness of vaccines. In addition, many pinners believe that doctors, pharmaceutical companies, and regulatory agencies are involved in a conspiracy to either distribute vaccines that do not work in order to create more revenue or to distribute vaccines that are known to hurt their recipients. Furthermore, these results point to a deep level of mistrust in government and medical authorities as it related to vaccines, and parents who do not vaccinate because of a lack of confidence in vaccines and those who manufacture and administer them are less likely to change their minds on vaccinating their children (C. Betsch, Korn, & Holtmann, 2015). These issues are of particular concern in the field of health communications because social media enables this type of misinformation to be spread quickly and widely.

Finally, and perhaps most importantly, this study shows that pediatric health organizations at this point do not respond to antivaccine concerns (or to any type of vaccine messaging) on Pinterest and barely mention the topic in their own pins. Public health organizations and pediatric health institutions need to take a more proactive role in ongoing discussion about vaccine safety on Pinterest so that rumors are contained and prevented from spreading further.

Conclusion, Practical Implications, and Future Directions

The results of this study confirm that vaccine conversations on Pinterest are primarily negative in stance, take place outside of usual health communication channels, and do not elicit responses from health communication and medical professionals. Furthermore, government and medical authorities are often seen as intentionally inflicting the harm that vaccines are perceived to cause, and pediatric health organizations with a presence on Pinterest seldom publish pins on the topic of childhood vaccines, let alone address this dynamic of fear and blame.

Future studies should first focus on determining how health communication professionals can participate in especially negative online vaccine conversations, both to address vaccine concerns and correct misinformation. In addition, messages for use in conversations on different types of social media platforms should be developed specifically for each platform and tested among relevant population segments. These messages should address the fears of both vaccine-adverse effects and in government and medical authorities who are perceived to intentionally create harm. Finally, considering the high level of conspiracy theories and assigned blame in these conversations, there may be a need to involve less traditional health communication pathways.

Note

1 Image type = 1.00, image stance = .77, caption stance = .81, story type = .77, conspiracy theory = .81, civil liberties = .81, type of website = .79, crisis responsibility = .85, Crisis origin = .91

References

Ache, K. A., & Wallace, L. S. (2008). Human papillomavirus vaccination coverage on YouTube. *American Journal of Preventive Medicine, 35*, 389–392. doi: 10.1016/j.amepre. 2008.06.029

Allen, A. (2007). *Vaccine: The controversial story of medicine's greatest lifesaver.* New York: W.W. Norton.

Betsch, C., Korn, L., & Holtmann, C. (2015). Don't try to convert the antivaccinators, instead target the fence-sitters. *Proceedings of the National Academy of Sciences, 112*(49), E6725–E6726.

Betsch, C., Renkewitz, F., Betsch, T., & Ulshöfer, C. (2010). The influence of vaccine-critical websites on perceiving vaccination risks. *Journal of Health Psychology, 15*, 446. doi: 10.1177/1359105309353647

Betsch, C., Ulshofer, C., Renkewitz, F., & Betsch, T. (2011). The influence of narrative v: Statistical information on perceiving vaccination risks. *Medical Decision Making, 31*, 742–753. doi: 10.1177/0272989X11400419

Bortree, D. S., & Seltzer, T. (2009). Dialogic strategies and outcomes: An analysis of environmental advocacy groups' Facebook profiles. *Public Relations Review, 35*(3), 317–319. doi: 10.1016/j.pubrev.2009.05.002

Boyce, T. (2007). *Health, risk and news: The MMR vaccine and the media.* New York: Peter Lang.

Briones, R. L., Nan, X., Madden, K., & Waks, L. (2012). When vaccines go viral: An analysis of HPV vaccine coverage on YouTube. *Health Communication, 27,* 478–485. doi: 10.1080/10410236.2011.610258

Coombs, W. T. (2007a). Attribution theory as a guide for post-crisis communication research. *Public Relations Review, 33,* 135–139. doi: 10.1016/j.pubrev.2006.11.016

Coombs, W. T. (2007b). Protecting organization reputations during a crisis: The development and application of situational crisis communication theory. *Corporate Reputation Review, 10*(3), 163–176. doi: 10.1057/palgrave.crr.1550049

Corner, J., Richardson, K., & Fenton, N. (1990). Textualizing risk: TV discourse and the issue of nuclear energy. *Media, Culture & Society, 12,* 105–124.

Davies, P., Chapman, S., & Leask, J. (2002). Antivaccination activists on the World Wide Web. *Archives of Disease in Childhood, 87,* 22–25.

DiStaso, M. W., & Messner, M. (2010). Forced transparency: Corporate image on Wikipedia and what it means for public relations. *Public Relations Journal, 4*(2), 1–23.

DiStaso, M. W., Messner, M., & Stacks, D. W. (2007). The wiki factor: A study of reputation management. In S. Duhé (Ed.), *New media and public relations* (pp. 121–133). New York: Peter Lang.

Godlee, F., Smith, J., & Marcovitch, H. (2011). Wakefield's article linking MMR vaccine and autism was fraudulent. *BMJ British Medical Journal, 342,* c7452.

Guidry, J. D., Carlyle, K., Messner, M., & Jin, Y. (2015). On pins and needles: How vaccines are portrayed on Pinterest. *Vaccine, 33,* 5051–5056.

Houts, P. S., Doak, C. C., Doak, L. G., & Loscalzo, M. J. (2006). The role of pictures in improving health communication: A review of research on attention, comprehension, recall, and adherence. *Patient Education and Counseling, 61,* 173–190. doi: 10.1016/j.pec.2005.05.004

Jin, Y., & Liu, B. F. (2010). The blog-mediated crisis communication model: Recommendations for responding to influential external blogs. *Journal of Public Relations Research, 22,* 429–455. doi: 10.1080/10627261003801420

Jin, Y., Liu, B. F., & Austin, L. L. (2014). Examining the role of social media in effective crisis management: The effects of crisis origin, information form, and source on publics' crisis responses. *Communication Research, 41*(1), 74–94. doi: 10.1177/0093650211423918

Kasperson, R. E., Renn, O., Slovic, P., Brown, H. S., Emel, J., Goble, R., . . . Ratick, S. (1988). The social amplification of risk: A conceptual framework. *Risk Analysis, 8*(2), 177–187.

Kata, A. (2012). Anti-vaccine activists, Web 2.0, and the postmodern paradigm: An overview of tactics and tropes used online by the anti-vaccination movement. *Vaccine, 30*(25), 3778–3789. doi: 10.1016/j.vaccine.2011.11.112

Keelan, J., Pavri, V., Balakrishnan, R., & Wilson, K. (2010). An analysis of the Human Papilloma Virus vaccine debate on MySpace blogs. *Vaccine, 28,* 1535–1540. doi: 10.1016/j.vaccine.2009.11.060

Keelan, J., Pavri-Garcia, V., Tomlinson, G., & Wilson, K. (2007). YouTube as a source of information on immunization: A content analysis. *JAMA: The Journal of the American Medical Association, 298,* 2482.

Kitta, A. (2012). *Vaccinations and public concern in history: Legend, rumor, and risk perception.* New York: Routledge.

Love, B., Himelboim, I., Holton, A., & Stewart, K. (2013). Twitter as a source of vaccination information: Content drivers and what they are saying. *American Journal of Infection Control, 41,* 568–570. doi: 10.1016/j.ajic.2012.10.016

Mansoor, L. E., & Dowse, R. (2003). Effect of pictograms on readability of patient information materials. *The Annals of Pharmacotherapy, 37*, 1003.

Michielutte, R., Bahnson, J., Dignan, M. B., & Schroeder, E. M. (1992). The use of illustrations and narrative text style to improve readability of a health education brochure. *Journal of Cancer Education, 7*(3), 251–260.

Offit, P. A., & Coffin, S. E. (2003). Communicating science to the public: MMR vaccine and autism. *Vaccine, 22*, 1–6. doi: 10.1016/S0264-410X(03)00532-2

Ołpiński, M. (2012). Anti-vaccination movement and parental refusals of immunization of children in USA. *Pediatria Polska, 87*, 381–385. doi: 10.1016/j.pepo.2012.05.003

Ottoni, R., Las Casas, D., Pesce, J. P., Meira, W. Jr, Wilson, C., Mislove, A., & Almeida, V. (2014, June). *Of pins and tweets: Investigating how users behave across image-and text-based social networks.* Paper presented at the Eighth International AAAI Conference on Weblogs and Social Media, Ann Arbor, MI.

Pinterest. (2015). Oh, how pinteresting! Retrieved from https://blog.pinterest.com/en/100-million-most-interesting-people-we-know

Poland, G. A. (2011). MMR vaccine and autism: Vaccine nihilism and postmodern science. *Mayo Clinic Proceedings, 86*(9), 869–871. doi: 10.4065/mcp.2011.0467

Poland, G. A., & Jacobson, R. M. (1994). Failure to reach the goal of measles elimination—Apparent paradox of measles infections in immunized persons. *Archives of Internal Medicine, 154*, 1815–1820.

ROI Research. (2012). Life on demand: Participant behavior and social engagement. Retrieved from http://www.slideshare.net/performics_us/performics-life-on-demand-2012-summary-deck

Rybalko, S., & Seltzer, T. (2010). Dialogic communication in 140 characters or less: How Fortune 500 companies engage stakeholders using Twitter. *Public Relations Review, 36*(4), 336–341. doi: 10.1016/j.pubrev.2010.08.004

Scott, W. A. (1955). Reliability of content analysis: The case of nominal scale coding. *The Public Opinion Quarterly, 19*, 321–325.

Smith, P. J., Chu, S. Y., & Barker, L. E. (2004). Children who have received no vaccines: Who are they and where do they live? *Pediatrics, 114*, 187.

Sugerman, D. E., Barskey, A. E., Delea, M. G., Ortega-Sanchez, I. R., Bi, D., Ralston, K. J., . . . Lebaron, C. W. (2010). Measles outbreak in a highly vaccinated population, San Diego, 2008: Role of the intentionally undervaccinated. *Pediatrics, 125*, 747–755. doi: 10.1542/peds.2009-1653

Taylor, B., Miller, E., Farrington, C. P., Petropoulos, M.-C., Favot-Mayaud, I., Li, J., & Waight, P. A. (1999). Autism and measles, mumps, and rubella vaccine: No epidemiological evidence for a causal association. *The Lancet, 353*, 2026–2029. doi: 10.1016/S0140-6736(99)01239-8

Tirkkonen, P., & Luoma-aho, V. (2011). Online authority communication during an epidemic: A Finnish example. *Public Relations Review, 37*(2), 172–174.

Wakefield, A. J., Murch, S. H., Anthony, A., Linnell, J., Casson, D. M., Malik, M., . . . Walker-Smith, J. A. (1998). RETRACTED: Ileal-lymphoid-nodular hyperplasia, nonspecific colitis, and pervasive developmental disorder in children. *The Lancet, 351*, 637–641. doi: 10.1016/S0140-6736(97)11096-0

SECTION IV-D
Areas of Application

Disaster

20

SOCIAL MEDIA USE DURING DISASTERS[1]

A Research Synthesis and Road Map

Julia Daisy Fraustino, Brooke Fisher Liu, and Yan Jin

Half of Americans rate the Internet as their preferred news source, a proportion that jumps to 75% for younger adults (Caumont, 2013). Individuals are even more active online during disasters, increasingly using social media in particular to seek and share information and support. However, publics use social media for more than information seeking or sharing during disasters. They increasingly expect emergency managers to monitor and respond to social media posts, often demanding action. Three quarters of American Red Cross (2010) survey respondents indicated they expected help to arrive within an hour of posting a social media request. Yet, another survey found the majority of emergency responders use social media for one-way information pushing rather than responding to and conversing with their publics (Su, Wardell, & Thorkildsen, 2013).

Given the increasingly important roles social media play during disasters and the apparent disparity in organizations' and publics' expectations, it is essential to understand what is known and remains to be tested about social media use during disasters. Otherwise, practitioners and policy makers risk making emergency communication decisions based on intuition or inaccurate information, and scholars leave important questions theoretically untapped. To that end, this chapter synthesizes existing research and gives a recommended road map for future research in this realm. First, it is important to establish baseline definitions of core concepts.

Disaster, Crisis, Disaster Communication, and Social Media

Disasters are sometimes equated with crises; however, researchers have singled out crises as organization based whereas disasters are community based (Seeger, Sellnow, & Ulmer, 1998). That is, a disaster is a "serious disruption of the functioning of a community or a society causing widespread human, material, economic or environmental losses which exceed the ability of the affected community or society to cope using its own resources" (National Science and Technology Council, 2005, p. 21). Despite a plethora of research on disasters and crises, the literature generally leaves disaster *communication* undefined. Consequently, proposing a definition here may be useful. Based on the given understanding of disasters, disaster communication deals with (a) disaster information disseminated to publics by governments, emergency management organizations, and disaster responders—often via traditional and social media, as well as (b) disaster information created and shared by journalists and affected or interested community members—often through word-of-mouth communication and social media.

In contrast to the lack of definitions surrounding disaster communication, studies often describe or define social media, taking a variety of perspectives. Here, social and emerging media are broadly understood as interactive digital or mobile websites, applications, platforms, or tools holding content that users may generate, manipulate, or influence. Social media are conducive to timely, interactive communication and can facilitate content exchange and dialogue among message consumers and creators (Wright & Hinson, 2013). Although many traditional media forms (e.g., newspapers, radio, and television) have been and remain important for disaster communication, they involve static, one-way information dissemination. The social media realm includes a multitude of two-way communication technologies, some of which are displayed with examples in Table 20.1.

TABLE 20.1 Social Media Types and Examples

Social Media Type	Examples
Blogs	Blogger, WordPress
Discussion forums	LiveJournal, ProBoards
Location tracking and displaying	Banjo, Foursquare
Microblogs	Tumblr, Twitter
Photo and video Sharing	Flickr, Instagram, Pinterest, Vine, YouTube,
Social bookmarking	Del.icio.us, Diigo
Social commerce and couponing	Groupon, Polyvore
Social discovery engines and news sources	Reddit, StumbleUpon
Social music sources	Pandora, Spotify
Social or professional networking	Facebook, LinkedIn
Social rating and reviews	AngiesList, Yelp
Social recruiting	Indeed, Glassdoor
Social travel	TripAdvisor, Tripline
Video and text Chatting	Google Hangouts, mobile texting, Skype, WhatsApp
Wikis	Wikipedia, Wikispaces

Social Media Use During Disasters

Research has begun to suggest the particular medium used to obtain disaster information can be as important as the information itself in influencing publics' responses (Jin & Liu, 2010; Schultz, Utz, & Göritz, 2011). Factors such as information form (i.e., the channel or medium used to communicate) and information source (i.e., the entity communicating) can impact receivers' acceptance of disaster messages and which media forms they choose for additional information (e.g., Austin, Liu, & Jin, 2012; Schultz et al., 2011). However, research has yet to consistently parse out individual and joint effects of various social media forms on publics' disaster information consumption and sharing, as well as the resulting behaviors.

Key Publics in Social-Mediated Disaster Communication

In understanding publics' disaster information seeking and sharing, research has begun to identify three publics that emerge during disasters: influential social media creators, social media followers, and social media inactives.

Influential social media creators perceive the disaster's importance and talk about it online (Liu, Jin, Briones, & Kutch, 2012). Influential social media creators (a) have more knowledge or experience regarding a specific disaster issue than others do or (b) are more interested in learning about a specific disaster issue than others are (Jin & Liu, 2010). Nagar, Seth, and Joshi (2012) analyzed tweets from the 2010 Philippines typhoon, 2011 Brazil flood, and 2011 Japan earthquake, finding more than 90% of tweeters were part of a connected group of influencers that emerged quickly after each disaster.

Social media followers are those who receive disaster information from influential social media content creators either directly or indirectly (Jin & Liu, 2010). Initial research points to the possibility that most who are active on social media during disasters are likely followers, given that publics primarily use social media to obtain or share rather than create disaster information (Hughes & Palen, 2009; Reynolds & Seeger, 2012).

Social media inactives do not use social media but may receive disaster information through offline word-of-mouth communication with social media followers and social media creators. Inactives tend to prefer traditional media for disaster information (Littlefield & Quenette, 2007; Seeger et al., 2003), but interpersonal communication is also important (Austin et al., 2012; Jin & Liu, 2010). Disasters may cause social media inactives to use social media for the first time, as documented during the 2011 Joplin tornado (William, Williams, & Burton, 2012).

Reasons Publics Use Social Media During Disasters

Overall, emerging research has revealed that individuals use social media differently during disasters than they do routinely. Scholars have called for more research on how publics make meaning during disasters—especially given that most crisis communication research instead focuses on organizations' information management (Liu & Fraustino, 2014). Some have started to answer this call, identifying why publics use and do not use social media for disaster communication. Largely, such research concludes that individuals use social media during disasters for the following reasons.

Because of Convenience

As discussed previously, social media provide nearly immediate access to up-to-date information, community interaction, and other support for publics during disasters (Liu, Jin, & Austin, 2013). Enhancing access to these features, nearly half of all Americans are smartphone owners (Smith, 2012), carrying in their pockets the capability to log on to a desired social media application with the tap of a finger. Free public library computer use, personal computers, laptops, tablets and e-readers, and mobile phones provide individuals previously unparalleled convenience in access to social media content.

Based on Social Norms

Social norms impact social media use in general, dictating that individuals are more likely to use a particular medium if (a) their friends and family frequently use it and (b) they trust and ascribe a high level of credibility to social media (Liu et al., 2013). A consistent research finding is that people turn to previously existing social networks during disasters (e.g., Spiro et al., 2012).

Based on Personal Recommendations

As just mentioned, individuals are more likely to use social media if their friends and family do, especially based on recommendations. Young adults have explained they might join Facebook groups to support disaster efforts if they saw their friends were doing the same (Liu et al., 2013). And when individuals receive recommendations to take up new social media during disasters and they do so, they often remain users even after the disaster ebbs (Hughes & Palen, 2009).

For Humor and Levity

Humor can motivate online disaster communication. Researchers found the most frequently shared tweets during three days of the 2011 Egyptian revolution fit into three categories: event updates, human-interest stories, and humor (Choudhary, Hendrix, Lee, Palsetia, & Lia, 2012). Positive emotions can be important coping mechanisms during and after disasters (Fredrickson, Tugade, Waugh, & Larkin, 2003). However, an important practical consideration is that some individuals consider humor inappropriate during disasters, such that humor can become a reason people report *not* using social media during disasters (Liu et al., 2013). Such perceived (in)appropriateness may vary based on disaster stage. For example, Fraustino and Ma (2015) found humor received positive audience attention and reception in basic disaster preparedness communication via social media, but Chew and Eysenbach (2010) found people posted fewer humorous comments about the 2009 H1N1 pandemic in particular as the seriousness of the situation increased.

For Information Seeking

Disasters often prompt high levels of uncertainty, spurring heightened information seeking, as seen in research on the September 11 terrorist attacks (Boyle, Schmierbach, Armstrong, & McLeod, 2004) and many other scenarios. When disasters occur, individuals might aim solely to find, not share or discuss, information (Hughes & Palen, 2009). Examining Twitter communication related to a major wildfire in 2011, researchers found some users were passive, only searching for and filtering information (Merrifield & Palenchar, 2012). Other reports, however, seem contradictory. For example, after the Hurricane Sandy in 2011, Fairfax County, Virginia, received 10,175 "likes" on their Facebook page, and more than 127,254 people shared Fairfax County's Sandy content on their own Facebook pages (Fairfax County, n.d.), effectively bringing these individuals' information seeking into the sharing realm as well.

For Timely Information

Social media provide real-time disaster information and thus can become a principal source of time-sensitive reports, especially when official sources are perceived as slow or unavailable (Spiro et al., 2012). During the 2007 California wildfires, publics turned to social media because they thought journalists and public officials were not providing relevant information quickly enough about their communities (Sutton, Palen, & Shklovski, 2008). Such time-sensitive information can be useful for officials. Analyzing more than 500 million tweets, Culotta (2010) found Twitter data forecasted future influenza rates with high accuracy during the 2009 pandemic, obtaining a 95% correlation with the national health statistics that had a typical lag time of one to two weeks for influenza reporting.

For Unique Information

Social media can often provide unique information (Caplan, Perse, & Gennaria, 2007). For example, individuals on the disaster scene may provide personal stories and give updates more quickly than traditional news sources and disaster response organizations, as was the case during the Boston Marathon bombings (Gilgoff &

Lee, 2013). During tornadoes in Tuscaloosa, residents turned to social media for volunteer opportunities (Stephens, 2011). And during the Elk River chemical spill contamination of 2014, West Virginia residents logged on to the grassroots Facebook group WV Clean Water Hub to share stories and information about access (or lack thereof) to clean drinking water, often questioning or refuting reports from more official sources (Fraustino, 2014).

For Unfiltered Information

To obtain crisis and disaster information, individuals often communicate with one another via social media rather than seeking a traditional news source or organizational website (Stephens & Malone, 2009). Research participants reported checking in with social media not only to obtain up-to-date, timely information unavailable elsewhere but also because they appreciate that information may be unfiltered by traditional media, organizations, or politicians (Liu et al., 2013).

To Determine Disaster Magnitude

People often log on to social media to stay apprised of a disaster's damage. They may turn to governmental or organizational sources for this information, but if publics do not receive the information they desire when they desire it, they or others will fill in the blanks (Stephens & Malone, 2009). For instance, several edited photos spread on Twitter during Hurricane Sandy inaccurately intensified the disaster magnitude (Kafka, 2012). On the flipside, when people believed emergency response officials were not disseminating enough information regarding the size and trajectory of the 2007 California wildfires, they used social media to track fire locations and notify residents potentially in danger (Sutton et al., 2008).

To Check in With Family and Friends

Social media can provide ways to ensure safety, offer support, and give and receive timely personal status updates (Procopio & Procopio, 2007; Stephens & Malone, 2009). Nearly half of respondents to an American Red Cross (2010) survey reported they would use social media to let loved ones know of their safety during a disaster. Correspondingly, after the 2011 earthquake and tsunami in Japan, people turned to a variety of social media to keep in touch with loved ones while mobile networks were down (Gao, Barbier, & Goolsby, 2011). In the wake of the 2015 Paris terrorist attacks, Facebook pledged to activate its Safety Check feature not only for natural disasters but also more human disasters (Deluca, 2015). Facebook's Safety Check allows and urges those within range of a particular disaster area to "check in" via the social networking site to inform friends of their safety.

To Share Relief Updates and Self-Mobilize

Publics may use social media to organize emergency relief efforts from near and far, for example, as "voluntweeters" (Starbird & Palen, 2011). Similarly, research has documented the role of Facebook and Twitter in disaster relief fundraising (PEJ New Media Index, 2010). Showcasing how social media can help identify and respond to urgent needs surrounding disasters, just two hours after the 2010 Haitian earthquake, Tufts University volunteers created Ushahidi-Haiti, a crisis map where disaster survivors and volunteers could send incident reports via text messages and tweets. In less than two weeks, 2,500 incident reports were sent to the map (Gao et al., 2011).

To Maintain a Sense of Community

During disasters, media in general and social media in particular may help provide a unique gratification: sense of community, even when scattered across a vast geographical area (Lev-On, 2011; Procopio & Procopio, 2007). Such online communities can be integral to recovery, perhaps particularly for physically displaced individuals (Reynolds & Seeger, 2012).

To Seek Emotional Support and Healing

Finally, disasters are often tragic, prompting individuals to seek human contact, conversation, and emotional care (Sutton et al., 2008). Social media are positioned to facilitate emotional support, allowing individuals to foster virtual communities and relationships, share information and feelings, and even demand resolution (Stephens & Malone, 2009). Plentiful research has found social media can aid healing during both natural (Procopio & Procopio, 2007) and person-made disasters (Perng et al., 2012).

Reasons Publics Might Not Use Social Media During Disasters

Not all individuals and publics use social media for disaster communication. Some reasons for avoidance include the following.

Privacy and Security Fears

Trepidation about privacy and security violations related to social media during disasters is pervasive (Mills, Chen, Lee, & Rao, 2009; Yates & Paquette, 2011). Although social media provide benefits in their ability to send important information across the globe with the press of a button, the flipside is personal communication can be spread just as quickly and broadly. Further, given the public nature of social media, some worry about criminals mining social media after disasters (Yates & Paquette, 2011).

Accuracy Concerns

Inaccuracy of disaster information is a concern that may lead to social media avoidance (Stephens & Malone, 2009; Veil, Buehner, & Palenchar, 2011). Such concerns are reasonable, considering existing research provides conflicting data, even when studying the same disaster. For example, Chew and Eysenbach (2010) found only a small minority of H1N1 pandemic-related tweets contained misinformation or speculation; but Scanfeld, Scanfeld, and Larson (2011) concluded the opposite when taking into account how misinformation reached a wide network of Twitter users. Of course, as noted previously, social media hoaxes remain real possibilities during disasters. More research is needed to evaluate the accuracy of social media content produced during disasters.

Access Issues

Discussion of social media use is predicated on an assumption that publics have access to the tools, but this is not always so. During disasters resulting in power outages, individuals who most need information and support can lose technical connections. Perhaps a more systemic barrier is the *digital divide*, characterized by the lack of access to the Internet and technology that individuals of low socioeconomic status may experience (Veil et al., 2011). As Veil and colleagues (2011) pointed out, free use is practically useless when lacking requisite technology.

Lack of Social Media Know-How

Finally, certain publics might not know how to use social media prior to disasters (Williams, Williams, & Burton, 2012). As a consequence, they are less likely to use social media during disasters (Reynolds & Seeger, 2012).

Research Gaps

The research on social media use during disasters is young but vibrant, yet there remain more knowledge gaps than answers.

Social Media Types and Functions

Research on social media use during disasters has overwhelmingly examined one social media type, such as Twitter, and researchers tend to generalize findings from that type to all social media. As a consequence, more research is needed to understand what, if any, unique roles various social media forms play, individually or even jointly, in publics' communication activities during disasters.

Primary Functions

Research has identified several reasons why publics use and do not use social media during disasters. Missing from the literature is research on whether users deem some functions as more important than others during disasters. Intuitively, different social media functions may vary in different situations, likely at least by disaster type and social media type, as well as user individual differences such as demographics and psychographics. Yet, existing research does not yet provide solid evidence-based guidance for identifying these possible differences.

Social Media Type

Academic scholarship tends to look at one or two types of social media at a time—often the popular longer-standing forms such as Facebook, Twitter, and blogs—with little regard for whether and how these sites act or are perceived differently. With the media landscape quickly evolving, the social media realm has experienced, for example, a marked increase in sites focused dominantly or solely on visuals (e.g., YouTube, Vimeo, Pinterest, Flickr, Instagram, Snapchat). Online Americans report massive use of visual-based sites such as YouTube for sharing and collecting news and information (Anderson, 2015), and citizen eyewitnesses of disasters now often provide the most breaking and viewed visual coverage of disaster information (Jurkowitz & Hitlin, 2013). These considerations prompt important research questions pertaining to whether particular platforms' inherent or perceived characteristic differences might impact usage and response and whether these platforms can be grouped into generalizable categories or instead must continue to be studied individually.

Disaster Type

Existing research lacks tests of how specific disaster types, such as severe weather events, health epidemics, and terrorist attacks, may result in different social media use needs or patterns, with limited exceptions (e.g., Liu, Fraustino, & Jin, 2015). Instead, research tends to examine one catastrophic event without comparison or contrast to other types. Examining different disaster types can strengthen the empirical record and provide a base for tailored communication recommendations.

Moving to Cause-Effect Explanation

Existing research does not comprehensively provide cause-effect explanations and evidence-based guidelines. Compounding the problem is dominant reliance on convenience samples, usually college students, for the few published experiments that do allow for causal explanations. Such student samples are valuable for establishing relationships among variables, but findings cannot be generalized to broader populations. The literature is also short on longitudinal studies, such as capturing social media use prior to a disaster, during the immediate response, and into recovery.

Developing Influence

Research must look at what motivates individuals to become influential in creating and distributing disaster information and others to perceive them as influential. It could be helpful in theory and practice to map the information flow among these influential social media creators and social media followers and inactives. Such mapping would allow for assessment of which sources, forms, and message features are most effective in facilitating disaster resilience and renewal.

The Road to Resilience Ahead

Ultimately, understanding what is not known about social media use during disasters is as important as knowing what has been scientifically validated. As this young research stream moves forward, more guidance will emerge to explain how various communication forms, sources, and content elements interact surrounding disaster information and, most crucially, to what extent those disaster messages influence communities' disaster recovery and resilience.

Note

1 This work was supported by the U.S. Department of Homeland Security Science and Technology Directorate under award number 2012ST061CS00, made to the National Consortium for the Study of Terrorism and Responses to Terrorism (START). The views and conclusions contained in this manuscript are those of the authors and should not be interpreted as necessarily representing the official policies, either expressed or implied, of the U.S. Department of Homeland Security or START.

References

American Red Cross. (2010). Social media in disasters and emergencies. Retrieved from http://www.redcross.org/wwwfiles/Documents/pdf/other/SocialMediaSlideDeck.pdf

Anderson, M. (2015, February 12). 5 facts about online video, for YouTube's 10th birthday. *Pew Research Center*. Retrieved from http://www.pewresearch.org/fact-tank/2015/02/12/5-facts-about-online-video-for-youtubes-10th-birthday/

Austin, L., Liu, B. F., & Jin, Y. (2012). How audiences seek out crisis information: Exploring the social-mediated crisis communication model. *Journal of Applied Communication Research, 40*(2), 188–207.

Boyle, M., Schmierbach, M., Armstrong, C., & McLeod, D. (2004). Information seeking and emotional reactions to the September 11 terrorist attacks. *Journalism and Mass Communication Quarterly, 81*(1), 155–167.

Caplan, S. E., Perse, E. M., & Gennaria, J. E. (2007). Computer-mediated technology and social interaction. In C. A. Lin & D. J. Atkin (Eds.), *Communication technology and social change: Theory and implication* (pp. 39–57). Mahwah, NJ: Lawrence Erlbaum.

Caumont, A. (2013, October 16). 12 trends shaping digital news. *Pew Internet.* Retrieved from http://www.pewresearch.org/fact-tank/2013/10/16/12-trends-shaping-digital-news/

Chew, C., & Eysenbach, G. (2010). Pandemics in the age of Twitter: Content analysis of tweets during the 2009 H1N1 outbreak. *PLoS ONE, 5*(11), 1–13.

Choudhary, A., Hendrix, W., Lee, K., Palsetia, D., & Liao, W.-K. (2012, May). Social media evolution of the Egyptian revolution. *Communications of the ACM, 55*(5), 74–80.

Culotta, A. (2010, July). *Towards detecting influenza epidemics by analyzing Twitter messages.* Proceedings of the First Workshop on Social Media Analytics, Washington, DC, Retrieved from http://dl.acm.org.proxy-um.researchport.umd.edu/citation.cfm?id=1964858&picked=prox

Deluca, M. (2015). Facebook broadens "safety check" feature after Paris attacks. *NBCNews.com.* http://www.nbcnews.com/storyline/paris-terror-attacks/facebook-broadens-safety-check-feature-after-paris-attacks-n464206

Fairfax County. (n.d.). Metrics report: Special edition: Hurricane Sandy. Retrieved from http://www.fairfaxcounty.gov/emergency/metrics/hurricane-sandy-metrics.pdf

Fink, S. (1986). *Crisis management: Planning for the inevitable.* New York: AMACOM.

Fraustino, J. D. (2014). Beyond image repair: Suggestions for crisis communication theory development. *Public Relations Review, 40*(3), 543–546.

Fraustino, J. D., & Ma, L. (2015). CDC's use of social media and humor in a risk campaign: "Preparedness 101: Zombie Apocalypse." *Journal of Applied Communication Research, 43*(2), 222–241.

Fredrickson, B. L., Tugade, M. M., Waugh, C. E., & Larkin, G. R. (2003). What good are positive emotions in crisis? A prospective study of resilience and emotions following the terrorist attacks on the United States on September 11th, 2001. *Journal of Personality and Social Psychology, 84*(2), 365–376.

Gao, H., Barbier, G., & Goolsby, R. (2011). Harnessing the crowdsourcing power of social media for disaster relief. *IEE Intelligent Systems.* Retrieve from http://wordpress.vrac. iastate.edu/REU2011/wp-content/uploads/2011/05/Harnessing-the-Crowdsourcins-Power-of-Social-Media-for-Disaster-Relief.pdf

Gilgoff, D., & Lee, J. J. (2013, April 15). Social media shapes Boston bombings response: Twitter and Facebook created national response, may help authorities. *National Geographic.* Retrieved from http://news.nationalgeographic.com/news/2013/13/130415-boston-marathon-bombings-terrorism-social-media-twitter-facebook/

Hughes, A. L., & Palen, L. (2009). Twitter adoption and use in mass convergence and emergency events. *International Journal of Emergency Management, 6*(3), 248–260.

Jin, Y., & Liu, B. F. (2010). The blog-mediated crisis communication model: Recommendations for responding to influential external blogs. *Journal of Public Relations Research, 22*(4), 429–455.

Jurkowitz, M., & Hitlin, P. (2013, May 22). Citizen eyewitnesses provide majority of top online news videos in Oklahoma tornado disaster. *Pew Research Center.* Retrieved from http://www.pewresearch.org/fact-tank/2013/05/22/citizen-eyewitnesses-provide-majority-of-top-online-news-videos-in-oklahoma-tornado-disaster/

Kafka, P. (2012, October 29). No, that amazing Hurricane Sandy photo isn't real. *All Things D.* Retrieved from http://allthingsd.com/20121029/no-that-amazing-hurricane-sandy-photo-isnt-real/

Lev-On, A. (2011). Communication, community, crisis: Mapping uses and gratifications in the contemporary media environment. *New Media Society, 14*(1), 98–116.

Littlefield, R. S., & Quenette, A. M. (2007). Crisis leadership and Hurricane Katrina: The portrayal of authority by the media in natural disasters. *Journal of Applied Communication Research, 35*(1), 26–47.

Liu, B. F., & Fraustino, J. D. (2014). Beyond image repair: Suggestions for crisis communication theory development. *Public Relations Review, 40*(3), 543–546.

Liu, B. F., Fraustino, J. D., & Jin, Y. (2015). How disaster information form, source, type, and prior disaster exposure affect public outcomes: Jumping on the social media bandwagon? *Journal of Applied Communication Research, 43*(1), 44–65.

Liu, B. F., Jin, Y., & Austin, L. L. (2013). The tendency to tell: Understanding publics' communicative responses to crisis information form and source. *Journal of Public Relations Research, 25*(1), 51–67.

Liu, B. F., Jin, Y., Briones, R., & Kuch, B. (2012). Managing turbulence in the blogosphere: Evaluating the blog-mediated crisis communication model with the American Red Cross. *Journal of Public Relations Research, 24*, 353–370.

Merrifield, N., & Palenchar, M. (2012, August). *Uncertainty reduction strategies via Twitter: The 2011 wildfire threat to Los Alamos National Laboratory.* Paper presented at the annual meeting of the Association for Education in Journalism and Mass Communication, Chicago, IL.

Mills, A., Chen, R., Lee, J., & Rao, H. R. (2009). Web 2.0 emergency applications: How useful can Twitter be for an emergency response? Retrieved from http://denman-mills. net/web_documents/jips_mills.etal._2009.07.22_finalsubmission.pdf

Nagar, S., Seth, A., & Joshi, A. (2012, April). *Characterization of social media response to natural disasters.* Paper presented at the International World Wide Web Conference, Lyon, France.

National Science and Technology Council. (2005, June). *Grand challenges for disaster reduction: A report of the Subcommittee on Disaster Reduction.* National Science and Technology Council, Executive Office of the President, Washington, DC. Retrieved from http:// www.sdr.gov/docs/SDRGrandChallengesforDisasterReduction.pdf

PEJ New Media Index. (2010, January 11–15). Social media aid the Haiti relief effort. *Pew Research Center's Project for Excellence in Journalism.* Retrieved from http://www.journalism.org/ index_report/social_media_aid_haiti_relief_effort

Perng, S.-Y., Halvorsrud, R., Buscher, M., Stiso, M., Wood, L., Ramirez, L., & Al-Akkad, A. (2012, April). *Peripheral response: Microblogging during the 22/7/2011 Norway attacks.* Proceedings of the 9th International ISCRAM Conference, Vancouver, Canada.

Procopio, C. H., & Procopio, S. T. (2007). Do you know what it means to miss New Orleans? Internet communication, geographic community, and social capital in crisis. *Journal of Applied Communication Research, 35*(1), 67–87.

Reynolds, B., & Seeger, M. (2012). Crisis and emergency risk communication. *U.S. Department of Health and Human Services Centers for Disease Control.* Retrieved from http:// emergency.cdc.gov/cerc/

Scanfeld, D., Scanfeld, V., & Larson, E. L. (2011). Dissemination of health information through social networks: Twitter and antibiotics. *American Journal of Infection Control, 38*(3), 182–188.

Schultz, F., Utz, S., & Göritz, A. (2011). Is the medium the message? Perceptions of and reactions to crisis communication via Twitter, blogs and traditional media. *Public Relations Review, 37*(1), 20–27.

Seeger, M. W., Sellnow, T. L., & Ulmer, R. R. (1998). Communication, organization, and crisis. *Communication Yearbook, 21*, 231–275.

Seeger, M. W., Sellnow, T. L., & Ulmer, R. R. (2003). *Communication and organizational crisis.* Westport, CN: Praeger.

Smith, A. (2012, March 1). Nearly half of American adults are smartphone owners. *Pew Internet & American Life Project.* Retrieved from http://pewinternet.org/Reports/2012/Smartphone-Update-2012/Findings.aspx

Spiro, E. S., Sutton, J., Greczek, M., Fitzhugh, S., Pierski, N., & Butts, C. (2012, June). *Rumoring during extreme events: A case study of Deepwater Horizon 2010.* Paper presented at WebSci 2012, Evanston, IL.

Starbird, K., & Palen, L. (2011, May). *"Voluntweeters": Self-organizing by digital volunteers in times of crisis.* Proceedings of the ACM 2011 Conference on Computer Human Interaction, Vancouver, BC, Canada.

Stephens, K. (2011, August 18). Tuscaloosa city schools turn to social media after the storms. *Idisaster 2.0.* Retrieved from http://idisaster.wordpress.com/2011/08/18/tuscaloosa-city-schools-turn-to-social-media-after-the-storms/

Stephens, K. K., & Malone, P. (2009). If the organizations won't give us information . . . : The use of multiple new media for crisis technical translations and dialogue. *Journal of Public Relations Research, 21*(2), 229–239.

Su, Y. S., Wardell, C., & Thorkildsen, Z. (2013, June). Social media in the emergency management field: 2012 survey results. *CNA.* Retrieved from http://www.cna.org/sites/default/files/research/SocialMedia_EmergencyManagement.pdf

Sutton, J., Palen, L., & Shklovski, I. (2008, May). *Backchannels on the front lines: Emergent uses of social media in the 2007 Southern California wildfires.* Proceedings of the 5th International ISCRAM Conference, Washington, DC.

Veil, S. R., Buehner, T., & Palenchar, M. (2011). A work-in-process literature review: Incorporating social media in risk and crisis communication. *Journal of Contingencies and Crisis Management, 19*(2), 110–122.

Williams, R., Williams, G., & Burton, D. (2012). The use of social media for disaster recovery. *University of Missouri Extension.* Retrieved from http://extension.missouri.edu/greene/documents/PlansReports/using%20social%20media%20in%20disasters.pdf

Wright, D. K., & Hinson, M. (2013). An updated examination of social and emerging media use in public relations practices: A longitudinal analysis between 2006 and 2013. *Public Relations Journal, 7*(3), article 1, 1–39. Retrieved from http://apps.prsa.org/Intelligence/PRJournal/past-editions/Vol7/No3

Yates, D., & Paquette, S. (2011). Emergency knowledge management and social media technologies: A case study of the 2010 Haitian earthquake. *International Journal of Information Management, 31,* 6013.

21

NATURAL DISASTERS, TWITTER, AND STAKEHOLDER COMMUNICATION

What We Know and Directions for Future Inquiry

Kenneth A. Lachlan, Patric Spence, and Xialing Lin

Background

Social media have, in a short period of time, forced scholars and practitioners alike to reconsider their assumptions about how to best reach audiences in times of crisis and emergency. Electronic resources such as Twitter and Facebook allow users to both create and disseminate content and facilitate shared understandings of content and subject matter across users and communities (O'Reilly & Battelle, 2009; Westerman, Spence, & Van Der Heide, 2012).

Twitter is an especially useful resource during crises and disasters, given its capacity for providing real-time updates to a large audience. The current chapter summarizes the state of what is known about Twitter use and effects during crises and emergencies. It also explores the possibility that the medium may be largely underutilized by first responders and provides recommendations for using the medium to mitigate crisis and disasters.

Review of Literature

A long history of media research has indicated that audiences are likely to seek out information concerning crisis and disasters in an effort not only to acquire information but also to restore order to an unknown, chaotic situation. Further research indicates that although initially dismissed as a novelty medium, Twitter is increasingly relied upon during these situations (Armstrong & Gao, 2010; Palser, 2009; Sutton, Palen, & Shklovski, 2008; Westerman et al., 2012; Westerman, Spence, & Van Der Heide, 2014). Numerous studies have indicated that the speed with which information is updated through Twitter is widely seen as an advantage during crises and that Twitter users strongly support the notion of local government and relief agencies using the medium to mitigate and respond to emergencies and disasters (Kavanaugh et al., 2011). The public will often turn to Twitter under circumstances in which they believe they are not receiving timely updates from traditional media or local officials (Sutton et al., 2008). Further evidence suggests that social media are commonly used in addition to more mainstream media and that users may rely upon Twitter for first alerts and basic information while turning to traditional media for detailed analysis and instruction (Jin & Liu, 2010; Lachlan, Spence, Lin, & Del Greco, 2014; Palen et al., 2010; Liu, Jin, & Austin, 2013).

The formal features of Twitter also allow for linking to URLs and other Web resources. Although critics often bemoan the 140-character limit of Twitter, in truth, the medium can be used to link to other, more detailed Web sources, either through live URLs, or through URL shortening services. A number of studies indicate that tweets stand a greater chance of being retweeted when they contain URLs, suggesting that users are able to identify and capitalize upon tweets that likely lead to more detailed information resources (Suh, Hong, Pirolli, & Chi, 2010). Further, past research has demonstrated that users take advantage of this capability during crises and disasters and that Twitter content associated with major events contains a higher proportion of tweeted and retweeted URLs than does more generalized Twitter content (Hughes & Palen, 2009).

Twitter Use During Crises and Disasters

In terms of specific application to crises and disasters, a small number of studies have attempted to examine the nature of Twitter content and the possible uses and dependencies that develop among Twitter users under conditions of great duress. Although there are only a handful of studies to this effect, they offer a glimpse into the human factors at play across Twitter and provide insights that can be used by government agencies and first responders. Numerous studies have suggested that social media may be especially useful for the purpose of connecting with others. One of the first studies to this effect revealed that during the Arab Spring, factual updates were less common than affective displays but that affective content became more intense and more frequent as the events unfolded (Papacharissi & de Fatima Oliveira, 2012). Twitter users were more likely to use the medium as a means of inducing emotional bonding and solidarity than they were to obtain actionable information.

Sutton and colleagues (2014) examined all public tweets sent by relevant government agencies during the 2012 Waldo Canyon fire in Colorado. Their results indicate that serial transmission (retweeting) of these messages was more likely to take place when the tweets were advisory (as opposed to instructive) and imperative or clear in sentence structure. Interestingly, neither the inclusion of a URL, nor the inclusion of specific evacuation instructions, predicted retweeting. Sutton and colleagues add that a comparison of the content of the tweets sent out by public officials with the criterion for serial transmission suggests that the organizations responding to the event were sending messages designed for very general audiences, when in fact they had an opportunity to engage with those who were directly affected.

Lachlan, Spence, Lin, and Del Greco (2014) examined the content of tweets after Hurricane Sandy, in this case looking at more general Twitter use by the public and the availability of information that users may have found useful in mitigating against and evacuating from the storm. Their line of research specifically looked at the available information during the prodromal stage of Hurricane Sandy (see Fink, 1986). Over 27,000 tweets were examined at specific intervals during the time leading up to the landfall of the storm. Their results indicated that information concerning specific behavioral recommendations was difficult to locate for anyone using the National Oceanic and Atmospheric Administration (NOAA) and the Centers for Disease Control and Prevention (CDC) prompted hashtag of #sandy. Moreover, as the storm progressed, the amount of useable information on Twitter became more difficult to obtain (Lachlan, Spence, Lin, & Del Greco, 2014). They also noted that this was troubling due to the fact that #sandy was a government-promoted hashtag. Therefore, citizens may have gone to #sandy looking for specific usable information, and that information was buried in a feed of tweets that had little to do with the storm itself, such as humorous tweets and expressions of fear and dread (Spence, Lachlan, Lin, & Del Greco, 2015).

Lachlan, Spence, Lin, Najarian, and Del Greco (2014) replicated and extended this research through examining a localized snow storm in the Boston area. In the follow-up research, the hashtags of #nemo and #bosnow were selected because #nemo was widely promoted by federal-level relief agencies, such as NOAA, whereas #bosnow was included as it was the hashtag promoted by the Boston Globe and other media outlets in southern New England. The results from the replication found similar results to the first study; however, they noted that the data suggested that localized hashtags may present a better place for an information-seeking public to look for crisis information.

This need for information under dire circumstances, and the ease and availability of information through Twitter, is also reflected in behavioral research on the matter. Notably, Sutton and colleagues (2008) reported that in a survey of those affected by a California wildfire, "information dearth" drove over half of the sample to mobile technologies. Although fewer reported using Twitter as a means of obtaining information, those who did were likely to have *discovered* the medium during their search. Although Twitter is much more widely used than it was at the time of that data collection, the authors pointed out that this is illustrative of the motivation to adopt new technologies in the face of grave threats and high consequence events; in this case, the desire for information was so great that it spurred technological adoption. Like Lachlan, Sutton and colleagues posited that although Twitter provides a promising platform for crowd-generated information, emergency managers should be concerned about the potential for misinformation and should participate in these "back-channel" communications in order to minimize its spread.

Underlying Processes

These findings, although informative, are also consistent with past research concerning the use of traditional, linear media (e.g., television and radio) during crises and disasters (Lachlan & Spence, 2007, 2010, 2014; Lachlan, Spence, & Seeger, 2009; Sandman, Miller, Johnson, & Weinstein, 1993). A long history of media research has indicated that audiences are likely to have specific affective and cognitive needs under these circumstances and that mediated information may enable individuals to make good decisions when these needs are addressed in a manner that both informs and motivates people to take remedial action. Much of this work has argued that a certain amount of fear or dread must be induced along with the information that is provided (Sandman, 2003). This affective appeal ideally is enough to motivate people to action but not so severe as to promote a sense of helplessness or outright panic. It may be the case that during times of extreme distress, such as political upheaval and natural disasters, Twitter may contribute to this process of both scaring people and calming them down. Although some have been quick to point out the lack of actionable information available through Twitter, any galvanizing effect or the enhancement of social capital may in and of itself be a functional phenomenon. If Twitter is able to help people attain a sense of rationality and bondedness, then individuals using the medium may be better able to respond to the more detailed information they receive from more traditional media outlets.

Across these studies, lessons can also be learned in terms of what we can expect in terms of media dependencies. Audiences likely have multiple outlets to which they can turn for information concerning crises and risks. Savvy Twitter users may know exactly what to expect from the medium and turn to it to meet those needs. Media dependency theory argues that as users become more accustomed to a resource and more satisfied with its utility, they will become more reliant on that medium to suit those goals and inherently place more credibility in the information received from those media to suit those goals. It stands to reason then that seasoned Twitter users would become comfortable with the primarily affective nature of the medium and use it for these more social purposes.

Of course, these dependency processes also lead us to the consideration of information literacy and the digital divide. If more savvy users are able to distinguish between Twitter and other media in terms of their functional utility under the circumstances, it may also be the case that less familiar users or those denied access will have less of an idea of what to expect from the medium. This is especially problematic given past research indicating that those audiences who are most at risk may possess limited access to varying media or find themselves in lower positions of information literacy.

At-Risk Populations

Access to Internet-based technology has seen a consistent increase to a level where a majority of American adults are Internet users (Pew, 2014), causing some to examine issues of motivation, norms of use, or personal characteristics rather than access to technology (DiMaggio, Hargittai, Celeste, & Shafer, 2004; Hargittai & Hinnant, 2008). Similarly, it may not be access to technology that makes a population at risk or vulnerable to disasters but these personal characteristics of technology use or technological or media literacy. Technological and media literacy is an area of research that is well situated for explaining how and why people obtain or do not access needed information. Thus, if people do not really know how to use Twitter, are they able to retrieve information from the site, particularly when that information is buried or grouped with thousands of other tweets using the same hashtag? Further, other areas that need to be examined include use by nonnative English-speaking populations (Spence, Lachlan, Burke, & Seeger, 2007) and use across socioeconomic statuses.

Practical Implications

Considering Dialogic Processes

Generally speaking, it appears as though Twitter is still largely used by emergency responders and management agencies as a broadcast medium. Messages concerning warnings and actionable information must compete with innumerable other messages for attention by the affected public. However, the real power of Twitter in these circumstances may be its ability to create dialogic processes. Although largely underutilized by emergency managers, social media like Twitter offer government agencies a chance to engage with the public and with those who are "on the ground" at the site of a disaster or incident; this dialogue can be used to build relationships with affected publics (Kietzmann, Hermkens, McCarthy, & Silvestre, 2011). Establishing some kind of dialogue with publics, or at least creating the impression that a dialogue is taking place, may be a distinct advantage offered by the medium and one that is consistent with past research in linear media. Numerous crisis communication scholars have posited that partnerships with the public and the sense of a dialogic exchange between community and agency is ideal for fostering trust and inducing prosocial behaviors during times of great duress (see Seeger, 2006).

This literature also suggests that listening to the concerns of the general public is essential not only in engendering trust in relief agencies but also in obtaining information from the ground that can help emergency managers make better decisions regarding relief, evacuation, and mitigation efforts. Twitter provides a means through which these agencies can obtain information from the public in real time and adjust their responses and strategies accordingly. By creating dialogue with affected publics, emergency management agencies can establish immediacy with those at risk and obtain critical information concerning the response that will best suit these communities (Lachlan, Spence, Edwards, et al., 2014).

Further, the media dependency literature would suggest that these dialogic processes could contribute positively to further relief efforts. As individuals are given the opportunity to have input into the relief messages they receive, they are likely to become more satisfied with the messages themselves and the accompanying relief efforts associated with them. If Twitter provides an outlet for emergency management to engage in these dialogic processes, then media dependency should lead individuals to place greater faith in both the medium and in the agency in question in future events. This seems especially useful for emergency management agencies that work in highly risk-prone areas. If common or repeated threats have to be dealt with (e.g., wildfires, floods, hurricanes) in a particular locale, then building dependencies through dialogic processes on Twitter may lead the public back to those agencies in the future and increase the likelihood that those audiences will believe the information they receive and respond to it appropriately.

However, this is all predicated on the assumption that those managing interactions with the general public have the appropriate social media training to manage these events in a dialogic manner. Emergency management agencies should invest in public information officers and staff members with an understanding of social media and new media technologies, including the facilitation of these types of interactions. This would not only help current and future crisis response but also bolster the image of the organization in a broader sense (Vultee & Vultee, 2011).

Best Practices and Conclusions

Social media, and Twitter in particular, present a particular set of challenges in the management of widespread crises and disasters. It also provides tremendous opportunity. If utilized well, the medium may allow government agencies to reach enormous groups of affected individuals with tremendous speed and simultaneously bolster the reputation of the agency by making this dialogue available through public time line. However, much of the extant behavioral and content analytic research on the matter suggests that this does not typically happen (see Sutton et al., 2014, for a detailed explication). This research argues that emergency management agencies still operate on principles more closely related to broadcasting information and minimizing misinformation—principles more germane to linear media. The findings in the extant literature are consistent with Waters and Williams's (2011) criticisms of Twitter use by government agencies. They argue that government organizations tend to tweet in the same manner as they would broadcast, instead of holding dialogues with stakeholders. At the same time, the sheer glut of information available on Twitter may make it difficult to reach those most directly affected and engage them in publicly observed dialogues.

Further, the medium is still underutilized. In 2010, it was ranked as the fourth most popular outlet for accessing emergency information (Lindsay, 2010). Given its popularity; the utility of widespread, crowdsourced messaging; and the capacity for engaging in direct dialogue with those affected, it provides an opportunity for communities, individuals, government agencies, and nongovernmental organizations to warn others of danger, take protective actions or evacuate, and respond. This strikes of the reinvention process commonly discussed in the literature on diffusion of innovations (Rogers, 2003). Reinvention involves changing the uses or application of a technology while still in the process of adopting it. Emergency management agencies using Twitter should open themselves to the reinvention process and partner with academics and applied researchers to develop new practices and techniques for reaching and satisfying those at risk while simultaneously building their credibility among others who may be affected in the future.

For example, it may be advantageous to consider the speed and repetition of risk messages to compete with the volume of information likely to be available along the same hashtags or search terms. It may also be advantageous to designate certain hashtags for emergency use only. For example, in the early 1970s, the U.S. Federal Communications Commission designated citizen's band channel 9 for emergency use only; this radio frequency is relied upon by police and first responders for monitoring and communicating information related to emergencies as they develop. Although it may prove difficult to enforce, designating particular hashtags as markers for official use would allow both first responders and everyday citizens to locate breaking, relevant information in an efficient manner. Developing and marketing searchable hashtag strategies that citizens in risk-prone areas are comfortable with and know how to use is one potential direction for future research and scholarship on the matter.

Further, little is known about the learning processes associated with obtaining emergency information from Twitter. As it is commonly argued in the literature, the public has a right to be made aware of risks as soon as they emerge, and emergency managers should aim to educate and motivate them under the circumstances (Nelson, Spence, & Lachlan, 2009; Seeger, 2006). The problem is that little is known about how much can be acquired, retained, and retransmitted under such trying psychological circumstances. Although we have a good understanding from the literature about the ways in which the public and different organizations use the medium, we have little empirical evidence concerning the impact the received information has on subsequent responses related to mitigation or relief.

Finally, future research efforts should investigate best practices for planning and implementing new media campaigns concerning developing crises. If relief agencies and government organizations are to respond to crises and disasters using Twitter and other social media, then they will have to conduct an initial examination of the social media landscape as these crises unfold; through researching what has been left behind by those affected, inferences derived from user-generated content may guide subsequent policy development (Spence, Lachlan, & Rainear, 2016). It may be advantageous to develop a set of policies and practices to be implemented during the prodromal stages of such crises, such as examining the specific hashtags, keywords, and search terms that are being used by the public to locate information. It may also be advantageous to identify key opinion leaders that emerge through serial transmission under the circumstances and to engage in dialogue with those individuals or agencies in order to reach the maximum number of individuals who are effected. The best means by which these steps can be taken have yet to be identified, and future research and practice should aim to develop a set of guidelines for these efforts.

References

Armstrong, C. L., & Gao, F. (2010). Now tweet this: How news organizations use Twitter. *Electronic News, 4*, 218–235.

DiMaggio, P., Hargittai, E., Celeste, C., & Shafer, S. (2004). Digital inequality: From unequal access to differentiated use. In K. Neckerman (Ed.), *Social inequality* (pp. 355–400). New York: Russell Sage Foundation.

Fink, S. (1986). *Crisis management: Planning for the inevitable.* New York, NY: AMACOM.

Hargittai, E., & Hinnant, A. (2008). Digital inequality: Differences in young adults' use of the Internet. *Communication Research, 35*, 602–621.

Hughes, A. L., & Palen, L. (2009). Twitter adoption and use in mass convergence and emergency events. *International Journal of Emergency Management, 6*(3–4), 248–260.

Jin, Y., & Liu, B. F. (2010). The blog-mediated crisis communication model: Recommendations for responding to influential external blogs. *Journal of Public Relations Research, 22*(4), 429–455.

Kavanaugh, A., Fox, E. A., Sheetz, S., Yang, S., Li, L. T., Whalen, T., . . . Xie, L. (2011, June). *Social media use by government: From the routine to the critical.* Proceedings of the 12th Annual International Conference on Digital Government Research, College Park, MD.

Kietzmann, J. H., Hermkens, K., McCarthy, I. P., & Silvestre, B. S. (2011). Social media? Get serious! Understanding the functional building blocks of social media. *Business Horizons, 54*(3), 241–251. doi: 10.1016/j.bushor.2011.01.005

Lachlan, K. A., & Spence, P. R. (2007). Hazard and outrage: Developing a psychometric instrument in the aftermath of Katrina. *Journal of Applied Communication Research, 35*(1), 109–123.

Lachlan, K. A., & Spence, P. R. (2010). Communicating risks: Examining hazard and outrage in multiple contexts. *Risk Analysis, 30*, 1872–1886.

Lachlan, K. A., & Spence, P. R. (2014). Does message placement influence risk perceptions and affect? *Journal of Communication Management, 18*(2), 122–130.

Lachlan, K. A., Spence, P. R., Edwards, A., Reno, K. M., & Edwards, C. (2014). If you are quick enough, I will think about it: Information speed and trust in public health organizations. *Computers in Human Behavior, 33*, 377–380. doi: 10.1016/j.chb.2013.08.014

Lachlan, K. A., Spence, P. R., & Lin, X. (2014). Expressions of risk awareness and concern through Twitter: On the utility of using the medium as an indication of audience needs. *Computers in Human Behavior, 35*, 554–559.

Lachlan, K. A., Spence, P. R., Lin, X., & Del Greco, M. (2014). Screaming into the wind: Examining the volume and content of tweets associated with hurricane sandy. *Communication Studies, 65*(5), 500–518.

Lachlan, K. A., Spence, P. R., Lin, X., & Najarian, K., & Del Greco, M. (2014). Twitter use during a weather event: Comparing content associated with localized and non-localized hashtags. *Communication Studies, 65*(5), 519–534.

Lachlan, K. A., Spence, P. R., & Seeger, M. (2009). Terrorist attacks and uncertainty reduction: Media use after September 11. *Behavioral Sciences of Terrorism and Political Aggression, 1*, 101–110.

Lindsay, B. R. (2010). Social media and disasters: Current uses, future options and policy considerations. *Journal of Current Issues in Media and Telecommunications, 2*, 287–297.

Liu, B. F., Jin, Y., & Austin, L. L. (2013). The tendency to tell: Understanding publics' communicative responses to crisis information form and source. *Journal of Public Relations Research, 25*(1), 51–67.

Nelson, L. D., Spence, P. R., & Lachlan, K. A. (2009). Learning from the media in the aftermath of a crisis: Findings from the Minneapolis bridge collapse. *Electronic News, 3*(4), 176–192. doi: 10.1080/19312430903300046

O'Reilly, T., & Battelle, J. (2009). Web squared: Web 2.0 five years on. Retrieved 1 February, 2013 from http://assets.en.oreilly.com/1/event/28/web2009_websquared-whitepaper.pdf

Palen, L., Anderson, K. M., Mark, G., Martin, J., Sicker, D., Palmer, M., & Grunwald, D. (2010). *A vision for technology-mediated support for public participation & assistance in mass emergencies & disasters*. Paper presented at the Proceedings of the 2010 ACM-BCS Visions of Computer Science Conference, Edinburgh, UK.

Palser, B. (2009). Hitting the tweet spot. *American Journalism Review, 31*, 54.

Papacharissi, Z., & de Fatima Oliveira, M. (2012). Affective news and networked publics: The rhythms of news storytelling on #Egypt. *Journal of Communication, 62*(2), 266–282.

Pew Research Center. (2014). *Internet user demographics*. Washington, DC. Retrieved 23 September, 2014 from www.pewinternet.org/data-trend/internet-use/lateststats/

Rogers, E. M. (2003). *Diffusion of innovations* (5th ed.). New York: Free Press.

Sandman, P. M. (2003, April). Four kinds of risk communication. *The Synergist, 26*–27.

Sandman, P. M., Miller, P. M., Johnson, B. B., & Weinstein, N. D. (1993). Agency communication, community outrage, and perception of risk: Three simulation experiments. *Risk Analysis, 13*, 585–598.

Seeger, M. W. (2006). Best practices in crisis communication: An expert panel process. *Journal of Applied Communication Research, 34*(3), 232–244. doi: 10.1080/00909880600769944

Spence, P. R., Lachlan, K. A., Burke, J. M., & Seeger, M. W. (2007). Media use and information needs of the disabled during a natural disaster. *Journal of Health Care for the Poor and Underserved, 18*, 394–404.

Spence, P. R., Lachlan, K. A., Lin, X., & Del Greco, M. (2015). Variability in Twitter content across the stages of a natural disaster: Implications for crisis communication. *Communication Quarterly, 63*(2), 171–186.

Spence, P. R., Lachlan, K. A., & Rainear, A. (2016). Social media and crisis research: Data collection and directions. *Computers in Human Behavior, 54*, 667–672.

Suh, B., Hong, L., Pirolli, P., & Chi, E. H. (2010, August). *Want to be retweeted? Large scale analytics on factors impacting retweet in Twitter network*. IEEE Intl Conference on Social Computing (pp. 177–184). Minneapolis, MN: IEEE.

Sutton, J., Palen, L., & Shklovski, I. (2008, May). *Backchannels on the front lines: Emergent uses of social media in the 2007 Southern California wildfires*. Proceedings of the 5th International ISCRAM Conference, Washington, DC.

Sutton, J., Spiro, E. S., Johnson, B., Fitzhugh, S., Gibson, B., & Butts, C. (2014). Warning tweets: Serial transmission of messages during the warning phase of a disaster event. *Information, Communication, & Society, 17*(6), 765–787.

Vultee, F., & Vultee, D. M. (2011). What we tweet about when we tweet about disasters: The nature and sources of microblog comments during emergencies. *International Journal of Mass Emergencies and Disasters, 29,* 221–242.

Waters, R. D., & Williams, J. M. (2011). Squawking, tweeting, cooing, and hooting: Analyzing the communication patterns of government agencies on Twitter. *Journal of Public Affairs, 11*(4), 353–363. doi: 10.1002/pa.385

Westerman, D. W., Spence, P. R., & Van Der Heide, B. (2012). A social network as information: The effect of system generated reports of connectedness on credibility and health care information on Twitter. *Computers in Human Behavior, 28,* 199–206.

Westerman, D. W., Spence, P. R., & Van Der Heide, B. (2014). Social media as information source: Recency of updates and credibility of Information. *Journal of Computer-Mediated Communication, 19*(2), 171–183.

22

VISUALIZING RESPONSE AND RECOVERY

The Impact of Social Media–Based Images in a Crisis

Melissa Janoske

Iconic photographs are often studied as performative models of citizenship; that is, the visual helps individuals better understand how to act, what to believe, or how to feel about a particular event, including crisis events (Hariman & Lucaites, 2007). With the rise of social media, one iconic photograph printed in every newspaper has been replaced with hundreds or thousands of images from professional and citizen journalists alike. With so many more photographs to choose from, visuals on social media can be used to exchange messages and share visual representation of the crisis as a form of meeting heightened information needs (Seeger, Venette, Ulmer, & Sellnow, 2002).

Visual understandings of crisis response and recovery are often overlooked in discussions of crises on social media, even though 56% of adult Internet users either post their own photos online or share photos taken by others, and 32% do both (Pew Research Internet Project, 2013). Additionally, a number of key research studies looking at communities and social media use during a crisis have focused on natural disasters (e.g., Macias, Hilyard, & Freimuth, 2009; Procopio & Procopio, 2007). By bringing visuals into the analysis, this study offers an important opportunity to build on and expand previous research in crisis communication.

Literature Review

This review examines areas important in understanding the impact of social media–based visuals on crisis communication, including the interconnectedness of crisis and emotion and how social media can build community during a crisis.

Crisis and Emotion

Publics have a variety of emotional responses to a crisis. Jin and Hong's (2010) survey found that publics have four major crisis coping strategies: rational thinking (making sense of the crisis), emotional venting (reduce stress through self-expression), instrumental support (others provide information or bolster current information), and action (self-support and engagement). They found that publics who engage in rational thinking, with or without instrumental support, are more likely to also engage in action and follow a plan to survive a crisis (Jin & Hong, 2010). Additionally, publics who emotionally vent with instrumental support (sharing how they feel with someone else or seeking advice on how to handle a situation) are also more likely to take action (Jin & Hong, 2010). Social media provide significant emotional support or coping strategies for the negative emotions associated with a crisis, including grief and shock (Bressers & Hume, 2012).

Social Media and Community

As a set of tools, social media share five characteristics: participation (everyone can create and respond to content), openness (everyone can post content and feedback), conversation (there is two-way interaction), communities (groups with similar interests find one another easily), and connectedness (there is strong linking to other content; Voit, 2008). *Community* is a term with multiple meanings, most centering around the idea of place and whether that place is physical or virtual, allowing community to potentially be defined "socially not spatially" (Wellman, 2005, p. 53).

Social media–based communities challenge a model of one-to-many communication that might occur via broadcast or print media (Enli, 2009). Individuals are increasingly turning to social media to search for and share information about a major event, where spreadability is a more conscious choice on the part of the public than simply letting something go viral (Enli, 2009).

People want to interact and engage, often in playful or entertaining ways, and they are looking to social media to find ways to make traditional content more engaging (Enli, 2009). Organizations may attempt to control what is expressed by moderating social media channels, but publics often add to and adapt the posted information to showcase their ideas and thoughts (Kent, 2010). Information sharing is easier via social media than more traditional media (Baron & Philbin, 2009), based on social media's ability to provide and gain access to that information anywhere (Procopio & Procopio, 2007) and to allow people to more easily take action based on that shared information (Murdock, 2010). The sharing of information through social media allows social media to act as a secondary or confirming source during crises (National Research Council, 2011).

Based on the understanding of the role emotion plays in a crisis, the power of social media to both form and nurture community, and the lack of knowledge about how visuals are used on social media to enhance crisis communication, the following research questions are posed:

RQ1: What types of visuals do individuals post to Facebook during and after Hurricane Sandy?

RQ2: How do individuals communicate the impact of seeing and interacting with Hurricane Sandy–based visuals on crisis response and recovery?

Case Background: Jersey Shore Hurricane News Facebook Page

Hurricane Sandy was a "superstorm" that hit the East Coast from October 29 to 31, 2012, causing approximately 100 deaths, a complete shutdown of the New York City subway system, and an estimated $29.4 billion in damage (Francescani, 2012; Keller, 2012). Justin Auciello created the Jersey Shore Hurricane News (JSHN) Facebook page in 2011 in response to Hurricane Irene and continued to build it as a place for the community to report and discuss future events, including Hurricane Sandy. As of October 6, 2014, the Facebook page had 225,929 likes, and 10,869 people had participated in conversation on the site (Jersey Shore Hurricane News, 2014). On the About section of the page, Auciello states that he has years of journalistic experience, both traditional reporting and social media based, and notes that the page is meant to be a "bottom-up, two-way news outlet . . . news for the people, by the people" and that it is also available to be used as a "community resource (events, missing people, lost animals, etc.)" (Jersey Shore Hurricane News, 2014).

According to the Pew Internet and American Life Project, in 2013, 73% of adult Internet users reported using a social networking site (Duggan & Smith, 2013). Additionally, Facebook has well over one billion monthly users and aims to "give people the power to share and make the world more open and connected" (Facebook, 2014). Other social media platforms offer visuals, but Facebook has both the broadest use and allows for text and visuals to be showcased together without character or space constraints, making it the best social media platform choice for this study.

According to *New York Magazine*, Hurricane Sandy created a "vortex in which the virtual community experienced the storm both in seclusion and all together" (Coscarelli, 2012, p. 1). Instagram, the photo sharing website, saw uploads of up to 10 images per second tagged with #Sandy during the storm (Laird, 2012). One function of all of this social media sharing is that not all of the pictures were real; fake sharks, ominous skies, and floods on the floor of the New York Stock Exchange all made the rounds, and all were eventually ousted as either not from the time of the storm, not from where Hurricane Sandy existed, or were crafted entirely on a computer (Coscarelli, 2012). Buzzfeed, a prominent social media website, discussed the impact of these rumors, eventually deciding that they were a small price to pay for having the platforms at all: "We end up with more facts, sooner, with less ambiguity" (Herrman, 2012, p. 1). Due to the extensive damage of the hurricane, the information-seeking needs of those impacted, and the role social media played in the recovery process, Jersey Shore Hurricane News was an excellent subject for this research.

Method

A qualitative content analysis was completed, an appropriate lens to study social media and crisis communication, as it showcases the constructs and understandings of the complex discourse surrounding the material (Berg, 2009). This case allowed the researcher to collect data within a real-life context, providing insights into complicated relationship links, interactions, and contexts (Yin, 2009). Crises are often studied in, and work well within, a case study context (May, 2006; Reierson, Sellnow, & Ulmer, 2009). Case studies also present an opportunity to gain a rich understanding of how individuals dealing with crises might use online communities by illuminating decisions made by those individuals (Schramm, 1971).

Data Collection

Three separate weeks of JSHN posts were chosen for study through a stratified purposive, within-case approach (Berg, 2009). This approach is common in crisis communication, as it allows for specific moments in time to be studied (Berg, 2009). The subgroups of weeks for data collection were the first week of the storm (October 29–November 6, 2012), a week at the six-month anniversary of the storm (April 28–May 6, 2013), and the one-year anniversary week of the storm (October 29–November 6, 2013). Collecting all posts from these three weeks resulted in 522 posts; this data set was then culled for every post that included a visual, resulting in 228 posts to be analyzed.

Data Analysis

Research questions were used to guide the analysis, and a grounded-theory approach appropriate for the exploratory nature of the study allowed for a constant comparative method of analyzing themes from the data (Corbin & Strauss, 2008). A coding sheet was developed, including a brief definition of codes; as the coding process moved forward, codes were adjusted, dropped, or added as necessary. Continuous inductive data analysis led to the final set of themes, as reported next (Glaser & Strauss, 1967).

Results

RQ1: What types of visuals are individuals posting to Facebook during and after Hurricane Sandy?

RQ1 looks to understand what sorts of visuals were actively being shown on JSHN and thus potentially impacting individuals. The images fell into categories including images of individuals involved in the crisis, destruction, reconstruction and restoration, symbols of renewal, and B-roll and other news images.

Individuals Involved in the Crisis

A number of pictures shown on JSHN included individuals, who may or may not be identified in the text of the post itself or in the comments that followed. Pictures tended to be uplifting, encouraging those reading to believe that help had arrived by showing pictures of utility workers arriving from other states or of a family who had driven in from Dallas with a truck full of supplies.

Other images showed those reading what things looked like for people who were venturing out after the storm. Multiple pictures showed people in line for gas, or at the store; others showcased people in line to get a permit to enter evacuated areas or to fill out paperwork about the amount of damage their home had taken in the storm. These pictures were often taken from such an angle that someone wanting to know if it was a good time to go or to compare differences in gas lines, for example, would have that information to aid their decision making.

Another common group of individuals shown were children, particularly those doing something related to the crisis. One woman posted a picture of her daughter covered by their giant Irish wolfhound, mentioning that because the heat had gone out in their home, they needed to be creative with how they were staying warm. Other children posed in their Halloween costumes, especially those who were dressed as utility or maintenance workers, with captions showing their appreciation for all that those workers did to help the community.

Other individuals showcased were a varied group—a picture of a public official, like New Jersey governor Chris Christie; people holding supportive signs thanking the volunteers; or individuals posing with buildings or spaces that were being reopened. One woman posted a picture of herself, jumping for joy, with the sign announcing that a local park was reopening.

Destruction

Although the pictures are sometimes cheerful, there were also a lot of pictures showcasing the destruction wrought by Hurricane Sandy. Often, this meant images of barely standing homes or restaurants, with something in the frame (like

FIGURE 22.1 A Fence in Union Beach, New Jersey, Shared With the Hope That This Is a Time for People to Come Together

a street sign) to help people establish where the picture was taken. Pictures showed the ocean flooding over piles of wreckage or what was left behind (like a haphazard pile of lumber) after the storm rolled through. The boardwalk was a particular area where people were anxious to see how it had fared; a number of pictures showed it in pieces or showed the attractions with water surrounding them. During the storm, there was a sense that JSHN posted any picture that it could get, such as pictures of people standing in flooded streets or rain-blurred shots showing bending trees and abandoned vehicles (see Figure 22.1). No pictures were of undamaged areas.

Reconstruction and Restoration

Once the storm itself was over, the pictures very quickly changed perspective to emphasize restoration and the speed of progress. Again, many pictures were of the boardwalk or of particular restaurants and shops that would be well known to a large number of people following JSHN.

Some of the pictures indicated how much things had changed over time. One particular series focused on a picture from the storm and would then layer over a picture taken six months later to showcase the changes and progress that had been made. Others looked at what was left behind or displayed how materials from a damaged building were being salvaged and utilized to build something new. These pictures often showcased people actively working on the restoration—driving construction equipment or hauling debris or lumber. Sometimes, like the picture shown in Figure 22.2, it was what the site looked like in previous years, as a way to see what something could be again in time.

FIGURE 22.2 Seaside Heights, New Jersey, Boardwalk

Symbols of Renewal

Many images on JSHN were of sunrises, the sun visible over the ocean, and even if there was destruction visible in the shot, it was not the focus. The images showcased beauty and the need for hope. These pictures always showed a calm ocean, with perhaps a sea gull or some waving sea grass. These visuals have an atmosphere of possibility, by showcasing what the area can look like when not in the middle of a hurricane. They could also include and overlap with the construction and progress pictures mentioned previously, also symbols of renewal, but these pictures seemed to be specifically chosen in order to bring a moment of peace and harmony to those participating in the site.

B-Roll and Other News Images

A number of images fell into the category of providing news and other information to people on the Facebook page. Some of these were the photographic equivalent of B-roll images, or stock footage used to supplement a news story. This might look like a soft-focus fire truck with an in-focus helmet in the foreground, or a photograph establishing place by showing road signs. Other news images presented included maps for traffic, maps for weather patterns, and maps for surveillance. These often provided necessary information on when things would be happening and where. One of the maps showed when the eye of Hurricane Sandy was expected to make landfall and the anticipated path of the storm. Others provided information that would be helpful during a hurricane, such as clarifying what a riptide is, and offering a picture of one. Infrequently, these visuals were accompanied by a link to another source; a picture of a school would include a link explaining that schools would remain closed for another week due to safety

concerns. In this way, the visual helped establish what the information was referring to, and the link was provided to offer additional detail.

In addition to understanding what the pictures showed, it is also important to
understand what those pictures were able to do in terms of aiding crisis response
and recovery, as discussed in RQ2.

> **RQ2:** How do individuals communicate the impact of seeing and interacting
> with Hurricane Sandy–based visuals on crisis response and recovery?

The visuals presented on JSHN offered a number of things to those who were
in the middle of crisis response and recovery, including an ability to hope, an emotional outlet, and another way to understand what was happening.

An Ability to Hope

People were interested in bolstering themselves and their emotions by being able
to see that the sun would rise again, especially evident in the pictures that were
promoting restoration and renewal. Commentary along with the sunrise photo
in Figure 22.3 encouraged people to "just sit on the edge of what's left of your
boardwalk and meditate, pray, or whatever makes you happy . . . enjoy the show."
Another person noted that it was still possible to find "beauty amidst destruction."
People were interested in being able to "share another hopeful photo . . . this is a
time for all of us to come together." One man mentioned that seeing the beach at
peace was "a sight for sore eyes" and that "another month n ill [*sic*] get to enjoy
it again." A picture like that was seen as "beautiful and shows hope and peace for
New Jersey. Great shot!"

An Emotional Outlet

Individuals were also able to use the visuals to process their emotions. One woman
mentioned that an image of the beach looking destroyed but with the sun shining
allowed her to acknowledge that "this is sooo sad, but I absolutely love this picture." Another woman commented that looking at the pictures made her feel like
she "was at a funeral saying goodbye to a piece of my life." Someone else noted
that photos, particularly of the rebuilding and progress made, "warm[ed] my heart
and soul." Pictures of the boardwalk encouraged people to note that they could
"smell funnel cakes" and that "that picture is classic . . . great to see it captured
like this." Others would tell stories about their connection to the location in the
photograph, noting that it was a chance to "share something that has always been
a special part of my life, whether I am there or 1000's [*sic*] of miles away. I will be
back there one day, and I hope you will too!"

Sometimes, these emotions took the form of venting or using the opportunity
to express frustration with a part of the process that could not be fixed at JSHN.

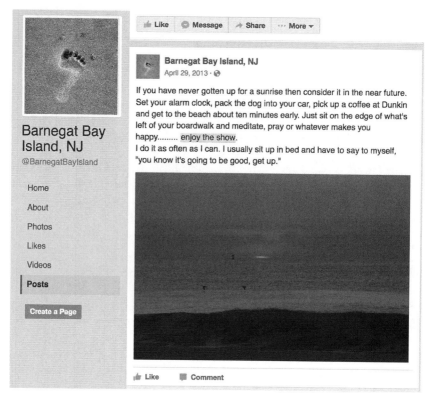

FIGURE 22.3 A Sunrise That Came With a Suggestion to Get Up Early and Enjoy the Show

However, individuals were glad to have a place to share those emotions with others who may be able to understand. One man expressed his frustration with the perceived slowness of restoring power by saying it was "good to see a picture of a parking lot full of trucks maybe now the only three poles that are down in Sayerwood South can be fixed after 8 days." Upon seeing a picture of Governor Christie, a woman commented that "government is not known for care, or speed or sense—this is another turf fight. Once the cameras left you did not have a prayer." This frustration could also be directed at JSHN, like the woman who commented, "gee, my mother is still waiting to get into Seaside Heights to take a picture of her house (that is, if she still has one), but I'm glad you got a picture of a cat. Yes I am being sarcastic."

Another Way to Understand

With storms as large and destructive as Hurricane Sandy, it can be difficult for people to have a sense of how long and at what pace construction and recovery will occur. The photographs showed that individuals were, in fact, working hard to rebuild and move forward and allowed people to see that they were actually making "great progress for one week!" Seeing much loved buildings and restaurants reopen, people often noted "that was my favorite." People mentioned that they wished there were "more pictures of home repairs moving forward" in order to answer "are they safe?" One woman talked about how the recovery was "not going well," even though "some of the restaurants in my town are open . . . but there's not many residents in town for them to serve." Another woman commented later, noting that "I am a waitress at a local diner and we have been extremely busy ever since we reopened on Saturday." Having a photograph to support that kind of discussion allowed people to bring up issues that might have otherwise never been mentioned.

Discussion and Critical Analysis

Photographs are a powerful way to quickly understand a situation and to get a sense of both emotion and need. Susan Sontag (2003) wrote that "in an era of information overload, the photograph provides a quick way of apprehending something and a compact form for memorizing it" (p. 22). Previously, everyone in a society shared common photographic images of an event and thus a common memory of a situation (Hariman & Lucaites, 2007). Previous events of national or international significance often had one main image burned into the cultural consciousness—a solitary man squaring off against a tank in Tiananmen Square, the raising of the flag on Iwo Jima or amid the rubble of September 11, a migrant mother and her children—these images help individuals remember that event or time period, remember how it made them feel, and discuss those reactions with others in ways that make sense to everyone involved. However, now that social media makes it possible for hundreds or thousands of images to circulate from one event, collective memory and experience may also be at risk, as individuals are less likely to be exposed to the same image.

As the individuals at JSHN have made clear, even multiple images still do offer us the chance to form a common memory, it just might be with a much smaller segment of society. Individuals are still looking to come together to express emotions, and they are using multiple photographs to enhance understanding of a crisis. Photographs and other images are still being used to showcase survival and the resilience of the human spirit; to marvel at destruction and what humans can endure; and to announce that we are in this together, regardless of just how much has been left behind.

As described in the literature review, Jin and Hong (2010) talked about four areas of emotional coping in a crisis: rational thinking, emotional venting, instrumental support, and action. Clearly, rational thinking was shown through photographs of both destruction and restoration, allowing people to see both what had happened and what the progress of rebuilding looked like. These visuals also helped people process that information as another way to understand what had happened and how it impacted their own lives. Emotional venting was also a large part of how people on JSHN used the images that were presented. Negative venting occurred, but also positive ideas of hope and recovery, the ability to see how much was changed, and reminders of what something used to look like all aided in guiding community members through the recovery process.

Having the opportunity to visualize individuals working to improve crisis recovery also made an impact on those following along via JSHN. That ability to hope because people were working to bring about renewal provided both instrumental support by bolstering information and action by encouraging engagement. This also typified Hariman and Lucaites's (2007) idea of the "individuated aggregate," or where an individual in a photograph is "used to depict collective experience" in a way that shows the need for both collective action and individual autonomy (p. 21). One individual in a hard hat, nailing down new boardwalk planks, thus has the opportunity to become a symbol of everything that is right, or wrong, with the recovery process. Individuals on JSHN were able to take one image and channel their ideas, fears, and emotions through that photograph and respond specifically to the image while also navigating their larger understandings and responses to the crisis and the recovery process in general. Due to this aggregated nature of the visual, having opportunities not only to post personal pictures but also to engage with the images as a community is becoming a salient and necessary part of crisis response and recovery.

Practical Implications for Social Media and Crisis Communication

Visuals in a crisis community like JSHN play particular roles for individuals. During the crisis, people were calling out for any picture they could find of what was happening. Images were another way to corroborate what was being said on television or the radio, or if the power was out and the television was no longer an option, most community members could access JSHN on a smartphone and feel like they were staying up to date on the crisis. Building a community on social media that shares their own photographs, and has a chance to discuss them, aids with that recovery process and thus should be utilized by crisis communicators. Most social media platforms are now either built around photographs (like Instagram or Pinterest) or have the capability to showcase photographs (like Twitter and Facebook), offering specific options for different types of communities.

Crisis communicators can use these communities, and the visuals they share, to improve understanding of the recovery process from the perspective of the people they aim to aid. If the reaction to pictures of construction is frustration at the bureaucracy of proceedings, communicators can work to get better or clearer information out to those hoping to rebuild. If the reaction focuses on hope and renewal, that is also important information for communicators to have and to build upon themselves in future messages. Increased knowledge of the needs and hopes of the people affected by the crisis offers myriad opportunities to crisis communicators: shared maps offer a look at where affected people are and the areas they think need significant recovery efforts; understanding which questions are asked and reasked offers insight into what information to present again; pictures of people making do with what they have clarifies what to suggest for emergency kits. Looking at visuals and online communities is a micro, detail-oriented way to understand how to best offer aid in a crisis, but it also can provide specific and significant help to those who need it, making it a useful relationship to build and maintain.

This chapter focused on a natural disaster, where plenty of people are involved who have the opportunity to take and post images; other crisis events like workplace violence or a food recall may not offer as many opportunities for this sort of logical and emotional response from the public. Postings that focus on text may generate response and engage a community, but visuals have a unique opportunity to allow for the expansion of logical and emotional responses, improving individual recovery from a crisis event. Crisis communicators looking to aid people dealing with a similar event would be wise to allow individuals both textual and visual means of processing their experience.

References

Baron, G., & Philbin, J. (2009, March). Social media in crisis communication: Start with a drill. Retrieved from http://www.prsa.org/SearchResults/view/7909/105/Social_media_in_crisis_communication_Start_with_a

Berg, B. L. (2009). *Qualitative research for the social sciences* (6th ed.). Boston: Allyn & Bacon.

Bressers, B., & Hume, J. (2012). Message boards, public discourse, and historical meaning: An online community reacts to September 11. *American Journalism, 29*(4), 9–33.

Corbin, J., & Strauss, A. (2008). *Basics of qualitative research* (3rd ed.). Thousand Oaks, CA: Sage.

Coscarelli, J. (2012, October 30). Hurricane Sandy: A perfect social media storm. *New York Magazine.* Retrieved from http://nymag.com/daily/intelligencer/2012/10/hurricane-sandy-perfect-social-media-storm.html

Duggan, M., & Smith, A. (2013, December 30). Social media update 2013. *Pew Internet & American Life Project.* Retrieved from http://pewinternet.org/Reports/2013/Social-Media-Update/Main-Findings.aspx

Enli, G. S. (2009). Mass communication tapping into participatory culture: Exploring strictly come dancing and Britain's got talent. *European Journal of Communication, 24*(4), 481–493. doi: 10.1177/0267323109345609

Facebook. (2014). *About.* Retrieved from http://www.facebook.com/facebook/info

Francescani, C. (2012). Chris Christie: Hurricane Sandy New Jersey damage will cost at least $29.4 billion. *Huffington Post.* Retrieved from http://www.huffingtonpost.com/2012/11/23/chris-christie-hurricane-sandy-new-jersey_n_2179909.html

Glaser, B. G., & Strauss, A. L. (1967). *The discovery of grounded theory.* Chicago: Aldine.

Hariman, R., & Lucaites, J. L. (2007). *No caption needed: Iconic photographs, public culture, and liberal democracy.* Chicago: The University of Chicago.

Herrman, J. (2012, October.) Twitter is a truth machine. *Buzzfeed*. Retrieved from https://www.buzzfeed.com/jwherrman/twitter-is-a-truth-machine?utm_term=.tv1WeerEN8#.kaaV885L94

Jersey Shore Hurricane News. (2014). *Facebook*. Retrieved from http://www.facebook.com/JerseyShoreHurricaneNews

Jin, Y., & Hong, S. Y. (2010). Explicating crisis coping in crisis communication. *Public Relations Review, 36*(4), 352–360. doi: 10.1016/j.pubrev.2010.06.002

Keller, J. (2012). Mapping Hurricane Sandy's deadly toll. *The New York Times*. Retrieved from http://www.nytimes.com/interactive/2012/11/17/nyregion/hurricane-sandy-map.html

Kent, M. L. (2010). Directions in social media for professionals and scholars. In R. L. Heath (Ed.), *The Sage handbook of public relations* (2nd ed., pp. 643–656). Thousand Oaks, CA: Sage.

Laird, S. (2012, October 29). Instagram users share 10 Hurricane Sandy photos per second. *Mashable*. Retrieved from http://mashable.com/2012/10/29/instagram-hurricane-sandy/

Macias, W., Hilyard, K., & Freimuth, V. (2009). Blog functions as risk and crisis communication during Hurricane Katrina. *Journal of Computer-Mediated Communication, 15*(1), 1–31. doi: 10.1111/j.1083-6101.2009.01490.x

May, S. K. (2006). *Case studies in organizational communication: Ethical perspectives and practices*. Thousand Oaks, CA: Sage.

Murdock, G. (2010). Shifting anxieties, altered media: Risk communication in networked times. *Catalan Journal of Communication & Cultural Studies, 2*(2), 159–176. doi: 10.1386/cjcs.2.2.159_1

National Research Council. (2011). *Public response to alerts and warnings on mobile devices: Summary of a workshop on current knowledge and research gaps*. Committee on Public Response to Alerts and Warnings on Mobile Devices: Current Knowledge and Research Gaps. Washington, DC: National Research Council.

Pew Research Internet Project. (2013). Social networking fact sheet. Retrieved from http://www.pewinternet.org/fact-sheets/social-networking-fact-sheet/

Procopio, C. H., & Procopio, S. T. (2007). Do you know what it means to miss New Orleans? Internet communication, geographic community, and social capital in crisis. *Journal of Applied Communication Research, 35*(1), 67–87.

Reierson, J. L., Sellnow, T. L., & Ulmer, R. R. (2009). Complexities of crisis renewal over time: Learning from the tainted Odwalla apple juice case. *Communication Studies, 60*(2), 114–129. doi: 10.1080/10510970902834841

Schramm, W. (1971, December). *Notes on case studies of instructional media projects*. Working paper for the Academy for Educational Development, Washington, DC.

Seeger, M. W., Venette, S., Ulmer, R. R., & Sellnow, T. L. (2002). Media use, information seeking, and reported needs in post crisis contexts. In B. S. Greenberg (Ed.), *Communication and terrorism: Public and media responses to 9/11* (pp. 53–63). Cresskill, NJ: Hampton Press.

Sontag, S. (2003). *Regarding the pain of others*. New York: Picador.

Voit, L. (2008). *Participation, openness, conversation, community, connectedness … yes that's what social media is all about!* Retrieved from http://www.isnare.com/?aid=595202&ca=Marketing

Wellman, B. (2005). Community: From neighborhood to network. *Communications of the ACM, 48*, 53–55.

Yin, R. K. (2009). *Case study research: Design and methods* (4th ed.). Thousand Oaks, CA: Sage.

SECTION IV-E

Areas of Application

Political

23

EXPLORING CRISIS MANAGEMENT VIA TWITTER IN THE AGE OF POLITICAL TRANSPARENCY

Lisa Gandy and Elina Erzikova

Introduction

The advent of the Internet has greatly increased transparency and information accessibility (Jahansoozi, 2006) and created new risks for politicians and public figures by making them more visible to their constituencies (Thompson, 2005). The uncontrolled nature of mediated visibility gives rise to new kinds of mediated events (Thompson, 2005, p. 39) that interrupt a carefully constructed flow of symbolic content and undermine the self-presentation of political leaders. Thus, the development of media and especially the Internet has changed relations between visibility and power (Thompson, 2005) and forced public relations practitioners to rethink the old paradigm of crisis management (Coombs, 2012).

Crisis communication is a rapidly growing area of public relations research (Coombs, 2014). Coombs and Holladay (2015) argued that although reactions (posts) on social media might not capture the opinions of all stakeholder, the messages nevertheless serve as a "rough real-time evaluation of how people are reacting to crisis responses" (p. 58). Coombs and Holladay (2015) also asserted that a crisis can be amplified through the process of retweeting. Analysis of recent studies shows that traditional media are the primary source of crisis-related information across all social media platforms (Austin & Jin, 2015). Therefore, strategies public relations specialists employ have the potential to influence the way reporters cover crises. A number of studies have shown a positive effect of stealing thunder (an organization talking about a crisis before media break the news) on the perceptions of crisis severity and guilt (Arpan & Roskos-Ewoldsen, 2005; Claeys & Cauberghe, 2012). Coombs and Holladay (2015) suggested that this old crisis communication timing strategy—stealing thunder—is still advisable in the digital age.

TABLE 23.1 Time Line of the Cain Sexual Harassment Scandal

Date	Event
May 21, 2011	Cain announces his candidacy as the Republican nominee for president of the United States in the 2012 election.
October 30, 2011	Politico reports that two women who were employed by the National Restaurant Association while Cain was the CEO complained of inappropriate behavior from Cain. Politico reports that both women received separation packages in the five figures.
November 2, 2011	The AP reports that a third woman who was employed by the National Restaurant Association had considered filing a complaint against Cain. She claimed that Cain made inappropriate remarks and gestures toward her.
November 7, 2011	A fourth woman, Sharon Bialek, holds a press conference and claims that Cain groped her while she was an employee at the National Restaurant Association when he was the CEO.
November 8, 2011	The first woman who accused Cain of sexual harassment identifies herself as Karen Kraushaar.
November 28, 2011	An Atlanta businesswoman, Ginger White, claims that she and Cain had a 13-year affair. Before White's claims are made public, Cain preemptively tells CNN that Ms. White's claim will be made and it is not true.
December 3, 2011	Cain suspends his bid for president.

This study focuses on Herman Cain's sexual harassment scandal that occurred in the middle of the 2012 Republican presidential primary. During this scandal (see a complete timeline in Table 23.1), several women claimed to have been verbally and physically harassed by Mr. Cain. These allegations presented a substantial public relations challenge for Mr. Cain's campaign.

Social media, especially Twitter, was a dominating force in promotion of all campaigns during the 2012 presidential election (Axelrod, 2013). Herman Cain himself was a popular figure on Twitter, having over 275,000 followers in 2011. In fact, in 2011, the Associated Press cited Herman Cain as the Republican most likely to be retweeted (Fouhy & Gillum, 2011). In this chapter we explore Cain's social media strategies before and during the sexual harassment scandal, specifically focusing on the social media platform Twitter.

Twitter and Political Involvement

In the past, Twitter has been a valuable tool in predicting the results of elections. Lamarre and Suzuki-Lambrecht (2013) found that congressional campaigns that used Twitter were more likely to win their elections. Importantly, the more followers a campaign had, the greater chance of winning the election, whereas the number of tweets sent by the candidate had no effect on the results.

According to the Pew Research Center, 73% of online adults in the United States use at least one social media platform and 42% of adults use multiple social media platforms (Duggan & Brenner, 2013). Further, 39% of all U.S. adults have engaged in at least one political activity (e.g., encouraging others to vote or posting comments about political issues) using social media (Rainie, Smith, Kay, Brady, & Verba, 2012).

In regards to political activity on social media, a study (Smith, Rainie, Shneiderman, & Himelboim, 2014) mapped conversations on Twitter and revealed that political conversations are usually polarized between liberals versus conservatives, and the split is especially evident in regards to controversial issues.

The Twitter Government and Elections Team (2014) recommends that political leaders be authentic (e.g., tweet personal facts and interests) because this tactic resonates with followers. The handbook also suggests engaging with audiences by bringing national attention to local issues, tweeting during popular televised events, and holding Twitter Q&As. These activities constitute an effort by the politician to establish a dialogue with constituents, a dialogue that involves risk, trust, mutuality, propinquity, empathy, and interaction (Kent & Taylor, 1998, 2002). Thus, the first objective of this study is to examine Herman Cain's strategy (or lack of thereof) in establishing a dialogue with his constituents before and during the crisis.

Political Scandals in the United States

The significance of political scandals' damage to the viability of politicians has increased in our post-Watergate age, largely due to the development of communication media, including social media (Thompson, 2005). However, despite growing scholarship, there are still more questions than answers about the effect of a scandal on public opinion.

There is an indication that if handled appropriately, a sexual harassment scandal does not always damage a politician's career. For example, in their widely cited study, Shah, Watts, Domke, and Fan (2002) argued that citizens strengthened their support for Clinton during the Lewinsky debacle because the media framed the sex scandal in terms of accusations of conservative elites. This implicit framing was complemented by Democrats' explicit questioning of the motive behind the Republicans' attacks on Clinton. Thus, Shah and colleagues (2002) concluded that Clinton's strong approval rating was sustained partly because of citizens' disagreement with the conservatives' attempts to remove a popular president over a seemingly private matter.

Public relations scholars recognize that the media's framing of a politician is crucial when forming a public relations strategy for a politician's campaign or in relation to a campaign crisis. Coombs (2007) notes that an attempt to change the media's frame in relation to a crisis might not be successful, and a public relations practitioner might be forced to manage the crisis situation within the frame created by the media. Coombs also notes that

> the same dynamic holds true when a crisis is based online. In these cases, people posting the information on the internet help to establish the crisis frame. If the media coverage or internet discussion provides no clear frame, the crisis manager will have an easier time establishing his/her own frame. (Coombs, 2007, p. 173)

Therefore, the second objective of this study is to look at whether Cain was able to generate his own frame on Twitter in order to respond to accusations made against him during the 2012 Republican presidential primary.

Method

Topsy, a social analytics platform, was used as a source to collect tweets. Although Twitter only allows access to the last 3,200 tweets that have been created by an individual tweeter, Topsy allows access to all tweets that originated from the beginning of Twitter (i.e., since 2006). Further, Topsy provides additional information such as whether a tweet is gaining or losing popularity (acceleration), among other features.

In the time frame of September 20, 2011, to December 10, 2011, a total of 498,190 unique tweets related to Herman Cain were written. The data include original tweets written by either Herman Cain or his social media team, as well as tweets shared by Cain but written by other tweeters. In addition, we gathered tweets from major news outlets and individuals that referenced news about Herman Cain. For comparison purposes, we divided the time frame of tweet collection into two periods—before Cain's sexual harassment scandal (September 20, 2011–October 29, 2011) and during the scandal (October 30, 2011–December 10, 2011). The breakdown of collected tweets in relation to time period and Twitter population is given in Table 23.2. We collected all tweets for the Herman Cain campaign official Twitter account (@THEHermanCain), as there were only

TABLE 23.2 Breakdown of All Collected Tweets

	Coded Tweets Before Crisis	Coded Tweets During Crisis	Total Tweets Before Crisis	Total Tweets During Crisis
Herman Cain campaign	95	133	95	133
Media and public	500	490	138,842	359,120

228 posts during the entire campaign period. The number of tweets *about* Herman Cain was 497,962. To make manual coding feasible, we trimmed down the number of tweets and examined the top 1,000 posts, before ($n = 500$) and during ($n = 490$) the crisis (the numbers for media and public tweets during the crisis became 490 due to 10 repeated tweets).

Both authors read posts authored by Herman Cain ($n = 228$) and tweets about Herman Cain ($n = 990$) to identify recurring patterns. A separate coding sheet for each group of tweets was created, as there was a little overlap between major themes. To refine the coding sheets, authors jointly coded 100 randomly selected tweets. The rest of the posts were coded independently. A manageable number of analyzed tweets—slightly over 1,000—made it possible to compare the outcomes of coding and settle all disagreements between coders by discussion.

Operational Definitions

Twitter

Twitter is a social networking site created in 2006. Specifically, it is an online social networking service that lets users create and have access to 140-character messages called "tweets." Users can subscribe to other users' tweets; this is called "following," and subscribers are called "followers." As of September 2014, Twitter has 271 million monthly active users and an average of 500 million tweets are sent per day.

Retweets

A retweet is a reposted or forwarded message on Twitter.

Acceleration

Acceleration is a measure created by Topsy, which scores whether a tweet is gaining in popularity (accelerating) or is losing interest (decelerating). The range for acceleration is −100 to 100, with 0 being neutral.

Sentiment

In this chapter, we define *sentiment* as a computationally derived measure of how positive or negative the emotional content of a tweet is. Sentiment was calculated by using the Nielsen sentiment dictionary (Nielsen, 2014). This dictionary gives words in the English language a negative and positive score between −5 and 5. For a given tweet, the sum of the word scores for individual words are tallied and then divided by the number of words in the tweet. The greater score (positive or negative) is then recorded as the sentiment score by using the algorithm given in Figure 23.1.

```
 1: procedure FINDSENTIMENT
 2:     words ← array of words from phrase
 3:     num_words ← number of words in phrase
 4:     i ← 0
 5:     pos_sent ← 0
 6:     neg_sent ← 0
 7:     num_pos ← 0
 8:     num_neg ← 0
 9: loop:
10:     if i>num_words then
11:         goto end
12:     if sentiment(words[i]) >= 3 then
13:         pos_sent ← pos_sent + sentiment(sentence[i])
14:         num_pos ← num_pos + 1
15:     if sentiment(words[i]) >= -3 then
16:         neg_sent ← neg_sent + sentiment(sentence[i])
17:         num_neg ← num_neg + 1
18:     i ← i + 1
19:     goto loop
20: end:
21:     if abs(pos_sent ÷ num_pos) > abs(neg_sent ÷ num_neg) then
22:         return pos_sent ÷ num_pos
23:     else
24:         return neg_sent ÷ num_neg
```

FIGURE 23.1 Algorithm for Sentiment Classification

Results

Herman Cain's Tweets

As discussed previously, Herman Cain and his team wrote and shared 228 unique tweets starting 40 days before ($n = 95$) the crisis and during ($n = 133$) the crisis. We calculated sentiment for each tweet using the algorithm in Figure 23.1, where a positive tweet is one that has a score of 3 to 5, a negative tweet has a score of −3 to −5, and all other tweets are regarded as neutral. As shown in Table 23.3, Herman Cain's strategy regarding negative and positive tweets changed slightly after the crisis broke. Cain's tweets became more emotional, with more positive and negative tweets during the crisis, and fewer neutral tweets. However, both before and during the crisis Cain posted more positive than negative tweets. The mean sentiment score of Cain's tweets before the crisis was 0.32 and during the crisis the mean sentiment score of tweets was 0.52.

Careful analysis revealed eight major themes in the collected tweets (Table 23.4). Two of the topics—*media appearances* and *emotional appeal*—considerably increased

TABLE 23.3 Sentiment Before and During the Crisis for Cain's Tweets

	Positive Tweets	Neutral Tweets	Negative Tweets
Before crisis (N = 95)	18% (n = 17)	75% (n = 71)	7% (n = 7)
During crisis (N = 133)	23% (n = 31)	68% (n = 91)	8% (n = 11)

TABLE 23.4 Themes Detected in Herman Cain and His Team's Tweets Before and During the Sexual Harassment Scandal, October 30–December 10, 2011

Theme	Number of tweets and percentage				Examples
	Before crisis		During crisis		
	#	%	#	%	
Media appearances★★	16	16.8	37	27.8	Be sure to watch Mr. Cain on FOX News Happening Now today at 11:15am ET.
Emotional appeal★★	8	8.4	21	17.3	America is the greatest & most exceptional nation in the world. We got here not because of government but in spite of it.
Success update	16	16.8	16	12.8	Great to hear that I won the West Alabama Straw Poll today with over 50% of the votes cast!
Foreign policy	5	5.3	13	9.8	My message to Iran: if you mess with Israel, you're messing with the USA.
Call for action	4	4.2	11	8.3	Click this link to sign up now for your local 999 Meetup on Nov 9. I need you to act today to help us win!
Economy★	22	23.2	8	6.0	Uncertainty is what's killing this economy! 1st #999 then unwind Fannie Mae and Freddie Mac!
Thank-you note	2	2.1	7	5.3	Thank you to all who donated & made the #IowaFund money bomb more successful than we ever imagined!
Sexual harassment scandal	NA	NA	7	5.3	Those who know Mr. Cain the best also know the suspiciously timed allegations are completely FALSE!
Other	22		10		

★Statistically significant results, p >.05.
★★Statistically significant results, p > .01.

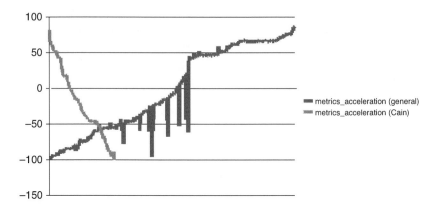

FIGURE 23.2 Acceleration of Cain's Tweets Versus the General Community From October 30 to December 10, 2011

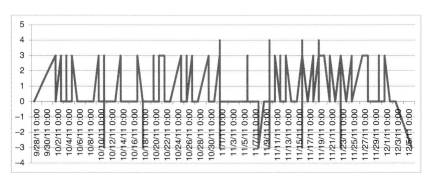

FIGURE. 23.3 Sentiment of Tweets Written by Cain From October 30 to December 10, 2011

in frequency during the crisis, whereas the number of tweets concerning the economy significantly decreased during that period. Importantly, only 7 out of 133 tweets during the crisis addressed the sexual harassment allegations against Cain.

The most retweeted tweet by Cain before the crisis was "I'm 100% pro-life. End of story" ($n = 1,111$). During the crisis, Herman Cain's most popular tweet was "My message to Iran: if you mess with Israel, you're messing with the USA," which was retweeted 809 times.

Our analysis shows that although acceleration of Cain's tweets significantly decreased (Figure 23.2) during the crisis, the sentiment of his tweets became more positive (0.32 vs. 0.52) (Figure 23.3).

Twitter Community's Tweets

Looking at tweets starting 40 days before the crisis to the day Cain announced his campaign suspension (September 20, 2011–December 10, 2011), we collected

TABLE 23.5 Sentiment Before and During the Crisis for the General Public's Tweets

	Positive Tweets	Neutral Tweets	Negative Tweets
Before crisis ($N = 500$)	16% ($n = 78$)	61% ($n = 304$)	24% ($n = 118$)
During crisis ($N = 490$)	6% ($n = 30$)	68% ($n = 331$)	26% ($n = 129$)

990 tweets that mentioned Herman Cain. In Table 23.5 we show the breakdown of positive, neutral, and negative sentiment before and during the crisis. The tone of tweets before the crisis was either neutral or negative, and after the crisis broke, the sentiment of tweets became even more negative.

The most popular post produced by an individual tweeter before the crisis, "Herman Cain spent $100k in campaign cash on his own books, putting donor money in his own pocket," was retweeted 80,756 times.

Analysis of the most retweeted tweets ($n = 500$) before the crisis revealed two popular themes: Cain's so-called 999 plan and his race (African American), which constituted 14% and 8% of tweets, respectively. For example, one tweeter posted, "It's 9–9–9 Herman Cain time." Another one said, "So I get it now. The GOP loves Herman Cain bc he can bash Obama in a way that the rest of them can't bc he's black too. Fail."

During the crisis, the theme of sexual misconduct dominated the Twitter community discourse (44.8%). The majority of tweets were quite sarcastic. One tweeter said, "With third female accuser coming forward, Herman Cain's campaign announced his 9-1-1 plan." Another echoed, "Might save time if only the women Herman Cain DIDN'T sexually harass came forward."

During the crisis, the overall sentiment score for tweets dropped from −0.22 to −0.71 (Figure 23.4).

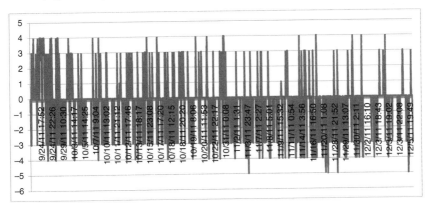

FIGURE 23.4 Sentiment of Tweets Written by the General Community From October 30 to December 10, 2011

The most popular tweet, "Herman Cain: 'Homosexuality is a "personal choice", and I respect their choice.' What a guy. In return, I respect his choice to be black," was retweeted 7,865 times during the crisis.

As mentioned before, mainstream media remain the primary source of information about crises across all social media platforms. This makes intuitive sense: reporters are professionally trained in creating messages and media organizations are considered legitimate information disseminators. However, the present study suggests that tweets posted by U.S. comedians (e.g., Andy Borowitz, Joy Behar, Neal Brennan, Conan O'Brien, Jason Whitlock, Albert Brooks) were more popular than tweets produced by mainstream media. For example, based on our analysis of the 490 most popular tweets during the crisis (October 30–December 10, 2011), tweets authored by a comedian, Andy Borowitz ($n = 39$) outnumbered tweets produced by the Associated Press ($n = 10$), CNN ($n = 9$), and Huffington Post ($n = 4$) taken all together. Overall, whereas the media were informing tweeters about the scandal (e.g., "Herman Cain admits he quoted Pokemon in campaign speeches"), comedians were both informing *and* entertaining (e.g., "Herman Cain is quoting Pokemon. Shouldn't that be Poke-woman?"). Further research is needed to determine whether social media users visit Twitter for entertainment reasons, news consumption, or both.

Discussion

Coombs (2012) argued that "social media is about interaction and control, not being fed information" (p. 25). Our analysis of tweets posted by Cain and his social media team before and during the scandal showed that Herman Cain's efforts to interact with and control tweeters were rather poor and even his attempt to "feed" information to them did not resonate much with his audience (based on a relatively low number of retweets).

Furthermore, our study revealed that the Twitter community focused mainly on economy and race before the scandal and primarily focused on the scandal after it arose. The crisis generated a more active discussion regarding Herman Cain. Most notably, the Twitter community had a quite negative feeling toward Cain from the beginning (before the crisis), and the discussion became even more negative after initial allegations of sexual misconduct were reported. In contrast, Cain's tweets were positive from the beginning and became even more positive after the crisis broke. In addition, Herman Cain ignored the scandal by saying very little and continued to focus on his economic policies.

There was a significant difference between the popularity of tweets written by the general community about Cain and tweets written by Cain himself. During the crisis, tweeters rather ignored Cain and conversed with each other. We call this outcome a drowning effect, or a phenomenon of an actor's message being "drowned out" because of increasing public discourse surrounding the actor that does not further the actor's platform (Figure 23.2).

Overall, our analysis of Herman Cain's tweets demonstrated a rather poor effort to use the dialogic potential of Twitter and engage with stakeholders. Cain's strategies were mostly asymmetrical because he tended to inform followers instead of listening to them, reaching out, and conversing. He underutilized the opportunities provided by Twitter to establish a dialogue, mobilize public support, and influence public opinion.

Implications for Public Relations and Crisis Management

This study found that reporters kept normalizing Twitter (Singer, 2005) by fitting it into their existing norms and practices during the 2012 Republican presidential primary. In other words, journalists did not use the "freewheeling nature of blogging" (Lasorsa, Lewis, & Holton, 2011, p. 21) to its full potential, failing to share opinions and engage with the audience. In short, reporters from traditional media represented a lesser threat to the campaign than, for example, comedians. In fact, their tweeting activities appeared to normalize Twitter as well. Yet, comedians' business as usual had a profound effect on the campaign. Whereas in the past public relations practitioners worried about traditional media as a damaging force, our study shows that comedians (the entertainment industry) were much more damaging to Herman Cain's campaign. Basically, the entertainment industry, not traditional media, "drowned" his campaign on Twitter.

As mentioned, our analysis of the most retweeted tweets showed that comedians' humorous and sarcastic posts enjoyed a high degree of popularity. It appeared they were *influential social media creators* or individuals who post information for others to consume, as opposed to *followers* and *inactives* who consume crisis information directly or indirectly (Liu, Jin, & Austin, 2013). Moreover, comedians' tweets energized the Twitter community and served as a remedy against political fatigue. This finding suggests a new direction of research to examine whether public relations practitioners should consider utilizing humor on social media during crisis communication and under what conditions this might be appropriate.

Another lesson learned from this study is that a candidate's popularity on Twitter (e.g., a large number of followers) should be checked against the Twitter community's overall sentiment toward the candidate. As mentioned before, Herman Cain had a large number of followers in fall 2011, yet the prevalence of an overall negative sentiment on Twitter might have been the factor that amplified the crisis.

The demographic makeup of Twitter might explain why Cain was unable to reach the Twitter audience effectively. For example, the Pew Research Center found that more tweeters are young liberals (Pew Research Center, 2014). In contrast, Herman Cain's usual supporters tended to be conservative and older (Pew Research Center, 2012). A recent study of ideological segregation on Twitter showed that the level of political polarization (conservatives vs. liberals) increases when the issue is clearly political (e.g., presidential elections; Barbera, Jost, Nagler, Tucker, & Bonneau, 2015).

The usage of such a crisis communication strategy as stealing thunder has been found effective during some political sex scandals. In particular, politicians who told their own bad news before the story broke in the media had less news coverage and fewer negative frames (Wigley, 2011). Wigley (2011) argued that this effect could be explained by Brock's (1968) commodity theory—the abundance of information decreases its value.

Apparently, Herman Cain increased the value of information about his past by failing to provide a clear response to Politico, a news organization that requested a comment about his alleged inappropriate behavior (Palmer, Martin, Haberman, & Vogel, 2011). Even after being cued about an upcoming story, Cain did not steal thunder by self-disclosing the damaging information on traditional or social media. Instead, based on the analysis of Cain's tweets, his social media team adopted a "let it die" approach as the main response strategy. Moreover, the team did not actively question the strategic motive behind the accusations against Cain and did not promote their frames and interpretation of the issue. In other words, they did not capitalize on the experience in crisis management gained by political strategists, for example, during the Lewinsky debacle.

Yet, after failing to steal thunder, the "let it die" strategy could have been the only approach in this crisis situation, where several women (not just one) kept coming out with similar accusations. In addition, it is hard to predict what reaction the Twitter community would have had if Cain had been more active in denying the accusations. Such a strategy might have hurt his reputation even more. In light of Cain's statement about a possible run for the presidency in 2016 (Bobic, 2014), although he did not in fact run in 2016, the campaign's suspension in 2011 did not seem like an exit strategy but rather part of a long-term plan to resurface in a few years.

Conclusion

Our study offers invaluable insight into the dynamics of crisis communication on Twitter during a political campaign. We discover the presence of a "drowning effect" where the entire platform of the candidate is drowned out because his past misbehavior becomes the center of discussion. A recommendation is to use the old crisis communication approach—stealing thunder—to mitigate the crisis and possibly decrease a number of negative frames. We assume that stealing thunder might be first step to reduce the drowning effect on social media. This proposition should be further tested.

This study has some limitations. First, Twitter users only account for 18% of Internet users, and their demographic profile does not reflect the overall adult population (Smith et al., 2014). Second, this study is a snapshot of a single campaign, and future research to explore a drowning effect in a different type of crisis is necessary (e.g., corruption). It is also important to look at how Twitter usage patterns will change in the future and what effect it will have on future campaign dynamics.

Despite its limitations, our study is helpful to public relations practitioners who are running campaigns on social media platforms. In addition, our study also provides lessons learned in regards to Herman Cain's failure to manage public opinion about the sexual harassment scandal on Twitter in this new era of political transparency.

References

Arpan, L. M., & Roskos-Ewoldsen, D. R. (2005). Stealing thunder: Analysis of the effects of proactive disclosure of crisis information. *Public Relations Review, 31*(3), 425–433.

Austin, L., & Jin, Y. (2015). Approaching ethical crisis communication with accuracy and sensitivity: Exploring common ground and gaps between journalism and public relations. *Public Relations Journal, 9*. Retrieved from http://apps.prsa.org/Intelligence/PRJournal/Documents/2015v09n01AustinJin.pdf

Axelrod, D. (2013). Election overview. In K. H. Jamieson (Ed.), *Electing the President, 2012: The insiders' view* (pp. 19–47). Philadelphia: University of Pennsylvania.

Barbera, P., Jost, J. T., Nagler, J., Tucker, J., & Bonneau, R. (2015). Tweeting from left to right: Is online political communication more than an echo chamber? *Psychological Science, 26*(10), 1531–1542.

Bobic, I. (2014, May 31). Herman Cain says he might run for president again in 2016. *The Huffington Post.* Retrieved from http://www.huffingtonpost.com/2014/05/31/herman-cain-2016_n_5424710.html

Brock, T. C. (1968). Implications of commodity theory for value change. In A. G. Greenwald, T. C. Brock, & T. M. Ostrom (Eds.), *Psychological foundations of attitudes* (pp. 243–275). New York: Academie.

Claeys, A. S., & Cauberghe, V. (2012). Crisis response and crisis timing strategies, two sides of the same coin. *Public Relations Review, 38*(1), 83–88.

Coombs, W. T. (2007). Protecting organization reputations during a crisis: The development and application of situational crisis communication theory. *Corporate Reputation Review, 10,* 163–176.

Coombs, W. T. (2012). *Ongoing crisis communication: Planning, managing, and responding* (3rd ed.). Thousand Oaks, CA: Sage.

Coombs, W. T. (2014). State of crisis communication: Evidence and the bleeding edge. *Research Journal of the Institute for Public Relations, 1*(1). Retrieved from http://www.instituteforpr.org/state-crisis-communication-evidence-bleeding-edge

Coombs, W. T., & Holladay, S. (2015). Digital naturals and crisis communication. In W. T. Coombs, J. Falheimer, M. Heidi, & P. Young (Eds.), *Strategic communication, social media and democracy* (pp. 54–62). New York: Routledge.

Duggan, M., & Brenner, J. (2013). Social media update 2013. Retrieved from http://www.pewinternet.org/2013/12/30/social-media-update-2013/

Fouhy, B., & Gillum, J. (2011, October 31). AP analysis: Candidates' Twitter use varies widely. *The Associated Press.* Retrieved from http://news.yahoo.com/ap-analysis-candidates-twitter-varies-widely-071935068.html

Jahansoozi, J. (2006). Relationships, transparency, and evaluation: The implications for public relations. In J. L'Etang & M. Pieczka (Eds.), *Public relations: Critical debates and contemporary practice* (pp. 61–91). Mahwah, NJ: Lawrence Erlbaum.

Kent, M. L., & Taylor, M. (1998). Building dialogic relationships through the World Wide Web. *Public Relations Review, 24*, 321–334.

Kent, M. L., & Taylor, M. (2002). Toward a dialogical theory of public relations. *Public Relations Review, 28*(1), 21–37.

Lamarre, H. L., & Suzuki-Lambrecht, Y. (2013). Tweeting democracy? Examining Twitter as an online public relations strategy for congressional campaigns. *Public Relations Review, 39*, 360–368.

Lasorsa, D. L., Lewis, S. C., & Holton, A. E. (2011). Normalizing Twitter. *Journalism Studies, 13*(1), 19–36.

Liu, B. F., Jin, Y., & Austin, L. (2013). The tendency to tell: Understanding public's communicative responses to crisis information form and source. *Journal of Public Relations Research, 15*, 51–67.

Nielsen, F. (2014). Nielsen sentiment dictionary. Retrieved from http://www2.imm.dtu.dk/pubdb/views/publication_details.php?id=6010, 2014.

Palmer, A., Martin, J., Haberman, M., & Vogel, K. P. (2011). Exclusive: 2 women accused Cain of inappropriate behavior. Retrieved from http://www.politico.com/story/2011/10/exclusive-2-women-accused-cain-of-inappropriate-behavior-067194

Pew Research Center. (2012). Politics fact sheet. Retrieved from http://www.pewinternet.org/fact-sheets/politics-fact-sheet

Pew Research Center. (2014, January). Social networking fact sheet. Retrieved from http://www.pewinternet.org/fact-sheets/social-networking-fact-sheet

Rainie, L., Smith, A., Kay, K. L., Brady, H., & Verba, S. (2012). Social media and political engagement. Retrieved from http://pewinternet.org/Reports/2012/Political-Engagement.aspx

Shah, D. V., Watts, M. D., Domke, D., & Fan, D. P. (2002). News framing and cueing of issue regimes: Explaining Clinton's public approval in spite of scandal. *Public Opinion Quarterly, 66*(3), 339–370.

Singer, J. B. (2005). The political J-blogger: "Normalizing" a new media form to fit old norms and practices. *Journalism, 6*(2), 173–198.

Smith, M. A., Rainie, L., Shneiderman, B., & Himelboim, I. (2014). *Topic networks: From polarized crowds to community clusters.* Retrieved 29 May, 2014 from www.pewinternet.org/2014/02/20/mapping-twitter-topic-networks-from-polarized-crowds-to-community-clusters/?_ga=1.256212555.1916574829.1400599181

Thompson, J. B. (2005). The new visibility. *Theory, Culture & Society, 22*(6), 31–51.

Twitter Government and Elections Team. (2014). *The Twitter government and elections handbook.* San Francisco, CA: Twitter, Inc.

Wigley, S. (2011). Telling your own bad news: Eliot Spitzer and a test of the stealing thunder strategy. *Public Relations Review, 37*, 50–56.

24

FROM BASHTAGS TO GEOBOMBING

Modern-Day Digital Guerrilla Tactics

Patricia Swann

Introduction

Historically, political and social activism has faced an uphill battle. Individuals, groups, and movements intent on challenging governments, corporations, and other powerful opponents have relied on limited, traditional methods. Although their tactics have met with some success, activists have been, for the most part, the underdog.

Through the use of sophisticated electronic communication made possible first by the rise of the Internet and the World Wide Web and enhanced by the introduction of social media and other information-sharing tools, activists are now able to level a playing field once dominated by those individuals and structures that used their power to protect their position and secure the status quo by preventing the release of information.

Activist power not only pressures an organization to change but also may damage an organization's reputation and hamper an organization's ability to prosper or survive. *Crisis*, as defined by T. W. Coombs (2014), is a "significant threat to organizational operations or reputations that can have negative consequences for stakeholders and/or the organization if not handled properly" (para. 10).

Review of the Literature

Activists push for change by promoting or hindering an organization or industry's ability to do something. Smith and Ferguson (2010) noted that activists are involved in social, political, economic, and environmental issues. J. E. Grunig and L. A. Grunig (1992) describe activist groups as activist publics: "two or more individuals who organize in order to influence another public or publics through action that may include either symmetrical or asymmetrical approaches such as education, compromise, persuasion, pressure tactics, or force" (p. 504). Coombs and Holladay (2012) found that activists usually have three goals: pressure or hinder change, seek public policy or regulatory changes, and change social norms.

Because activists have historically lacked authority or power, they have interacted with "corporations to achieve a possible compromise" in order to gain social changes (J. E. Grunig & L. A. Grunig, 1989). When power and influence are not evenly distributed, however, activists often use asymmetrical approaches. J. E. Grunig (1997) acknowledged that activists may need to use asymmetrical tactics if the organization does not wish to collaborate with activists.

Later, J. E. Grunig (2001) changed the excellence theory typology to include both symmetrical and asymmetrical (mixed-motive) elements, but this still assumed that activist groups and organizations would "accommodate the interests of the other" (p. 15). A contingency interpretation of the model allowed that organizations and activist publics may have separate and conflicting interests (Grunig, Grunig, & Dozier, 2002).

To better explain the need for the asymmetrical tactics by activist publics, other theoretical perspectives of public relations are emerging from critical, cultural, rhetorical, functionalist, or multidisciplinary disciplines (Botan & Hazleton, 2006; Botan & Taylor, 2004; Curtin & Gaither, 2005; Demetrious, 2013; Dozier & Lauzen, 2000; Edwards, 2006; Hallahan, Holtzhausen, van Ruler, Vercic, & Sriramesh, 2007; Holtzhausen, 2000, 2007, 2012; Leitch & Neilson, 1997; Marsh, 2008; McKie, 2001; Motion & Leitch, 1996; Pal & Dutta, 2008; Pompper, 2005; Weaver, 2001). Another approach, the cocreational approach, accommodates plural realities and views many publics as cocreators of meaning (Yang & Taylor, 2010). Critical postmodern views of public relations (Demetrious, 2013; Holtzhausen, 2012) are calling for public relations and communication workers to become activists within their own organizations and become change agents to ensure their "organizations' survival and effectiveness" (Holtzhausen, 2000). Activist publics not only have separate and conflicting interests from their corporate targets but also may eschew any accommodation or compromise, especially when the stakes are high in matters of public health and the environment (Demetrious, 2013; Stokes & Rubin, 2010) or other social and political causes.

Social Media

Brian Solis, social media expert, defined *social media* as "the democratization of information, transforming people from content readers into publishers. It is the shift from a broadcast mechanism, one-to-many, to a many-to-many model, rooted in conversations between authors, people, and peers" (Solis, 2010). However, Merriam-Webster's definition adds the concept of online communities: social media are "forms of electronic communication . . . through which users create online communities to share information, ideas, personal messages, and other content (as videos)" (Merriam-Webster, n.d.).

As of January 2014, 74% of all U.S. Internet users are using social networking, with the heaviest users aged 18–29 at 89% (Pew Research Internet Project, 2014). The most frequently used form of social media was Facebook, used by 71% of online adults, followed by LinkedIn, 22%; Pinterest, 21%; Twitter, 18%; and Instagram, 17% (Pew Research Internet Project, 2014).

Activism, Social Media, and Crisis

Many activists today are using the Internet and social media platforms to raise awareness, present evidence, criticize opponents, activate and nurture supporters, and build resources to achieve their goals. Internet-based public relations strategies and tactics can be effective in conducting traditional public relations activities, not only for raising awareness and media relations, but also in raising funds, organizing members, and strengthening social networks and coalition building (Bimber et al., 2005; Coombs & Holladay, 2012; J. E. Grunig, 1997; Jenkins, 1983; Kent, Taylor, & White, 2003; Reber & Kim, 2006; Smith & Ferguson, 2001; Sommerfeldt, 2011; Taylor, Kent, & White, 2001; Taylor & Sen Das, 2010; Yang & Taylor, 2010).

Uysal and Yang (2013) found activists could be successful "active agencies" through effective mass self-communication tactics characterized by their constant flow of communication in their social networks. They concluded that compromise or accommodation may not be desirable when they have the power to force corporations to change.

Coombs (2014) said the often-used phrase "social media crisis" is not really a crisis. He defined it as a *paracrisis*, which is a situation that appears "or is amplified by social media" in the areas of customer service, venting, and charges of irresponsible behavior by an organization (p. 7). For example, angry customers who vent on organizational websites about bad service are risks and need a communication response, but this does not rise to the level of a crisis. Untended, this situation could grow into a crisis especially if the underlying problem is not corrected.

Method

This chapter examines numerous examples of social media activism to describe the current landscape of activism. Specifically, these examples seek to describe the "how" of activism—how activists are using social media and digital tools to achieve their goals using grounded theory's principles of developing theory first by collecting and assessing data within the substantive area (Glaser & Strauss, 1967).

Social Media Activism

Two brief examples of activists using Facebook and YouTube illustrate the power of social media to galvanize grassroots support: the 2011 Egyptian revolution and Kony 2012.

When photos of a young blogger's beaten dead body were circulated in 2010 on the Internet, Egyptian activist Wael Ghonim anonymously created a Facebook protest page called "We Are All Khaled Said" (Wallace-Wells, 2012). Protesting Said's death, purportedly at the hands of Egyptian security officials, the site called for an end to corruption and torture by President Hosni Mubarak's government. The site also proposed a protest on January 25, 2011, an official Egyptian holiday, Police Day. His Facebook page had 365,000 members before the outbreak of the mass revolt, which led to the 18-day uprising that ousted Mubarak. Ghonim (2012) said his Facebook page provided strength in numbers and helped reduce people's fears enough for them to become active in the silent street protests (Ghonim, 2012, p. 142). The first silent protests drew 8,000 people (Reuters, 2010).

A 26-year-old Egyptian woman, Asmaa Mahfouz, one of the founders of the Egyptian youth movement, created a video call to action on January 18, 2011, posted on her Facebook page, and later to YouTube by another poster after which it went viral (more than 70,000 views by March 2011; El-Naggar, 2011; Wall & Zahed, 2011). It, and another video posted on the eve of the massive January 25, 2011, protest, received more than 140,000 views within two months (Wall & Zahed, 2011). These videos helped draw the first large prodemocracy crowds to Cairo's Tahrir Square, which led to the 18-day uprising that ousted Mubarak (Fadel, 2011). Mahfouz's willingness to identify herself publicly in a video post on Facebook inspired many other Egyptians to do the same and build a movement (DemocracyNow.com, 2011). Part of Mahfouz's first video message included the following:

> I, a girl, am going down to Tahrir Square, and I will stand alone. And I'll hold up a banner. Perhaps people will show some honor . . . I'm making this video to give you one simple message: we want to go down to Tahrir Square on January 25th. If we still have honor and want to live in dignity on this land, we have to go down on January 25th. We'll go down and demand our rights, our fundamental human rights. (El-Baghdadi, 2011)

A more controversial social media phenomenon, Kony 2012, involved a 30-minute film, produced by the San Diego–based nonprofit Invisible Children, Inc., that sought to raise awareness and support for the capture and arrest of Joseph Kony, an African cult and militia leader (Cohen, 2012). He abducted and used children as soldiers in his Lord's Resistance Army. The film, available on Facebook, You-Tube, Vimeo, and the Invisible Children's website on March 5, 2012, reached 100 million views in six days (Invisible Children, 2014). The campaign was also aided by heavy Twitter traffic using the hashtag #Kony2012, which was tweeted 2.4 million times in the campaign's first month (Dewey, 2014). The effort garnered $3.7 million in pledges of support for efforts to arrest Kony, which resulted in $16 million in donations (Invisible Children, 2014). Although criticized for oversimplifying and misrepresenting key facts (Cohen, 2012) and its heavy programming costs, the campaign demonstrated social media's ability to raise awareness and motivate action quickly.

Social media and digital tools are helping to level the playing field. In particular, free, open-source tools such as TWiki and Crabgrass, which provide collaboration platforms, Off-the-Record Messaging, which provides instant messaging chats that are encrypted and authenticated, and Sukey, a mobile app that helps street protesters steer clear of trouble spots and barricades, can help mobilize people and resources, share information, and build public awareness about issues to grow support for their causes. Social media also allow activists to upload and share information controlled by target organizations as evidence supporting the activists' causes through sites such as WikiLeaks and GlobaLeaks. Digital software tools, such as Tor, help activists operate undetected in the Internet sphere so they can evade authorities to organize, communicate, and protest. Sharable platforms such as Creative Commons provide simple legal licenses for users to remix or reproduce creative work such as research, photographs, and graphics.

Public relations research about how social media are used to pressure organizations for change needs to expand beyond Facebook and Twitter, although both are important in activist causes. Social media platforms such as YouTube, Instagram, Pinterest, Tumblr, and other software applications should be investigated to understand how these digital tools are being used to achieve activist goals. This article investigates some of the lesser known digital and social tools and tactics used by activists to organize, raise funds, build awareness, and share knowledge, as well as encourage dialogue and strengthen relationship building for social, environmental, and political movements.

Activists' Tools and Strategies

Mobilizing Organizational and Financial Resources

Although most activists' organizations have some kind of identity and organization through their websites, nurturing members as most traditional organizations do can be challenging. Free, open, online constituent relationship-management software platforms such as the Action Network, Corporate Action Network, CiviCRM (n.d.), Causes, and Empowered.org provide the framework to grow and manage efficient organizations and member relations. Users can create petitions, events, forms, e-mails, fundraisers, reports, and other organizing needs (Action-Network, 2014). The Action Network, for example, helps organize and mobilize protests by Walmart employees on Black Friday for living wages (ActionNetwork, 2014). To a lesser degree, platforms such as Meetup and Eventbrite are used for online communities to mobilize for activist causes. Occupy Wall Street activists' recognition of the need for collaborative decision-making mobile software during street protests inspired the application Loomio (Rushkoff, 2014). It helps organizations discuss issues virtually and then offer a proposal for a vote. The Alliance for Direct Democracy in Greece uses Loomio to cultivate more direct citizen participation (Chao, 2014).

Social media brings otherwise disparate people and groups together around a common interest or cause. Although activists' websites have been used for raising funds, crowdsourcing, or micropatronage, is another way that nonprofit activist organizations can raise money for their causes. Similar to the Kickstarter model that supports fundraising for creative projects (Kickstarter, n.d.), crowdsourcing sites such as GlobalGiving, Crowdrise, StartSomeGood, and Indiegogo allow non-profits and individuals to fundraise. GlobalGiving, for example, has funded nearly 11,000 projects and raised more than $151 million since 2002 (About Global-Giving, n.d.) An antifracking activist Henry Boschen for Concerned Chippewa Citizen crowdsourced $2,000 using Indiegogo to purchase a drone-like mobile camera (Aerial Fracking Photos, 2014) to take aerial still images and videos of environmental problems associated with fracking that he publishes on his website (Concerned Chippewa Citizen, 2014).

Mobilizing People for Action

Although social media, such as Facebook and YouTube, are used for many causes, such tactics are not without their critics. The terms "slacktivism" and "clicktivism" have emerged to describe the passive, low-risk nature of simply clicking the "like" button on a Facebook page or retweeting a Twitter post; these actions so easily made are soon forgotten. After all, most social, political, and environmental causes still need the old fashioned "boots on the ground" approach. Still, *Huffington Post* blogger Avi Sholkoff (2014) called hashtag activism "a centerpiece of our culture," and the *Washington Post* blogger Caitlin Dewey (2014) said hashtag activism tactics provide "profound benefits" by "amplification of minority voices" that historically have been ignored. When the U.S. Federal Communications Commission was considering Internet "fast lanes," social media were used to create a coalition of organizations to mobilize for net neutrality. The coalition of 27 organizations called Battle for the Net (Battle for the Net, n.d.) developed an Internet Slowdown Day as an action day. Using downloadable website widgets that illustrated how users would be affected and an app that connected individuals to their Congressional representatives' contact information, the FCC and government were swamped with comments (Sweetland Edwards, 2014).

One of the easiest ways to galvanize public opinion is through online petitions such as Change.org, SignOn.org, or iPetition.com. "Prosecute the killer of our son, 17-year old Trayvon Martin" was one of the largest Change.org petitions. It received more than 2.2 million signatures and helped bring about charges of second-degree murder against George Zimmerman, the neighborhood watch captain (Change.org, 2012). Another Change.org petition started in 2011 by 22-year-old Molly Katchpole urged signers to "Tell Bank of America: No $5 Debit Card Fees." The petition's 300,000 signatures, including that of U.S.

President Barack Obama, led to national media coverage and Bank of America dropping the fee (Change.org, 2011). Another petition, "Southwest Airlines: Stop Promoting SeaWorld Animal Cruelty," needed just 27,000 signatures to convince Southwest Airlines to end its 26-year promotional partnership with SeaWorld (Sasso & Palmeri, 2014) to see its famed orcas.

Social media attacks and hijackings occur when social media platform systems are either hacked with implanted activist messages or when activists appropriate an individual's or organization's social media platform for their own messages.

Twitter hashtags, begun in 2007 and formally adopted by Twitter in 2009 (MacArthur, n.d. a), are how Twitter users create conversations around a single topic that are fed to a Twitter page (MacArthur, n.d. b) Hashtags are embedded in tweets and start with the pound sign or hashtag symbol (#) followed by a hyperlinked word or phrase. The 2011 Egyptian revolution's #egypt hashtag, used 1.4 million times, followed by #jan25, with 1.2 million mentions in the first three months of 2011, mobilized support for action. The hashtag #egypt was the most popular hashtag of 2011 (Schonfeld, 2011) and was the most significant activist hashtag effort at the time (Larsen, 2011; Twitter's top 2011 hashtags, 2011). Until then, Twitter hashtags were used primarily for breaking news, celebrity gossip, and to add humor or "meta-commentary" to a tweet (Parker, 2011).

In the United States, one of the first major Twitterstorms that used hashtags for activism formed in 2012 when the Susan G. Komen Foundation, which annually contributed $680,000 to Planned Parenthood for breast exams and mammograms, announced plans to cut off that funding. The decision was largely political, which outraged Planned Parenthood supporters (Swann, 2014a). By February 3, 2012, more than 100,000 people had tweeted hashtags like #singon, #standwithpp, and #stopthinkingpink (Rothschild, 2012), and Komen restored funding. An analysis of the 100,000 tweets during the first four days of the controversy showed that 25 of the 28 hashtags related to the controversy were pro-Planned Parenthood (Rothschild, 2012).

The shooting death of 17-year-old Michael Brown by police in Ferguson, Missouri, provides several examples of the use of hashtags to mobilize people for protests. The day after the shooting and before street protests began in Ferguson, a Twitter activist called Feminista Jones organized a campaign for a national moment of silence for recent victims of police brutality using the hashtag #NMOS14; it attracted tens of thousands of protesters in more than 20 vigils around the country (Donovan, 2014; Jones, 2014).

"Bashtags" are hashtags appropriated by activists for their own purposes, such as when the New York City Police Department asked Twitter followers to submit favorite photos of themselves with police officers using the hashtag #myNYPD. Occupy Wall Street activists used the hashtag to flood the Twitter account with photos of alleged police brutality (Swann, 2014b).

Geographical location data called geotags can be applied to anything in digital form (websites, blogs, photos, videos, or RSS feeds) with global positioning system software (BetterEvaluation, n.d.) such as Google Maps and Google Earth, a virtual globe based on sophisticated satellite imagery. Activists use this technology to showcase or build evidence for a cause. Activists tag events to certain locations and track the progression of events or their size, such as oil spills, deforestation (Amazonas Sustainable Foundation, n.d.; WWF & Eyes on the Forest, n.d.), and slum growth (Shelter Associates, n.d.)

Tunisian activists used geotagging to "geobomb" the Tunisian presidential palace's location on Google Earth with links to video testimonies of Tunisian political prisoners and human rights defenders after the government blocked access to video-sharing websites (Global Voices, 2008).

Organizations such as Anonymous, a loosely affiliated group of computer hackers known as hacktivists, use common social media platforms plus Internet forums and websites to mobilize members for a variety of Web-based attacks on websites (Chen, 2011; Fitri, 2011). These tactics, which often violate website user policies or are illegal, use easy-to-find Internet tools such as LOIC (low-orbit ion canon) to execute denial of service attacks. Distributive denial of service (DDoS) attacks, the most common cyberattack, flood targeted websites with requests to access it and effectively shut the site down (Joyce, 2010). Some groups illegally hack into computer systems and expose sensitive data, such as user account information that can include credit card numbers, e-mails, and other personal data. Anonymous was widely credited with the attack on Sony that took down the PlayStation Network for nearly a month (Swann, 2014a). Soon after an unarmed 18-year-old African-American resident was killed by a Ferguson, Missouri, police officer, the Ferguson City Hall website went down from a DDoS attack by members of Anonymous. They also urged people to protest in the streets (Hunn, 2014). These digital street protesters can inflict different types of attacks beyond DDoS attacks, including website defacements, such as replacing or manipulating information on a webpage to convey a specific message. Susan G. Komen's homepage was defaced by hackers during the funding controversy with Planned Parenthood (Johnson, 2012). Activists have also redirected users to other websites, in a tactic called a site redirect.

Sharing Resources

As mentioned earlier, there are many free, open-source digital tools that can be customized for activists' causes and other digital resources that offer basic, no-frills services. Additionally, there are online resources to help activists share their expertise through sharable training programs. Witness, a nonprofit human rights organization, is training activists how to gather effective visual evidence of misbehavior or illegal activities of individuals, organizations, and governments. Witness has worked with YouTube to develop a dedicated human rights channel for user-generated videos on human rights (Witness, n.d.). Witness's sharable training program via YouTube teaches activists how to create effective videos, including how to conduct interviews and preserve and label (adding metadata on who, what, where, and when) the videos so they meet evidentiary requirements of the courts.

A joint project of Witness and the Guardian Project has developed Informa-Cam, which allows activists to transmit material to a trusted recipient (Guardian Project, n.d.) This software allows the recipient, such as a news editor, to determine who has seen and handled the file or who might have tampered with it with metadata tagging. This tool allows journalists and courts to judge the trustworthiness of the citizen media.

Activists often need to encrypt their online communication to evade detection from authorities about their activities. The Electronic Frontier Foundation has developed guides for activists to secure information and circumvent online censorship (Electronic Frontier Foundation, n.d.). The Tor Project software, a free, open-source software tool, makes online video and phone calls more secure from surveillance (Tor: Overview, n.d.). It encrypts the original data, including the destination IP address, and sends it through a virtual circuit multiple times via randomly selected Tor relays that change the IP address.

Instead of encrypting information to protect activists from discovery, sometimes information needs to be liberated for all to see. Activists and whistleblowers use platforms such as WikiLeaks and GlobaLeaks to publish original source materials from organizations and governments that provide evidence of wrongdoing. Even eliminating artificial paywalls to information helps activists build support for their issue. RECAP, a joint project of the Center for Information Technology Policy at Princeton University and the Free Law Project, is a digital tool that allows free access to legal documents relating to thousands of federal court cases from Public Access to Court Electronic Records (PACER).

Building Awareness and Pressure

Building awareness for an activist cause still involves traditional public relations tactics such as news releases, media interviews, testimonials, pamphlets, posters, and events. Social media platforms allow activists to disseminate these information tactics to their members, journalists, and others. In addition to these, some new methods have emerged that build awareness and disseminate visual information.

Activists functioning as citizen journalists can upload videos to social media sites such as Facebook, YouTube, and Instagram to show aspects of activities such as street protests or human rights violations. Live-streaming software tools, such as Bambuser, Livestream, and Ustream or Facebook's live-streaming feature, allow activists to broadcast real time to their own social networks from their smartphones or other digital devices. These digital sharing services are important because street protesters can have their cell phones and other recording devices confiscated before they have the opportunity to upload their information. Examples of live streaming by activists include democracy protesters in Hong Kong (Ukrstream, 2014), social and economic equality protests of the Occupy Wall

Street movement (Occupy Wall Street: Watch Live, 2011), and marches protesting the police shooting of Michael Brown in Ferguson, Missouri (I am Mike Brown Live from Ferguson, Mo, 2014).

Beyond traditional videos and photos, there are two other types of sharable data methods that use visual data for causes: memes and infographics. Dawkins (1989) said memes are small parts of our culture that have been modified and spread from person to person. Memes are a type of participatory media culture that parody, mimic, or recycle bits of culture in humorous, mocking, and serious ways (Kuipers, 2005; Shiftman, 2013). Memes can function as a reaction to dominant media messages (Kempe, Kleinberg, & Tardos, 2003). The Human Rights Campaign's equal rights logo was turned into a popular Facebook meme when a pink version of its equal sign logo began appearing in avatars and profile pictures throughout the Internet as the U.S. Supreme Court considered two marriage equality cases (Akel, 2013).

Infographics are graphical displays that condense large amounts of information into an easy-to-understand format (Tufte, 2001). Miller and Barnett (2010) found that "a combination of text and graphics may aid in the understanding of complex material" (p. 62). Free software such as Piktochart, Easel.ly, and others make creation of infographics easy. These images are often circulated through Facebook, Tumblr, and other social media platforms. Infographics often combine text and multiple graphics. When a U.S. Supreme Court decision denying health coverage for contraceptives was issued, one organization turned it into an infographic, "The True Cost of Birth Control" (2014), depicting the expense of different forms of birth control (Kutner, 2014). Other activist organizations, such as People for the Ethical Treatment of Animals (PETA, n.d.) and environmental groups, create infographics to distill long or complex messages visually. Restore the Mississippi River Delta, for example, posted an infographic titled "#4 Years Later" that was circulated on social media sites to explain the negative effects of the BP gulf oil spill (Rastegar, 2014).

Lessons for Crisis Managers

Activists who are organized, powerful, and good communicators can inflict harm to an organization's reputation and bottom line as seen from this chapter's examples. Many of Coombs's (2014) general crisis communications recommendations are appropriate for dealing with crisis situations that involve activists: be the first to release information about a crisis; use the organization's available online channels to communicate and do so frequently; when people are endangered by a crisis, communicate how they can protect themselves physically. Additionally, for those affected by the crisis, the organization should help people cope psychologically with the situation.

Because social media works best when communication flows like a conversation rather than like stilted corporate speak, Swann (2014b) suggested that organizations should talk like real people do. And when an organization makes a serious mistake, the organization should "own it" and fix the problem.

In his book *Crisis Communication: Practical PR Strategies for Reputation Management and Company Survival*, Anthonissen (2008) recommends to "keep [communication] open and honest" during a crisis while on the Internet (p. 175).

Organizations should also monitor social media mentions of their name and brands, dedicate a response team to deal with emerging social media issues and track their growth, and act quickly.

References

ActionNetwork. (n.d.). Walmart workers take action: Black Friday 2014. Retrieved from https://actionnetwork.org/event_campaigns/walmart-workers-strike-black-friday-2014

ActionNetwork, The. (2014). The toolset. Retrieved from https://actionnetwork.org/toolset

Aerial Fracking Photos. (2014). Retrieved from http://www.indiegogo.com/projects/aerial-fracking-photos

Akel, J. (2013, March 29). Fighting for equality, one meme at a time. *Salon.com*. Retrieved from http://www.salon.com/2013/03/29/fighting_for_equality_one_meme_at_a_time_partner/

Amazonas Sustainable Foundation. (n.d.). Retrieved from http://www.google.com/earth/outreach/stories/fas.html

Anthonissen, P. F. (2008). *Crisis communication: Practical PR strategies for reputation management and company survival.* London: Kogan Page.

Battle for the Net. (n.d.). We're in the battle for the net. Retrieved from http://www.battleforthenet.com

BetterEvaluation. (n.d.). Geotagging. Retrieved from http://betterevaluation.org/evaluation-options/mapping_geo_tagging

Bimber, B., Flanagin, A., & Stohl, C. (2005). Conceptualizing collective action in the contemporary media environment. *Communications Theory, 15*(4), 365–388.

Botan, C. H., & Hazleton, V. (2006). *Public relations theory II.* Mahwah, NJ: Lawrence Erlbaum Associates.

Botan, C. H., & Taylor, M. (2004). Public relations: State of the field. *Journal of Communication, 54*(4), 645–661.

Change.org. (2011, November). Tell Bank of America: No $5 debit card fees. Retrieved from http://www.change.org/p/tell-bank-of-america-no-5-debit-card-fees

Change.org. (2012, April). Prosecute the killer of our 17-year-old Trayvon Martin. Retrieved from http://www.change.org/p/prosecute-the-killer-of-our-son-17-year-old-trayvon-martin

Chao, R. (2014, March 13). The largest Loomio project yet. Retrieved from http://techpresident.com/news/wegov/24818/loomios-largest-project-yet

Chen, C. (2011, August 15). Anonymous hackers use social media to mobilize for tonight's BART protest. *SFWeekly.com*. Retrieved from http://www.sfweekly.com/thesnitch/2011/08/15/anonymous-hackers-use-social-media-to-mobilize-for-tonights-bart-protest

CiviCRM. (n.d.). About CiviCRM. Retrieved from https://civicrm.org/what/whatiscivicrm

Cohen, N. (2012, March 11). A video campaign and the power of simplicity. *New York Times*. Retrieved from http://www.nytimes.com/2012/03/12/business/media/kony-2012-video-illustrates-the-power-of-simplicity.html?_r=0

Concerned Chippewa Citizen. (2014). Retrieved 15 October, 2014 from http://wisair.wordpress.com/

Coombs, W. T. (2014). State of crisis communication: Evidence and the bleeding edge. *Research Journal of the Institute for Public Relations*, 1(1). Retrieved from http://www.instituteforpr.org/state-crisis-communication-evidence-bleeding-edge

Coombs, W. T., & Holladay, S. J. (2012). Fringe public relations: How activism moves critical PR toward mainstream. *Public Relations Review, 38*, 880–887.

Curtin, P., & Gaither, T. (2005). Privileging identity, difference, and power: The circuit of culture as a basis for public relations theory. *Journal of Public Relations Research, 17*, 91–115.

Dawkins, R. (1989). *The selfish gene* (2nd ed.). New York: Oxford University.

Demetrious, K. (2013). *Public relations, activism, and social change: Speaking up.* New York: Routledge.

DemocracyNow. (2011, February). Asmaa Mahfouz and the YouTube video that helped spark the Egyptian uprising. Retrieved from https://www.democracynow.org/2011/2/8/asmaa_mahfouz_the_youtube_video_that

Dewey, C. (2014, May 8). #Bringbackourgirls, #Kony2012, and the complete, divisive history of "hashtag activism." *Washington Post*. Retrieved from http://www.washingtonpost.com/news/the-intersect/wp/2014/05/08/bringbackourgirls-kony2012-and-the-complete-divisive-history-of-hashtag-activism

Donovan, T. (2014, August 20). Michael Brown, Gaza and a crowd-sourced record of abuse: In defense of "clicktivism." *Salon.com*. Retrieved from http://www.salon.com/2014/08/20/michael_brown_gaza_and_a_crowd_sourced_record_of_abuse_in_defense_of_clicktivism/

Dozier, D., & Lauzen, M. (2000). Liberating the intellectual domain from the practice: Public relations, activism, and the role of the scholar. *Journal of Public Relations Research, 12*, 3–22.

Edwards, L. (2006). Rethinking power in public relations. *Public Relations Review, 32*(3), 229–231.

El-Baghdadi, I. (2011, February 1). Meet Asmaa Mahfouz and the vlog that helped sparked the revolution. [Video file]. Retrieved from http://www.youtube.com/watch?v=SgjIgMdsEuk

Electronic Frontier Foundation. (n.d.). Surveillance self-defense. Retrieved from https://ssd.eff.org

El-Naggar, M. (2011, February 1). The female factor: Equal rights takes to the barricades. *New York Times*. Retrieved from http://www.nytimes.com/2011/02/02/world/middleeast/02iht-letter02.html?_r=0

Fadel, L. (2011, August 14). Asmaa Mahfouz, Egyptian youth activist, is charged by military prosecutor. *Washington Post*. Retrieved from http://www.washingtonpost.com/world/middle-east/asmaa-mahfouz-egyptian-youth-activist-is-charged-by-military-prosecutor/2011/08/14/gIQAuqihFJ_story.html

Fitri, N. (2011). Democracy discourses through the Internet communication: Understanding the hacktivism for global changing. *Online Journal of Communication and Media Technologies*, 1(2), 11–12. Retrieved from http://www.academia.edu/1438665/Hacktivism_for_Global_Changing_Nofia_Fitri_ojcmt.net_

Ghonim, W. (2012). *Revolution 2.0: The power of the people is greater than the people in power.* New York: Houghton Mifflin Harcourt.

Glaser, B., & Strauss, A. (1967). *The discovery of grounded theory.* Chicago: Aldine.

GlobalGiving. (n.d.). About global giving. Retrieved 15 October, 2014 from www.globalgiving.org/aboutus/

Global Voices. (2008, May 27). Human rights videos besiege the Tunisian presidential palace. Retrieved from http://advocacy.globalvoicesonline.org/projects/advocacy-20-guide-tools-for-digital-advocacy/geo-bombing-youtube-google-earth

Google Earth. (n.d. a). Shelter associates. Retrieved from http://www.google.com/earth/outreach/stories/shelter.html

Google Earth. (n.d. b). WWF & eyes on the forest. Retrieved from http://www.google.com/earth/outreach/stories/wwf.html

Grunig, J. E. (1989). Communication, public relations, and effective organizations: An overview of the book. In J. E. Grunig & L. A. Grunig (Eds.), *Public relations research annual* (Vol. 1, pp. 27–61). Hillsdale, NJ: Lawrence Erlbaum Associates.

Grunig, J. E. (1997). A situational theory of publics: Conceptual history, recent challenges and new research. In D. Moss, T. MacManus, & D. Vercic (Eds.), *Public relations research: An international perspective* (pp. 3–48). London: International Thomson Business Press.

Grunig, J. E. (2001). Two-way symmetrical public relations: Past, present and future. In R. L. Heath (Ed.), *Handbook of public relations* (p. 15). Thousand Oaks, CA: Sage.

Grunig, J. E., & Grunig, L. A. (1989). Toward a theory of public relations behavior of organizations: Review of a program of research. In J. E. Grunig & L. A. Grunig (Eds.), *Public relations research annual* (vol. 1, pp. 27–63). Hillsdale, NJ: Lawrence Erlbaum Associates.

Grunig, J. E., & Grunig, L. A. (1992). Models of public relations and communication. In J. E. Grunig (Ed.), *Excellence in public relations and communication management* (pp. 285–326). Hillsdale, NJ: Lawrence Erlbaum Associates.

Grunig, L. A. (1992). Activism: How it limits the effectiveness of organizations and how excellent public relations departments respond. In J. E. Grunig (Ed.), *Excellence in public relations and communications management* (pp. 503–530). Hillsdale, NJ: Lawrence Erlbaum Associates.

Grunig, L. A., Grunig, J. E., & Dozier, D. M. (2002). *Excellent public relations and effective organizations: A study of communication management in three countries.* Mahwah, NJ: Lawrence Erlbaum Associates.

Guardian Project. (n.d.). InformaCam: Verified mobile media. Retrieved from https://guardianproject.info/apps/informacam/

Hallahan, K., Holtzhausen, D., van Ruler, B., Vercic, D., & Sriramesh, K. (2007). Defining strategic communication. *International Journal of Strategic Communication, 1,* 3–35.

Holtzhausen, D. R. (2000). Postmodern values in public relations. *Journal of Public Relations Research, 12,* 93–114.

Holtzhausen, D. R. (2007). Activism. In E. L. Toth (Ed.), *The future of excellence in public relations and communication management: Challenges for the next generation* (pp. 357–379). Mahwah, NJ: Lawrence Erlbaum Associates.

Holtzhausen, D. R. (2012). *Public relations as activism: A postmodern approach to public relations theory and practice.* New York: Taylor & Francis/Routledge.

Hunn, D. (2014). How anonymous hackers changed Ferguson, Mo., protests. Retrieved from http://www.govtech.com/local/How-computer-hackers-changed-the-Ferguson-protests.html

I am Mike Brown Live from Ferguson, Mo. (2014). [Video file]. Retrieved from http:// new.livestream.com/accounts/9035483/events/3271930

Invisible Children. (2014). Retrieved from http://invisiblechildren.com/kony-2012/

Jenkins, J. C. (1983). Resource mobilization theory and the study of social movements. *Annual Review of Sociology, 9*, 527–553.

Johnson, L. (2012, February 2). Susan G. Komen Foundation website apparently hacked by Planned Parenthood controversy. Retrieved from http://www.huffington post.com/2012/02/02/susan-g-komen-foundation-website-hacked-planned-parenthood_n_1250647.html

Jones, F. (2014, August). National moment of silence #NMOS14. Retrieved from https:// storify.com/FeministaJones/national-moment-of-silence-nmos14

Joyce, M. (2010). *Digital activism decoded: The new mechanics of change* [ebook]. New York: International Debate Education Association.

Kempe, D., Kleinberg, J., & Tardos, É. (2003, August). *Maximizing the spread of influence through a social network.* International Conference on Knowledge Discovery and Data Mining, Washington, DC.

Kent, M. L., Taylor, M., & White, W. J. (2003). The relationship between web site design and organizational responsiveness to stakeholders. *Public Relations Review, 29*, 63–77.

Kickstarter. (n.d.). Seven things to know about Kickstarter. Retrieved from http://www. kickstarter.com/hello

Kuipers, G. (2005). "Where was King Kong when we needed him?" Public discourse, digital disaster jokes, and the functions of laughter after 9/11. *The Journal of American Culture, 28*(1), 70–84. doi: 10.1111/j.1542-734X.2005.00155.x

Kutner, J. (2014). Why Hobby Lobby is still a disaster, in one short infographic. *Salon.com.* Retrieved from http://www.salon.com/2014/08/28/why_hobby_lobby_is_still_a_disaster_in_one_short_infographic/

Larsen, R. (2011, August 22). Civil movements: Facebook and Twitter in the Arab Spring. *Arab Social Media Report, 1*(2). Retrieved from http://journalistsresource.org/wp-content/uploads/2011/08/DSG_Arab_Social_Media_Report_No_2.pdf

Leitch, S., & Neilson, D. (1997). Reframing public relations: New directions for theory and practice. *Australian Journal of Communication, 24*, 17–32.

MacArthur, A. (n.d. a). *The history of hashtags: Shedding some light on the history of hashtags and how we've come to use them.* Retrieved from http://twitter.about.com/od/Twitter-Hashtags/a/The-History-Of-Hashtags.htm

MacArthur, A. (n.d. b). Overview of hashtags on Twitter. [Video file]. Retrieved from http://video.about.com/personalweb/Overview-of-Hashtags-on-Twitter.htm#vdTrn

McKie, D. (2001). Updating public relations: "New science," research paradigms, and uneven developments. In R. L. Heath (Ed.), *Handbook of public relations* (pp. 75–92). Thousand Oaks, CA: Sage.

Marsh, C. (2008). Postmodernism, symmetry, and cash value: An Isocratean model for practitioners. *Public Relations Review, 34*, 237–243.

Merriam-Webster. (n.d.). Social media. Retrieved from http://www.merriam-webster. com/dictionary/social%20media

Miller, B. M., & Barnett, B. (2010). Understanding of health risks aided by graphics with text. *Newspaper Research Journal, 31*(1), 52–68.

Motion, J., & Leitch, S. (1996). A discursive perspective from New Zealand: Another worldview. *Public Relations Review, 22*, 297–309.

Occupy Wall Street: Watch Live. (2011). Retrieved from http://www.truth-out.org/article/item/3425:occupy-wall-street-watch-live

Pal, M., & Dutta, M. (2008). Theorizing resistance in a global context: Processes, strategies, and tactics in communication scholarship. *Communication Yearbook, 32,* 41–87.

Parker, A. (2011, June 10). Twitter's secret handshake. *New York Times.* Retrieved from http://www.nytimes.com/2011/06/12/fashion/hashtags-a-new-way-for-tweets-cultural-studies.html?pagewanted=all&_r=0

People for the Ethical Treatment of Animals (PETA). (n.d.). [Facebook]. Retrieved from https://www.facebook.com/officialpeta

Pew Research Internet Project. (2014, January 8). Social media sites, 2012–2013. Retrieved from http://www.pewinternet.org/2013/12/30/social-media-update-2013/social-media-sites-2012-2013/

Pompper, D. (2005). "Difference" in public relations research: A case for introducing critical race theory. *Journal of Public Relations Research, 17,* 139–169.

Rastegar, R. (2014, April 17). BP oil spill 4 years later [Infographic]. Retrieved from http://www.mississippiriverdelta.org/?s=infographic

Reber, B. H., & Kim, J. K. (2006). How activist groups use websites in media relations: Evaluating online press rooms. *Journal of Public Relations Research, 18,* 313–334.

Reuters. (2010, June 23). Autopsy says Egypt activist choked, protest planned. Retrieved from http://af.reuters.com/article/egyptNews/idAFLDE65M22620100623?pageNumber=2&v

Rothschild, D. (2012, February). The Twitter users who drove the furor over Komen and Planned Parenthood. *Yahoo! News.* Retrieved from https://www.yahoo.com/news/blogs/signal/twitter-users-drove-furor-over-komen-planned-parenthood-160326208.html

Rushkoff, D. (2014, March 19). Loomio: The occupy inspired app for consensus. Retrieved from http://www.shareable.net/blog/loomio-the-occupy-inspired-app-for-consensus-decision-making

Sasso, M., & Palmeri, C. (2014, July 31). Southwest, SeaWorld end partnership after animal petition. *Bloomberg.* Retrieved from http://www.bloomberg.com/news/2014-07-31/southwest-seaworld-end-partnership-after-animal-petition.html

Schonfeld, E. (2011, December 5). The top Twitter hashtags of 2011. Retrieved from http://techcrunch.com/2011/12/05/top-twitter-hashtags-2011/

Shiftman, L. (2013). *Memes in digital culture.* London: MIT Press.

Sholkoff, A. (2014). Hashtag activism is here to stay. *Huffington Post.* Retrieved from http://www.huffingtonpost.com/avi-sholkoff/hashtag-activism_b_5737184.html

Smith, M. E., & Ferguson, D. P. (2001). Activism. In R. L. Heath & G. Vasquez (Eds.), *The handbook of public relations* (pp. 291–300). Beverly Hills, CA: Sage.

Smith, M. E., & Ferguson, D. P. (2010). Activism 2.0. In R. L. Health (Ed.) *The Sage handbook of public relations* (pp. 395–407). Thousand Oaks, CA: Sage.

Solis, B. (2010, January 7). Defining social media: 2006–2010. Retrieved from http://www.briansolis.com/2010/01/defining-social-media-the-saga-continues/

Sommerfeldt, E. J. (2011). Activist online resource mobilization: Relationship building features that fulfill resource dependencies. *Public Relations Review, 37,* 429–431. doi: 10.1016/j.pubrev.2011.03.003

Stokes, A., & Rubin, D. (2010). Activism and the limits of symmetry: The public relations battle between Colorado GASP and Philip Morris. *Journal of Public Relations Research, 22*(1), 26–48.

Swann, P. (2014a). *Cases in public relations management.* New York: Routledge.

Swann, P. (2014b, July 15). NYPD blues: When a hashtag becomes a bashtag. *Public Relations Strategist.* Retrieved from http://www.prsa.org/Intelligence/TheStrategist/Articles/view/10711/1096/NYPD_Blues_When_a_Hashtag_Becomes_a_Bashtag#.VFFHcPnF-So

Sweetland Edwards, H. (2014, September 10). Net neutrality campaign claims victory in "Battle for the Net." *Time.* Retrieved from http://time.com/3319344/net-neutrality-congress-fcc/

Taylor, M., Kent, M. L., & White, W. J. (2001). How activist organizations are using the Internet to build relationships. *Public Relations Review, 27,* 263–284.

Taylor, M., & Sen Das, S. (2010). Public relations in advocacy: Stem cell research organizations' use of the Internet in resource mobilization. *Public Relations Journal, 4*(4). Retrieved from http://apps.prsa.org/Intelligence/PRJournal/Documents/2011TaylorDas.pdf

TorProject. (n.d.). Tor: Overview. Retrieved from http://www.torproject.org/about/overview

The true cost of birth control. (2014, August 27). [Facebook]. Retrieved from http://www.facebook.com/thisispersonalcampaign/photos/pb.358538020891738.-2207520000.1414627215./723923441019859/?type=3&theater

Tufte, E. (2001). [1983]. *The visual display of quantitative information* (2nd ed.). Cheshire, CT: Graphics Press.

Twitter's top 2011 hashtags: #egypt and #tigerblood. (2011, December 6). *BBC.* Retrieved from http://www.bbc.com/news/technology-16047918

Ukrstream. (2014). Protests in Hong Kong. [Video file]. Retrieved from http://ukrstream.tv/en/stream/protests_in_hong_kong_live_stream#.VFO_fBYcOJk

Uysal, N., & Yang, A. (2013). The power of activist networks in the mass self-communication era: A triangulation study of the impact of WikiLeaks on the stock value of Bank of America. *Public Relations Review, 39,* 459–469.

Wall, M., & El Zahed, S. (2011). "I'll be waiting for you guys": A YouTube call to action in the Egyptian revolution. *International Journal of Communication, 5.* Retrieved from http://ijoc.org/index.php/ijoc/article/viewFile/1241/609

Wallace-Wells, B. (2012, January 22). The lonely battle of Wael Ghonim. *New York Magazine.* Retrieved from http://nymag.com/news/features/wael-ghonim-2012-1

Weaver, C. K. (2001). Dressing for battle in the new global economy: Putting power, identity, and discourse into public relations theory. *Management Communication Quarterly, 15*(2), 279–288.

Witness. (n.d.). What is video metadata? [Video file]. Retrieved from http://www.youtube.com/user/Witness

Yang, A., & Taylor, M. (2010). Relationship-building by Chinese ENGOs' websites: Education, not activation. *Public Relations Review, 36*(4), 342–351.

SECTION IV-F
Areas of Application

Sports

25

SPORTS, CULTURE, AND FINANCIAL CRISIS

A Cross-Cultural Comparison of the Social Media Responses of Struggling Sports Associations in the United States and the United Kingdom

Audra Diers-Lawson and Stephen M. Croucher

Practice in corporate communications—especially public relations—has been changed because of social media's emergence, its centrality to strategy, and the corresponding power of social media users to engage with organizations (Diers, 2012; Freberg, 2012; Smith, 2010; Waters, Tindall, & Morton, 2010; Winchell, 2010). However, researchers and practitioners must better understand the changing global media landscape because it affects a modern understanding of communication. Interactions between organizations and their stakeholders in social media are redefining approaches to public relations (Winchell, 2010). Across contexts (see, e.g., Hartmann, 2012; Hayden, 2011; Hyun, 2012; Luck & Buchanan, 2008; Metzgar & Maruggi, 2009; Murphy & White, 2007; Rollason, 2011; Rowe & Gilmour, 2009; Weber, Erickson, & Stone, 2011; Wilson, 2011), the findings are all very clear—examining crisis response within the social media landscape is essential if we are to build, test, and apply theory in crisis communication.

This is particularly true in today's uncertain economic environments. However, critics of public relations practice and research argue scholars have too long ignored the influence of economics on organizational communication despite the reality that economic problems are often more characteristic of communication problems rather than technical problems (Jameson, 2009). Although the global financial crisis has renewed some interest in the influence of economics on public relations, Lawniczak (2009) argues the economic context is often ignored.

In addition, despite arguments and analysis indicating that, in an increasingly global world, conflicts and crises within a nation can have transnational implications, very little crisis-response research has addressed the role national culture might have on the crisis-response messages created and disseminated (Molleda, Connolly-Ahern, & Quinn, 2005; Moore, 2004). This need to develop cultural knowledge in crisis response is only amplified by the use of the Internet (Krishnamurthy & Kucuk, 2009).

Taking these factors together, one of the most logical contexts to analyze modern crisis response is in the sports industry because it is one of the world's largest industries, with revenues of more than $100 billion dollars worldwide (Anonymous, 2005; Espinoza, 2010) and because it is inextricably linked with culture, cultural domination, and cultural diffusion (Hartmann, 2012; Murphy & White, 2007; O'Callaghan, 2011; Rollason, 2011; Rossol, 2010; Rowe & Gilmour, 2009). Unfortunately, sport also remains one of the least studied organizational contexts in communication. For example, as Helland (2007) also points out, analyses of sport and media are often neglected. However, the Internet and social media have both introduced more powerful means by which sports organizations can communicate with their fans and have also changed the ways many fans can consume sports (Crolley, 2008). For these reasons, the present study concentrates on social media response to crises as we also explore the concepts of cross-cultural crisis response in one of the world's dominant industries—the sports industry.

Literature Review

Researchers and practitioners must better understand the changing global media landscape because it affects a modern understanding of crisis response. Interactions between organizations and their stakeholders in social media are redefining approaches to public relations (Winchell, 2010).

Crisis Communication

Though crisis communication scholarship has addressed crisis type as an important variable for consideration (Coombs & Holladay, 1996, 2004), research analyzing organizational events—a category that includes economic downturns—show mixed findings regarding the types of responses that organizations are likely to employ. For example, some research suggests organizations facing these situations would likely use strategies that explained or worked to get ahead of the crisis (Coombs & Holladay, 1996). Other research focusing more directly on economic downturns (Diers & Tomaino, 2010) found organizations focused on present-oriented strategies that essentially focused on a 'business as usual' approach to responding to managing crises resulting from economic downturns. Still other research emphasizes the importance of communicating competency, honesty, concern for employees, and the organization's stability (Anonymous, 2008; Quirke, 2009), but there remains little research evaluating how organizations managing economic crises respond.

Although a perfect list of strategies may not exist (Coombs, 2007), Coombs and Holladay (1996) offer the most comprehensive set of predictions about an organization's strategic choices in responding to crises. For example, the authors argue that in events where the onus of responsibility is ambiguous—such as with many organizational events—organizations should frame the crisis and its severity, emphasizing the denial of responsibility. However, depending on theoretical perspective, analyses of crisis-response strategies range from considering a handful (Benoit, 1997, 2004; Coombs, 2006) of tactics to including more than 40 distinctive response tactics (Diers, 2009; Mohamed, Gardner, & Paolillo, 1999). However, in the social media context in which organizations are directly engaging public stakeholders, less is known about the effectiveness of crisis response (Coombs & Holladay, 2012; Freberg, 2012). Thus, the most open assessment of crisis response considers 40 individual tactics categorized into eight broad tactic groupings (see Diers & Tomaino, 2010), including the following: self-enhancement, routine communication, responses that frame the crisis, responses that frame the organization, responses that are defensive or antisocial, responses that are accommodative, excellence or renewal responses, and responses focusing on organizational relationships (see Appendix A). These tactic groupings offer academics and practitioners a complete set of tactics on which to base analyses, identify strategies, and compare the emergence of those strategies across crises, industries, and time. By beginning with a more inclusive list of tactics and categories, we argue we can more effectively build theory with regard to financial crises. Therefore, we pose the following research question:

RQ1: How do organizations facing financial crises respond via social media to those crises?

APPENDIX A Taxonomy of Crisis Response Tactics Potentially Used By Organizations

Strategy Category	Strategy	Strategy Description
Self-enhancement (SE)	Marketing	Emphasizing product quality, prices, safety, and promotions
	Image advertising	Providing information to make the organization look positive; framing an issue for the stakeholders
Routine communication (RC)	Communication of mission or vision	Communication emphasizing organizational goals; mentioning the mission or vision
	Annual reports	Reporting monetary assets, liabilities, future liabilities, or interest in cooperation to increase market value
	Newsletters	Reporting monetary gains; attending to stakeholder concerns
Framing the crisis (FC)	Accounts	Developing a dominant narrative; using narrative to explain the problem

(Continued)

Strategy Category	Strategy	Strategy Description
	Information dissemination	Delivering information regarding the issue to educate, often with the goal of increasing stakeholders' sense of empowerment
	Issue salience	Communicating importance, often using risk or fright factors or scientific discourse
	Preconditioning	Influencing stakeholders to the organization's position on a crisis and their opinions about the organization by downplaying damage, putting the act in a more favorable context, or attacking accusers
Framing the organization (FO)	Ingratiation	Creating a positive image by reminding stakeholders of past good works or qualities
	Organizational promotion	Presenting the organization as being highly competent, effective, and successful
	Issues management	Diagnosing issues; using advocacy advertising
	Supplication	Portraying the organization as dependent on others in an effort to solicit assistance
	Organizational handicapping	Making task success appear unlikely in order to have a ready-made case for failure
	Bolstering	Separating the organization from the crisis by emphasizing past accomplishments; stressing good traits
Antisocial or defensive (D)	Noncompliance	Choosing not to act
	Disclaimers	Giving explanations prior to an action that might be embarrassing to ward off negative implications to image
	Defensive compliance	Indicating that actions are driven by compliance or requirements
	Evasion of responsibility	De-emphasizing the role in blame by emphasizing a lack of control over events, emphasizing the accident, or emphasizing good intentions
	Shifting the blame	Shifting or minimizing responsibility for fault, the most defensive strategy
	Simple denial	Denying the organization performed the act
	Strategic ambiguity	Not releasing many details; keeping stories consistent
	Intimidation	Representing the organization as powerful or dangerous, willing and able to adversely affect those who oppose its efforts
	Minimization	Emphasizing that the act or event is not serious
	Transcendence	Emphasizing more important considerations

Strategy Category	Strategy	Strategy Description
Accommodative (A)	Corrective action or compensation	"Correcting" actions adversely affecting others, including announcements of recall or offers of compensation
	Apologia	Communicating contrition or admission of blame, including remorse and requests for pardon or mortification
	Compassion	Communicating concern over well-being or the safety of the public; helping people psychologically cope with the crisis
	Offering reassurances	Asserting that problems are corrected: "This will never happen again."
	Eliciting sympathy	Asking stakeholders to feel sorry for the organization because of what happened
	Transparency	Emphasizing complete compliance; openness to inquiry and information seeking
	Volunteering	Seeking stakeholder involvement with the organization as a means of resolving the crisis
Excellence or renewal	Dialogic	Emphasizing openness and a willingness to engage about the issue
	Exemplification	Portraying the organization as having integrity, social responsibility, and moral worthiness
	Prosocial behavior	Engaging in actions to atone for transgression; persuading stakeholders of positive identity
Interorganizational relationships (IOR)	Blaring others	Identifying a negative link to an undesirable other
	Blasting	Exaggerating negative features of an undesirable other
	Burying	Obscuring or disclaiming a positive link to an undesirable other
	Blurring	Obscuring or disclaiming a negative link to a favorable other
	Belittling	Minimizing traits or accomplishments of a negatively linked other; attacking accuser's credibility
	Boosting	Minimizing undesirable features of a positively linked other
	Boasting	Proclaiming a positive link to a desirable other
	Burnishing	Enhancing desirable features of a positively linked other
	Collaboration	Emphasizing a desire to change and working with other organizations to resolve the crisis

National Culture

In recent years, there has been an increased recognition that national identity matters in crisis response (see, e.g., Chen, 2009; Molleda et al., 2005; Rovisco, 2010). This suggests we must look beyond case analyses in individual nations to better understand crisis response in a global communication environment because culture and crisis communication are likely linked at all levels from the decisions about what to communicate to the content of the messages communicated (Marra, 1998). In one of very few cross-cultural comparisons of crisis response, Haruta and Hallahan (2003) found meaningful differences in the use of apology, media strategies, and litigation concerns between the two countries. This suggests we should expect differences; however, because of the dearth of comparisons, we still do not have a sufficient understanding of the finer influence of culture on crisis response.

Certainly, we should expect differences in crisis response when cultures are vastly different; however, a better evaluation of the influence of culture would be to compare similar cultures—like those of the United States (U.S.) and United Kingdom (UK)—because it may effectively demonstrate the relative strength or weakness that culture has on crisis response. In one of few direct comparisons of these cultures' influences on communication style, Croucher and colleagues (2010) found national identity was a significant predictor of argumentativeness citing differences between the United States and the United Kingdom, despite focusing on differences based on religion.

Because research has found differences in crisis response exist and because there are demonstrated differences between American and British communication styles, we posit the following hypothesis:

> **H1:** There are differences between American and British crisis-response strategies in social media.

However, because there are few indications as to what those differences might be, we propose the following research question:

> **RQ2:** How do organizations representing different national cultures respond to financial crises in social media?

Sporting Organizations and National Culture

One issue that makes it challenging to identify the "national" character of crisis response is the industry to which an organization belongs. Industry has long been posited as a factor that would likely influence an organization's reaction to crises (Arpan, 2002; Brooks & Waymer, 2009; Glynn, 2000; Millar, 2004). As such, identifying a "national" identity in crisis response seems challenging. However,

Rowe and Gilmour (2009) argue that in Western cultures, professional sports are an important form of popular culture "shaped by constantly mutating interactions between the media and sport industries and established and evolving fan cohorts on which they depend" (p. 172).

Today sports are widely regarded as a "cultural subsystem of modern society" (Hopwood, 2005, p. 175). As such, there are important communicative implications because, to keep fans loyal, sports clubs must engage in relationship-building and maintaining activities (Hopwood, 2005). Hopwood argues managing two-way symmetric communication, like social media engagement, is essential for both dominant and secondary sports because it builds fan engagement. Luck and Buchanan (2008) found that open communication is vital to the success of sporting organizations, particularly in the face of economic downturns, because it meets their expectations for information and organizational engagement. In this way, the sports industry serves two masters—the corporate interests running them and the community that supports them (Boyd & Stahey, 2008). Thus, although sports teams may represent sites for practicing ritualized local identity, we do not have a clear understanding regarding the degree to which sports organizations use broader cultural memes to communicate with their stakeholders. Therefore, we pose the following research question:

RQ3:   Do social media–based crisis responses from sports organizations reflect elements of "national identity"?

Methods

Beginning in January 2010, a research team of 14 identified organizational crises viable for this study based on the following criteria: (a) each crisis had to be judged as substantial enough to receive news coverage and organizational attention for the following eight weeks of data collection, (b) each had to be relevant at the time of data collection so that new media information would be readily available, and (c) at least two organizations from the same industry but different nations had to be identified. The team's goal was to identify an exhaustive group of unique statements from official organizational representatives across new and traditional media sources. The result was 10 crises in five different industries from the United States and the United Kingdom with 419 unique messages to analyze. Included in the analysis were misdeeds with injuries, including accusations against The Who's Peter Townshend for child pornography ($n = 20$) emerging before their 2010 Super Bowl performance; economic downturns, including the study's focus— professional sports teams' financial struggles with Portsmouth Football Club's (FC) debt crisis ($n = 63$) and the Women's National Basketball Association's (WNBA) financial struggles ($n = 150$), Morris Publishing's financial struggles ($n = 37$), and the automobile manufacturing industry's financial struggles with General Motors ($n = 42$); and finally, the team also identified events outside of the organization's control, including the devastating Haiti earthquake focusing on the American and British Red Cross's responses to the crisis ($n = 107$). For our two struggling sports teams, we exclusively evaluated social media engagement in order to focus on direct efforts at fan engagement about the organizations' financial crises.

Coding Scheme

Single messages (i.e., press release, Twitter post, unique Facebook post, etc.) were coded because previous studies of crisis-response messages (Benoit & Czerwinski, 1997; Elsbach, 1994; Greer & Moreland, 2003; Henderson, 2003; Kauffman, 2001) emphasize that when studying crisis communication, examining the interplay of tactics employed affords researchers more information about an organization's strategy (see Appendix A).

Seven team members coded the entirety of one organization's crisis-response messages. Following procedures to establish intercoder reliability used by Molleda and colleagues (2005), 10% of the sample was randomly selected and independently coded by another member of the research team. An overall intercoder reliability analysis was conducted finding the coding scheme to be reliable ($\alpha = .87$) with individual analyses also reliable (The Who: $\alpha = .83$; Portsmouth: $\alpha = .91$; WNBA: $\alpha = .87$; Morris Publishing: $\alpha = .85$; General Motors: $\alpha = .89$; British Red Cross: $\alpha = .84$; and American Red Cross: $\alpha = .88$). The coding scheme is based on manifest content for each variable (see Diers & Tomaino, 2010). Evidence of the presence of each crisis-response tactic was coded as binary data with its presence or not noted.

Results

These data suggest there are significant differences between American and British sports responses to financial crises. However, more importantly, these data suggest a strong cultural effect for crisis response.

Social Media Response to Financial Crises by Sports Teams

RQ1 and 2 focused on the structure of crisis response by the sports teams in social media. The five dominant tactics used by the WNBA were self-enhancement, routine communication, excellence and renewal, image oriented, and defensive information (see Tables 25.1 and 25.2). Emergent image-oriented strategy (self-enhancement and framing the organization; $n = 34$) appeared 16% of the time when the WNBA was communicating. Self-enhancement alone was used 33% of the time. Defensive information management (routine communication, frame the organization, and defensive) was used three times (1% of the time)—all three times that the antisocial or defensive strategy was used. Routine communication was used the remaining 16% of the time. Excellence or renewal was used 9% of the

TABLE 25.1 Correlations Between Social Media Tactics Used in the United States by the WNBA

Variables Correlated[1]	1	2	3	4	5	6	7	8
1. Self-enhancement	—							
2. Routine communication	−.42**	—						
3. Frame the crisis	N/A	N/A	—					
4. Frame the organization	.21**	.19**	N/A	—				
5. Defensive or antisocial	−.08	.18*	N/A	.25**	—			
6. Accommodative	N/A	N/A	N/A	N/A	N/A	—		
7. Excellence or renewal	−.16*	−.15*	N/A	−.01	−.06	N/A	—	
8. Interorganizational relationships	−.10	−.17*	N/A	−.08	−.05	N/A	−.09	—

[1] $N = 213$, N/A indicates there were no cases of the tactic being used by the WNBA.
* $p < .05$.
** $p < .01$ (two-tailed).

TABLE 25.2 Frequency of Social Media Tactics and Strategies Used in the United States by the WNBA

Tactic	Observed N	Expected N	X^2 Value	Single-Tactic Strategy	Multiple-Tactic Strategy
Self-enhancement	136	106.5	71.60**	70	66
Routine communication	67	54	18.30**	35	32
Frame the crisis	0	43.2	237.53**	N/A	N/A
Frame the organization	40	47.1	5.98*	3	37
Defensive or antisocial	3	12.3	32.74**	0	3
Accommodative	0	15.4	72.90**	N/A	N/A
Excellence or renewal	45	38.6	5.70**	19	26
Interorganizational relationships	27	37	14.44**	9	18
Image oriented	34	24.6	16.92***	—	—
Defensive information management	3	2.4	.81	—	—

$N = 213$, N/A indicates there were no cases of the tactic being used by the WNBA, df for all = 1.
* $p < .05$.
** $p < .01$.

TABLE 25.3 Correlations Between Social Media Tactics Used in the United Kingdom by Portsmouth FC

Variables Correlated[1]	1	2	3	4	5	6	7	8
1. Self-enhancement	—							
2. Routine communication	−.04	—						
3. Frame the crisis	.06	.08	—					
4. Frame the organization	−.13	.00	.25★	—				
5. Defensive or antisocial	−.09	.07	−.19	.14	—			
6. Accommodative	−.12	.17	−.19	−.05	−.18	—		
7. Excellence or renewal	−.05	−.06	−.27★	−.21	−.15	.30★	—	
8. Interorganizational relationships	.06	.16	.04	.29★	.06	.17	.04	—

[1] $N = 63$, N/A indicates there were no cases of the tactic being used by Portsmouth FC.
★ $p < .05$.
★★ $p < .01$ (two-tailed).

time. These were often used in combination. Taken together, the dominant strategies were used 75% of the time by the WNBA. The remaining 25% represents a combination of messages not appearing enough to be significantly correlated or being used more often than expected. As such, these represent the dominant talking points.

The Portsmouth strategy was a nuanced approach to responding to the crisis with both dominant strategies, as well as different themes communicated (see Tables 25.3 and 25.4). There are four dominant response strategies. Framing the crisis was used on its own 25% of the time. Corporate social responsibility (CSR) was used 6% of the time. An explanative strategy (framing the crisis and framing the organization) was used 33% of the time. Finally, an effort to situate the organization (interorganizational relationships, framing the organization) was used 17% of the time. Taken together, this represents 71% of the messages from Portsmouth. However, there were additional themes emerging across all of Portsmouth's messaging. For example, appeals to interorganizational relationships were typically used in combination with other tactics or strategies 16% of the time; however, the specific strategies and tactics were not predictable. Even more importantly, accommodation—an effort to demonstrate goodwill and corporate social responsibility—was used in 25% of Portsmouth's messaging but did not significantly correlate with any particular tactic or strategy aside from the CSR strategy itself. Finally, the most dominant response theme was the team's effort to frame the crisis—used significantly within the explanative strategy and on its own; however, an effort to control the public's understanding of the situation was the single dominant message communicated by Portsmouth, used in an additional 30% of the time.

TABLE 25.4 Frequency of Social Media Tactics Used in the U.K. by Portsmouth

Tactic	Observed N	Expected N	X^2 Value	Single-Tactic Strategy	Multiple-Tactic Strategy
Self-Enhancement (M = 1.03)	2	31.5	71.60**	0	2
Routine Communication (M = 1.05)	3	16	18.30**	0	3
Frame the Crisis (M = 1.89)	56	12.8	237.53**	16	40
Frame the Organization (M = 1.33)	21	13.9	5.98*	0	21
Defensive/Anti-Social (M = 1.21)	13	3.7	32.74**	2	11
Accommodative (M = 1.32)	20	4.6	72.90**	1	19
Excellence/Renewal (M = 1.08)	5	11.4	5.70**	0	5
Emphasizing IOR's (M = 1.33)	21	11.0	14.44**	1	20
Corporate Social Responsibility (M = 1.09)	4	.9	14.89**	–	–
Explanative (M = 1.75)	21	2.9	144.89**	–	–
Situating the Organization (M = 1.26)	11	3.1	28.03**	–	–

N = 63
$\star = p < .05, \star\star = p < .01$

RQ2 asked about the structure of response between the U.S. and UK sports teams. By focusing on the dominant strategies, we identified the central talking points the teams communicated based on a combination of significant correlations combined with a chi-square analysis of the occurrences of strategies combined. These data reveal (see Table 25.5) the WNBA focused almost exclusively on an image-based approach to talking about the organization—essentially ignoring the financial struggles and focusing on self-promotion. In fact, even in their routine communication strategy, image advertising, organizational promotion, bolstering, and transcendence were all image-based talking points within the strategy that the organization used to talk about its day-to-day events. Further, the distinctive lack of defensive responses coupled with the overall promotional messaging seems to build the argument that the organization simply needs to be better promoted in order to solve its financial struggles.

TABLE 25.5 Construction of Talking Points in the WNBA's Social Media Response

Strategy	Message	Correlation	Observed	Expected	X^2
Self-enhancement	SE Marketing	.46★★★	61	39.6	45.20★★★
	SE Image advertising	.59★★★	83	53.6	73.44★★★
	RC Newsletters	−.44★★★	17	37.0	41.19★★★
	FO Organizational promotion	.24★★★	36	26.2	12.62★★★
	IOR Burnishing	−.18★★	2	5.7	7.06★★
Routine communication	SE Image advertising	−.30★★★	12	26.4	18.96★★★
	RC Communication of mission or vision	.42★★★	16	5.0	37.70★★★
	RC Newsletters	.90★★★	58	18.2	173.68★★★
	FO Ingratiation	.21★★	8	3.5	9.16★★
	FO Organizational promotion	.16★	19	12.9	5.22★
	FO Bolstering	.14★	2	.6	4.40★
	D Transcendence	.18★★	3	.9	6.63★★
	ER Dialogic	−.16★	2	6.8	5.43★
	IOR Burnishing	−.14★	12	26.4	18.96★★★
Excellence or renewal	SE Marketing	−.26★★★	3	13.1	13.92★★★
	RC Newsletters	−.19★★	5	12.3	7.48★★
	ER Dialogic	.62★★★	21	4.7	80.44★★★
	ER Exemplification	.67★★★	23	4.9	96.26★★★
Image oriented	SE Marketing	.60★★★	17	5.8	38.22★★★
	SE Image advertising	.80★★★	26	8.7	67.81★★★
	RC Communication of mission or vision	.39★★★	11	4.5	15.74★★★
	FO Ingratiation	.44★★★	9	2.9	20.56★★★
	FO Organizational promotion	1.00★★	34	11	105.00★★★
	FO Bolstering	.20★	2	.6	4.26★

★ $p < .05$.
★★ $p < .01$.
★★★ $p < .001$.

TABLE 25.6 Construction of Talking Points in Portsmouth FC's Social Media Response

Strategy	Message	Correlation	Observed	Expected	X^2
Framing the crisis	FC Information dissemination	1.00***	56	49.8	63.00***
	D Transcendence	−.36**	0	.9	8.13**
	ER Exemplification	−.51***	0	1.8	16.53***
Explanative	FC Information dissemination	1.00***	21	15.8	28.00***
	FO Ingratiation	.58***	14	10.5	9.33**
	ER Exemplification	−.48**	0	1.5	6.46*
Situating the organization	FO Ingratiation	.82***	8	2.0	28.59***
	FO Organizational promotion	.38*	2	.5	6.10*
	FO Supplication	.38*	2	.5	6.10*
	D Shifting the blame	.36*	3	1.0	5.66*
	IOR Blaring	.45**	4	1.3	8.80**
	IOR Collaboration	.55***	4	1.0	12.83***
Accommodative	FC Preconditioning	.33**	3	1.0	6.77**
	A Corrective action	.52***	7	2.2	16.93***
	A Compassion	.33**	3	1.0	6.77**
	A Eliciting sympathy	.64***	10	3.2	25.56***
	ER Exemplification	.27*	2	.6	4.44*
Interorganizational relationships	FO Ingratiation	.27*	8	4.7	4.59*
	FO Supplication	.26*	2	.7	4.13*
	IOR Blaring others	.39***	6	2.3	9.72**
	IOR Blasting	.37**	4	1.3	8.54**
	IOR Boasting	.37**	4	1.3	8.54**
	IOR Collaboration	.54***	8	2.7	18.33***

* $p < .05$.
** $p < .01$,.
*** $p < .001$.

Conversely, the Portsmouth FC (see Table 25.6) response focused on directly addressing the crisis, addressing concerns, and addressing the club's relationships with other organizations. Although there were elements of promotion within most of the major talking points, these were not overly emphasized. In fact, although we see an emphasis on moving on, making amends, explaining the situation, and defending the organization, we do not see the overly promotional approach to dealing with the financial crisis.

Significant Differences Between U.S. and UK Financial Crisis Responses

These data indicate that on all major talking points used by the WNBA and Portsmouth FC (see Table 25.7), except defensive information management, there were significant differences between the social media strategies used by the two organizations. We see substantially different approaches to communicating with each organization's stakeholders—even outside of the central driving messaging. Therefore, H1 is confirmed.

Can We Build a National Character of Crisis Response Based on These Findings?

These data (see Table 25.8) suggest the findings comparing the U.S. and the UK responses to financial crises to be characteristic of American versus British responses to crises in general. Once the data were controlled for industry, channel, and crisis type—all of which were significant—these data demonstrate American

TABLE 25.7 Comparisons (*t*-Test) for Social Media Strategies Used by U.S. and UK Sports Teams

Variable	US		UK		
	M	*SD*	*M*	*SD*	*t*
Self-enhancement	1.64	0.48	1.03	0.18	15.24★★★
Routine communication	1.31	0.47	1.05	0.22	6.38★★★
Framing the crisis	1.00	0.00	1.89	0.32	−22.27★★★
Accommodative	1.00	0.00	1.32	0.47	−5.37★★★
Excellence or renewal	1.21	0.41	1.08	0.27	2.98★★
Interorganizational relationships	1.13	0.41	1.33	0.48	−3.22★★
Image oriented	1.32	0.47	1.00	0.00	7.06★★★
Defensive information management	1.02	0.15	1.00	0.00	1.75
Corporate social responsibility	1.00	0.00	1.09	0.28	−2.07★
Explanative	1.00	0.00	1.75	0.44	−9.00★★
Situating the organization	1.02	0.14	1.26	0.44	−3.46★★★

Note. U.S.: *n* = 213, UK: *n* = 63. Equal variances not assumed.
★ *p* < .05,
★★ *p* < .01,
★★★ *p* < .001

TABLE 25.8 Significant Between-Subjects Tests for the Influence of Nation on Crisis Response

Dependent Variable	Independent Variable	Est. Marginal Means	df	F	p	Partial η^2
Self-enhancement	U.S.	1.55	1, 507	97.11	.00[1,2]	.16
	UK	1.08				
Routine communication	U.S.	1.33	1, 507	12.62	.00[3]	.02
	UK	1.16				
Excellence or renewal	U.S.	1.25	1, 507	15.48	.00[1,3]	.03
	UK	1.09				
Image oriented	U.S.	1.36	1, 288	66.25	.00[1,3]	.19
	UK	0.95				
Framing the crisis	U.S.	1.24	1, 507	37.60	.00[3]	.07
	UK	1.53				
Explanative	U.S.	1.18	1, 341	4.85	.03[1,3]	.01
	UK	1.29				
Situate the organization	U.S.	1.01	1, 343	26.15	.00	.07
	UK	1.17				
Accommodative	U.S.	1.07	1, 507	36.87	.00[1,2,3]	.07
	UK	1.28				
Interorganizational relationships	U.S.	1.08	1, 507	23.69	.00[1,2,3]	.05
	UK	1.24	1, 507			

[1] Industry significant.
[2] Channel significant.
[3] Crisis type significant.

crisis response focuses much more strongly on self-enhancement, routine messaging, excellence and renewal, and image orientation, whereas, British crisis response focuses much more strongly on framing the crisis, explaining the situation, situating the organization within a larger context, being accommodative, and invoking interorganizational relationships.

Discussion and Conclusions

Based on these data, there are two instrumental findings for researchers and practitioners. First, in the case of American and British sports organizations, we found significant differences in the nature of response. The WNBA focused on an image-oriented approach to crisis recovery whereas Portsmouth FC focused on an engagement-oriented approach to crisis recovery. Second, comparing these findings to organizations in different industries and facing different types of crises, these findings were indicative of "typical" American and British responses to organizational crises. These findings are significant because by comparing the responses of organizations in two countries that are very similar on Hofstede's (2001) dimensions of culture, but focusing on the communicative forms where culture is communicated—their language and narratives (Trice & Beyer, 1993)—we have identified important cultural norms in crisis response. Additionally, the findings identifying that the cultural norms in crisis response within sports are consistent with crisis response across industries, channels, and types of crises provide direct support for previous researchers' arguments (e.g., Rowe & Gilmour, 2009) that sports represent popular culture. These data support previous research suggesting that organizations must reach out using different media (Freberg, 2012); in particular, ensuring engagement in social media using a synchronized or coordinated response is likely to be not only a useful crisis-response approach (Diers & Donohue, 2013) but also a culturally grounded one as well.

British Excellence in Crisis Response

For British crisis response, it reveals cultural norms of tackling crises directly—working to help stakeholders understand the crisis, explaining the situation, placing the organization's actions within the context of the situation and other actors, and trying to accommodate criticisms to show that the organization is meaningfully working to address the problem. This is a well-grounded and strongly recommended approach to managing crises for three reasons. First, focusing on restoring the organization's legitimacy is a core component to crisis recovery (Allen & Caillouet, 1994; Boyd, 2000; Elsbach, Sutton, & Principe, 1998). Second, the messaging is stakeholder centered, demonstrating a commitment to engagement and renewal (Alpaslan & Mitroff, 2009; Seeger & Ulmer, 2002; Sung-Un, Minjeong, & Johnson, 2010). Third, the content of the messaging reflects a "genuine" effort toward image repair (Benoit, 1997; Elsbach, 1994; Taylor, Ungureanu, & Caldiero, 2006) and acceptance of responsibility as necessary (Carroll, 2009; Pace, Fediuk, & Botero, 2009) but a lack of fear in defending themselves against what they view are inappropriate criticisms (Oles, 2010). These findings communicate a British crisis communication culture centered on openness, dialogue, and engagement.

America's Consumer Culture Personified in Crisis Response

The findings are not so complimentary in what they reveal about American public culture. They reveal message strategies focused on brand identity, idealizing the brand identity, and blanket self-promotion against the reality that the organization was financially struggling. Although the WNBA did communicate an interest in dialogue in two of their talking points, the majority of the communication was unidirectional and relatively superficial. It could be summarized as promotionalism

(Knight & Greenberg, 2002) without the essential component of social responsibility that made Nike successful in managing allegations of sweatshop labor abuses. Another way to think of the American crisis-response approach is conspicuous consumption. Conspicuous consumption represents purchasing consumer products as a way of signaling income or social status (Giacomo & Olivier, 1997). McCracken (1986) explains consumption has important cultural implications—advertising, fashion, and consumption rituals transmit cultural values. Those cultural values become a part of consumption and can over time influence personal values as is evidenced by the strength of consumerism in North America. This process has not simply emerged overnight; we see it in the inadvertent socialization of American children where parents, educators, and business interests acculturate children into different consumer identities (Milner, 2006). As such, from an early age, Americans define themselves and their peers based on consumption. The challenge for American crisis communication is that conspicuous consumption may adequately reflect some underlying American values, but based on the last couple of decades of research, it represents poor crisis response, yet it seems to be a consistently employed approach to managing crises for American companies.

Certainly, this research raises several questions. For example, how do competing cultural values (e.g., consumerism and social responsibility) compare in terms of crisis-response effectiveness? Although cultures may hold some popular cultural values, during crisis situations these may not be the most effective memes to communicate. Therefore, future research needs to directly examine stakeholder reactions to different models of crisis response. For example, it may well be that the British approach to crisis response is also culturally more appropriate for an American audience compared to the image focused and fairly superficial approach evidenced in this research.

Though there are questions that must still be answered, this research remains an important next step in understanding crisis communication, viable contexts of study, and the role of culture in crisis response. Future research should develop cultural typologies for crisis response among Western nations and identify if these methods are appropriate for non-Western societies as well. These data indicate that as organizations try to manage crises in an increasingly virtual and shrinking world, they cannot underestimate the power and influence of culture. These data also suggest it is a mistake to only compare vastly different cultures—we must focus our analyses on both very similar and very different cultures in order to better understand the influence of culture on crisis response.

References

Allen, M. W., & Caillouet, R. H. (1994). Legitimation endeavors: Impression management strategies used by an organization in crisis. *Communication Monographs, 61*, 44–64.

Alpaslan, C. S. G., & Mitroff, I. (2009). Corporate governance in the context of crises: Towards a stakeholder theory of crisis management. *Journal of Contingencies & Crisis Management, 17*(1), 38–49.

Anonymous. (2005). The business of soccer. *Business Reference Services*, (3/4). The Library of Congress Science, Technology, and Business Division. Retrieved from http://www.loc.gov/rr/business/BERA/issue3/soccer.html

Anonymous. (2008). Communicating with employees during the current financial crisis. 8. Retrieved from http://www.watsonwyatt.com/news/pdfs/2008-WT-0066.pdf

Arpan, L. M. (2002). When in Rome? The effects of spokesperson ethnicity on audience evaluation of crisis communication. *The Journal of Business Communication, 39*(3), 314–339.

Benoit, W. L. (1997). Image repair discourse and crisis communication. *Public Relations Review, 23*(2), 177–187.

Benoit, W. L. (2004). Image restoration discourse and crisis communication. In D. P. Millar & R. L. Heath (Eds.), *Responding to crisis: A rhetorical approach to crisis communication* (pp. 263–280). Mahwah, NJ: Lawrence Erlbaum Associates.

Benoit, W. L., & Czerwinski, A. (1997). A critical analysis of U.S. Air's image repair discourse. *Business Communication Quarterly, 60*(3), 38–57.

Boyd, J. (2000). Actional legitimation: No crisis necessary. *Journal of Public Relations Research, 12*(4), 341–353.

Boyd, J., & Stahey, M. (2008). Communitas/Corporatas tensions in organizational rhetoric: Finding a balance in sports public relations. *Journal of Public Relations Research, 20*, 251–270. doi: 10.1080/10627260801962707

Brooks, K. P. de, & Waymer, D. (2009). Public relations and strategic issues management challenges in Venezuela: A discourse analysis of Crystallex International Corporation in Las Cristinas. *Public Relations Review, 35*, 31–39.

Carroll, C. (2009). Defying a reputational crisis—Cadbury's salmonella scare: Why are customers willing to forgive and forget? *Corporate Reputation Review, 12*(1), 64–82.

Chen, N. (2009). Institutionalizing public relations: A case study of Chinese government crisis communication on the 2008 Sichuan earthquake. *Public Relations Review, 35*, 187–198.

Coombs, W. T. (2006). The protective powers of crisis response strategies: Managing reputational assets during a crisis. *Journal of Promotion Management, 12*(3/4), 241–260. doi: 10.1300/J057v12n03•13

Coombs, W. T. (2007). Attribution theory as a guide for post-crisis communication research. *Public Relations Review, 33*(2), 135–139.

Coombs, W. T., & Holladay, S. J. (1996). Communication and attributions in a crisis: An experimental study in crisis communication. *Journal of Public Relations Research, 8*(4), 279–295.

Coombs, W. T., & Holladay, S. J. (2004). Reasoned action in crisis communication: An attribution theory-based approach to crisis management. In D. P. Millar & R. L. Heath (Eds.), *Responding to crisis: A rhetorical approach to crisis communication* (pp. 95–115). Mahwah, NJ: Lawrence Erlbaum Associates.

Coombs, W. T., & Holladay, S. J. (2012). The paracrisis: The challenges created by publicly managing crisis prevention. *Public Relations Review, 38*, 408–415. doi:10.1016/j.pubrev.2012.04.004

Crolley, L. (2008). Using the Internet to strengthen its identity: The case of Spanish football. *Sport in Society: Cultures, Commerce, Media, Politics, 11*(6), 722–738. doi:10.1080/17430430802284003

Croucher, S. M., Oommen, D., Hicks, M. V., Holody, K. J., Anarbaeva, S., Yoon, K., . . . Aljajli, A. I. (2010). The effects of self-construal and religiousness on argumentativeness: A cross-cultural analysis. *Communication Studies, 61*(2), 135–155. doi: 10.1080/10510971003603994

Diers, A. R. (2009). *Strategic crisis response: The strategic model of organizational crisis communication*. Germany: VDM Verlag.

Diers, A. R. (2012). Reconceptualizing mass communication as engagement: The influence of social media. *Mass Communication and Journalism, 2*(1). Retrieved from https://www. omicsgroup.org/journals/reconceptualizing-mass-communication-as-engagement-the-influence-of-social-media-2165-7912.1000e104.pdf. doi: 10.4172/2165-7912.1000e10

Diers, A. R., & Donohue, J. (2013). Synchronizing crisis responses after a transgression: An analysis of BP's enacted crisis response to the Deepwater Horizon crisis in 2010. *Journal of Communication Management, 17*(3), 252–269.

Diers, A. R., & Tomaino, K. (2010). Comparing strawberries and quandongs: A cross-national analysis of crisis response strategies. *Observatorio, 4*(2), 21–57.

Elsbach, K. D. (1994). Managing organizational legitimacy in the California cattle industry: The construction and effectiveness of verbal accounts. *Administrative Science Quarterly, 39*, 57–88.

Elsbach, K. D., Sutton, R. I., & Principe, K. E. (1998). Averting expected challenges through anticipatory impression management: A study of hospital billing. *Organization Science, 9*(1), 68–86.

Espinoza, J. (2010). Global sports revenue set to rise. *The Wall Street Journal*, NA. Retrieved from http://online.wsj.com/article/SB10001424052748704717004575268741492537 062.html

Freberg, K. (2012). Intention to comply with crisis messages communicated via social media. *Public Relations Review, 38*, 416–421. doi: 10.1016/j.pubrev.2012.01.008

Giacomo, C., & Olivier, J. (1997). Conspicuous consumption, snobbism, and conformism. *Journal of Public Economics, 66*(1), 55–71. doi: 10.1016/S0047-2727(97)00016-9

Glynn, M. A. (2000). When cymbals become symbols: Conflict over organizational identity within a symphony orchestra. *Organization Science, 11*(3), 285–298.

Greer, C. F., & Moreland, K. D. (2003). United Airlines' and American Airlines' online crisis communication following the September 11 terrorist attacks. *Public Relations Review, 29*, 427–441.

Hartmann, D. (2012). Beyond the sporting boundary: The racial significance of sport through midnight basketball. *Ethnic and Racial Studies, 35*(6), 1007–1022. doi: 10.1080/ 01419870.2012.661869

Haruta, A., & Hallahan, K. (2003). Cultural issues in airline crisis communications: A Japan-US comparative study. *Asia Journal of Communication, 13*(2), 122–150.

Hayden, C. (2011). Beyond the "Obama Effect": Refining the instruments of engagement through U.S. public diplomacy. *American Behavioral Scientist, 55*(6), 784–802. doi: 10.1177/0002764211400571

Helland, K. (2007). Changing sports, changing media. *Nordicom Review, 28*(Jubilee Issue), 105–119.

Henderson, J. C. (2003). Communicating in a crisis: Flight SQ 006. *Tourism Management, 24*, 279–287.

Hofstede, G. (2001). *Culture's consequences: Comparing values, behaviors, institutions and organizations across nations*. Thousand Oaks, CA: Sage.

Hopwood, M. K. (2005). Applying the public relations function to the business of sport. *International Journal of Sports Marketing & Sponsorship, 6*(April), 174–188.

Hyun, K. D. (2012). Americanization of web-based political communication? A comparative analysis of political blogospheres in the United States, the United Kingdom, and Germany. *Journalism and Mass Communication Quarterly, 89*(3), 397–413. doi: 10.1177/1077699012447919

Jameson, D. A. (2009). Economic crises and financial disasters: The role of business communication. *Journal of Business Communication, 46*(4), 499–509.

Kauffman, J. (2001). A successful failure: NASA's crisis communications regarding Apollo 13. *Public Relations, 27*(4), 437–449.

Knight, G., & Greenberg, J. (2002). Promotionalism and subpolitics: Nike and its labor critics. *Management Communication Quarterly, 15*(4), 541–570.

Krishnamurthy, S., & Kucuk, S. U. (2009). Anti-branding on the Internet. *Journal of Business Research, 62*, 1119–1126.

Lawniczak, R. (2009). Re-examining the economic roots of public relations. *Public Relations Review, 35*(4), 346–352. doi: 10.1016/j.bbr.2011.03.031

Luck, E., & Buchanan, E. (2008). Sporting organisations: Do they need to communicate with members? *Journal of Community, Citizen's, and Third Sector Media and Communication, 4*(August), 45–60.

McCracken, G. (1986). Culture and consumption: A theoretical account of the structure and movement of the cultural meaning of consumer goods. *Journal of Consumer Research, 13*(1), 71–84.

Marra, F. J. (1998). Crisis communication plans: Poor predictors of excellent crisis public relations. *Public Relations Review, 24*(4), 461–475.

Metzgar, E., & Maruggi, A. (2009). Social media and the 2008 U.S. Presidential election. *Journal of New Communications Research, 4*(1), 141–165.

Millar, D. P. (2004). Exposing the errors: An examination of the nature of organizational crises. In D. P. Millar & R. L. Heath (Eds.), *Responding to crisis: A rhetorical approach to crisis communication* (pp. 19–35). Mahwah, NJ: Lawrence Erlbaum Associates.

Milner, M. J. (2006). *Freaks, geeks, and cool kids: American teenagers, schools, and consumption.* New York: Routledge.

Mohamed, A. A., Gardner, W. L., & Paolillo, J. G. P. (1999). A taxonomy of organizational impression management tactics. *Advances in Competitiveness Research, 7*(1), 108–128.

Molleda, J. C., Connolly-Ahern, C., & Quinn, C. (2005). Cross-national conflict shifting: Expanding a theory of global public relations management through quantitative content analysis. *Journalism Studies, 6*(1), 87–102.

Moore, S. (2004). Disaster's future: The prospects for corporate crisis management and communication. *Business Horizons, 47*(1), 29–36.

Murphy, K., & White, A. (2007). Watching the directive: Sports rights and public culture in the United Kingdom and the Republic of Ireland. *International Journal of Media and Cultural Politics, 3*(3), 253–269. doi: 10.1386/macp.3.3.253/1

O'Callaghan, L. (2011). The red thread of history: The media, Munster rugby and the creation of a sporting tradition. *Media History, 17*(2), 75–88. doi: 10.1080/13688804.2011.554729

Oles, D. L. (2010). Deny, delay, apologize: The Oprah Winfrey image-defense playbook. *Northwest Journal of Communication, 39*(1), 37–63.

Pace, K., Fediuk, T. A., & Botero, I. C. (2009). The acceptance of responsibility and expressions of regret in organizational apologies after a transgression. *Corporate Communications: An International Journal, 15*(4), 410–427. doi: 10.1108/13563281011085510

Quirke, B. (2009). Steering leaders out of a crisis using effective communication. *Strategic Communication Management, 14*(1), 24–27. doi: 1930082341

Rollason, W. (2011). We are playing football: Seeing the game on Panapompom, PNG. *Journal of the Royal Anthropological Institute, 17*, 481–503.

Rossol, N. (2010). Performing the nation: Sports, spectacles, and aesthetics in Germany, 1926–1936. *Central European History, 43*, 616–638. doi: 10.1017/S0008938910000737

Rovisco, M. (2010). One Europe or several Europes? The cultural logic of narratives of Europe views from France and Britain. *Social Science Information*, *49*(2), 241–266. doi: 10.1177/0539018409359844

Rowe, D., & Gilmour, C. (2009). Global sport: Where Wembley way meets Bollywood boulevard. *Continuum: Journal of Media and Cultural Studies*, *23*(2), 171–182. doi: 10.1080/10304310802710512

Seeger, M., & Ulmer, R. R. (2002). A post-crisis discourse of renewal: The cases of Malden Mills and Cole Hardwoods. *Journal of Applied Communication Research*, *30*(2), 126–142.

Smith, B. G. (2010). Socially distributing public relations: Twitter, Haiti, and interactivity in social media. *Public Relations Review*, *36*(4), 329–335.

Sung-Un, Y., Minjeong, K., & Johnson, P. (2010). Effects of narratives, openness to dialogic communication, and credibility on engagement in crisis communication through organizational blogs. *Communication Research*, *37*(4), 473–497. doi: 10.1177/0093650210362682

Taylor, M., Ungureanu, L., & Caldiero, C. (2006, June). *Telling the story in your words: The value of news releases in image repair*. Paper presented at the International Communication Association, Dresden, Germany.

Trice, H. M., & Beyer, J. M. (1993). *The cultures of work organizations*. Upper Saddle River, NJ: Prentice Hall.

Waters, R. D., Tindall, N. T. J., & Morton, T. S. (2010). Media catching and the journalist-public relations practitioner relationship: How social media are changing the practice of media relations. *Journal of Public Relations Research*, *22*(3), 241–264. doi: 10.1080/10627261003799202

Weber, M., Erickson, S. L., & Stone, M. (2011). Corporate reputation management: Citibank's use of image restoration strategies during the U.S. banking crisis. *Journal of Organizational Culture, Communication and Conflict*, *15*(2), 35–55. doi: 2439571401

Wilson, J. (2011). Playing with politics: Political fans and Twitter taking in post-broadcast democracy. *Convergence: The Journal of Research into New Media Technologies*, *17*(4), 445–461. doi: 10.1177/1354856511414348

Winchell, K. (2010, February). Writing the conversation: How social media is redefining PR's content creation. *Public Relations Tactics*. Public Relations Society of America. Retrieved from http://www.prsa.org/intelligence/tactics/articles/view/8509/1007/writing_the_conversation_how_social_media_is_redef

26

THE ROLE OF INFLUENCERS

An Analysis of Social Media Discussion Across Platforms Through a Sustained Crisis

Tina McCorkindale and Marcia W. DiStaso

Introduction

For the past couple of years, controversy surrounding the National Football League (NFL) team name of the Washington Redskins has heated up as high-profile influencers have weighed in about whether the name should be changed. In 2014, the U.S. Patent and Trademark Office canceled the trademark of the name claiming it was "disparaging of Native Americans" (Rovell, 2014, para. 1). This sustained crisis has two polarized sides as evidenced by a 2014 WTOP poll that found 61% of respondents in the Washington area supported keeping the Redskins name whereas others wanted it changed. A strong voice in the contro-versy is team owner Dan Snyder, who has been an outspoken proponent of the name, even creating a Native-American foundation, although Native-American groups and tribes, including the Oneida Nation, have chastised the name publicly through appearances and advertisements.

Crisis research typically has focused on crises that have a clearly defined begin-ning, middle, and end that often go through the five stages of crisis: detection, prevention and preparation, containment, recovery, and learning (Fearn-Banks, 2011). Although these five stages do apply in many cases where a sudden crisis appears, such as a natural disaster, in a sustained crisis, such as with the Washington Redskins name controversy, these same rules may not apply. This is especially likely in a social media environment where influencers are likely to elevate engagement around a crisis.

Therefore, the purpose of this chapter is to explore a sustained crisis to identify if it follows the traditional crisis stages and to explore the trends of engagement through the lens of agenda setting. Special attention is paid to the trends in engagement across multiple social media platforms and news media, highlighting influencers and "triggering" events.

Literature Review

Washington Redskins Controversy

The Washington Redskins were founded in 1932, and their name changed from the "Braves" to the "Redskins" in 1933 (Washington Redskins History, n.d.). When the team relocated from Boston to Washington, DC, the Washington Redskins franchise began. Currently, their games are played at FedExField sponsored by the global courier services company FedEx.

Since 1999, the majority ownership of the team belongs to Dan Snyder. With 5 league championships and Super Bowl Championships (1937, 1942, 1982, 1987, 1991) under their belt, they have also had 5 conference championships, 13 division championships, and 23 playoff appearances (with the most recent in 2012; Washington Redskins History, n.d.).

The team logo is a picture of a Native American inside a yellow circle with two feathers hanging on the side (see Redskins.com, n.d., to view the logo; logo not shown here for copyright reasons).

Some consider the name and logo of the Washington Redskins to be racist (Blackhorse, 2013), even though they have been constant for the past 81 years. Concern over the name is not new, however. In 1992, a group of Native Americans filed a petition to have the team's trademark revoked. Ultimately, in 1999 the Washington Redskins won on appeal in federal court (Nuckols, 2014).

Unlike in 1999, there is now a groundswell of support against the name. In 1992, support for the Washington Redskins name was 89% and that dropped to 79% in April 2013 (Nuckols, 2014). The measure of amount of support does vary depending on what survey or poll is discussed, but consistently, those numbers are trending lower than in 1992. Although this can be considered a high level of support, it is important to remember the number of people that want the name to change. Assuming a representative random sample was used, this indicates that 21%–39% of the population wants the name changed, depending on the source of the poll.

Native-American groups and other high-profile individuals have campaigned against the team name. In October 2013, President Obama joined the conversation in an interview with the Associated Press when he said, "If I were the owner of the team and I knew that there was a name of my team—even if it had a storied history—that was offending a sizeable group of people, I'd think about changing it" (Nakamura, 2013). Then, in an attempt to force a name change, in May 2014, 50 Democratic members of the U.S. Senate sent letters to NFL Commissioner Roger Goodell urging him and the league to endorse a change of the Washington Redskins' name (Maske, 2014). All of this led to the U.S. Patent and Trademark Office canceling six Washington Redskins trademarks in June 2014. Following this, the Washington Redskins hired public relations firm Burson-Marsteller in June 2014 to help battle the criticism (Clarke, 2014).

One point of note is that in May 2013, Washington Redskins owner Dan Snyder told *USA Today*, "We'll never change the name. It's that simple. NEVER—you can use caps" (Brady, 2013). This quote was shared on Facebook and Twitter from the article nearly 4,000 times. Even more than a year later, it is still used in news stories to demonstrate Snyder's unwavering position.

Influencers

According to the *Dictionary of Public Relations Measurement and Research* (Stacks & Bowen, 2013) *influence* is defined as "an outcome of engagement based on proactive messaging that seeks to sway attitudes or behaviors" (p. 15). More specifically, the Word of Mouth Marketing Association (WOMMA) defines influence as "the ability to cause or contribute to a change in opinion or behavior" (2003, p. 6). From this, a *key influencer* is "a person or group of people who possess greater than average potential to influence due to attributes such as frequency of communication, personal persuasiveness or size of and centrality to a social network, among others" (p. 15).

Influencers are especially important; research has found that influencers reach over twice as many people as the average consumer (Keller, Fay, & Berry, 2007). There are two distinct states of influence to consider: (a) the potential to influence and (b) observed influence (WOMMA, 2013). Both are important, but during a crisis observed influence is what organizations need to measure while keeping an eye out for potential influencers.

Social Media Engagement

According to Paine (2011), "engagement means that someone has taken an additional step beyond just viewing what you tossed out there" (p. 5). This can include basic actions such as "liking" or "sharing" Facebook posts or retweeting on Twitter, along with more involved actions such as commenting on social media sites, tweeting, posting on a discussion board, and writing or commenting on a blog.

Engagement is beneficial to organizations for a variety of reasons. Brodie and Hollebeek (2011) indicate that the benefits are especially important as related to customers in that engagement is positively related to brand relationship outcomes such as satisfaction, trust, and loyalty. It is likely that a relationship exists between a company and customers or fans before they seek a form of online engagement (Algesheimer, Dholakia, & Herrmann, 2005).

Social media sites like Facebook and Twitter are typically considered to be the best tools for engagement and subsequently where most social media engagement takes place with companies (Avery et al., 2010). One of the biggest advantages of engagement on social media is connecting with people of similar opinions. However, this can lead to a spiral of silence effect with people being less likely to speak up when they believe their opinion is not widely shared (Hampton et al., 2014).

Crisis Communication Theory

Whereas some may argue that the Washington Redskins name controversy does not meet the definition of a crisis, we argue that it does. According to Coombs (2011), a *crisis* is defined as "a significant threat to operations that can have negative consequences if not handled properly" (p. 1). Coombs explained a crisis can create three related threats: public safety, financial loss, or reputation loss. With the Washington Redskins, threats can relate to both reputation and financial loss, including declining ticket sales or loss of fans. Due to the crisis, the Washington Redskins have been the subject of boycotts by organizations such as the Oneida Nation, as well as intense media scrutiny (Brady, 2014). Even though the crisis has not resulted in significant loss of sponsorships, this is a possibility.

There are several characteristics of this crisis that make it interesting to study. First, the crisis has been sustained for several years, and in the past year, there has been a jump in conversation and news stories surrounding it. Second, other than the apathetic public, the Washington Redskins debate has two polarized sides. In 2014, a WTOP sports poll found 61% of respondents in the Washington area supported keeping the Washington Redskins name. Others want to see it changed. Third, high-profile celebrities and athletes have weighed in on the discussion. Fourth, owner Dan Snyder is an outspoken proponent of the name whereas Native-American groups and tribes, including the Oneida Nation, have chastised the name publicly through appearances and in advertisements. Fifth, influencers have played a critical role in contributing to the spikes in discussion during this crisis and, in many cases, have escalated the crisis. Therefore, this crisis provides a unique perspective through an analysis into the increases and dips in social media conversation and engagement throughout a crisis.

Method

Sample and Data Collection

Using data analysis techniques, this study analyzed how the Washington Redskins crisis has been presented across social media platforms. Using a platform from a service provider devoted to advanced social media intelligence, conversation was captured related to the Washington Redskins naming strategies on social media.

After constructing a Boolean search, we used the platform to collect content from forums, discussion boards, blogs, Twitter, and Facebook for eight months, from January 1, 2014, to August 31, 2014. To compare volume differences, data were also collected from 2013 but not analyzed in terms of themes, sentiment, tone, and so on. News and mainstream media were collected separately as a point of comparison. This broad collection of data from various platforms allowed for a collection of robust and rich consumer-generated content.

For most of the platforms a census of data was collected, but this was not possible for Twitter due to the extremely high volume of content. The only way to access 100% of Tweets in real time is via the Twitter "Firehose," for which companies have to pay a premium fee. Therefore, this analysis used a standard "spritzer," or 1% of Twitter content.

Analysis

Volume was calculated by totaling the number of content across all the platforms for each day over the eight months. For comparison purposes, the total number of content was also collected for eight months prior, but these data were only reviewed to identify spikes in engagement and it was not included in the chapter analysis.

To code for sentiment, Lexalytics sentiment was used, which is an automated system of scoring the "emotion" or tone of a post into positive, negative, or neutral. One benefit to machine scoring is the ability to code a large set of messages using an optimized algorithm because manually coding hundreds of thousands of messages is not practical. However, it is possible that sometimes machine scoring may result in posts being coded incorrectly.

Net sentiment was calculated as the percentage of positive engagement minus the percentage negative engagement.

Social media analysis offers many advantages. Consumers use various social media platforms as a tool or a voice for their opinion on a topic. Plus, social media can be "raw" or in the moment, so many times when consumers take to social media, they are sharing their experience as it is happening. Plus, data can be captured instantaneously. Social media are also beneficial for tracking "themes" or obtaining immediate feedback about campaigns or events. Observers can find out why stakeholders may not be responding to a certain product or service or what pain points they may be experiencing. Social media can also report what stakeholders think and feel about a specific topic.

Analysis and Discussion

Eight months of data were analyzed from January 1, 2014, to August 31, 2014, for a total of 556,910 posts across social media platforms that referenced the Washington Redskins crisis.

Engagement Volume Analysis

In addition to the data collected for the first eight months of 2014, volumes for the last eight months of 2013 were collected as a point of comparison. The number of posts about the Washington Redskins name controversy increased by 542%, as May 2013 through December 2013 saw 86,729 posts compared to 556,910 posts from

January 2014 to August 2014. This indicates more people were discussing it on social media. In October 2013, several high-profile influencers spoke out about the crisis. President Obama, NBC commentator Bob Costas, ESPN sportswriter Chris Broussard, and the Oneida Nation publicly said the Washington Redskins team name is offensive to Native Americans. That same month, former football player Joe Theismann said the Washington Redskins name was a tribute to Native Americans. These declarations drew a spike in coverage to 10,000 posts in October 2013.

Sentiment

The volume of engagement was calculated on a monthly basis (see Figure 26.1). This trend line was then compared to the trend line of net sentiment. Net sentiment was calculated as the percentage of positive discussion minus the percentage of negative discussion; therefore, the higher the net sentiment score, the better. During the first eight months of 2014, the Washington Redskins crisis only generated negative net sentiment. At the beginning of 2014, the volume of social media discussion about the Washington Redskins crisis started to slowly increase until May 2014, when U.S. senators (all Democrats) signed a petition urging NFL commissioner Roger Goodell to change the name, which increased discussion. Then, in June 2014, the largest spike of discussion volume occurred when the U.S. Patent and Trademark Office canceled the U.S. trademark for the Washington Redskins. After this, net sentiment declined and then slightly rose in subsequent months. As noted in the figure, discussion volume and net sentiment did not follow a clear line. Instead, they are both characterized by spikes and drops.

Crisis Triggering Events

Fearn-Banks (2011) identified that organizations progress through five crisis stages: detection, prevention and preparation, containment, recovery, and learning.

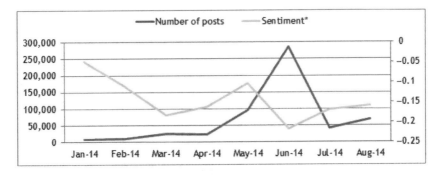

FIGURE 26.1 Volume of Posts and Net Sentiment (% of Positive Engagement – % of Negative Engagement) Related to the Washington Redskins Naming Crisis

Although these five stages do apply in many cases where a sudden crisis appears, such as a natural disaster, it is likely that sustained crises do not follow the same rules. In the case of the Washington Redskins, traditional media outlets are often the ones responsible for thrusting the crisis into the spotlight as other traditional outlets and posters on social media pick up the story. In some cases, engagement on social media has been responsible for causing discussion spikes on social media. Following a spike, social media engagement and news coverage will decline, and then a "triggering" event may generate another surge of engagement and coverage.

Figure 26.2 highlights the daily trend of discussion volume on social media and online news to demonstrates the highs and lows in conversation. Drilling down into a daily versus monthly trend line helps identify the specific triggers of social media discussion. The figure shows how social media discussion typically follows quick spikes, or bursts of social media discussion, followed by quick falls. On an average day during the first eight months of 2014, a total of 2,291 posts appeared on social media and 273 stories were written in online news media outlets regarding the Washington Redskins crisis; the median was 773 posts on social media and 142 in online news. Influencers played a vital role in spreading discussion of the crisis.

As evidenced by the figure, the Washington Redskins crisis has been sustained over a period of time and does not have a clear beginning, middle, and end, compared to typical accidental and victim crises. Instead, some ongoing crises experience peaks and drops in discussion as is the case with the Washington Redskins crisis. Outside of an apathetic public, the analysis allowed for an identification of two clear publics: (a) Native Americans and others who want to change the name because it is racist and (b) Washington Redskins fans and others who often cite "honor" and "tradition" as to why the name should not be changed.

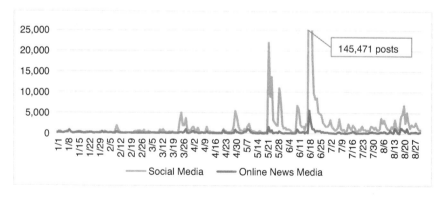

FIGURE 26.2 Daily Trend of Engagement Volume of Social Media and Online Media Relating to the Washington Redskins Crisis

There is some overlap of who fits into what category, as some Native Americans do not want the name changed and some fans want the name changed, but the basic composition of each category remains. Overall, influencers from either side of the crisis have helped to generate discussion spikes, maintain the crisis, and influence social media discussion.

Little research has demonstrated the influence of an individual triggering conversation on social media. In this case, high-profile athletes, coaches, and commentators have influenced consumer discussion surrounding the crisis. Comments that fall outside the norm have also had an impact. For example, former Washington Redskins kicker Mark Moseley said, "Somebody would have to drop a bomb on FedExField to get us to change [the Redskins name]" (Steinberg, 2014, para. 2). This extreme statement earned headline coverage on online media sites.

It is important to note that Washington Redskins owner Dan Snyder has also helped keep the crisis in the media by his public persona and interjecting himself into the spotlight. On March 24, 2014, news broke that Snyder was opening a foundation for Native Americans, which some sources said was an attempt to diffuse criticism about his team name (Beusman, 2014). This resulted in a 3,247% increase in posts, from 95 social media posts on March 23, to 3,206 social media posts on March 24. March 25 saw another 54% increase from the previous day; then the number of social media posts fell the following day by 61%. The Washington Redskins–branded account also tweeted on March 25 about the foundation, which helped boost the increase. Only 15% of posts that tracked sentiment (vs. neutral posts) were positive, indicating support for Snyder's efforts. The gesture was more likely to spur negative posts from those who thought the gesture was hollow and who called for Snyder to change the name. Endorsements from influencers helped spur retweets on Twitter, including one from writer Teju Cole who tweeted to his 167,000 followers, "Please give up this ridiculous name RT @Redskins: It's not enough to celebrate the values and heritage of #Native Americans, we must do more." Cole's tweet was retweeted more than 100 times.

The convergence among broadcast, online media, and social media was demonstrated on Comedy Central's *The Colbert Report*. The crisis started on March 27 when *The Colbert Report* tweeted a controversial tweet that Stephen Colbert was going to start a foundation for Asians in a humorous attempt to mock Snyder's foundation for Native Americans. Because the tweet was outside the context of his television show, people were offended. On March 28, social media discussion surged (3,695 social media posts and 958 online posts), as some thought the tweet was racist, which led to a popular hashtag, #CancelColbert. The Washington Redskins crisis was referenced in 1,814 stories across social media with the #CancelColbert hashtag, 84% of which were published within seven days after the Colbert crisis surfaced. Of the posts that tracked sentiment, 92% were negative, thanks in part to the term "cancel."

Political leaders also played a role in elevating both the social media and online discussion. Another spike in discussion volume occurred on April 30 (5,395 social media posts and 889 online news posts) after U.S. Senate Majority Leader Harry Reid called on the NFL to force the change of the Washington Redskins name that he deemed to be "racist." This request was influenced by the Los Angeles Clippers owner crisis in which the National Basketball Association (NBA) banned Donald Sterling for making racist remarks. Ninety percent of posts with sentiment for that day were negative. Soon after, on May 22 (21,939 social media posts and 1,614 online news posts), half the U.S. Senate, all Democrats, urged NFL Commissioner Roger Goodell to change the Washington Redskins' name. On May 24, one of the few cases where positive discussion outweighed negative was when Washington Redskins president Bruce Allen sent a letter to Sen. Reid that said the team's name was "respectful" to Native Americans. Most social media posts shared during this time were shares about news rather than original commentary from posters. Of the posts that earned sentiment, 74% were positive.

Although influencers kept the story in the news and on social media, the U.S. Patent and Trademark Office played a significant role in elevating the crisis. This was evidenced by the amount of social media conversations and news coverage generated on June 18. The largest spike (145,471 social media posts and 5,586 online news posts) of the analyzed time period occurred as the U.S. Patent and Trademark Office canceled the Washington Redskins trademark. Eighty-eight percent of social media conversation that tracked sentiment was negative. Some of the negative terms used in these stories included "stripped," "canceled," and "racial slur." Soon after the initial spike, discussion waned quickly, as on June 20, two days after the initial story broke, discussion had fallen on social media by 88% and by 80% on news sites. Prominent news outlets, including the *Wall Street Journal*, the *Washington Post, Time*, ESPN *SportsCenter*, and others, shared the story on social media, spreading the news. *The Onion* even tweeted a satirical piece to its six million followers with a story that earned 713 retweets and 631 favorites.

The Washington Redskins crisis died down until influencers once again sparked a discussion about the crisis. On August 20, former Chicago Bears coach Mike Ditka said about the "stupid" Washington Redskins debate that "it's so much horse s★★★, it's incredible" (6,803 social media posts and 721 online news posts). What should be noted about this spike is that online news did not see a comparable shift in discussion, as this story was primarily shared on social media. The counterpart to this happened two days prior, when an online news spike on August 18 regarding CBS analyst Phil Sims refusing to use the Washington Redskins name was noted but not discussed as much on social media.

Engagement Platforms

As demonstrated in Figure 26.3, crises are not platform specific, and with media convergence, the lines delineating content reserved to only one platform have been blurred. Even though Twitter accounts for 80% of social media discussion (news sites excluded) surrounding the Washington Redskins crisis in the first eight

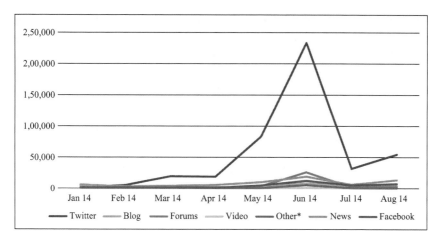

FIGURE 26.3 Monthly Trend Comparing the Volume of Posts Between Various Types of Social Media and Online News

months of 2014, the other 20% was found on other platforms such as blogs, Facebook, forums, video sites, and so forth. Although it may still be the case that the media sets the agenda based on agenda-setting theory, nonmedia sources and influencers are also playing a role. The time gap between news media and consumers sharing the content has been shortened with social media. The figure demonstrates there is little lag between media content and consumer reaction. Engagement, though, on the topic is generally spurred by media-driven stories. Across platforms, though, the conversation follows, for the most part, the same trend pattern.

Due to the variety of content being posted across various platforms, researchers must look at the set of platforms rather than focusing on only one social media site through a microscopic lens. For example, in March 2014, Twitter saw a greater lift in volume compared to other platforms. This was due to people tweeting links to stories on the ESPN.com and NFL.com websites that "Redskins announced foundation to aid Native Americans." Also, it is not enough to only look at quantitative statistics on social platforms; researchers must also look at the verbatim, or quoted, material to get a sense of what consumers are saying along with the sentiment of the posts. This will give a stronger and more accurate analysis of consumer reaction.

Conclusion

This chapter explored the impact of a sustained crisis, the Washington Redskins naming controversy, as it played out across social media platforms (forums, discussion boards, blogs, Twitter, and Facebook) in 2014. It demonstrates how this ongoing crisis experienced peaks and drops in social media engagement, indicating the true nature of a sustained crisis, thus challenging the traditionally understood characteristics of a crisis that were identified before social media played such a monumental role in creating, elevating, and maintaining a crisis.

References

Algesheimer, R., Dholakia, U. M., & Herrmann, A. (2005). The social influence of brand community: Evidence from European car clubs. *Journal of Marketing, 69,* 19–34.

Avery, E., Lariscy, R., Amador, E., Ickowitz, T., Primm, C., & Taylor, A. (2010). Diffusion of social media among public relations practitioners in health departments across various community population sizes. *Journal of Public Relations Research, 22*(3), 336–358.

Beusman, C. (2014, May). Redskins owner opens foundation for Native Americans, won't drop slur. *Jezebel.* Retrieved from http://jezebel.com/redskins-owner-opens-foundation-for-native-americans-w-1551398273

Blackhorse, A. (2013, March). Why the R*dsk*ns need to change their name. Retrieved from http://www.huffingtonpost.com/amanda-blackhorse/washington-nfl-name-change_b_2838630.html

Brady, E. (2013, May). Daniel Snyder says Redskins will never change name. *Washington Post.* Retrieved from http://www.usatoday.com/story/sports/nfl/redskins/2013/05/09/washington-redskins-daniel-snyder/2148127

Brady, E. (2014, June). Church group latest to boycott Redskins over name. Retrieved from http://www.usatoday.com/story/sports/nfl/redskins/2014/06/14/church-of-christ-boycott-washington-redskins-name/10524269/

Brodie, R. J., & Hollebeek, L. D. (2011). Advancing and consolidating knowledge about customer engagement. *Journal of Service Research, 14*(3), 283–284.

Clarke, J. (2014, July). Redskins hire PR firm Burson-Marsteller amid fight over name. Retrieved from http://www.reuters.com/article/2014/07/30/us-nfl-redskins-burson-id USKBN0FZ2FV20140730

Coombs, T. (2011). Crisis management and communications. Institute for PR. Retrieved from http://www.instituteforpr.org/crisis-management-and-communications/

Fearn-Banks, K. (2011). *Crisis communication: A casebook approach* (4th ed.). New York: Routledge.

Hampton, K., Rainie, L., Lu, W., Dwyer, M. Shin, I, & Purcell, K. (2014, August). Social media and the "spiral of silence." Retrieved from http://www.pewinternet.org/2014/08/26/social-media-and-the-spiral-of-silence/

Keller, E., Fay, B., & Berry, J. (2007). Leading the conversation: Influencers' impact on word of mouth and the brand conversation. Retrieved from http://www.kellerfay.com/wp-content/uploads/2011/01/KellerFay_WOMMA-Influencers-Paper-11-13-07.pdf

Maske, M. (2014, May). Senate Democrats urge NFL to endorse name change for Redskins. Retrieved from http://www.washingtonpost.com/sports/senate-democrats-urge-nfl-to-endorse-name-change-for-redskins/2014/05/22/f87e1a4c-e1f1-11e3-810f-764fe508b82d_story.html

Nakamura, D. (2013, October). Obama: "I'd think about changing" Washington Redskins team name. *Washington Post.* Retrieved from https://www.washingtonpost.com/politics/obama-id-think-about-changing-washington-redskins-team-name/2013/10/05/e8d5cb4a-2dcd-11e3-b139-029811dbb57f_story.html

Nuckols, B. (2014, May). AP-GfK poll: 4 in 5 Americans say don't change Redskins nickname; 11 percent say change it. Retrieved from http://ap-gfkpoll.com/featured/our-latest-story-2

Paine, K. D. (2011). Lies and consequences in KD Paine's PR Measurement Blog. Retrieved from http://kdpaine.blogs.com/

Redskins.com. (n.d.). The official site of the Washington Redskins. Retrieved from http://www.redskins.com/

Redskins History. (n.d.). Retrieved from http://www.redskins.com/team/history.html

Rovell, D. (2014, June). Patent office: Redskins "disparaging." Retrieved from http://espn.go.com/nfl/story/_/id/11102096/us-patent-office-cancels-washington-redskins-trademark

Stacks, D., & Bowen, S. (2013). Dictionary of public relations measurement and research (3rd ed.). Retrieved from http://www.instituteforpr.org/dictionary-public-relations-measurement-research-third-edition/

Steinberg, D. (2014, August). Mark Moseley: "Somebody would have to drop a bomb on FedEx Field to get us to change" the name. *Washington Post*. Retrieved from https://www.washingtonpost.com/news/dc-sports-bog/wp/2014/08/12/mark-moseley-somebody-would-have-to-drop-a-bomb-on-fedex-field-to-get-us-to-change-the-name

WOMMA. (2013). Influencer guidebook 2013: What makes an influencer? Retrieved from http://www.aaaa.org/wp-content/uploads/legacy-pdfs/WOMMA-%20Influencer%20Guidebook%20-%202013-05.pdf

WTOP. (2014). Study shows range of views about Redskins' name change. Retrieved from http://www.wtop.com/363/3654236/Poll-Range-of-views-on-Redskins-name

Emerging Frameworks and Future Directions

27

DIGITAL DIALOGUE

Crisis Communication in Social Media[1]

Øyvind Ihlen and Abbey Levenshus

Introduction

Most studies conclude that organizations seldom utilize the technological potential of social media to its fullest in their attempts to establish dialogue with stakeholders (Etter, 2013; Lovejoy, Waters, & Saxton, 2012). Organizations typically carry on with one-way communication and do not dedicate enough time or resources to implement their social media strategy. In addition, much of the literature has focused on dialogue in a rather narrow sense, seeing it as functional interactivity and feedback loops (Kelleher, 2009). Dialogic opportunities are said to take the "form of email lines, live chat opportunities, and links to others with similar interests" (Stephens & Malone, 2012, p. 391). Albeit important, we argue that dialogue involves something more and that the notion is often poorly defined in the literature on crisis and social media or it is equated with an exchange or two-way symmetrical communication (Theunissen & Wan Noordin, 2012). Thus, we want to examine a more sophisticated philosophical take on what dialogue is. That is, writings that discuss dialogue as a quality of communicating and relating with others or an ideal to strive for. Typical keywords are mutuality, reciprocity, and difference. Still, this dialogue ideal has been formulated on the interpersonal level. In the chapter we also discuss the challenges that arise when the concept is transferred to the organizational context where a different rationality reigns. The following research questions are formulated:

RQ1: What can dialogue theory contribute in the context of social media and crisis?

RQ2: What challenges arise for the dialogue ideal in an organizational setting?

The next section provides a short overview of how dialogue has been discussed in the literature on social media and crisis. In the following section we turn to the literature on dialogue and the use of dialogue in organizations. A section discussing the problems of the dialogue ideal then follows. The final section draws some conclusions and points to further avenues for research.

Social Media, Crisis, and Dialogue

Scholars have identified challenges and opportunities facing crisis communicators, also related to social media use (e.g., Schultz, Utz, & Göritz, 2011; Veil, Buehner, & Palenchar, 2011). Much of the early research connecting crisis communication and social media focused on social media use after a crisis (e.g., Procopio & Procopio, 2007; Sweetser & Metzgar, 2007; Taylor & Perry, 2005). Whereas social media can help facilitate information and opinion sharing, social media communication can also facilitate the quick spread of rumors, misinformation, and negative opinions and emotions (e.g., Liu, Jin, Austin, & Janoske, 2012; Macias, Hilyard, & Freimuth, 2009). As such, crisis managers may lose control of the official message as traditional media rely more heavily on citizen-generated social media content rather than on official organizational sources during a crisis (Wigley & Fontenot, 2010). Despite the focus on social-mediated crisis response, in an early piece on Internet-based crisis management, Perry, Taylor, and Doerfel (2003) wrote, "Organizations that bring in new media tactics and engage publics in proactive discussions before, during, and after a crisis exemplify an important movement from one-way communication to two-way interaction between the public and an organization" (p. 230). For example, crisis managers should incorporate social media into pre-crisis planning, including ongoing monitoring and engagement with online sites and users (Wigley & Fontenot, 2010). The social-mediated crisis communication (SMCC) model offers guidance for crisis managers built on best practices and knowledge related to social media's role as a channel, source, or origin of information and rumor, engagement, opinion, or emotional expression (Liu et al., 2012). Organizational and community resilience and renewal can also be enhanced by using social media to aid information sharing, reconnection, and resource acquisition following a crisis (Chewning, Lai, & Doerfel, 2012).

Another general research-based tenet is that organizations should establish dialogue with stakeholders well before a crisis occurs and regardless of whether a risk is manifested. Social media tools should be incorporated into risk and crisis management policies and plans but should also be integrated into everyday communication activities (Veil et al., 2011). Initiating dialogue before risks manifest or crises occur can help an organization navigate a crisis (Veil et al., 2011). Should a crisis occur or risk manifest, empowering relevant publics to develop and use emergency responses can help mitigate crisis outcomes (Palenchar, 2009). In this sense, social media have been recognized for their self-efficacy potential. Hence dialogic efforts are crucial for crisis communication, and social media can be of great value by making the "community part of the actual crisis communication response" (Veil et al., 2011, p. 110).

The literature has pointed to the possibility of creating feedback loops (Kent & Taylor, 1998) and to the importance of using a conversational voice to build a positive relationship with stakeholders (Kelleher, 2009). It has also been argued that organizations that utilize "dialogic voice" are better able to understand the preferences and expectations that stakeholders have (McAllister-Spooner, 2009). "Dialogic voice" could probably be equated with what Macnamara (2013) has dubbed an *architecture of listening*, defined as "a framework with appropriate policies, structures, resources and facilities that enable voice to matter by gaining attention, recognition, consideration and response" (Macnamara, 2013, p. 168). An organization's framework and orientation may play into what Romenti, Murtarelli, and Valentini (2014) call "dialogue history." A focus on monitoring and utilizing social media to enhance dialogue with key stakeholders leaves out the need for critical context, such as the organization's dialogue history, that is necessary to actually foster dialogue (Romenti et al., 2014).

Despite acknowledgments of social media's influence and key role postcrisis, existing literature focuses more often on using social media to provide crisis information and manage a crisis in order to benefit the organization's reputation and survival (Waymer & Heath, 2007). This focus may be part of the overall "generic managerial bias" in the crisis communication literature that has marginalized voices and deemphasized views of powerless stakeholders who may be the victims of the crises being managed (Waymer & Heath, 2007, p. 95). Kim and Dutta (2009) have also identified crisis communication research's managerial bias, functionalist orientation, and marginalization of voices.

Although dialogue's potential effects are addressed, dialogue itself—including what it entails—is not well defined in the strategic communication literature and related crisis communication research.

Dialogue and Organizations

Whereas much of the literature on social media, dialogue, or crisis has focused on functionality and related aspects, the literature on dialogue typically equates dialogue with an *attitude* or an *orientation*, rather than a technique (Johannesen, 1971). Varying conceptualizations of dialogue are found in different disciplines, ranging from philosophy to conversation analysis (see Anderson, Baxter, & Cissna, 2003b; Anderson, Cissna, & Arnett, 1994). Most of the philosophical approaches are seen as "holistic and tensional" and "communicative events are described as multidimensional rather than as simply products of rationality, as dynamic rather than static, as emergent rather than defined in advance, as context-dependent, and as processual" (Stewart, Zediker, & Black, 2003, p. 37).

One prominent approach relies on the work of philosopher Martin Buber (1999) and implies that dialogue is a process and a quality of communication.

Dialogic communication is, for instance, characterized by availability and willingness to be held responsible and accountable. Participants "meet" each other and the dialogue can result in change. Humans relate to their surroundings with two distinct attitudes, either as "I–thou," as in face-to-face meetings, or as "I–it," seeing the existent as a passive object. This attitude has also been labeled "duality-in-unity," as both attitudes are present (Clark as cited in, Czubaroff, 2000). Still, the problem Buber points to relates to how Western culture has lost the balance and is primarily focused on the I–it world, treating others as discrete objects. I–thou, however, does not objectify but is focused on relations between two subjects (for an overview, see Biemann, 2002).

Buber is said to be first among the prescriptive dialogue theorists (Stewart et al., 2003), something that perhaps could explain why his work has gotten some traction within public relations. For instance, Nigel de Bussey (2010) has suggested operationalizing stakeholder dialogue as listening, treating other people as goals and not ends, and showing willingness to change. Still, the first extensive treatment of dialogue in public relations literature (i.e., Pearson, 1989) primarily relied on Jürgen Habermas and discourse ethics (Habermas, 1984, 1987). Pearson posited dialogue as an ethical imperative for public relations practitioners and presented some "rules" that could help foster dialogic systems between organizations and their stakeholders. For instance, he argued that participants should agree on the rules for response time, ability to suggest topics or change topics, and when a response could be considered a response.

Lately, the most extensive theory of dialogue in public relations has been suggested by Michael Kent and Maureen Taylor (1998, 2002; Taylor & Kent, 2014). Building on Buber and others, they discuss dialogue as an orientation pointing to five particular traits:

1. Reciprocity: A recognition that organizations and their stakeholders are closely intertwined through their relationship and therefore have to find a way to cooperate. This attitude stretches beyond negotiations and compromises.
2. Propinquity: Organizations must engage in dialogue with stakeholders in the present and over time.
3. Empathy: An organization will attempt to recognize and understand its stakeholders' situation.
4. Risk: Organizations should interact with stakeholders even if this makes the organization vulnerable and the consequences of the dialogue are unknown.
5. Commitment: Organizations need to be committed to genuine dialogue, interpretation, and understanding in their meeting with stakeholders.

Kent and Taylor (2002) suggested that organizations should implement this orientation in their development of interpersonal relationships, mediated relationships, and the procedural dialogue rules developed by Pearson.

Another effort to use Habermas's theory of communicative action (1984, 1987) for the purpose of stakeholder dialogue is found in the work of Esben Rahbek Pedersen (2006). Pedersen points to five dimensions that have to be in place to make dialogue work: all relevant stakeholders have to be included (inclusion); all issues should be possible to discuss (openness); views should not be suppressed (tolerance); stakeholders should be able to influence the structure, process, and outcome of the dialogue (empowerment); and stakeholders should have access to information about the outcome after the dialogue has ended (transparency).

Taken together, there are suggestions in the public relations literature for seeing dialogue as an orientation and for developing procedural rules for such dialogues. Still, it has been argued that the literature is underdeveloped and lacking the sophistication found in disciplines like political science and organizational communication. The argument goes that more attention has to be paid to the philosophical discussions and traditions concerning dialogue (Taylor & Kent, 2014; Theunissen & Wan Noordin, 2012). Such attention, it is argued, might also lead to questioning whether social media really offers the positive potential that it is often made out to provide. The latter decision is really in the hands of the dialogue participants (Theunissen & Wan Noordin, 2012). Critics have cautioned against seeing social media as a dialogic panacea (e.g., Kent, 2010).

Benefits and Challenges of "Dialogue" and Dialogue

The literature often points to the organizational benefits of using a dialogic orientation. Through dialogue, organizations can learn about issues they would not otherwise hear about. Dialogue can help organizations cope with public pressure, social change, and complexity (Burchell & Cook, 2008; Gergen, Gerne, & Barrett, 2004). If the organization does not engage in dialogue, it also runs the risk of only asking questions that have pleasant answers for the organization. Without seeking alternative and perhaps critical views, organizations risk reinforcing existing perspectives that might not benefit the organization (or society) in the long run. Thus, it could be argued, ethical, dialogic principles and practices must be part of everyday organizational activities and reinforced in a bottom-up and top-down capacity in order to cultivate a dialogic culture. And, as already stated, such a dialogic culture has to be in place before a crisis hits. The number one rule for building trust is to listen to public concerns and get involved if demanded (Renn, 2009).

Taylor and Kent (2014) argued that public relations is "dedicated to truth and understanding" and that "dialogue represents a model with much closer correspondence to the lived reality of public relations" (p. 389) rather than a propaganda or monologue model. It is easy to concur with this as an ethical ideal, although public relations is often accused of running counter to such an ideal (e.g., Miller & Dinan, 2008). The next section identifies general problems with dialogue for public relations:

First, there is the very *practical* problem that dialogue theorists maintain that dialogue is a phenomenon that "exists in moments rather than extended states, [and] it cannot be planned precisely or made to happen" (Anderson, Baxter, & Cissna, 2003a, p. 15). This poses a challenge for public relations given the field's preoccupation with modernist planning and prescriptive and linear understandings of strategy (Raupp & Hoffjann, 2012). One suggested possibility here then would be to build on other types of strategic thinking that would give more flexibility and possibilities to adapt to emerging situations. Organizations might engage in scientific planning and prescriptive decision making. When a crisis hits, the organization will, nonetheless, not likely be able to control the situation and the driving factors of the crisis. Hence, organizations would be better off if they learned how to improvise and adapt to the ambiguity and uncertainty created by unpredictable crisis situations (Gilpin & Murphy, 2008). It seems inevitable that dialogue would also occupy a crucial role in precrisis periods and that this would have a potential long-term positive effect.

Second, and related to the aforementioned, dialogue theorists see *risk* as a fundamental trait of dialogue. In a true dialogue, judgments and assumptions are set in play (Golob & Podnar, 2011). As many commentators have remarked, however, dialogue runs counter to an organizational preoccupation with power and control (Gilpin & Murphy, 2008). Given that dialogue has transferred into a "God term" designating "the ultimate motivation" (Burke, 1945/1969, p. 355), organizations are, however, likely to engage in "dialogue," which leads to the next problem.

Third, there is the problem of a misappropriation of the word "dialogue." In other words, the term "dialogue" may be used but not in the fuller sense outlined previously. There are examples of how "dialogue" is used to defuse criticism, to privatize the debate, or co-opt critical stakeholder groups (Deetz & Simpson, 2003). These references then would not be characterized as authentic dialogue by any of the dialogue theorists that see authenticity as a crucial value (Stewart et al., 2003).

Fourth, and related to the last problem, dialogue can be *instrumentalized* as a tool for predefined organizational goals. Organizations might be tempted to cut the time-consuming dialogue efforts short and impose a deadline not mutually agreed upon, thus violating crucial procedural demands of the dialogue ideal (Rowell, 2002). In short, as critics have pointed out, many of the "current planning processes and a focus on achieving specific end results do not support the philosophy of dialogue" (Theunissen & Wan Noordin, 2012, p. 12).

Fifth, the idea that participants should come together on common ground often functions to *privilege understandings that are already dominating* (Dempsey, 2011). A willingness to change is, however, a dialogue hallmark and "predetermined outcomes [should be] set aside momentarily" (Theunissen &

Wan Noordin, 2012, p. 8). Thus, the type of criticism that is often leveled at the symmetry theory can be rehearsed here, too (Roper, 2005). Neither symmetry nor dialogue can be reduced to an organizational attitude of willingness to listen and adapt one's behavior.

If the dialogue ideal is conditioned on a harmony model of society, it is worth recalling that an alternative view built on a conflict perspective does exist. Here, organizations in general are seen as competing and seeking to position themselves with the help of public relations (Ihlen, 2009).

These problems of dialogue are intertwined and linked to the particular instrumental rationality that organizations in general, and corporations in particular, are based on. Dialogue is difficult enough to achieve in interpersonal relations. As already mentioned, dialogue theorists do not really see it as something that can be made to happen and argue that dialogue in general "exists in moments" (Anderson et al., 2003a, p. 15). The challenge grows bigger when talking about organizations that operate within an economic system where stakeholders become means to achieve organizational goals and not ends in themselves.

When organizations are responding to a crisis, they may be especially likely to focus on reputation and control as opposed to true dialogue. As Veil and colleagues (2011) noted, a balance must be struck between social media engagement and the organization's effort to control information. This balance may further narrow an organization's overall embrace of dialogue as a philosophy or orientation. This may be especially true for corporations that have an extremely limited perspective on nature. It is argued that they cannot really "handle concepts of value beyond instrumentality" (Fisher & Lovell, 2003, p. 281). This limitation, as pointed out previously, also means that corporations inevitably run the danger of instrumentalizing dialogue with stakeholders, thus running against the grain of dialogue theory in general.

The previous argument that organizations are bound by a limited rationality hinges on a particular sociological perspective on agent, structure, and agency. Building on Pierre Bourdieu and his theory of practice (Bourdieu, 1977), the three concepts of habitus, field, and capital are suggested as a useful compass to understand this relationship (Ihlen, 2009). In brief, *habitus* is conceptualized as a cognitive structure of durable dispositions that constrain actors. Still, habitus is an open system that produces and reproduces society at the same time, but a system that can also be modified as a consequence of reflection. It is also a concept that has a dialectical relationship with *field*. The latter is defined as a social space where relationships are determined by different positions, which, in turn, are anchored in amounts of different types of capital that are appreciated in a particular field. In the business field, economic capital is typically most valued. As already stated, organizations thus find themselves in struggles over positions and use public relations to get ahead.

The flexibility of this theoretical framework aids understanding of the motivating forces that see organizations being driven by their goal rationality, while at the same time being able to modify this rationality. As an example, dialogue, like corporate social responsibility (CSR), does not *necessarily* have to be conducted from a singular profit motive. The market will "allow" CSR-based companies if the niche is big enough (Vogel, 2005). As such, practitioners have some flexibility in pursuing ethical goals and conducting dialogue within various public relations functions, including crisis communication. There are, however, limitations to such actions rooted in the goal-driven rationality of organizations.

The major implication of the aforementioned is that tension exists between the dialogue ideal and the system in which organizations are situated. In the final section we conclude the discussion and explore its effect for public relations, crisis communication, and dialogue in social media.

Conclusion

In the preceding sections, we reviewed research on social media, crisis and dialogue, the dialogue literature itself, and the literature discussing dialogue in an organizational setting.

Although we pointed to some problems of implementing the dialogue ideal in public relations, there are dialogue scholars that maintain that it *is* feasible for organizations to engage in dialogue. For instance, Theunissen and Wan Noordin (2012) argue that

> an organization may create an environment where dialogic moments can be nurtured but the success of these moments will depend on the extent to which organizations embrace its underlying philosophy and whether they afford appropriate resources to creating such an environment. (p. 11)

The organizational impetus for moving in such a direction would be to avoid limiting the organizational perspective, avoid producing "incomplete and inadequate decision-relevant information," and avoid doing "violence to those 'others' whose positions are often already institutionally and culturally marginalized" (Deetz & Simpson, 2003, p. 157). In other words, there are both pragmatic and ethical reasons to engage in dialogue in the philosophical sense of the term as discussed previously. Organizations seeking to avoid or mitigate crisis are indeed encouraged to implement a dialogue orientation. Social media would be a "natural" part in a communication policy and communication strategy built on dialogic principles and insights from the theory seeing dialogue as an orientation.

Still, we have to acknowledge the trade-offs and reality facing many practitioners. Is "dialogue" a slipping, sliding continuum? Crisis sometimes necessitates one-way, direct messages (Sellnow & Sellnow, 2010). Indeed, dialogue theorists do not suggest that dialogue is "the only valid model for communication, [but] it is a crucial one" (Anderson et al., 2003a, pp. 15–16). Still, precrisis and long-term programs always have the potential to foster more engagement—though it is unrealistic to say all voices will be equally engaged or heard.

As mentioned, in Bourdieu's treatment of the habitus concept, he argued that although this cognitive structure is durable, it can also be modified. We argue that a crucial way to modify the habitus would be to adapt a "warts and all" perspective that acknowledges both the good and the bad of public relations and its use of dialogue (Ihlen & Verhoeven, 2012). As stated by Fawkes, public relations has to come to grips with its shadow side and accept the internal dualities (Fawkes, 2014). This approach, then, would also tie in with theories like Buber's (1999) that emphasize the dual orientation of humans toward their surroundings.

In sum, the use of dialogue, not "dialogue," is constrained by some systemic limitations that are poorly understood in public relations theory in general. Still, dialogic potential exists, partially rooted in the perspective of enlightened self-interest, and partially rooted in the development of a professional ethic looking beyond the limited goal rationality of organizations. If we cannot really demand that organizations have "true and pure" ethical motives in the Kantian sense, we can at least encourage that they do "the right thing." This would involve cultivating a dialogue culture and orientation and employing both digital and nondigital media for this purpose. And it also involves recognizing the limits to dialogue, digital or not, in the organizational setting.

Note

1 The chapter extends on Ihlen, Ø., & Levenshus, A. (2017, in press). Panacea, placebo or prudence: Perspectives and constraints for corporate dialogue. Public Relations Inquiry.

References

Anderson, R., Baxter, L. A., & Cissna, K. N. (2003a). Texts and contexts of dialogue. In R. Anderson, L. A. Baxter, & K. N. Cissna (Eds.), *Dialogue: Theorizing difference in communication studies* (pp. 1–17). Thousand Oaks, CA: Sage.

Anderson, R., Baxter, L. A., & Cissna, K. N. (Eds.). (2003b). *Dialogue: Theorizing difference in communication studies.* Thousand Oaks, CA: Sage.

Anderson, R., Cissna, K. N., & Arnett, R. C. (Eds.). (1994). *The reach of dialogue: Confirmation, voice, and community.* Cresskill, NJ: Hampton Press.

Biemann, A. D. (2002). *The Martin Buber reader: Essential readings.* New York: Palgrave Macmillan.

Bourdieu, P. (1977). *Outline of a theory of practice* (R. Nice, Trans.). Cambridge, UK: Cambridge University Press.

Buber, M. (1999). *I and thou* (W. Kaufmann, Trans.). New York: Simon & Schuster.

Burchell, J., & Cook, J. (2008). Stakeholder dialogue and organisational learning: Changing relationships between companies and NGOs. *Business Ethics: A European Review, 17*(1), 35–46. doi: 10.1111/j.1467-8608.2008.00518.x

Burke, K. (1945/1969). *A grammar of motives*. Berkeley, CA: University of California Press.

Bussey, N. D. (2010). Dialogue as a basis for stakeholder engagement: Defining and measuring the core competencies. In R. L. Heath (Ed.), *The Sage handbook of public relations* (pp. 127–144). Thousand Oaks, CA: Sage.

Chewning, L. V., Lai, C.-H., & Doerfel, M. L. (2012). Communication technologies to rebuild communication structures. *Management Communication Quarterly, 27*(2), 237–263. doi: 10.1177/0893318912465815

Czubaroff, J. (2000). Dialogical rhetoric: An application of Martin Buber's philosophy of dialogue. *Quarterly Journal of Speech, 86*(2), 168–189.

Deetz, S., & Simpson, J. (2003). Critical organizational dialogue. In R. Anderson, L. A. Baxter, & K. N. Cissna (Eds.), *Dialogue: Theorizing difference in communication studies* (pp. 141–158). Thousand Oaks, CA: Sage.

Dempsey, S. E. (2011). NGOs as communicative actors within corporate social responsibility efforts. In Ø. Ihlen, J. Bartlett, & S. May (Eds.), *Handbook of communication and corporate social responsibility* (pp. 445–466). Oxford, UK: Wiley Blackwell.

Etter, M. (2013). Reasons for low levels of interactivity. *Public Relations Review, 39*(5), 606–608. doi: 10.1016/j.pubrev.2013.06.003

Fawkes, J. (2014). *Public relations ethics and professionalism: The shadow of excellence*. London: Routledge.

Fisher, C., & Lovell, A. (2003). *Business ethics and values*. Harlow, UK: Financial Times/Prentice Hall.

Gergen, K. J., Gerne, M. M., & Barrett, F. J. (2004). Dialogue: Life and death of the organization. In D. Grant, C. Hardy, C. Oswick, & L. L. Putnam (Eds.), *The Sage handbook of organizational discourse* (pp. 39–59). London: Sage.

Gilpin, D. R., & Murphy, P. J. (2008). *Crisis management in a complex world*. New York: Oxford University Press.

Golob, U., & Podnar, K. (2011). Corporate social responsibility communication and dialogue. In Ø. Ihlen, J. Bartlett, & S. May (Eds.), *Handbook of communication and corporate social responsibility* (pp. 231–251). Oxford, UK: Wiley Blackwell.

Habermas, J. (1984). *The theory of communicative action* (Vol. 1). Cambridge, UK: Polity Press.

Habermas, J. (1987). *The theory of communicative action* (Vol. 2). Cambridge, UK: Polity Press.

Ihlen, Ø. (2009). On Pierre Bourdieu: Public relations in field struggles. In Ø. Ihlen, B. van Ruler, & M. Fredriksson (Eds.), *Public relations and social theory: Key figures and concepts* (pp. 71–91). New York: Routledge.

Ihlen, Ø., & Verhoeven, P. (2012). A public relations identity for the 2010s. *Public Relations Inquiry, 1*(2), 159–176.

Johannesen, R. L. (1971). The emerging concept of communication as dialogue. *Quarterly Journal of Speech, 57*(4), 373–382.

Kelleher, T. (2009). Conversational voice, communicated commitment, and public relations outcomes in interactive online communication. *Journal of Communication, 59*(1), 172–188. doi: 10.1111/j.1460-2466.2008.01410.x

Kent, M. L. (2010). Directions in social media for professionals and scholars. In R. L. Heath (Ed.), *The Sage handbook of public relations* (pp. 643–656). Thousand Oaks, CA: Sage.

Kent, M. L., & Taylor, M. (1998). Building dialogic relationships through the World Wide Web. *Public Relations Review, 24*(3), 321–334. doi: 10.1016/s0363-8111(99)80143-x

Kent, M. L., & Taylor, M. (2002). Toward a dialogic theory of public relations. *Public Relations Review, 28*, 21–37.

Kim, I., & Dutta, M. J. (2009). Studying crisis communication from the subaltern studies framework: Grassroots activism in the wake of Hurricane Katrina. *Journal of Public Relations Research, 21*(2), 142–164.

Liu, B. F., Jin, Y., Austin, L. L., & Janoske, M. (2012). The social-mediated crisis communication model: Guidelines for effective crisis management in a changing media landscape. In S. C. Duhe (Ed.), *New media and public relations* (2nd ed., pp. 257–266). New York: Peter Lang.

Lovejoy, K., Waters, R. D., & Saxton, G. D. (2012). Engaging stakeholders through Twitter: How nonprofit organizations are getting more out of 140 characters or less. *Public Relations Review, 38*(2), 313–318. doi: 10.1016/j.pubrev.2012.01.005

Macias, W., Hilyard, K., & Freimuth, V. (2009). Blog functions as risk and crisis communication during Hurricane Katrina. *Journal of Computer-Mediated Communication, 15*(1), 1–31.

McAllister-Spooner, S. M. (2009). Fulfilling the dialogic promise: A ten-year reflective survey on dialogic Internet principles. *Public Relations Review, 35*(3), 320–322.

Macnamara, J. (2013). Beyond voice: Audience-making and the work and architecture of listening as new media literacies. *Continuum, 27*(1), 160–175. doi: 10.1080/10304312.2013.736950

Miller, D., & Dinan, W. (2008). *A century of spin: How public relations became the cutting edge of corporate power.* London: Pluto Press.

Palenchar, M. J. (2009). Historical trends of risk and crisis communication. In R. L. Heath & D. O'Hair (Eds.), *Handbook of risk and crisis communication* (pp. 31–52). New York: Routledge.

Pearson, R. (1989). Business ethics as communication ethics: Public relations practice and the idea of dialogue. In C. H. Botan & V. Hazelton Jr. (Eds.), *Public relations theory* (pp. 111–131). Hillsdale, NJ: Lawrence Erlbaum.

Pedersen, E. R. (2006). Making corporate social responsibility (CSR) operable: How companies translate stakeholder dialogue into practice. *Business and Society Review, 111*(2), 137–163.

Perry, D. C., Taylor, M., & Doerfel, M. L. (2003). Internet-based communication in crisis management. Management *Communication Quarterly, 17*(2), 206–232.

Procopio, C. H., & Procopio, S. T. (2007). Do you know what it means to miss New Orleans? Internet communication, geographic community, and social capital in crisis. *Journal of Applied Communication Research, 35*(5), 67–87.

Raupp, J., & Hoffjann, O. (2012). Understanding strategy in communication management. *Journal of Communication Management, 16*(2), 146–161. doi: 10.1108/13632541211217579

Renn, O. (2009). Risk communication: Insights and requirements for designing successful communication programs on health and environmental hazards. In R. L. Heath & D. O'Hair (Eds.), *Handbook of risk and crisis communication* (pp. 80–98). London: Routledge.

Romenti, S., Murtarelli, G., & Valentini, C. (2014). Organisations' conversations in social media: Applying dialogue strategies in times of crises. *Corporate Communications: An International Journal, 19*(1), 10–33.

Roper, J. (2005). Symmetrical communication: Excellent public relations or a strategy for hegemony? *Journal of Public Relations Research, 17*(1), 69–86.

Rowell, A. (2002). Dialogue: Divide and rule. In E. Lubbers (Ed.), *Battling big business: Countering greenwash, infiltration and other forms of corporate bullying* (pp. 33–43). Totnes, UK: Green Books.

Schultz, F., Utz, S., & Göritz, A. (2011). Is the medium the message? Perceptions of and reactions to crisis communication via Twitter, blogs and traditional media. *Public Relations Review, 37*(1), 20–27. doi: 10.1016/j.pubrev.2010.12.001

Sellnow, T. L., & Sellnow, D. D. (2010). The instructional dynamic of risk and crisis communication: Distinguishing instructional messages from dialogue. *The Review of Communication, 10*(2), 111–125.

Stephens, K. K., & Malone, P. (2012). New media for crisis communication: Opportunities for technical translation, dialogue, and stakeholder responses. In W. T. Coombs & S. J. Holladay (Eds.), *The handbook of crisis communication* (pp. 381–395). Malden, MA: Wiley-Blackwell.

Stewart, J., Zediker, K. E., & Black, L. (2003). Relationships among philosophies of dialogue. In R. Anderson, L. A. Baxter, & K. N. Cissna (Eds.), *Dialogue: Theorizing difference in communication studies* (pp. 21–38). Thousand Oaks, CA: Sage.

Sweetser, K. D., & Metzgar, E. (2007). Communicating during crisis: Use of blogs as a relationship management tool. *Public Relations Review, 33*, 340–342.

Taylor, M., & Doerfel, M. (2003). Building interorganizational relationships that build nations. *Human Communication Research, 29*(2), 153–181.

Taylor, M., & Kent, M. L. (2014). Dialogic engagement: Clarifying foundational concepts. *Journal of Public Relations Research, 26*(5), 384–398. doi: 10.1080/1062726X.2014.956106

Taylor, M., & Perry, D. (2005). Diffusion of traditional and new media tactics in crisis communication. *Public Relations Review, 31*(2), 209–217.

Theunissen, P., & Wan Noordin, W. N. (2012). Revisiting the concept "dialogue" in public relations. *Public Relations Review, 38*(1), 5–13. doi: 10.1016/j.pubrev.2011.09.006

Veil, S. R., Buehner, T., & Palenchar, M. J. (2011). A work-in-process literature review: Incorporating social media in risk and crisis communication. *Journal of Contingencies and Crisis Management, 19*(2), 110–122. doi: 10.1111/j.1468-5973.2011.00639.x

Vogel, D. (2005). *The market for virtue: The potential and limits of corporate social responsibility.* Washington, DC: Brookings Institution.

Waymer, D., & Heath, R. L. (2007). Emergent agents: The forgotten publics in crisis communication and issues management research. *Journal of Applied Communication Research, 35*, 88–108.

Wigley, S., & Fontenot, M. (2010). Crisis managers losing control of the message: A pilot study of the Virginia Tech shooting. *Public Relations Review, 36*(2), 187–189.

28

SOCIAL MEDIA ENGAGEMENT FOR CRISIS COMMUNICATION

A Preliminary Measurement Model

Hua Jiang and Yi Luo

Introduction

The eruption of a crisis makes salient the digital influence by the online publics in framing the perceptions of crisis responsibility and behavioral reactions (Liu, 2010; Meer, 2014). The interactive nature of social media platforms provides a socially mediated space for organizations to engage with their online publics (e.g., Yang, Kang, & Johnson, 2010). The question of how organizations can optimize their *online engagement* with publics, especially during crisis, has not been intensively probed (Neiger, Thackeray, Burton, Giraud-Carrier, & Fagen, 2013; Ott & Theunissen, 2015).

Particularly, this study conceptualizes an engagement model to systematically measure how effectively an organization can engage with its online publics during crisis communication. Based on existing literature on public relations, crisis communication, consumer studies, and business, we have proposed a hierarchical measurement model of engagement in crisis. Specifically, crisis engagement can be measured at four hierarchical dimensions: (a) crisis involvement (e.g., providing timely and accurate information, cultivating offline involvement and awareness), (b) crisis interaction (e.g., requesting real-time information, sharing credible sources, creating credible media content), (c) crisis intimacy (e.g., empathy, attending to the emotional needs of the affected publics), and (d) crisis influence (e.g., constant multimedia-enhanced conversations, content forwarding, a multidirectional communication network).

This chapter starts with a general discussion on crisis communication and then moves to the use of social media in crisis communication and existing scholarship on measuring social media use in crisis management. After providing the general context of social media use in crisis communication, this chapter links engagement with social media, discusses public relations engagement, explains engagement in crisis communication, and presents the proposed conceptual measurement model of engagement. Finally, implications for crisis managers and researchers are also addressed.

Crisis Communication

Few situations jeopardize an organization's reputation and financial health as intensely as a crisis (Coombs, 2007a, p. 164). The ability to shape crisis perceptions, ensuing behaviors, and crisis impact constitutes a critical component of crisis communication (Coombs, 1999; Gray, 2003; Stephens & Malone, 2009). Scholars have approached crisis communication from different perspectives. Sellnow and Seeger (2001) defined *crisis communication* as an enactment function of framing the fundamental meaning of a crisis. Coombs and Holladay (2002) viewed crisis communication as strategic communication plans to limit and repair reputation damage. Fearn-Banks (2010) defined *crisis management* as strategic initiatives aimed to remove risk and uncertainty in order for the focal organization to be in great control. Clearly a common theme of the aforementioned definitions lies in the strategic goal of enabling an organization to diminish the negative consequences (e.g., negative perceptions, reputation damage, and uncertainty) in a crisis.

The unique characteristics of social media (e.g., interactivity, broad reach, immediacy) have empowered stakeholders in terms of increasing the exposure of contested issues (e.g., Bridgeman, 2008; Coombs & Holladay, 2012), participating in issue framing (e.g., Meer & Verhoeven, 2013; Veil, Buehner, & Palenchar, 2011), and demanding organizational transparency (Rawlins, 2009). It is paramount for organizations to integrate social media into crisis communication management (Coombs, 2012; Jin, Liu, & Austin, 2014).

Research in crisis communication started from a rhetorical perspective (e.g., Hearit, 2001; Huxman & Bruce, 1995; Ryan, 1982) with a primary focus on apologia (i.e., "the speech of self-defense," Ware & Linkugel, 1973, p. 273), seeking to identify persuasive counterdescriptions to defend an organization during crises (Hearit & Courtright, 2004). Some communication scholars (e.g., Arpan & Roskos-Ewoldsen, 2005; Dean, 2004) advocated for a shift to an evidence-based management approach to prescribe effective crisis-response strategies for communication managers. The situational crisis communication theory (SCCT) (Coombs, 1999; Coombs & Holladay, 2005; Coombs, 2007a) emerged as a dominant paradigm in this management approach.

Building upon attribution theory (Weiner, 1985, 1986, 2006) and image restoration theory (Benoit, 1995), SCCT asserts that stakeholder perceptions of crisis responsibility, organizational crisis history, and prior relationship reputation create reputational threat for an organization in crisis. How stakeholders perceive crisis responsibility of the organization results in affective consequences (e.g., anger, resentment), which in return trigger behavioral intentions (e.g., supportive, destructive; Coombs, 2012). Additionally, the degree of reputational threat from the crisis directly affects stakeholder behavioral intentions. By matching the crisis types (i.e., victim, accidental, or preventable) with the level of perceived crisis responsibility, the SCCT model proposes nine reputation-repair strategies: *attacking the accuser* (attacking the claim against the organization), *denial* (i.e., denying the existence of crisis), *scapegoating* (i.e., blaming the third party), *excuse* (i.e., emphasizing that the factors causing the crisis are out of control), *justification* (i.e., minimizing the perceived damage), *reminder* (i.e., praising the organization's past good deeds), *ingratiation* (i.e., touting stakeholders' support), *compensation* (i.e., compensating victims), and *apology* (i.e., admitting fault).

Social Media and Crisis Communication

Social media are "a group of internet-based applications that build on the ideological and technological foundations of Web 2.0 and that allow the creation and exchange of user-generated content" (Kaplan & Haenlein, 2010, p. 61). Based on disaster and crisis communication literature, Alexander (2014) identified seven major functions of social media use during crisis: listening to the voices of its stakeholders, monitoring the situation, integrating social media into crisis management, crowdsourcing and collaborative development, creating social cohesion and promoting therapeutic effects, promoting social causes, and conducting research. Existing research linking social media use with crisis communication has focused on the following key areas: crisis responses, emotional coping, and crisis framing.

Crisis Responses

Theoretical frameworks of crisis responses center on the SCCT (Coombs, 1998, 2007b, 2012; Coombs & Holladay, 2005) and the social-mediated crisis communication (SMCC) model (Jin et al., 2014; Liu, Jin, Briones, & Kuch, 2012). Studies applying the SCCT model probed how communication programs on various social media manifested the crisis-response strategies in the SCCT model (see Brown & Billings, 2013; Ki & Nekmat, 2014 for examples).

Whereas the SCCT model prescribes the optimized crisis-response strategies, the influence of medium channels (e.g., traditional vs. social or new media) and information source (e.g., organization vs. the third party) on crisis responses are not accounted for (Jin & Liu, 2010; Schultz, Utz, & Göritz, 2011). The SMCC model (Austin, Liu, & Jin, 2012; Jin et al., 2014; Liu, Austin, & Jin, 2011) emerges as an alternative to address the insufficiency in the SCCT model. Originally developed in the context of crises in blogosphere, the blog-mediated crisis communication (BMCC) model (Jin & Liu, 2010) helps crisis managers monitor, respond, and determine the appropriate crisis-response strategies. Particularly, the BMCC model suggests that crisis managers should engage with influential bloggers during crisis communication. These influential blog leaders have direct impact (relaying information and addressing emotional needs) on blog followers and indirect impact on non-blog followers through providing information to mass media and offline word-of-the-mouth communication. To counting the influence of many emerging social media platforms (e.g., Facebook, Twitter), Jin and her colleagues revised the model to the SMCC model (see Jin et al., 2014). Empirical testing of SMCC (Austin et al., 2012; Jin et al., 2014; Liu et al., 2011) revealed two key findings. First, information form (traditional vs. social media vs. word of mouth) and source (organization vs. third party) affected publics' emotional responses during crisis. Second, organizations should strategically integrate traditional and social media in crisis communication.

Emotional Coping

Another popular focus of crisis communication centers on the impact of social media use in addressing the emotional reactions of publics. A crisis creates threats and interruptions to the well-being and expectations to an organization's publics and surrounding community (Coombs, 2007a; Heath, 2006). Such interruptions are likely to generate strong emotional reactions from publics who are affected (Choi & Lin, 2009; Jin et al., 2012; McDonald & Härtel, 2000). Especially, when publics perceive an organization to be highly responsible for a crisis, strong negative emotions such as anger or schadenfreude (i.e., drawing pleasure from the pain of others) are triggered (Coombs, Fediuk, & Holladay, 2007; Coombs & Holladay, 2005). These negative emotions in turn tend to result in negative behavior (e.g., boycott) against the target organization (Coombs & Holladay, 2004).

Humans have an innate tendency to share and express their emotions following an emotional event such as a crisis, especially sharing negative feelings (Rime, 2009). During crises, various social media platforms with dynamic interactive functions thus serve as a socially supportive space for users to form emotional connections (e.g., Macias, Hilyard, & Freimuth, 2009; Smith, 2010), find emotional and community support (e.g., Saffer, Sommerfeldt, & Taylor, 2013; Stephens & Malone, 2009), and alleviate negative emotions (e.g., Neubaum, Rösner, der Pütten, & Krämer, 2014). Brummette and Sisco (2015) recommended that crisis managers use social media platforms (i.e., Twitter) to identify the affected stakeholders' collective sentiment and then match appropriate crisis responses to address those emotional needs. It is not only strategic but also ethical for the target organization in a crisis to engage the affected publics on social media to address their emotional needs.

Despite the vast evidence on linking the impact of social media use on coping with publics' negative emotions during crises, caution needs to be exercised when studying the linkage between social media use and emotional coping. For example, Jin and colleagues' (2014) study yielded mixed results. Particularly, contrary to the hypothesis, internal crisis origin with high organizational responsibility, instead of external crisis origin, induced more attribution-independent emotions (e.g., fear, anxiety). More research needs to be conducted to explore publics' emotional reactions as a result of different crisis origins. Culture may appear as another situational factor that creates challenge to this linkage. In An, Park, Cho, and Berger's

(2010) study, participants from a highly collectivistic culture (i.e., South Korea) exhibited more negative emotions and attitudes toward the target organization than U.S. participants from a highly individualistic culture in a crisis caused by individuals (e.g., employee mistakes).

Crisis Framing

The participatory nature of social media has empowered the public to be a vital force in shaping the interpretation (i.e., framing) of a crisis (Castells, 2007), which has a significant influence on organizational reputation (Coombs, 2007a, 2012) and reducing public confusion or ambiguity (Liu & Kim, 2011; Meer & Verhoeven, 2013). A crisis interrupts the previously held expectations for an organization (Schultz, Kleinnijen-huis, Oegema, Utz, & Atteveldt, 2012), which activates the process of sense making (Schultz & Raupp, 2010; Weick, 1998) among the affected groups.

Given the varying interests and goals from individuals and groups, interpre-tations (i.e., framing) of an event (e.g., crisis) are likely to diverge (Liu, 2010; Hellsten, Dawson, & Leydesdorff, 2010). Crisis framing development follows a dynamic and unstable process (Scheufele, 1999; Steinberg, 1998). In the initial stage, publics, media, and the target organization tend to apply their own iden-tities, beliefs, or knowledge to make sense of the crisis based on external cues (Cornelissen, Carroll, & Elving, 2009; Scheufele, 1999). This difference occurs as the involved parties (e.g., publics, media) use similar information, apply different criteria, selectively filter information, and assign different meanings to informa-tion (Leydesdorff & Hellsten, 2005). At this stage, it is critical for crisis managers to provide credible narratives to reach coherence on the issue among competing frames in order to protect reputation from damage and prevent further loss to the organization (Hellsten et al., 2010).

However, humans also have a need for meaning coherence, which motivates the affected parties to move toward one another (Meer, Verhoeven, Beentjes, & Vliegenthart, 2014). Such collective sense making may lead to mutual under-standing, though not a complete overlap, of the crisis, thus resulting in the next stage: crisis frame alignment. Nevertheless, such alignment is temporary. In the third stage, publics tend to personalize their crisis frame, choosing a crisis-specific interpretation away from the shortly achieved alignment (Coombs, 2010; Meer & Verhoeven, 2013). The dynamic shift of framing during crises necessitates crisis managers to develop crisis narratives at different framing stages to avoid misfram-ing and help the involved parties engage in crisis meaning construction.

Measuring Effectiveness of Social Media Use in Crisis Communication

Research on the impact of social media in crisis communication is still at its nascent stage (Alexander, 2014; Coombs, 2012; Jin et al., 2014; Schultz, et al.,

2011). Few studies have systematically developed metrics to measure the effectiveness of social media use in crisis communication. Nevertheless, the yardstick for gauging the effectiveness of social media use in crisis communication has appeared sporadically in some studies, as outlined next.

Measuring Interactivity

Interactivity refers to the perceived satisfaction of interaction and the degree of rapport built in the process (Rafaeli, 1998). Assessing interactivity in social media use encompasses two dimensions: "distal interactivity" (Kelleher & Sweetser, 2012, p. 107) and contingency interactivity (Kelleher, 2009). *Distal interactivity*, also termed as functional interactivity (Sundar, Kalyanaraman, & Brown, 2003), refers to the technical functions afforded by the medium itself to facilitate dialogic communication, such as site maps, chat boards, search boxes, e-mail links, or feedback forms (McAllister & Taylor, 2007; Taylor & Perry, 2005). Having these dialogic features does not necessarily yield dialogue without fostering contingency interactivity and actual back-and-forth conversations between organizations and their online users (Kelleher, 2009; Rafaeli & Ariel, 2007). The dimension of functional interactivity does not address whether user messages are responded to or associated with one another (Sundar et al., 2003). Contingency interactivity, however, involves one-to-many and many-to-many relations, requiring participants to respond to each other (Stromer-Galley, 2004) and post messages "contingent on the content of previous messages" (Kelleher, 2007, pp. 10–11).

The more the conversations are "intertwined and cumulative," the higher the level of interactivity of the process (Walther, Gay, & Hancock, 2005, p. 641). The impact of interactivity on the effectiveness of crisis communication has been measured in Facebook (e.g., Ki & Nekmat, 2014) and blogs (Yang et al., 2010). Yang and colleagues' (2010) study discovered that contingent interactivity-related conversations online improved blog users' perceptions of closeness and engagement with the target organization during crises. Ki and Nekmat's (2014) study on Fortune 500 companies' use of Facebook during crises revealed that involving online users in contingent interactivity (e.g., two-way communication) was associated with the users' positive tone about the target organizations and their crisis responses.

Measuring Effectiveness of Messages

Crisis communication scholars in public relations have not systematically probed the question of what constitutes an effective crisis message on social media (Freberg, Saling, Vidoloff, & Eosco, 2013b). The value model proposed by Freberg and colleagues represented a pioneering attempt to bridge this gap by proposing a matrix to identify the most important messages to monitor and communicate.

Freberg and colleagues borrowed problem definition and analysis techniques used in systems engineering (Kossiakoff, Sweet, Seymour, & Biemer, 2011) to develop the value model that involves three steps. First, *the functional requirements analysis* aims to identify the general function or purpose, representing an action or activity that must be implemented to reach "a desired outcome" (Parnell, Driscoll, & Henderson, 2011, p. 315). The overall function thus refers to the overarching end purpose of the system. Subfunctions are then further categorized. The next step involves *developing a qualitative value model* that "reflects the key stakeholder values regarding the [system]" (p. 327). The information developed in the previous functional analysis needs to be considered to create objectives and value measures for the model. The objectives determine the optimal value for a specific function and demonstrate what the ideal system should generate in the corresponding category (p. 188). The value measure thus renders a benchmark to rank alternatives in comparison to the ideal system. The third step is *to develop a quantitative value model* to gauge how well the proposed solutions to the problem satisfy stakeholder expectations.

Engagement as an Integral Part of Measurement Metrics

As reviewed previously, a daunting challenge resides in establishing codes of effectiveness and measurement metrics to assess how an organization's social media efforts can translate into tangible organizational outcomes (Loechner, 2014). To further examine engagement as part of public relations measurement, researchers and practitioners need to conceptualize what engagement actually is and how it can be measured (Calder, Malthouse, & Schaedel, 2009).

Engagement in Public Relations

Engagement as a multidimensional construct offers scholars and practitioners a great perspective to looking into behavioral outcomes in public relations campaigns (Slater, Chipman, Auld, Keefe, & Kendall, 1992), community building (Heath, Bradshaw, & Lee, 2002), organization-public relationship (OPR) management (Bortree, 2011), and stakeholder participation (Heath, 2011). More recently, researchers have started to define engagement as a new theoretical paradigm in public relations (Johnston, 2014): (a) engagement as an *orientation* can influence the way organizations interact with their strategic internal and external publics (Taylor & Kent, 2014); (b) engagement as publics' *psychological or behavioral state* in their interactions with an organization consists of multiple dimensions (Kang, 2014; Men & Tsai, 2014); (c) engagement as a form of *publics' behavior* has been linked to cultivating OPRs (Bortree, 2011; Devin & Lane, 2014); and (d) engagement should be examined as a strong predictor of prosocial relationships (Mersey, Malthouse, & Calder, 2012; Smitko, 2012).

Social Media Engagement as a Behavioral Process

In this book chapter, we define engagement as a *behavioral process* rather than a cognitive or affective *state* (Doorn et al., 2010). Engagement describes publics' positive and negative *behavioral manifestations* toward an organization over time (Javornik & Mandelli, 2012).

A Review of Previous Research on the Behavioral Approach

Previous social media engagement literature largely operationalized its behavioral outcomes in a constricted and inconsistent manner. For instance, Bijmolt and colleagues (2010) identified word of mouth, customer cocreation, and complaining behavior as key behavioral manifestations of customer social media engagement. Customer social media engagement as a *cycle* consists of connection, interaction, satisfaction, retention, commitment, advocacy, and engagement as distinct stages (Sashi, 2012). To predict stakeholders' active and passive use of social media, Pagani and Mirabello (2011) differentiated two types of engagement: *personal engagement* (with intrinsic drivers) and *social-interactive engagement* (with extrinsic drivers). Through personal engagement, online users often look for stimulation and inspiration, share online content, seek input and feedback, and find a site fun and attractive if they perceive the site reflects their personal values. As for social-interactive engagement, users benefit from socializing online and through participating in the community. In performing these engagement activities, they receive useful information for making more informed decisions. Moreover, engagement represents publics' behavioral investment in their interactions with a specific brand (Hollebeek, 2011), online community interactions (Jang, Olfman, Ko, Koh, & Kim, 2008), relationship building (Kietzmann, Hermkens, McCarthy, & Silvestre, 2011), and stakeholders' intrinsic motivation to be involved in an online brand community (OBC) (Wirtz et al., 2013). Importantly, engagement also means to create conversations and engage audiences (Neiger et al., 2013).

Building a Theoretical Framework for Studying Social Media Engagement From the Behavioral Perspective

Researchers have attempted to build *a theoretical framework* for social media engagement research (Hollebeek, 2011; Paine, 2008, 2011; Taylor & Kent, 2014). The relationship marketing (RM) theory and the service-dominant (S-D) logic account for the notion of engaged stakeholders' proactive contributions, whereas the social exchange theory (SET) explains their intrinsic motivation for making such contributions (Hollebeek, 2011).

Prior studies examined customer social media engagement from the RM theory and the S-D logic approach (Hollebeek, 2011). Customers who are *engaged* in constant interactions with organizations tend to proactively participate in cocreating value congruency with the organizations (Carter, 2008). With its conceptual foundation rooted in the RM theory and the S-D logic, customer social media engagement reflects the dynamics of interactive activities or behaviors that involve multiple agents: customers, organizations, and other strategic stakeholders (Palmatier, Dant, Grewal, & Evans, 2006).

Taking a broad perspective, the SET scholars further explained *why* stakeholders are no longer *passive information recipients* but proactive contributors to dynamic interactions with an organization and *why* it is critical to conceptualize social media engagement as *behavioral manifestations* that stakeholders demonstrate (Hollebeek, 2011). Based on Blau's (1964) SET, stakeholders are likely to exhibit favorable attitudes and behaviors toward an organization if they perceive benefits from the relationship with an organization (Hollebeek, 2011). In particular, they can fully devote their physical, emotional, and cognitive resources when they perceive they are benefiting from their relationship with an organization (Higgins & Scholer, 2009). This *cost-reward logic* is in congruence with the *interactive-dialogic* nature of social media engagement (Hollebeek, 2011).

The Conceptualization of Social Media Engagement in Public Relations Literature

Based on the dialogic theory (e.g., Taylor & Kent, 2014), some scholars have defined social media engagement as a construct consisting of the following components: online and offline interaction with organizations; stakeholders' sharing of experiences, needs, and counsel with organizations; and stakeholders' active role in building a fully functioning community. Others (e.g., Paine, 2008, 2011; Scoble, 2006) conceptualized engagement as stakeholders' cognitive and behavioral responses to mediated experiences on social media platforms. We define *social media engagement* in this chapter as the presence of a meaningful dialogue between an organization and its stakeholders and the ability of the organization to predict those stakeholders' behavior by measuring their *signs of engagement* on a social media site.

Assessment of Social Media Engagement Behaviors

To manage social media effectively strategies to engage audiences must be developed, and evaluation standards and metrics must be applied (Neiger et al., 2012, 2013). As one of the first organizations that have developed such standards, the #SMMStandards coalition (i.e., Conclave)[1] proposed six key priorities for standardization: (a) content sourcing and methods, (b) reach and impressions, (c) engagement, (d) influence and relevance, (e) opinion and advocacy, and (f) impact and value (#SMMStandards, 2013). In particular, engagement should be measured at three levels: low, medium, and high (#SMMStandards, 2013). Unlike the aforementioned prior studies centered on the classification of engagement behaviors,

Neiger and colleagues (2012, 2013) described social media engagement behaviors as *hierarchical* and developed the evaluation metrics of Twitter use in health promotion settings.

Low Engagement

Neiger and colleagues (2013) identified the lowest level of engagement in terms of (a) the number of tweets posted by the organization, (b) the number of tweets directed to specific users with the @username syntax, (c) the number of the organization's followers, and (d) the number of second-level followers (i.e., followers of followers; p. 160).

Medium Engagement

Neiger and colleagues (2013) claimed that medium engagement measurement typically focused on how organizations help build appealing online conversations for audiences to get involved. Key performance indicators in Twitter metrics include (a) mutual relationships (the percentage of users in the following list that are also followers), (b) the number of tweets that have been retweeted, (c) the number of users that have retweeted, (d) the number of followers of those who have retweeted the user's messages, (e) the number (or percentage) of retweets made by nonfollowers, (f) the number of @ mentions (excluding retweets and questions), (g) the number of followers responding to a question posed by the organization, (h) the number of questions asked directly of the user (@username), (i) the number of direct (private) messages, and (j) the number of followers who follow each other (p. 160).

High Engagement

Finally, they argued that high engagement relates to audiences' online or offline involvement with an organization either as a partner or participant (Neiger et al., 2013, p. 161). Neiger and colleagues (2013) provided three typical examples of high Twitter engagement: (a) the number of Twitter followers who engage in formative research with and about the organization (e.g., online or offline participation with data-collection procedures to provide consumer feedback to an organization's specific programs); (b) the number of Twitter followers who engage with the organization in the delivery or support of programs, services, or activities (e.g., online or offline volunteerism, cause promotion, donation, etc.); and (c) the number of Twitter followers who engage with the organization as participants in programs, services, or activities (e.g., online or offline participation in organizational offerings; pp. 160–161).

In a similar vein, public relations scholars also proposed a *hierarchical* view of evaluating social media engagement (Marklein & Paine, 2012; Paine, 2008, 2011).

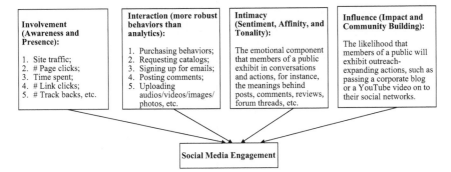

Involvement (Awareness and Presence):	Interaction (more robust behaviors than analytics):	Intimacy (Sentiment, Affinity, and Tonality):	Influence (Impact and Community Building):
1. Site traffic; 2. # Page clicks; 3. Time spent; 4. # Link clicks; 5. # Track backs, etc.	1. Purchasing behaviors; 2. Requesting catalogs; 3. Signing up for emails; 4. Posting comments; 5. Uploading audios/videos/images/photos, etc.	The emotional component that members of a public exhibit in conversations and actions, for instance, the meanings behind posts, comments, reviews, forum threads, etc.	The likelihood that members of a public will exhibit outreach-expanding actions, such as passing a corporate blog or a YouTube video on to their social networks.

Social Media Engagement

FIGURE 28.1 A Tentative Measurement Model of Social Media Engagement for Future Development

Adapted from Paine, 2008; and Scoble, 2006.

For example, based on the conceptualization by Scoble (2006), Paine (2008) proposed the following social media engagement evaluation model (with both tangible and intangible factors; see Figure 28.1):

1. *Involvement*[2] (i.e., awareness and presence) includes Web analytics—for example, site traffic, page views, time spent, link clicks, and track backs.
2. *Interaction* (i.e., dialogic actions) consists of some more robust actions that stakeholders take, such as purchasing behaviors; requesting catalogs; signing up for e-mails; posting comments; and uploading audios, videos, and photos.
3. *Intimacy* (i.e., sentiment, affinity, and tonality) refers to the emotional component that stakeholders of an organization exhibit in conversations and actions—for instance, the meanings behind posts, comments, reviews, and social media threads.
4. *Influence* (i.e., impact and community building) addresses the likelihood that members of a public will exhibit outreach-expanding actions, such as passing a corporate blog or a YouTube video on to their social networks (families, friends, acquaintances, and even strangers) and making purchasing recommendations to them.

Levels of Social Media Engagement in Crisis Communication[3]: Involvement, Interaction, Intimacy, and Influence

When crises occur, responsible parties are expected to take speedy actions—disseminate information, maintain interactions with affected publics in all means, attend to their emotional needs, abide by ethical standards, and retain or rebuild key stakeholders' trust and confidence (Freberg, Palenchar, & Veil, 2013a; Freberg et al., 2013b; Heath, 2004). The way an organization handles a crisis largely determines whether it can take a more positive or negative direction to develop (Freberg et al., 2013a, 2013b).

Engagement as an Important Social Media Strategy for Crisis Communication

With its pervasive presence in today's public relations practices, social media creates both opportunities and challenges in crisis communication (Prentice & Huffman, 2008). Organizations can share initial information, updates, explanations, and decisions on social media (Smith, 2010; Sutton, Palen, & Shklovski, 2008). Organizational social media engagement behaviors may lead to closer connections with affected communities, stronger bonds of social support, and greater control over crisis development (Hsu, Ju, Yen, & Chang, 2007; Marken, 2007; Shklovski, Burke, Kiesler, & Kraut, 2010). At the same time, the extensive use of social media by both stakeholders and organizations in crisis communication creates great challenges (Freberg et al., 2013a, 2013b; Liu et al., 2012). During crisis, on-site and online crisis-related behaviors often happen spontaneously and simultaneously (Palen, Vieweg, Sutton, Liu, & Hughes, 2007). Organizations need to proactively monitor all user-generated content related to a particular crisis and how it is created and shared among these users, social media followers and consumers of information, social media inactives, and even traditional media organizations who constantly look for information subsidies on social media (Liu et al., 2012; Veil et al., 2011). In addition, affected parties turn to a greater variety of information channels during a crisis (González-Herrero & Smith, 2008). Social media engagement strategies for crisis management are therefore much more needed than ever (Deragon, 2008; Veil et al., 2011).

Social Media Engagement for Crisis Communication

Although a widely acknowledged framework for social media engagement in crisis communication is still developing, some preliminary tenets for managing social media in crisis communication have emerged across the extant crisis communication literature (e.g., Bruns, Burgess, Crawford, & Shaw, 2012; Freberg et al., 2013a, 2013b; Gordon, 2007; Liu et al., 2012):

1. Involvement (i.e., awareness and presence) in crisis communication: Organizations need to provide timely and accurate information to cultivate a high level of online involvement and awareness among affected communities. The level of achieved awareness and presence can be measured by site traffic; page views; time spent; link clicks; and track backs on Facebook, Twitter, Google+, Instagram, Pinterest, YouTube, and so forth. Other examples include the number of posts about the crisis, the number of comments about the crisis, and the number of unique visitors.

2. Interaction (i.e., dialogic actions) in crisis communication: Organizations need to monitor and facilitate engaging interactions. The effectiveness of such organizational dialogic actions is measured by the extent to which all affected and interested parties can easily request real-time information (e.g., the number of RSS subscribers, the number of crisis-related links to and from other sites), share messages with credible sources, create and curate unfiltered yet truthful eyewitness and reaction media content (e.g., videos, photos, texts), and so on.

3. Intimacy (i.e., sentiment, affinity, and tonality) in crisis communication: Rumor, empathy, and sympathy management is key to organizational crisis management. Affected communities' emotional needs should be well considered so that they can exhibit constructive actions conducive to problem solving and decision making. It is measured via the meanings behind posts, comments, reviews, and social media threads.

4. Influence (i.e., impact and community building) in crisis communication: Affected and interested individuals, groups, and organizations coconstruct an online crisis community characterized by constant multimedia-enhanced conversations, content forwarding, and a multidirectional communication network (e.g., one to one, one to many, and many to many). The assessment focuses on the outreach-expanding actions that the affected parties exhibit, such as passing a corporate tweet or a YouTube video on to their social networks (families, friends, acquaintances, and social media followers, among others).

Conclusions and Implications

Over the past decades, public relations researchers and practitioners have been discussing the importance of establishing measurement standards and metrics (Anderson, Hadley, Rockland, & Weiner, 2009; Coalition for Public Relations Research Standards, 2014; Eisenmann, 2012; #SMMStandards, 2013; Watson & Likely, 2013). Common themes of measurement have been covered in the discussion, including measurement toward intangible outcomes (e.g., relationship management and return on investment [ROI]), measurement of public relations outputs (i.e., measurement of production, message exposure, audience awareness, audience attitudes, and audience action), consistency and credibility of metrics, and the social media measurement standards that the Conclave established in 2013 (i.e., content and sourcing, reach and impressions, engagement and conversation, influence, opinion and advocacy, and impact and value).

This study adds to the existing measurement metrics a tentative model for social media engagement during crisis communication (see Figure 28.2). Here are some important implications of the measurement model for research and practice:

1. Based on the existing social media engagement metrics (Marklein & Paine, 2012; Neiger et al., 2012, 2013; Paine, 2008, 2011; Scoble, 2006), the proposed

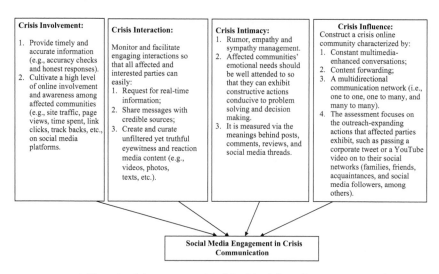

Crisis Involvement:	Crisis Interaction:	Crisis Intimacy:	Crisis Influence: Construct a crisis online community characterized by:
1. Provide timely and accurate information (e.g., accuracy checks and honest responses). 2. Cultivate a high level of online involvement and awareness among affected communities (e.g., site traffic, page views, time spent, link clicks, track backs, etc., on social media platforms.	Monitor and facilitate engaging interactions so that all affected and interested parties can easily: 1. Request for real-time information; 2. Share messages with credible sources; 3. Create and curate unfiltered yet truthful eyewitness and reaction media content (e.g., videos, photos, texts, etc.).	1. Rumor, empathy and sympathy management. 2. Affected communities' emotional needs should be well attended to so that they can exhibit constructive actions conducive to problem solving and decision making. 3. It is measured via the meanings behind posts, comments, reviews, and social media threads.	1. Constant multimedia-enhanced conversations; 2. Content forwarding; 3. A multidirectional communication network (i.e., one to one, one to many, and many to many). 4. The assessment focuses on the outreach-expanding actions that affected parties exhibit, such as passing a corporate tweet or a YouTube video on to their social networks (families, friends, acquaintances, and social media followers, among others).

Social Media Engagement in Crisis Communication

FIGURE 28.2 A Tentative Measurement Model of Social Media Engagement for Social Media

Adapted from Marklein and Paine, 2012; Neiger and colleagues, 2012, 2013; Paine, 2008, 2011; Scoble, 2006; and #SMMStandards, 2013.

model operationalizes social media engagement in crisis communication into four distinct dimensions: involvement, interaction, intimacy, and influence.

2. It extends the current interactivity- and message effectiveness–dominated measurement framework in social media for crisis communication by reinforcing *engagement* as a critical metric in social media measurement (see #SMMStandards, 2013).

3. It moves beyond the basic "engagement counts"[4]—"likes, comments, shares, votes, +1s, links, retweets, video views, content embeds, etc." (#SMMStandards, 2013, p. 6)—by adding the *intimacy* (i.e., sentiment, affinity, and tonality) and *influence* (i.e., impact and community building) elements into the measurement of social media use in crisis communication. Specifically, the demonstrated online and offline emotional needs of affected communities should be adequately measured.

4. Finally, it provides a more systematic and inclusive model that not only identifies stakeholders' social media engagement practices in crises but also helps explain how the measurement of social media engagement may be related to management's future strategic decision making and crisis management.

Notes

1 A broad coalition of individuals representing business-to-business and business-to-consumer companies, public relations and social media agencies, and industry associations, including

the Institute for Public Relations, the International Association for Measurement and Evaluation of Communications, the Council of Public Relations Firms, the Digital Analytics Association, the Public Relations Society of America, the Word of Mouth Marketing Association, the International Association of Business Communicators, the Chartered Institute of Public Relations, Federation Internationale des Bureaux d'Extraits de Presse, the Global Alliance for Public Relations and Communications Management, and the Society for New Communications Research; research and communication leaders from Dell, Ford Motor Company, General Motors, McDonald's, Procter & Gamble, SAS, Southwest Airlines, and Thomson Reuters, as well as many major communications agencies *(#SMMStandards, 2013,* p. 1), such as Porter Novelli and Edelman.

2 As performance or behavioral indicators of social media engagement, *involvement* measures the early stage of social media implementation (i.e., the outcome of establishing a social media awareness or presence). *Interaction*, emphasizing stakeholders' feedback and responses (or some type of change or progression), is rooted in the dialogic theory. *Intimacy* and *influence*, as two higher engagement indicators, focus on stakeholders' more meaningful involvement with organizations' social media programs, with both emotional and behavioral components.

3 In our adapted engagement model, we use the term "crisis engagement" to represent levels of social media engagement in crisis communication.

4 Basically, the involvement and interaction parts of the four-dimensional model.

References

Alexander, D. E. (2014). Social media in disaster risk reduction and crisis management. *Science and Engineering Ethics, 20,* 717–733.

An, S.-K., Park, D.-J., Cho, S., & Berger, B. (2010). A cross-cultural study of effective organizational crisis response strategy in the United States and South Korea. *International Journal of Strategic Communication, 4,* 225–243.

Anderson, F. W., Hadley, L., Rockland, D., & Weiner, M. (2009, September). Guidelines for setting measurable public relations objectives: An update. *The Institute for Public Relations.* Retrieved from http://www.instituteforpr.org/setting-measurable-objectives/

Arpan, L. M., & Roskos-Ewoldsen, D. R. (2005). Stealing thunder: An analysis of the effects of proactive disclosure of crisis communication. *Journal of Public Relations Research, 8,* 279–295.

Austin, L., Liu, B. F., & Jin, Y. (2012). How audiences seek out crisis information: Exploring the social-mediated crisis communication model. *Journal of Applied Communication Research, 40,* 188–207.

Benoit, W. L. (1995). *Accounts, excuses, and apologies: A theory of image restoration.* Albany, NY: State University of New York Press.

Bijmolt, T. H. A., Leeflang, P. S. H., Block, F., Eisenbeiss, M., Hardie, B. G. S., Lemmens, A., & Saffert, P. (2010). Analytics for customer engagement. *Journal of Service Research, 13*(3), 341–356.

Blau, P. (1964). *Exchange and power in social life.* New York: Wiley.

Bortree, D. S. (2011). Mediating the power of antecedents in public relationships: A pilot study. *Public Relations Review, 37,* 44–49.

Bridgeman, R. (2008). Crisis communication and the net: Is it just about responding faster . . . or do we need to learn a new game? In P. F. Anthonissen (Ed.), *Crisis communication: Practical PR strategies for reputation management and company survival* (pp. 169–177). London: Kogan Page.

Brown, N. A., & Billings, A. C. (2013). Sports fans as crisis communicators on social media websites. *Public Relations Review, 39,* 74–81.

Brummette, J., & Sisco, H. F. (2015). Using Twitter as a means of coping with emotions and uncontrollable crises. *Public Relations Review, 41,* 89–96.

Bruns, A., Burgess, J., Crawford, K., & Shaw, F. (2012). #qldfloods and #QPSMedia: Crisis communication on Twitter in the 2011 South East Queensland Flood: ARC center of excellence for creative industries & innovation (CII) media ecologies project. Retrieved from http://www.cci.edu.au/floodsreport.pdf

Calder, B. J., Malthouse, E. C., & Schaedel, U. (2009). An experimental study of the relationship between online engagement and advertising effectiveness. *Journal of Interactive Marketing, 23*(4), 321–331.

Carter, T. (2008). Customer engagement and behavioral considerations. *Journal of Strategic Marketing, 16,* 21–26.

Castells, M. (2007). Communication, power and counter-power in the network society. *International Journal of Communication, 1,* 238–266.

Choi, Y., & Lin, Y.-H. (2009). Consumer responses to Mattel product recalls posted on online bulletin boards: Exploring two types of emotions. *Journal of Public Relations Research, 21,* 198–207.

Coalition for Public Relations Research Standards. (2014, September). PR measurement standards: Do's and don'ts for PR practitioners. Retrieved from http://www.institute-forpr.org/wp-content/uploads/Standards-dos-and-donts-09302014.pdf

Coombs, W. T. (1998). An analytic framework for crisis situations: Better responses from a better understanding of the situation. *Journal of Public Relations Research, 10,* 177, 191.

Coombs, W. T. (1999). *Ongoing crisis communication: Planning, managing, and responding.* Thousand Oaks, CA: Sage.

Coombs, W. T. (2007a). Attribution theory as a guide for post-crisis communication research. *Public Relations Review, 33,* 135–139.

Coombs, W. T. (2007b). Protecting organization reputations during a crisis: The development and application of situational crisis communication theory. *Corporate Reputation Review, 10,* 163–176.

Coombs, W. T. (2010). Parameters for crisis communication. In W. T. Coombs & S. J. Holladay (Eds.), *The handbook of crisis communication* (pp. 17–53). Chichester, UK: Wiley-Blackwell.

Coombs, W. T. (2012). *Ongoing crisis communication: Planning, managing, and responding* (3rd ed.). Thousand Oaks, CA: Sage.

Coombs, W. T., Fediuk, T. A., & Holladay, S. J. (2007). *Further explorations of post-crisis communication and stakeholder anger: The negative communication dynamic model.* Paper presented at the International Public Relations Research Conference, Miami, FL.

Coombs, W. T., & Holladay, S. J. (2002). Helping crisis managers protect reputational assets: Initial tests of the situational crisis communication theory. *Management Communication Quarterly, 16,* 165–186.

Coombs, W. T., & Holladay, S. J. (2004). Reasoned action in crisis communication: An attribution theory-based approach to crisis management. In D. P. Millar & R. L. Heath (Eds.), *Responding to crisis: A rhetorical approach to crisis communication* (pp. 95–115), Mahwah, NJ: Lawrence Erlbaum Associates.

Coombs, W. T., & Holladay, S. J. (2005). Exploratory study of stakeholder emotions: Affect and crisis. In N. M. Ashkanasy, W. J. Zerbe, & E. E. J. Hartel (Eds.), *Research on emotion in organizations: Volume 1: The effect of affect in organizational settings* (pp. 271–288). New York: Elsevier.

Coombs, W. T., & Holladay, S. J. (2012). The paracrisis: The challenges created by publicly managing crisis prevention. *Public Relations Review*, *38*, 408–415.

Cornelissen, J. P., Carroll, C., & Elving, W. J. L. (2009). Making sense of a crucial interface: Corporate communication and the news media. In C. Chouliaraki & M. Morsing (Eds.), *Media, organization and identity* (pp. 1–22). Hampshire: Palgrave McMillan.

Dean, D. H. (2004). Consumer reaction to negative publicity: Effects of corporate reputation, response, and responsibility for a crisis event. *Journal of Business Communication*, *41*, 192–211.

Deragon, J. (2008). Leveraging social media for business purposes. Retrieved from http://www.slideshare.net/jderagon/Leveraging-Social-Media-for-Business

Devin, B. L., & Lane, A. B. (2014). Communicating engagement in corporate social responsibility: A meta-level construal of engagement. *Journal of Public Relations Research*, *26*(5), 436–454.

Doorn, J. van, Lemon, K. N., Mittal, V., Nass, S., Pick, D., Pirner, P., & Verhoef, P. C. (2010). Customer engagement behavior: Theoretical foundations and research directions. *Journal of Service Research*, *13*(3), 253–266.

Eisenmann, M. (2012, December). PR measurement: The pursuit of consistent and credible metrics. Retrieved from http://www.ipra.org/itl/12/2012/pr-measurement-the-pursuit-of-consistent-and-credible-metrics

Fearn-Banks, K. (2010). *Crisis communications: A casebook approach* (4th ed.). New York: Routledge.

Freberg, K., Palenchar, M. J., & Veil, S. R. (2013a). Managing and sharing H1N1 crisis information using social media bookmarking services. *Public Relations Review*, *39*, 178–184. doi: http://dx.doi.org/10.1016/j.pubrev.2013.02.007

Freberg, K., Saling, K., Vidoloff, K. G., & Eosco, G. (2013b). Using value modeling to evaluate social media messages: The case of Hurricane Irene. *Public Relations Review*, *39*, 185–192. doi: http://dx.doi.org/10.1016/j.pubrev.2013.02.010

González-Herrero, A., & Smith, S. (2008). Crisis communications management on the web: How Internet-based technologies are changing the way public relations professionals handle business crises. *Journal of Contingencies and Crisis Management*, *16*(3), 143–153.

Gordon, J. (2007). The mobile phone and the public sphere: Mobile phone usage in three critical situations. *Convergence*, *13*, 307–319.

Gray, G. M. (2003, May). *The risk communication challenge*. Paper presented at the Conference from Cad Cow to Acrylamide to Listeria: The Art of Effective Risk Communication, Boston, MA.

Hearit, K. M. (2001). Corporate apologia: When an organization speaks in defense of itself. In R. L. Heath (Ed.), *Handbook of public relations* (pp. 501–511). Thousand Oaks, CA: Sage.

Hearit, K. M., & Courtright, J. L. (2004). A symbolic approach to crisis management: Sears' defense of its auto repair policies. In D. P. Millar & R. L. Heath (Eds.), *Responding to a crisis: A rhetorical approach to crisis communication* (pp. 201–212). Mahwah: Lawrence Erlbaum Associates.

Heath, R. L. (2004). Telling a story: A narrative approach to communication during crisis. In D. P. Millar & R. L. Heath (Eds.), *Responding to crisis: A rhetorical approach to crisis communication* (pp. 167–187). Mahwah, NJ: Erlbaum.

Heath, R. L. (2006). Best practices in crisis communication: Evolution of practice through research. *Journal of Applied Communication Research*, *34*, 245–248.

Heath, R. L. (2011). External organizational rhetoric: Bridging management and sociopolitical discourse. *Management Communication Quarterly*, *25*(3), 415–435. doi: 10.1177/0893318911409532

Heath, R. L., Bradshaw, J., & Lee, J. (2002). Community relationship building: Local leadership in the risk communication infrastructure. *Journal of Public Relations Research, 14,* 317–353. doi: 10.1207=S1532754XJPRR1404_2

Hellsten, I., Dawson, J., & Leydesdorff, L. (2010). Implicit media frames: Automated analysis of public debate on artificial sweeteners. *Public Understanding of Science, 19,* 590–608.

Higgins, E. T., & Scholer, A. A. (2009). Engaging the consumer: The science and art of the value creation process. *Journal of Consumer Psychology, 19,* 100–114.

Hollebeek, L. (2011). Exploring customer brand engagement: Definition and themes. *Journal of Strategic Marketing, 19*(7), 555–573. doi: 10.1080/0965254X.2011.599493

Hsu, M.-H., Ju, T. L., Yen, C.-H., & Chang, C.-M. (2007). Knowledge sharing behavior in virtual communities: The relationship between trust, self-efficacy, and outcome expectation. *International Journal of Human-Computer Studies, 65*(2), 153–169.

Huxman, S., & Bruce, D. (1995). Toward a dynamic generic framework of apologia: A case study of Dow Chemical, Vietnam, and the napalm controversy. *Communication Studies, 46,* 57–72.

Jang, H., Olfman, L., Ko, I., Koh, J., & Kim, K. (2008). The influence of on-line brand community characteristics on community commitment and brand loyalty. *International Journal of Electronic Commerce, 12*(3), 57–80.

Javornik, A., & Mandelli, A. (2012). Behavioral perspectives of customer engagement: An exploratory study of customer engagement with three Swiss FMCG brands. *Journal of Database Marketing and Customer Strategy Management, 19*(4), 300–310.

Jin, Y., & Liu, B. F. (2010). The blog-mediated crisis communication model: Recommendations for responding to influential external blogs. *Journal of Public Relations Research, 22,* 429–455.

Jin, Y., Liu, B. F., & Austin, L. (2014). Examining the role of social media in effective crisis management: The effects of crisis origin, information form, and source on publics' crisis responses. *Communication Research, 41,* 74–94.

Jin, Y., Pang, A., & Cameron, G. T. (2012). Toward a publics-driven, emotion-based conceptualization in crisis communication: Unearthing dominant emotions in multi-staged testing of the integrated crisis mapping (ICM) model. *Journal of Public Relations Research, 24,* 266–298. http://dx.doi.org/10.1080/1062726X. 2012.676747

Johnston, K. A. (2014). Public relations and engagement: Theoretical imperatives of a multidimensional concept. *Journal of Public Relations Research, 26*(5), 381–383. doi: 10.1080/1062726X.2014.959863

Kang, M. (2014). Understanding public engagement: Conceptualizing and measuring its influence on supportive behavioral intentions. *Journal of Public Relations Research, 26,* 399–416.

Kaplan, A. M., & Haenlein, M. (2010). Users of the world, unit! The challenges and opportunities of social media. *Business Horizons, 53,* 59–68.

Kelleher, T. (2007). *Public relations online: Lasting concepts for changing media.* Thousand Oaks, CA: Sage.

Kelleher, T. (2009). Conversational voice, communicated commitment, and public relations outcomes in interactive online communication. *Journal of Communication, 59,* 172–188.

Kelleher, T., & Sweetser, K. (2012). Social media adoption among university communicators. *Journal of Public Relations Research, 24,* 105–122.

Ki, E.-J., & Nekmat, E. (2014). Situational crisis communication and interactivity: Usage and effectiveness of Facebook for crisis management. *Public Relations Review, 35,* 140–147.

Kietzmann, J. H., Hermkens, K., McCarthy, I. P., & Silvestre, B. S. (2011). Social media? Get serious! Understanding the functional building blocks of social media. *Business Horizons, 54*(3), 241–251.

Kossiakoff, A., Sweet, W. N., Seymour, S., & Biemer, S. M. (2011). *Systems engineering principles and practice.* New York: Wiley.

Leydesdorff, L., & Hellsten, I. (2005). Metaphors and diaphors in science communication mapping the case of stem cell research. *Science Communication, 27*(1), 64–99.

Liu, B. F. (2010). Distinguishing how elite newspapers and A-list blogs cover crises: Insights for managing crises online. *Public Relations Review, 36*, 28–34.

Liu, B. F., Austin, L., & Jin, Y. (2011). How publics respond to crisis communication strategies: The interplay of information form and source. *Public Relations Review, 37*, 345–353.

Liu, B. F., Jin, Y., Briones, R., & Kuch, B. (2012). Managing turbulence in the blogosphere: Evaluating the blog-mediated crisis communication model with the American Red Cross. *Journal of Public Relations Research, 24*, 353–370.

Liu, B. F., & Kim, S. (2011). How organizations framed the 2009 H1N1 pandemic via social and traditional media: Implications for U.S. health communicators. *Public Relations Review, 37*, 233–244.

Loechner, J. (2014). Can you measure engagement? *Media Post.* Retrieved from http://www.ana.net/miccontent/show/id/kp-mediapost-can-you-measure-engagement

McAllister, S., & Taylor, M. (2007). Community college web sites as tools for fostering dialogue. *Public Relations Review, 33*, 230–232.

McDonald, L., & Härtel, C. E. J. (2000). *Applying the involvement construct to organizational crises.* Australian and New Zealand Marketing Academy Conference Proceedings, Visionary Marketing for the 21st Century: Facing the Challenge, Department of Marketing, Griffith University, Gold Cost, Australia, pp. 799–803.

Macias, W., Hilyard, K., & Freimuth, V. (2009). Blog functions as risk and crisis communication during Hurricane Katrina. *Journal of Computer-Mediated Communication, 15*, 1–31.

Marken, G. A. (2007). Social media . . . The hunted can become the hunter. *Public Relations Quarterly, 52*(4), 9–12.

Marklein, T., & Paine, K. D. (2012). *The march to standards: #SMMStandards progress and roadmap.* Paper presented at the Fourth European Summit on Measurement, Dublin, Ireland. Retrieved from http://www.slideshare.net/tmarklein/march-tostandards-smmstandards-progress-and-roadmap

Meer, T. G. L. A. van der. (2014). Organizational crisis-denial strategy: The effect of denial on public framing. *Relations Review, 40*, 537–539.

Meer, T. G. L. A. van der, & Verhoeven, P. (2013). Public framing organizational crisis situations: Social media versus news media. *Public Relations Review, 39*, 229–231.

Meer, T. G. L. A. van der, Verhoeven, P., Beentjes, H., & Vliegenthart, R. (2014). When frames align: The interplay between PR, news media, and the public in times of crisis. *Public Relations Review, 40*, 751–761.

Men, L. R., & Tsai, W.-H. S. (2014). Perceptual, attitudinal, and behavioral outcomes of organization-public engagement on corporate social networking sites. *Journal of Public Relations Research, 26*(5), 417–435.

Mersey, R. D., Malthouse, E. C., & Calder, B. J. (2012). Focusing on the reader engagement trumps satisfaction. *Journalism & Mass Communication Quarterly, 89*, 695–709.

Neiger, B. L., Thackeray, R., Burton, S. H., Giraud-Carrier, C. G., & Fagen, M. C. (2013). Evaluating social media's capacity to develop engaged audiences in health promotion settings: Use of Twitter metrics as a case study. *Health Promotion Practice, 14*(2), 157–162.

Neiger, B. L., Thackeray, R., Van Wagenen, S. A., Hanson, C. L., West, J. H., Barnes, M. D., & Fagen, M. C. (2012). Use of social media in health promotion: Purposes, key performance indicators, and evaluation metrics. *Health Promotion Practice, 13*(2), 159–164.

Neubaum, G., Rösner, L., der Pütten, A. M. R., & Krämer, N. C. (2014). Psychosocial functions of social media usage in a disaster situation: A multi-methodological approach. *Computers in Human Behavior, 3,* 28–38.

Ott, L., & Theunissen, P. (2015). Reputations at risk: Engagement during social media crises. *Public Relations Review, 41,* 97–102.

Pagani, M., & Mirabello, A. (2011). The influence of personal and social-interactive engagement in social TV Web sites. *International Journal of Electronic Commerce, 16*(2), 41–67.

Paine, K. D. (2008, March). Are we engaged yet? Social media measurement: Engagement in social media: Web stats, visitor behavior, and relationship theory. Retrieved from http://kdpaine.blogs.com/themeasurementstandard/2008/03/are-we-engaged.html

Paine, K. D. (2011). *Measure what matters: Online tools for understanding customers, social media, engagement, and key relationships.* Hoboken, NJ: John Wiley & Sons.

Palen, L., Vieweg, S., Sutton, J., Liu, S. B., & Hughes, A. (2007, October). *Crisis informatics: Studying crisis in a networked world.* Paper presented at the Third International Conference on e Social Science, Ann Arbor, MI. Retrieved from http://www.itr-rescue.org/pubs/upload/922_Palen2010.pdf

Palmatier, R. W., Dant, R. P., Grewal, D., & Evans, K. R. (2006). Factors influencing the effectiveness of relationship marketing: A meta-analysis. *Journal of Marketing, 70*(4), 136–153.

Parnell, G. S., Driscoll, P. J., & Henderson, D. L. (2011). *Decision making in systems engineering management.* Hoboken, NJ: John Wiley & Sons.

Prentice, S., & Huffman, E. (2008, March). *Social media's new role in emergency management.* Idaho Fall, ID: Idaho National Laboratory.

Rafaeli, S. (1998). *New media technology: Cultural and commercial perspectives* (2nd ed.). Boston: Allyn & Bacon.

Rafaeli, S., & Ariel, Y. (2007). Assessing interactivity in computer-mediated research. In A. N. Joinson, K. Y. A. McKenna, T. Postmes, & U.-D. Reips (Eds.), *The Oxford handbook of Internet psychology* (pp. 71–88). Oxford, UK: Oxford University Press.

Rawlins, B. (2009). Giving the emperor a mirror: Toward developing a stakeholder measurement of organizational transparency. *Journal of Public Relations Research, 21*(1), 71–99.

Rime, B. (2009). Emotion elicits the social sharing of emotion: Theory and empirical review. *Emotion Review, 1,* 60–85.

Ryan, H. R. (1982). Kategoria and apologia: On their rhetorical criticism as a speech set. *Quarterly Journal of Speech, 68,* 254–261.

Saffer, A. J., Sommerfeldt, E. J., & Taylor, M. (2013). The effects of organizational Twitter interactivity on organization-public relationships. *Public Relations Review, 39,* 213–215.

Sashi, C. M. (2012). Customer engagement, buyer-seller relationships, and social media. *Management Decision, 50*(2), 253–272.

Scheufele, D. A. (1999). Framing as a theory of media effects. *Journal of Communication, 49,* 103–122.

Schultz, F., Kleinnijenhuis, J., Oegema, D., Utz, S., & van Atteveldt, W. (2012). Strategic framing in the BP crisis: A semantic network analysis of associative frames. *Public Relations Review, 38,* 97–107.

Schultz, F., & Raupp, J. (2010). The social construction of crises in governmental and corporate communications: An inter-organizational and inter-systemic analysis. *Public Relations Review, 36,* 112–119.

Schultz, F., Utz, S., & Göritz, A. (2011). Is the medium the message? Perceptions of and reactions to crisis communication via Twitter, blogs and traditional media. *Public Relations Review, 37,* 20–27.

Scoble, R. (2006). New audience metric needed: Engagement. Retrieved from http://scobleizer.com/2006/10/25/new-audience-metric-needed-engagement/

Sellnow, T. L., & Seeger, M. W. (2001). Exploring the boundaries of crisis communication: The case of the 1997 Red River Valley flood. *Communication Studies, 52*(2), 153–167.

Shklovski, I., Burke, M., Kiesler, S., & Kraut, R. (2010). Technology adoption and use in the aftermath of Hurricane Katrina in New Orleans. *American Behavioral Scientist, 53,* 1228–1246.

Slater, M. D., Chipman, H., Auld, G., Keefe, T., & Kendall, P. (1992). Information processing and situational theory: A cognitive response analysis. *Journal of Public Relations Research, 4,* 189–203.

Smith, A. (2010, April). *Government online: The Internet gives citizens new paths to government services and information.* Washington, DC: Pew Internet & American Life Project.

Smith, B. G. (2010). Socially distributing public relations: Twitter, Haiti, and interactivity in social media. *Public Relations Review, 36,* 329–335.

Smitko, K. (2012). Donor engagement through Twitter. *Public Relations Review, 38,* 633–635.

#SMMStandards. (2013). About #SMMStandards. Retrieved from http://www.smmstandards.com/about/

Steinberg, M. W. (1998). Tilting the frame: Considerations on collective action framing from a discursive turn. *Theory and Society, 27,* 845–872.

Stephens, K. K., & Malone, P. (2009). If the organizations won't give us information . . . : The use of multiple new media for crisis technical translations and dialogue. *Journal of Public Relations Research, 21,* 229–239.

Stromer-Galley, J. (2004). Interactivity as process and interactivity as product. *The Information Society, 20*(5), 391–394.

Sundar, S. S., Kalyanaraman, S., & Brown, J. (2003). Explicating Web site interactivity: Impression formation effects in political campaign sites. *Communication Research, 30,* 30–59.

Sutton, J., Palen, L., & Shklovski, I. (2008, May). *Backchannels on the front lines: Emergent uses of social media in the 2007 Southern California wildfires.* Proceedings of the 5th International ISCRAM Conference, Washington, DC.

Taylor, M., & Kent, M. L. (2014). Dialogic engagement: Clarifying foundational concepts. *Journal of Public Relations Research, 26*(5), 384–398.

Taylor, M., & Perry, D. C. (2005). Diffusion of traditional and new media tactics in crisis communication. *Public Relations Review, 31,* 209–217.

Veil, S., Buehner, T., & Palenchar, M. J. (2011). A work-in-progress literature review: Incorporating social media in risk and crisis communication. *Journal of Contingencies and Crisis Management, 19*(2), 110–122.

Walther, J. B., Gay, G., & Hancock, J. T. (2005). How do communication and technology researchers study the Internet? *Journal of Communication, 55,* 632–657.

Ware, B. L., & Linkugel, W. A. (1973). They spoke in defense of themselves: On the generic criticism of apologia. *Quarterly Journal of Speech, 59*(3), 273–283.

Watson, T., & Likely, F. (2013). Measuring the edifice: Public relations measurement and evaluation practices over the course of 40 years. In K. Sriramesh, A. Zerfass, & J.-N. Kim (Eds.), *Public relations and communication management* (pp. 143–162). New York: Routledge.

Weick, K. E. (1998). Enacted sense making in crisis situations. *Journal of Management Studies, 25*, 305–317.

Weiner, B. (1985). An attributional theory of achievement motivation and emotion. *Psychology Review, 92*, 548–573.

Weiner, B. (1986). *An attributional theory of motivation and emotion.* New York: Springer Verlag.

Weiner, B. (2006). *Social motivation, justice, and the moral emotions: An attributional approach.* Mahwah, NJ: Lawrence Erlbaum Associates.

Wirtz, J., den Ambtman, A., Bloemer, J., Horváth, C., Ramaseshan, B., van de Klundert, J., . . . Kandampully, J. (2013). Managing brands and customer engagement in online brand communities. *Journal of Service Management, 24*(3), 223–244.

Yang, S.-U., Kang, M., & Johnson, P. (2010). Effects of narratives, openness to dialogic communication, and credibility on engagement in crisis communication through organizational blogs. *Communication Research, 37*, 473–497.

29

CRISIS COMMUNICATION IN A CHANGING MEDIA ENVIRONMENT

A Review of the Theoretical Landscape in Crisis Communication and Research Gaps

Lucinda Austin, Julia Daisy Fraustino, Yan Jin, and Brooke Fisher Liu

Crisis communicators facing high-stakes threats have an increasing need for evidence-based guidelines for communicating crisis information, in terms of both response form and content (Coombs, 2006), to ensure the safety and welfare of publics and organizations and aid in crisis recovery. When it comes to crisis-response, crisis communication literature points to the need to "be quick, be consistent, and be open" (Coombs, 2006, p. 172). The "be quick" lesson, according to Coombs (2006), has its roots in media frames. The selection process of mass media frames the story, influences its interpretation, and thus defines how a message is perceived (Hallahan, 1999). The prevalence and ubiquity of digital and social media in creating and spreading crisis information have not only changed the definition of "quickness" but also merged the process of information production and selection from both social and traditional media. Indeed, some have argued that this prevalence and ubiquity have led us to become increasingly dependent on the Internet for our daily information consumption and production needs (Ball-Rokeach, 1998). During crises, this dependency can heighten, particularly when at-risk publics face health and safety threats (Tai & Sun, 2007).

Thus, communicating about crises via a complex media landscape affects how audiences learn about and, ultimately, recover from crises. Although crisis communication theories have evolved from a rich literature, the catalytic impact of social media—in combination with joint effects with traditional media—make the case for more thorough, in-depth examination of mass communication theory to provide road maps for research and theory development. Consequently, the purpose of this chapter is to examine theories that inform understanding of how information flows during crises, including both theories directly tested in crisis communication research and those not yet tested but that show great promise for future research. Doing so will highlight directions for crisis communication scholarship in a changing media landscape.

The social-mediated crisis communication (SMCC) model is an emerging framework describing the current landscape and environment for crisis communication and is one of the first theoretical frameworks to explain the relationship between an organization, key publics, social media, traditional media, and offline word-of-mouth communication before, during, and after crises. This chapter highlights how the SMCC model was developed through incorporation of mass communication theory and suggests research directions for future model testing and improvement.

The Theoretical Tool Kit—and Missing Tools

This section groups crisis-relevant mass communication theories into four categories: (a) audience and stakeholder theories and models, (b) form or medium influence-based theories and frameworks, (c) source influence-based theories and frameworks, and (d) content influence-based theories and frameworks. After reviewing theories within each grouping, and the extent to which they have been or could be examined in crisis information-flow scholarship, we conclude with recommendations for future research.

Audience and Stakeholder Theories and Frameworks

To investigate how mass communication theory must adapt to more fully describe and predict crisis communication flow in a changing media landscape, a perhaps obvious place to begin is with the audience. Audience and stakeholder theories and frameworks center on how individuals, publics, stakeholders, and audiences seek, share, and create crisis communication. Theoretical perspectives in this grouping include (a) uses and gratifications theory (UGT) and channel complementarity theory, (b) media dependency theory, and (c) spiral of silence theory.

Uses and Gratifications Theory (UGT) and Channel Complementarity

One such theory that focuses on media users' motivations is UGT. UGT explains how and why audience members and stakeholders seek out specific information based on the satisfaction of specific needs. Users pursue particular types of information based on their known needs, such as the need for information, relaxation, social interaction, diversion, or escape (Blumler & Katz, 1974). UGT represents one of the first shifts away from thinking about audiences as passive consumers of media but, instead, as active seekers of information (Ruggiero, 2000), shifting away from traditional media effects studies and toward thinking about individual users and their needs and preferences. As research on UGT suggests, individuals may use media forms that meet a larger number of combined needs, including information seeking, socialization, and emotional support (Urista, Qingwen, & Day, 2009).

As Lev-On (2012) noted, "the study of media uses and gratifications is particularly important in emergency and crisis situations, which magnify needs and make them more acute" (p. 101). Particularly in crises, emotional needs are high, such as needs for support and emotional outlets (Perse et al., 2002). For example, studying the response to Hurricane Katrina, Macias, Hilyard, and Freimuth (2009) found blogs fulfilled the following key functions: communicating with others, political, information, and helping. After September 11, Dutta-Bergman (2006) found online participation provided support for publics and helped to build community, a finding supported by Lev-On (2010, 2012) in a study of evacuees of Gush Katif, Israel.

Scholars have called for reexamination of UGT in light of advancements in computer-mediated communication (Ruggiero, 2000). Addressing the changing media climate and answering this call, Dutta-Bergman (2004, 2006) proposed channel complementarity theory. Drawing from selective exposure research and UGT, this theory suggests that audiences select certain media types based on personally relevant functions. It further asserts that audiences select multiple forms of media, complementary to the forms they already use to fulfill functional needs (Dutta-Bergman, 2004, 2006), explaining congruence between traditional and social media use. Users select media forms that are readily available and tend to reinforce existing beliefs.

Channel complementarity theory has been explored in the context of social media and crises and offers some explanation for why audiences prefer certain forms of communication. Liu, Jin, and Austin (2013) found that forms of interpersonal communication both online and offline (e.g., Facebook and word-of-mouth communication) were most used during crises compared to traditional media forms and sources. Audiences sought channels of information based on the perceived functions these channels served. Additionally, Austin, Liu, and Jin (2012) suggested channel complementarity might be influenced further by the channel and source of information by which audiences first learn about a crisis, in turn affecting further crisis information seeking from congruent channels and sources. In crises, audiences use various media forms together for different purposes, and use of certain media may reinforce use of other media. Accordingly, Lev-On (2012, p. 98) mentioned the need to understand UGT from a perspective of mass media and "small media" (i.e., media with a local or limited reach) combined.

Media Dependency Theory

Similar to uses and gratifications theory, media dependency theory posits that the media fulfill audiences' psychological needs, including surveillance needs, through media information-seeking behavior (Ball-Rokeach, 1985; Ball-Rokeach & DeFleur, 1976). However, media dependency theory goes a step further, positing that media can reinforce or change audience members' attitudes and behaviors and that media are interdependent with social and political systems (Ball-Rokeach, 1985). Research has repeatedly confirmed that media dependencies occur when people face high-threat, ambiguous situations such as crises (e.g., Hirschburg, Dillman, & Ball-Rokeach, 1986; Lin & Lagoe, 2013; Lowrey, 2004; Tai & Sun, 2007). For example, Lin and Lagoe (2013) found media dependency predicted audiences' perceptions of their personal risk of contracting H1N1 during the 2009 H1N1 pandemic. Also, after the September 11 terrorist attacks, media dependency predicted donations to charities supporting victims and expressing patriotism (Lowrey, 2004).

Researchers have begun to investigate how type or form of media dependencies might impact audiences differently during crises. On one hand, multiple studies have pointed to the Internet as playing a strong role in media dependency during crises, particularly when information is not readily available in mainstream media and audiences have Internet access (e.g., Lin & Lagoe, 2013; Lowrey, 2004; Tai & Sun, 2007). Yet, other research found TV media dependency predicted behavioral intentions, such as to obtain an emergency vaccination, but Internet (and newspaper) news dependency did not (Lin & Lagoe, 2013).

Scholars have called for more research on crisis media dependency in light of social media (Lin & Lagoe, 2013), which have the potential to lower people's dependencies on traditional media. Yet, this call has been unanswered by media dependency theorists, demonstrating the need for additional research on the impact of crisis information form, as proposed by the SMCC model and networked crisis communication (NCC) model (e.g., Austin et al., 2012; Jin, Liu, & Austin, 2014; Schultz, Utz, & Göritz, 2011; Utz, Schultz, & Glocka, 2013), elaborated here in later sections.

Furthermore, media dependency theorists have called for research that considers audiences' individual differences in media dependencies, such as gender (Lachlan, Spence, & Nelson, 2010), which researchers have started to investigate (Lachlan et al., 2010). Finally, media dependency researchers have not tested the impact of crisis information source (e.g., government, organization in crisis, citizen journalist), despite the fact that a growing body of research on social media and crisis communication confirms that source affects how audiences consume and respond to crisis information (e.g., Jin et al., 2014; Liu, Fraustino, & Jin, 2015), as expanded upon later under source influence-based frameworks.

Spiral of Silence Theory

Research applying the spiral of silence theory has lent insight into the changing climate of communication. Spiral of silence theory describes the process of how opinions and voices of those perceived as the majority become dominant over the opinions and voices of those perceived as the minority, as the minority fears the threat of social isolation. Noelle-Neumann (1984, 1991) introduced the spiral of silence theory more than 40 years ago in a drastically different media climate;

however, recent studies have shown that social media communication has not broken the spiral of silence, counter to assumptions that social media may bring forth more minority voices (Hampton et al., 2014; S. Kim, H. Kim, & Oh, 2014).

Researchers have proposed that anonymous forms of online communication could affect the opinion climate in ways that other forms cannot, and a few studies provide support for this notion (Ho & McLeod, 2008; Liu & Fahmy, 2011). These studies found that fear of isolation was more prevalent in face-to-face versus anonymous online communication, the latter of which allows posters to be more candid about their minority viewpoints. However, even for anonymous online message posting, studies have shown that participants are still more likely to post online messages when expressing a majority rather than a minority viewpoint (Yun & Park, 2011). Although anonymous posting may be somewhat more freeing than in-person, face-to-face communication, posters nonetheless face unpleasant outcomes—such as personal attacks and online flaming—from other users when sharing an unpopular viewpoint, discouraging expression of minority viewpoints (Yun & Park, 2011). Further, for social media sites including Facebook and Twitter, which are not anonymous, researchers found users were even less likely to share minority opinions than they were in face-to-face communication (Hampton et al., 2014). Individuals' willingness to share their opinions was influenced by their level of knowledge, the intensity of their opinions, and their involvement with the topic.

These few studies have given some insight into effects of the changing media climate on expression of opinions; however, findings remain somewhat inconsistent and more research is needed as to how social media and other forms of online communication further reproduce the spiral of silence, particularly in times of crisis communication, where scholarship is largely lacking (e.g., Shaia & Gonzenbach, 2007). As Neuwirth (2010) contended, pressures to conform to dominant opinions may be stronger during major crises or for highly contentious issues.

Form or Medium Influence-Based Theories and Frameworks

When examining how existing theory must be refined or adapted, or new theory generated, to account for crisis communication in today's multifaceted media environment, discussion of the effects and influences of media form (cf. medium or channel) is markedly warranted. In that vein, this conceptual grouping examines established and newer theoretical perspectives from (a) media richness theory (MRT), (b) the limited capacity model for motivated mediated message processing (LC4MP), and (3) the NCC model.

Media Richness Theory (MRT)

According to MRT, originally deriving from organizational and business communication, *media richness* refers to a communication form's ability to create shared meaning (Daft & Lengel, 1986). When communicating about uncertainty or ambiguity, shared meaning is best achieved through communication via forms that are considered highly rich. The richer the form, the more opportunity for visual and social cues like gestures, such as through videos or pictures, posited to reduce message-related ambiguity, equivocality, and uncertainty. Word-of-mouth (WOM) communication through face-to-face interaction, thus, may be considered highly rich, whereas communication through static documents is deemed quite lean (D'Urso & Rains, 2008). MRT has not to date been empirically tested in crisis or disaster communication. However, crisis communication scholars have asserted that it follows from this theory that rich forms of crisis information could reduce receivers' uncertainty and speed up their information-seeking actions— and thus lead to quicker (potentially lifesaving) behavioral responses to the crisis (Liu, Fraustino, & Jin, 2015).

That is, through a process that disaster sociologists refer to as milling, publics who are at risk for or are experiencing a negative event engage in heightened efforts to seek information to confirm or disconfirm initial news and reduce uncertainty (Mileti & Sorensen, 1990). While milling, publics often share with others the information they find (Liu, Fraustino, & Jin, 2016). Scholars have asserted that social and mobile media contribute to rapid information seeking and sharing— such as seen in milling—before, during, and after crises, but particularly during the crisis event. Yet, it could also be the case that the milling process is drawn out when audiences seek and share information via social media, as messages within these outlets are often brief and incomplete. Liu and colleagues (2016) posited that such message brevity might be understood through the lens of MRT, a contention deserving of additional research.

Indeed, considering milling in conjunction with media richness complicates any idea of a simple flow of information from a source to a receiver who then has a response. Instead, during crises' inherent uncertainty, those who seek or receive information from forms they find insufficiently rich may continue milling, perhaps attempting to find satisfying information from richer forms before settling on response(s) to the information. These ideas may be able to help inform effects of crisis information form on receivers' likelihood to seek and share additional information from a variety of places, questions that are examined by, for instance, the SMCC model, as discussed here in a later section, and channel complementarity as reviewed previously.

Limited Capacity Model for Motivated Mediated Message Processing (LC4MP)

Perhaps particularly relevant to the new and social media popularity of platforms based on audio and visual communication (e.g., Pinterest, Flickr, Instagram, Snapchat, Periscope, YouTube) is LC4MP. Founded in cognitive psychology, LC4MP researchers have produced a robust record explaining and predicting message receivers' restricted capacities to cognitively process mediated messages (e.g., Lang, 2000, 2006; Lang, Bolls, Potter, & Kawahara, 1999; Lang, Bradley, Park, Shin, & Chung, 2006). The LC4MP framework is based on ideas about how people actively process information; that is, they "perceive stimuli, turn them into mental representations, do mental work on those representations, and reproduce them in the same or in an altered form" (Lang, 2000, p. 47). And further, people do not have infinite resources for that processing (i.e., they have a "limited capacity"). Media consumers enact three iterative cognitive subprocesses during consumption—encoding, storage, and retrieval—with two related mechanisms: orienting behavior and resource allocation. Simply put, what people leave with after message exposure is based on how much they initially encode, how well they store the encoded information, and then how much of the encoded and stored information they can ultimately retrieve. These processes may vary as a function of orienting to the message, as well as ability or desire to allocate resources to it.

Research in and outside of health or emergency contexts has uncovered orienting-inducing message features. For example, viewers may orient to structural components of television, such as the cuts and movements of commercials or news broadcasts (e.g., Lang et al., 1999). Listeners may also orient to structural features of audio (e.g., Lang et al., 2006). And media audiences can orient to messages on the basis of content as well, particularly negative emotional content in video images (e.g., Lang, Newhagen, & Reeves, 1996; Lang et al., 1999). However, particularly relevant for crisis communication, increased structural features (which alone are generally automatically processed and relatively unlikely to contribute to cognitive overload) along with increased arousing content can indeed contribute to cognitive overload (Lang et al., 1999). Overload decreases encoding, storage, and retrieval capabilities—and thus message recall.

In a setting such as a crisis, the level of arousal produced by a related message is likely strong, and visual or audio depictions of a crisis event may maintain or increase that arousal. Thus higher levels of certain visual or audio orienting cues in crisis communication could decrease message recall (and, in turn, accurate protective-action taking) in ways that the same types of visual or audio cues would not in a neutral or positive context. Yet to be studied from a strategic mass crisis communication approach, this idea has both theoretical and practical implications for videos, B-roll, podcasts, and radio spots intended to reach audiences with crisis information, particularly via visual- and audio-based media platforms.

Networked Crisis Communication (NCC) Model

A newer theoretical examination of form- or medium-influence hailing from crisis communication literature is the NCC model, a framework to incorporate new media into a structure to explain and predict mediated crisis information outcomes. With perhaps McLuhan-esque underpinnings (i.e., the medium is the message), Utz and colleagues' (2013) NCC model "challenges classical crisis communication theories by showing that the medium used affects the impact of crisis communication" (p. 41). Moving away from one-way traditional-media approaches, the model attempts to illuminate a many-to-many model of crisis communication that social media may afford.

The handful of studies to date developing the NCC model have predominately examined effects of various crisis communication strategies via different media on organizational reputation and certain stakeholder behavioral outcomes that could harm the organization (e.g., Schultz, Utz, & Göritz, 2011; Utz et al., 2013). NCC research investigates effects of media type on crisis message effectiveness, looking at both communicative behavioral intentions (e.g., information sharing) and noncommunicative behavioral intentions (e.g., boycotting and product or service purchase intent). Yet, like much of the crisis communication literature, the young scholarship in this area has focused on how organizations use media to mitigate potential negative outcomes (e.g., boycotts and negative WOM communication) rather than prosocial outcomes such as taking recommended protective actions (e.g., evacuate or check on family and friends' safety; Liu & Fraustino, 2014). This functionalist organizational perspective renders the model able to provide fewer implications for broad mass communication theory than can other perspectives reviewed herein, such as the SMCC model discussed in the next grouping.

Source Influence-Based Theories and Frameworks

Researchers have recommended more investigation into sources of information, in addition to forms or channels (Rains & Ruppel, 2016; Ruppel & Rains, 2012). McQuail (2000) advocated for the need to develop new theory for new media. According to McQuail's categorization of "new media"—interpersonal communication media, interactive play media, information search media, and collective participatory media—social media seem to encompass features of all four. Related to influence of sources on news, "media of all kinds depend on having a readily available supply of source material . . . Relations with news sources are essential to news media and they often constitute a very active two-way process" (McQuail, 2000, p. 287). McQuail further pointed out that "trust in and respect for the source can be conductive to influence," research on which has primarily focused on "relationships between sender (or message sent) and receiver" (p. 432). Therefore, the grouping of perspectives addressing crisis information sources in an evolving mediascape include (a) two-step flow of communication model, (b) cocreational framework and dialogic communication theory (DCT), and (c) social amplification of risk (SARF).

Two-Step Flow of Communication and Credibility

The two-step flow of communication and opinion leadership is a theoretical tradition in media effects (Jeffres, Neuendorf, Braken, & Atkin, 2008). This strain of scholarship studies opinion leaders, who have a higher tendency and likelihood to obtain information from the media and then pass it to others through interpersonal channels (e.g., Yang & Stone, 2003). Given that the two-step flow model highlights the role individuals play in mediating information flow between mass media and the public (Yang & Stone, 2003), to further understand how opinion leadership exerts influence in online and social media contexts credibility of source and channels needs fuller examination. Kelleher (2009) argued for the importance of investigating how interactive media and online communication are related to different relational outcomes, including trust, satisfaction, commitment, and control mutuality. In differentiating two types of interactivity, Kelleher (2009) pointed out that the concept of functional interactivity focuses on the features of media, whereas the concept of contingency interactivity focuses on a process in which the interchange of media, messages, and users make interactivity more fully occur.

Related to trust, Kiousis (2001) explicated the concept of source credibility, one key factor of opinion leadership in the two-step flow process in interpersonal, organizational, and mass-mediated contexts. Medium (cf. channel, form) credibility, on the other hand, is a concept centered on both the source of the message and the medium transmitting the message (Thorson & Moore, 1996). Kiousis (2001) argued that researchers must examine perceived credibility as "primarily a function of both source and channel characteristics" (p. 388).

To further understanding of source credibility in the context of influential social media and its role in a social-mediated two-step flow process, Jin and Liu (2010) posited that the effectiveness of online WOM lies in the opinion leader's lack of material interest, genuine care for others' well-being, and their knowledge and experience. For instance, when bloggers' perceived trustworthiness is high, their argument quality has a greater impact on brand attitudes than when their perceived trustworthiness is low (Chu & Kamal, 2008). For publics not exposed to influential external blogs, unless the organization discloses the crisis information directly to the public through other venues, traditional mass media tend to be the main source of information (e.g., Littlefield & Quenette, 2007; Seeger, Sellnow, & Ulmer, 2003). Although message source and form credibility have been studied extensively in mass communication and somewhat broadly in crisis communication, the role social media play in crisis communication source and form credibility, along with their relationships with traditional media and offline communication channels, remain open territory to be explored.

Cocreational Framework and Dialogic Communication Theory (DCT)

Another perspective that may complicate notions of source and influence considerations in crisis communication (especially digital or online efforts) is related to the cocreational framework and DCT. Botan and Taylor (2004) observed two main research themes in public relations research: a functional perspective and a cocreational perspective. Whereas a functional perspective views publics and communication as ways to achieve organizational goals, a cocreational perspective "sees publics as cocreators of meaning and communication as what makes it possible to agree to shared meanings, interpretations, and goals" (p. 652).

One example of a theory reflecting a cocreational perspective relevant to mediated crisis communication is DCT. Kent and Taylor (2002) proposed that dialogue, an end in itself rather than a means to an end, is essential to an ethical, two-way organization-public relationship open to creation of shared meaning. These scholars asserted that dialogic features include mutuality, propinquity, empathy, risk, and commitment. Applying principles of dialogue can guide creation of a dialogic loop via online or digital organizational communication efforts (Kent & Taylor, 1998).

In suggesting future directions in social media for public relations professionals and scholars, Kent (2010) argued for recognizing the power of relationships for fostering trust and loyalty and the importance of incorporating dialogue in relationship building via social media, especially given the capability of social media to provide access to dialogue for individuals. Therefore, effective organization-public communication on social media needs to have the capacity for practitioners to communicate with individuals as valued and trusted companions. Merritt, Lawson, Mackey, and Waters (2012) further echoed that dialogue is a relational process and product rather than a series of steps, and building authentic relationships online and in social media requires following dialogic principles. Kent (2013) then proposed that to use social media for relationship building, organizations need to (a) develop media spaces that allow organizational members to communicate with individuals, (b) allow organizational members and publics to freely interact and collaborate, (c) make the identity of participants public and verifiable, (d) provide clear rules for social media participation, (e) seek out and invite experts to participate, and (f) nurture and encourage divergent voices to participate.

Although the cocreational framework has been adopted in strategic communication research and DCT has been studied and tested in organization-stakeholder relationship studies, the main focus has been on how practitioners interact and connect with publics via different media forms according to DCT principles. Neither the cocreational perspective nor DCT has been tested in crisis communication research. Questions remain in terms of (a) to what degree crisis communicators should follow DCT principles to engage publics, given the risk of escalating a conflict by overengaging with emotionally charged publics on sensitive topics with legal and regulatory confinements, and (b) whether and how an organization and its publics can work together during crises to genuinely cocreate effective and ethical crisis information, particularly via media that allow real-time conversation listening and exchanges.

The Social Amplification of Risk Framework (SARF)

Adding to understanding of how individual, organizational, and other social sources impact information flow, particularly across a multilayered media environment, is SARF. SARF focuses on the processes that underlie how a risk event generates an assessment of the risk, which is then amplified or attenuated through engagement with psychological, social, institutional, and cultural processes (Kasperson et al., 1988). A five-stage model unravels what happens after the risk event has occurred. Namely, sources of amplification use channels of amplification, which transmit signals that are decoded by social or individual stations of amplification, resulting in behavioral responses to the risk, which can lead to ripple effects at various levels of the social ecosystem.

SARF has been applied as a framework for risk-communication researchers to study the heightening or softening of risk perception related to a range of environmental (e.g., Bakir, 2005) and health crises (Lewis & Tyshenko, 2009). For example, in analyzing how different "amplification" stations (e.g., newspapers, scientists) use metaphors, statistics, and other devices to elicit expectations and actions related to the impending avian influenza, Nerlich and Halliday (2007) observed "the process of amplification occurs when the situation of use (in this case the newspaper articles using information gleaned from scientific journals and interviews with experts) is exploited intentionally in order to enrich the interpretation of utterances" (p. 55).

The linear conceptualization of the risk amplification process has been noted by researchers (e.g., Bakir, 2005) as one of the shortcomings of SARF. Although Kasperson and colleagues' (1988) original model had accounted for this potential critique by pointing out the dynamism of the risk amplification process, this criticism has remained. From a mass communication perspective, the linearity of SARF and its proposed communication effects on risk perceptions and behavioral outcomes imply organization-centric, top-down risk-communication practices prevalent at the time when the model was conceptualized. However, social media technologies provide the ability to more objectively document, not only communication events (e.g., Twitter feeds), but also an analysis of these events using scientific methods (e.g., sentiment analysis) and track their transmission through digital networks. In the case of communication about an infectious disease outbreak, the use of social media–based "infoveillance" techniques (Chew & Eysenbach, 2010, p. 1) might allow researchers to generate more objective measures of risk perception and situate these communication measures against clinical levels of an outbreak's risk to the population.

The nature and ever-expanding capacity of social media have allowed various risk information sources and publics to interact via content cocreation, sharing, and influence exertion on traditional media online and offline. The integration of the amplification of risk perception based on SARF and the emphasis on multiple sources, media, and communication channels, such as channel complimentary theory discussed earlier, could help refine crisis communication theory building.

Content Influence-Based Theories and Frameworks

With audience-based perspectives considered and the influences of source and form discussed, an important category to round out understanding of crisis communication flow is an examination of scholarship related to crisis message content. Theories of key relevance to this category are (a) framing theory and (b) situational crisis communication theory (SCCT), including evolving research focused particularly on crisis-related emotions.

Framing Theory

Framing research hails from psychology and sociology but has been adapted and applied by communication and media scholars for nearly half a century. Many perspectives at several levels of analysis exist, yet perhaps the most commonly cited definition explains, "To frame is to select some aspects of a perceived reality and make them more salient in a communicating text, in such a way as to promote a particular problem definition, causal interpretation, moral evaluation, and/or treatment recommendation" (Entman, 1993, p. 52).

That is, frames generally can be thought of as techniques that media content creators and influencers use to characterize an issue and its context through selected packaging of information, symbols, metaphors, and visuals (Gamson & Modigliani, 1989; Hallahan, 1999). Through this suggested interpretation or meaning (intentional or not) via packaging of written, spoken, and visual information, framing can have powerful implications for audiences' acquisition of beliefs, attitudes, and impressions about an issue (Iyengar, 1993; Kahneman & Tversky, 1979; Pan & Kosicki, 1993). Thus, framing theory points to the idea that mass media content not only ascribes saliency but also plays a role in constructing meaning for content consumers. Although framing theory has been examined extensively in political and journalistic contexts, especially for civic and economic issues, it has been explored with less breadth and depth in crisis communication. In light of the host of potentially detrimental outcomes for organizations, communities, and individuals inherent in crisis situations, the construction of meaning based on the presentation of crisis information becomes apparent.

In existing crisis-related framing research, crisis news coverage has been found to exhibit various crisis-relevant frames—such as attribution of responsibility, conflict, and morality, among others—along with varying levels of responsibility (i.e., individual level or organizational level), all of which may vary based on crisis type (An & Gower, 2009). Research has shown that crisis message framing in the form of response strategies from organizations can impact audience perceptions of the crisis, especially related to organizational reputation, blame, and secondary crisis communication, such as negative WOM and boycotting (e.g., Claeys & Cauberghe, 2012; Coombs, 2015). Only recently have such findings begun to be tested in the digital and social media realm, often focusing on an organizational strategy perspective (e.g., DiStaso, Vafeiadis, & Amaral, 2015). Potentially fruitful territories for crisis scholarship include: (1) expanding research to delve into crisis message framing in the online environment—especially looking at established mass media framing sets such as gain versus loss (Kahneman & Tversky, 1979) and episodic versus thematic (Iyengar, 1993), and (2) widening operationalizations of frames beyond organizational strategies to mitigate their reputational and financial harm (cf. Freberg, 2012).

Situational Crisis Communication Theory (SCCT)

With partial roots in framing research, Coombs's (2015) SCCT, one of the most prominent crisis communication theories, focuses on the content of organizations' crisis responses in combination with audiences' perceived crisis responsibility and level of reputational threat involved. SCCT posits that organizational crisis responses and messages should be matched to publics' perceptions in crisis situations by surveying attribution of crisis responsibility and assessment of crisis types.

SCCT first advises that organizations prioritize protecting impacted publics from harm through providing two types of message content: instructing information and adjusting information (Coombs, 2015). *Instructing information* informs publics about how to protect themselves from physical threats, whereas *adjusting information* helps publics cope with resulting psychological threats (Coombs, 2015). Adjusting information may also provide publics with emotional support.

After providing necessary instructing and adjusting information to impacted publics, organizations then select from four response postures for reputation management—deny, diminish, rebuild, or reinforce—with various content strategies within each option (Coombs, 2007a, 2007b, 2010; Heath & Coombs, 2006). Crisis-response strategies for reputation management can range on a continuum from defensive to accommodative strategies (Jin, 2010).

Defensive strategies separate the blame for the crisis from the organization and often include a combination of attacking the accuser, denial, scapegoating, ignoring, excusing, justifying, and separating. Conversely, accommodative strategies emphasize image repair, which is needed as image damage increases, and include bolstering, ingratiation, victimage, endorsement, compensation, transcendence, and full apology (for a full description of these response options, see Coombs, 2015; Jin & Liu, 2010). SCCT and related research (Coombs, 2007a, 2010, 2015; Jin, Pang, & Cameron, 2012; Jin & Liu, 2010; Jin et al., 2014) provide suggestions for when and how organizations should respond based upon attribution of responsibility. Factors that influence publics' crisis responsibility attribution include crisis type, crisis history, and prior relationship. SCCT has been widely applied in understanding SMCC research and practice among public relations scholars (e.g., Austin & Jin, in press; Coombs, 2007a, 2007b; Jin & Liu, 2010).

Crisis Emotions and SCCT

Coombs (2015) highlighted the importance of studying emotions in crisis communication research, as crises create high-stakes situations where organizations need to consider their publics' emotional well-being prior to addressing financial losses and mitigating blame. Scholars have recognized the need to address emotions in crisis decision making (Coombs & Holladay, 2005; Pfau & Wan, 2006; Turner, 2006; Wang, 2006).

Grounded in SCCT and crisis communication frameworks, crisis researchers (e.g., Choi & Lin, 2009; Jin, Liu, & Austin, 2014; Jin, Pang, & Cameron, 2007, 2012) advocated that developing effective crisis responses lies in a deeper understanding of human emotions and how they are integrated with cognitive processes and crisis responsibility attribution. Specific emotions have been tied to undesirable crisis outcomes. For instance, anger has been found to predict reduced purchase intentions and negative WOM communication (Coombs, 2006, 2007b). Fear leads to negative WOM communication for crises that have internal causes (McDonald, Sparks, & Glendon, 2010). Grounded in Lazarus's (1991) cognitive appraisal theory, Jin and colleagues (2007, 2012) examined four primary crisis emotions (i.e., anger, sadness, fright, and anxiety) in their integrated crisis mapping (ICM) model.

To understand the relationship between attributions and emotions, Choi and Lin (2009) proposed two types of emotions, attribution-independent emotions and attribution-dependent emotions, as outcomes of how publics attribute crisis responsibility. Choi and Lin (2009) suggested crisis emotions, such as anger and contempt, are likely to be elicited from the attribution process, whereas other types of emotions (such as fear) without clear direction of attribution or blame may be categorized as attribution-independent crisis emotions. For attribution-dependent emotions, anger has been studied extensively in crisis communication (e.g., Coombs & Holladay, 2005; Jin, 2014). For instance, more anger was reported as perceptions of crisis responsibility increased (Coombs & Holladay, 2005). For attribution-independent emotions such as fear, Jin (2009) found that low perceived crisis controllability and high uncertainty contributed to more fear. Jin (2009, 2010) also suggested that publics tended to feel more anxiety, another type of attribution-independent emotion, when they perceived the crisis situation as uncertain yet somewhat controllable.

Choi and Lin (2009) further suggested the need for research about whether crisis emotions may change according to different types of crises, depending on the locus of control (internal or external) and attribution of crisis responsibility. To echo this, Jin and colleagues (2014) selected nine negative emotions based on crisis emotions literature (e.g., Choi & Lin, 2009; Jin, 2009, 2010) to investigate the likelihood of feeling each of the selected emotions in different organizational crisis situations. Three clusters of crisis emotions were rendered: (a) attribution-independent (AI) emotions, consisting of anxiety, apprehension, and fear;

(b) external attribution-dependent (EAD) emotions, consisting of disgust, contempt, and anger; and (c) internal attribution-dependent (IAD) emotions, consisting of embarrassment, guilt, and shame. Whereas the first two clusters of crisis emotions were in accordance with Choi and Lin's (2009) argument of grouping crisis emotions as attribution-dependent and independent ones, emotions in the third cluster indicated an additional attribution process—how individuals felt about themselves as publics associated with a given organization after learning about the crisis situation.

Based on the crisis attribution theoretical framework, Jin, Liu, Anagondahalli, and Austin (2014) developed a multiple-item scale for measuring publics' crisis emotions, examining the conceptualization and operationalization of attribution-independent crisis emotions versus attribution-dependent crisis emotions: (a) attribution-independent (AI) crisis emotions; (b) external attribution-dependent (EAD) crisis emotions; and (c) internal attribution-dependent (IAD) crisis emotions. This recent study and scale enriched the study of crisis emotions in SCCT research by providing a valid and reliable psychometric tool for researchers and crisis managers to measure publics' different emotions that are relevant to a crisis situation, as a result of the appraisal of crisis attribution.

Social-Mediated Crisis Communication (SMCC) Model

Finally, and perhaps the most comprehensive approach to crisis communication theorizing in a multisource, multimedia environment, is the SMCC model. SMCC is an emerging framework describing the current landscape and environment for crisis communication and is one of the first theoretical frameworks to explain the relationship between an organization, key publics, social media, traditional media, and offline WOM communication before, during, and after crises. It provides a framework for understanding crisis communication among organizations, news media, and online and offline publics (Liu, Jin, Austin, & Janoske, 2012; Liu, Jin, Briones, & Kuch, 2012). The conceptual model sheds light on interrelationships among social media, traditional media, and WOM communication, explaining and, in some instances, predicting crisis communication flow across organizations, news media, and publics. Given continual leaps in Internet, digital media, and social media consumption among American adults of all ages (Duggan & Smith, 2013); scholars' appeals for stronger theory development in crisis research (e.g., An & Cheng, 2010; Liu & Fraustino, 2014); and fears about traditional mass media theory being, at least partially, inadequate to account for today's increasingly decentralized media landscape (Chaffee & Metzger, 2001), the burgeoning SMCC model is particularly suited to inform future mass communication research. In fact, in development of the initial blog-mediated crisis communication (BMCC) model, later renamed SMCC upon incorporation of new media forms and sources, mass communication theories played essential roles in conceptualizing relevant constructs and paths, such as WOM communication, opinion leadership, and agenda setting (e.g., Jin et al., 2014; Jin & Liu, 2010; Liu, Jin, & Austin, 2012; Liu, Jin, Austin, & Janoske, 2012).

The SMCC model consists of two parts or stages (Liu, Jin, Austin, et al., 2012). The first shows ways publics seek and distribute crisis information based on a variety of factors. The second gives guidance on how the organization experiencing a crisis can use knowledge from the first part to effectively respond to publics. More specifically, the model's first part asserts that three key publics communicate crisis information: (a) *influential social media content creators*, who communicate about the crisis via social media; (b) *social media followers*, who communicate about the crisis by posting *creators'* crisis information online and otherwise communicating the content to others both on- and offline; and (c) *social media inactives*, who communicate about the crisis by garnering information from traditional media and conveying it via WOM with both the social media content creators and followers, who may in turn communicate this content online and offline. These three publics may seek or share crisis information with similar individuals, other publics, organizations, and news media outlets. Research on the model has also given suggestions for identifying and measuring online influencers as part of regular environmental scanning for potential issues before, during, and after crises (Jin & Liu, 2010; Liu, Jin, & Austin, 2012; Liu, Jin, Austin, & Janoske, 2012).

The model's second part adapts SCCT (e.g., Coombs, 2015), rumor psychology (e.g., DiFonzo, 2007), and best practices in crisis and risk communication to provide organizations with suggestions for communicating with publics during social-mediated crises. It offers organizations recommended message strategies for crisis response via social media, traditional media, and WOM communication. Such responses frame messages with varying levels of accommodation based on publics' levels of blame attributed to the organization, along with their negative crisis-related emotions, existing relationship with the organization, and perceptions of whether the organization has a similar crisis history (for more on the model's second part, see Austin et al., 2012; Jin & Liu, 2010; Liu, Jin, Austin, et al., 2012).

Despite the SMCC model's infancy, work has posited, tested, and extended several of these relevant constructs. Examinations of SMCC constructs thus far have focused on how information form (i.e., channel or medium), source, message characteristics, and context impact a variety of cognitive, affective, and intended communicative or behavioral responses (Austin et al., 2012; Jin & Liu, 2010; Jin et al., 2014; Liu, Austin, & Jin, 2011; Liu et al., 2015; Liu et al., 2013). SMCC studies have been theoretical (e.g., Liu et al., 2012) and empirical, with the latter dominantly using quantitative experiments (e.g., Liu et al., 2015) and qualitative interviews (e.g., Liu, Jin, Briones, et al., 2012). As Liu, Jin, Austin, and Janoske (2012) summarized, early in the model's development, research pointed to five areas posited to impact the flow of information among organizations, media outlets, and publics: (a) *crisis origin* (i.e., who or what caused the crisis; internal vs. external), (b) *crisis type* (i.e., how the crisis took form and the related extent of perceived organizational blameworthiness), (c) *organizational infrastructure* (i.e., the extent to which organization-wide response is warranted; centralized vs. localized), (d) *crisis message strategy* (i.e., crisis communication content), and (e) *crisis message form* (i.e., the communication channel used to distribute the message: social media, traditional media, or WOM; p. 261). Scholarship has begun to flesh out and provide empirical evidence for this list.

Collectively, this body of work has looked at crisis information flow in the context of for-profit organizations, nonprofit organizations, and government and has investigated how crisis information form, information source, crisis type, and past experiences with a similar crisis may impact outcomes such as reported involvement in the situation, perceived information credibility, perceived information complexity, likelihood to seek and share more information, attributions of crisis responsibility, a host of discrete crisis-related emotions, and intentions to take a variety of protective actions (e.g., Austin et al., 2012; Jin et al., 2014; Liu et al., 2011; Liu et al., 2015, 2016; Liu et al., 2013). Findings have revealed that no particular form or source consistently outperforms others in terms of generating positive responses for the organization, individual, or community. Yet, nuanced significant differences among several subsets of variables have emerged, pointing to the importance of incorporating a richer understanding of the multiple communication possibilities and realities of the modern media landscape.

Discussion and Conclusions

The aforementioned is a synthesis and critique of a current tool kit available to crisis communication scholars interested in advancing theory to account for changing media realities. Several research gaps and opportunities emerged. Our related recommendations and areas for future research directions follow.

Shift From an Organizational to Cocreational Focus

Currently crisis communication theory focuses on how organizations communicate about crises (Liu & Fraustino, 2014), which is also true for theories that have attempted to reflect or predict effective crisis communication in the changing media landscape (e.g., the NCC and SMCC models). Audience and stakeholder perspectives reviewed here could provide fresh viewpoints on how voices outside of organizations shape and form crisis information before, during, and after crises—ultimately guiding how organizations and others respond. Indeed, research on theories such as UGT, spiral of silence, media dependency, and rumor psychology have for decades examined how active audiences and stakeholders engage with media. Little research exists testing and extending these theories during crises, when audiences are especially active information creators, seekers, and sharers (Liu et al., 2012). Furthermore, much of the theory-driven research that attempts to capture active audiences and stakeholders, such as in DCT and the SMCC model, still focuses on organizational messaging.

As such, much more research is needed to describe and predict crisis communication thoughts, emotions, and behaviors independent of organizations. Research questions could include (a) what motivates individuals to become especially active social media content creators and sharers?; (b) what factors predict when individuals will become active versus passive social media users and why?; and (c) what crisis communication strategies are especially effective for individuals influencing other individuals to prepare for, respond to, or recover from crises?

Furthermore, research needs to build theory on audience and stakeholder crisis communication independent of a specific event. Here, SARF could provide a starting point given the dearth of research on this topic. To date, research has not captured or theorized the role of social media in preparing the public for crises in the absence of a specific, imminent threat. Research questions could include (a) what factors motivate individuals to prepare for crises?; (b) what communicative strategies are most effective in motivating individuals to prepare for crises?; and (c) what role can and do social media play in motivating individuals to prepare for crises?

Message and Source Credibility

Message and source credibility have been studied minimally in crisis communication, mostly through the SMCC model (e.g., Jin et al., 2014). Research suggests that when credibility and trustworthiness of bloggers is perceived as high, their argument quality has a greater impact on the reception of messages by their audiences (Chu & Kamal, 2008). This finding has great implications for communicating messages during crises, if the same findings hold true in crisis settings. However, source and message credibility during crises have remained largely unexplored. Initial research from the SMCC model has begun to suggest that third-party information can aid in enhancing credibility of information on social media in times of crisis (Austin et al., 2012), although traditional media remain a more credible source of information during times of crisis than social media. This credibility can affect message processing, seeking of additional crisis information, and intentions to perform protective actions; as such, credibility will be an incredibly important factor for crisis managers to consider moving forward in crisis communication via social media.

More broadly, the roles digital and social media play in crisis communication, along with traditional media and offline communication channels, remain wide open for exploration. Research questions could include (a) how does news content related to social media crises affect individuals who are not online or active via social media?; (b) how do crisis information creators, including organizations, news media, and influential online sources, obtain their original information and further generate and disseminate information?; and (c) how do different sources and the relationships among them influence crisis information followers' and sharers' perceptions, attitudes, emotions, and behaviors toward the crisis and the organization(s) experiencing the crisis?

Expanded Social and Digital Media Focus

Finally, social and digital media research in crisis contexts tends to look at one or two media types and then generalize to all social and digital media (Austin & Jin, 2016). Perhaps even more problematic, scholars have not kept pace with newer media tools popular for crisis communication, particularly still and moving visual-based tools such as Instagram, Pinterest, Snapchat, and YouTube. Also, as stated previously, Lev-On (2012) mentions a need for understanding mass media versus small media (media with more local or limited reach), and social media might fall into multiple categories.

The mass communication theory reviewed here, particularly LC4MP and MRT, could enhance understanding of how crisis information visualization and presentation in itself affects message processing and subsequent behaviors. For instance, LC4MP research asserted media consumers may allocate cognitive processing in varying amounts dependent on message form and content, impacting message recall (e.g., Lang et al., 1999). It follows that if audiences receive messages formed in ways that prompt cognitive overload, they will be less likely to encode, store, and be able to retrieve important crisis protection–related information. As higher levels of visual or audio orienting cues might decrease message recall and protective actions in crises versus other positive or neutral contexts, paying careful attention to message forms and content in crises will be increasingly important for crisis managers and communicators.

Research could also explore how the crisis information form and its richness and orienting features interact with other factors found to influence crisis information flow, such as source, crisis type, and crisis severity (e.g., Jin et al., 2014; Schultz et al., 2012). Further, study of crises through the lens of the spiral of silence holds potential to explore how some online voices become dominant and influential and others do not. As Neuwirth (2010) suggested, future research on spiral of silence theory will be especially important in emotionally charged crises. Additionally, as spiral of silence research suggests that people are more likely to share minority opinions via anonymous online communication, more dissenting voices and unpopular opinions may emerge in crises that represent problems or opportunities for crisis managers (Yun & Park, 2011), although, pressure to conform to majority opinion is higher in times of major crisis (Neuwirth, 2010). This presents problems for organizations trying to repair their reputations after crises; if majority opinion about an organization is negative, audiences and stakeholders may be less likely to speak positively on social media on its behalf.

Thus, research questions in this realm might include (a) how can the concepts of social and digital media be explicated such that research on individual platforms may generalize to other platforms in the same category and be distinguished from other platform categories?; (b) where is the cognitive overload threshold for crisis visual cues and arousing crisis information content on social and digital media, and does the threshold vary as a function of platform or crisis type?; and (c) how do some social media users become influential crisis information sources, and what contributes to the lack of influence of other users?

Conclusion

In conclusion, this chapter suggests integration and, in some instances, adaptation of mass communication, organizational communication, strategic communication, risk communication, and social and cognitive psychology theories to augment understanding of crisis communication in a changing media climate. Doing so can enhance the scope and utility of crisis communication theory and research. Such work can build additional bridges between mass communication and crisis communication scholars. Specifically, areas of mass communication theory considered for inclusion in social media and crisis communication research include (a) audience and stakeholder theories and frameworks, (b) form or medium influence-based theories and frameworks, (c) source influence-based theories and frameworks, and (d) content influence-based theories and frameworks.

Although the emerging SMCC model described here begins to integrate these areas of focus, including audience and stakeholder perspectives, form and medium, source, and content, this review of theory highlights how inclusion of mass communication theory in these particular areas may aid understanding of gaps in current theory and research on social media and crisis communication. Particularly, this chapter recommends including aspects of the following mass communication theories. Within audience and stakeholder theories and frameworks considered are (a) UGT and channel complementarity theory, (b) media dependency theory, and (c) spiral of silence theory. Within form and medium influence-based theories and frameworks are (a) MRT, (b) LC4MP, and (c) NCC. Within source influence-based theories and frameworks are (a) the two-step flow of communication model, (b) the cocreational framework and DCT, and (c) SARF. Within content influence-based theories and frameworks are (a) framing theory and (b) SCCT.

Particularly, informed by these theories, shifting from a focus on organizations in times of crisis to a cocreational approach to communication will provide a fuller picture of crisis communication and response for crisis managers. Inclusion of research here on DCT, UGT, spiral of silence, and media dependency can help to understand factors affecting audiences' communication during crises, as well as how audiences and stakeholders can help to become cocreators of crisis messages via social media. Additionally, considering credibility of message sources (e.g., organizations, audiences themselves, third parties), as well as the perceived credibility of the message form (e.g., traditional media vs. social media), is important for future crisis communication research, as informed by the two-step flow of communication model and the SMCC model. Last, this chapter recommends an expanded social and digital media focus. Although most prior research has examined one or more forms of social media (e.g., Facebook, Twitter, Instagram,

Pinterest), understanding what factors may be universal across social media platforms can aid in crisis communication recommendations for social media as a broader category, as informed by MRT, LC4MP, and NCC. Additionally, distinguishing what factors are not universal, but are platform specific, will aid in strategic communication for different platforms during crises.

References

An, S.-K., & Cheng, I.-H. (2010). Crisis communication research in public relations journals: Tracking research trends over thirty years. In W. T. Coombs & S. Holladay (Eds.), *The handbook of crisis communication* (pp. 65–90). Malden, MA: Wiley-Blackwell.

An, S.-K., & Gower, K. K. (2009). How do the news media frame crises? A content analysis of crisis news coverage. *Public Relations Review, 35*(2), 107–112. doi: 10.1016/j.pubrev.2009.01.010

Austin, L., & Jin, Y. (2016). Social media and crisis communication: Explicating the social-mediated crisis communication model. In A. Dudo and L. A. Kahlor (Eds.), *Strategic communication: New agendas in communication* (pp. 163–186). New York: Routledge.

Austin, L., Liu, B. F., & Jin, Y. (2012). How audiences seek out crisis information: Exploring the social-mediated crisis communication model. *Journal of Applied Communication Research, 40*, 188–207. doi: 10.1080/00909882.2012.654498

Bakir, V. (2005). Greenpeace v. Shell: Media exploitation and the Social Amplification of Risk Framework (SARF). *Journal of Risk Research, 8*, 679–691. doi: 10.1080/13669870500166898

Ball-Rokeach, S. J. (1985). The origins of individual media-system dependency: A sociological framework. *Communication Research, 12*, 485–510. doi: 10.1177/009365085012004003

Ball-Rokeach, S. J. (1998). A theory of media power and a theory of media use: Different stories, questions, and ways of thinking. *Mass Communication and Society, 1*, 5–40. doi: 10.1080/15205436.1998.9676398

Ball-Rokeach, S. J., & DeFleur, M. L. (1976). A dependency model of mass media effects. *Communication Research, 3*, 3–21. doi: 10.1177/009365027600300101

Blumler, J. G., & Katz, E. (Eds.). (1974). *The uses of mass communication: Current perspectives on gratifications research.* Beverly Hills, CA: Sage.

Botan, C. H., & Taylor, M. (2004). Public relations: State of the field. *Journal of Communication, 54*, 645–661. doi: 10.1111/j.1460-2466.2004.tb02649.x

Chaffee, S. H., & Metzger, M. J. (2001). The end of mass communication? *Mass Communication & Society, 4*, 365–379. doi: 10.1207/S15327825MCS0404_3

Chew, C., & Eysenbach, G. (2010). Pandemics in the age of Twitter: Content analysis of tweets during the 2009 H1N1 outbreak. *PLoS ONE, 5*(11), e14118. doi: 10.1371/journal.pone.0014118

Choi, Y., & Lin, Y.-H. (2009). Consumer responses to Mattel product recalls posted on online bulletin boards: Exploring two types of emotion. *Journal of Public Relations Research, 21*, 198–207. doi: 10.1080/10627260802557506

Chu, S., & Kamal, S. (2008). The effects of perceived blogger credibility and argument quality on message elaboration and brand attitudes: An exploratory study. *Journal of Interactive Advertising, 8*(2), 26–37. doi: 10.1080/15252019.2008.10722140

Claeys, A. S., & Cauberghe, V. (2012). Crisis response and crisis timing strategies, two sides of the same coin. *Public Relations Review, 38*, 83–88. doi: 10.1016/j.pubrev.2011.09.001

Coombs, W. T. (2006). Crisis management: A communicative approach. In C. H. Botan & V. Hazleton (Eds.), *Public relations theory II* (pp. 171–197). Mahwah, NJ: Lawrence Erlbaum.

Coombs, W. T. (2007a). Attribution theory as a guide for post-crisis communication research. *Public Relations Review, 33,* 135–139. doi: 10.1016/j.pubrev.2006.11.016

Coombs, W. T. (2007b). Protecting organization reputation during a crisis: The development and application of situational crisis communication theory. *Corporate Reputation Review, 10,* 163–176. doi: 10.1057/palgrave.crr.1550049

Coombs, W. T. (2010). Pursuing evidence-based crisis communication. In W. T. Coombs & S. J. Holladay (Eds.), *The handbook of crisis communication* (pp. 719–725). New York: Wiley-Blackwell.

Coombs, W. T. (2015). *Ongoing crisis communication: Planning, managing, and responding* (4th ed.). Thousand Oaks, CA: Sage.

Coombs, W. T., & Holladay, S. J. (2005). An exploratory study of stakeholder emotions: Affect and crises. *Research on Emotion in Organizations, 1,* 263–280. doi: 10.1016/S1746-9791(05)01111-9

Daft, R. L., & Lengel, R. H. (1986). Organizational information requirements, media richness and structural design. *Management Science, 32,* 554–571. doi: 10.1287/mnsc.32.5.554

DiFonzo, N. (2007). *Rumor psychology: Social and organizational approaches.* Washington, DC: American Psychological Association.

DiStaso, M. W., Vafeiadis, M., & Amaral, C. (2015). Managing a health crisis on Facebook: How the response strategies of apology, sympathy, and information influence public relations. *Public Relations Review, 41,* 222–231. doi: 10.1016/j.pubrev.2014.11.014

Duggan, M., & Smith, A. (2013). Social media update 2013: 42% of online adults use multiple social networking sites, but Facebook remains the platform of choice. *Pew Research Internet Project.* Retrieved from http://www.pewinternet.org/2013/12/30/social-media-update-2013

D'Urso, S. C., & Rains, S. (2008). Examining the source of channel expansion: A test of channel expansion theory with new and traditional communication media. *Management Communication Quarterly, 21,* 1–20. doi: 10.1177/0893318907313712

Dutta-Bergman, M. J. (2004). Interpersonal communication after 9/11 via telephone and Internet: A theory of channel complementarity. *New Media & Society, 6,* 659–673. doi: 10.1177/146144804047086

Dutta-Bergman, M. J. (2006). Community participation and Internet use after September 11: Complementarity in channel consumption. *Journal of Computer-Mediated Communication, 11,* 469–484. doi: 10.1111/j.1083-6101.2006.00022.x

Entman, R. M. (1993). Framing: Towards clarification of a fractured paradigm. *Journal of Communication, 43,* 51–58. doi: 10.1111/j.1460-2466.1993.tb01304.x

Freberg, K. (2012). Intention to comply with crisis messages communicated via social media. *Public Relations Review, 38,* 416–421. doi: 10.1016/j.pubrev.2012.01.008

Gamson, W. A., & Modigliani, A. (1989). Media discourse and public opinion on nuclear power: A constructionist approach. *American Journal of Sociology, 95,* 1–37. doi: 10.1086/229213

Hallahan, K. (1999). Seven models of framing: Implications for public relations. *Journal of Public Relations Research, 11,* 205–242. doi: 10.1207/s1532754xjprr1103_02

Hampton, K. N., Rainie, L., Lu, W., Dwyer, M., Shin, I., & Purcell, K. (2014). *Social media and the "spiral of silence."* Washington, DC: Pew Research Center. Retrieved from http://www.pewinternet.org/2014/08/26/social-media-and-the-spiral-of-silence

Heath, R. L., & Coombs, W. T. (2006). *Today's public relations.* Thousand Oaks, CA: Sage.

Hirschburg, P. L., Dillman, D. A., & Ball-Rokeach, S. J. (1986). Media system dependency theory: Responses to Mt. St. Helens. In S. J. Ball-Rokeach & M. G. Cantor (Eds.), *Media, audience, and social structure* (pp. 117–126). Beverly Hills, CA: Sage.

Ho, S. S., & McLeod, D. M. (2008). Social-psychological influences of opinion expression in face-to-face ad computer-mediated communication. *Communication Research, 35*, 190–207. doi: 10.1177/0093650207313159

Iyengar, S. (1993). *Is anyone responsible? How television frames political issues.* Chicago: University of Chicago.

Jeffres, L. W., Neuendorf, K., Braken, C. C., & Atkin, D. (2008). Integrating theoretical traditions in media effects: Using third-person effects to link agenda-setting and cultivation. *Mass Communication and Society, 11*, 470–491. doi: 10.1080/15205430802375303

Jin, Y. (2009). The effects of public's cognitive appraisal of emotions in crises on crisis coping and strategy assessment. *Public Relations Review, 35*, 310–313. doi: http://dx.doi.org/10.1016/j.pubrev.2009.02.003

Jin, Y. (2010). Making sense sensibly in crisis communication: How publics' crisis appraisals influence their negative emotions, coping strategy preferences and crisis response acceptance. *Communication Research, 37*, 522–552. doi: 10.1177/0093650210368256

Jin, Y. (2014). Examining publics' crisis responses according to different shades of anger and sympathy. *Journal of Public Relations Research, 26*, 79–101. doi: 10.1080/1062726X.2013.848143

Jin, Y., & Liu, B. F. (2010). The blog-mediated crisis communication model: Recommendations for responding to influential external blogs. *Journal of Public Relations Research, 22*, 429–455. doi: 10.1080/10627261003801420

Jin, Y., Liu, B. F., Anagondahalli, D., & Austin, L. (2014). Scale development for measuring publics' emotions in organizational crises. *Public Relations Review, 40*(3), 509–518. doi: 10.1016/j.pubrev.2014.04.007

Jin, Y., Liu, B. F., & Austin, L. (2014). Examining the role of social media in effective crisis management: The effects of crisis origin, information form, and source on publics' crisis responses. *Communication Research, 41*, 74–94. doi: 10.1177/0093650211423918

Jin, Y., Pang, A., & Cameron, G. T. (2007). Integrated crisis mapping: Towards a publics-based, emotion-driven conceptualization in crisis communication. *Sphera Publica, 7*, 81–96. Retrieved from http://www.redalyc.org/articulo.oa?id=29720421006

Jin, Y., Pang, A., & Cameron, G. T. (2012). Toward a publics-driven, emotion-based conceptualization in crisis communication: Unearthing dominant emotions in multi-staged testing of the Integrated Crisis Mapping (ICM) model. *Journal of Public Relations Research, 24*, 266–298. doi: 10.1080/1062726X.2012.676747

Kahneman, D., & Tversky, A. (1979). Prospect theory: An analysis of decision under risk. *Econometrica: Journal of the Econometric Society, 47*, 263–291. doi: 10.2307/1914185

Kasperson, R. E., Renn, O., Slovic, P., Brown, H. S., Emel, J., Goble, R., . . . Ratick, S. (1988). The social amplification of risk: A conceptual framework. *Risk Analysis, 8*, 177–187. doi: 10.1111/j.1539-6924.1988.tb01168.x

Kelleher, T. (2009). Conversational voice, communicated commitment, and public relations outcomes in interactive online communication. *Journal of Communication, 59*, 172–188. doi: 10.1111/j.1460-2466.2008.01410.x

Kent, M. L. (2010). Directions in social media for professionals and scholars. In R. Heath (Ed.), *The Sage handbook of public relations* (pp. 643–656). Thousand Oaks, CA: Sage.

Kent, M. L. (2013). Using social media dialogically: Public relations role in reviving democracy. *Public Relations Review, 24*, 321–334. doi: 10.1016/j.pubrev.2013.07.024

Kent, M. L., & Taylor, M. (1998). Building dialogic relationships through the World Wide Web. *Public Relations Review, 24*, 321–334. doi: 10.1016/S0363-8111(99)80143-X

Kent, M. L., & Taylor, M. (2002). Toward a dialogic theory of public relations. *Public Relations Review, 28*, 21–37. doi: 10.1016/S0363-8111(02)00108-X

Kim, S., Kim, H., & Oh, S. (2014). Talking about genetically modified (GM) foods in South Korea: The role of the Internet in the spiral of silence process. *Mass Communication and Society, 17*, 713–732. doi: 10.1080/15205436.2013.847460

Kiousis, S. (2001). Public trust or mistrust? Perceptions of media credibility in the information age. *Mass Communication and Society, 4*, 381–403. doi: 10.1207/S15327825MCS0 404_4

Lachlan, K. A., Spence, P. R., & Nelson, L. D. (2010). Gender differences in negative psychological responses to crisis news: The case of the I-35W collapse. *Communication Research Reports, 27*, 38–48. doi: 10.1080/08824090903293601

Lang, A. (2000). The limited capacity model of mediated message processing. *Journal of Communication, 50*, 46–70. doi: 10.1111/j.1460-2466.2000.tb02833.x

Lang, A. (2006). Using the limited capacity model of motivated mediated message processing to design effective cancer communication messages. *Journal of Communication, 56*, 557–580. doi: 10.1111/j.1460-2466.2006.00283.x

Lang, A., Bolls, P. D., Potter, R., & Kawahara, K. (1999). The effects of production pacing and arousing content on the information processing of television message. *Journal of Broadcasting and Electronic Media, 43*, 451–475. doi: 10.1080/08838159909364504

Lang, A., Bradley, S. D., Park, B., Shin, M., & Chung, Y. (2006). Parsing the resource pie: Using STRTs to measure attention to mediated messages. *Media Psychology, 8*, 369–394. doi: 10.1207/s1532785xmep0804_3

Lang, A., Newhagen, J., & Reeves, B. (1996). Negative video as structure: Emotion, attention, capacity, and memory. *Journal of Broadcasting & Electronic Media, 40*, 460–477.

Lazarus, R. S. (1991). *Emotion and adaptation.* New York: Oxford University.

Lev-On, A. (2010). Engaging the disengaged: Collective action, media uses and sense of (virtual) community by evacuees from Gush Katif. *American Behavioral Scientist, 53*, 1208–1227. doi: 10.1177/0002764209356251

Lev-On, A. (2012). Communication, community, crisis: Mapping uses and gratifications in the contemporary media environment. *New Media and Society, 14*, 98–116. doi: 10.1177/1461444811410401

Lewis, R. E., & Tyshenko, M. G. (2009). The impact of social amplification and attenuation of risk and the public reaction to mad cow disease in Canada. *Risk Analysis, 29*, 714–728. doi: 10.1111/j.1539-6924.2008.01188.x

Lin, C. A., & Lagoe, C. (2013). Effects of news media and interpersonal interactions on H1N1 risk perception and vaccination intent. *Communication Research Reports, 30*, 127–136. doi: 10.1080/08824096.2012.762907

Littlefield, R. S., & Quenette, A. M. (2007). Crisis leadership and Hurricane Katrina: The portrayal of authority by the media in natural disasters. *Journal of Applied Communication Research, 35*, 26–47. doi: 10.1080/00909880601065664

Liu, B. F., Austin, L. L., & Jin, Y. (2011). How publics respond to crisis communication strategies: The interplay of information form and source. *Public Relations Review, 37*, 345–353. doi: 10.1016/j.pubrev.2011.08.004

Liu, B. F., & Fraustino, J. D. (2014). Beyond image repair: Suggestions for crisis communication theory development. *Public Relations Review, 40*, 543–546. doi: 10.1016/j. pubrev.2014.04.004

Liu, B. F., Fraustino, J. D., & Jin, Y. (2015). How disaster information form, source, type, and prior disaster exposure affect public outcomes: Jumping on the social media bandwagon? *Journal of Applied Communication Research*, *43*, 44–65. doi: 10.1080/ 00909882.2014.982685

Liu, B. F., Fraustino, J. D., & Jin, Y. (2016). Social media use during disasters: How information form and source influence intended behavioral responses. *Communication Research*, 43(5), 626–646. doi: 10.1177/0093650214565917

Liu, B. F., Jin, Y., & Austin, L. L. (2013). The tendency to tell: Understanding publics' communicative responses to crisis information form and source. *Journal of Public Relations Research*, *25*, 51–67. doi: 10.1080/1062726X.2013.739101

Liu, B. F., Jin, Y., Austin, L. L., & Janoske, M. (2012). The social-mediated crisis communication model: Guidelines for effective crisis management in a changing media landscape. In S. Duhé (Eds.), *New media in public relations* (2nd ed., pp. 257–266). New York: Peter Lang.

Liu, B. F., Jin, Y., Briones, R., & Kuch, B. (2012). Managing turbulence in the blogosphere: Evaluating the blog-mediated crisis communication model with the American Red Cross. *Journal of Public Relations Research*, *24*, 353–370. doi: 10.1080/1062726X.2012.689901

Liu, X., & Fahmy, S. (2011). Exploring the spiral of silence in the virtual world: Individuals' willingness to express personal opinions in online versus offline settings. *Journal of Media and Communication Studies*, *3*, 45–57. doi:10.5897/JMCS/58558A711227

Lowrey, W. (2004). Media dependency during a large-scale social disruption: The case of September 11. *Mass Communication and Society*, *7*, 339–357. doi: 10.1207/s15327825 mcs07035

McDonald, L. M., Sparks, B., & Glendon, A. I. (2010). Stakeholder reactions to company crisis communication and causes. *Public Relations Review*, *36*, 263–271. doi: http:// dx.doi.org/10.1016/j.pubrev.2010.04.004

Macias, W., Hilyard, K., & Freimuth, V. (2009). Blog functions as risk and crisis communication during Hurricane Katrina. *Journal of Computer-Mediated Communication*, *15*, 1–31. doi: 10.1111/j.1083–6101.2009.01490.x

McQuail, D. (2000). *McQuail's mass communication theory* (4th ed.). Thousand Oaks, CA: Sage.

Merritt, S., Lawson, L., Mackey, D., & Waters, R. D. (2012). If you blog it, they will come: Examining the role of dialogue and connectivity in the nonprofit blogosphere. In S. Duhe (Ed.), *New media and public relations* (2nd ed., pp. 157–168). New York: Peter Lang.

Mileti, D. S., & Sorensen, J. H. (1990). *Communication of emergency public warnings: A social science perspective and state-of-the-art assessment*. Oak Ridge, TN: Oak Ridge National Laboratory, U.S. Department of Energy.

Nerlich, B., & Halliday, C. (2007). Avian flu: The creation of expectations in the interplay between science and the media. *Sociology of Health & Illness*, *29*, 46–65. doi: 10.1111/j.1467-9566.2007.00517.x

Neuwirth, K. (2010). Risk, crisis, and mediated communication. In R. L. Heath & D. O'Hair (Eds.), *Handbook of risk and crisis communication* (pp. 398–411). New York: Routledge.

Noelle-Neumann, E. (1984). *The spiral of silence: Public opinion-our social skin*. Chicago: University of Chicago.

Noelle-Neumann, E. (1991). The theory of public opinion: The concept of the spiral of silence. In J. A. Anderson (Ed.), *Communication yearbook* (Vol. 14, pp. 256–287). Newbury Park, CA: Sage.

Pan, Z., & Kosicki, G. M. (1993). Framing analysis: An approach to news discourse. *Political Communication*, *10*, 59–79. doi: 10.1080/10584609.1993.9962963

Perse, E., Signorielli, N., Courtright, J. A., Samter, W., Caplan, S. E., Lambe, J. L., & Cai, X. (2002). Public perceptions of media functions at the beginning of the war on terrorism. In B. S. Greenberg (Ed.), *Communication and terrorism* (pp. 39–52). Cresskill, NJ: Hampton.

Pfau, M., & Wan, H. (2006). Persuasion: An intrinsic function of public relations. In C. H. Botan & V. Hazleton (Eds.), *Public relations theory II* (pp. 101–136). Mahwah, NJ: Lawrence Erlbaum.

Rains, S., & Ruppel, E. K. (2016). Channel complementarity theory and the health information-seeking process: Further investigating the implications of source characteristic complementarity. *Communication Research, 43*(2), 232–252. doi: 10.1177/0093650 213510939

Ruggiero, T. E. (2000). Uses and gratifications theory in the 21st century. *Mass Communication and Society, 3*, 3–37. doi: 10.1207/S15327825MCS0301_02

Ruppel, E. K., & Rains, S. A. (2012). Information sources and the health information-seeking process: An application and extension of channel complementarity theory. *Communication Monographs, 79*, 385–405. doi: 10.1080/03637751.2012.697627

Schultz, F., Utz, S., & Göritz, A. (2011). Is the medium the message? Perceptions of and reactions to crisis communication via Twitter, blogs and traditional media. *Public Relations Review, 37*, 20–27. doi: 10.1016/j.pubrev.2010.12.001

Seeger, M. W., Sellnow, T. L., & Ulmer, R. R. (2003). *Communication and organizational crisis.* Westport, CT: Praeger.

Shaia, J. S., & Gonzenbach, W. J. (2007). Communications with management in times of difficulty and crisis: Silence explained. *International Journal of Strategic Communication, 1*, 139–150. doi: 10.1080/15531180701434777

Tai, Z., & Sun, T. (2007). Media dependencies in a changing media environment: The case of the 2003 SARS epidemic in China. *New Media and Society, 9*, 987–1009. doi: 10.1177/1461444807082691

Thorson, E., & Moore, J. (1996). The circle of synergy: Theoretical perspectives and an evolving IMC agenda. In E. Thorson & J. Moore (Eds.), *Integrated communication: Synergy of persuasive voices* (pp. 333–354). Mahwah, NJ: Lawrence Erlbaum.

Turner, M. M. (2006). Using emotion in risk communication: The anger activism model. *Public Relations Review, 33*, 114–119. doi: http://dx.doi.org/10.1016/j.pubrev.2006.11.013

Urista, M., Qingwen, D., & Day, K. (2009). Explaining why young adults use MySpace and Facebook through uses and gratifications theory. *Human Communication, 12*, 215–229. Retrieved from http://www.uab.edu/Communicationstudies/humancommunication/07_Urista_final.pdf

Utz, S., Schultz, F., & Glocka, S. (2013). Crisis communication online: How medium, crisis type and emotions affected public reactions in the Fukushima Daiichi nuclear disaster. *Public Relations Review, 39*, 40–46. doi: 10.1016/j.pubrev.2012.09.010

Wang, X. T. (2006). Emotions within reason: Resolving conflicts in risk preference. *Cognition and Emotion, 20*, 1132–1152. doi: 10.1080/02699930500387428

Yang, J., & Stone, S. (2003). The powerful role of interpersonal communication in agenda setting. *Mass Communication and Society, 6*, 57–74. doi: 10.1207/S15327825MCS0601_5

Yun, G. W., & Park, S.-Y. (2011). Selective positing: Willingness to post a message online. *Journal of Computer-Mediated Communication, 16*, 201–227. doi: 10.1111/j.1083-6101.2010.01533.x

30

CONCLUSION

Yan Jin and Lucinda Austin

As the first edited scholarly volume on social media and crisis communication, this book attempts to provide crisis scholars and managers with a comprehensive overview of (a) the current theoretical foundations and frameworks in crisis that have been adapted or developed to examine crisis communication in a complex media network intertwining social media and traditional media; (b) crisis communication strategies for using social media differently in varied practice areas with specific contexts, issues, and stakeholders; and (c) pathways toward "evidenced-based crisis communication research," as Coombs and Holladay (2012) advocated for in *The Handbook of Crisis Communication*, in situations where a crisis was initiated, mediated, or escalated through social media. The ultimate goal of these areas of research are to provide insights for crisis managers to effectively, efficiently, and ethically help organizations prepare for, respond to, and recover from crises.

Beyond what is provided here in this book, we propose the following areas and directions for future crisis communication and social media research. These future directions, based on recommendations and observations from fellow crisis scholars, are aimed at providing social science–generated insights that can be used by crisis managers to guide and enhance practice.

First, scholars should continue applying established crisis communication theories, such as Coombs's situational crisis communication theory (SCCT) (e.g., Coombs, 2007), Benoit's image-repair theory (e.g., Benoit, 1997, 2004), and Cameron and colleagues' contingency theory of strategic conflict management (e.g., Cancel, Cameron, Sallot, & Mitrook, 1997), to study the role of social media (both content and form) in effective crisis communication practice. Given the rapidly changing features of media technology and new opportunities for crisis information content creation and dissemination strategies, new components, factors, and propositions might emerge in the process of testing existing crisis theories. Additionally, scholars should consider developing social media–specific crisis communication theories and frameworks to explain crisis communication practice, identify stakeholder engagement patterns, and predict responses to and outcomes of crisis communication. Thus far, the only theoretical framework proposed and developed specifically for crisis communication in a social media–centered network is the social-mediated crisis communication (SMCC) model (Austin & Jin, 2016), proposed by the editors of the book and colleagues, which has been systematically tested since the conceptual paper was first published in 2010 (Jin & Liu, 2010). We hope to see more efforts and endeavors in this direction, prescribing strategic solutions and recommendations for crisis managers who look for science-based insights tailored for a relatively focused and specialized crisis communication arena.

Second, scholars need to continue addressing the research needs Chang and Cameron's chapter identified in reviewing existing literature in social media and crisis communication research, including applying more global approaches, improving sampling frames, emphasizing different crisis communication phases, and improving metrics and measures of effectiveness. More research is needed on how multinational companies can strategically use culture-specific social media platforms in the context of different media systems and cultural contexts, in order to create and disseminate crisis information and engage local audiences effectively via sensitive and culturally appropriate dialogues. For instance, to deal with organizational crises in China, where Facebook and Twitter are not accessible to the general public, a crisis manager must be familiar with the popular social media platforms (e.g., WeChat, Weibo) and competent in communicating with and engaging a wide variety of stakeholder groups. Additional factors should also be examined, including how to measure effectiveness of social-mediated crisis communication, identify indicators of crisis recovery, and define outcomes of social-mediated crisis communication efforts. For example, should outcome measures address long-term reputation repair or should information seeking and sharing on social media, together with the level and valence of stakeholder engagement, be measured? Other social science approaches, in addition to interviews, experiments, and surveys, need to be incorporated in future social media and crisis communication research. Social network analysis, for example, will be an important research method and analysis approach to tap into social media data, monitor the social conversation at a macro level, and identify patterns in crisis issue discussions and the networks of opinion leaders on different platforms and across platforms.

Third, future volumes on social media and crisis communication might expand research insights and practice recommendations by including different types of crises, with contextual factors and influencing issues more fully examined. The current volume covers crisis in a broad sense, including both organizational crises and natural disasters. Under organizational crisis, we look at social media and crisis communication practiced by the private sector (e.g., corporate crisis management), nonprofit organizations, and government agencies. Some crises, such as disasters (natural disasters or man-made disasters), have multiple layers, involving both threats to an organization's reputation and operations if the organization does not help relieve the disaster in a timely and effectively manner, as well as severe damage to the safety and well-being of the community. Effective crisis communication using social media is thus pivotal in public health crises, terrorist attacks, and natural disasters, such as earthquakes, where an organization (e.g., a government agency) is not directly responsible for what happened but is held accountable for relief and rescue due to the roles and responsibilities ascribed to the organization. In addition, social media and crisis communication–specific guidelines for ethical communication and stakeholder engagement need to be further developed and tailored, when possible, for different contexts and issues.

Fourth, current theories and frameworks included in this volume reflect a functional perspective of crisis communication, although the focus has shifted from a more organization-centered approach to a public-centered approach in the last decade (e.g., the focus on stakeholder engagement and dialogic communication). Botan and Taylor (2004) proposed a cocreational approach to public relations research, focusing on the values and meanings of messages exchanged between publics and organizations and showing a genuine interest and intention from the organization to involve publics and reflect their needs for effective communication approaches and messages. The editors of this book recently attempted to integrate a cocreational framework in social-mediated crisis communication in a forthcoming book chapter in Botan's edited volume on strategic communication. Whether this type of paradigm shift, from a functional to cocreational approach, is likely to change how crisis communication should be practiced, when possible and feasible, remains an emerging area for scholars to explore further. It is especially critical to understand, appreciate, and be mindful of crisis emotions in times of crisis and how audiences and publics express their feelings toward multiple entities, including organizations, victims, and others. It is important not only to mitigate negative crisis emotions such as anger, anxiety, fear, and sadness, but also to foster genuine positive and constructive emotions in crisis messages and actions, such as hope, relief, and compassion. How crisis messages can be improved by effectively creating and sharing information using visual social media such as Pinterest, Instagram, and Snapchat is another important area, as Guidry and Messner pointed out in their chapter. The power of visuals in crisis and how to utilize them effectively and ethically is yet to be fully studied.

To summarize, this volume is a first step toward a promising journey, reflecting collective research endeavors of prominent crisis scholars across the globe. We hope this book will be a helpful teaching tool, facilitating students' learning about social media and crisis communication. We also hope that crisis communication practitioners and media professionals will find the insights this book provides helpful in facilitating their daily practice and strategic decision making in the ever dynamic field of managing changes, uncertainties competition, and conflicts in crisis communication.

References

Austin, L. L., & Jin, Y. (2016). Social media and crisis communication: Explicating the social-mediated crisis communication model. In A. Dudo & L. A. Kahlor (Eds.), *Strategic communication: New agendas in communication* (pp. 163–186). New York: Routledge.

Benoit, W. L. (1997). Image repair discourse and crisis communication. *Public Relations Review, 23*(2), 177–186.

Benoit, W. L. (2004). Image restoration discourse and crisis communication. In D. P. Millar & R. L. Heath (Eds.), *Responding to crisis: A rhetorical approach to crisis communication* (pp. 263–280). Mahwah, NJ: Lawrence Erlbaum.

Botan, C. H., & Taylor, M. (2004). Public relations: State of the field. *Journal of Communication, 54*(4), 645–661.

Cancel, A. E., Cameron, G. T., Sallot, L. M., & Mitrook, M. A. (1997). It depends: A contingency theory of accommodation in public relations. *Journal of Public Relations Research, 9*(1), 31–63.

Coombs, W. T. (2007). Protecting organization reputation during a crisis: The development and application of situational crisis communication theory. *Corporate Reputation Review, 10*, 163–176.

Coombs, W. T., & Holladay, S. (2012). *The handbook of crisis communication.* Malden, MA: Wiley Blackwell.

Jin, Y., & Liu, B. F. (2010). Strategic responses to influential external blogs: A model for managing blog-mediated crisis communication. *Journal of Public Relations Research, 22*(4), 429–455. doi: 10.1080/10627261003801420

INDEX